Critical Acclaim for
Gerald Posner and *Case Closed*

Case Closed

CASE CLOSED

Lee Harvey Oswald and the Assassination of JFK

GERALD POSNER

ANCHOR BOOKS

DOUBLEDAY

New York London Toronto Sydney Auckland

AN ANCHOR BOOK
PUBLISHED BY DOUBLEDAY
a division of Bantam Doubleday Dell Publishing Group, Inc.
1540 Broadway, New York, New York 10036

ANCHOR BOOKS, DOUBLEDAY, and the portrayal of an
anchor are trademarks of Doubleday, a division of Bantam
Doubleday Dell Publishing Group, Inc.

Case Closed was originally published in hardcover by Random
House in 1993. The Anchor Books edition is published by
arrangement with Random House.

Library of Congress Cataloging-in-Publication Data
Posner, Gerald L.
    Case closed : Lee Harvey Oswald and the assassination of JFK /
Gerald Posner. — 1st Anchor Books ed.
        p.   cm.
    Originally published : New York : Random House, 1993.
    Includes bibliographical references and index.
    1. Kennedy, John F. (John Fitzgerald), 1917–1963—
Assassination. 2. Oswald, Lee Harvey.   I. Title.
    [E842.9.P67   1994]
    364.1'524—dc20   94-6602
                                                              CIP

To
Bob Loomis, my editor,
who nurtured this project from its inception,
and to
Trisha, my wife, my partner, my life

Contents

Author's Note

The response to the hardcover publication of this book surprised both me and my publisher, Random House. We were initially worried that the book might be lost in the publicity surrounding the publication of other books espousing convoluted theories. But we had underestimated the extent to which, after thirty years of virtually unchallenged conspiracy conjecture, the conclusion that Oswald acted alone in assassinating JFK had evolved, ironically, into the most controversial position. While the media's response was overwhelmingly positive, the reaction from the conspiracy community was the opposite—not simply negative, but often vitriolic. There was little effort to study my overall evidence and conclusions with anything that approached an open mind. Indeed, there was a concerted counterattack to discredit both the book and its author.

There were panel discussions at conspiracy conventions in Boston and Dallas and special publications focused solely on contesting the book. A conspiracy-based "research center" in Washington, D.C., issued a "media alert" about *Case Closed*. The release consisted of five pages alleging the book was misleading and flawed, but the alert misstated my arguments and distorted the evidence in the case. Harold Weisberg, one of the deans of the conspiracy press, found his first publisher (he had previously self-published six conspiracy books) to bring out a book titled *Case Open*, a broadside attack attempting to diminish the impact of my work.

Other conspiracy buffs launched personal attacks. It was, as one journalist commented, as if overnight I had become the Salmon Rushdie of the assassination world. I was accused of treason by a buff who ran a Dallas "research center," and my wife and I were subjected to several months of harassing telephone calls and letters. At an author's luncheon, pickets protested that I was a dupe of the CIA. Faxes and letters to the media also charged I was a CIA agent, or that the CIA had written my book, or that I was part of a conscious effort to deceive the public and hide the truth. (Some critics even expanded the accusations to my first book about Nazi doctor Josef Mengele, contending that I whitewashed the Mengele investigation, when actually that book was the first to detail Mengele's entire life on the run, including his time in U.S. captivity and the Israeli and German bungling of his capture.) Television and radio producers were harassed by callers attempting to have my appearances cancelled. Some reviewers who wrote favorably about the book received intimidating calls or letters. My publisher was subjected to the same treatment, and even my editor, Bob Loomis, was publicly accused of being a CIA agent.

Although I had expected that individuals who had invested their adult lives into investigating JFK conspiracies might react angrily to a book that exposed the fallacies in their arguments, the vehemence of these personal attacks surprised me. I had mistakenly expected a debate on the issues. It took little time to discover, however, the extent to which many people who believe in a JFK conspiracy do so with almost a religious fervor and are not dissuaded by the facts.

Case Closed was probably subjected to greater scrutiny by more "critics" than any other book published in recent years. Several emendations in this book are the result of what some charged as fraudulent omissions in my discussion of various aspects of the case. Because *Case Closed* attempted to deal with all the major issues in the assassination, plus countless arguments raised by conspiracy critics in the three decades following the Warren Commission, many of these, especially those addressed in footnotes, were condensed. To fit all of my research into a single, manageable volume, I did not have the luxury of presenting and explaining each nuance of every issue, but instead focused only on primary arguments. For instance, in a few pages I addressed the theory that JFK's corpse was stolen from Air Force One and medically altered, although the author of that theory took over seven hundred pages to present it. Obviously, not every point raised in his book could be dealt with in *Case Closed*.

In the first edition, I acknowledged that "any of a dozen issues could have been the subject of a separate book, including, among others, Oswald's time in Russia, Jack Ruby's story, or the actual assassination." However, there was not one aspect of the assassination in which I did not study *all* of the available evidence before reaching any conclusion. Conspiracy critics, often complained that I had omitted some information that they contended contradicted one or another of my conclusions. In this edition, I have reinstated material included in earlier drafts but cut for the sake of brevity, to further explain the layers of intricacies in this case.

The remainder of the updated text in this edition has nothing to do with contentions raised by conspiracy buffs, but rather is the result of new scientific evidence or documents uncovered since the hardcover publication. Some of the information is critical, including the first confirmation that two of Oswald's fingerprints have now been identified on the trigger guard of his rifle, the one ballistically proven to have fired the bullets that killed JFK. Also, new disclosures about Oswald's visit to Mexico City provide important insights into the extent of his instability only two months before JFK's visit to Dallas. These, and other significant discoveries, such as a 1962 CIA debriefing of Oswald, have been added to the book.

The updated and restored information in this edition has only strengthened the book's original conclusion that Oswald and Ruby acted alone. Government files will continue to be released for the next few years. Not only am I familiar with the content of many already released, but I have spoken to individuals who are familiar with the still-classified documents. None of the government documents to be released alters the judgment reached in *Case Closed*.

Time and technology have caught up to the conspiracy critics. Some of their most important contentions have collapsed; for example: Photographic tests reveal that the backyard photos of Oswald holding his weapons, contested as fakes, are authentic; ballistics and computer studies confirm the so-called magic bullet theory, long derided by conspiracy theorists as impossible; and neutron activation tests provide the final link that Oswald tried to assassinate General Edwin Walker, a crime for which many considered Oswald innocent. After thirty years of studying the case the critics have failed to produce a single, cogent, alternate scenario of how the alleged conspiracy happened or who was involved.

There is more than enough evidence available on the record to draw conclusions about what happened in the JFK assassination. But apparently most Americans, despite the strength of the evidence, do not want to accept the notion that random acts of violence can change the course of history and that Lee Harvey Oswald could affect our lives in a way over which we have no control. It is unsettling to think that a sociopathic twenty-four-year-old loser in life, armed with a $12 rifle and consumed by his own warped motivation, ended Camelot. But for readers willing to approach this subject with an open mind, it is the only rational judgment.

Preface

More than two thousand books have been written about the assassination of President John Kennedy. Most have attacked the conclusion of the government-appointed Warren Commission that a lone assassin, Lee Harvey Oswald, killed JFK. Many not only assail the Warren Report but also propose myriad suspects —including the CIA, anti-Castro Cubans, the FBI, and the mafia—for ever-expanding conspiracy theories.

Writers have identified nearly thirty gunmen, by name, as the second or—depending on the theory—the third, fourth, or fifth shooter at Dealey Plaza, the site of the assassination. In the critical literature, Lee Harvey Oswald has evolved from being the lone killer to being part of a conspiracy to being an innocent patsy to being a hero who vainly tried to save the President by warning the FBI of the plot.

The public has been particularly receptive to conspiracy theories in this case. Oswald's curious past, especially his defection to the Soviet Union and his apparent pro-Communist philosophy in the middle of the cold war, showed the alleged assassin was anything but ordinary. Nightclub owner Jack Ruby's killing of Oswald within forty-eight hours of the assassination raised the suspicion he had been silenced. Within days of Oswald's death, public opinion polls confirmed that two thirds of those queried doubted he acted alone.

Besides the skepticism over Oswald's murky background and

his murder, strong psychological reasons prompted the public's early embrace of conspiracy theories. The notion that a misguided sociopath had wreaked such havoc made the crime seem senseless and devoid of political significance. By concluding that JFK was killed as the result of an elaborate plot, there is the belief he died for a purpose, that a powerful group eliminated him for some critical issue. Public receptivity to the theories is also fed by suspicions that politicians lie and cover up misdeeds while intelligence and military officials plot against the nation they are supposed to protect.

Books and movies promoting conspiracy theories have reinforced and expanded the early public doubts. Today, the Warren Report is almost universally derided, mostly by people who have never read it. The debate is no longer whether JFK was killed by Lee Oswald acting alone or as part of a conspiracy—it is instead, which conspiracy is correct?

The early critics used the Warren Commission's work as the springboard for their own efforts. They dissected the twenty-six volumes of testimony and exhibits and raised questions about its conclusions by highlighting inconsistencies and errors. The next generation of critics used the doubts sown by the initial writers and went far beyond the issues addressed by the Commission. Focusing on matters such as the history of the mafia or clandestine CIA operations, many of these books championed complex theses involving dozens of conspirators.

Forgotten in most recent studies of the assassination is Oswald. He is referred to only briefly and often presented as a sterile figure. With Oswald stripped of character, the reader is seldom given any insight into understanding him. His intricate personality and temperament are obscured under a deluge of technical details about trajectory angles and bullet speeds.

During the past three decades, hundreds of questions have been raised about the assassination. Few books provide answers. No single volume can deal with all the published contentions. However, the truth in the case can be uncovered by reviewing original documents and testimony and interviewing those involved. Despite a seemingly intractable quagmire of conflicting evidence, it is possible to find reliable and accurate information about the assassination and, by so doing, answer the riddle of what really happened as well as what motivated Lee Harvey Oswald and Jack Ruby.

The breadth of the issues in the Kennedy assassination dissuades many reputable journalists from pursuing the subject. Others are discouraged because the JFK murder has, regrettably, become an entertainment business, complete with board games and shopping-mall "assassination research centers" stuffed with souvenir T-shirts and bumper stickers.

As in every famous case, people have come out of the woodwork for their fifteen minutes of fame. Some publicity seekers have even implicated themselves in the murder conspiracy. If someone is willing to make a statement, no matter how outrageous, it is too often printed as "proof." These more sensational claims may sell books, but they bring us no closer to understanding what really happened.

The only casualty is truth, especially in a society where far too many people are content to receive all their knowledge on an important issue from a single article or a three-hour movie. In this book, Oswald's life is investigated in some detail, and to a lesser extent, so is the life of Ruby. As the story progresses, arguments raised by the leading conspiracy critics, such as Anthony Summers, Mark Lane, Jim Marrs, and others, are resolved in the text or in footnotes. Also, beyond the human stories, there are separate chapters about the medical and ballistics issues, the Warren Commission and its critics, and the late New Orleans district attorney Jim Garrison.

Many people, understandably, believe that the truth in the Kennedy assassination will never be discovered. But the troubling issues and questions about the assassination can be settled, the issue of who killed JFK resolved, and Oswald's motivation revealed. Presenting those answers is the goal of this book.

Case Closed

1

"Which One Are You?"

President John F. Kennedy had been dead less than an hour. J. D. Tippit, only the third Dallas policeman in a decade to die in the line of duty, was killed shortly after the President. Rumors swept the city. Dealey Plaza, the site of the presidential assassination, was in pandemonium. Dozens of witnesses sent the police scurrying in different directions in futile search of an assassin. While most police mobilized to hunt the President's killer, more than a dozen sped to Dallas's Oak Cliff, a quiet middle-class neighborhood, to search for Tippit's murderer.

At 1:46 P.M., after an abortive raid on a public library, a police dispatcher announced: "Have information a suspect just went in the Texas Theater on West Jefferson." Within minutes, more than six squad cars sealed the theater's front and rear exits. Police armed with shotguns spread into the balcony and the main floor as the lights were turned up. Only a dozen moviegoers were scattered inside the small theater. Officer M. N. McDonald began walking up the left aisle from the rear of the building, searching patrons along the way. Soon, he was near a young man in the third row from the back of the theater. McDonald stopped and ordered him to stand. The man slowly stood up, raised both hands, and then yelled, "Well, it is all over now."[1] In the next instant, he punched McDonald in the face, sending the policeman's cap flying backward. McDonald instinctively lurched forward just as his assailant pulled a pistol from his waist. They tumbled over the seats as other police rushed to subdue the gunman. The gun's hammer clicked as the man pulled the trigger, but it did not fire.[2]

After the suspect was handcuffed, he shouted, "I am not resisting arrest. Don't hit me anymore."[3] The police pulled him to his feet and marched him out the theater as he yelled, "I know my rights. I want a lawyer."[4] A crowd of nearly two hundred had gathered in front of the building, the rumor circulating that the President's assassin might have been caught. As the police exited, the crowd surged forward, screaming obscenities and crying, "Let us have him. We'll kill him! We want him!" The young man smirked and hollered back, "I protest this police brutality!"[5] Several police formed a wedge and cut through the mob to an unmarked car. The suspect was pushed into the rear seat between two policemen while three officers packed into the front. Its red lights flashing, the car screeched away and headed downtown.

The suspect was calm. Again he declared, "I know my rights," and then asked, "What is this all about?"[6] He was told he was under arrest for killing J. D. Tippit. He didn't look surprised. "Police officer been killed?" he asked. He was silent for a moment, and then he said, "I hear they burn for murder." Officer C. T. Walker, sitting on his right side, tried to control his temper: "You may find out." Again, the suspect smirked. "Well, they say it just takes a second to die," he said.[7]

One of the police asked him his name. He refused to answer. They asked where he lived. Again just silence. Detective Paul Bentley reached over and pulled a wallet from the suspect's left hip pocket. "I don't know why you are treating me like this," he said. "The only thing I have done is carry a pistol into a movie."[8]

Bentley looked inside the wallet. He called out the name: "Lee Oswald." There was no reaction. Then he found another identification with the name Alek Hidell. Again no acknowledgment. Bentley said, "I guess we are going to have to wait until we get to the station to find out who he actually is."[9]

Shortly after 2:00 P.M., the squad car pulled into the basement of the city hall. The police told the suspect he could hide his face from the press as they entered the building. He shrugged his shoulders. "Why should I hide my face? I haven't done anything to be ashamed of."[10]

The police ran him into an elevator and took him to a third-floor office. He was put into a small interrogation room, with several men standing guard, as they waited for the chief of homicide, Captain Will Fritz. Suddenly, another homicide detective, Gus Rose, entered the room. He had the suspect's billfold in his hand, and he pushed two plastic cards forward. "One says Lee Harvey Oswald and one says Alek Hidell. Which one are you?"

A smirk again crossed his face. "You figure it out," he said.

For the past thirty years historians, researchers, and government investigators have tried to deal with Oswald's simple challenge. Although the identity of the suspect remained in doubt for only a few more minutes at that Dallas police station, the search has continued for the answer to the broader question of who Lee Harvey Oswald was. Understanding him is the key to finding out what happened in Dallas on November 22, 1963.

Oswald was born on October 18, 1939, into a lower-middle-class family in a downtrodden New Orleans neighborhood. His father, Robert Edward Lee Oswald, died two months before his birth. His mother, Marguerite, was a domineering woman, consumed with self-pity both over the death of her husband and because she had to return to work to support Lee, his brother, Robert, and a halfbrother, John Pic, from the first of her three marriages.[11] Marguerite played an important role in Oswald's development, and conspiracy critics cast her in a positive light. Jim Marrs, author of *Crossfire*, one of two books upon which the movie *JFK* was based, downplays Oswald's formative years: "Despite much conjecture, there is little evidence that Lee's childhood was any better or any worse than others."[12] Anthony Summers, in his best-selling *Conspiracy*, quotes a relative describing Marguerite as "a woman with a lot of character and good morals, and I'm sure that what she was doing for her boys she thought was the best at the time."[13]

The truth is quite different. Robert described his mother as "rather quarrelsome" and "not easy to get along with when she didn't get her own way."[14] According to Robert, Marguerite tried to "dominate" and "control" the entire family, and the boys found it "difficult . . . to put up with her."[15] John Pic developed a "hostility" toward her and felt "no motherly love."[16] Although she wanted to rule her sons' lives, she was unable to cope with them following the death of her husband. High-strung, and failing to keep any job very long,* she committed Robert and John Pic to an orphanage.[17] She wanted also to send Lee, but he was too young to be accepted. Instead, she shuttled him between her sister and an assortment of housekeepers and baby-sitters.[18] The temporary arrangement did not work. Marguerite had let a couple move into her home to help care for Lee, but had to fire them when she discovered they had been whipping him to control his "unmanageable" disposition.[19] She admitted it "was difficult with Lee," juggling different jobs and homes (they moved five times before Lee was three). The instability had its effect on Oswald. Years later, in an introductory note to a manuscript, he wrote: "Lee Harvey Oswald was born in Oct 1939 in New Orleans, La. the son of a Insuraen [sic] Salesman whose early death left a far mean streak of indepence [sic] brought on by negleck [sic]."[20]

The day after Christmas 1942, Marguerite finally placed three-year-old Lee into the orphanage, where he joined his two brothers.[21] Nearly one hundred youngsters lived at the Bethlehem Children's Home. The atmosphere was relaxed, and Lee's older brothers watched out for him during his stay there, which was quite uneventful. In early 1944, Marguerite unexpectedly checked her sons out of the Bethlehem Home and moved to Dallas. She relocated there because of her personal interest in a local businessman, Edwin Ekdahl, whom she had met six months earlier in New Orleans.[22] They married in May of the following year. Lee's new stepfather worked for a utility company and extensive travel was part of his job. Robert and John Pic were placed in a military boarding school and Marguerite and Lee traveled with Ekdahl.[23] The business trips and short relocations were so extensive that Lee missed most of his first

---

* She admitted in her Warren Commission testimony to holding more than a dozen jobs and being fired from half of them.

year of school, but by late October, they settled in Benbrook, Texas, a suburb of Fort Worth. Just after his sixth birthday, Lee was admitted to Benbrook Common Elementary.[24]

But young Oswald was no longer concerned about the frequent moves or his absence from school because he had found a friend in his stepfather. Lee's halfbrother, John Pic, recalled, "I think Lee found in him the father he never had. He had treated him real good and I am sure that Lee felt the same way. I know he did."[25] Soon after the marriage, however, Marguerite and Ekdahl began arguing. "She wanted more money out of him," recalls Pic. "That was the basis of all arguments."* The fights increased steadily in vituperation and intensity. Ekdahl often walked out, staying at a hotel, and in the summer of 1946, Marguerite moved with Lee to Covington, Louisiana.[26] But Ekdahl and Marguerite soon reunited. Lee was ecstatic when his stepfather moved back in, but he hated the fighting and separations.[27] "I think Lee was a lot more sensitive than any of us realized at the time," recalled his brother, Robert.[28]

The uncertainty in the marriage prevented Lee from ever settling into a single neighborhood and school. In September 1946, he enrolled in a new school, Covington Elementary, but was again in the first grade, because he had not completed the required work at Benbrook. After five months, Marguerite withdrew him from Covington and they moved back to Fort Worth, where Lee enrolled in his third school, the Clayton Public Elementary. He finally finished the first grade, but soon after he was registered for the second grade in the fall, they moved again.[29] A schoolmate at Clayton, Philip Vinson, recalled that while Oswald was not a bully, he was a leader of one of three or four schoolyard gangs.[30] Since he was a year older than his classmates, "they seemed to look up to him because he was so well built and husky . . . he was considered sort of a tough-guy type."[31] Vinson also noted, however, that none of the boys in Oswald's gang ever played with him after school or went to his

---

* Marguerite was always concerned about money. After the assassination, she almost always refused to give an interview or sit for photographs unless paid. Marina, Lee's wife, said, "She has a mania—only money, money, money." Her son John Pic said in 1964 that money was "her god."

home. "I never went to his house, and I never knew anybody who did," said Vinson.[32]

In January 1948, Ekdahl moved out permanently, and he started divorce proceedings in March. Soon after, Marguerite moved to a run-down house in a poor Fort Worth neighborhood, adjoining railroad tracks.[33] Lee was enrolled in another school, the Clark Elementary, his fourth. Unable to afford the tuition at military boarding school for her other two sons, Marguerite moved them in with her and Lee. Robert Oswald and John Pic described the new home as "lower-class" and "prisonlike," and they found Lee even less communicative than when they had previously left the household, often "brooding for hours" at a time.[34] Lee had always been a quiet child. But with the constant moving, he did not easily fit in with his schoolmates and seldom made friends.

In June 1948, the bitter divorce proceedings came to trial. Lee was brought to court to testify, but refused, saying he would not know the truth from a lie. While the divorce dragged along, he stayed home alone with a pet dog, a gift from a neighbor.[35] His brother noticed that he seemed to withdraw further into himself.

That summer, Marguerite and her sons moved once again to Benbrook, Texas. By the autumn they returned to Fort Worth, the thirteenth move since Lee's birth. He was enrolled in the third grade at Arlington Heights Elementary. With her marriage over, Marguerite now gave Lee all her attention, spoiling and protecting him. "She always wanted to let Lee have his way about everything," recalled her sister, Lillian Murret.[36] Afraid he could be hurt in physical activities like sports, she instead encouraged gentler pursuits like tap dancing, but he preferred to stay home by himself or with her.[37] Until he was almost eleven years of age, Lee often slept in the same bed with his mother.[38]

According to Pic, who admittedly resented his mother more than Robert did, Marguerite's attitudes made the home atmosphere depressing.[39] She was jealous of others, resented what they had, and constantly complained about how unfairly life treated her. "She didn't have many friends and usually the new friends she made she didn't keep very long," recalled Pic. "I remember every time we moved she always had fights with the neighbors or something or another."[40] Pic felt so strongly about her that after the assassination he said that if Lee was guilty, then he "was aided with a little extra push from his mother in the living conditions that she presented to him." Even Lee's wife, Marina, later said that "part of the guilt" was with Marguerite, because she did not provide him the correct education, leadership, or guidance.

She did not encourage him to attend school when Lee whined that he did not like it. Instead, his mother told him he was brighter and better than other children, and reinforced his feeling that he learned more at home by reading books than from listening to his teachers. "She told me that she had trained Lee to stay in the house," Marguerite's sister, Lillian, recalled, "to stay close to home when she wasn't there; and even to run home from school and remain in the house or near the house. . . . He just got in the habit of staying alone like that."[41] Oswald's cousin Marilyn Murret said that Marguerite thought it was better for him to stay at home alone than to "get in with other boys and do things they shouldn't do."[42]

When Lee visited the Murrets during this period, Lillian found "he wouldn't go out and play. He would rather just stay in the house and read or something." She did not think it was healthy for him to be inside all the time, so the Murrets took him out, but immediately noticed "he didn't seem to enjoy himself." "He was obviously very unhappy," his aunt concluded.

Neighbors noticed the odd relationship between the overbearing mother and the introverted youngster. Mrs. W. H. Bell, a neighbor in Benbrook, remembered Lee as a loner who did not like to be disciplined.[43] Myrtle Evans, a good friend of Marguerite, said she "was too close to Lee all the time."[44] Evans said Lee was "a bookworm" even at seven years of age, and that his mother "spoiled him to death."[45] "The way he kept to himself just wasn't normal," Evans recalled.[46]

Another neighbor, Hiram Conway, lived two doors away from Lee in Fort Worth. He noticed something else about him: "He was quick to anger." Conway noticed that on the way home from school, Oswald looked for other children to throw stones at. They got out of his way. "He was vicious almost. . . . He was a bad kid," recalled Conway.[47] Conway's impressions were formed from watching Lee from the age of nine to almost thirteen. He believed the young Oswald was smarter than most his age, but also "very strange."[48]

Otis Carlton, a neighbor in Benbrook, was in the Oswalds' living room one evening when Lee, gripping a butcher knife, ran through chasing John Pic. Lee hurled the knife at Pic, in front of a startled Carlton, but it missed and struck the wall. According to Carlton, Marguerite calmly said, "They have these little scuffles all the time and don't worry about it."[49]

In September 1949, Lee transferred to his sixth school, Ridglea West Elementary, just in time to start the fourth grade. As in his other schools, his grades were mediocre. On an IQ test he recorded an unexceptional 103.* He remained there for the next three years, his longest stay at a single school. One of his teachers, Mrs. Clyde Livingston, never saw him make friends or come out of his shell.[50]

In January 1950, John Pic left the house to join the Coast Guard. Robert joined the Marines in July 1952. Lee, who had grown closer to Robert than anyone else in the family, bought a copy of the Marine Corps handbook. Although only twelve, "he was going to keep up with me, to learn everything I was learning," recalled Robert.[51]

With both her older sons gone, in August 1952 Marguerite moved with Lee to New York City, where John Pic was stationed. They temporarily moved in with Pic, his wife of one year, Marge, and their newborn son, who were staying at Pic's mother-in-law's small apartment, at 325 East 92nd Street in Manhattan. Pic, who took a week's leave from the Coast Guard to tour New York with his younger brother, recalled that Lee "was real glad to see me." But he soon realized Marguerite had no intention of moving and finding her own apartment. Tension in the household grew as Pic's wife and Marguerite often argued. Lee added to the strained atmosphere by fighting loudly with his mother and often striking her.[52] One day, Marge asked Lee to lower the volume on the television, and instead he pulled out a knife and threatened her. When Marguerite rushed into the

---

* When committed to Youth House in New York several years later, Oswald scored 118 on an IQ test.

room and told him to put it away, he punched her in the face.[53] The Pics immediately asked Marguerite and Lee to move. "After I approached Lee about this incident," recalled Pic, "his feelings toward me became hostile and thereafter [he] remained indifferent to me and never again was I able to communicate to him in any way."[54]* Pic stayed in contact with his mother but felt helpless as he witnessed her gradual loss of control over Lee.[55]

While he was at the Pics', Lee enrolled in Trinity Evangelical Lutheran School, but was only there several weeks before moving with Marguerite to a one-room basement apartment in the Bronx. There, he entered Public School 117, a junior high. He hated the New York schools, where he was teased by other students for his Southern drawl and shabby clothes, primarily jeans and T-shirts. At P.S. 117, he missed forty-seven of sixty-four school days and was failing most of his courses when his mother pulled him out.[56] In January 1953, they moved again in the Bronx, their third time in five months. Lee was enrolled in a new school, P.S. 44, but refused to attend. Two hearings regarding Oswald's truancy were set, but Marguerite and Lee did not show up. In April, a judge declared him a truant and remanded him to Youth House for three weeks of psychiatric evaluation.[57] Social workers noted he made no effort to mix with the other children while there. The probation officer assigned to the case, John Carro, remembered it because it was unique. "This was not

---

*Testifying before the Warren Commission, Marguerite could still find no fault with her son despite the knife incident. She said, "He did not use the knife—he had an opportunity to use the knife. But it wasn't a kitchen knife, or a big knife. It was a little knife."

People who present Lee as fairly stable overlook the incident when he punched his mother and threatened Pic's wife with a knife. Harold Weisberg, in the first of his six self-published books attacking the Warren Commission, does not even inform the reader that Marguerite and Lee lived with the Pics. He covers the entire period by writing: "In August 1952, Oswald and his mother moved to New York City, where an older, married son by her first marriage also lived" (*Whitewash I*, p. 9). Henry Hurt, in his best-seller *Reasonable Doubt*, not only omits the knife incident but covers all of Oswald's life from birth to New York in one innocuous sentence: "Born in New Orleans in 1939, Oswald and his domineering, eccentric mother lived in various places, including New York City and Fort Worth" (*Reasonable Doubt*, p. 195). Bestselling authors like Anthony Summers, Jim Garrison, Mark Lane, Josiah Thompson, and Robert J. Groden and Harrison Livingstone do not mention the New York City period.

the usual hooky playing type . . . the type of boy who does not
go to school, to truant with his other friends, to go to the park,
fish, play, or whatever it is," recalled Carro. "This [Oswald] was
a boy who would not go to school just to remain home, not do
anything."[58] Carro found that Oswald "did not want to play with
anybody, he did not care to go to school."[59] In the few classes
Oswald attended at P.S. 117, Carro discovered he had been dis-
ruptive.

At Youth House, Oswald told Evelyn Strickman, his
caseworker, that he felt his mother "never gave a damn" about
him. In her report, Strickman wrote that Lee "feels almost as if
there's a veil between him and other people through which they
cannot reach him, but he prefers this veil to remain intact."[60]
After the social workers interviewed Lee, he was sent to the
staff psychiatrist, Dr. Renatus Hartogs, a Ph.D. in clinical psychology and an M.D. He vividly remembered Oswald eleven
years later when he testified before the Warren Commission.
Hartogs gave seminars for other professionals in which he discussed interesting and unusual cases discovered at Youth
House. One week, he chose Oswald as the seminar subject. The
reason Hartogs considered him so interesting was "because he
came to us on a charge of truancy from school, and yet when I
examined him, I found him to have definite traits of dangerous-
ness. In other words, this child had a potential for explosive,
aggressive, assaultive acting out which was rather unusual to
find in a child who was sent to the Youth House on such a mild
charge as truancy from school." Hartogs thought Oswald "in full
contact with reality" but "intensely self-centered."[61] He also said
the thirteen-year-old "showed a cold, detached outer attitude"
and "talked about his situation" in a "nonparticipating fashion."[62] Hartogs found it "difficult to penetrate the emotional wall
behind which this boy hides."[63] He perceived that Oswald had
"intense anxiety, shyness, feelings of *awkwardness* and insecu-
rity" as the main reasons for his withdrawal tendencies (emphasis in original). Oswald told him his main goal was to join the
Army, although Hartogs noticed he had developed a "vivid fantasy life, turning around the topics of omnipotence and
power."[64]

Oswald admitted that he became very angry with his mother

whenever she returned home without having brought food for supper, and confessed he occasionally hit her. He also told the psychiatrist, "I don't want a friend and I don't like to talk to people." When asked if he preferred the company of boys or girls, he responded, "I dislike everybody."

Hartogs's diagnosis was "personality pattern disturbance with schizoid features and passive-aggressive tendencies. Lee has to be seen as an emotionally, quite disturbed youngster who suffers under the impact of really existing emotional isolation and deprivation, lack of affection, absence of family life and rejection by a selfinvolved and conflicted mother."[65] Although Hartogs thought he "was quite clear" in emphasizing Oswald's potential for violence by "the diagnosis of passive-aggressive," he did not explicitly state it since that would have mandated institutionalization. Instead, he recommended that Oswald be placed on probation so long as he was under guidance, preferably from a psychiatrist.*

The New York Domestic Relations Court considered Hartogs's diagnosis serious enough that it assigned a probation officer to Oswald and tried for the next nine months to find appropriate treatment for the disturbed youngster. Meanwhile, Lee was at his ninth school, P.S. 44. On several occasions, Marguerite refused to bring him to court, claiming he had returned and adapted well to school. Instead, his grades were low, sometimes

---

* A few critics have denigrated Hartog because in some of his Warren Commission testimony, and in a subsequent book, he went beyond the conclusions of his original 1953 report by describing Oswald as an even more disturbed youngster with a far greater disposition for violence. But he is not even listed in books written by Mark Lane, Josiah Thompson, Jim Garrison, John Davis, Robert J. Groden and Harrison Livingstone, Robert Blakey, Henry Hurt, David Scheim, or David Lifton. Among those who mention the tests, Jim Marrs disingenuously says: "The results were essentially inconclusive. They showed him to be a bright and inquisitive young man who was somewhat tense, withdrawn, and hesitant to talk about himself or his feelings."

Harold Weisberg tells of the tests but does not quote any of Hartogs's conclusions. Sylvia Meagher, in her acclaimed book *Accessories After the Fact*, writes, "There is, then, no basis in any of the available medical or psychiatric histories for allegations that Oswald was psychotic, aberrant, or mentally unsound in any degree." Meagher's conclusion is contradicted not only by Hartogs but also by two Soviet psychiatrists who evaluated Oswald after his failed suicide attempt in Moscow in 1959 (see page 51).

failing, and comments from his teachers noted he was "quick-tempered," "constantly losing control," and "getting into battles with others."[66] Oswald refused to do his homework or salute the American flag during the class's normal recital of the Pledge of Allegiance.[67] One of his teachers, H. Rosen, said, "When we spoke to him about his behavior, his attitude was belligerent. I offered to help him, he brushed out with, 'I don't need anybody's help!' "[68] John Carro, his probation officer, believed that Marguerite was part of the reason Lee was not getting better: "[S]he may have been as disturbed as the boy. . . . [S]he seemed so preoccupied with her own problems at the time that I do not think she really had an awareness as to the boy's own problems and fears."[69] "If she had faced it," said Robert, "if she had seen to it that Lee received the help he needed—I don't think the world would ever have heard of Lee Harvey Oswald."[70]

By November 1953, Judge Sicher ordered Oswald be placed in a home for disturbed boys and that he be given mandatory psychiatric care. Placing him was difficult since most of the residence homes for which he qualified were overcrowded. Marguerite was now convinced that New York and the court system were the sources of her son's problems. "In New York, if you are out of school one day you go to children's court," she told the Warren Commission. "In Texas the children stay out of school for months at a time." At the start of 1954, to avoid Lee's placement in an institution, she fled the jurisdiction and returned with him to New Orleans. Carro recalled, "I wrote to her . . . and the letter was returned 'Moved, address unknown.' . . . There is very little one can really do. We don't have extra-state jurisdiction, and we didn't even know where she had gone."[71]

Marguerite briefly moved in with her sister, Lillian, who saw that Lee was still a "lonely boy" and that no matter what he did, Marguerite "didn't think her child could do anything wrong . . ."[72] But the Oswalds left the Murrets' after several weeks and rented an apartment owned by Marguerite's friend Myrtle Evans. Evans had not seen the Oswalds in several years. She immediately noticed changes in Lee, who was fourteen. Although still withdrawn, he had become abusive toward his mother. "He was more spoiled," Evans said. "He wanted his way . . . he was very difficult."[73] Lee returned from school each day, stood at the head of the stairs, and screamed for his mother to fix him something to eat. Marguerite dropped whatever else she was doing to take food to his room, where he locked himself away to listen to records and read books. "[H]e was a lot more difficult this time to understand or control than he was when he was younger. . . . He was a hard one to figure out," Evans recalled. Lee had developed a "loud and quite disturbing voice" and used it to order Marguerite around the house; although Lee "was getting a little unbearable," his mother obligingly acquiesced to his dictates.[74]

Evans's husband, Julian, also noticed that Lee had changed, "was arrogant. . . . Real demanding, and loud. . . . Nobody liked him. . . . He didn't associate with anybody. Stayed mostly in the apartment."[75] Julian was surprised by the "insolent" manner with which Lee spoke to his mother. Once Julian took Lee, with some other children, to fish at a small pond. Oswald did not talk to the others, insisting on fishing by himself. The other children either threw small fish back into the pond or kept the larger ones to eat later. Lee just laid everything he caught in a row at his feet and then, when he tired of fishing, walked away, leaving them dying on the bank. "We couldn't understand that at all," says Julian. "It just showed how totally inconsiderate he was of everything. It was a good example of how he acted, and his general attitude."[76] Julian tried to get Lee to socialize, but could not get through to him. "I don't think anybody did. I don't think anybody even came close to it, because the way he was, nobody could figure him out. It was hard to get to him or to understand him. He didn't want you to get too close to him . . ." Frustrated by Lee's coldness, Julian abandoned his efforts. "I thought he was a psycho," said Julian. "I really did."[77]

Lee was now enrolled at Beauregard Junior High, his tenth school. Bennierita Sparacio, a classmate, said, "I could remember him so much because he was always getting in fights . . ."[78] Soon after enrolling, Oswald had a bloody fight with two brothers, which attracted a crowd from the school. A couple of days later, a football player surprised Lee and smashed him in the mouth, knocking out a tooth. Edward Voebel and several other classmates tried to "fix him up" in the bathroom. "That's when our friendship" began, Voebel said.[79] But he soon learned that

Lee "didn't make friends. It was just that people and things just didn't interest him generally. He was just living in his own world . . ." According to Voebel, Lee was "bitter" and thought he had a raw deal out of life. "He didn't like authority," he recalled.[80]

Voebel discovered Oswald was an avid reader, and they shared a mutual interest in guns. Lee owned a plastic model of a .45 caliber pistol, but he wanted a real revolver. Voebel was startled when Oswald hatched a plan to steal a Smith & Wesson automatic from a local store. "He [Oswald] came out with a glasscutter . . . [and] finally told me his complete plans . . ."[81] Oswald convinced him to help case the downtown store, but Voebel noticed a strip around the window and warned Lee that if he cut the window, it would set off an alarm. Oswald abandoned his plan.

Another Beauregard student who spent time with Lee was William Wulf, the astronomy club president. Wulf soon discovered that Oswald shared his interest in history, and one day at Wulf's house, they had a conversation that eventually "got around to communism."[82] "I think Oswald brought it up," Wulf recalled, "because he was reading some of my books in my library, and he started expounding the Communist doctrine and saying that he was highly interested in communism, that communism was the only way of life for the worker, etc., and then came out with the statement that he was looking for a Communist cell in town to join but he couldn't find any."[83] Wulf was surprised by Oswald's radicalism and argued with him. As their voices raised, Wulf's father, having heard Oswald's philosophy, "politely put him out of the house."

Wulf was convinced that Oswald was a "self-made communist. . . . He just learned it on his own." The extent of his commitment startled Wulf. It struck him odd that he was so adamant at such a young age. "His beliefs seemed to be warped but strong . . . he seemed to me a boy that was looking for something to belong to. . . . He had very little self-identification . . . he just happened . . . to latch on to this particular area to become identified with. . . . He impressed me as a boy who could get violent over communism . . . ."[84]

By the end of the 1955 school year, the ninth grade, which

was marked again by mediocre grades, Oswald filled in a personal-history form. As for plans after high school, he checked off both "Military Service" and "Undecided."[85] Although he was briefly a member of the Civil Air Patrol and thought of joining the astronomy club, when asked if he had any close friends, Oswald answered "none."[86]

In the fall of 1955, Oswald enrolled in his eleventh school, Warren Easton High. But after a month he forged his mother's name and wrote school authorities a note saying they were moving to San Diego and that he "must quit school now."[87] Oswald's aunt, Lillian Murret, later explained: "Lee didn't think he had to go to school. He said that he was smart enough and that he couldn't learn anything at school, that nobody could teach him anything." Having dropped out days before his sixteenth birthday, Oswald then asked his mother to lie about his age so he could enlist in the Marines.* She agreed in the hope it might provide some direction for what had become an increasingly rebellious and aimless life-style. But though his mother gave her help, the Marines realized he was underage and rejected him. Oswald was furious. He further isolated himself, assiduously avoiding his few acquaintances, and thought only of enlisting as soon as he turned seventeen.[88] He studied the Marine Corps handbook so much that eventually "he knew it by heart."[89]

After leaving school, Oswald kept himself busy with clerical and messenger jobs at several companies. Palmer McBride, who worked as a messenger for Pfisterer Dental Laboratory, met Oswald, who was working there in the same capacity. Because both enjoyed classical music, on several occasions Oswald went to his home and they listened to records in McBride's bedroom. During their first get-together, the discussion turned to politics. After McBride commented that he thought Eisenhower "was doing a pretty good job," Oswald bristled that Ike "was exploiting the working people" and that if he had the opportunity, he would like to kill Eisenhower.[90] McBride did not report the threat because he did not think Oswald would act on it. But he

---

* Several years earlier, Oswald's halfbrother, sixteen-year-old John Pic, had joined the Marine Corps Reserve by using his mother's false affidavit that he was seventeen (WC Vol. XI, p. 32). (Note to reader: An explanation of abbreviations used in footnotes appears on page 507.)

had no doubt Lee was a committed Communist. On other occasions, Oswald lectured McBride about the "virtues of Communism," how "the workers in the world would one day rise up and throw off their chains," and he often praised Khrushchev.[91] At times, he encouraged McBride to join the Communist party with him. McBride once accompanied Oswald to his apartment, and there Lee "seemed quite proud" to have library copies of *Das Kapital* and the *Communist Manifesto*.[92] Years later, Lee's Dallas friend George de Mohrenschildt asked him, "Who told you to read the Marxist books?" Oswald bragged, "Nobody, I went by myself. I started studying it all by myself."[93]* Oswald also later confirmed to a correspondent, Aline Mosby, that he had studied Marxism from the age of fifteen, when an elderly woman in New York handed him a pamphlet about the Rosenberg case.[94] But he said it was not until he arrived in New Orleans that he discovered *Das Kapital* on a library bookshelf. "It was like a very religious man opening the Bible for the first time," he recalled. "I continued to indoctrinate myself for five years."†

In July 1956, Marguerite and Lee moved for the twenty-first time since his birth. Expecting that Lee would join the Marines on his seventeenth birthday, she decided to return to Fort Worth. In September, Oswald enrolled at Arlington Heights, his twelfth school. For a few weeks, he sporadically attended classes before dropping out.[95] He bought his first real gun, a Marlin bolt-action .22 caliber rifle, which he later sold to his brother, Robert.[96] He also continued devouring library books about Communism. Within days of leaving school, he wrote a letter to the Socialist Party of America and announced, "I am sixteen years of age and would like more information about your youth League, I would like to know if there is a branch in

---

* Marguerite later admitted to the Warren Commission that Lee had books about Communism at their house. But she still defended her deceased son: "I knew he was reading it. But if we have this material in the public libraries, then certainly it is all right for us to read."

† Oswald's early fascination with Communism is a difficult issue for the conspiracy critics, and many ignore his early attraction to Marxism/Leninism. Despite the fact that Oswald was fifteen years old and living with his mother, Harold Weisberg writes that his attraction to Communism only makes sense when "the possibility of Oswald's being somebody's agent is considered."

my area, how to join, ect. [sic], I am a Marxist and have been studying Socialist principles for well over fifteen months."[97]

Why did Oswald, a dedicated leftist, want to join the Marines? Ideology did not control him at that young age, and his desire to enlist preceded his interest in Communism. Oswald had talked of joining the Marines since grammar school.[98] And those who knew him best, his mother and brothers, never had any doubts about his reasons. Robert acknowledged that Lee idolized him, and said, "I feel very surely that the reason that Lee joined the United States Marine Corps was because of my service . . ."[99] Even when he was a truant in New York and virtually uncontrollable, Lee wore his brother's Marine ring as a sign of honor.[100] Oswald later told a reporter: "I joined the Marine Corps because I had a brother in the Marines."[101]

But Oswald's halfbrother, John Pic, perceived an additional motive beyond emulation of Robert. "He did it for the same reasons that I did it and Robert did it . . . to get from out and under . . . [t]he yoke of oppression from my mother."[102] Even Robert admitted that Lee "had seen us escape from Mother that way. To him, military service meant freedom."[103]

At sixteen, Oswald had a strong interest in Communism, but he was not prepared to stand on principle and refuse to join the Marines, which would have meant staying in Fort Worth, friendless and still under his mother's control.* The Marine Corps offered a new start, and if it had worked for Robert, who returned very satisfied with the service, Oswald was convinced it could work the same magic for him. Lee turned seventeen on October 18, 1956, and joined the Marines one week later.

* If nothing else, being in the Marines provided Oswald the opportunity to break away from his mother. After enlisting, he wrote her infrequently, and saw her only sporadically during the remaining seven years of his life. When she arrived at the police headquarters on the night of November 22, 1963, Marguerite did not even know Lee and his wife, Marina, had a second child.

2

"The Best Religion Is Communism"

Oswald reported for duty at the Marine Corps recruit depot in San Diego on October 26, 1956, and was assigned to the Second Training Battalion. There, he was given a series of aptitude tests and scored slightly below average.[1] He was also trained in the use of the M-1 rifle.[2] On December 21, 1956, after three weeks of training, he shot 212, two points over the score required for a "sharpshooter" qualification, the second highest in the Marine Corps.[3] Such a score indicated that from the standing position, he could hit a ten-inch bull's-eye, from a minimum of 200 yards, eight times out of ten.[4] Shortly before he left the Marine Corps, in May 1959, Oswald again certified himself on a firing range. Although he then had no motivation and his disgust for the Marines was high, he still managed to score 191, enough to qualify as a "marksman."[5] Sgt. James Zahm, the NCO in charge of the marksmanship training unit, said, "In the Marine Corps he is a good shot, slightly above average . . . and as compared to the average male . . . throughout the United States, he is an excellent shot."[6]*

---

* Harold Weisberg stated that "Oswald's marksmanship . . . was poor . . ." Jim Garrison is merciless in his attack on Oswald's rifle ability, saying he was "terrible," a "notoriously poor shot," and had "an abysmal marksmanship record in the Marines." A fellow Marine, Nelson Delgado, is often cited by critics as saying that Oswald drew "Maggie's Drawers" on the firing range, meaning that Oswald completely missed his targets. But Delgado was not posted with

Oswald left San Diego in January 1957, and through that summer he proceeded from infantry training at Camp Pendleton to an introductory course on radar at Jacksonville, Florida, to basic instruction in aircraft surveillance at Keesler Air Force Base in Biloxi, Mississippi.[7] In early May, he was routinely promoted to private first class and given a clearance to handle confidential material.*

His progress in the Marines appeared normal on paper, but he had already developed a reputation as an eccentric among the other men. Allen Felde, a fellow recruit who served with him at both San Diego and Camp Pendleton, said he was a "left-winger" who was not popular with the other recruits and was avoided by most of them.[8] Daniel Powers, a senior Marine at Keesler, recalled, "My first impression . . . is that he was somewhat, to use the term, [a] 'loner.' "[9] Powers thought he was "meek . . . could easily be led," and "his general personality would alienate the group against him."† Other Marines unmercifully razzed him "as the frail little puppy in the litter," and he was nicknamed Ozzie Rabbit, because of his meekness. He used weekend passes to escape, returning the almost one hundred miles to his native city of New Orleans.[10]

Oswald when Lee qualified as a sharpshooter. Those in charge of the marksmanship branch who were familiar with Oswald's record praised his ability and said he was easily capable of carrying out the JFK assassination. It "was an easy shot for a man with the equipment he had and his ability," said Sgt. Zahm. Major Eugene Anderson, of the marksmanship branch, said the assassination shots "were not particularly difficult" and that, based on his Marine record, "Oswald had full capabilities to make this shot."

* Oswald had the lowest-level security clearance, "confidential." Two fellow Marines believed he had a "secret" clearance, though they admitted it was merely a hunch and not based on direct knowledge. The House Select Committee on Assassinations investigated the question in the late 1970s, reviewing all relevant military files, and concluded Oswald did not have a higher clearance.

† Powers was perhaps the first person, but certainly not the last, to think Oswald was homosexual. "He had a lot of feminine characteristics," he recalled. Another Marine, David Christie, stayed away from him because he thought he was gay. Although he seldom went to bars with other Marines, several recall that while stationed in Japan, Oswald visited a transvestite bar in Yamato, a club with which he seemed familiar. When stationed in California, Oswald once crossed with a group of Marines to Tijuana, Mexico. There, he took them to a run-down gay bar, the Flamingo. Several recalled that Oswald seemed to know the place and people.

Oswald did not easily adjust to the Corps. Kerry Thornley, a Marine who knew him well, recalled, "Well, definitely, the Marine Corps was not what he had expected it to be when he first joined. Also, he felt that the officers and the staff NCO's at the Marine Corps were incompetent to give him orders."[11] Convinced he had great talent and intelligence, Oswald was frustrated that his superior officers did not recognize it.[12] He soon griped about the strict discipline, and even got into a fight in the barracks.[13] But in July 1957, his fortunes changed when he was transferred to the Marine Corps Air Station in El Toro, California, and was informed he was to be sent in six weeks to Japan. The foreign posting opened a new vista for him, one he felt he deserved.

He arrived at Yokosuka on September 12 and was posted to the Marine Air Control Squadron One (MACS-1), based at Atsugi, about twenty miles west of Tokyo.[14] Atsugi served as the base for the U-2 spy plane. Most of the Marines had seen the strange-looking plane either take off or land, as had many of the townspeople. But Oswald was not intimately associated with the U-2. He worked in a radar bubble, and although he and other radar operators sometimes heard requests for wind speeds at 90,000 feet, giving them an idea of the startling altitude the plane achieved, they knew little else about it. None of the operators in the MACS-1 unit were involved in the U-2 reconnaissance flights.*

Slightly over a month after arriving at Atsugi, Oswald shot himself in the left arm while playing with a .22 caliber derringer he had purchased a few months earlier.[15] One of his fellow Ma-

---

*Some critics try to tie Oswald to the U-2, assuming such a relationship might have intelligence overtones. Yet he never showed any interest in the plane. Of the more than two hundred Marines spoken to by researchers, only one claimed Oswald ever mentioned the plane, and his testimony is suspect. Lieutenant John Donovan, the officer in charge of Oswald's radar team, said he remembered one day when Oswald discussed the U-2's radar blips with him. Yet other Marines in Oswald's unit do not recall any radar operations at the time Donovan claims the incident happened, at Cubi Point in the Philippines. Moreover, Donovan testified before the Warren Commission in 1964 and never mentioned the U-2 incident in fourteen pages of detailed testimony. He told the U-2 story for the first time in the 1970s, as if his memory had improved during the intervening decade.

rines, Paul Murphy, remembered: "I heard a shot in the adjoining cubicle. I rushed into the cubicle to find Oswald sitting on a foot locker looking at a wound in his arm. When I asked what happened, Oswald very unemotionally responded, 'I believe I shot myself.' "[16] Three other Marines were nearby when the accident happened. Pete Connor admitted that he and some others had been baiting Oswald and initially thought he had fired the shot to scare them. However, all were later convinced it was a mistake. Daniel Powers said the "feeling of the group was . . . Ozzie screwed up again." Oswald was taken by ambulance to the U.S. Navy hospital in nearby Yokosuka, where he recuperated for more than two weeks.* He was released just in time to ship out on November 20, bound for the Philippines. Although the Marines intended to bring court-martial charges against him for possessing an unauthorized gun, they postponed the proceedings until he returned to Japan.

Oswald's unit finished its Philippine maneuvers in four weeks, but did not immediately return to Atsugi since the internal war in Indonesia had heated up. Instead, it established a temporary radar installation at Subic Bay.† While there, Oswald passed a test for promotion to the rank of corporal.[17] But his dissatisfaction intensified as he was assigned to KP (kitchen)

---

* Oswald's shooting accident has been seized upon as "arranged" so that he could be absent from his unit and engage in intelligence work. Henry Hurt, in *Reasonable Doubt*, ignores the testimony of the four Marine witnesses, and asserts that Oswald's wound was "contrived" and there "was a general assumption that Oswald had shot himself intentionally." Anthony Summers says the ailments "could conceivably have been excuses to get Oswald out of circulation for another purpose." He concludes, "The sickness ploy, it turns out, is a standard intelligence technique." But they have no supporting evidence. Even Summers admits he is indulging in "some very cautious speculation," and Hurt confesses, "Such evidence of espionage activities is, of course, speculative and circumstantial." Military records show that Oswald was confined to a hospital for his entire recuperation.

† On January 5, 1958, one of Oswald's fellow Marines, Martin Schrand, was killed at Subic Bay in an accident during guard duty when his gun dropped and discharged. Summers alleges that an unnamed Marine, after the assassination, "heard a rumor" that Oswald was involved in Schrand's death. According to Summers, if that hearsay is true it could have provided the CIA a "handle" to force Oswald into intelligence work. After extensive speculation, Summers finally concedes, "There is no hard evidence that Lee Oswald really was involved in the death of Marine Schrand . . ."

duty for the duration, a punishment for the derringer incident. His deteriorating attitude was reflected in his semiannual performance rating of 3.9, slightly below the minimum required for an honorable discharge.[18] Oswald later wrote to his brother, Robert, about his Philippine posting: "I remember well the days we stood offshore at Indonesia waiting to surpress [sic] yet another population, when they were having a revolution there in Mar. 1958. I can still see Japan and the Philippines and their puppet governments."[19]* The Indonesia crisis did not cool until March, when Oswald's unit finally returned to Atsugi.

Within a month, on April 11, a summary court-martial was brought against him for the unregistered weapon with which he had wounded himself.[20] He was found guilty, given twenty days' hard labor (suspended for six months if his behavior was good), fined $50, and demoted to the rank of private (negating his passing mark for corporal). Oswald was infuriated, convinced he had been singled out for enough punishment with three months of KP duty. To others, he seemed more irritated than usual. A Marine colleague, Paul Murphy, remembered that in the Philippines, and upon the return to Atsugi, Oswald was "self-contained and withdrawn."[21] This was the time that Oswald later admitted he first thought of defecting to Russia. The more dissatisfied he became with the Marine Corps, the more he looked for another horizon for fulfillment, and the Soviet Union was increasingly the likely candidate.

He may have been influenced by Japanese Communists who encouraged him to defect. George de Mohrenschildt, later his only friend in Dallas, quoted him as saying: "I had met some Communists in Japan and they got me excited and interested, and that was one of my inducements in going to Soviet Russia, to see what goes on there."[22] Oswald also told de Mohrenschildt that the evidence to bolster his Marxist beliefs was manifest throughout Japan. "He said that while he was in Japan he saw tremendous injustice. . . . the poverty of the Japanese working class or the proletariat, as he called them, and the rich people of Japan. He said it was more visible than anywhere else."[23]

---

*Oswald appears to have been dyslexic. Because of his extensive misspellings, when any of his writing is further quoted herein, the author has omitted "[sic]" after the errors.

His contact with Japanese Communists may have come through a hostess at Tokyo's Queen Bee, one of the three most expensive nightclubs in the capital. The club was frequented by officers and foreign businessmen who ogled the one hundred beautiful hostesses, some of whom were informants for Japanese and foreign intelligence agencies.[24] An evening at the Queen Bee cost anywhere from $60 to $100. Oswald only made $85 a month, and he was extremely tightfisted. By the time he defected in the fall of 1959, he had saved $1,500, nearly 75 percent of his Marine salary during two years of service.[25] That makes it unlikely Oswald bought any dates at the Queen Bee. But some of his fellow Marines saw him with a striking and well-dressed Japanese woman on several occasions, and later during his stay in Japan, he was seen with a Eurasian woman who reportedly spoke Russian.*

Oswald did not discuss his personal life with his fellow Marines, and the more he refused to fit in, the worse he was treated. Corporal Thomas Bagshaw recalled Oswald "was almost frail, shy and quiet," when he arrived at Atsugi. He felt sorry for him because so many other Marines picked on him.[26] When Oswald spent his liberties reading instead of bar-hopping and chasing women, others ridiculed him. They taunted him as "Mrs. Oswald," threw him in the shower fully clothed, and provoked him in every possible way. Fellow Marine Dan Powers recalled, "He was a different individual. . . . He was quiet . . . feminine . . . and a lot of times you felt sorry because the rest of the guys were most of the time picking on him . . ."[27] When Oswald had been in school, since he was a year older than his classmates, he was larger than most, and he often bullied them. In the Marines, he was far from the toughest and, at five feet nine inches, hardly the biggest in his unit. Initially, he did not fight back, instead walking away from any provocation, the anger bottled inside.

After a couple of abusive months, Oswald decided to mix with his fellow Marines. Initially, he tried to be funny, thinking it

---

* Oswald later told Marina that he had had eight sexual relationships while in Japan, though he described only three of the women in detail—one nearly twice his age, one extremely thin and promiscuous, and the last one a fat woman who also cooked for him.

might allow him to be accepted. But those who knew him said he was absolutely humorless and failed completely.[28] He then began socializing, visiting nearby bars, drinking for the first time in his life, and even having his first sexual experience with a bar girl as some of his newfound buddies cheered him on.[29]*

Despite his efforts, Oswald was never completely accepted. Slowly, he became more aggressive, using his knowledge of current affairs to belittle others, especially officers. John Donovan recalled, "He would listen interestedly, ask questions in an interested manner, and then . . . point out a dozen places they didn't know what they were talking about."[30] Nelson Delgado, one of Oswald's fellow Marines, said Oswald tried to "cut up anybody" in those arguments and "make himself come out top dog."[31] Powers noticed that Ozzie Rabbit had changed at Atsugi: "[H]e had started to be more aggressive . . . he took on a new personality, and now he was Oswald the man rather than Oswald the rabbit."[32] Peter Connor remembered that the new Oswald got into several fights and began responding to orders from officers "with insolent remarks."[33] John Heindel said Oswald started drinking a good deal and "was often in trouble for failure to adhere to rules and regulations and gave the impression of disliking any kind of authority."[34]

His anger found a partial release in June 1958, when Oswald confronted Sgt. Miguel Rodriguez, the man he blamed for his long stint on KP duty during the Philippine posting. At the Bluebird Cafe in Yamato, Oswald poured a drink on Rodriguez and challenged him to fight. Military police broke it up before the two went outside. This prompted a second court-martial, on June 27, where Oswald was sentenced to twenty-eight days in the brig and fined $55.[35] His suspended sentence of twenty days from the first court-martial was reinstated. In a performance review, he was given his lowest rating since joining the Marines,

---

* In the autumn of 1958, Oswald was treated for a mild case of venereal disease. The Marine file has a notation "in line of duty, not due to own misconduct." Jim Marrs, without any citation, charges this is "strong evidence that his extracurricular activities had the blessings of the military, if not of the CIA." The truth is much simpler. The doctor who treated him said that such notations were made routinely to avoid having the person's pay jeopardized.

and a previously granted extension of overseas duty was canceled.[36]*

The brig was meant to be punishing. Conversation was prohibited. Except while eating and sleeping, prisoners stood at attention. Even asking to go to the bathroom required standing at attention and repeatedly screaming a request until a guard gave permission. When Oswald was released, other Marines noticed he had changed. He abandoned his unsuccessful attempts to be accepted by them. Joseph Macedo found him cold, withdrawn, and bitter.[37] According to Daniel Powers, his attitude was: "All the Marines did was to teach you to kill, and after you got out of the Marines you might be good gangsters."[38] He remarked he "was tired of getting kicked around."[39]†

---

* Henry Hurt alleges that when Oswald was in the brig, "his fellow Marines . . . were out of touch with him . . . and cannot testify that he was actually confined." Hurt implies the incarceration may have been a cover story so Oswald could continue purported intelligence work. But another Marine, confined in the brig at the same time, confirmed that he remembered seeing Oswald in a single cell during his imprisonment.

As for the general proposition that Oswald was recruited by the CIA while he was a Marine stationed in Japan, the evidence is unconvincing. James B. Wilcott, a former CIA finance officer, claimed that while stationed in Japan after the assassination, he heard that Oswald had worked for the CIA under a special code designation and had been paid from a secret fund for deep cover operations (*Conspiracy*, p. 129). Wilcott admitted he never reported the allegations because he considered the information unreliable hearsay (HSCA Rpt., p. 199). When questioned by the House Select Committee in 1978, he could not remember Oswald's special cryptonym or the project name from which the disbursements allegedly came. CIA employees who served with Wilcott testified Oswald had no contacts to the Agency, and they repudiated Wilcott's tale (HSCA Rpt., pp. 199–200). An intelligence analyst with whom Wilcott claimed to have had a conversation about Oswald was not even posted overseas at the time. The Select Committee concluded: "Based on all the evidence . . . Wilcott's allegation was not worthy of belief" (HSCA Rpt., p. 200). Another source pointing to a possible Oswald intelligence connection during his Marine service is Gerry Patrick Hemming, who served with Oswald in Japan and was himself recruited by the CIA. Hemming, a self-promoter who has provided other outlandish and unproven "disclosures" about the JFK assassination, says that while Oswald never said he was an agent, Hemming had a hunch he was. Hemming's intuition is the extent of his evidence (Marrs, *Crossfire*, p. 104).

† Because of his sullen and changed attitude when released from the brig, Jim Marrs raises the astonishing speculation that Oswald may have been swapped with an identical imposter. He writes, "It may well be right here that a new Oswald—an entirely different man—was substituted for the New Orleans–born Marine." Michael Eddowes, a British author, later wrote an entire

Within two months, on September 14, 1958, Oswald sailed with his unit to Taiwan. A few days after arriving, the constant razzing from his colleagues and his overall frustration at the Marine Corps resulted in a breakdown. One evening while on guard duty, Oswald started firing his M-1 rifle at shadows in the woods. By the time his commanding officer reached him, he was on the floor, slumped against a tree, "shaking and crying."[40] As they walked Oswald back to his tent, he kept repeating that he could no longer bear guard duty. He was sent to Japan to recuperate, returning to Atsugi by October 5. The following day he was transferred out of MACS-1 and placed on general duty.[41] He was reassigned to the Marine squadron at Iwakuni, an air base 430 miles southwest of Tokyo. Owen Dejanovich, who had gone to radar school with him, was stationed at the same base, and immediately noticed that Oswald, now called Bugs by his fellow Marines, referred to them as "you Americans" and spoke of U.S. "imperialism" and "exploitation."[42] Other Marines ignored him.

On November 2, Oswald ended his fourteen-month tour of duty in Japan and sailed for the States. He spent a one-month leave in Fort Worth with his mother and brother, Robert, with whom he went hunting.[43] On December 21, he boarded a bus and reported for his new Marine assignment, the Air Control Squadron Nine, at El Toro, California.[44] It was there that Oswald, disgusted with the Marines, flaunted his Russian studies and Communist leanings. Court-martialed twice, he seemed no longer to care what the Marines did to him.

At El Toro, Oswald subscribed to a Russian-language newspaper that he painstakingly tried to read with the help of a Russian-English dictionary, and played Russian records "so loud that one could hear them outside the barracks."[45] While some Marines continued to call him Ozzie Rabbit, most now dubbed him Oswaldskovich, and he liked it so much that he asked peo-

---

book contending that Oswald had been switched with a KGB assassin while in the Soviet Union. He led an effort to exhume Oswald's corpse, winning the support of Lee's mother and wife. In 1981, the body was dug up from its Texas grave, and forensic pathologists confirmed it was Oswald. Incredibly, the issue still lives, as some conspiracy buffs now claim the body of the real Oswald was swapped back into the grave before the exhumation.

ple to call him that.[46] He peppered his conversations with *da* and *nyet*. Every time a friend played a record containing classical Russian music, Oswald ran to his tent, inquiring, "You called?"[47] Whenever he played chess, he used a set with red pieces to represent the "Red Army." Some Marines kidded him that he was a Russian spy. He liked that.[48] He walked around the camp with his hat pulled so low over his eyes that he could barely see. Extremely sloppy, with unshined shoes and his shirt partially hanging out, looking like a caricature of the cartoon character Beetle Bailey, he bid "Hello, Comrade" to acquaintances.

Fellow Marine Nelson Delgado became friends with Oswald soon after his arrival at El Toro. It was then that Castro was leading his revolutionary army toward Havana. Oswald and Delgado shared a mutual respect for Castro, so much so that they eventually spoke about going to Cuba to fight in the revolution.[49] Oswald kept pressing Delgado for information on how he could get to Cuba, and finally Delgado recalled, "I started getting scared. He started actually making plans . . ."[50] Delgado's enthusiasm waned as Castro's commitment to Communism was exposed in the press. But Oswald told him the U.S. media was full of propaganda that distorted Castro's position. The more he listened to Oswald, Delgado found him a "devout atheist" who preached that the U.S. "was not quite right." He told Delgado that Socialism was the best choice for most people, and complained about how he "hated the military."[51] Among Oswald's reading materials, Delgado saw *Das Kapital*, *Mein Kampf*, and George Orwell's *Animal Farm*.*

Another Marine who knew Oswald even better was Kerry

---

* Delgado tried to deflect Oswald's interest in Cuba by telling him to write to the Cuban embassy in Washington, D.C. Oswald later told Delgado he had been in contact with the Cuban consulate in Los Angeles, but Delgado thought he was lying until he saw a letter in Oswald's belongings with a gold seal on it and assumed it was from the Cubans. On another occasion, Oswald received a visitor at the base, and although Delgado did not see the person and did not even know if it was a man or woman, he assumed it might be someone from the Cuban government. He never asked Oswald. Although Delgado's speculation has no factual foundation and is only his hunch, some critics use it to assert Oswald may have had a Cuban intelligence connection. The Cuban government has officially denied having had any contact with Oswald in 1959.

Thornley. When Thornley met him, around Easter 1959, "he [Oswald] had lost his clearance previously, and if I remember, he was assigned to make the coffee, mow the lawn, swab down decks, and things of this nature." Thornley enjoyed debating philosophy, politics, and religion with him. Thornley, who described himself as "an extreme rightist," thought Oswald such an unusual character that he wrote a preassassination novel based on him (it was not published until 1991).[52] Over the course of half a dozen discussions, Thornley was convinced Oswald believed that capitalism exploited workers and that "Communism was the best system in the world." Oswald was also "quite sure that Castro was a great hero."[53] Once, Thornley recounted, "he looked at me and he said, 'What do you think of communism?' And I replied I didn't think too much of communism, in a favorable sense, and he said, 'Well, I think the best religion is communism.' "[54] Thornley found it difficult to debate issues regarding the Soviet Union since Oswald challenged any information "on the grounds that we were probably propagandized in this country and we had no knowledge of what was going on over there."

Thornley thought he was "emotionally unstable" and "unpredictable." "He got along with very few people," he recalled. "He seemed to guard against developing real close friendships."[55] Before long, Thornley and Oswald had a falling out, when Oswald griped about a march they were scheduled to be in. Thornley commented, "Well, comes the revolution you will change all that." Oswald's voice cracked as he screamed at Thornley. He put his hands in his pockets, pulled his cap low over his eyes, and sat by himself. He never spoke to Thornley after that. "Well, at the time I just thought," recalled Thornley, "well, the man is a nut. . . . He had a definite tendency toward irrationality at times, an emotional instability." He also found Oswald "impulsive," burdened by a "persecution complex," and said that he never showed any affection to anyone, and nobody ever showed any in return.[56] By the end of their relationship Thornley thought Oswald was "pathetic."[57]*

---

* Jim Garrison provides snippets of quotes from seven Marines saying they never heard Oswald talk about Communism, the Soviet Union, or Cuba. He

There is, of course, the question of why the Marines tolerated Oswald's flagrant study of Russian and subscription to Russian-language newspapers as well as leftist publications like *The Worker*. None of his fellow Marines reported that he proselytized Communism during basic training or during his fourteen months in Japan. He complained about the Marines, but that was not thought to be unique. Oswald did study the Russian language, but not in the conspicuous way that he did later at El Toro. Even one of his commanding officers in Japan studied the language. While he may have been considered a Russophile, he gave the Marines no reason to believe he might be a security threat.

Only after arriving at El Toro, and following his two court-martials and nervous breakdown while on guard duty, did Oswald flaunt his controversial and brazen behavior. By then, he had been busted to buck private, had spent time in the brig, and was already known as an eccentric troublemaker. Instead of working as a trained radar operator, he had been reduced to doing janitorial work around the base.[58]

Only one officer is known to have taken him seriously. When an El Toro mailroom clerk informed his operations chief, Captain Robert E. Block, that Oswald was receiving leftist literature, Block confronted him. Oswald dissembled that he was merely trying to indoctrinate himself in the enemies' philosophy, according to Marine Corps policy. Although skeptical, Block dropped the matter. Except for Block, others viewed Oswald as peculiar but harmless.

Near the end of his tour of duty, Oswald began a series of

---

concludes, "The statements of Oswald's other associates at the Marine base were almost uniform in their agreement that he had no inclination in the direction of communism or anything leftwing" (*On the Trail of the Assassins*, pp. 52–53). Garrison writes that Thornley "had not served with Oswald as long as a number of others and had not even lived on the same part of the base. . . . The other Marines' affidavits . . . overwhelmingly contradicted Thornley's claims." But Thornley did live on the same part of the base as Oswald, though they were in different Quonset huts (WC Vol. XI, p. 85). The other Marines' affidavits did not contradict Thornley's testimony—they only said Oswald did not talk to them about the same things he discussed with Thornley. Thornley is not even listed in the indexes for books by Robert Groden and Harrison Livingstone, Henry Hurt, John Davis, David Scheim, Mark Lane, and Josiah Thompson.

maneuvers intended to sever his Marine ties and prepare for his defection to the USSR. In March 1959, he applied for admission to a small liberal arts school in Churwalden, Switzerland, the Albert Schweitzer College.[59] After a discharge from the Marines, Oswald was expected to fulfill a three-year inactive-reserve commitment.[60] During that period, foreign travel was only allowed for a valid reason. Attending a Swiss school would qualify him for overseas travel. He lied extensively on the school application, and he was accepted.*

On August 17, Oswald submitted a request for a dependency discharge on the ground that his mother needed his support.[61] A candy jar had fallen off a shelf while Marguerite was at work and hurt her nose. Although several doctors could find nothing wrong with her, she claimed she was totally disabled and finally found a physician who agreed.[62] She sent her own affidavit, as well as affidavits from a doctor and two friends, attesting to her injury and maintaining she could not support herself.[63] Oswald's request for a dependency discharge was approved two weeks later. On September 4, 1959, he was transferred to another squadron, the H&H, in preparation for his release.[64] That day he also applied at the superior court of Santa Ana, California, for a passport. Citing the primary purpose of his trip as attending Albert Schweitzer College in Switzerland and Turku University in Finland, he also listed England, France, Germany, Russia, Cuba, and the Dominican Republic as places of intended travel.[65] The passport was routinely issued six days later.[66]

Oswald was discharged from the Marines on September 11, 1959, and he traveled by bus to Fort Worth, where he arrived at his mother's house in the early morning hours of September 14. The next day he shocked Marguerite by informing her that he was about to board a ship and was going to work for an import-export business.[67] He withdrew $203 from his only bank account, at the West Side State Bank, gave $100 to his mother, and left for New Orleans on September 16.[68] There, he purchased a

---

* On the application, he said he intended to take a summer course at the University of Turku in Finland. He never contacted that school. However, since he intended to apply for a Soviet visa in the less-trafficked consulate in Helsinki, the statement on the application provided him an excuse for traveling to Finland.

one-way ticket for passage on the freighter *Marion Lykes*, scheduled to leave for Le Havre, France, on September 18.[69] During his final night in New Orleans, he wrote his mother and warned her: "Just remember above all else that my values are different from Robert's or your's. It is difficult to tell you how I feel, Just remember this is what I must do. I did not tell you about my plans because you could hardly be expected to understand."[70]

Although completely ignorant of his intent to defect, two Marine acquaintances would not have been entirely surprised if they had known. Mack Osborne recalled: "I once asked Oswald why he did not go out in the evening like the other men. He replied that he was saving his money, making some statement to the effect that one day he would do something which would make him famous." Kerry Thornley had also heard Oswald talk of fame. "He wanted to be on the winning side so that 10,000 years from now people would look in the history books and say, 'Well, this man was ahead of his time.' . . . He wanted to be looked back upon with honor by future generations. He was concerned with his image in history. . . . He expected the Russians to accept him on a much higher capacity . . . to invite him to take a position in their government, possibly as a technician. . . . He then felt he could go out into the Communist world and distinguish himself . . ."[71]

Two days behind schedule, on September 20, 1959, the *Marion Lykes* left for Europe.

3

The War of the Defectors

In June 1962, a thirty-five-year-old KGB officer attached to the Soviet disarmament delegation in Geneva approached an American diplomat and offered to trade information for money. That request was the beginning of one of the most controversial episodes in CIA history, the case of Yuriy Nosenko,* a key to unlocking important pieces of the Oswald puzzle.

Nosenko sought permanent asylum in the U.S. in January 1964, only two months after the Kennedy assassination. His story stunned the CIA. He claimed to be a lieutenant colonel responsible for compromising Americans visiting Moscow. That meant Oswald was under his jurisdiction when the Marine first defected to the Soviet Union. After the assassination, he was temporarily assigned to investigate whether there was ever any KGB-Oswald relationship. According to Nosenko, although Soviet intelligence kept Oswald under surveillance, it viewed him as mentally unfit, had not debriefed him, and had no relationship with him. If that was true, it meant the KGB and the Soviet Union were absolved of any complicity in JFK's murder. If it was false, Nosenko could be a phony defector, intended, among other things, to deflect the Warren Commission from focusing

---

*The transliteration of names from the Russian Cyrillic alphabet used herein is the same system utilized by American intelligence and regarded as academically correct by the CIA's Soviet Division. It results in spellings that are often different from popular ones.

on evidence of the real Soviet role with Oswald. The overall question of whether he was a bona fide defector or a KGB plant became the most divisive issue within the Agency since its establishment: Is Nosenko a bona fide defector, and is his information about Oswald reliable?

When Nosenko contacted an American diplomat in 1962, the CIA was immediately notified. It dispatched thirty-seven-year-old Tennant "Pete" Bagley and an agent fluent in Russian, George Kisevalter, to meet Nosenko four times at a safe house near Geneva's center.[1] Nosenko said he was dissatisfied with the Soviet system and asked for some money in exchange for information. He refused to be contacted inside the USSR for fear of exposure.[2]

CIA transcripts reveal that at those meetings, Nosenko provided critical leads on a number of intelligence cases. Among other disclosures, he exposed KGB spies in the U.S. embassy in Moscow, the British admiralty, and in the U.S. Army;[3] revealed new Soviet surveillance technologies; pinpointed the location of hidden microphones in the U.S. embassy; and startled his CIA contacts by claiming that both Canadian ambassador John Watkins and prominent U.S. newspaper columnist Joe Alsop were homosexuals who were compromised by the KGB.[4]*

Bagley was ecstatic with the information, and not only considered Nosenko bona fide but the most important Soviet agent ever recruited by the CIA.[5] However, Bagley was shocked when he returned to CIA headquarters because the chief of counterintelligence, James Jesus Angleton, was convinced that no matter what Nosenko said, he was a KGB plant.

The reason for Angleton's distrust was another defector who had arrived in America six months earlier, Anatoliy Golitsyn. Golitsyn had told the extremely cynical Angleton that the CIA was penetrated by a high-ranking KGB agent code-named Sasha. The possibility that the CIA was compromised, as British intelligence had been by Kim Philby, was Angleton's worst fear.

---

* Because Alsop was a good friend of President Kennedy, the CIA's assistant deputy director for plans ordered those references cut from the Nosenko interview tapes.

Accepting Golitsyn's revelations without hesitation, he embarked the CIA on a twenty-year hunt for a phantom mole that destroyed careers of good officers and split the Agency.

Not only was Angleton convinced the mole existed, but Golitsyn further warned him that the KGB would send "defectors" intended to deflect the interest in Sasha. That is how they viewed Nosenko. When Nosenko was asked if there was a KGB mole in the CIA, he said no. Told of his reply, Golitsyn reached an instant conclusion: "This is disinformation. The KGB wants me to appear bad to you. This is going to damage my leads."[6] Bagley, too, was soon convinced Nosenko was a plant. His information was dismissed either as stale or as exposing expendable KGB operations.

Completely unaware the CIA thought he was a double agent, Nosenko prepared for his eventual goal, defection. For the remainder of 1962 and all of 1963, he committed to memory the details of more than three hundred new leads and almost two thousand names for the Agency.[7] In January 1964, Nosenko arrived in Geneva as part of the Soviet disarmament delegation and immediately used his prearranged signal to call a meeting with the CIA. The same two agents who had met him in 1962, Bagley and Kisevalter, flew in from Washington.[8]

Nosenko first surprised the agents by announcing, "Gentlemen, I am not going back, so how about that?"[9] Bagley, convinced Nosenko was a fake, tried to dissuade him from defecting, encouraging him to stay in the Soviet Union even though Nosenko had disclosed his knowledge about Oswald.[10] At a second meeting, a week later, the disagreement over his defection continued, with Nosenko increasingly concerned the KGB might uncover his treachery. Five days later, in the final meeting, Nosenko announced he had received a cable ordering him home immediately. He feared the KGB had unmasked him and his return meant arrest and execution.[11] "Gentlemen," he told the two CIA agents, "I don't know about you, but this hour, this minute, I have defected. I am not going back."[12] The story of the cable left the CIA with little choice since the Agency feared the repercussions of losing an agent who might have information about

Oswald. Headquarters authorized his defection, and within days he passed through Germany and was in the U.S.*

Nosenko's statement about the recall cable and his declaration that he had been promoted to lieutenant colonel are central issues used to contest his credibility. There was no recall cable. Confronted with this fact, Nosenko explained he fabricated the story because he feared that otherwise Bagley would not allow him to defect.[13] The story about the cable accomplished its purpose, forcing the CIA to spirit him to the West. "To this day, I do not regret making that false statement," he says.† "Without that 'cable,' they would have brushed me off."[14] If he had been a plant, the KGB would almost have certainly provided him with a cable to keep his cover story intact.

The questions raised about his declaration that he was a lieutenant colonel are more complex. Many assassination-conspiracy books say that CIA document experts determined that Nosenko could not have held the rank or position he claimed in the KGB and that travel papers he had in his possession had been concocted to give his defection credibility.[15] Are these doubts about his veracity warranted?

When Nosenko first contacted the CIA in 1962 he was indeed a captain. In the spring of 1963, however, he was appointed to lieutenant colonel by his close friend Major General Oleg Gribanov, the director of the Second Chief Directorate.‡ Although his rank was approved by the Party Committee and Personnel Directorate, Nosenko had to wait for the KGB chairman's annual approval of all promotions. His travel document did say he was a lieutenant colonel, but since he defected before the chairman's

---

* Since Nosenko defected less than two months after the assassination, some believe the two events are connected. Nosenko is adamant that defection was his goal since 1962 but that 1964 was his first opportunity. Disarmament negotiations were postponed twice in 1963. "If there had been a meeting as scheduled in the spring of 1963, I would have defected then, six months before the assassination," he says. "I had always planned to defect in 1963."

† In this book, when a person is quoted in the present tense, it indicates that the statement was obtained during an interview by the author. The past tense is used for quotations from other sources.

‡ Later defectors revealed that Gribanov was dismissed after Nosenko's defection and ended his life as a drunk, wandering Moscow's bars with a KGB handler.

approval, the CIA could not verify that rank.[16] The Agency mistakenly assumed the higher rank was part of a false legend prepared for Nosenko.

When Nosenko first arrived in the U.S., he was placed in a safe house. He did not know that his CIA debriefers were only interested in exposing him as a liar. However, when J. Edgar Hoover learned about him, he immediately obtained access for the FBI. A deep-cover FBI informant at the Soviet mission to the United Nations, code-named Fedora, personally confirmed to Hoover that Nosenko was bona fide and that his defection had caused an uproar in the highest Kremlin circles.

The FBI believed Nosenko about Oswald and supported his request to testify before the Warren Commission. But Angleton outmaneuvered them. Richard Helms, then deputy director of plans, met privately with Earl Warren on June 24, 1964, and informed him the CIA doubted Nosenko's credibility.[17] Helms warned that if the Commission used his information and it was a lie, it would ruin the rest of their work.[18] Nosenko did not testify and is not even mentioned in the Commission's twenty-six volumes.

Helms did not tell the Chief Justice that since early April, with the backing of attorney general Robert Kennedy, Nosenko had been under hostile interrogation, treated as a captured spy rather than a voluntary defector. The FBI was denied access to him, and his CIA jailers expected him to crack within a few weeks. Robert Kennedy called frequently to discover whether he had confessed yet.

Nosenko's ordeal had started on April 4, 1964, when he was driven to a three-story safe house in a Washington suburb. He was given a medical exam and then strapped to a polygraph machine.[19] The operator, Nick Stoiaken, knew the CIA thought Nosenko was a liar. After an hour of questions, Stoiaken made a big show of discussing the prearranged results with some of the CIA personnel. Then Bagley appeared and denounced Nosenko as a "liar." Several guards rushed into the room. Nosenko was stripped, inspected inside his mouth, ears, and rectum, and then marched into the house's tiny attic, which would serve as his prison for more than a year.

The windows were boarded over. The only furniture was a

metal bed fastened to the middle of the floor. Guards watched him twenty-four hours a day through a wire mesh screen built into the door. The room had no heat or air-conditioning, and during the oppressive Washington summers it was like a furnace. Nosenko was given little food, allowed to shower only once a week, and not allowed a toothbrush or toothpaste.* Human contact was banned. There was no television, radio, reading material, exercise, or cigarettes. He was told he would be kept like that for twenty-five years. The interrogations, which began within days, were extremely aggressive. He was constantly attacked as a KGB plant and told his only chance for freedom was to confess. Over the months, the CIA agents became increasingly frustrated that he refused to admit he was a bogus defector. Robert Kennedy had long since stopped telephoning for an update, and the Warren Commission had released its report. Nosenko was a forgotten man, a prisoner of the CIA.

On August 13, 1965, after sixteen months closeted in the attic, Nosenko was moved by the CIA to a new prison, a top-secret facility constructed especially for him. Located on the grounds of the CIA's training facility, Camp Peary, it made the attic seem luxurious. On a heavily wooded site on the ten-thousand-acre compound, Nosenko was locked inside a ten-foot-by-ten-foot windowless concrete bunker. A single bare bulb illuminated the room's only piece of furniture, a metal bed so small that his feet hung over the edges. The luxuries from the attic—a pillow, sheet, and blanket—were gone. The bunker accentuated the weather, either brutally hot or freezing cold.[20] A ceiling camera monitored him. His allotted food was lowered to the subsistence level. Documents reveal that while the government spent $1.5 million to construct and man the prison, it spent less than a dollar a day feeding him.

After four months, he was finally allowed to walk in a small enclosed yard that had been constructed outside his jail. It was the first time in nearly two years he had seen daylight or been in fresh air. The yard was encircled with a twelve-foot-high chain-

---

*Because he was deprived of dental care for nearly two years, he later suffered severe gum disease, which led to the loss of most of his teeth.

link fence, and several feet beyond was an eighteen-foot-high fence of solid material.[21] The CIA did not want anyone, even at Camp Peary, to see what had become of him.

He tried to keep his sanity in a variety of ways. When his jailers finally allowed him to brush his teeth after two years in captivity, he was so starved for something to read that he secretly kept a printed piece of paper from the toothpaste package. Though it was only a list of ingredients, he kept rereading it until his guards saw him and confiscated it. Another time he painstakingly created a makeshift deck of cards from shreds of paper napkins. The guards watched him for several weeks and destroyed it on the day he completed it. The same happened to a chess set he fashioned from pieces of lint.[22]

Meanwhile, each subsequent Soviet defector who knew of the Nosenko case vouched for his bona fides.[23]* Most of them, like Colonel Oleg Gordievskiy, were quite surprised to learn that the CIA thought Nosenko was a plant, and told the Agency of the KGB's panicked reactions when he had fled to the West.[24] Nosenko had been tried in absentia and was to be executed on his recapture.† But to Angleton and Golitsyn, the moment a defector vouched for Nosenko's bona fides, it branded that defector as a plant. Angleton concluded that in the decade after Golitsyn, the Soviets sent twenty-two phony defectors to the U.S.[25] Today, the CIA and FBI consider every one of those defectors as bona fide.[26]

Instead of being persuaded by growing evidence that Nosenko might be authentic, Angleton and Bagley grew increasingly impatient and debated drugging him to hasten his breakdown. Internal documents show an assortment of drugs were considered, including a so-called truth serum, an amphetamine, and even LSD. Nosenko is positive he was drugged, recalling injec-

---

* Every Soviet defector to the U.S. who was in a position to know about the Nosenko case confirmed his bona fides. Of the fifteen who have confirmed Nosenko, the following are considered by CIA officials to be the ten most important (their year of defection is in parentheses): Yuriy Loginov (1961); Igor Kochnov (1966); Oleg Lyalin (1971); Rudolf Herrmann (1980); Ilya Dzhirkvelov (1980); Vladimir Kuzichkin (1984); Viktor Gundarev (1985); Vitaliy Yurchenko (1985); Ivan Bogattyy (1985); and Oleg Gordievskiy (1985).

† The KGB had no intention of returning Nosenko to Russia. Plans had been preapproved to liquidate him once he was found.

tions by CIA doctors, followed by days of panic and terror. "Once, following an injection, I couldn't breathe," he remembers. "I was dying."[27] His guards dragged him to a shower, where they ran alternating hot and cold water to revive him.[28]

In October 1966, two and a half years after he was placed into solitary confinement, and shortly after the incidents with drugs, a second polygraph was administered. Nosenko recalls it was "even uglier than the first."[29] Without any warning, the same doctor who had examined him in April 1964 conducted a physical. During the exam, the doctor inserted a gloved finger inside Nosenko's rectum and, over his protests, wriggled it around for some ten minutes.[30] The doctor suggested he liked the degradation. Nosenko is certain this was done to anger him and stimulate his blood pressure, a key factor in affecting polygraph readings.[31]

After the "exam," he was immediately hooked to the machinery. The same operator, Nick Stoiaken, conducted the test. But instead of asking yes and no questions as on the first test, he spent an hour calling Nosenko a "liar" and asking demeaning questions about alleged homosexuality.[32] Then Stoiaken took a lunch break, leaving Nosenko strapped to the machine. Guards ensured he did not move.

When Stoiaken returned a couple of hours later, he continued the questioning for another two hours.[33] No matter how Nosenko responded or what the polygraph showed, Stoiaken said he was a liar. It was conducted so he would fail. Shortly after the test, Bagley presented him a fake confession that admitted he was a plant and there were moles inside the CIA. Nosenko took a pencil and turned to the last page. Summoning his last reserves of strength, he scrawled near the signature line, "Not true."[34]

Bagley was infuriated. His desperation was evident when he soon made a list of how the festering case could be closed. Included among the choices were "liquidate the man," "render him incapable of giving [a] coherent story (special dose of drug, etc)," or committing him to a "loony bin without making him nuts."[35]

After the second polygraph, Nosenko was at his lowest point since defecting. But unknown to him, his fortunes were about to improve. In June 1966, Richard Helms became the Agency's director.[36] Although undecided about Nosenko's bona fides, he knew the matter had to be resolved. Within several months of Helms's taking office, he assigned a complete review to Bruce Solie, a sixteen-year veteran and the Agency's most experienced spycatcher. To offset Helms's moves, Angleton and Bagley produced a nine-hundred-page report detailing why Nosenko was a plant.

Without deciding whether Nosenko was bona fide, it took Solie six months to determine that the Angleton/Bagley work was seriously flawed, more an unchallenged prosecutor's brief than an impartial report. As a result of Solie's preliminary conclusions, CIA guards entered the concrete bunker, blindfolded, handcuffed, and shackled Nosenko, and stuffed him into the backseat of a car. He thought they were finally going to kill him. Instead, they drove him to a small CIA safe house in a Washington suburb. After three and a half years, he was no longer in solitary confinement. He was soon moved to a farmhouse, where he was given a comfortable bedroom, ate normal meals, and could exercise. However, he was still the Agency's prisoner, and during 1968 Solie interviewed him, often six days a week. He found a very different man than the one portrayed by Angleton and Bagley.

In early 1968 the Soviet Division of the CIA, technically responsible for defectors, received a new director, Rolfe Kingsley, and he ordered a complete review of his department's Nosenko files. In debriefing files tucked away in a safe, he was astonished to discover the defector had provided six solid leads about Soviet penetration of European allies. When the information was turned over to foreign governments, Soviet spies were arrested.[37] Angleton dismissed them as disposable KGB assets.

In August 1968, after eight months of interviews with Solie, Nosenko had a third polygraph, the only valid test he was ever given. It was monitored by several Agency departments. He passed it, including those questions about whether he was telling the truth about Lee Harvey Oswald.[38] One month later, Solie submitted his final 283-page report. It was the first CIA document to accept Nosenko as a bona fide defector. J. Edgar Hoover received a copy and dispatched FBI agents to interview

Nosenko for the first time in over four years. They discovered nine new counterintelligence cases and seventy-five leads on pending cases.[39]

After Solie's report, Nosenko's conditions significantly improved. Although still confined to the farmhouse, he was allowed to read books and newspapers and given a small black-and-white television. Starved for news, he asked for the 1964–67 copies of the *World Almanac*. In December, almost five years after his arrival in the U.S., he was allowed to visit public places, as long as CIA handlers accompanied him.[40]

While Angleton watched with frustration, the Soviet Division's independent review also declared Nosenko a bona fide defector. In March 1969, Helms employed him as an independent consultant on the KGB, at a salary of $16,500 per year, and arranged for limited compensation for his illegal imprisonment. By April, five years after he was locked into an attic, he was released from all security restrictions. He changed his name and married within a year.

All six directors of Central Intelligence who followed Helms agreed that Nosenko was a bona fide defector.[41] The FBI never wavered from its initial determination of his bona fides. The official CIA position today is that Nosenko is the most valuable KGB defector to come to the West as of 1964.

Yet despite the gross injustice done to him, and the historical correction at the CIA, some still disparage his bona fides. Anthony Summers, in *Conspiracy*, dubs the Nosenko information about Oswald "a fairy story from the KGB" and, in particular, terms his testimony that the KGB had not questioned Oswald about his military service a "blithe assertion."[42] The first two polygraph results are sometimes used to malign his credibility, without any description about the conditions in which the tests were conducted. Edward Epstein, in *Legend*, says CIA "experts . . . carefully analyzed" the results and "[a]ccording to the evaluation by the Office of Security, Nosenko had failed his first lie detector test."[43] In *Crossfire*, Jim Marrs covers the barbaric multiyear treatment in three sentences.[44] He then concludes: "Toward the end of the ordeal, Nosenko was given at least two lie detector tests by the CIA. He failed both."

Assassination critics are not the only ones to use the first polygraph results to impugn Nosenko's bona fides. The House Select Committee on Assassinations, in 1977–78, was the first government body, independent of the intelligence community, to study the case and was "unable to resolve the Nosenko matter."[45] The committee stated that his earlier handling by the CIA "virtually ruined him as a valid source of information about the assassination."[46] Moreover, it was certain Nosenko had lied about Oswald, either to the FBI and CIA in 1964 or to the committee in 1978, or to both. There were two reasons for its finding.

First, it commissioned an independent polygraph expert, Richard Arther, president of the Scientific Lie Detection, Inc., to evaluate Nosenko's three polygraph tests. He concluded the second test (the most abusive exam) was "valid and reliable."[47] Yet Arther did not interview any of the participants, did not know of the hostile conditions surrounding the test, was not aware that Nosenko was strapped to the machine for nearly six hours, and was not given any of the operator's tape recordings or handwritten notes. He reached his conclusion solely by reviewing the official, typed reports of the test.[48]

Second, the Select Committee used Nosenko's statements from hostile interrogations to impeach his current testimony. In its own investigation in 1967, the CIA discovered there were massive errors in the translation of the interviews conducted before and during Nosenko's imprisonment.[49] Not only did the interrogators often misunderstand his broken English, but Bagley and Angleton further distorted the record by overlaying their own interpretations into the transcript. Those were the answers often used by the Select Committee to establish whether Nosenko's 1978 testimony was consistent and truthful. While Nosenko pleaded that the hostile interrogations not be used against him, the committee's counsel persisted. Finally, Nosenko refused to answer any more questions and the interview abruptly ended.

"I had expected a fair hearing from a congressional committee," Nosenko told the author. "I was terribly disappointed. They seemed to have made up their minds before I ever spoke to them. The staff had been impressed by Golitsyn, and then by Angleton. No matter what I said, it wasn't going to affect their decision. But they still performed their duty by talking to me. From the beginning, I sensed the hostility."

Nosenko has been questioned twice about his CIA treatment, but the interview he granted for this book is the first that focused on Oswald. Although he is no longer a full-time counterintelligence consultant for the Agency, there are still paramount concerns for Nosenko's security. Nothing about him can be reported, particularly personal details that might compromise his new identity. When Edward Jay Epstein briefly interviewed him in the mid-1970s, the same restrictions applied. At one point Epstein asked Nosenko where he had been relocated. Nosenko claims that after swearing him to secrecy, he revealed the state. Epstein printed it. "He blew me," Nosenko remembers angrily. "It was treachery."*

In 1964, the CIA drafted 130 questions it intended to ask Nosenko about Oswald but never did. In the interview for this book, those questions were put to him, and the substance of his answers are included in this and the following chapter. Also included are the revelations reported in an extensive four-part series in 1992 by *Izvestiya* about Oswald's KGB file, No. 31451, domiciled in Minsk. The *Izvestiya* series not only provided details from the file but included interviews with those in Minsk who knew Oswald. That both supplements and confirms the information from Nosenko.†

When Oswald defected in 1959, a foreigner could not visit the USSR without a visa and the purchase of a preset package tour. That ensured all foreigners were in regular contact with personnel of the Soviet tourist agency, Intourist, which, according to Nosenko, was an organization made up entirely of KGB informants or agents.[50] An Intourist guide, Rima Shirokova, played an important role in Oswald's first weeks in Russia.

---

* The author tried to obtain a comment from Epstein regarding Nosenko's accusation, but Epstein never returned the author's telephone calls.

† In the summer of 1992, the chairman of the Belorus KGB, Eduard Shirkovskiy, denied reports that the Oswald file was available to the highest bidder, and claimed he had been offered, and rejected, $50 million for it. Yet by the fall the KGB had reportedly reached an arrangement (the terms undisclosed) with Norman Mailer for access to the file.

Oswald arrived in Helsinki on October 10, 1959, and applied for his visa from the Soviet consulate on October 12. He purchased $300 of Intourist vouchers.[51] The Soviets issued his visa in two days,[52] and it was valid until October 20, allowing him to take one trip of not more than six days to the Soviet Union.[53] Questions have been raised about the speed with which the visa was issued. Summers says, "Oswald's easy access had encouraged the belief that the Soviets were expecting him."[54] According to Nosenko, that speculation shows no understanding of how the Soviet tourist system worked. Nosenko should know, since he was deputy chief of the KGB's Tourist Division in the Second Chief Directorate. Thousands of tourist applications were processed annually, and only a cursory review was given the forms, with the names checked against a security watch list. Also, the Soviet consul in Helsinki, Gregory Golub, had the authority to give Americans an instant visa if he was convinced the tourist was "all right."[55]

In Oswald's case, he was nineteen years old, did not list his Marine service or any current employer, and said he was a student traveler.[56] "There was nothing of interest on his visa application," remembers Nosenko.[57] It was routinely approved, and since Helsinki was not as busy as London, Paris, or other major European capitals, its visa processing was quick. Two days was well within the ordinary time for that consulate.[58]

Oswald arrived in Moscow on October 16. He was taken by an Intourist representative to the Hotel Berlin.[59] Since the KGB had no inkling that he was anything but a student visitor, it had absolutely no interest in him until his Intourist guide, Rima Shirokova, informed them that, on his second day in Moscow, Oswald had told her he wanted to defect and become a Soviet citizen.

Oswald's defection to Russia seemed so well planned that some refuse to believe he accomplished it by himself. Garrison puts the word *defection* in quotation marks and Jim Marrs says Oswald was a "fake defector." But in fact Oswald had carefully planned for his defection. His disciplined savings from his Marine Corps salary, maneuvers for an early discharge, and rudimentary study of the Russian language all suggest long-term preparation. He confirmed this after his arrival in Moscow, writing to his brother, Robert, that he had thought of defecting for over a year.[60] To a reporter in Moscow, Aline Mosby, he admitted even longer: "For two years I've had it in my mind, don't form any attachments, because I knew I was going away. I was planning to divest myself of everything to do with the United States."[61]

He boasted of his reasons for defecting, telling his brother that Communism was the wave of the future: "Look at a world map! America is a dieing country, I do not wish to be a part of it, nor do I ever again wish to be used as a tool in its military aggressions."[62] Aline Mosby and another correspondent in Russia, Priscilla Johnson, were both impressed that his reasons were strictly ideological, and Johnson found his commitment to Communism "extraordinary" in light of his age.[63] Mosby remembered that as he spoke of *Das Kapital*, "his eyes shone like those of a religious enthusiast."[64] For two hours he lectured her that "capitalism has passed its peak," that "the Soviet Union has always been my ideal, as the bulwark of communism," and that he was sick of the American "hysteria . . . hating communists or niggers."[65]

"He appeared totally disinterested in anything but himself," Mosby recalled. "He talked almost non-stop like the type of semi-educated person of little experience who clutches what he regards as some sort of unique truth."[66]

His Intourist guide, Shirokova, was instructed to assist Oswald in his dealings with the government and to help him draft a letter to the Supreme Soviet formally requesting citizenship.[67] October 18, two days after he arrived in Russia, was his twentieth birthday. Shirokova gave him Dostoevski's *The Idiot* and inscribed it: "Dear Lee, Great Congratulations! Let all your dreams come true!"[68]

One of Nosenko's subordinates, Major Rastrusin, prepared a small file, including statements about Oswald from the Intourist and hotel informants.[69] From that moment Nosenko took charge of the matter. Although Oswald had declared his intention to defect, Nosenko is adamant the KGB did not interrogate him. Summers charges that "is transparent nonsense." Garrison said,

"The newcomer [Oswald] underwent extensive interrogation, although when, where, and under what circumstances have never been revealed."[70]

"Not true," insists Nosenko. "The KGB was not at all interested in him. I cannot emphasize that enough—absolutely no interest."[71] But what of Oswald's Marine background and his service at Atsugi, where the U-2 spy plane was based? The Soviets had made the U-2 a top priority and finally shot one down on May 1, 1960, less than seven months after Oswald's arrival. "People who raise this point do not understand intelligence work," he says. "I am surprised that such a big deal is made of the fact that he was a Marine. Even the House Select Committee kept saying to me, 'But he was a Marine—that must have interested the KGB.' I was astonished at their naiveté. So what is the big deal that he was in the Marines? First, he wasn't in the Marines any longer, but even if he had come to us in a uniform, we still would have had no interest. What was he in the Marine Corps—a major, a captain, a colonel? We had better information already coming from KGB sources than he could ever give us.

"If he had been a Marine guard at the U.S. embassy, then we would have been very interested. But that wasn't the case with Oswald.

"As for Atsugi, we didn't know he had been based there. The media section of the KGB would have seen Oswald's public interviews, but they would not necessarily have transferred that information to us. Even if we knew about Atsugi, it is unlikely we would have spoken to him. Our intelligence on the U-2 was good and had been for some time."[72] The Soviets already had considerable knowledge about the plane. They had often tracked its path, speed, and altitude. Intelligence experts on the U-2 concur that Oswald could not have contributed to its eventual downing, as some have suggested.[73]

Though Oswald was not interrogated in depth, he was questioned by KGB informants, including Shirokova. On October 19, he was interviewed by Radio Moscow correspondent Lev Setyayev. While the purported reason was to record Oswald's impressions as a tourist for broadcast overseas, Setyayev was also an informant for the KGB.[74] Based on the information it received, Nosenko's department vetoed Oswald's request for citizenship. "We had no reason to let him stay," remembers Nosenko. "Soviet citizenship was not something lightly given out to foreigners and there was certainly no reason to make an exception for Oswald.

"We did not have many defectors that wanted to live in Russia.* We were realistic about living conditions in Russia. [Robert] Webster, another defector who had arrived shortly before Oswald, was happy for three or four months, but then he missed the conveniences of home and wanted to go back to America. It was an unusual person who decided to defect as a civilian to Russia. And, of course, we could never totally dismiss the idea that any of these defectors might be a provocation from American intelligence. In the case of Oswald, we simply didn't want him and thought it best to send him home."

On October 21, Oswald was called to the Ministry of Foreign Affairs. There was only one day left on his six-day visa. The official was discouraging about his chance for obtaining citizenship but said he would check on extending his visa. Later that afternoon, Oswald's citizenship request was officially denied and he was told he must leave Moscow within two hours.[75]

Nosenko later learned the details of what happened next. "His Intourist guide went to the Berlin Hotel to pick him up. He was late by ten minutes, and then by twenty minutes, so she went to the duty clerk on his floor.† The clerk did not have his key, which meant he was still in the room. She got the manager of the hotel and told him she was worried about Oswald, and together they went to his room. They knocked and called his name and received no answer. When they entered the room [with an extra key], they found Oswald with his wrist cut and blood all over."[76]

In his diary, Oswald wrote what happened after he received the news that his citizenship request was rejected: "I am stunned. . . . Eve. 6.00 Recive word from police official. I must

---

* Records show that fourteen Americans defected to Communist countries from 1958 through 1960. Two went to China, one to East Germany, and the remaining eleven to Russia, four of those with their wives.

† Each floor at the main Soviet tourist hotels had a clerk, termed the *dezhurnaya*. When a tourist left his room, he was required to give the key to the clerk for safekeeping. Nosenko says all such clerks were KGB informants.

leave country tonight at. 8.00 P.M. as visa expirs. I am shocked!!
My dreams! I retire to my room. I have $100 left. I have waited
for 2 year to be accepted. My fondes dreams are shattered because of a petty offial; because of bad planning I planned too
much! 7:00 P.M. I decide to end it. Soak rist in cold water to
numb the pain. Than slash my left wrist. Than plaug wrist into
bathtub of hot water. I think 'when Rimma comes at 8. to find
me dead it wil be a great shock. somewhere, a violin plays, as I
wacth my life whirl away. I think to myself. 'how easy to die'
and 'a sweet death, (to violins)."[77]*

Oswald was rushed by ambulance to nearby Botkinskaya Hospital. Blood transfusions stabilized him. Nosenko reports:
"When Oswald regained consciousness, he was asked why he
did it. He said, 'I'm not leaving here.' "[78] Oswald's KGB file reveals that a note written in English was discovered on the table
near his bed in his hotel room. It read: "Did I come here just to
find death? I love life."[79]

Prompted by his suicide attempt, the KGB ordered a mental
evaluation. Oswald was transferred to a psychiatric ward at
Botkinskaya, where he was kept for three days.[80] "We had two
psychiatrists, neither of whom was a KGB doctor, examine
him," recalls Nosenko. "One was on the Botkin staff and the
other came in from outside. I read their reports. Both concluded
he was 'mentally unstable.' It made us feel one hundred percent
that he should be avoided at all costs." A transcript, maintained
in the KGB files, of a conversation with the doctor who sewed
up Oswald's slashed wrist indicated that he was capable of
more irrational acts.[81]

The KGB certainly knew it was right not to grant Oswald citizenship, but now it was faced with the difficult decision of what

---

* Oswald calls the document his Historic Diary, and it is an account of his
time in Russia. There is not an entry for each day, and sometimes a single
entry will cover a month or more. The early entries seem to be written after
the events described, but the later ones, reflecting life in Minsk, appear contemporaneous. Robert Groden, in *High Treason*, declares the diary "clearly a
fake." He maintains the spelling is too good to belong to Oswald, a terrible
speller. But the diary is replete with misspellings and Oswald's trademark
transpositions. Handwriting experts used by both the Warren Commission and
the House Select Committee determined the diary was written by Oswald.

to do with him. There were two choices—to force him onto a plane for coerced deportation, or allow him to stay temporarily without granting him citizenship. Oswald's timing could not have been better.

"The Foreign Ministry decision on what to do with Oswald was really influenced by the larger political climate," says Nosenko. On September 26 and 27, when Oswald had traveled to Europe for his defection, President Eisenhower and Premier Khrushchev were meeting in the Maryland woods in what became known as "the spirit of Camp David." After Khrushchev's return, the Soviets were acutely aware of how the treatment of visiting Americans might affect the new relationship between the countries. Because of his suicide attempt, Oswald gained the attention of the USSR's leaders. His KGB file shows that senior Politburo member Anastas Mikoyan personally gave orders that Oswald's request for asylum be given careful consideration. "After years of cold relations between the superpowers, they were just starting to warm up," recalls Nosenko. "We didn't want to do anything to hurt this new atmosphere or to give a pretext to those who wanted to ruin better relations. By telling Oswald he had to leave, he was so unstable he might try and succeed in killing himself. Then we would be criticized for a KGB murder of an American tourist. If we forced him onto a plane for deportation, there was still the image of a student being manhandled by the Soviet security forces. Considering the options, we decided to let him stay. He seemed harmless enough. We could decide where he worked and lived, and maintain surveillance over him to ensure he did not cause any trouble or was not an American sleeper agent."[82]

Oswald was released from Botkinskaya Hospital on October 28, and Shirokova checked him into a new hotel, the Metropole.[83] Nosenko's department took more than two months to decide finally what to do with him. Meanwhile, Oswald continued to try to impress his new hosts with his zeal for the Russian system and his distaste for America. On Saturday, October 31, after three days in which he stayed in his hotel room waiting futilely for word from Soviet officials, he stormed into the American embassy and tried to renounce his U.S. citizenship. He declared he was a Marxist, tossed his passport across the consul's desk, and said he intended to give the Soviets all the information he had acquired as a Marine radar operator.[84] American consul Richard Snyder was still smarting from a recent would-be defector who had quickly changed his mind afterward.[85] Snyder knew Oswald's act would be irrevocable, and thought he was too young at twenty to make such a permanent decision. He put him off by claiming it was too late in the day and the paperwork could not be finished in time. Oswald left in a huff. Although Snyder told him to return Monday to finish the revocation, he did not. He was apparently satisfied that his bravado had adequately impressed the Soviets, and wrote in his diary that he was "elated" by his scene at the embassy.[86]

In the belief his mail might be read by the Soviets, Oswald was explicit in denouncing the U.S. when writing to his family. He told his brother, Robert, that the United States was "a country I hate,"[87] and that he would like to "see the present capitalist government of the U.S. overthrown."[88] He condemned "American propaganda" and a government based on economic exploitation and war, and bragged "I fight for communism" (emphasis in original).[89] He warned his brother: "In the event of war I would kill any american who put a uniform in defense of the american government—any american—"(emphasis in original).[90]*

His diatribes against America and praise for the Russian system did not impress the KGB. While Oswald ended the year in

---

*Despite his attempt to renounce his citizenship and his threat to tell the Soviets about U.S. military secrets, the CIA did not open a file on Oswald, termed a 201, until December 9, 1960, almost a year after his defection. It was created in response to a State Department request about defectors in general. Robert Groden and Harrison Livingstone call the 201 a personnel file and claims it proves Oswald was a CIA employee. But a 201 is actually opened on anyone in whom the CIA takes interest. That there was no Agency file on Oswald prior to December 1960 is further evidence he had no connection to U.S. intelligence through the time of his defection to Russia.

The FBI, on the other hand, had started a file in November 1959, a month after Oswald's defection, and the Marine Corps had reversed his honorable discharge to undesirable a year after he left the service.

Moscow spending most of his time studying Russian in his hotel room, the KGB decided his fate.[91] On January 4, 1960, he was summoned to the passport office and given an identity document for stateless persons, No. 311479.[92] He was told he was being immediately relocated to Minsk, an industrial city of five hundred thousand people, 450 miles southwest of Moscow. "It wasn't Moscow, of course, but it was a provincial capital and not a little farming village," says Nosenko.

The local KGB in Minsk was ordered to monitor Oswald once he arrived there. "Surveillance was typical in the case of any foreigner who was allowed to live in Russia at that time," Nosenko recalls. "The Minsk KGB was prohibited from any 'active surveillance' of Oswald. They could not detain or arrest him, blackmail him, or attempt to recruit him without the permission of the chief of the Second Directorate, as well as the chairman of the KGB. Under no conditions could any officer establish an operative relationship with Oswald. They could not approach him except in the course of their surveillance. In those days no KGB agent would think of violating an order from Moscow. It meant the end of your career."[93]

While the Minsk KGB kept Oswald under detailed surveillance and his file grew, Nosenko, who had been transferred to another department, lost track of the Marine defector. He thought he had heard the last of Lee Harvey Oswald. Then on Friday, November 22, 1963, he was working late at KGB headquarters at Dzerzhinsky Square when somebody ran in with the news that President Kennedy had been shot. Turning on the radio, Nosenko and several other agents monitored the reports until the confirmation of the President's death. "We were all shocked," he recalls. "The Russian people truly liked Kennedy. He was just starting to warm up relations. It was not good news."

But if Nosenko was shocked by the assassination, his biggest surprise was yet to come. "Soon they announced that Lee Harvey Oswald killed Kennedy." According to Nosenko, that news sent shock waves through the KGB and the Kremlin. What would be made of the fact that Oswald had lived in the Soviet Union for nearly three years? "Immediately, I remembered him," says Nosenko. "Then, in minutes, General Gribanov, the section chief, called me and asked me to contact the KGB in Minsk and get the entire file to Moscow by military plane. Gribanov also told me to find out if anyone in the Minsk KGB had any unauthorized relation with Oswald."[94]

Nosenko telephoned the Minsk headquarters and had them retrieve the file and read him a summary sheet. He was initially relieved, because it appeared the local KGB had followed its orders of only conducting surveillance on Oswald. Within two hours, file 31451 arrived in Nosenko's department.

"It consisted of five to six file folders, each about four to five inches thick," he remembers.* "Together, they filled a suitcase. In the KGB, the first file is always the most important. The other files were just the ordinary reports of the local surveillance. But the first would show if there was any intelligence approach to Oswald. Not only the KGB, but also any contact by GRU [Soviet military intelligence], or even Cuban Intelligence, would be revealed in that file."[95]

Nosenko became concerned when he noticed a line in the first file that the Minsk KGB had attempted "to influence Oswald in the right direction."[96] That greatly disturbed General Gribanov as well. Later, Nosenko was relieved to discover it referred to a lieutenant colonel in the MVD, the local militia—he was an uncle of Marina, the woman Oswald had married.† Marina's uncle had contacted Oswald shortly before the couple departed for America, and warned him not to speak disparagingly of the Soviet Union upon his return to the U.S.[97] Nosenko spent about an hour and a half with Oswald's file, then several agents from the First Department, the American section, came in and demanded the paperwork. "They were the most important department in the KGB," according to Nosenko. "Gribanov knew they would

---

* Nosenko's memory on the files is good. KGB case No. 31451 actually consists of five thick volumes and a thin folder tied together with shoelaces.

† Marina lived with her aunt and uncle before marrying Oswald. Some exaggerate her uncle's position to suggest an intelligence connection for either Marina or Lee. Robert Groden and Harrison Livingstone write that Marina's uncle, "it is believed, [was] with the KGB." Nosenko dismisses the suggestion. "He was MVD," he says. "It's like being a local policeman, nothing more. He was completely unimportant."

write a better report for the government. There was no way we could refuse them. Before I could review those containing the routine surveillance on Oswald, the First Department had left with the files."[98]

But not before Nosenko had reached a firm opinion about whether Oswald had any KGB connection. "Absolutely none," he adamantly says. "The files were clear. The KGB didn't want Oswald from day one."[99]*

---

*While Nosenko concluded that Soviet intelligence had no relationship with Oswald, Vladimir Semichastny, then chairman of the KGB, later reached a conclusion as to whether Oswald worked for American intelligence. "Would the FBI or CIA really use such a pathetic person to work against their archenemy?" asked Semichastny. "I had always respected the CIA and FBI, and we knew their work and what they were capable of. It was clear Oswald was not an agent, couldn't be an agent, for the U.S. secret services, either the CIA or the FBI" ("Inside the KGB," NBC, May 25, 1993).

4

"The Lesser of Two Evils"

The day after Oswald received his Soviet identity document, a government agency called the Red Cross gave him 5,000 rubles (about $500).* He paid his hotel bill of 2,200 rubles and used 150 to buy a rail ticket to Minsk.[1] He arrived in the provincial capital on January 7 and was met by Roza Kuznetsova, an Intourist worker who would become a friend. There, he discovered that as the only American defector in the city, he was a minor celebrity. The next day he met the mayor and was promised a rent-free apartment, something that normally took years to achieve.[2] On January 13, Oswald began his job as a metalworker at the Belorussian Radio and Television Factory, an enormous complex that employed over five thousand workers. He was initially disappointed with his work, since he had told Soviet officials he was instead interested in going back to school to study economics, philosophy, and politics.[3]†

---

  * Although called the Red Cross, it was not part of the international aid society of the same name. In his diary, Oswald wrote that he believed the money was authorized by the Soviet Interior Ministry to reward him for his anti-American statements.

  † Oswald's transfer to Minsk is sometimes cited as evidence that he had a special relationship with the Soviets. Some contend he was put to work in Shop Number 25, an experimental plant in a restricted area. But Shop Number 25 did not become a restricted plant for almost two years after Oswald left Russia (*Izvestiya*, August 11, 1992, p. 3). Summers also notes there was a Soviet intelligence school in Minsk, with the inference there is a connection

Oswald's discontentment with his factory job faded through the spring and summer of 1960. His monthly income, between his salary and a Red Cross subsidy, was a very comfortable $150.[4] By March, extraordinarily fast by Soviet standards, he was placed in a one-room apartment in a middle-class complex at 4 Kalinin Street. Although his room had no telephone or television and neighbors described it as sparsely furnished and dismal, it was in a good building and afforded a fine view from two small balconies of the Svisloch River.[5] Henry Hurt says Oswald received "extraordinary VIP treatment,"[6] and Jim Marrs claims he had a "lavish lifestyle."[7] But his conditions, while better than those of the average Soviet worker, were not different from those of other defectors. "There was nothing special about his arrangement," says Nosenko.

As an American defector at the height of the cold war, he was an oddity, and Russians, who called him Alik, because Lee sounded too Chinese, went out of their way to ask him questions about America and to help him settle into his new homeland. He liked the attention.[8] Oswald was more social and contented than at any other time in his life. From his first days at the factory, he formed a friendship with the plant's deputy engineer, Alexander Ziger, a Polish Jew who had immigrated to Argentina in 1938, and then to Russia in 1955. Ziger spoke English, and he and his wife, Maria, often entertained Oswald at their home. Eventually Lee briefly dated the Zigers' daughters, Anita and Eleonora.[9]

For several months, Oswald took Roza Kuznetsova, the Intourist worker who also acted as his interpreter, to the movies, opera, or theater almost every night.[10] He formed two friendships with contemporaries. One was Pavel Golovachev, a young co-worker and son of a highly decorated World War II pilot; also, Kuznetsova introduced him to Ernst Titovets, a medical student who spoke English.[11] By the summer, he bought a 16-gauge shotgun, joined a hunting club, and went on several ex-

with Oswald. Epstein believes that Oswald may have received Soviet training in propaganda and street demonstrations while there. Oswald's KGB file, documenting every day of his life in Minsk, does not support such suppositions (*Izvestiya*, August 7, 8, 11, 13, 1992).

cursions in the countryside. "I am living big and am very satis-fied," he wrote in his diary.[12]

Not all of those who befriended him did so because they liked him. Some, like Kuznetsova, were KGB informants. Within two weeks of meeting Oswald, KGB agent Aleksandr Kostyukov approached eighteen-year-old Golovachev outside his apart-ment building and pressured him to meet with agents several times a week to supply information about Alik.[13] Oswald's KGB file, No. 31451, reveals that he was code-named Likhoy and that the local KGB kept him under constant surveillance.* To deter-mine whether he was a foreign spy, Oswald's reactions were observed when he was put in contact with people who pre-tended to possess secret information.[14] At other times the KGB used informants to engage him in anti-Soviet conversations.[15] When Oswald went hunting in the nearby woods, KGB agents followed to ensure he did not try to observe military or re-stricted sites.[16] Even drugs may have been used. Eduard Shirkovskiy, the current chairman of the KGB in Belorus, said, "Well, maybe they did drop a few tablets in his glass, but just the kind to make him let down his guard and be a little more talkative."[17] Local operative Kostyukov said that as many as twenty agents were used to shadow Oswald, bug his apartment, and check informants at the factory and his apartment building. "The KGB of Belorussia conducted more surveillance of Os-wald than was probably necessary," says Yuriy Nosenko. "But, for the local KGB, Oswald was an extraordinary case. They never worked on an American case by themselves, and this one belonged to them."[18]

Although Oswald was oblivious to the extent of the surveil-lance, he suspected that the KGB watched him (Golovachev says he warned Oswald to be careful).[19] He seemed more con-scious of the KGB's interest as he had some second thoughts about his defection as early as summer 1960. "He tried hard to adapt to this country," Ernst Titovets told the author, "but he never did. When you know someone, you can tell how they feel.

---

* *Likhoy* is Russian for "valiant" or "dashing" and was a play on the names Lee Harvey. Before his arrival in Minsk, the KGB external surveillance in Mos-cow had code-named Oswald *Nalim*, a Russian fish.

He was never really in touch with Russia, never really part of it."[20] His diary reflects his changing attitudes as he complained that he was becoming "increasingly concious of just what sort of a sociaty" he lived in.[21]*

Part of his early disillusionment was that after six months, the novelty of his defection had worn off, and he had lost his celebrity status. He heard nothing about his request to attend a university, and the factory work had become tedious. Max Clark, a Russian immigrant who befriended Lee when he returned to America, recalled: "He didn't want to be among the common people; he wanted to stand out. He wanted everybody to know he was the defector. . . . While he was in Russia . . . he was completely disgruntled by the fact they only made him a common sheet metal worker; that he thought since he was a defector and a former Marine Corpsman that he would be given special attention . . ."[22] Valentina Ray, another Russian acquaintance in the U.S., recalled, "When he defected to Russia . . . he expected them to give [him the] presidency job; he was [an] American and should have a job like that and I think his hopes went down the drain."[23] George de Mohrenschildt, Oswald's closest friend in Dallas, noted, "He was a fellow who needed attention, he was a new fellow in Minsk, a new American, so they were all interested in him. And they lost interest in him eventually. So he became nothing again. So he got disgusted with it."[24]

---

* Titovets made tape recordings of Oswald in order to help his own study of English. Titovets gave Oswald passages by Hemingway and Shakespeare, among others, to record on the tape. He also interviewed Oswald in improvised, mock dialogue. In one interview, Lee enthusiastically played the role of a killer.

TITOVETS: "Will you tell us about your last killing?"

OSWALD: "Well, it was a young girl under a bridge. She came in carrying a loaf of bread and I just cut her throat from ear to ear."

TITOVETS: "What for?"

OSWALD: "Well, I wanted the loaf of bread of course."

TITOVETS: "And what do you think to be your most famous murder?"

OSWALD: "Well, the time I killed eight men on the Bowery, on the sidewalk there. They were just standing there loafing around and I didn't like their faces, so I just shot them all with a machine gun. It was very famous. All the newspapers carried the story."

But Oswald's personal fortunes suddenly took an upturn in June 1960, when he met a co-worker, Ella Germann. In his diary, he described her as "a silky, black haired Jewish beauty with fine dark eyes, skin as white as snow, a beautiful smile, and a good but unpredictable nature." He later said he "perhaps fell in love with her the first minute" he saw her.[25] They dated through the fall of 1960 and spent New Year's Eve of 1961 with her family. As he wrote in his diary, "Passing the river homeward, I decide to propose to Ella."[26] She shocked him by saying no. "Standing on the doorstep I propose's," he wrote in his diary entry for January 2, 1961. "She hesitates than refuses, my love is real but she has none for me. . . . I am stunned she snickers at my awkarness in turning to go (I am too stunned too think!) I realize she was never serious with me. . . . I am misarable!"[27]

Ella's refusal highlighted many nagging problems, including the bitterly cold winter, the drudgery of his work, and the dullness of Minsk. It was another of his failures, following on the footsteps of school and the Marines. His diary entry for January 4, only two days after Ella's rejection, reveals his disillusionment with Russia was now pronounced. "I am stating to reconsider my disire about staying The work is drab the money I get has nowhere to be spent. No nightclubs or bowling allys no places of recreation acept the trade union dances I have have had enough."[28] That same day the Minsk visa authorities, to update their files, asked if he still wanted Soviet citizenship. He told them no, asking only that his temporary papers be extended a year.[29]

His changing opinions about the Soviet Union were reflected in his deteriorating performance at the factory. The KGB file reveals that while initially Oswald was productive and industrious, his supervisors soon noted he had an attitude problem, and his work was unsatisfactory. Over several months Oswald became increasingly lazy, and took to propping his feet on a table and complaining about not being paid enough.[30] In his diary, he whined about the trade-union meetings and the compulsory mass gymnastics, attendance at political lectures, and weekend crop work.[31] Always rebellious against authority, he slowly discovered the Soviet system was much more regimented than he had ever imagined. Expecting to find a classless society, the fulfillment of Marxist theory, he instead recognized that the Soviets promoted a privileged Communist party class while forcing most of the population into compliant workers' collectives. Oswald later griped that the oppressive discipline "turn to stone all except the hard-face communists with roving eyes looking for any bonus-making catch of inattentiveness on the part of any worker."[32] He railed against the central ministries, the power of the state, and the crippling bureaucracy.[33]

But instead of abandoning his Communist philosophy, he merely concluded that the Soviet system was a perversion of Marxist goals. For the rest of his life, his only identity was as a "Marxist." He considered himself the pure ideologue, not corrupted by petty desires for privilege and material accumulation.

As Russia's luster dimmed, Oswald found America less objectionable than when he had defected. In early February 1961, a month after Germann's devastating rejection, Oswald wrote the American embassy in Moscow, stating, "I desire to return to the United States."[34]* He had completely reversed himself from a letter to his brother, a year earlier, when he adamantly announced, "I will not leave this country, the Soviet Union, under any conditions, I will never return to the United States which is a country I hate."[35] The same young man who had attempted to renounce his citizenship now urged the embassy to do everything it could to help him since he was still an "American citizen."[36]

On February 28, consul Richard Snyder wrote Oswald, informing him that he should come personally to the embassy to discuss the matter.[37] Oswald answered a week later, March 5, saying he could not leave Minsk without Soviet approval and requesting that everything be resolved through the mail.[38] On March 24, the embassy again wrote that he would have to visit Moscow.[39] The State Department, already notified of Oswald's change of heart, had decided to return his passport only if he

---

* The undated letter arrived at the American embassy on February 13. In it, Oswald referred to an earlier letter he said he had sent to the embassy, but none was ever received. When the Soviets intercepted his February letter, Oswald's Red Cross subsidies were terminated. The only person he informed of his plans was his friend Alexander Ziger, who advised him not to tell any of his other acquaintances.

personally appeared at the embassy and the consular staff was satisfied, after talking to him, that he had not renounced his U.S. citizenship.[40]*

It was during the period Oswald was exchanging letters with the embassy that he met his soon-to-be wife. In his diary entry for March 17, he wrote: "I and Ernst went to trade union dance. Boring but at the last hour I am introduced to a girl with a French hair-do and red-dress with white slipper I dance with her. . . . Her name is Marina. We like each other right away."[41] Marina Prusakova was a striking nineteen-year-old pharmacology student who worked at a local hospital. Born out of wedlock, she remained unsure of her father's real identity throughout her childhood. Her mother died when Marina was fifteen, and unable to endure a terrible relationship with her stepfather, Marina had moved from Leningrad to Minsk in August 1959.

Marina's comments about her first encounter with Oswald have mistakenly raised suspicion that he must have had "official" help to be so fluent in the Russian language. Summers says that when they first met, "Oswald spoke Russian so well . . . she thought he merely came from another part of the Soviet Union."[42] Marrs says after Marina and Lee spoke Russian, she thought he was a "Soviet citizen."[43] Did he have government help to learn such a difficult language, perhaps a "crash course" at the U.S. Army's Monterey Language School (now the Defense Language Institute)? Such conjecture was fueled when Lee Rankin, the Warren Commission's chief counsel, once indicated he was trying to "run down" a report that Oswald had studied at the Monterey School. After investigation, the Commission was convinced Oswald had never been there. The Monterey School is not an intelligence facility, and its student rosters show

---

*Some mistakenly assume that since Oswald had defected, it was difficult for him to obtain permission to return to the U.S. But the process was routine. Records show that within two months of Oswald's return, two other American defectors to Russia also returned. One of the Americans, Robert Webster, was an even more extreme case than Oswald in that Webster had successfully renounced his American citizenship. He was repatriated as a Soviet alien under the USSR's immigration quota for 1962 and his application to return to the U.S. took less time than Oswald's (*The Washington Post*, June 9, 1962, p. A7). By 1963, thirty-six defectors to Communist countries had come back to the U.S.

Oswald was never enrolled there and never attended a single class.

Since the autumn of 1957, however, when he was in the Marines, he had been studying the language, sometimes with the help of an officer in his unit who shared his interest.[44] This coincides with the time he initially thought of defecting. By the end of 1958, Oswald was so disillusioned with his Marine service that he flaunted his interest in Russian while posted to the El Toro air base. On February 25, 1959, seventeen months after he began his "crash course," Oswald took an Army Russian equivalency examination. In reading, writing, and understanding the language, he scored "poor" in all categories, with his overall language marks also "poor."[45] When he took the Russian exam, he also took an extensive aptitude test. He finished in the bottom of the lowest category.

Oswald redoubled his efforts at Russian after the dismal test results. He often sat in the barracks testing himself against the dictionary, a Russian paper, or a textbook.[46] But even another half year of study made little difference. By the time of his defection in October 1959, two years of efforts produced meager results. Richard Snyder, the embassy consul, said, "He did not know very much Russian. I don't think he could have gotten along on his own in Russian society. I don't think he could have done more than buy a piece of bread, maybe."[47] Correspondent Priscilla Johnson recalled, "He indicated considerable helplessness in the language," and he told Aline Mosby, "I can get along in restaurants but my Russian is very bad."[48]

Oswald's own diary reveals the remedy for his shortcomings. From the middle of November to the end of December 1959, while in Moscow, he wrote, "I have bought myself two self-teaching Russian Lan. Books I force myself to study 8 hours a day I sit in my room and read and memorize words."[49]* After he

* During this six-week period, the KGB file, informants' statements, and Oswald's own writings confirm he stayed in his central Moscow hotel and worked on improving his Russian. For some, however, this period remains suspicious. Summers mistakenly writes: "There are no details of where the Russians kept Oswald for a period of at least six weeks, beginning around the end of November 1959. . . . During this early period Oswald was most probably interviewed by KGB officials, repeatedly and in depth."

was sent to Minsk, his Intourist friend Roza Kuznetsova gave him lessons.[50] But his studies produced mixed results. It was not until the fall of 1960, nearly a year after his arrival, that Oswald wrote in his diary that his Russian was improving.[51] But even after two and a half years in Russia, his language ability was limited. In Minsk, his upstairs neighbor Mayya Gertsovich said he spoke Russian poorly.[52] Ernst Titovets told the author that his Russian was "rather inadequate, only several hundred words, really nothing."[53] Titovets spoke to him as much as possible in English.

But what of the reports that Marina thought Oswald spoke so well she believed he was a Russian when she first met him in 1961? What Marina told the author was that she did not know Oswald was from America and that she thought he might be from one of the Baltic states, because "they speak with accents and do not speak Russian."[54] According to Marina, those from the Baltics "don't speak Russian very well, they have different nationalities than Russians."[55]

Although Marina may not have been impressed by Oswald's command of Russian, she liked him. The day after the dance, Oswald was admitted to a hospital to have his adenoids removed. He asked Marina to visit, and feeling sorry for him, she stopped by daily. Her association with a foreigner carried a certain prestige, and she liked the attention from her friends. When he was released, she started seeing him regularly. A month after they met, Oswald proposed. They were married twelve days later, April 30, 1961, in the Minsk registry office. The speed of the marriage has, of course, prompted suspicions. Henry Hurt writes "Nothing about Oswald's time in the Soviet Union is more peculiar and beguiling than his marriage to Marina. . . . The extraordinary haste with which they married . . . raises the question of whether Marina might have played some intelligence role in terms of Oswald."[56] The KGB file, however, does not show she was even an informant, much less an operative.*

---

*Some cite a vacation she once took to visit an acquaintance. Marina's friend lived in the same apartment complex as another American defector. But Marina had no contact with the other defector. Henry Hurt admits, "It could, of course, be mere coincidence . . ."

Furthermore, the marriage is only "peculiar" if the personal motives and emotions of Marina and Lee are ignored. Oswald was on the rebound from Ella. He confided to his diary that he married Marina "to hurt Ella," and even after their marriage wrote, "The trasition of changing full love from Ella to Marina was very painfull esp. as I saw Ella almost every day at the factory but as the days and weeks went by I adjusted more and more [to] my wife mentaly."[57] It was not until June, two months after he married Marina, that he wrote in his diary, "We draw closer and closer, and I think very little now of Ella . . ."[58] As for Marina, marrying Oswald was a move up the Minsk social ladder.[59] While she says she liked him more than any of her other boyfriends, she admits that a great inducement was that he had his own apartment.[60] Priscilla Johnson said the "great lottery of Soviet life was to find a man you loved—who had an apartment."[61] Until she married Oswald, Marina never even had a room of her own. George de Mohrenschildt, Oswald's good friend, later said, "She [Marina] said it was her dream some day to live in an apartment like that. . . . [It] was one of the greatest things she desired . . . and she finally achieved her dream. It sounds ridiculous, but that is how in Soviet Russia they dream of apartments rather than of people."[62] De Mohrenschildt's wife, Jeanne, said Marina also had larger goals than a small Minsk apartment. "She was always dreaming to come to the United States. She looked at those pictures with big, big houses and everything."[63] Two of Oswald's Minsk friends, Titovets and Golovachev, accuse Marina of being a sly woman who, while she pretended she did not want to go to America, at the same time encouraged Oswald to leave Russia.[64]

Marina denies she married Oswald for a passport, although she admits, "Maybe I was not in love with Alik as I ought to have been."[65] She says he lied to her that he intended to stay in Russia. At the time they met in March, Oswald had already written the U.S. embassy a month earlier requesting to return to America. In his diary, he says he finally told Marina about his plans at the end of June, and that she was "slightly startled."[66] But he had written the U.S. embassy in mid-May, informing them he had married and that his wife wanted to accompany him home.[67] In that letter, he also asked for assurances that he would not be prosecuted for any crimes if he returned to the U.S.

Around the time that Oswald told Marina of his intention to return home, she had begun complaining about him to some friends. She confided to her neighbor Mayya Gertsovich that he was a tyrant, fought constantly with her, brought home little money from his job, and was demanding in peculiar ways.[68] He refused to allow her to wear makeup and was obsessed that she stay ultra-thin, almost boyish, in her figure.[69]* She felt he did not love her.[70]

But those early problems were temporarily diverted when Marina discovered in June that she was pregnant. Oswald was elated and for the first time said he loved her. Yet the pregnancy strained their relationship in other ways. Marina had learned about Ella, felt ambivalent about having the child, was repulsed by sex with him, and thought she had made a mistake by marrying. In their first serious argument he asked if she wanted a divorce. Marina said, "Maybe." "I ought to have married Ella after all," Oswald retorted.[71]

His changeable nature was evident not only in his relationship with Marina but even in small matters. While in Russia, he initially attended dances with Ernst Titovets, and then tired of them.[72] He bought a camera, started developing a photo hobby, and then just as quickly dropped the project. Oswald purchased a radio so he could listen to Voice of America (which was not being jammed at the time), but his listening became sporadic over the months.† He was extremely enthusiastic when he had purchased a single-barreled TOZ shotgun and joined the plant's hunting club.[73] But after a few outings, he tired of the sport and sold the gun to a secondhand store for 18 rubles.‡

---

* Oswald told Marina he had once slept with a peasant girl, Nella, and "there was so much of her" that it made him physically sick. When he saw a girl he liked, he commented to Marina, "She'd suit me fine. I could feel all her bones."

† When his radio broke, Oswald could not repair it, although his friends fixed it by adjusting a small plate. To KGB counterintelligence, that meant the former Marine did not even grasp the fundamentals of simple radio devices and could not have had any intelligence training.

‡ The KGB file reveals that his fellow workers considered Oswald a poor shot when he failed to shoot a rabbit during his one hunting excursion. After

The one issue on which he did not change his mind during this time was his desire to leave Russia and return to the States. By the beginning of July, the embassy had still not answered his May letter disclosing his marriage and his wife's desire to join him. Oswald decided to visit Moscow, obtained Soviet permission to travel, and unexpectedly arrived at the embassy on Saturday, July 8, 1961. It was the same day of the week he had arrived in 1959 to try and revoke his U.S. citizenship, and again he was asked to return Monday. This time he did.

Oswald telephoned Marina in Minsk, and she joined him in Moscow,* waiting outside the embassy while he met with American consul Richard Snyder, the same official who had encountered him in 1959.[74] Snyder found him remorseful. Unknown to Snyder, Oswald told him several lies—that he had never applied for Soviet citizenship, had not made derogatory statements about the U.S., and was not a member of the factory trade union. He truthfully told Snyder that he had never given the Soviets any military information and that the KGB had not debriefed him.

Convinced Oswald had learned his lesson, Snyder had him fill out an application for renewal of his American passport. The renewal was necessary since his passport was set to expire on September 10, 1961, and Snyder considered it very unlikely that the Soviets would issue an exit visa in the next two months. On the questionnaire, Oswald repeated that he was still an American citizen.†

---

returning to the U.S., Oswald complained to his brother, Robert, that the firing pin on his rifle was defective. "I went hunting with Lee plenty of times," says Robert. "He was a good shot who always got his game."

* Unknown to Oswald, Marina, frustrated by their unsatisfying sexual contact since her pregnancy, slept with a former suitor, Leonid, on the day Oswald had left for the embassy (McMillan, *Marina and Lee*, p. 129).

† Some question why Snyder approved Oswald based upon his answers on the carbon copy of the questionnaire. At the bottom of the form, four acts were listed that would indicate a person had forfeited his American citizenship. All the prohibitions related to actions in a foreign state, including swearing allegiance, serving in the armed forces or the government, or voting in an election. Next to these prohibitions were the words *have* or *have not*. On Oswald's form, *have not* was apparently stricken, indicating he had committed one or more of the prescribed acts. In approving Oswald, therefore, it appeared that Snyder had bent the rules. The real explanation is more mundane

Satisfied Oswald was still a U.S. citizen and had not violated any prohibitions, Snyder returned his passport, stamped with the restriction: "This passport is valid only for direct travel to the United States."[75] Although he had physical possession of the travel document, Oswald could not use it until the State Department also gave its approval and the Soviets granted him an exit visa. Independent of Snyder's decision, Bernice Waterman, an employee for thirty-six years in the Passport Office in Washington, later reviewed Oswald's file and also decided he had not expatriated himself and was entitled to the passport renewal. Waterman's decision was further reviewed and approved by the chief of the Passport Office's foreign operations division, as well as the legal division.[76]

On the next day, Tuesday, July 11, Oswald reappeared at the embassy, this time with Marina. She completed the paperwork necessary to start the process for obtaining an entrance visa to the U.S. Her interview with Snyder's assistant, John McVickar, was routine and centered on three issues: 1) was she the wife of an American; 2) had she voluntarily joined any Communist organizations; and 3) would she become a "public charge" if allowed into the U.S.[77] Marina was a member of Komsomol, the Communist youth league, but at Lee's insistence, she lied to McVickar, denying her Komsomol affiliation.[78] Even if Marina had told the truth, it was not an automatic disqualification, as some Russian wives of American citizens had previously been admitted to the U.S. although they were Komsomol members.[79] As for Marina's membership in a Communist trade union, McVickar concluded it was mandatory and did not adversely affect her application.[80]*

—a typing error. According to Snyder, the strikeout is between the *have* and *have not*, and only on the carbon is it directly over the *have not* (WC Vol. V, pp. 282–83). The author tried to examine both the original and the carbon at the National Archives in 1993, but neither could be located by the archive's staff. But, in any case, Snyder had Oswald fill out a supplementary questionnaire, and his more detailed answers showed he had not violated any of the disqualifications (CE 938; WC Vol. XVIII). In any conflict between the short form and the questionnaire, the longer answers control (WC Vol. V, pp. 359-60).

*Marrs repeats an old allegation by Epstein that Marina was issued a new birth certificate on July 19, 1961, raising the possibility the KGB had furnished her with fresh documents for her trip to America. Marina needed a birth certif-

Oswald wrote to his brother, Robert, on the same day Marina visited the embassy. He informed him that they were doing everything possible to leave the Soviet Union.[81] Marina and Lee returned to Minsk on July 14 and then began the work of obtaining permission to leave the country from Soviet authorities. When the news of their effort spread in Minsk, Marina was pressured to change her mind. Only four days after their joint appearance at the U.S. embassy, Oswald wrote to the embassy, complaining "there have been some unusual and crude attempts on my wife at her place of work. . . . Then there followed the usual, 'enemy of the people' meeting, in which . . . she was condemned and her friends at work warned against speaking with her."[82] In his July 15 diary entry, Oswald was upset that Marina had received a "strong browbeating. The first of many indoctrinations."[83] The Komsomol expelled her that same month.

The Soviet bureaucratic obstacles were formidable. Besides an exit visa, Marina also needed a passport. The Russian officials had reams of forms to fill out, all in triplicate, and Marina recalls that her apparently dyslexic husband had to bring five or six blank forms home for each one he managed to complete error-free. It took him a month to complete the twenty forms. In his diary he wrote, "On August 20th we give the papers out they say it will be 3½ months before we know wheather they let us go or not. . . . We only hope that the visas come through soon."[84]

After submitting his paperwork, Oswald tried to speed the process by repeatedly visiting the passport and visa office, the Ministry of Foreign Affairs, and the Ministry of Internal Affairs. "I extrackted promises of quick attention to us."[85] For his diary entry for September through mid-October, he wrote, "No word from Min [Ministry]. (They'll call us.")"[86]

By October, Oswald pleaded with the American embassy to intervene with Soviet authorities to expedite the exit visas. Calling upon his "lawful right" as an American citizen, he asked that the embassy make an official inquiry to the Russian Interior

icate for the U.S. authorities, and the "new" one was merely an official copy of her original.

Ministry, "since there have been systematic and concerted attempts to intimidate my wife into withdrawing her application for on visa."[87] Marina's uncle, who worked in the local militia, feared the loss of his job, apartment, and pension if his niece was branded an "enemy of the state" for wanting to go to America. Two of her aunts tried to scare Marina by telling her that the U.S. was racked with poverty and unemployment. "You'll cry," said her aunt Polina, "and no one will hear you."[88]

On his twenty-second birthday, on October 18, which he celebrated alone because Marina was visiting an aunt in the Ural Mountains, Oswald worried about whether the Soviets would allow him to leave Russia with his wife and expected child. In his diary entries for November and December, he wrote: "Now we are becoming anoid about the delay Marina is beginning to waiver about going to the US. Probably from the strain . . ."[89] Marina was increasingly nervous and depressed, often sobbing at night as she fretted about her decision to leave Russia.[90]* In December, Oswald wrote a letter to Senator John Tower of Texas, seeking his assistance in budging the Soviets. "[T]he Soviets refuse to permit me and my Soviet wife . . . to leave the Soviet Union. . . . I bessech you, Senator Tower, to rise the question of holding by the Soviet Union of a citizen of the U.S., against his will and expressed desires."[91] But by the time Tower's office received the letter, on January 26, 1962, the Soviets had informed the Oswalds their exit visas were approved. Oswald marked the event in his diary, Christmas Day, 1961: "It's great (I think!)."[92] Vladimir Semichastny, then chief of the KGB, was unequivocal as to why the Soviets agreed to grant him an exit visa: "We realized that Oswald was a useless man." Yuriy Nosenko commented on the Soviet decision to grant Marina a visa: "There was no reason to keep her. She was not the daughter of a prominent family or a government official. She was not considered so wonderful herself . . ."[93]

A little over a month after the news of Soviet approval, Ma-

---

* Oswald's frustration over the Soviet delay was evidently so great that he startled his KGB watchers by taking steps to build two small, rudimentary bombs. Some in the KGB thought Oswald might try to use the bombs to force the issue of his exit visas. But he abandoned his project shortly after receiving permission to emigrate.

rina gave birth to a daughter, June. Although Oswald had told no one at the factory but his friend Golovachev about Marina's pregnancy, all his co-workers knew of the birth, congratulated him, and even gave him a box of baby clothes. As he concentrated on his daughter, his mania to return to the States subsided, and in February and March his regular flow of letters to the U.S. embassy dropped to only one.*

Although the Soviets had given their approval for the Oswalds to leave the country, the process for approving Marina's U.S. immigration visa was still under way. After she interviewed with consul John McVickar at the embassy in July, he recommended to the State Department on August 28, 1961, that her visa application be approved.[94] His decision was prompted "principally because she was the wife of an American citizen."[95]†

The State Department conducted a security check on Marina through the CIA and FBI. Two months later, October 1961, State informed the U.S. embassy in Moscow that Marina was eligible for an immigrant visa. Despite this October approval, the State Department later gave Oswald a difficult time over the possibility that she might become a public charge once she was in the U.S. After considerable correspondence, all of which further embittered him about American bureaucracy, State decided to accept affidavits from Oswald and his mother's Texas employer to guarantee Marina's support in the U.S.[96] The Immigration and Naturalization Service (INS), the final U.S. agency that had to approve Marina's visa, did not receive her file from the State Department until October 1961. State told INS that it "believes it is in the interest of the U.S. to get Lee Harvey Oswald and his family out of the Soviet Union and on their way to this country soon. An unstable character, whose actions are entirely unpredictable, Oswald may well refuse to leave the USSR or subsequently attempt to return there if we should make it impossible

---

* June's birth showed Marina another unusual aspect of her husband. When Marina ran a fever and had too much breast milk, he offered to suck the milk. She was startled, but he convinced her it was "quite natural." She was further surprised when he swallowed it instead of spitting it out as she expected.

† Since 1953, through the time of Marina's pending application, more than eight hundred Russian relatives of American citizens had left the USSR for the U.S. A defector's wife fell into that group.

for him to be accompanied from Moscow by his wife and child."[97] INS gave its final approval in May 1962.[98]

A frequent misconception is that Marina and Lee had an easy and rapid repatriation, and that it is evidence of intelligence connections with one or both governments. In point of fact, their approval to come to the U.S. was not easily obtained from either government, nor was it speedy. Instead of providing evidence of conspiracy, it is a classic study of how bureaucracies strictly follow narrowly drafted regulations, mixed with some blunders and inefficiency. From the time Oswald visited the U.S. embassy in Moscow, it took nearly a year before he returned with his family to the States. That was well within the normal range. It took Marina six months to get an American visa, and since 1953, the average time for Soviet citizens seeking to immigrate had been between three and six months. The Soviet exit visas for both of them also took six months, with the average being four months. Oswald was frustrated by what seemed to him a snail's pace. He frequently complained, blaming both Russian and American bureaucratic incompetence.

Several weeks after the INS approval, the State Department granted Oswald's request for a repatriation loan so he could pay for transportation to the States. On June 1, he signed a promissory note for $435.71.[99]*

On that same day, Oswald, Marina, and June left by train for

_____

* Oswald had unsuccessfully sought a grant of $1,000 from the International Rescue Committee of the Red Cross. The State Department loan, together with $200 he had saved, was almost the exact amount needed for train and sea travel to America, the cheapest form of transportation. Oswald was disgruntled that he could not travel home by aircraft.

A lookout card, a warning tag attached to a person's passport file, should have been posted to Oswald's when he received the loan, to make sure he repaid it. One was not placed in his file. After the assassination, the State Department's legal adviser, Abram Chayes, admitted that it was a bureaucratic mistake, which some view as evidence of wrongdoing and even conspiracy.

Garrison charges the loan was a sham since a prerequisite was that Oswald's loyalty to the U.S. had to be proven "beyond question." But that was not even considered in his case. Instead, State Department files show the loan was approved under a special clause covering situations that are "damaging to the prestige of the United States Government." The State Department held the clause applied to Oswald since his "unstable character and prior criticisms of the United States" made his presence in the USSR damaging to U.S. prestige.

Rotterdam, from where they had reserved passage on a ship to the U.S.[100] The Zigers and Pavel Golovachev went to the train station to see them off. Before he left Minsk, Oswald handed his neighbor Mayya Gertsovich a note that said, "Build communism by yourselves! You do not even know how to smile like human beings here!"[101] Marina also received some advice from her uncle, who warned her about the fickle Oswald. "He flits from side to side and is unhappy everywhere. Maybe he'll go back and not like it there and then he'll want to come back here. But he'll never be allowed to come back. People are tired of nursing him over here."[102]

Even their return trip to America has prompted questions. Summers says, "The record of their journey is shot through with nagging inconsistencies."[103] Marina's passport was stamped at Helmstedt, West Germany, but Oswald's passport had no stamp. Summers speculates that Oswald stopped over in West Berlin—without Marina—and then continued west on his own.[104] The divergence is because Berlin "had long served as an intelligence crossroads, and as a haven for operatives coming in from the cold."[105] But a comparison of the visa stamps at border crossings shows the Oswalds entered and exited Poland, Germany, and the Netherlands together. They share the same visa stamps, with the exception that his passport is not marked on the entry to the West, at Helmstedt.[106] Marina's passport, a Soviet document, would automatically be stamped at a crossing to the West. As for Oswald's American passport, the decision to stamp it was at the discretion of the border guards. Moreover, Marina said Oswald was never out of her sight. "We traveled by train to Rotterdam [from the Soviet Union], and he didn't leave, I mean there is no way you can leave anyway on the train. He was present all the time . . . except when he went, you know, for the bathroom and things like that."[107] She testified to the House Select Committee that Lee was with her when they crossed Helmstedt. Senator Dodd asked her, "There is no question in your mind about that?" "Yes, sir, he was with me all the time."*

---

* Summers and Marrs also allege that when the Oswalds arrived in Rotterdam, they stayed, without paying, at a house that may have been connected to U.S. intelligence. There is no evidence that happened, and Marina rebuts it.

During their nine-day voyage on the SS *Maasdam*, Marina recalls they did not often go on deck because she was poorly dressed and Oswald was ashamed of her. He was indifferent toward her for most of the journey, but occasionally they argued, with Marina again feeling he did not love her.[108] They finally arrived at Hoboken, New Jersey, on June 13, 1962, in the midst of a heavy downpour. They were met by Spas T. Raikin, a representative of the Traveler's Aid Society, which had been contacted by the State Department. He helped walk them through customs. Then, since the Oswalds only had $63 left, he put them in contact with the New York Department of Welfare, which found them a hotel room near Times Square. The next day, with a $200 wire transfer from his brother, Robert, they left by air for Texas.*

Oswald was severely dismayed at not attracting media attention on his arrival. He was as deflated as when the Russians initially ignored him after his defection. In Russia, he had boasted to Marina that a "whole bunch" of reporters would meet them in New York.[109] Marina recalls his face showed his dejection both in New York and again in Texas.[110] Robert and his family met them at the Fort Worth airport. Robert recalled, "He seemed, perhaps the word is, disappointed, when there were no newspaper reporters around. . . . I believe his comment was something, 'What, no photographer or anything?' "[111]

Oswald wanted to tell the press that his return did not mean he had reversed himself and become pro-American. He wanted to announce his discovery that Russia was as bad as the U.S. Oswald later wrote his own questions and answers, the ones he had hoped to be asked.† Two are particularly revealing:

She testified to the Select Committee that they stayed in a cheap boarding-house, and Oswald paid for the stay.

* Garrison says Raikin was the secretary-general of the American Friends of the Anti-Bolshevik Nations, "a private anti-communist operation with extensive intelligence connections." There is no citation for the allegation. Raikin was actually chosen because he was a native Russian, and the State Department, unsure of the quality of Oswald's Russian, thought it best to have a translator meet Marina. Raikin stayed with the Oswalds only long enough to send them on to the New York Department of Welfare.

† Oswald wrote two sets of questions and answers, one truthful and one facetious. The answers listed above are the truthful ones.

"7A Are you a communits? Yes ~~have~~ basically, allthough I hate the USSR and socialist system I still think marxism can work under different circumstances. 8. What are the othestanding dif” ferants between the USSR and USA? None . . ."[112]

When he had returned Oswald's passport, consul Richard Snyder wrote the State Department: "Twenty months of realities of life in the Soviet Union have clearly had a maturing effect on Oswald. He stated frankly that he had learned a hard lesson the hard way and that he had been completely relieved of his illusions about the Soviet Union, at the same time that he acquired a new understanding and appreciation of the United States and the meaning of freedom."[113]

Snyder had been fooled. In notes made during his return voyage to America, Oswald wrote: "But how many of you have tryed to find out the truth behind the cold-war clic'es!! ~~I liv no man~~ I, have lived under both systems, I have <u>sought</u> the answers and although it would be very easy to dupe myself into believing one system is better than the other, I know they are not. I despise the representatives of both systems weather they be socialist or cristan democrates, weath they be labor or conservative they are all products of the two systems"[114] (emphasis and strikeout in original).

In a draft of a speech extremely critical of the United States, he said, "In returning to the U.S. I have done nothing more or less than select the lesser of two evils."[115]

At twenty-two years of age, and angry over his Russian experience, Oswald began thinking beyond mere criticism. He wanted fundamental change and ruminated that a new world order would "become effective only <u>after</u> conflict between the two world systems leaves the ~~world~~ country without defense or foundation of government . . ."[116] He speculated about the effects of anarchy: "I wonder what would happen it somebody was to stand up and say he was utterly opposed not only to the governments, but to the people, too the entire land and complete foundations of his socially."[117] His rebellious convictions against government and authority were slowly evolving toward violence and revolution.[118]

5

"I'll Never Go Back to That Hell"

Short on money, and without a job, Lee moved with Marina and June into Robert's Fort Worth home. The brothers had a "tacit" agreement not to discuss politics, and Robert said they got along well, almost as though Lee had "not been to Russia."[1] Marina, who spoke no English,* was introduced to American novelties, like her first hair permanent and a pair of shorts that would have been scandalous in Russia. She was given a whirlwind tour of Dallas by Robert and his wife, Vada. Marguerite arrived Friday, the day after Marina and Lee settled in. She told Lee she intended to write a book about his defection, and they were arguing before the end of the weekend. "She thinks that she did it all," Lee complained to Marina. "She thinks she's the one who got us out."[2]

Four days after arriving in Fort Worth, Oswald appeared at the office of a public stenographer, Mrs. Pauline Bates. He located Bates through the Yellow Pages and wanted her to type a manuscript from scraps of paper on which he had scribbled his recollections of the USSR. Oswald had smuggled the notes out of Russia, and told her he wished to publish them as a mem-

---

* Through the assassination, seventeen months later, Marina understood and spoke very little English. Despite the prodding of acquaintances and his family, Oswald steadfastly refused to teach her, claiming he was afraid he would lose his weak mastery of Russian.

oir.[3]* She was intrigued by the young man just returned from the Soviet Union and discounted her normal fees for him. For the next three days, Oswald sat in her office helping her decipher his writing. When Bates had typed ten pages, about a third of his notes, he said he was out of money, but turned down her offer of continuing the work for nothing. "No, I don't work that way. I've got $10," she recalled him saying. "And he pulled a $10 bill from his pocket and walked out."[4] About the three days they spent together, Bates said, "If you got ten words out of him at a time, you were doing good."[5] She also noticed that he never showed any emotion and "he had the deadest eyes I ever saw."[6]

The manuscript, titled *The Collective*, is a dreary and pedestrian commentary on the lives of average Russian workers. Oswald's discontent with the USSR is evident throughout. To obtain some feedback on his "memoirs," he found Peter Gregory, a Russian-born petroleum engineer who worked part-time as a language teacher at the Fort Worth Public Library. Dressed in a poorly cut heavy flannel Russian suit, he visited Gregory twice at his office, not only to show his memoirs, but also to inquire about possible work as a translator. Through Gregory, Oswald's presence became known to a local Russian community of émigrés, most of them middle- or upper-middle-class, politically conservative, and staunchly anti-Communist. There were a couple of dozen families living between Fort Worth and Dallas, and most of them attended the area's single Eastern Orthodox church. They were always curious about current conditions inside the USSR, and after Oswald met Gregory, the word quickly spread that an American who had lived there for a couple of years had returned with a young Russian wife and baby. Within a week, Gregory and his son, Paul, visited Marina and arranged for her to earn some money by giving Paul Russian-language lessons over the summer.

---

*The notes he had Bates transcribe were in addition to the writing he kept in his diary. On the application for Albert Schweitzer College, Oswald listed his vocational interest: "To be a short story writer on contemporary American life." He also told a reporter in Moscow that he wanted to write about the Soviet Union. But five months after having Bates type the notes, the fickle Oswald told an acquaintance that he had no intent to publish his memoirs, as they were not meant for people to read.

Members of the émigré community were not the only ones talking about the couple from Russia. Oswald was right that the local media would be interested in him. A week before he arrived in Fort Worth, the *Star-Telegram* had run a story titled "Ex-Marine Reported on Way Back from Russia," based on information released by the U.S. embassy in Moscow. Several journalists called Oswald after he settled into Robert's home, but he refused to be interviewed, still piqued because no one had met him at the airport. But he received another call during the first week that was more difficult to refuse. It was from the FBI. They wanted to see him at the Fort Worth office Tuesday, June 26.*

The FBI had opened a file on Oswald when he defected. Special agents John Fain and B. Tom Carter conducted the two-hour interview. According to Fain, the purpose of interviewing him was "to determine whether or not he had been contacted by the Soviet Intelligence Agencies, whether he had been given an assignment or not, whether they had made any deal with him, and whether . . . for permitting his wife to accompany him . . . the Soviets had demanded anything of him in return . . ."[7] Fain found Oswald "kind of drawn up, and rigid." When asked why he went to Russia, Oswald "got white around the lips and

---

* For years the CIA officially denied that it debriefed Oswald. The House Select Committee on Assassinations concluded that while the CIA's Domestic Contact Division considered interviewing him, it finally decided against it, since he was of "marginal importance." Between 1958 and 1963, the CIA did not automatically debrief returning defectors, instead allowing the FBI to report significant results from its interviews. Of the twenty-two American defectors who returned to the U.S. during those five years, the CIA only interviewed four, and all interviews related to particular intelligence matters. However, in 1993, documents discovered at the National Archives indicated that the Domestic Contact Division, through a CIA employee, Andy Anderson, had probably debriefed Oswald in 1962. As of early 1994, neither the interview notes nor Anderson had been located. Yet other CIA employees confirmed they knew of the debriefing and those familiar with its contents described it as innocuous, showing that Oswald knew nothing about Soviet intelligence. After the death of JFK, the CIA evidently feared that any pre-assassination contact with Oswald might be embarrassing and therefore denied the existence of the file. As discussed further in Chapter 17, the desire to protect their reputations led both the CIA and the FBI to often hide or destroy the extent of their early contacts to Oswald, actions that were later misinterpreted by critics as the cover-up of a murder conspiracy.

tensed up, and I understood it to be a show of a temper . . . and he stated he did not care to relive the past."[8]* The agents questioned him on the contents of State Department reports about his activities in Russia. Oswald denied he had had any contacts with the KGB or that he had threatened to disclose military secrets, and even disavowed his attempt to renounce his citizenship.[9] He also flatly disowned any effort on his part to become a Soviet citizen, and promised to inform the FBI if any Soviet agents approached him in America.

Fain was not entirely satisfied with these answers. He found Oswald's demeanor "arrogant, cold, and inclined to be just a little insolent."[10] Carter thought Oswald was uncooperative and evasive.[11] Fain recommended he be interviewed again.[12]

Oswald was both furious and nervous about the confrontational interview with the FBI. He resented authority and its interference in his life. He did not tell Marina or his relatives about the meeting.

Just two days before the FBI interview, Oswald had hit Marina for the first time in one of their fights. He had been rude over the telephone to one of the local Russians, Gali Clark. At the dinner table with Robert and Vada, Oswald told Marina of the call, and she was angry with him. He kept smiling and told her in Russian that he did not want Robert to know they were fighting. When she walked away from the table, he rushed after her and had a cold look in his eyes she had never seen before.[13] He slapped her hard around the face and threatened to kill her if she spoke a word to Robert or Vada. Marina was so stunned she ran from the house and wandered the neighborhood for two hours, wondering what to do. Since she spoke no English, she had to return to Robert's house. It was the first time she ever feared Lee.[14]

Marina excused Lee's outburst because she felt that without a high school diploma and with no job skills, he was under tre-

---

* Unknown to the FBI agents, Oswald was afraid his answers would be used against him in a criminal prosecution. Some contend that Oswald must have had U.S. government backing, since the Justice Department never charged him with any crime. But there was no evidence he ever gave military information to the Soviets—there was only his threat to do so when he first defected. His unsubstantiated assertion was not enough to build a case against him.

mendous pressure to find work. To make things worse, his mother showed up again after he had been at Robert's a month and announced she had given up her job and rented a small Fort Worth apartment that Marina and Lee could move into. She intended to live with them, sleeping in the living room and paying the rent. Lee was "not overjoyed" at the thought, Robert recalled, "but Mother had made up her mind, and when she made up her mind nobody could change it."[15] The Oswalds moved into Marguerite's two-room apartment on July 14. Only three days later, after being referred by the Texas Employment Commission, Lee finally landed a job as a sheet-metal worker for the Louv-R-Pak division of Leslie Welding Company, a manufacturer of louvers and ventilators.[16] He hated the menial work, and his foreman later remembered he never mixed with any of the other workers.[17]

Relationships in the small apartment quickly deteriorated.[18] Lee, as usual, was very cool to his mother, but she now blamed Marina for alienating her son. She also suspected Marina really spoke more English than she indicated and speculated that her daughter-in-law, and maybe even her son, had become Russian spies. When Marina and Lee played a Russian version of tic-tac-toe, Marguerite worried they were passing secret codes. She began arguing with Marina, accusing her, "You took my son away from me!"[19] Lee reacted by completely ignoring his mother, exacerbating a tense situation, and less than a month after they moved in with Marguerite, the Oswalds left. On the day Robert picked them up, August 10, Marguerite screamed and cried in front of the house, even chasing the car down the street as it drove away. Marina feared she might have a heart attack, but Lee coldly told her, "She'll be all right. It's not the first time."[20]

They moved into a bungalow at 2703 Mercedes Street.* Those who saw it described it as a "decrepit shack," a "horrible" place to live.[21] They had barely settled in when the FBI came to interview him again. On the evening of Thursday, August 16, agents

---

* When Marguerite visited them at their new apartment, Lee ordered Marina not to let his mother into the house. Marina refused to obey him. On one occasion, after she had let his mother in, he exploded and slapped Marina about the face and head. Marguerite noticed her black eye, and asked Lee about it. He told her, "Mother, that is our affair" (WC Vol. I, p. 140).

John Fain and Arnold Brown drove to the end of the block on which Oswald lived and waited for him to return from work. At 5:30, as they saw him walking home, the agents slowly drove alongside. Fain rolled down the window and said, "Hi, Lee. How are you? Would you mind talking to us for a few minutes?"[22] Oswald reluctantly got into the rear seat.*

The agents quizzed him for an hour. Fain noticed he had changed since the first interview, seven weeks earlier. He had "settled down . . . wasn't as tense. . . . [and] he seemed to talk more freely with us."[23] They covered the same questions as in their first meeting. Although Oswald still refused to say why he had defected to the USSR, he again promised to contact them if he heard from Soviet agents. Based upon his answers, together with information in reports from two confidential informants that Marina and Lee had nothing to do with the local Communist party, Fain recommended the case be closed. He recalled, "Even though he [Oswald] was arrogant and cold, from his answers, I couldn't see any potential for danger or violence at that point."[24] Since cases were easy to reopen, Fain had no compunction in closing the file.†

Oswald had no idea the FBI was essentially through with him.

----

*The agents had decided not to interview Oswald at work for fear it might cost him his job. Fain later said he did not want to upset Oswald's wife by talking to him in the house, so the car was the only alternative. FBI agents sometimes talk to informants in their cars. But the FBI agents parked the car directly in front of Oswald's house and conducted the interview in full view of the neighborhood, not a very effective means of protecting an alleged informant. The House Select Committee, which reviewed the question of whether Oswald was ever an FBI informant, concluded there was no evidence the FBI even considered it, much less proposed it to Oswald. In spite of this, Robert Groden flatly claimed in his 1993 book: "He [Oswald] became an official FBI informant beginning in September 1962."

† After the assassination, J. Edgar Hoover was furious with the Bureau's handling of the case. Seventeen agents were secretly reprimanded for the preassassination investigation of Oswald. When some of the agents protested to Hoover that Oswald did not meet the criteria for the FBI's security index, he replied "no one in full possession of all his faculties" could make such a claim. Hoover believed that agents with early contact to Oswald too willingly accepted his word that he was not in touch with Soviet agents or subversive elements and, at the very least, he should have been the subject of a more rigorous investigation. But Hoover kept this criticism private since he feared its disclosure would hurt the Bureau's reputation.

Instead, the second interview put him into a funk. He ate little at dinner that night and sullenly told Marina about the Bureau's interest: "Now it's begun. Because I've been over there [the USSR], they'll never let me live in peace. They think anyone who's been there is a Russian spy."[25] He began to wonder if he had made a mistake by coming home. Perhaps he should even go back to the Soviet Union. He wrote the Soviet embassy in Washington asking where he could obtain subscriptions to *Pravda* and *Izvestiya*, and requested the embassy send periodicals and bulletins published for the benefit of "your citizens living, for a time, in the U.S.A."[26]

Oswald's reactions to the FBI interviews had an effect on his marriage as well. With Oswald more tense and withdrawn than usual, the arguments and his physical abuse of Marina increased. Their sexual activity was infrequent. Marina said: "I would say immediately after coming to the United States Lee changed. I did not know him as such a man in Russia. He helped me as before, but he became a little more of a recluse. . . . He was very irritable . . ."[27] Robert Oswald saw Marina with a black eye but did not say anything. Marguerite, who knew Lee was beating Marina, later defended her deceased son to the Warren Commission: "There may be times a woman needs to have a black eye."[28]

Paul Gregory had begun taking language lessons from her, and because of the deteriorating home life, Marina looked forward to their twice-a-week meetings.[29] Even in his brief contact with Oswald, Gregory realized he had a "bad temper," was "mixed up," and "seemed to be a small person that is always ready to flare up."[30] Gregory once took the Oswalds on a tour of Dallas and, after passing through a wealthy neighborhood, had to endure a lecture from Lee about the horrors of capitalism. He told Gregory, "Well, I never want to be rich like that."[31]

Gregory and other émigrés tolerated Oswald because they liked Marina and felt sorry for her predicament. At a dinner party on Saturday, August 25, the senior Gregorys invited the Oswalds for dinner. Also present were Anna Meller and George Bouhe, two other émigrés. Bouhe, a fifty-eight-year-old businessman originally from St. Petersburg, was the unofficial leader of the émigré community. He had hesitated about meeting a defector from the Soviet Union, but he wanted to hear from the Oswalds what was happening in Russia.

At the dinner party, no one discussed Lee's politics or his defection. Since Marina had lived in Bouhe's birthplace, she told him what she could about the city since his departure. Frail and caring constantly for her infant daughter, she evoked both sympathy and affection. As for Oswald, they found him well mannered but cold.[32] In Russia, Oswald had, for a time, been the center of attention. The Soviets were initially fascinated to hear his stories about the U.S. But now the émigrés' interest in Russia was satisfied by Marina. They avoided his favorite subject, politics, and he had no use for them.

After the dinner party, Bouhe telephoned other émigrés. Katya Ford remembered, "I had heard of them [the Oswalds] . . . from Mr. George Bouhe . . . who had told us that there was a young Russian girl came to Fort Worth. . . . And she had a baby and so forth."[33] Soon, the émigrés appeared regularly at the Oswalds' residence, bringing Marina small gifts for June, as well as stocking her refrigerator and helping her get new clothes.

Their efforts seemed to challenge Oswald's ability to care for his own family: "He passed a remark shortly after the second or third visit to their house," recalled Bouhe, "when the ladies and I brought the clothes to Marina and such . . . that is where I saw him for the first time trying to show his displeasure over me."[34] Bouhe had brought him two shirts. He refused them. "I don't need any," he said.[35] Another time he objected when Bouhe bought groceries for Marina. Elena Hall, another émigrée, was at the Oswald home and says he got "real mad" and yelled at Bouhe and Marina.[36] Anna Meller, another Russian, also saw Oswald get "mad [as] people tried to help Marina. . . . He was against everything . . ."[37] Once Oswald came home when Bouhe arrived with a playpen for the baby. "He was furious," Meller recalled, "why we did all that and buy all that and he said, 'I don't need [it]'; he was in a rage . . ."[38]

It was evident among the émigrés there were problems with Lee Oswald. Katya Ford told others that he was "unstable. . . . Something was rather wrong with the man."[39] "[He was] a mental case. . . . We all thought that at some point."[40] Meller, who had seen him explode at Bouhe, thought he was "absolutely sick. I mean mentally sick; you could not speak with him about anything."[41] The most authoritative opinion probably belonged to Bouhe, who felt Oswald "had a mind of his own, and I think it was a diseased one."[42]

The Russian community also became disturbed by Oswald's politics. Paul Gregory reported that during his Russian lessons, Lee sat on the sofa reading Lenin and later praised both Khrushchev and Castro.[43] Meller, on her third visit, noticed *Das Kapital* and Communist literature on a small table. "It caught my eye and I was real upset," she remembered.[44] Bouhe saw an assortment of Communist books, including works by Marx and Lenin. He was "aghast," and flipped open the covers and noticed some were Fort Worth Public Library books.[45]

All of this only created more sympathy among the émigrés for Marina. They thought that it would punish Marina if they cut him out of the community, and none of them wanted to do that. Gossip had already spread that Lee beat Marina. Anna Meller noticed Marina had "a terrible blue spot over her eye." Marina told Meller she had walked into the door during the middle of the night, but Meller knew the "girl [was] trying to hide something . . ."[46] George Bouhe also saw Marina with a black eye, but when he asked what happened, she told him that Lee hit her.[47] He was shocked, and discussed what to do with the other Russians. Max Clark, an attorney, remembered his advice to his fellow Russians: "I said, 'In my opinion he is a defector and you know what he is. You should not hold that against the girl Marina. She's having a hard time. He's beating her up, everything is strange to her, she can't speak the language, I don't think you should ostracize her because of Oswald.' Most of them had absolutely no use for Oswald and they discussed all the time [how] they hated to let this girl get beat up and kicked around by this Oswald without at least trying to look after her."[48]

It was about this time, in mid-September, that Oswald first met another of the émigrés, someone on the fringe of the Russian group, George de Mohrenschildt. De Mohrenschildt simply stopped at the Mercedes Street apartment and introduced himself. He remembered the Oswalds lived in "the slums of Ft. Worth"; their house was "very poorly furnished, decrepit, on a dusty road."[49] Marina greeted him with a baby who appeared sickly: "It was kind of a big head, bald big head, looked like Khrushchev, the child—looked like an undergrown Khrushchev."[50] He admitted his initial attraction to the couple was out of sympathy.[51] But eventually he was the only person who grew to like the introverted youngster. "I liked the fellow, and I pitied him all the time," said de Mohrenschildt. As opposed to many others who met Oswald, de Mohrenschildt never found him arrogant. Because he was nice to Oswald, he saw a side no one else did. "There was something charming about him, there was some—I don't know. I just liked the guy—that is all."[52]

De Mohrenschildt and Oswald seemed a most unlikely pair of friends. Oswald had a ninth-grade education, was humorless and introverted, and, at the age of twenty-two, had a provincial view of the world despite his time in Japan and Russia. For most people, it was difficult to get more than a few sentences out of him during a conversation, and he disliked socializing. De Mohrenschildt, an oil geologist, was a handsome six-foot-two-inch, fifty-one-year-old sportsman and adventurer who had been involved in diverse business ventures on five continents. Perennially tanned, he was a womanizer and partygoer who also happened to hold numerous university degrees and had the right to call himself a baron since he was born into an aristocratic Russian family. Married four times, friends of the Bouvier family, including the parents of Jacqueline Kennedy, he was loud and boisterous, able to drink heavily without ever showing the effect, and had a wild sense of humor. De Mohrenschildt made a lasting impact on all who met him.

Why would the aristocratic baron waste his time in a friendship with Lee Oswald? There is also the question of de Mohrenschildt's alleged intelligence connections—that he might have controlled Oswald for the CIA (or, depending on the theory, maybe for the KGB).* Summers says there was "speculation" that de Mohrenschildt had worked for the Nazis during World War II, while he claimed he worked for French intelligence against the Germans.[53] Following a 1957 geological survey in

---

* The KGB informed this author in 1992 that it had no file on de Mohrenschildt or his wife, Jeanne, indicating neither had worked for it.

Yugoslavia, the CIA's Domestic Contact Division (DCD) interviewed him.* The DCD agent, J. Walton Moore, liked him and
contacted him on several other occasions after de Mohrenschildt's extensive trips abroad. Summers postulates that de
Mohrenschildt monitored Oswald for the CIA, at Moore's request.[54] De Mohrenschildt himself said that he asked Moore in
1962 if it was all right to know Oswald, and Moore told him that
Oswald was "a harmless lunatic."[55] But that seems unlikely because Moore apparently did not see or speak to de Mohrenschildt after 1961, more than a year before Oswald even returned to the U.S.[56]

A closer look at de Mohrenschildt reveals understandable,
rather than sinister, motivations for his friendship with Oswald.
Although extremely different on the surface, the two men had a
similar rebellious streak that often made them outsiders. De
Mohrenschildt liked being provocative. Émigrés remember that
if he was talking to someone who was a right-winger, he advo-
cated Communism, and in front of leftists, he praised fascism.[57]
He knew his friends the Voshinins hated Hitler, so he constantly
greeted them with a "Heil Hitler." At a local Dallas social club,
whose members included some of the city's most prominent
Jewish businessmen, he gave a speech where he praised the
Nazi SS chieftan Heinrich Himmler.[58] Katya Ford said he was
"an oddball . . . [who] was always doing something unusual."
George Bouhe said he came "from an excellent family . . . [but
is] a nonconformist, meaning if you invited him to formal [black-
tie] dinner, he might arrive there in a bathing suit and bring a
girl friend which is not accepted."[59] Sometimes de Mohrenschildt dropped into parties uninvited, bare-chested and without
shoes.[60] He and his wife, Jeanne, often walked Dallas streets, or
drove their convertible, attired only in bathing suits, even during
the winter months.[61] Paul Raigorodsky, a friend of de Mohrenschildt, said he acted like an immature adolescent, "liable to do
anything," and would "never grow old."[62] Igor Voshinin found
him "neurotic," "extremely bitter . . . toward life," and "abso-

---

* De Mohrenschildt's relationship with the Domestic Contact Division is not
evidence of a relationship with the CIA. The DCD was an overt CIA branch
and annually interviewed over twenty-five thousand U.S. travelers who visited
Communist-bloc countries during the cold war.

lutely unpredictable."[63] Mrs. Voshinin said he was constantly trying to pose as "a big shot" and she normally discounted 30 to 40
percent of what he said because of exaggeration, and some 90
percent of his wife's stories.

Instead of being the aristocratic baron portrayed in many
books, totally at odds with the lowly Oswald, it is evident that
de Mohrenschildt shared with Oswald an outcast's perspective
on life. And the politics of both de Mohrenschildt and his wife
was another common bond with Oswald. Not only were the de
Mohrenschildts aggressive atheists,[64] but Igor Voshinin considered both of them leftists.[65] Declan Ford, the husband of
émigrée Katya Ford, said de Mohrenschildt had "a reputation for
being a leftwing enthusiast . . ."[66] In his own Warren Commission testimony, de Mohrenschildt admitted he was politically the
furthest left of the Dallas Russians.[67] He said that Communism
"is a system that can work and works, and possibly for a very
poor man, and a very undeveloped nation it may be a solution.
. . . I have seen through my life that communism in certain
places has developed into a livable type of an economy, a way
of life."[68]

Oswald took to de Mohrenschildt as he had no other person.
Marina said he quickly became Lee's best friend.[69] De Mohrenschildt was his mentor, almost a political and social guide whom
Oswald respected. Oswald had never had anyone of such status
pay attention to him. He relished the opportunity to talk to
someone he viewed as his intellectual equal. And de Mohrenschildt cultivated Oswald by doing something few had ever done
—he was attentive to him. "He [Oswald] was a fellow who
needed attention," de Mohrenschildt later said. "If somebody expressed an interest in him, he blossomed, absolutely blossomed.
If you asked him some questions about him, he was just out of
this world. . . . I think that is his main characteristic. He
wanted people to be interested in him, not in Marina."[70] While
the rest of the émigrés fawned over Marina and shunned Oswald, de Mohrenschildt had time for both, especially Lee. He
noticed Oswald was egocentric, and "that is probably the reason
he was clinging to me. . . . He would call me. He would try to
be next to me—because let's face it, I am a promoter and a
salesman. So I know how to talk to people. . . . I am interested

in them. And he appreciated that in me. The other people considered him, well, he is just some poor, miserable guy, and disregarded him."[71]

De Mohrenschildt, of course, also noted less admirable sides of Oswald's nature. "He was not particularly nice with her [Marina]," he noted. "He didn't kiss her. It wasn't a loving husband. . . . He was just indifferent with her."* As he talked with Oswald about politics and social issues, he discovered not only an atheist and "idealistical Marxist," but someone who desired power.[72] "One conversation I had with him—I asked him, 'Would you like to be a commissar in the United States,' just teasing him. And he said—he sort of smiled—you could see that it was a delightful idea. To me, it was a ridiculous question to ask. But he took me seriously."[73] De Mohrenschildt said Oswald "was a semi-educated hillbilly," and thought he was "an unstable individual, [and] mixed-up."[74] When asked after the assassination if Oswald could have been an intelligence agent, de Mohrenschildt dismissed the thought: "I never would believe that any government would be stupid enough to trust Lee with anything important."[75]

De Mohrenschildt was the one bright spot for Oswald during his first months in the U.S. The strain continued in his marriage, he disliked the émigrés, and he thought his job was demeaning. Oswald wanted a change, and the opportunity came in early October. Several of the émigrés, and Marguerite, dropped by on a weekend. Oswald said that he was behind in his rent and complained he couldn't find a higher-paying job. They advised him that Dallas would have better prospects than Fort Worth.[76] Before the day had finished, Elena Hall invited Marina and June to stay in her home while Oswald looked for work in Dallas. (He later told Marina he was discharged from Leslie Welding, but instead he just failed to appear after Tuesday, October 9.) Marina and June moved to Hall's home, while Oswald went to Dallas looking for work.†

---

* Although de Mohrenschildt later speculated whether Oswald's lack of attention to Marina was because he was homosexual, he concluded that instead he was asexual.

† He stayed at the YMCA at 605 North Ervay for part of the time he was in Dallas, but thought it too expensive at $2.25 a night (WR, pp. 718–19). Near

When Elena Hall first met Marina, she had noticed "black and blue over half of her face and I didn't ask at that time . . ." But when Marina moved into Hall's home, she inquired, " 'What was that on your face?' And she told me that he beat her."[77] During the following week Marina confided in Hall as she had to no one since arriving in America. Hall learned that Oswald was "cruel to her, and they would argue for nothing, just nothing. And he would beat her all the time."[78] Marina seemed relieved to be able to talk about her problems. Living in a strange country, unable to speak the language, and without her family, she felt trapped. Now she told Hall of how "cold" Lee was to her, and that she never wanted another child with him. Marina admitted they "very seldom" had sex, and concluded Lee was "not a man . . . not a complete man."[79] On October 16, Hall took Marina to an Eastern Orthodox church in Dallas to baptize June. Marina assumed Lee would oppose it, and decided to do it before they reunited. Two days later, Hall was hospitalized from an auto accident. Over the next two weeks, Oswald spent weekends at Hall's house with Marina and June.

Both de Mohrenschildt and Bouhe tried to find work for the unskilled Oswald. But even with their wide business contacts, they were unable to help. Oswald scored well on tests given by the Texas Employment Commission, indicating aptitude for clerical work. Knowing he needed money badly, Helen Cunningham, a counselor in the commission's clerical and sales division, decided to get him any job she could find.[80] She sent him first to an architect's firm to be a messenger, but he was not hired. On October 11, she referred Oswald to Jaggars-Chiles-Stovall Co., a graphic-arts company, to fill the post of a photoprint trainee. He was hired, and was delighted since he had a longstanding interest in photography. He began work the following day, October 12, at $1.35 an hour.

His employment at Jaggars-Chiles-Stovall has created considerable controversy. The company prepared advertisements for newspapers, magazines, and trade publications and was also un-

---

the YMCA, in the Oak Cliff section of Dallas, there are many small rooming houses, where owners rent rooms at daily or weekly rates. Although he probably stayed at one of those houses, he never told Marina which one.

der contract to the Army's Map Service. Jim Garrison said that Oswald thus "had access to a variety of classified materials."[81] Oswald did write the term *micro-dots* next to Jaggars's listing in his address book.[82]

But Jaggars's work for the government was almost entirely unclassified.[83] The small percentage that was confidential involved the setting of words, letters, and figures for maps, but at no time did the company have any idea of what the material correlated to—the actual maps were never at Jaggars.[84] The employees who worked in the map section had security clearances. Oswald did not have one, did not work with the Army maps, and never had access to that section.[85] Jaggars never did work involving microdots.[86]

Garrison is correct that Oswald learned a good deal about photographic techniques at Jaggars, but mistakenly assumes it was for an intelligence employer. Oswald worked hard, but his efforts were part of a fantasy world he slowly invented, one that made it increasingly difficult for him to differentiate reality from illusion. When he lived in Russia, he once told Marina he "would love a life" of a spy. "I'd love the danger," he told her.[87] He also daydreamed about being a secret agent.[88] "I think that he had a sick imagination," Marina recalled. "I already considered him to be not quite normal . . ."[89] Back in the States, he digested a steady stream of Ian Fleming espionage novels. One of the émigrés, Lydia Dymitruk, once noticed a book, *How to Be a Spy*, on his living room table.[90] According to his brother, Robert, Lee loved intrigue and mystery.[91]*

At Jaggars, Oswald set out to fulfill his fantasy world. He asked another co-worker, Dennis Ofstein, to teach him advanced photographic techniques. He constantly requested overtime, and tried to stay late on many days to practice with the plant's equipment. At first, he tried his talents at making calling cards for himself and de Mohrenschildt.[92] Then he created sam-

---

*Robert recalled that as a youngster, Lee's favorite television program was *I Led Three Lives*, about an FBI informant who posed as a spy. "Lee's imagination and love of intrigue was a lot like Mother's," he recalled. "She's always had a wild imagination and I think it influenced Lee's view of the world. Even now, she still sees a spy behind every door and tree" (Robert Oswald, *Lee: A Portrait*, p. 47).

ples of his work and sent them to two leftist publications to which he had subscribed shortly after his return to the U.S., *The Worker*, the Communist party newspaper, and *The Militant*, the Socialist Workers party paper. He offered his services to both. *The Worker* thanked him and said it would occasionally call on him.[93] Oswald tried to join the Socialist Workers party, but it did not have a Texas branch.

After months of honing his skills, and enrolling in an evening typing course, he was ready to try more sophisticated applications.[94] Although there is no direct evidence, it appears likely that it was at Jaggars, where he had the necessary equipment, that he could produce poor forgeries of a Selective Service Notice of Classification and Marine Corps Certificate of Service, both in the name of Alek Hidell.[95]* It was a play on the Russians' nickname for him, Alik, and the surname of a Marine with whom he had served, Heindel. The document experts who examined the forgeries said Oswald had made photographic reproductions of his own Selective Service and Certificate of Service cards, blotted out the information he did not want, made new copies on which he typed the Hidell data, and prepared another print as the final copy. Oswald feared the FBI had him under surveillance, but he felt safe using Hidell and the supporting documents whenever he thought his own name might attract government scrutiny that he wished to avoid.†

---

* The signature of Alek J. Hidell on the notice of classification was later determined by handwriting experts to be Oswald's, and document experts concluded that the forgeries "did not require great skill" and only an elementary knowledge of photography.

† Oswald also apparently altered his Uniformed Services Identification and Privilege Card (DD-1173), issued on the date he was discharged from the Marines, September 11, 1959. That card granted some medical and PX privileges. Since the 1960s, a DD-1173 has only been issued to reservists if they suffered an injury while on active duty, or were a civilian employee overseas. Although some critics try to attach importance to the card by questioning why it was issued to Oswald, they usually omit that such cards were routinely issued to reservists through most of 1959, the year of Oswald's discharge. That Oswald was given such a card is more evidence that he had no relation to any U.S. intelligence agency, none of which could afford to risk exposing an undercover agent with a military privileges card valid for three years. Oswald used his DD-1173 to apply for his original passport, and it was his best legitimate form of identification (he did not have a driver's license). It appears he later changed the card's photo to one taken of him in Minsk, the same one he put

From his instructional book *How to Be a Spy*, Oswald began to adopt the trappings of the espionage world in which he fantasized himself. He rented a post-office box, and in Dallas, in the fall of 1962, began a habit that was to carry through during his later stay in New Orleans, the occasional use of false addresses.* In his job applications before he landed the Jaggars work, he used Bouhe and Meller as character references, without their knowledge, and he gave a false address for Bouhe.[96] He later told Bouhe he was temporarily staying at the Carolton Boarding House in Oak Cliff, but records show he was never there. It was part of what Bouhe later said was Oswald's "incessant mysterymaking."[97]

On Friday, November 2, Oswald called Marina and told her he had found an apartment for them at 604 Elsbeth Street, in the Oak Cliff section of Dallas. The next day, the Oswalds, with the help of de Mohrenschildt's daughter, Alexandra, and son-in-law, Gary Taylor, packed their meager belongings at Hall's house. Alex Kleinlerer, who also arrived to help, witnessed yet another outburst aimed at Marina. Oswald noticed Marina's skirt zipper was not completely closed. He summoned her "in a commanding tone of voice just like . . . you would call a dog," recalled Kleinlerer.[98] He screamed at her in Russian and, while she had the baby in her arms, slapped her twice, hard across the face. Kleinlerer recalls, "I was very much embarrassed and also angry but I had long been afraid of Oswald and I did not say anything."[99]

On Sunday, November 3, the Oswalds moved to Elsbeth Street. Marina, who called it a pigsty, so hated the new apartment that when she first saw it she almost refused to move in.

---

on his forged Hidell Selective Service Notice of Classification. The DD-1173 also has an added stamped date, "October 23 [or 28] 1963," as well as "JUL," both of which give the appearance of extending the expiration date of December 7, 1962. Since the dates are clumsily stamped within a circle, some have interpreted them as part of a postmark, but they appear to have been done with Oswald's cheap rubber-stamping kit. Since the original card is now in such poor condition, it is impossible to definitely settle forgery questions.

* As for his post-office boxes, Oswald could have been following the Communist Fair Play for Cuba Committee dictum that "a P.O. Box is a must . . . to guarantee the continued contact with the national [headquarters] even if an individual should move or drop out" (WC, Lee Exhibit 3).

The Taylors, who had come along in the rented van, thought the place was terrible. But Oswald persuaded her to try it—they could fix it up, and it was three rooms for only $68 a month. They started fighting almost immediately. On Monday, November 5, they had a violent argument and Marina ran from the house. From a nearby gas station, she called Anna Meller and, sobbing, pleaded for help. The Mellers paid for a taxi to bring her to their one-bedroom apartment. Marina arrived with June, and "was very nervous . . . shaking." She told the Mellers that Oswald had beaten her. The following day, the émigrés held a conference regarding Marina's predicament. Bouhe told her that if she left Lee, the community would help her, but if she went back, she was on her own. "I'll never go back to that hell," she promised herself.[100]

De Mohrenschildt—probably the only person who could even have attempted it—drove to the Elsbeth Street apartment the next morning to fetch Marina and June's belongings. Lee greeted his friend by telling him, "By God, you are not going to do it [move Marina]. I will tear all her dresses and I will break all the baby things."[101] De Mohrenschildt got angry and said, "If you don't behave, I will call the police." Oswald threatened him in return, "I will get even with you." It was the first time de Mohrenschildt had ever seen him angry, but it drove de Mohrenschildt to even greater fury. Eventually, Oswald "submitted to the inevitable." Before de Mohrenschildt finished packing Marina's goods, Oswald even helped. De Mohrenschildt again showed his affinity for Oswald by later being the only person to take his side in the marital abuse: "Having had many wives, I could see his point of view. She was annoying him all the time— 'Why don't you make some money?,' why don't they have a car, why don't they have more dresses, look at everybody else living so well, and they are just miserable flunkies. She was annoying him all the time. Poor guy was going out of his mind."[102]* Ac-

---

*In de Mohrenschildt's first marriage, his wife successfully sued on several grounds, including his physical cruelty to her. Regarding his statement that Marina nagged Lee, Marina told the author, "It's a lie. I never asked Lee for those types of material things. They weren't important to me then or now. All I kept asking him was to stay in work, because we had so little money, we couldn't even afford to buy milk for June sometimes."

cording to de Mohrenschildt, Marina sometimes ridiculed Oswald by saying, "He sleeps with me just once a month, and I never get any satisfaction out of it."[103]

After five days with the Mellers, during which time a doctor examined her and found she was undernourished, Marina left for the larger home of Katya and Declan Ford. Three days later, Oswald began telephoning. Marina was initially hesitant to speak to him, but Katya Ford said Marina finally took the phone to tell him "not to call on her again, and not to bother, she was not going to return to him."[104] Marina confessed to the Fords how badly Lee mistreated her and told Katya that she originally "felt sorry for Oswald because everybody hated him, even in Russia."[105] There was talk of divorce. After a week with the Fords, Marina and June moved to the home of an émigré couple, Frank and Valentina Ray. That same day, Oswald called Mrs. Ray and asked if he could come to their house and visit Marina. She acquiesced. He arrived in the late afternoon, and Marina and Lee went into a guest bedroom and spoke for an hour. Oswald begged her to return. "He cried, and you know a woman's heart," Marina recalled. "He said he didn't care to live if I did not return." Marina relented. Before leaving the Rays', the Oswalds stayed for dinner. Lee engaged Frank Ray in a discussion on economics, and eventually gave Ray a lecture about the shortfalls of capitalism. "My husband just came in huffing, puffing, and said he never met anybody dumber in his life, doesn't understand simple economics or how anything works in this country," recalled Valentina Ray. "He considered him a complete idiot."[106]

The reunion was not a happy one. Within days, they were fighting again. "It seems to me that it was at that time that Lee began to talk about his wanting to return to Russia," remembered Marina. "I did not want that and it is why we had quarrels."[107] Although he now liked his job, he did not get along with most of his co-workers, had completely alienated the local Russian community, and had concluded, according to Marina, that "it was very hard for him here [in the U.S.]."[108] He took his frustrations out on her. Mrs. Mahlon Tobias, a next-door neighbor of the Oswalds, remembered there was an "awful lot of trouble."[109] As the apartment complex's manager, Tobias's husband often listened to other tenants complaining they could hear thumping sounds "as if Mrs. Oswald was hitting the floor."[110] Tobias had to replace a window after Oswald smashed it when shoving Marina around the rooms, and another time rushed to their apartment when a neighbor excitedly reported, "I think that he's really hurt her this time."[111] Marina, with a black eye and bruised cheek, answered the door clutching her housecoat.[112]

Marina admitted that Lee became more violent as the weeks passed in Dallas, at times being "brutal" and "cruel."[113] She told de Mohrenschildt that Oswald threatened to kill her.[114] He beat her if he caught her smoking.[115] He punched and slapped her one night when she had not drawn his bath.[116] Marina was even more distraught because now she had lost the support of the émigrés by returning to him. "George Bouhe said he was not going to help them anymore," recalled Katya Ford. "He was through, since Marina, he tried to help her very hard, and she did not hold her word about not going back to him. So he said since she went back, so now it is her problem."[117] Oswald still refused to teach her English, and that made her feel more dependent on him. "And I did not have any choice, because he was the only person that I knew and I could count on," she said, "the only person in the United States."[118]

Toward the close of 1962, the Oswalds' only remaining friends were the de Mohrenschildts. Jeanne told Katya Ford that "she felt it was their duty now since everybody else dropped them and they needed help."[119] But even their visits were less frequent, down to every other week.[120] For Thanksgiving, Oswald tried to break out of the isolation by reaching out to his own family. Marina, Lee, and June went to Robert and Vada's house for the holiday, and Lee saw and spoke to John Pic for the first time in ten years.[121] It was the last time Pic ever saw him, and Robert would not see Lee again until after the assassination.

De Mohrenschildt brought the embattled couple to a December 28 celebration of the Russian New Year at the Fords' house. For the provocative de Mohrenschildt, it was an ideal way to crash the party. They arrived late in the evening, and George Bouhe recalled, "I could almost hear a gasp among some of the people who were around me."[122] Marina tried to mingle, but no one was warm to her. Oswald spent most of the night talking to Yaeko Okui, a Japanese woman who had been brought to the party by Lev Aronson, the first cellist of the Dallas Symphony Orchestra. Oswald talked to her about Japan and briefly discussed economics with Aronson. After the party, Aronson commented, "My God, what an idiot that is."[123]

On New Year's Eve, Oswald went to bed at 10:00 P.M., leaving Marina alone, sobbing in the bathroom. That night she wrote an old boyfriend in Russia, complaining how Lee had changed, that she was lonely, and that she wished she had married him instead. The letter was returned within a week for insufficient postage and Oswald discovered it. He was enraged and again battered her.[124] "I'll never trust you again," he told her. Marina's future letters had to be approved by Lee before he gave her postage money.

One note that had his full approval arrived at the Soviet embassy in Washington, D.C., at the end of the year. It was a holiday card written in Russian. It wished the embassy staff New Year's greetings and wishes for "health, success and all of the best." The card was signed "Marina and Lee Oswald."[125]

6

"Hunter of Fascists"

January 1963 was a good start to the new year for Oswald. On the twenty-fifth, he sent two postal money orders, totaling $106, to the State Department as the final installment on his repatriation loan.[1] He also made the final payment on the $200 loan his brother, Robert, had given him the previous October.* Free of debt for the first time in America, he turned his attention to things he had wanted for some time. On January 28, he sent a mail-order coupon with $10 in cash to the Los Angeles–based Seaport Traders and ordered a Smith & Wesson .38 special revolver. The balance of $19.95 was to be paid C.O.D. when delivered to his post-office box.[2] The order form was signed by A. J. Hidell, and the line requiring a witness by D. F. Drittal. Hidell was the third authorized name to receive mail at the post-office box, the others being Marina and Lee. After the assassination, handwriting experts confirmed Oswald had signed both Hidell and Drittal.[3]

January also started well for Marina, free of Oswald's marital

---

* How did the Oswalds manage to repay the State Department and Robert when Lee was only earning $1.35 an hour? "We lived very modestly," Marina testified. "Perhaps for you it is hard to imagine how we existed. . . . He worked and we paid out the debt. Six or seven months we were paying off this debt" (WC Vol. I, p. 62). It actually took them eight months to repay the loans. Copies of Oswald's tax returns show he had little money left after paying monthly expenses.

abuse. But when the beatings resumed, they were with increased intensity. He no longer just slapped her, but now delivered multiple punches to her head.[4] Marina remembered that late in January he began arguing over "trifling reasons" and was "very unrestrained and very explosive . . ."[5] Whenever he wanted sex, he forced himself on her. Once when she called him "crazy," he grabbed her by the throat and threatened to kill her if she ever called him that again.[6]

Their first night away from their flat was on February 13, when the de Mohrenschildts invited them to a dinner party at their house. Oswald spent the evening talking to a young German geologist, Volkmar Schmidt. De Mohrenschildt was surprised to see them getting along at all since he had expected that Schmidt, a right-winger, would antagonize Oswald. Schmidt later commented that based upon their political conversation, Oswald "appeared to be a violent person."[7]

When de Mohrenschildt drove the Oswalds home from the party, Lee expressed astonishment at meeting a fascist. De Mohrenschildt gave him a lecture about the dangers posed by people like Schmidt and other right-wing fanatics. Marina thought Oswald acted differently after the conversations that evening. No one in Dallas had political sway over him except de Mohrenschildt, whose opinion he respected. Marina later believed that de Mohrenschildt had "influenced Lee's sick fantasy."[8]

The next day, Oswald saw a front-page story in the *Dallas Morning News* that seemed a prime example of what de Mohrenschildt had warned about. The *News* had extensive coverage that General Edwin Walker had joined right-wing evangelist Billy James Hargis in Operation Midnight Ride, a five-week national tour to fight the threat of Communism. Walker disturbed Oswald.[9] General Edwin Walker had been the commanding officer of the 24th Army Division under NATO, but President Kennedy relieved him of his post in 1961 for distributing right-wing literature to his troops. Walker resigned from the Army and returned to his native Texas. He was a virulent anti-Communist and strict segregationist who quickly became a prominent voice in the right-wing John Birch Society. Between well-planned speaking tours and high-profile incidents such as his

1962 efforts to prevent James Meredith from enrolling as the first black student at the University of Mississippi, Walker became a moving force for the political right.* The endemic conservatism of Texas, coupled with fears engendered by the cold war and the 1962 Cuban Missile Crisis, in which Russia and the U.S. came close to nuclear confrontation, all boosted Walker's public standing. In 1962, he ran for governor of Texas, and while he lost in a six-man primary to John Connally, he received over 138,000 votes.[10] Following the press coverage of Operation Midnight Ride, the papers and local radio and television had additional stories about the general, focusing on his radical anti-Castro stance.

De Mohrenschildt never hid his own distaste for the John Birch Society and people like Walker. "I don't like that movement personally," he said. "I dislike it very much. . . . I get sometimes into heated discussion and sometimes I say things which maybe you don't think."[11] De Mohrenschildt's attitude was so evident that Katya and Declan Ford, as well as Marina, shared the feeling that he had said to Oswald in mid-February that anyone who "knocked off Walker" would be doing society a favor.[12]

A couple of weeks after his order for the revolver, and near the time of the de Mohrenschildt party, Marina noticed Lee spent several evenings in the kitchen, poring over maps of Dallas and a bus schedule. When she asked him what he was doing, he said he was trying to find the quickest route from his job at Jaggars to the typing course in which he had enrolled. That satisfied Marina, but it was a lie. The typing institute was only a few blocks from Jaggars, a walk of less than five minutes.

That same day, February 14, when Oswald read the news coverage about Walker's Operation Midnight Ride, he and Marina also celebrated their daughter June's first birthday. The next day, Marina told Oswald she was pregnant. While he was temporarily pleased with the news, it did not stop him from instituting a new punishment for her. "Anytime I did something which didn't please him, he would make me sit down at a table and

---

* Walker's segregationist stance was another factor that must have infuriated Oswald. De Mohrenschildt described Oswald as a "ferocious . . . advocate of integration."

write letters to the Soviet Embassy stating that I wanted to go back to Russia," she said. "He liked to tease me and torment me in this way."[13] Two days later he forced her to write the first letter. Marina's great stress showed in the sloppy Russian handwriting, uncharacteristic of her; she told the embassy she wanted to return to the USSR to "again feel a full-fledged citizen," and pleaded, "I beg you once more not to refuse my request."[14] Marina hated her life with Oswald, but she liked America, and since her family had warned her that she would be terribly unhappy in the U.S., she was too embarrassed to ask them for help. Oswald recognized Marina's predicament and knew the threat of sending her back to Russia was one that further tormented her.

On Friday evening, February 22, the Oswalds attended a small dinner party given by Everett Glover and his roommate, Volkmar Schmidt. Schmidt was curious about Oswald, and Glover remembered "it was a gathering for a fairly specific reason, to look at this fellow and let some other people look at him and see what they made of him . . ."[15] The de Mohrenschildts were also at the dinner, as were several of Glover's friends who were studying Russian, including Ruth Paine, a thirty-one-year-old beginner in the Russian language, whom Glover had met through a madrigal singing group from the local Unitarian church. Despite the language barriers, Ruth spent most of the evening trying to talk to Marina. Ruth Paine was a Quaker, scrupulously honest, with a strong conscience. Although she could not always understand her, Marina immediately liked her sincere and direct approach. Ruth and her husband, Michael (who missed the party because of a cold), were ACLU members, and in 1963 Texas they were part of a liberal political minority.* The Paines would eventually become the Oswalds' closest acquaintances in the months before the assassination.

But on that night, the attention was turned to Lee. Glover remembered: "He was pretty much flattered that someone else would take an interest in him, and I think he ate this up to be questioned about something by somebody who might have some

---

*Michael Paine was a research engineer at Bell Helicopter. Although the Paines were temporarily separated, they remained very friendly and saw each other frequently.

status in society where he didn't have any."[16] Oswald spoke about his time in Russia and some of his general political thoughts. The de Mohrenschildts left early; they had heard Lee expound often before. Oswald told the group he was a Marxist who had failed to find the ideal society. By the end of the evening, his listeners were not impressed. "He was poorly adjusted as far as his whole living was concerned," remembered Glover. "He certainly was very immature."[17] Although Ruth "didn't like" Lee, she wanted to know more about Marina and took her address.[18]

The dinner party did not provide Marina much of a break from Lee's abuse. Although he knew she was pregnant, he continued to pummel her for the slightest infraction. Marina later reported that the week after she had been forced to write the Soviet embassy was the most violent of their marriage.[19] He seemed to hit her harder and with greater anger than ever before. On the next night, Saturday, Oswald flew into a rage over Marina's inability to cook a Southern dish, red beans and rice, which he demanded for dinner. The fight ended in their bedroom, with Oswald choking her and threatening, "I won't let you out of this alive."[20] When June started crying, it stemmed Oswald's fury. As he tended to the baby, Marina looked at her bruised face in a mirror and decided her life was useless. She later told Katya Ford she felt she had no way out.[21] Within a few minutes she had taken the clothesline rope, climbed onto the toilet seat, and looked for a place to hook the rope. But Lee returned to find her fumbling with the cord. "At my attempt at suicide, Lee struck me in the face and told me to go to bed and I should never attempt to do that," she recalled. "Only foolish people would do it."[22]

Ever since their fights had attracted the attention of neighbors, Oswald had resolved to move. He occasionally spent free time looking in the neighborhood for a new apartment, and finally found one near the end of February, at 214 West Neely Street. Only a block away from their current apartment, it had a balcony and a small private room he could make into a study, and cost eight dollars less a month. They walked their goods over on Saturday, March 2. A few days later a letter arrived for Marina, a rare occurrence. It had been forwarded from the Elsbeth Street address and was from Ruth Paine, requesting permission to visit.[23] Marina wrote a short note to Ruth, providing the new address and welcoming her. Oswald was not there when Ruth arrived mid-morning Tuesday, March 12. She and Marina took a walk in a nearby park, and Marina confided her pregnancy. "I was impressed, talking with her in the park, with what I felt to be her need to have a friend," Ruth recalled. They departed with Ruth promising to visit occasionally.

The Soviet embassy replied to Marina's request for a return to Russia on March 8. It asked for complete applications, a biography, letters to the Soviet ambassador, passport photos, several letters from Marina's relatives living in the USSR, and some indication of professional interest, all in triplicate. Five to six months was given as the minimum processing time.[24] In the midst of their quarrels, Oswald even went further and had Marina prepare a response, an application, and a biography to at least start her file, all of which she finally sent on March 17.[25]

Meanwhile, he began promoting his political philosophy. The results were evident in a letter published in the March 11 issue of *The Militant*. The letter, signed "L.H." was listed under the heading "News and Views from Dallas." In it he lauded the paper as "the most informative radical publication in America."[26]* Near the time *The Militant* published his letter, Oswald visited the vicinity of General Walker's Dallas home. He took at least two photos of the back of Walker's house, and one that depicted an entrance to the general's driveway from a back alley. Two other photos show rail tracks about half a mile from the Walker home.[27]† In his fantasy espionage world, Oswald had placed the "enemy" under surveillance.

---

*Some contest whether the letter was written by Oswald since it is only signed "L.H." and refers to an independent Senate campaign in Massachusetts, about which he supposedly would not have any knowledge. But the campaign in question, of H. Stuart Hughes, was covered in the September 7, 1962, issue of *Time*, to which Oswald subscribed. Others claim that Oswald did not write the letter since it does not have his trademark misspellings. But *The Militant* did not have the original, and admitted its policy was to edit for syntax, grammar, and spelling.

† FBI photo experts later determined the pictures were taken by Oswald's Imperial Reflex camera. He may have taken other photos that day, but only those five have survived.

The day after his Walker vigil, Monday, March 12, he clipped a coupon from the February issue of *American Rifleman* and sent a $21.45 money order to a Chicago-based mail-order house, Klein's Sporting Goods. He ordered, under his alias A. Hidell, an Italian military rifle, a 6.5mm Mannlicher-Carcano, complete with a four power (4x) scope.[28]* Most critics disparage the Carcano rifle as a poor choice for eventual use in an assassination. Robert Sam Anson says it "had a reputation for being notoriously inaccurate" and that the Italians had dubbed it "the humanitarian rifle" since it never was known to hurt anyone.[29] Mark Lane alleges the Carcano is "universally condemned as inaccurate and slow" and the ammunition was "old and unreliable."[30] Besides the fact that Oswald would not have known this, firearms experts say the opposite. When the FBI ran Oswald's gun through a series of rigorous shooting tests, it concluded "it is a very accurate weapon."[31] It had low kickback compared to other military rifles, which helped in rapid bolt-action firing.[32] With a 4x scope, even an untrained shooter could fire at a target like a marksman. As the FBI firearms expert Robert Frazier said, "It requires no training at all to shoot a weapon with a telescopic sight," and that particular sight needed virtually no adjustment at less than 200 yards, the range of the eventual assassination shots.[33] The Carcano is rated an effective battle weapon, good at killing people, and as accurate as the U.S. Army's M-14 rifle.[34] The Carcano's bullets, 6.5 millimeter shells, are 30 to 50 percent heavier than the average bullet of that diameter, and travel with the same velocity, 2,100 feet per second, as the Russian AK-47 assault rifle.[35] "The 6.5mm bullet, when fired, is like a flying drill," says Art Pence, a competitions firearms expert.[36] Some game hunters use the 6.5mm shell to bring down animals as large as elephants. The bullets manufactured for Oswald's Carcano were made by Western Cartridge Company, and the FBI considered them "very accurate . . . [and] very dependable," never having misfired in dozens of tests.[37] The FBI's Frazier concluded the Carcano was a good rifle for the assassination.[38]

Oswald was anxious for his rifle, and the pistol he had or-

---

* Treasury Department and FBI document experts later confirmed that the hand-printing on the coupon, as well as the addresses on the envelope, were done by Oswald.

dered in January, to arrive. Starting the week of March 18, he left Jaggars early enough each evening to check his post-office box for the packages.[39] That same week, Marina was cleaning the apartment and came across photos of a house she did not recognize. She asked Lee what they were, but he didn't answer, and later kept his study clean himself so she would not have to enter.[40] She thought little of it. Lee had always been secretive; even in Russia he closeted himself to one side of the apartment and scribbled notes about his Soviet experiences, refusing to share any of them with her. She did not know he had ordered a revolver or rifle or that he had forged identifications in another name.

By coincidence, the rifle from Klein's and the revolver from Seaport Traders were shipped on the same day, March 20. Five days later Oswald left work early. He went first to the post office, where he picked up the rifle, and then traveled across town for the revolver that was sent to the offices of REA Express.[41] Marina saw the rifle for the first time later that week. It was leaning against the corner of Lee's study, a raincoat partially hiding it. She asked why he had it, and he said he might go hunting sometime.[42] "And this was not too surprising because in Russia, too, we had a rifle," she recalled. Marina did not like a gun in the house, but when she objected, she remembered his answer: "That for a man to have a rifle—since I am a woman, I don't understand him, and I shouldn't bother him. A fine life."[43] She stopped complaining because it could easily lead to another beating.

Oswald increasingly spent time locked in his small study. There, unknown to Marina, he compiled a blue looseleaf folder, an operations manual for an action he was planning against Walker. It was filled with photographs of the general's house and a safe place to stash a rifle, as well as maps of a carefully designed escape route. Later, when Marina discovered its existence, he told her it was "a complete record so that all the details would be in it. He told me that these entries consisted of the description of the house of General Walker, the distances, the location, and the distribution of windows in it."[44] Oswald also wrote two political documents during this time—one the rationale for his coming act against Walker, and the other his proposals for a future society. In his justification, he condemned the U.S. and USSR as reprehensible: "No man, having known, having lived, under the Russian Communist and American capitalist system, could possibly make a choice between them, there is not choice, one offers oppresstion the other poverty. Both offer imperialistic injustice, tinted with two brands of slavery. . . . There <u>are</u> two world systems, one twisted beyond recognition by its misuse, the other decadent and dying in its final evolution."[45] He also damned the American Communist party for being a tool of the USSR. But most of the vitriolic paper condemned the U.S. and the capitalist system: "It is ~~fairly~~ readily forseeable that a coming economic, political or military crisis . . . will bring about the final destruction of the capitalist system . . ."[46] In his proposals for a future system, he wrote "Fascism [must] be abolished."[47] Calling himself a "radical futurist," he spoke of the time "after the military debacle of the United States," with the goal of replacing the U.S. government with a "separate, democratic, pure communist sociaty." [48]

While Oswald compiled his book of plans for Walker, he temporarily stopped fighting with Marina. She had an opportunity to develop her budding friendship with Ruth Paine. Ruth stopped by to visit the Neely Street apartment again on March 20, and the following week took Marina and June for a visit to her house in Irving, a Dallas suburb. With the recent letter to the Soviet embassy fresh in her mind, Marina told Ruth about Lee's insistence she return to Russia and her desire to stay in America.[49] That disclosure, coupled with Lee's refusal to teach Marina English, angered Ruth.[50] Since her command of Russian was poor, Ruth decided to put her thoughts into Russian in a letter instead of struggling through a conversation. For over a week she carefully prepared a letter for Marina. She decided to invite Marina to live with her, so there would be another option besides staying with Oswald or returning to Russia. But Ruth never sent it. She even carried it with her on another visit to Neely Street, but did not give it to Marina. "I didn't want to get into a position of competition with Lee for his wife. I thought about that, and thought he might be very offended. . . . It is possible he even might have been violent . . ."[51]

On Sunday afternoon, March 31, Marina was in the small

fenced-in backyard hanging up diapers when Lee asked her to take a picture. She protested that she had never taken a photo in her life, but he assured her it was simple. He returned to the apartment and in a few minutes emerged dressed all in black, a revolver tucked into the waist of his pants, a rifle held in one hand, and a camera and some newspapers in the other hand.* Marina broke into laughter: "I asked him then why he had dressed himself up like that . . . I thought he had gone crazy, and he said he wanted to send that to a newspaper. I thought that Lee [was] . . . just playing around."[52] But he was absolutely serious, and angry that she thought it was funny. Marina became a "little scared" as she worried about taking the pictures correctly and whether anyone in the neighborhood could see him.[53] "It was quite embarrassing the way he was dressed," she recalled.[54] He posed and she snapped the shutter. Then he walked over and reset the shutter and she did it again, and again.† Oswald developed the photos himself, probably the next day when he returned to work. He brought one back to Marina and inscribed on the back: "For Junie from Papa." Marina was flabbergasted and asked why June would want a picture of him holding guns. "To remember Papa by sometime," Oswald said.[55]

The backyard photos have become one of the most debated issues in the conspiracy press. The critics are led by self-appointed photo expert Jack White, who has made a small busi-

---

* Some claim the newspapers, *The Militant* and *The Worker*, were issues dated after Marina said the photos were taken. Oswald subscribed to both papers. Through enhancements and blowups, photo experts determined that *The Worker* was the March 24, 1963, issue, which had been mailed from New York on March 21, and *The Militant* was the March 11, 1963, issue (which contained the letter from Oswald), mailed on March 7. Both were sent second class and should have arrived in Dallas in six to seven days, well in time for the March 31 photos.

† Marina took at least three different pictures that day, since three different poses exist. It is unrealistic to think that anyone making a composite photograph would make three versions, thereby allowing photo experts more basis for comparison in uncovering any fake. Some critics have used the number of photos to attack Marina's credibility since she originally said she took one, then later admitted to two or more. "I was very nervous that day when I took the pictures," she told the author. "I can't remember how many I took, but I know I took them and that is what is important. It would be easier if I said I never took them, but that is not the truth."

ness from producing videos, booklets, and lecture series on why he believes the photos are fake. His primary arguments are alleged shadow inconsistencies, conflicting body proportions, a variant chin, and suggestion of a grafting line between the mouth and the chin.[56] While the Warren Commission's FBI photo experts concluded the shots were real and there was no evidence of retouching, the technology did not exist in 1964 to settle the issue dispositively. However, by the time of the House Select Committee on Assassinations (HSCA) in the late 1970s, science could resolve the matter. Twenty-two of the nation's leading experts studied the backyard photos, utilizing sophisticated photo enhancements and measurements to determine their validity. Because of microscopic frame edge marks and scratches left by a camera on a negative, they concluded that Oswald's Imperial Reflex took the photos, to the exclusion of any other camera ever made.[57] Once it was determined Oswald's camera took the shots, the photo experts tested to see if the photos were composites. Using five tests, Calvin McCamy, speaking for the photographic panel, said, "We found no evidence whatsoever of any kind of faking in these photographs."[58]* The HSCA panel addressed twenty-one issues raised by the critics and scientifically disproved each.[59] The panel also settled the issue of whether the rifle in the photos was the same as that found on the sixth floor of the Texas School Book Depository on the day of the President's assassination. Twenty-one photos, revealing fifty-six different and unique marks on the rifle found at the depository, were compared to enhancements of the photo of the rifle Oswald held in the backyard shots, and the panel concluded the rifle was the same, to the exclusion of all others.[60] Finally, HSCA handwriting experts determined that Oswald's handwriting was present in an inscription on the back of one of the originals.[61]

Even committed conspiracy buffs like Anthony Summers, after reviewing the HSCA report on the backyard photos, admitted

---

* The tests used were photogrammetry, varying exposures, digital image processing, vanishing point analysis, and stereoscopic viewing of the pictures. A digital computer enhancement showed a grain pattern unique to each photo. When the entire print is scanned, any disruption in the minute pattern is clear evidence of fakery. There was none.

"they are probably genuine pictures of Oswald," but Summers added that "his purpose in posing for them remains mysterious."[62] But Oswald's motivation is only "mysterious" if one ignores his personality and his expressed desires to Marina about the photos. From the prints he developed, Oswald told Marina he intended to send one to *The Militant*.[63]* He was proud of his guns and his activism, saying he wanted the newspaper to have his photo to prove he was "ready for anything."[64] On the back of another photograph, which de Mohrenschildt turned over to federal investigators years after the assassination, was the inscription "Hunter of Fascists, ha, ha, ha."†

By coincidence, on the day Oswald had Marina take the photographs, March 31, FBI special agent James Hosty recommended that the Oswald file be reopened. He had picked up information that Oswald was on a mailing list for *The New York Daily Worker* and had reports that he was drinking heavily and beating his wife (the drinking reports were wrong).[65] Later, Hosty learned that a confidential informant, identified in FBI reports only as T-2, reported that Oswald had been in contact with the Communist and pro-Castro organization Fair Play for Cuba. According to the informant, Oswald told Fair Play for Cuba that he had passed out pamphlets in Dallas on its behalf while wearing a sign around his neck proclaiming, "Hands Off Cuba, Viva Fidel."[66]‡ Hosty intended to visit Oswald within

---

* After the assassination, *The Militant* checked its files but claimed not to find any photo of Oswald. In 1993, two former *Militant* staffers reportedly admitted that one of Oswald's backyard photos had indeed arrived at their office before the assassination. It vanished after JFK's death.

† That inscription is in Cyrillic, written by a pen traced over pencil, and because of its condition, handwriting experts could not positively identify who wrote it. However, Marina, while not certain, believes it is her writing. That photo, together with some English-Russian language records, was apparently sent to de Mohrenschildt from New Orleans sometime after May 4, 1963, the date that House Select Committee handwriting experts determined Oswald had inscribed on the rear.

‡ The Dallas police reported an incident of chasing a pro-Castro demonstrator around this time but not catching him. In an undated letter to Fair Play for Cuba's national headquarters in New York, Oswald wrote, "I stood yesterday for the first time in my life, with a placard around my neck, passing out fair play for Cuba pamplets . . ." He said he had been "cursed as well as praised" and requested forty to fifty more of Fair Play's leaflets. Oswald could have carried out his demonstrations on any day from Sunday, April 7, until the

forty-five days of the reopening of the file, but when he checked at Neely Street in the middle of May, he found they had moved, with no forwarding address. Hosty did not know what happened to Oswald until June, when the New Orleans FBI contacted Dallas, "advising that one Lee Oswald, was apparently in New Orleans, and [they] requested information on him."[67]

The very day Oswald likely processed the prints of the backyard photos at Jaggars, April 1, appears to be the day he was also fired and given a week's notice. The quality of his work had deteriorated since the beginning of the year, when Jaggars tried to give him more responsibility. According to Robert Stovall, one of the founders of the company, Oswald "was a constant source of irritation because of his lack of productive ability . . ."[68] Stovall called his work "inefficient [and] . . . inept."[69] Grumbling about him had spread to management. The area in which they worked was small and required that workers be considerate of each other as they moved about the room. Instead, Oswald charged around the shop, constantly knocking into other workers and never uttering an apology. Finally, some became so frustrated with his "selfish and aggressive" actions they almost had fistfights with him.[70] Oswald was also spotted reading a Russian paper, *Krokodil*, in the firm cafeteria, and his supervisor, John Graef, had enough. He privately informed Oswald that he was fired. It was the only job he had ever liked, and since he had spent almost everything he earned, the dismissal was crushing news. Graef recalled his reaction: "And there was no outburst on his part. He took this whole time looking at the floor . . . and after I was through, he said, 'Well, thank you.' And he turned around and walked off."[71] He internalized the anger, appearing on the surface to be calm and collected.

That evening he did not tell Marina he was fired. He did confide in a co-worker, Dennis Ofstein, that he had been dismissed. Ofstein asked him what he intended to do. Oswald said "he would look around and if he didn't find anything else he could always go back to the Soviet Union . . ." recalled Ofstein.[72] He

---

afternoon of Wednesday, April 10. Although he practiced with his rifle and also conducted some surveillance at General Walker's house on those days, he had time to distribute the pamphlets.

again sought help from the Texas Employment Commission, but it was unable to find him new work.

The day after Oswald was informed of his discharge, Tuesday, April 2, he and Marina went to dinner at Ruth Paine's house. Michael, Ruth's husband, drove to Neely Street to pick them up. It was his first meeting with the Oswalds, and he was immediately "shocked" by Lee's "cruel" conduct toward Marina. Although Paine could not understand Russian, by Lee's tone and attitude he could tell that Marina was "a vassal to him."[73] While they waited for Marina to get ready, Paine had a half-hour political conversation with Oswald. Paine's father had been an avid Trotskyite, and Michael was intensely interested in politics. Lee's defection to Russia was one of the reasons Paine wanted to meet him. That half-hour talk was the most open and informative he ever had with Oswald.[74] Lee told him of his early attraction to Marxism, "without ever having met a communist," and his search for the "paradise of the world" when he defected to Russia. He expressed his anger at both the U.S. and the Soviet Union, and "great resentment" at capitalism's "exploitation of man by man." "It seemed to me, he was critical of almost everything that occurs in this country," Paine recalled.[75]

When Paine tried to have a debate with Oswald, he found it was not possible. "He was quite dogmatic," he recalled. "[He thought] he knew the truth and therefore I was just spouting the line that was fed to me by the power structure."[76] That night at dinner, Oswald closed off any discussion with the Paines once they challenged his ideas. In a conversation about religion, Michael remembers that "when he couldn't answer he would just state . . . the Communist line . . . [and then] instead of supporting further his view . . . he just restated it." Michael recalls that they all "seemed to agree . . . the far right was unfortunate in its thoughts." Soon, the conversation turned to Dallas's most prominent far right representative, General Edwin Walker. "He was familiar with Walker . . . quite familiar."[77] But Oswald did not say anything about his recent surveillance of the general's house.

The evening ended on the sour note, again, of Lee's mistreatment of Marina. "He spoke loudly to her," said Michael. "Spoke surprisingly harshly especially in front of a guest . . . he would slap her down verbally." After the supper, Ruth informed her husband that Lee had been calling Marina a "fool" during dinner and telling her that she did not know anything. Michael thought Marina was in "bondage and servitude," but he did not express his distaste to Oswald.[78] They instead spoke of politics during the car ride home.

Three days later, Friday, Lee checked out of work a few minutes after 5:00 P.M., and as he approached the apartment in a rush, he ran into Marina outside with the baby carriage. He disappeared inside the flat for a moment, and when he returned she noticed he was carrying his rifle, hidden under his Marine Corps raincoat.[79] She was startled and asked what he was doing. "Target practice," he replied. At the bus stop, they argued, with Marina telling him not to come home and that she hoped the police caught him.[80] She saw him get on a bus marked LOVE FIELD. When he returned at 9:00 P.M., Marina again warned him about the police, but he told her not to worry since no one could hear him where he practiced.[81] The FBI later studied the Love Field bus route and found that a five-minute ride took Oswald within walking distance of a protected levee.[82] Marina once noticed a box of ammunition at the apartment and saw him clean his rifle on four or five nights, but she does not believe he shot the gun on each occasion.[83] But he did not need much practice to be proficient with the Carcano. Firearms experts testified after the assassination that a marksman such as Oswald would need to fire only ten rounds to adjust the scope and become familiar with the peculiarities of that rifle.

Around April 4 or 5, Jeanne de Mohrenschildt stopped by for an afternoon visit. It was her first visit to the Neely Street apartment, as the de Mohrenschildts had been busy preparing to move from Dallas to Haiti, where George had another of his ambitious business projects in the works. While Marina showed Jeanne around the apartment, she opened a clothes closet and the rifle was leaning against the corner. Jeanne recalls, "She just said, we are so short of money, and this crazy lunatic buys a rifle."[84] She was probably the only person besides Marina to see the rifle before the presidential assassination.

Lee's last day at work was Saturday, April 6. He still had not told Marina he had been fired almost a week earlier. On the following day, he left the apartment with his rifle, and when he returned home that evening, he no longer had it.[85] Oswald had begun to put his Walker plan into action. He later told Marina that he buried the Carcano near some railroad tracks only some minutes' walk from Walker's house, probably the same tracks he had photographed.[86] On Monday, April 8, Oswald left in the evening on a bus, which Marina assumed was to take him to his typing course, but she did not know he had already quit the class. Instead, he traveled to Walker's house, where he intended to assassinate the general. But he later told Marina he discovered that the Mormon church whose parking lot was adjacent to General Walker's home had services scheduled for Wednesday evening, providing him a better chance of not standing out in the otherwise quiet neighborhood. On Tuesday, Oswald continued the charade over his job, telling Marina that it was a holiday. In the evening, he was kind to her for the first time in months.

On Wednesday, April 10, Oswald finally told Marina he had been fired. She recalled he had tears in his eyes, blaming the FBI for inquiring about him and costing him the position. "When will they leave me alone?" he asked.[87] She actually felt sorry for him as he left that day. He was home for an early dinner and Marina noticed "he was tense . . . I could tell by his face."[88] He left immediately after supper. By the time she put June to bed, between 8:00 and 9:00, she wondered why he was not home. There was no one to call. She paced between the rooms, and on a supposition, opened the door to his small study. There, she found a piece of paper on the desk, with a key on top. Immediately, she thought he had left her. She picked it up and read it (the translation from the Russian does not include any of Oswald's original misspellings or grammatical mistakes):

1. Here is the key to the post office box, which is located in the main post office downtown on Ervay Street, the street where there is a drugstore where you always used to stand. The post office is four blocks from the drug-

store on the same street. There you will find our mailbox. I paid for the mailbox last month so you needn't worry about it.

2. Send information about what has happened to me to the [Soviet] Embassy and also send newspaper clippings (if there's anything about me in the papers). I think the Embassy will come quickly to your aid once they know everything.

3. I paid our rent on the second so don't worry about it.

4. I have also paid for the water and gas.

5. There may be some money from work. They will send it to your post office box. Go to the bank and they will cash it.

6. You can either throw out my clothing or give it away. Do not keep it [emphasis in original]. As for my personal papers (both military papers and papers for the factory), I prefer that you keep them.

7. Certain of my papers are in the small blue suitcase.

8. My address book is on the table in my study if you need it.

9. We have friends here and the Red Cross will also help you.

10. I left you as much money as I could, $60 on the second of the month, and you and Junie can live for two months on $10 a week.

11. If I am alive and taken prisoner, the city jail is at the end of the bridge we always used to cross when we went to town (the very beginning of town after the bridge).

Marina started shaking. "I couldn't understand at all what can he be arrested for," she recalled.[89] She was frantic by the time Oswald returned at 11:30.[90] He was pale and out of breath from walking quickly. "I showed him the note and asked him, 'What is the meaning of this?' . . . And he told me not to ask him any questions," she said. "He only told me that he had shot at General Walker."[91] She was horrified. She asked about the rifle, and he said he had buried it. "Don't ask any questions," he commanded her.[92] He flipped on the radio but was disappointed as there was no news. "When he fired, he did not know whether he had hit Walker or not," Marina said. Oswald could not understand that the radio was silent about the assassination. Frustrated there was no coverage, he went to bed within the hour. "I didn't sleep all night," said Marina. "I thought that any minute now, the police will come."[93] She was also petrified of tracking dogs, and expected they would follow Lee's scent from the shooting to Neely Street.

Although Marina was appalled that Lee had tried to kill someone, she never seriously thought of turning him in to the police. Not only was she completely dependent on him, but her Russian upbringing made her fear the police. She worried what would happen to her, alone in the U.S., if her husband was charged with murder. There was no way she could have imagined that by postponing any decision on the Walker shooting, she would find herself in seven months in the very situation she hoped to avoid, only with a much more prominent victim.* Marina finally fell asleep in the early morning hours.

It was a fluke that Walker was not dead. The general had been sitting behind a desk in his dining room, working on his income taxes, when the shot was fired. Oswald had likely taken a position inside Walker's backyard fence, leaning against the general's station wagon to brace himself for the shot.[94] He was less than one hundred feet away from the window, which had no covering to block his view into the brightly lit room. "I heard a blast and crack right over my head," recalled Walker. "I thought possibly somebody had thrown a firecracker, that it exploded right over my head through the window right behind me."[95] Walker stood up from the desk, looked around the room, and noticed a hole in the wall, just left of where he had been sitting. He went upstairs to get a gun and it was several minutes before he noticed his right forearm was bleeding, the result of bullet fragments.[96] What saved Walker's life was the wooden frame across the middle of the double window. Upon close examination, it turned out that the bullet had passed through a wire

---

* Even after the Kennedy assassination, she did not tell the FBI about the Walker shooting until the Bureau confronted her with the incriminating note that was discovered among Oswald's belongings.

screen, then grooved along the bottom of the wooden bar, and then through the glass. When it struck the wooden frame, the bullet was deflected so minutely that it passed through Walker's hair instead of into his skull.* "He [Oswald] couldn't see from his position any of the latticework either in the windows or in the screens because of the light," said Walker. "It would have looked like one big lighted area, and he could have been a very good shot and just by chance he hit the woodwork."[97]†

When Marina awoke, Oswald was bent over a radio. "I missed," he said disgustedly. She was immensely relieved. "He said only that he had taken very good aim, that it was just chance that caused him to miss," Marina remembered.[98] Now she felt relaxed enough to ask him questions about Walker. He told Marina that he had planned the Walker assassination for two months, and then he showed her his operations book, crammed with photographs of Walker's residence, a map, and pages of handwritten notes.[99] Marina was shocked. She thought he had been writing his memoirs, as he had when they lived in Russia. "He said that this was a very bad man, that he was a fascist, that he was the leader of a fascist organization, and when I said that even though all of that might be true, just the same he had no right to take his life, he said if someone had killed Hitler in time it would have saved many lives. I told him that this is no method to prove your ideas, by means of a rifle. . . . I told him he had no right to kill people in peacetime, he had no right to take their life because not everybody has the same ideas as he has."[100] Marina thought he was "sick" and "not a stable-minded person."[101]

He left the apartment to purchase the local newspapers, which carried front-page stories about the failed assassination.

* The author personally examined the window and damaged frame, still in General Walker's possession, shortly before Walker died in November 1993.

† The bullet, recovered in another room of the house, was so badly damaged that ballistics experts could not match it to Oswald's rifle to the exclusion of all others, but they did conclude, based on the visible markings, there was a good probability that it was fired from Oswald's Carcano. The House Select Committee utilized an advanced technique to subject the bullet to neutron-activation tests, and determined the Walker slug was a Western Cartridge Company 6.5mm bullet, the same type of bullet, made by the same manufacturer, as that used later in President Kennedy's assassination.

In the initial reports the police mistakenly identified the mangled bullet as a .30-06. A Walker aide said he had seen an unlicensed car near the general's house several nights before the shooting. A fifteen-year-old neighbor, Walter Kirk Coleman, said he saw two cars speed away from the scene right after the shooting. According to Marina, those errors made Lee laugh heartily. He called them fools over the bullet. Regarding the false reports of getaway cars, he said, "Americans are so spoiled, it never occurs to them that you might use your own two legs."[102]*

Marina said Lee was "very sorry that he had not hit him," and she worried he might try again—she made him promise that he would not. "I asked him to give me his word that he would not repeat anything like that," she recalled. "I said that this chance shows that he [Walker] must live and that he should not be shot at again. I told him that I would save the note and that if something like that should be repeated again, I would go to the police and I would have the proof in the form of that note."[103] Marina hid the note in a cookbook. Then she asked him what he intended to do with his notebook of Walker photos and assassination plans. He said he wanted to save it "as a keepsake."[104]† She

---

*Walter Coleman was playing with a friend in the back room of his house when he heard "a car backfire" between 9:00 P.M. and 10:00 P.M. He looked into the parking lot of the Mormon church. Contrary to press reports that he saw two men get into separate cars and race away, he told the FBI that he only saw one car leave, and it moved at a normal rate of speed. At least six other cars were in the parking lot at the same time. Other neighbors contradicted Coleman's story, saying no cars left after the noise. If he did see a departing car, it was probably because church services had just finished. The pastor told the FBI that on Wednesdays, services began at 7:30 and finished at 9:00, leaving the area busy with people. Oswald's original plan was to mix with that crowd.

† An issue was later created when the Warren Commission showed Marina one of the surviving five photographs Lee had taken of the Walker residence, of a car parked in front of the house. There was a hole in the print in the area of the license plate. Marina said the hole had not been there when Lee had shown it to her. But Marina may be mistaken. A photo of evidence taken from Oswald's flat after the assassination shows the hole was in the print at that time. (The photo in question was reproduced in a 1969 book, *JFK Assassination File*, by Dallas police chief Jesse Curry. Many critics contend there is no hole visible in that reproduction, but upon close examination, it is evident that a similarly toned piece of paper, lying underneath the Walker photo, is actually

was furious and told him it was evidence that could be used against him. But he initially ignored her and saved the book.[105] Marina was convinced there was only one guarantee that Oswald would not try again to kill Walker. "And then I insisted that it would be better for him to go to New Orleans where he had relatives," she said. "I insisted on that because I wanted to get him further removed from Dallas and Walker, because even though he gave me his word, I wanted to have him further away, because a rifle for him was not a very good toy—a toy that was too enticing."[106]

For two days after the Walker attack, Marina reported that Lee suffered convulsive anxiety attacks during his sleep, but without waking up.[107] By Friday, he tried to return to a normal routine, filing a claim for unemployment benefits. Saturday, the Oswalds spent a quiet day at the Neely Street apartment. They had just gone to bed that night when there was loud pounding at the front door. Marina's heart jumped, as she feared it was the police, until she heard George de Mohrenschildt's deep voice. She vividly recalled what happened next. "As he opened the door, he said, 'Lee, how is it possible that you missed?' I looked at Lee. I thought he had told de Mohrenschildt about it. And Lee looked at me, and he apparently thought I had told. . . . I noticed that his [Lee's] face changed, that he almost became speechless."[108] De Mohrenschildt knew about Oswald's distaste for Walker, and his wife, Jeanne, had informed him just a week ago that she saw a rifle at the Oswald apartment.* It was his idea of a joke, but he could immediately tell he had hit a target.

---

filling in the hole around the license plate.) Also, the photo was taken from such a distance that the license plate of the car would not have been legible in any case, and it was later determined the car belonged to a Walker aide, Charles Klihr.

* In their testimony to the Warren Commission, the de Mohrenschildts mistakenly recalled one visit to Neely Street, April 13. But Jeanne had forgotten about her solo visit to Marina on April 4 or 5. She confused the sighting of the rifle and the joke her husband made about the shooting and thought they both happened on April 13. George de Mohrenschildt gave the same testimony. The Warren Commission believed their version. But Marina is clear about two separate visits, and more important, Oswald did not retrieve his rifle until Sunday, April 14, a day after the de Mohrenschildts' visit. So Mrs. de Mohrenschildt could not have seen the rifle on April 13 as she thought, but only on the earlier visit on either April 4 or 5.

"He sort of shriveled," de Mohrenschildt recalled, "when I asked this question. Became tense, you see, and didn't answer anything, smiled . . . made a peculiar face. [It] had an effect on him."[109] That surprise visit, the evening before Easter, was the last time the de Mohrenschildts ever saw the Oswalds. The de Mohrenschildts moved from Dallas five days later.*

The following day, Easter Sunday, April 14, Oswald thought the manhunt for Walker's shooter had slackened and that it was safe to retrieve his rifle. Less than an hour after his return with it, he decided Marina was right about his operations book for the Walker assassination. Marina smelled burnt matches and walked into the bathroom. Lee was burning most of the evidence over the washbasin.[110]†

By April 17, Oswald had told Marina he was ready to move to New Orleans.[111] The decision seemed to improve his mood, which had been miserable after his failure to kill Walker a week earlier. The Oswalds even joined Ruth Paine and her two chil-

---

* On March 29, 1977, de Mohrenschildt told Edward Jay Epstein that the CIA had asked him to keep tabs on Oswald in Dallas during 1962. Several hours later, de Mohrenschildt killed himself with a shotgun blast to the head. However, most books fail to disclose that de Mohrenschildt was quite mad by the time he gave his final interview. For nearly a year before his death, he was paranoid, fearful that the "FBI and Jewish mafia" were out to kill him. He twice tried to kill himself with drug overdoses, and another time cut his wrists and submerged himself in a bathtub. After he began waking in the middle of every night, screaming and beating himself, his wife finally committed him to the Parkland Hospital psychiatric unit, where he was diagnosed as psychotic and given two months of intensive shock therapy. After his treatment he said he had been with Oswald on the day of the assassination, though he was actually with dozens of guests at the Bulgarian embassy in Haiti the day JFK was killed. Despite de Mohrenschildt's imbalance, Epstein and others still quote the final interview as though it were an uncontested fact.

† Henry Hurt writes in *Reasonable Doubt* that there is no evidence "that this mild-mannered young man [Oswald] had ever committed an act of serious violence," and he dismisses the Walker shooting in two sentences, concluding "the evidence [was] . . . of the flimsiest kind." John Davis, in more than six hundred pages of *Mafia Kingfish*, covers the shooting in a single sentence, and rejects it as unproven. David Scheim, in *Contract on America*; Jim Garrison, in *On the Trail of the Assassins*; and David Lifton, in *Best Evidence*, do not even mention the Walker shooting. Even the House Select Committee on Assassinations dropped the entire Walker incident into a single footnote because it could not find any accomplices to fit into its eventual conclusion of an overall conspiracy.

dren for a picnic on Sunday, April 21. But as soon as Marina began to relax over the Walker episode and Lee's receding temper, another incident sent her into a panic. When Oswald read the Monday morning paper, its front-page headline was NIXON CALLS FOR DECISION TO FORCE REDS OUT OF CUBA. Marina said, "Then he got dressed and put on a good suit. I saw that he took a pistol. I asked him where he was going, and why he was getting dressed. He answered, 'Nixon is coming. I want to go and have a look.' I said, 'I know how you look.' "[112] She did not know who Nixon was, but was determined that Lee should not leave the house with the pistol. She asked him to join her in the bathroom, and when he entered she jumped out and slammed the door shut. Bracing her feet against the nearby wall, she struggled as hard as she could to keep the door closed against his efforts to push out. "I remember that I held him," she said. "We actually struggled for several minutes and then he quieted down. I remember that I told him that if he goes it would be better for him to kill me than to go out."[113] Some have questioned whether Marina could have prevented Oswald from leaving the bathroom. "He is not a big man," remarked Marina. "When he is very upset, my husband . . . is not strong and when I want to and when I collect all my forces and want to do something very badly I am stronger than he is."[114] She reminded him of her pregnancy and that the excitement could cause a miscarriage. At first he was furious, but as he calmed, Oswald agreed to strip to his underwear, and stayed home reading the remainder of the day. They quarreled often that afternoon, with Marina reminding him of his promise, and saying she was sick about "all these pranks of his."[115] He gave Marina the pistol and she hid it under the mattress, but he took it back that evening. The next day he informed her that Nixon had not come to town after all.*

---

* Nixon was not in Dallas on the day Oswald packed a pistol and set out to meet him. Vice-President Lyndon Johnson was due in Dallas within a day, but Marina is certain the name was Nixon. Oswald was dyslexic and could have confused the news about Nixon's anti-Castro plans with the visit of the "Vice-President," a title still used to refer to Nixon. Also, Nixon may have just been the excuse given to Marina, and it is possible Oswald had second thoughts about agreeing to let Walker live. The fact that Oswald could not physically fulfill his stated mission does not extirpate the seriousness of the incident, and again highlights his increasing instability.

Two days later, Wednesday, April 24, Ruth Paine, with her two children, drove to the Oswald apartment. She was expecting to spend the morning visiting Marina and instead was shocked to see Lee Oswald fully packed and ready to move. "I was evidently expected," Ruth recalls. "I and my car, because he asked if I could take these bags and duffel bags, suitcases, to the bus station for him."[116] Oswald merely told her that he was unable to find work in Dallas and had decided to try his native New Orleans, and Marina would stay in the Neely Street flat until he had found a job and an apartment. She helped him load her 1955 Chevrolet station wagon and drove him to the downtown bus station. When Oswald went to buy the tickets, Ruth said, "I was thinking, while he was in the bus station, and suggested that it would be a very difficult thing for a pregnant woman with a small child to take a 12-hour, 13-hour bus trip to New Orleans, and suggested that I drive her down with June."[117] Ruth said that instead of Marina returning to the Neely Street apartment, she was welcome to stay with her until she left for New Orleans. He readily accepted the offer. He stopped briefly at his post-office box to pick up fifty leaflets sent to him on April 19 by the Fair Play for Cuba Committee. Adding those to his luggage, he was set for the overnight bus trip home to New Orleans.

7

"Hands off Cuba"

Early in the morning of Thursday, April 25, Lee Oswald called his aunt, Lillian Murret, from the New Orleans bus station.

"Hello, Aunt Lillian?"

"Who is this?"

"This is Lee."

"Lee?"

"Yes."

"When did you get out? When did you get back? What are you doing?" Murret did not even know he had returned from Russia. She had not heard from him in six years.

"I have been back since about a year and a half now."

"Well, I am glad you got back."

"I am married, and I got a baby. I am down here trying to find a job; would you put me up for a while?"

"Well, we will be glad to, Lee."[1]

He took a streetcar to the Murrets', and when he arrived, Lillian says he was "very poorly dressed" and she felt sorry for him. He told Lillian, and his uncle, Charles "Dutz" Murret, that he wanted quickly to find a job and have his wife and daughter join him.[2]*

The next morning he visited the Louisiana Division of Em-

---

* Henry Hurt, in *Reasonable Doubt*, tries to add mystery to the start of the New Orleans period by writing, "He [Oswald] arrived in New Orleans on April 25, 1963, and—after several days that have never been accounted for—moved

ployment Security Office, listed his availability for work, and noted his skill as "photography."[3] His aunt said he was diligent in searching for a job. He read the help-wanted section in each day's newspaper, and left mid-morning to visit the ads he had checked as promising. "I had supper anywhere from 5:30 to 6:00," Murret recalled, "and he was there on time every day for supper, and after he didn't leave the house."[4] After watching television, Oswald went to bed early each evening.*

Three days after his arrival, Lee asked his aunt, "Do you know anything about the Oswalds?" She had only known his father, and once met an uncle. He was disappointed. "Well, you know, I don't know any of my relatives. You are the only one I know."[5] He had been embarrassed in Russia when asked about his own family. Later that day he visited the cemetery where his father was buried and a groundskeeper helped him find the tombstone.[6] Back at the Murrets' he pored over the telephone book, calling every Oswald until he found an aunt by marriage, Hazel. When he called on her in the late afternoon, she gave him a photo of his father and said that only two aunts and some cousins where still alive in New Orleans.† Although she invited him to visit again, he did not.

Monday, he filed an appeal to Texas's decision to deny him unemployment benefits since his wages at Jaggars were too low to qualify.[7]‡ He continued searching for work, filling out applications on which he sometimes listed false names and addresses as references, invented previous jobs, and lied about personal details.[8]

---

in temporarily with relatives . . ." In fact, Oswald moved in with the Murrets the same morning he arrived at the bus station.

* While Oswald was at the Murrets' for two weeks, and then with Marina after she arrived in New Orleans, there was only a single night (August 9, when he was in jail for a pro-Castro street demonstration) out of four months that he was not home and early to bed. His quiet home life, attested to by his wife and relatives, contradicts numerous postassassination tales of Oswald's supposed late-night cavorting with anti-Castro Cubans, homosexuals, or soldiers of fortune.

† He never showed Marina the photo of his father. After Lee's death, it was not found among his belongings.

‡ Oswald filed his appeal on April 29, and by May 8 the unemployment commission ruled in his favor, awarding him the maximum benefit of $369, payable at $33 per week.

On May 3, Oswald wrote Marina saying that while he still had no work, he was receiving "15 to 20 dollars" a week from the unemployment office, and that was enough money on which to live. Without rent or food costs, he saved more than when he supported his family in Dallas on his small salary. His uncle Dutz had offered a $200 loan, but Oswald declined.[9]

He found a job on May 9, two weeks to the day after he arrived in New Orleans. Lillian Murret recalled, "One morning he saw this job with the Reily Coffee Co., and he went down and applied and he got the job, and he came home waving the newspaper, and he grabbed me around the neck, and he even kissed me, and he said, 'I got it; I got it!' "[10] He was hired as a maintenance man, responsible for greasing and oiling the fittings on the company's machinery, at $1.50 an hour.* When Lillian asked how much he earned, he said, "It don't pay much, but I will get along on it." She suggested he return to school and "learn a trade," since "you are really not qualified to do anything too much." "No, I don't have to go back to school," he answered. "I don't have to learn anything. I know everything."[11]

His application at the Reily company was filled with lies. He listed his address as 757 French Street, the Murrets' house, and said he lived there "23 yrs. continu." He claimed his last job was "active duty" in the Marines and that he was a high school graduate and currently a college student. For references, he listed John Murret, a cousin, without his permission, and then added fictitious names, Sgt. Robert Hidell, and Lt. J. Evans, both of whom were on active duty, complete with false addresses.[12]

With the security of a job, Oswald searched for an apartment. He returned to a building where he had once lived, and his former landlady, Myrtle Evans,† looked at him closely for a few minutes, and said, "I know you, don't I?" "Sure, I am Lee Os-

---

* Jim Garrison charges that an Oswald imposter filled in all the applications for jobs in New Orleans, including the one at Reily. He asserts that job was arranged by American intelligence because it wanted Oswald to be nearby to an ex–FBI agent, Guy Banister. But handwriting experts confirmed the writing on all the applications was Oswald's, and witnesses later identified him as the applicant in each case. Oswald also spoke of his job hunting to both his aunt and wife.

† The fictitious reference on his job application earlier that day, Lt. J. Evans, was probably based on Myrtle's husband, Julian Evans.

wald," he said. "I was just waiting to see when you were going to recognize me."[13] She thought he was still "in Russia." He explained he had returned with a Russian wife and daughter, and intended to bring them to New Orleans if Evans could help him find an apartment. Although she did not have any for rent, she made some calls and soon Oswald had given a $5 deposit toward a $65-a-month ground-floor apartment in a two-story house at 4907 Magazine Street.[14] He even lied to his new landlady, Mrs. Jesse Garner, saying that he worked for the Leon Israel Company. It was a real company, but not the one that hired him.

He returned to have lunch with Myrtle Evans, and they discussed Marina and his daughter as well as his reasons for settling in New Orleans. "New Orleans is my home," he said. "I just felt like I wanted to come back." Evans said she would like to meet his family, and he said, "Just come anytime." She never did.

That night Oswald telephoned Marina to tell her about the Reily job and the new apartment. Marina, who worried she might not hear from Lee for some time, was excited about joining him so quickly. The next day, Friday, May 10, Ruth Paine, her two children, and Marina and June set off in Paine's station wagon. Oswald had begun working at Reily the same day. The supervisor who showed him his work duties, Charles Le Blanc, said that from the start Oswald was "just one of these guys that just didn't care whether he learned it or he didn't learn it." Oswald found his new job even more demeaning than his previous ones.

The next day, Saturday, Marina and Ruth arrived at the Murret's, and they spent an hour talking to Oswald's aunt and uncle. Initially, Marina thought the Murret home was the place Lee had rented, and she was very pleased. But when he took her to their new apartment on Magazine Street, she was disappointed to find it dark and dirty, with little ventilation, and cockroach-infested.[15] Ruth slept in the living room with her children while the Oswalds took the only bedroom. She noticed they did not have a pleasant reunion. "He was very discourteous to her," Ruth recalled, "and they argued most of that weekend. I was very uncomfortable in that situation, and he would tell her to shut up, tell her, 'I said it, and that is all the discussion on the subject.' "[16] Their fighting so poisoned the atmosphere that Ruth returned to Dallas on Tuesday, May 14, a day earlier than planned.

On the day Ruth left for Texas, Oswald wrote the Fair Play for Cuba headquarters in New York and notified them of his new mailing address, and he did the same for the Soviet embassy in Washington a few days later.[17] He had requested that his Dallas post-office box mail be forwarded to his Magazine Street apartment, and two of his subscriptions, *The Militant* and a Communist daily subsidized by the USSR, *Soviet Belorussia*, soon arrived. He also received a letter from the Socialist Workers Party of America. It had taken five months to respond to his request for some leftist pamphlets and an English translation to the revolutionary anthem "Internationale."[18]

On May 22, just over a month after he moved to New Orleans, settled with a job and apartment, Oswald began preparing for a new phase of his activist politics. He went to the New Orleans public library and borrowed *Portrait of a Revolutionary: Mao Tse-tung.* Four days later he wrote Vincent (V. T.) Lee, the president of the Fair Play for Cuba Committee, requesting formal membership and saying he wanted to open a Fair Play branch office in New Orleans. He noted that "a picture of Fidel, suitable for framing would be a welcome touch."[19] Although Oswald had expressed admiration for Castro even when he was in the Marines, Marina contended his attraction to Castro peaked in New Orleans. "Well, I knew for a long time that Fidel Castro was his hero," she recalled. "He was a great admirer of him, so, he was in some kind of revolutionary mood at that period of time. He thought that maybe he would be, I mean, he would be happy to work for Fidel Castro causes or something like that."[20] Since the USSR had failed his Marxist theories, the mercurial Oswald now viewed Cuba as the pure embodiment of Communist ideology.[21] Also, Oswald's attraction to Fair Play for Cuba as an instrument for exercising his pro-Castro sentiments fit with his view of Marxism/Leninism. Marina and Ruth and Michael Paine said Oswald was a Trotskyite Marxist.[22] Trotskyites were the heart of the Socialist Workers Party, the key element in the Fair Play for Cuba Committee.[23]

Without waiting for a formal reply from the national office, Oswald acted as though he had permission to start an independent chapter. Picking up where he left off with his Dallas demonstration on behalf of Fair Play, he decided to begin passing out leaflets in New Orleans, but on a grander scale. On Wednesday, May 29, he went to the Jones Printing Company, opposite the side entrance of the Reily company. Using the name Lee Osborne, he said he needed a thousand handbills. He handed the receptionist an 8-by-10-inch sheet of paper on which he had written:

HANDS
OFF
CUBA!
Join the Fair Play for
Cuba Committee
New Orleans Charter
Member Branch
Free Literature, Lectures
Location:
Everyone Welcome![24]

Again under the alias Osborne, he ordered five hundred copies of a yellow, 4-by-9-inch membership application for his Fair Play for Cuba "chapter" from the Mailers' Service Company on Magazine Street.[25] Next, also with Mailers' Service, he placed an order for three hundred $2\frac{1}{2}$-by-$3\frac{1}{2}$-inch membership cards.[26]* By June 4, when Oswald picked up the thousand handbills from the Jones Printing Company, he had received a response from Fair

---

* The question of how Oswald could afford such large printing orders on his minimal income has led some to suggest he had secret sources of funding. Oswald paid cash for all the orders. The 1,000 flyers cost $9.89; the 500 membership applications were $9.34; and the 300 membership cards cost $3.50. The $22.73 printing costs came in a month in which Oswald's total income was $157.58, and with only $44 on housing for the prorated month, he had more than enough for the printing costs (WC Report, App. XIV; Burcham Ex. 1, WC Vol. XIX, p. 192).

Play. In a warm May 29 letter, V. T. Lee sent Oswald an official membership card, and in a three-page typewritten letter offered him advice regarding a possible New Orleans chapter.[27] V. T. Lee told Oswald, "We are certainly not at all adverse to a very small Chapter" and "in fact, we would be very, very pleased to see this take place and would like to do everything possible to assist in bringing it about."[28] Also enclosed were copies of the Fair Play for Cuba Committee's bylaws and constitution. But V. T. Lee also told Oswald that a review of the committee's records indicated there were probably "too few members . . . in the New Orleans area" to make a successful chapter. The letter also warned that Fair Play work would place Oswald under "tremendous pressures" as "we do have a serious and often violent opposition." V. T. Lee's response was the friendliest Oswald ever received to any of his letters to leftist organizations, and it strengthened his faith in Fair Play for Cuba.

Meanwhile, Oswald's preoccupation with Fair Play led him to neglect Marina. She could not have a normal relationship with him while his obsession was Castro. "Mostly—most of the conversations [we had] were on the subject of Cuba," Marina said.[29] On May 25, Marina complained in a letter to Ruth Paine, "My mood currently is that I don't feel much like anything! As soon as you left all 'love' stopped, and I am very hurt that Lee's attitude toward me is such that I feel each minute that I bind him. He insists that I leave America, which I don't want to do at all. . . . And again Lee has said to me that he doesn't love me. . . . How will it all end?"[30] Even when he went out with her, to visit the Murrets for lunch, for instance, she later had to listen to him complain, "Well, these are just bourgeois, who are only concerned with their own individual welfare."[31] Marina said his mood was "gloomy," and overall she considered the marriage a succession of "tears and caresses, arguments and reconciliations."[32]

Although he no longer beat her (she was five months' pregnant), their arguments were fierce, and Marina was frequently heard sobbing.[33] It was not long before their New Orleans neighbors were talking about the bad relationship between the new couple.[34] When they had sex, Oswald would sometimes roll over when finished, turn his back to Marina, and say, "Don't touch me, and don't say a word. I'm in paradise now. I don't want my good mood spoiled."[35] After receiving a letter from Ruth with details of her own marital difficulties with Michael, Marina answered, "It is very sad news . . . as it is the same story with Lee. . . . In many ways you and I are friends in misfortune." In another letter, Marina told Ruth, "You know that Lee either yells at me or is silent, but never talks. It is oppressive."[36]

Although there was little communication, Marina still became aware of some of Oswald's political activities. On Tuesday, June 4, the same day a letter arrived from the Soviet embassy suggesting she travel to Washington to discuss her request to return to the USSR, Lee involved her in his fantasy political world. When he returned that evening from work he "wrote this [A. J. Hidell] down on a piece of paper and told me to sign it on this card," Marina recalled, "and said that he would beat me if I didn't sign . . ."[37] She signed the "Hidell" as the chapter president for Lee's Fair Play for Cuba membership card, as well as on a couple of blank cards. Marina asked him who Hidell was, and Oswald admitted he did not exist. She said, " 'You just have two names?' and he said, 'Yes.' " Unaware of his Marine colleague Heindel, Marina assumed the alias was a rhyme for Fidel. "I said, 'You have selected this name because it sounds like 'Fidel' and he blushed and said, 'Shut up, it is none of your business.' . . . I taunted him about this and teased about this . . . and he said . . . 'I would have to do it this way, people will think I have a big organization' and so forth."[38] "He always brought his pamphlets home," she recalled. "I was kind of pleased that the papers weren't as bad an occupation as playing with the rifle so I couldn't see any harm in that."[39]

Unknown to Marina, two days after he had her sign his Fair Play membership card, he took a government printed form entitled "International Certificates of Vaccination or Revaccination against Smallpox," wrote his name at the top, and then stamped it, with a 98-cent rubber-stamping kit he had bought from a local variety store, with the name Dr. A. J. Hideel [sic].[40] Oswald wanted to travel and planned to apply for a passport, and apparently thought the vaccination certificate might be needed for visas to some countries. On this occasion, instead of threatening to send her to Russia on her own, he insisted he would join her in the Soviet Union. "I'll go to Cuba, then China, and you will wait for me in Russia," he told Marina. "I love to travel and with you, I can't" (he thought her pregnancy hindered her).[41] Oswald rented a new post-office box on June 3 and signed Hidell's name as one of those authorized to use it. Besides himself and Hidell, he listed Marina as well, giving a false home address for all three.[42]

As Oswald began to implement his Fair Play for Cuba activities, he slacked off at his work at Reily. Charles Le Blanc, his supervisor, was increasingly dissatisfied with Oswald's performance. Le Blanc would drop him off on a floor to grease and oil the machinery and then "about a half hour or 45 minutes or so, I would go back up and check how he is doing . . . and I wouldn't find him . . . So I would start hunting all over the [five-story] building . . ."[43] When Le Blanc found Oswald, "I asked him, I said, 'Well, where have you been?' And all he would give me was that he was around. I asked him, 'Around where?' He says, 'Just around,' and he would turn around and walk off." Le Blanc later estimated that Oswald probably spoke one hundred words to him during his two and a half months at Reily. But on one of the few occasions when Oswald spoke to Le Blanc, Lee asked him, "Do you like it here?" Le Blanc, thinking Oswald was referring to the Reily Coffee Company, told him yes, that he had been employed there for eight years. "Oh, hell, I don't mean this place," Oswald said. Le Blanc asked what he meant. "This damn country," replied Oswald.[44] When Le Blanc said he "loved it," Oswald again just turned around and walked away without saying anything else.

As he had on other jobs, he stayed to himself, ate lunch alone, and made no friends among the workers.[45] Some remembered that during their coffee breaks he often sat in a chair and stared blankly into space.[46] Oswald further alienated his co-workers, recalled Le Blanc, by walking past and aiming his forefinger at them. "He would go, 'Pow!' and I used to look at him, and I said, 'Boy, what a crackpot this guy is!' "[47]

On the occasions when Le Blanc could not find him, Oswald had often gone to the neighboring Crescent City Garage. It was run by Adrian Alba, a gun enthusiast, who subscribed to *American Rifleman, Field and Stream, Argosy,* and National Rifle Association magazines. Oswald sat in the garage reading these and often borrowed the magazines overnight. Alba remembered Oswald as inquisitive about guns and specifically about which caliber bullet was the most deadly on a human target.[48] Alba had ordered a .30-06-caliber rifle and Oswald offered to buy it sight unseen. On another occasion, he saw a Japanese rifle at the garage, and again wanted it, but Alba would not sell. He also asked Alba if he "knew of a place where you could discharge firearms . . . without getting the car and riding for hours."[49] Alba told him about the River Road levee, but warned he could be arrested if discovered shooting there.

Among other customers, Alba's garage serviced cars for the Secret Service and FBI. He later told a story, repeated by many conspiracy writers, that he saw Oswald approach a car occupied by an FBI agent from Washington. According to Alba, Oswald then "bent down as if to look in the window and was handed what appeared to be a good-sized envelope . . . I think he put it under his shirt . . . and the car drove off."[50] A few days later he saw Oswald again meet the car and briefly talk to the same FBI agent. If true, Alba's story is the critical link to establish a covert government connection to Oswald. Although Alba was interviewed immediately after the assassination, on at least three occasions by the FBI, and later extensively testified to the Warren Commission, he never mentioned this story. He did not disclose it publicly until 1978, fifteen years after it allegedly happened, when interviewed by Anthony Summers. Alba's excuse for not mentioning the story earlier was that he claimed he forgot it until his memory was triggered years after the incident, while watching a television commercial.[51] The 1970 commercial was for a local furniture store and portrayed an elderly man walking up to a car, leaning over toward the window, and inviting the driver into the store. "That's when I remembered Oswald doing the same thing," he says.[52]* After talking to Summers,

---

* During a conversation with the author, Alba claimed "it was a fact" that Robert Kennedy had personally selected Lee Harvey Oswald to kill Castro, and when Oswald instead killed his brother, Robert Kennedy went around the Justice Department wailing, "Oh God, I killed my brother, I killed my brother." He

Alba testified before the House Select Committee on Assassinations and it thoroughly investigated his claim, discovering that no FBI agents checked a car out of his garage during all of 1963 and concluding that he was of "doubtful reliability."[53]

Although the only part of the workday he found enjoyable was the time spent at Alba's garage, Oswald needed the income and had no choice but to stay at Reily. On June 8, he was reminded of his weak finances when he could not afford to provide for Marina's prenatal care. On that day, he took her to the New Orleans Charity Hospital, but since she had not lived long enough in Louisiana to qualify as a resident, they refused to treat her free of charge. After arguing with a doctor for nearly an hour, Lee left with Marina. He was furious about the American emphasis on money. "Everything is money is this country," he yelled at Marina. "Even the doctors are businessmen. You can't have a baby without money."[54] It was the first time she saw his anger mixed with tears. The hospital rejection highlighted his distaste for capitalism. Although Marina never recalled him saying anything bad about President Kennedy, she said that shortly after the hospital incident, he complained that "his papa bought him the Presidency. Money paves the way to everything here."[55]

Oswald now focused his attention more than ever on politics. He wrote to *The Worker* requesting more Communist party literature, announcing his formation of a local chapter of Fair Play for Cuba, and sent honorary membership cards to "those fighters for peace" Benjamin Davis and Gus Hall, leaders of the American Communist party.[56]* On Sunday, June 16, he put his activism into practice, appearing at the Dumaine Street Wharf, where the U.S.S. *Wasp*, an aircraft carrier, was docked. There, he distributed his Fair Play for Cuba propaganda. In the late

admitted he was always worried, even in 1992, that people who telephoned were FBI or other federal agents trying to pry information from him (Interview with Adrian Alba, March 20, 1992).

* From Dallas, in December, 1962, Oswald had also sent the Hall-Davis Defense Committee some of the posters he made while at Jaggars-Chiles-Stovall, and offered his photographic services. The lawyer for the Defense Committee was John Abt, the legal counsel Oswald requested five months later, when he was arrested for killing the President.

afternoon, the officer of the deck aboard the ship complained to harbor patrolman Girod Ray, who found Oswald and asked if he had permission to distribute the leaflets.[57] Oswald said he did not need it, and would distribute his pamphlets wherever he desired. Ray told him that he was on port authority property and without authorization he had to leave, but Oswald argued with him. Finally, when Ray threatened to arrest him, he left.[58] Oswald was exhilarated by his demonstration, later boasting in a letter to Fair Play president Vincent Lee, "We also manged to picket the fleet when it came in and I was surprised at the number of officers who were interested in our literature."[59]*

Oswald's interest in Cuba now included Marina. He asked her if she liked Cuba and "Uncle Fidel" and said that his demonstrating "will help make people be on the side of Cuba. Do you want them attacking little Cuba?"[60] He pasted a photo of Castro, clipped from the Soviet magazine *Ogonyok*, on their living room wall.

On Monday, June 24, he visited the U.S. passport office and applied for a new passport (one that he never used before his death). His passport had expired exactly one year earlier. Oswald said he intended to travel as a tourist, starting in October, for three months to a year. Destinations included England, France, Germany, Holland, Finland, Poland, Italy, and the USSR.[61] He listed the Lykes shipping line, the same he took during his 1959 defection, as his means of transportation. He also gave his date of marriage to Marina as the nonexistent April 31, 1961, and said his occupation was "photographer." The New Orleans office issued his passport the following day.[62]†

---

* Oswald used "we" when writing to the Fair Play national headquarters since he often wanted to impress them that his local chapter had attracted more volunteers than just him. Officer Ray said Oswald was alone on the day he confronted him on the wharf.

† Since Oswald was a defector, was the overnight processing for his passport unusual? Jim Marrs says that the ease with which Oswald obtained his passport is key evidence "pointing to Oswald's involvement with spy work" (*Crossfire*, pp. 189–90). But only a few months earlier, in order to speed up passport applications, the New Orleans office had instituted a state-of-the-art teletype to Washington. The local newspapers covered the innovation as a major technological advance. When Oswald applied, one-day turnarounds were typical (WC Vol. V, p. 335). All that was required was for the field office, in this case New Orleans, to telex the names of the applicants, together with

Oswald did not tell Marina about his passport. But he did begin talking about how dissatisfied he was with the United States. "Little by little he became gloomier, or disillusioned," recalled Marina.[63] One day she found Oswald sobbing uncontrollably in a darkened kitchen. He said he was lost, and she tried to console him by saying they could stay together in America and still make a better life. But he refused, telling her it was too difficult for him in the U.S.[64] "He was extremely upset," Marina recalled. "He appeared to be very unhappy and he said that nothing keeps him here [in the U.S.], and that he would not lose anything if he returned to the Soviet Union, and that he wants to be with me. And that it would be better to have less and not be concerned about tomorrow. . . . I don't think he was too fond of Russia, but simply he knew that he would have work assured him there, because he had—after all, he had to think about his family."[65] "Would you like me to come to Russia, too?" he asked. A year after returning to the U.S., filled with hatred for the USSR, the mercurial Oswald had second thoughts as his life in the U.S. seemed in a quagmire over which he had lost control.

Less than a week after getting his new passport, Oswald had Marina write another letter to the Soviet embassy.[66] A letter from the embassy had arrived on June 4, asking Marina to visit in person or to send a detailed explanation of why she wanted to return to Russia. She excused the delay in answering due to "certain family problems," expressed "homesickness" for Russia, and asked for financial help for a return to the Soviet Union. "But things are improving," she wrote, "due to the fact that my

their place and date of birth, to the Department of State. Then Washington checked through a lookout-card file, and if there was no card for that person, it automatically authorized the field office to issue a passport. There was no lookout card for Oswald, and legally there was no reason to deny him a passport (WC Vol. V, p. 317). Oswald had repaid his repatriation loan to the State Department, his defection to the USSR was not a bar, and there was no indication in the file that he was under criminal indictment, wanted by the police, or a member of the Communist party (WC Vol. V, pp. 317, 329–30, 376). "They [the State Department] could not have refused a passport," said Abram Chayes, the State Department legal adviser in 1964, "based on the information in the Oswald file" (WC Vol. V, pp. 317). Near the time of Oswald's application, another defector to a Communist country, Paul David Wilson, applied for a passport and it was also routinely issued (WC Vol. V, pp. 338–39; WC Vol. XI, pp. 204–5).

husband expresses a sincere wish to return together with me to the USSR. I earnestly beg you to help him in this. There is not much encouraging for us here and nothing to hold us. . . . My husband is often unemployed. It is very difficult for us to live here. We both urgently solicit your assistance to enable us to return and work in the USSR. . . . Please do not deny our request. Make us happy again, help us to return that which we lost because of our foolishness. I would like to have my second child, too, to be born in the USSR." Enclosed with the letter was an application completed by Lee for permission to enter the Soviet Union.[67] He also included a short note, in English, asking that Marina's visa be "rushed" so she could have the baby, due in four months, in Russia, and that his request should be considered "separtably."[68]

Although Oswald was still demanding and abrupt, their fighting temporarily subsided. He spent his evenings quietly reading books from the public library.* The Oswalds wrote to friends in the Soviet Union, like Ziger and Titovets, telling them they planned to return to the USSR. One answered him saying that he should be sure he wanted to return, as his next Atlantic crossing was likely to be the last the Soviets allowed him.[69]

Marina again wrote the Soviet embassy on July 8, emphasizing their "impatience" with the delay over visas and asking for expedited service.[70] A few days later, Marina received a letter from Ruth Paine, who was unaware of Lee's recent change of mind about returning to Russia. Ruth invited Marina to live with her if Lee still insisted she return to the Soviet Union. "Marina, come to my home the last part of September [just before the baby was due] without fail," Ruth wrote. "Either for two months or two years. And don't be worried about money."[71] Ruth soon sent another letter, reiterating that Marina should not be concerned about the money, because Michael was financially secure and would gladly help them.[72]

Yet just as things seemed to stabilize, Oswald was fired from Reily, on July 19.[73] It was the third job dismissal in less than a

---

* He read a broad range of books, including science fiction, spy novels, volumes about Communism, and even two books involving John Kennedy—William Manchester's biography, *Portrait of a President,* and Kennedy's *Profiles in Courage.*

year. To worsen his sense of failure, his sedulous efforts to find another job through the help-wanted ads met with constant rejection. In order to continue collecting unemployment benefits of $33 per week, he had to visit the Louisiana Employment Commission personally every Tuesday and report on his job-hunting progress. He let his fantasies run free and not only listed scores of employers to which he never applied, including NASA, but he also lied extensively on the applications he did submit for work.[74]

Several days after Oswald was fired, Marina received another letter from Ruth Paine, offering to visit New Orleans in mid- to late September, at the end of a long vacation, and then take Marina back to Dallas to have her baby.[75] Paine's offer now looked more acceptable in case Lee could not find work, but he did not relish the idea of Marina returning to Dallas and the Russian community that so disliked him.

The succession of unsettling news continued. On July 25, Oswald was notified that his 1962 demand for a review of his undesirable Marine Corps discharge was rejected.[76] He was infuriated. The Marine Corps had initially given him an honorable discharge and then belatedly changed it to an "undesirable" discharge, based upon his defection to Russia and anti-American statements he made to the press.[77] Oswald had written letters, in January 1962, to John Connally, the former secretary of the Navy, and the Department of the Navy, saying his defection to the USSR was "much in the same way E. Hemingway resided in Paris."[78] He was convinced his defection should have no bearing on his Marine service.

That Saturday, Marina and Lee traveled to Mobile, Alabama, with Lillian and Dutz Murret, to visit his cousin Eugene Murret, who was training to be a Jesuit priest. Eugene had invited Oswald by letter to speak to the students about "contemporary Russia and the practice of Communism."[79] Oswald gave a half-hour talk that evening. Those present later described him as "very tense and high-strung." He confirmed he was a Marxist, although he admitted that he was disillusioned with the USSR.[80] In fact, he said he was against most forms of organized government. "Capitalism doesn't work, communism doesn't work. In the middle is socialism, and that doesn't work either."[81]

Back in New Orleans, he tried to have another three thousand "Hands off Cuba" flyers printed, but for reasons that are unclear, he was turned away from the print shop. On August 1, the New Orleans *Times-Picayune* ran a front-page story saying that federal agents had seized a ton of dynamite and other materials on a raid of an anti-Castro paramilitary group planning operations against Cuba. That same day Oswald wrote to Vincent Lee, Fair Play's president.[82] The letter is almost a complete fabrication. He claimed that he had attracted "great interest" in his local chapter, that anti-Castro agitators were attacking him and ruining his base of popular support, and that he had distributed "thousands of circulars." There was one sentence, however, that later caused considerable debate: "I rented an office as I planned and was promptly closed three days later for some obscure reasons by the renters." Oswald stamped addresses for his fictional chapter of the Fair Play for Cuba Committee on the printed leaflets. Most were marked "L. H. Oswald, 4907 Magazine Street" or "A. J. Hidell, P.O. Box 30016" (the dyslexic Oswald transposed the last two digits of his post-office box, as it should have been 30061). But some were stamped "544 Camp St."

If Oswald had an office, even briefly, at 544 Camp, it could be significant, for as Jim Marrs writes, "It was at 544 Camp Street in an old, three-story office building that the paths of Lee Harvey Oswald, the FBI, the CIA, anti-Castro Cubans, and organized crime figures all crossed."[83] That address was the office of Guy Banister, a highly decorated ex–FBI agent who maintained a relationship with Naval Intelligence as well as doing investigative work for G. Wray Gill, an attorney for New Orleans crime boss Carlos Marcello.[84] Another frequent Camp Street visitor was David Ferrie, a rabid anti-Communist who worked with Banister, for some of the most radical anti-Cuban groups, and also for the attorney for Marcello.[85]

Ferrie and Banister were a strange and memorable pair of associates. Ferrie was a self-ordained ultra-orthodox Catholic bishop and an amateur hypnotist and cancer researcher.[86] This self-proclaimed fighter pilot and soldier of fortune was eccentric but brilliant. He suffered from alopecia totalis, a rare disease that left him totally hairless. He wore a badly fitted red wig and sometimes glued on tufts of synthetic fabric for eyebrows.[87] Banister, former agent-in-charge of the Chicago FBI office and then deputy police chief of New Orleans, established his own detective agency in 1958.[88] He was an obsessive crusader against Communism and belonged to several radical right-wing groups, including the John Birch Society and the paramilitary Minutemen. He even published his own virulently racist journal, *The Intelligence Digest.*[89]

Many claim Banister was possibly the middleman linking the CIA and the mafia in a plot to kill the President. But the only Oswald-Banister connection is 544 Camp Street. Most ignore that the FBI and Secret Service conducted an extensive investigation in December 1963 to determine whether Oswald was ever at 544 Camp. None of the building's five tenants, or the janitor who lived there, recalled ever seeing Oswald visit there, much less rent an office as a tenant.[90] None ever heard of the Fair Play for Cuba Committee or saw any propaganda from the organization. Sam Newman, the building's owner, personally rented all office space and was adamant he never met or saw Oswald, never rented space to anyone from the Fair Play for Cuba Committee, and indeed did not rent any of 544 Camp's three empty offices during the summer of 1963.[91] A militant anti-Castro organization, the Cuban Revolutionary Council, had rented an office at 544 Camp but had moved out more than a year before Oswald arrived in New Orleans.[92] Such testimony seemed to settle the issue, and allowed the Warren Commission to conclude "investigation has indicated that neither the Fair Play for Cuba Committee nor Lee Harvey Oswald ever maintained an office at that address."[93]

The House Select Committee on Assassinations, however, re-examined the issue in the late 1970s.* Two witnesses now told

---

* The investigator on the 544 Camp Street issue, as well as the question of any Oswald relationship to either Guy Banister or David Ferrie, was Gaeton Fonzi. Fonzi seems an unusual choice for an inquiry that claimed to be impartial, as he was a committed believer in a conspiracy, having written his first article critical of the Warren Commission in 1966. After the House Select Committee finished its work and concluded that Oswald shot JFK as part of a conspiracy, Fonzi wrote a scathing 80,000-word article in *The Washingtonian* attacking the committee for not going far enough in its conspiracy conclu-

the Select Committee they saw Oswald at 544 Camp Street with Banister. One was Jack Martin, a former private investigator who sometimes worked with Banister. But Martin was an admitted drunk who had previously given statements to the FBI that he had never seen Oswald at 544 Camp Street.[94] Hubie Badeaux, the former chief of the New Orleans police intelligence division, knew both Banister and Martin. "Jack drank, took pills, and had a criminal record," Badeaux told the author. "He was goofy to begin with, and lied all the time."[95] The Select Committee concluded Martin's testimony was so "contradictory . . . [that] credence should not be placed in Martin's statements to the committee."[96] The second witness was Guy Banister's former secretary, Delphine Roberts. In one interview, she told the committee that Oswald had never visited 544 Camp, but in a subsequent one she said he had been in Banister's office several times.[97] The Select Committee concluded that because of the contradictions in Roberts's statements "and lack of independent corroboration . . . the reliability of her statements could not be determined." The Select Committee questioned six other individuals who worked for Guy Banister during the summer of 1963, and none of them recalled seeing Oswald at 544 Camp.[98]

Anthony Summers interviewed Roberts in 1978, and she told him a different, and wilder, story than the one she gave to the Select Committee. Roberts said that Oswald had come to 544 Camp Street and she interviewed him to become "one of Banister's agents," that he maintained an office on the floor above them, and that he often visited privately with Banister.[99] Summers interviewed Roberts's daughter, also named Delphine, who claimed she used an upstairs room for photographic work. She said that Oswald kept his pro-Castro pamphlets in an office at 544 Camp and he came there often and knew Banister.[100] Many subsequent conspiracy writers, as well as Oliver Stone in the film *JFK*, have relied heavily on these statements.*

The author located both Delphine Roberts and her daughter

---

sions, and setting forth his own hypothesis of how renegade CIA agents masterminded JFK's death.

*Some critics use less credible witnesses to establish an Oswald link to Camp Street. Garrison, during his investigation, found a local resident, David Lewis, who claimed he often saw Oswald in Mancuso's Restaurant on the

in New Orleans. The mother is still a rabid anti-Communist and racist who rails against the U.N. Charter and "niggers." She says, "Jesse Jackson is a satan in the skin of a human" and contends that every Japanese "should have been wiped off the face of the earth."[101] She claims to be related to the "king and queen of Wales [sic] and Mary Queen of Scots," as well as "being one of the very few, since the beginning of the world, who has ever read the sacred scrolls that God himself wrote and gave to the ancient Hebrews for placing in the Ark of the Covenant. . . . I think I have been the last person to see them."[102] Roberts asserts there was "Communist involvement" in the JFK assassination, talks vaguely of a dead pigeon being brought to her by a stranger, which was then sent off to JFK as a threat, and claims she is writing a book about the assassination, "although it will also tell the story of the Creation." She warmly remembers that she first met Guy Banister when she was demonstrating in downtown New Orleans "for states' rights, and against the niggers," with a Confederate flag draped behind her. She said she not only became Banister's secretary but his mistress as well.*

As for Anthony Summers, Delphine Roberts admits, "I didn't tell him all the truth." She claims the only reason she told him the story she did was that Summers, then shooting a television documentary, paid her money. Roberts, who lives with her daughter, survives on welfare. "He [Summers] said our information wasn't worth much," she says. "He did give us $500 eventually, and they did take us to dinner. We did enjoy the dinner." John Lanne, a former Banister friend and attorney, acknowledges that Roberts refused to speak to Summers unless she was paid.[103]†

---

ground floor of Camp Street. The problem was that Lewis swore he saw Oswald there in early 1962, when Lee was still in Russia.

* Two of Banister's closest friends, John Lanne and Hubie Badeaux, confirmed to the author that Roberts was Banister's mistress. They both said that after Banister's unexpected death by heart attack in 1964, his wife took possession of all of her husband's files and barred Delphine from the office, leaving her extremely bitter.

† Anthony Summers told the author that he had met with Delphine Roberts at John Lanne's office. There, Lanne, whom Summers "thought to be fairly mad, certainly odd," pulled a pistol from his desk, waved it in the air, and told

As unreliable as Delphine Roberts is regarding the Oswald–544 Camp Street issue, her daughter spins an equally untenable tale. She told the author that Oswald did not have an office at 544 Camp, but rather that "he lived there, had an apartment there, for two or three months."[104] Oswald came to 544 Camp at night and left every morning, she said, during the same period that Marina said he was never away from their house for a single evening (except his overnight stay in jail). She also says she met Oswald's mother and that "she was lovely." Marguerite lived in Texas during 1963. When Oswald finally abandoned his "apartment," Delphine claimed he left behind "boxes and boxes of pamphlets, everything, just everything."[105]

The House Select Committee did not go far enough in branding Roberts's testimony as unreliable. Summers caveated Delphine Roberts's story by writing, "It is by no means certain that [she] has told the whole truth . . ." and attempted to buttress her testimony by citing her daughter.[106] There simply is no credible evidence that Oswald ever had an office at 544 Camp Street or, much less, that he knew Guy Banister.

But what of Oswald's stamp "544 Camp Street" on some of his Fair Play for Cuba leaflets? There are several nonsinister explanations. When Oswald worked at Reily, he was only a block away from 544 Camp Street and his weekly visits to the unemployment commission took him directly past the address. He easily could have seen the FOR RENT signs at the small corner building. The offices at 544 Camp started at $30 a month, too much for Oswald on his minimal income, and his letter to Vincent Lee that he had rented an office and then was told to leave after three days is certainly a fabrication (as were many other

---

Summers he could not interview his client, Delphine. Summers drove Delphine home from that meeting, and during the ride, "she suddenly, more or less, broke up, put her hands to her face, and said, 'Mr. Summers, look, why should I bottle this up?'" She then told him the story he wrote in his book. Following that discussion, Summers told Roberts that he wanted to do an interview for television. He says that "several days later, at the urging of her daughter, Delphine Jr., a big fat lady, she agreed to do the interview, not for $500, but if I rightly recall, for $250 to $300." Summers says, "Just so you know, the general tariff I make is that I do not pay people to do interviews for the book, ever, but I do regard television interviews as a different thing" (Interview with Anthony Summers, May 31, 1993).

statements he used to enhance his importance to the national headquarters). However, there is evidence he may have actually stopped by to see an office at 544 Camp. The building's janitor, James Arthus, who lived in the basement, told the FBI after the assassination that someone had attempted to rent an office, but he had discouraged him.[107] Arthus could not identify the man. But there is a possibility that it was Oswald who talked to Arthus about an office and, if so, that was the extent of his contact to the building, though he still stamped it on some of his leaflets as the "official" office address for Fair Play. Another explanation is advanced by Ross Banister, Guy's brother, who is convinced that Banister, who monitored Communist agitators, would have been very interested in Oswald's Fair Play activities.[108] Banister's office and his anti-Communist crusade were well known in New Orleans, and a year before Oswald moved to New Orleans, 544 Camp Street was the headquarters for a radical anti-Castro group, the Cuban Revolutionary Council.[109] Some of its propaganda still carried the old Camp Street address even when Oswald lived in New Orleans. It is possible that Oswald, who had used phony addresses on dozens of applications and forms, had decided when settling on a false address for his imaginary Fair Play chapter that it should embarrass his nemesis, the extreme right wing and the city's anti-Castro militants.

The issue of whether Oswald associated with the adventurer David Ferrie during the summer of 1963 is equally important, since Ferrie had extensive anti-Castro Cuban contacts and also did some work for an attorney for Carlos Marcello, the New Orleans godfather. According to the House Select Committee and its investigator Gaetón Fonzi, the two most credible pieces of information linking Oswald and Ferrie are Oswald's 1955 Civil Air Patrol service, when Ferrie was allegedly the commanding officer, and a 1963 incident in Clinton, Louisiana, where six witnesses identified Ferrie, Oswald, and a third person, New Orleans businessman Clay Shaw.*

When Oswald was fifteen, he briefly joined the New Orleans

---

* Jim Garrison also found another witness, Perry Raymond Russo, who claimed to be at a party where Ferrie, Oswald, and Shaw discussed their plans to assassinate Kennedy. The problem is that Russo only remembered the story when given drugs and asked leading questions while under hypnosis. He later

Civil Air Patrol (CAP), at a time the House Select Committee believed Ferrie was the squadron captain. Several witnesses told the Select Committee, twenty-three years after the event, that they thought they recalled Ferrie as the group leader in 1955 when Oswald was in CAP. Summers suggests Oswald may have been the object of Ferrie's homosexual advances or, at the very least, his political influence.[110] Garrison charges that through Oswald's attendance at several CAP meetings, Ferrie initiated him into the CIA.[111] Ferrie was interviewed by the FBI on November 27, 1963, and denied ever knowing Oswald in the Civil Air Patrol.[112]* CAP records show that while Ferrie was a member through 1954, he was disciplined because he gave unauthorized political lectures to the cadets.[113] When he submitted his 1955 renewal, he was rejected.[114] Ferrie was not reinstated until December 1958.[115] Although he was not even supposed to be in the Civil Air Patrol when Oswald was a member in 1955, he may have continued to attend CAP events with a unit in Metarie (a New Orleans suburb). A photo produced in 1993 purported to show Ferrie and Oswald standing on opposite sides of a small group at a CAP cookout. Another photo, yet to be published, shows Oswald and Ferrie talking to each other.† If the photos are legitimate, they show that Ferrie ignored his official CAP suspension. Yet, even if the two met in 1955 when Oswald was fifteen years old, the question then is whether the two rekindled any association in 1963, only months before JFK's assassination.

The evidence for a later Oswald-Ferrie relationship is the testimony of witnesses from Clinton, Louisiana. The witnesses were found by Jim Garrison's investigators, in 1967, when they

---

contradicted himself numerous times, then finally recanted. For more on Russo, see Chapter 18.

* The FBI's interview of Ferrie was prompted by two rumors, later repeated in Garrison's investigation. One was that Ferrie's New Orleans library card had been found in a search of Oswald's house in Dallas after the assassination. That was false, and Ferrie produced his library card for the FBI agents in the November 27 interview. The second rumor was that Ferrie was to use his plane as a getaway vehicle for Oswald. The FBI discovered that his single-engine four-passenger monoplane had not been airworthy since 1962.

† These photos have not yet been tested for their authenticity. During the late 1960s probe by Garrison, two other photos that purported to show Oswald and Ferrie together in CAP were unmasked as composites.

interviewed more than three hundred people in Clinton and the neighboring township of Jackson, some 20 percent of the local population. From this enormous dragnet they produced six witnesses.[116] The allegation is that in early September 1963, Oswald conspicuously appeared in Clinton, a dusty, backwater town of fifteen hundred people, some ninety miles from New Orleans. At the time of the supposed appearance, the Congress of Racial Equality (CORE) was organizing blacks to register to vote in the still-segregated South. According to the way the witnesses now tell the story, on the same day that a long line of black residents waited to sign forms at the registrar's office, a large, expensive car pulled into Clinton and parked near that office. It attracted considerable attention in the poor rural town.[117]

One young man got out and joined the line of blacks waiting to register. That man was identified as Oswald. According to Garrison, since Oswald was the only white man in the long line, the witnesses found his face and the scene "unforgettable."[118] One of the other passengers in the car was identified as David Ferrie. Garrison says "There was no doubt that this was David Ferrie."[119]* Other Clinton witnesses say that Oswald got a haircut while there and asked about obtaining a job at a local mental hospital.[120]

Not only is the Clinton episode used to establish the Oswald-Ferrie link, but some give it greater significance. Summers says it might be "connected with the FBI's infamous Counterintelligence Program, better known as COINTELPRO," a program to infiltrate political groups like CORE.[121] History professor Philip H. Melanson says that the incident "might even be part of an illegal CIA domestic spying effort on leftist organizations like CORE."[122]

The House Select Committee interviewed six Clinton wit-

---

* The car's driver was allegedly identified by all the witnesses as Clay Shaw, the tall, distinguished businessman from the International Trade Mart. Jim Garrison used the Clinton evidence in his unsuccessful 1969 trial against Shaw, trying to tie him to Oswald. However, few critics now believe that the third man was Shaw. As Anthony Summers says, the case against Shaw "was extremely weak," so "many investigators now favor the theory that the car's driver was in fact Guy Banister." Except for their both having white hair, Shaw and Banister did not look alike.

nesses and found their testimony, fifteen years after the event, "credible and significant."[123] The committee concluded they were "telling the truth" and "[t]herefore, [is] inclined to believe that Oswald was in Clinton, La., in late August, early September 1963, and was in the company of David Ferrie, if not Clay Shaw."[124] While the Select Committee sealed the testimony of the Clinton witnesses under the confidentiality cloak of executive sessions, it firmly established an Oswald-Ferrie connection as part of the historical record.[125]

Since Garrison's investigators uncovered the Clinton witnesses, evidently no researcher has gained access to the witnesses' original statements. The author, however, obtained affidavits, handwritten statements, and summary memoranda to Garrison regarding the initial stories the witnesses told the investigators.* Their original statements reveal substantial confusion, and only after extensive coaching by the Garrison staff did the witnesses tell a cohesive and consistent story. By the time they testified to the Select Committee, they had told their story so often that they had ironed out fundamental contradictions. The following discussion is based on the witnesses' original statements.

The first problem arises over the time of the purported visit. Summers says the episode took place "in early September."[126] It is imperative that the alleged visit not have taken place later because Oswald permanently left New Orleans and Louisiana on September 24. But Edward McGehee, the Jackson town barber who claimed to have cut Oswald's hair and advised him about a job at the local mental hospital, said it "was kind of cool" on the day he saw Oswald. He remembered the air conditioner was not on in his shop. Reeves Morgan, the state representative for the parish, said Oswald visited him at his home to inquire about obtaining the hospital job. There was a chill in the air, and Morgan recalled lighting the fireplace.[127] Review of U.S. Weather Bureau records for the period through September 24 show daily temperatures above 90 degrees, with only a few days dipping into the eighties, with high humidity.[128] There was certainly no

---

* All of the papers were in the files of the late Edward Wegmann, one of Clay Shaw's defense lawyers.

day that was "cool" or required a burning fireplace. The registrar of voters, Henry Palmer, felt very strongly that the visit was
the "first week of October, possibly around the 6th or 7th."[129]
Oswald was in Dallas then.

In their testimony at the Shaw trial, and in subsequent statements, all the witnesses described a black Cadillac entering the
town. Summers says that "everyone agrees" the car was a black
Cadillac.[130] In his statement to Garrison's investigators, Corey
Collins, the local CORE chairman, said it was a big, black, ex-
pensive-looking car, with four doors, and not more than two
years old.[131] Edward McGehee described it as an old, dark-
colored, beat-up car, probably a Nash or Kaiser, but probably
not a station wagon.[132]

Since the Garrison trial, the witnesses have consistently described only three men—Oswald, Ferrie, and Shaw—in the car.
However, originally, they were not nearly as certain on the number of people, much less their identifications. Corey Collins said
the driver of the car (whom he later identified as Clay Shaw)
was about forty-five years old and wore a light hat that prevented Collins from seeing his hair.[133] John Manchester, the
town marshal, said the driver did not have a hat and his hair
was gray.[134] Henry Burnell Clark, a local resident, said the man
had no hat and "looked like a movie star."[135] McGehee, who
claimed Oswald sat in his barber chair staring at a photo of
Martin Luther King at a Communist training school, said a young
woman may have been the driver.[136]

McGehee also said that only Oswald and the young woman
were in the car, with a baby bassinet in the rear seat.[137]* Andrew
Dunn said there were four men and that one of them was Estes
Morgan, a local resident. "I knew Estes Morgan personally," said
Dunn.[138] At the Garrison trial, Dunn described only three men
and omitted Morgan.[139] Town marshal John Manchester said
there were only two men in the car and that about that time he
also saw Estes Morgan, whom he knew well, in the voter-regis-

---

* McGehee's testimony is so different from any of the others' that some
critics suggest Oswald visited the barber shop on a different day than when he
appeared in the voter registration line. Postulating a second Oswald car trip,
especially since he did not drive, compounds the critics' problems, since Marina testified he was in New Orleans every day during August and September.

tration line.[140] Corey Collins remembered two men in the car.[141] At the Garrison trial Collins identified three.[142] Henry Burnell Clark, on the other hand, said there was only one man in the car.[143] He said he saw Ferrie, "or his twin," on another day, and recognized him from photos because his hair was "bushy and stood up [in] all directions on his head like he had been out on a drunk all night."[144] Bobbie Dedon claimed she did not see the car but that she spotted Oswald at the nearby Louisiana State Hospital applying for a job. She also connected Oswald to Estes Morgan, but dropped that association during her trial testimony.[145] Another hospital employee, Maxine Kemp, testified she did not see Oswald, but saw a job application with his name on it. A thorough search of the hospital's records shows no such application existed or had been filed.[146]

Registrar of voters Henry Palmer, at the Garrison trial, gave the most potentially damaging testimony identifying Oswald. He said that when Oswald was attempting to register to vote, he had interviewed him. He later told Summers, "I asked him for his identification, and he pulled out a U.S. Navy ID card. . . . I looked at the name on it, and it was Lee H. Oswald with a New Orleans address."[147] But Palmer said much more than that in his 1967 statement to Garrison's office. Not only did he think the visit was in October, but he said there were only two white men in the voter-registration line that morning, and as a result they were very conspicuous. When he spoke to them, he learned one was Estes Morgan and the other was Lee Oswald. He said he interviewed both Morgan and Oswald separately in his office, and said Oswald produced a "cancelled Navy I.D. card" and that Oswald told him he had been living in Jackson for six months with a doctor from the hospital. Palmer could not remember the doctor's name. In his trial testimony and subsequently, he omitted Estes Morgan and the story of Oswald living with a local doctor for six months. He saw two men in the black car outside the voter-registration site and identified one as Ferrie, solely upon his "heavy eyebrows."[148] Palmer told the Garrison investigators that he only had a side angle of the driver and "could not positively identify him." Yet at the trial, under oath, he emphatically picked out Clay Shaw as the driver.

None of the Clinton witnesses had a good explanation for why they had not contacted the authorities if they thought they had seen Oswald. One, Reeves Morgan, testified he had called the FBI after the assassination. There is no record of such a call.[149] There is little doubt the Clinton witnesses are telling the truth as they now recall it. However, their original statements to Garrison's staff reveal considerable contradictions, so much so that the very heart of their story is invalidated. Oswald clearly was not in Clinton in October or when it was cold, nor was he there with Marina, nor did he live there for six months with a doctor, or apply for a job at the local mental institution. Garrison's staff realized that the local resident Estes Morgan had no connection to Oswald, Ferrie, and Shaw and therefore required the witnesses to drop their reference to Morgan being with Oswald. The evidence shows the witnesses saw Estes Morgan, whom they personally knew, with someone whom they later mistook to be Oswald. Garrison never mentioned Morgan because he did not support his hypothesis. (The author was unable to locate Morgan.)

It was almost six years after the alleged incident in Clinton that the witnesses first testified at the Garrison trial. Garrison's staff, when questioning the Clinton witnesses, had only presented photos of Oswald, Ferrie, and Shaw, and incorrectly said that others had already identified those as the people who had visited the town. This power of suggestion, and later coaching, developed the testimony that today has been repeated so often that the House Select Committee found it convincing.

Irvin Dymond, the New Orleans attorney who led the legal team that defended Clay Shaw in 1967, told the author that the Clinton testimony is "a pack of lies. What the motive of the Clinton witnesses is I do not know. But it is clearly and demonstrably false."[150]

There is no credible evidence that Oswald knew Guy Banister or had any association with David Ferrie during the critical months preceding the assassination. Marina cannot visualize him working with an accomplice. "I am not a psychiatrist . . . but living with a person for a few years you at least have some kind of intuition about what he might do or might not. He was not a trustworthy and open person. So, personally, I seriously doubt that he will confide in someone."[151] As Oswald moved toward more radical actions at the start of August 1963, he was acting quite alone.

8

"Our Papa Is out of His Mind"

Oswald's initial efforts on behalf of Fair Play for Cuba had not attracted a single recruit. While Marina found him somewhat disillusioned, he remained committed to his cause. But she was concerned because she thought he was increasingly disconnected from reality. He began telling her that he would be "prime minister" of the U.S. in twenty years, and she begged him to come down from his "castle of air."[1] Yet his exaggerated sense of self-worth received a boost during the first days of August, when he received a letter from Arnold Johnson, director of the Information and Lecture Bureau of the U.S. Communist party.[2] Johnson was responding to Oswald's letter in which he sent honorary Fair Play membership cards to Communist party directors Gus Hall and Benjamin Davis. Johnson enclosed Communist literature on Cuba and congratulated Oswald, saying, "It is good to know that movements in support of Fair Play for Cuba has [sic] developed in New Orleans . . ."[3] Johnson was one of the highest-ranking U.S. Communist officials ever to acknowledge one of Oswald's letters. Later, when Marina and Lee argued over his Fair Play activities and she contended, "Has one person come to you as a result of them [the leaflets]? People don't care about that here," his response was often a tearful reading of the Johnson letter aloud. "See this?" he demanded, shaking the letter. "These are people who understand me and think I'm doing useful work. If he respects what I'm doing, then it's important. He's the Lenin of our country."[4]

Convinced his work for Cuba was gaining the attention of national leftist leaders, Oswald was encouraged to embark on a new gambit. Having read only a week earlier about anti-Castro militants and their armed training camp, raided by federal agents across the river from New Orleans, Oswald was ready to infiltrate the "enemy." On Monday, August 5, he walked into a Cuban-owned general goods store, Casa Roca.* Behind the counter was the co-manager, Carlos Bringuier, a twenty-nine-year-old Cuban lawyer who also was the New Orleans delegate for the anti-Castro Cuban Student Directorate. Casa Roca served as the Student Directorate's unofficial headquarters, as well as a general clearinghouse for Cuban activities in New Orleans. Bringuier was explaining the Cuban fight against Castro to two fifteen-year-old Americans, Philip Geraci and Vance Blalock, when Oswald walked up to them. Geraci recalled that Oswald asked, "Is this the Cuban exiles' headquarters?"[5]†

"He started to agree with my point of view and he showed real interest in the fight against Castro," recalled Bringuier. "He told me that he was against Castro and that he was against Communism."[6] Then Oswald requested some literature, which Bringuier gave him. "After that, Oswald told me that he had been in

---

* Also on August 5, the Soviet embassy notified Marina that her request to enter the USSR had been forwarded to Moscow for processing. And unknown to the Oswalds, that same day, the FBI interviewed his landlady, Jesse Garner. She confirmed he was in the city. At that point, the New Orleans FBI office became chiefly responsible for Oswald. Special agent Milton Kaack was assigned to the matter.

† In his address book, Oswald had three addresses listed on the same page with Carlos Bringuier's name: 117 Camp, 107 Decatur, and 1032 Canal. Harold Weisberg claimed the first address was a formal-dress shop and the second did not exist. He then juggled the numbers and determined that if Oswald had meant 107 Camp and 117 Decatur, that would lead to two anti-Castro militants. It shows the extent to which some will speculate. In fact, Weisberg searched the addresses when he helped Jim Garrison in his 1967 investigation. Instead, a review of 1963 records reveals there is no mystery or mixup. 117 Camp was the Hispanic-American Discount House, owned by two prominent Cubans (it was only a dress shop when Weisberg saw it years later). 107 Decatur was Bringuier's Casa Roca. 1032 Canal was at the corner of Canal and Ramparts, the New Orleans Discount Center, owned by a Jewish Cuban. The addresses were part of Oswald's efforts to discover the headquarters of the Cuban exiles.

the Marine Corps and that he had training in guerilla warfare and that he was willing to train Cubans to fight against Castro," said Bringuier. "Even more, he told me that he was willing to go himself to fight against Castro."[7]

Bringuier rejected the offer. "I had nothing to do with military operations, and the paramilitary training camp across the river had just been raided a few days earlier," Bringuier says. "My first reaction was this guy could either be an FBI agent or an agent of Castro just trying to find out what we were doing. Something about his offer to train Cubans seemed strange to me."[8] Bringuier walked away from the counter, leaving Geraci and Blalock talking to Oswald. When they told Oswald they were interested in guerrilla warfare, he regaled them with stories of how to derail a train, blow up a bridge, and make a homemade pistol and gunpowder.[9]

The next day Oswald returned to Casa Roca. He left his Marine Corps training manual for Bringuier as evidence of his good faith.* But Bringuier remained uninterested in Oswald and did not try to contact him. Then, three days later, on Friday, August 9, one of his Cuban friends, Celso Hernandez, ran into the store. "He was upset and angry," says Bringuier, "because when he got off the bus at Canal Street, he had seen an American with a sign that said 'Viva Fidel! Hands off Cuba!' Celso's English was terrible, so he cursed the American in Spanish and then ran to tell me."[10] Bringuier grabbed a poster showing the Statute of Liberty with a knife in the back, proclaiming that "90 miles away Cuba lies in chains!" and left with Hernandez to find the American demonstrator. On the way, they stopped at a nearby restaurant and picked up another young Cuban, Miguel Cruz. "So the three of us went to Canal Street and couldn't find the guy," Bringuier says. "We went down the side streets, and no sign of him. We took a streetcar, even with our big sign, and stood up looking in every direction for that Communist, but he was nowhere."[11]

Bringuier returned to his store. A few minutes later Miguel Cruz dashed in with the news that the American was back at

---

* Bringuier still has the manual, and showed it to the author. It is inscribed in pen on the inside front cover: "Private Lee H. Oswald."

Canal and St. Charles. Again, they raced to confront him. "When the three of us approached him, the guy looked at me and I said, 'That's the same American who was in the store,'" says Bringuier. Oswald had a placard around his neck and was distributing Fair Play for Cuba leaflets. "He looked at me and smiled and he put his hand out to shake my hand, and I refused. I was angry and started to call him names, 'Why, you are a Communist! You traitor! What are you doing?' "[12] A crowd formed as the shouting started. Bringuier tried to incite the throng against Oswald, telling them he was a Communist who had pretended to befriend the Cuban movement when actually he was a friend of Castro. Some in the crowd began jeering at Oswald, telling him to go to Russia. The crowd's reaction further provoked Bringuier, who later said, "I lost control and I took my glasses off as I was going to hit him—he saw that and put his arms down and said, 'Hey, Carlos, if you want to hit me, hit me.' That made me stop. He was smart. That would have made me the aggressor and turned the crowd against me." Hernandez snatched the stack of Fair Play pamphlets from Oswald's hands and tossed them into the air. "Then Oswald got mad," says Bringuier. "But by that time the police had arrived. Oswald was accusing Celso of destroying his pamphlets, and the police just took all of us away."*

---

* Some suggest that the fight between Bringuier and Oswald was staged in order to enhance Oswald's "cover" identity as a pro-Castro activist. Summers raises suspicions by saying Bringuier had "past contact with the CIA." But it was with the Domestics Contact Division, which interviewed him *after* the assassination about a nephew who had defected from Cuba to America. "Except for that single interview," Bringuier says, "it is a lie to say I had any CIA contact" (Interview with Bringuier, March 16, 1992). According to Summers, Bringuier also published a right-wing newsletter backed by the CIA-sponsored Crusade to Free Cuba. "Absolutely false," Bringuier says. "Summers is mixed up. My paper was *Crusado*, but had nothing to do with the Crusade to Free Cuba, a completely different organization, to which I had no connection." Summers also cites New Orleans police lieutenant Francis Martello as concluding, "He [Oswald] seemed to have them set up to create an incident." "No, that is not true," Martello told the author. "That is a fabrication. That fight was not set up. I didn't believe it back then and I don't believe it now—no way" (Interview with Francis Martello, March 16, 1992). Although the fight was not staged, it was certainly prompted by Oswald, and it was intended to enhance his legitimate pro-Communist credentials. In a ten-page biographical sketch written in late August, meant to impress the Cuban officials in Mexico City to

At the jail, Bringuier was shocked to hear Oswald announce he was born in Cuba. Until his confrontation with Oswald, he had no idea that Fair Play was active in New Orleans—or that Oswald was its only member. Bringuier noticed that in the interrogation room, Oswald was "really cold-blooded. . . . [H]e was not nervous, he was not out of control, he was confident . . ."[13] The three Cubans raised the $25 bail money and were told to return to court for a hearing on Monday, but Oswald had to spend the night in jail.

The following morning, Saturday, Lt. Francis Martello, the former deputy commander of the New Orleans police intelligence division, saw one of Oswald's Fair Play leaflets and decided to interview him. Oswald lied throughout the interview, telling Martello that he had lived at Mercedes Street in Fort Worth since his honorable discharge from the Marine Corps in 1959. He said that besides Reily, he had worked at the city's largest brewery, Jax. As for the New Orleans Fair Play for Cuba chapter, Oswald said it had thirty-five members, met monthly at locations he refused to disclose, and that the first name of one of the members was "John," a student at Tulane University.[14]*

At the end of that interview, Oswald made the seemingly unusual request that Martello call the FBI. Oswald wanted to see an agent. Special Agent John Quigley arrived later that morning. Oswald had been worried about the FBI's interest in him since the first interview in Fort Worth, and was convinced it had cost him at least two jobs with its inquiries. He was certain he was under active surveillance. If the FBI did not know he was ar-

---

whom Oswald intended to apply for a visa, he wrote, "I infiltraled the Cuban Student directorite and then harresed them with information I gained . . ." (CE 93, WC Vol. XVI, p. 341).

* A leftist professor at Tulane, Leonard Reissman, under surveillance by the New Orleans Police Department's intelligence division, was later found to have one of Oswald's handbills in his car. A Tulane graduate student, Harold Gordon Alderman, who had been involved in Fair Play activities elsewhere, had one of Oswald's leaflets taped to his front door. Reissman and Alderman denied ever meeting Oswald. Another Tulane student, Vereen Alexander, thought she had met Oswald at a party with other pro-Castro students in the summer of 1963, but no one else confirmed her story. Though Oswald told his aunt that he visited a language professor at Tulane, subsequent investigations by the New Orleans police and the FBI could not uncover any evidence that he visited Tulane.

rested, he thought, it would shortly, and Oswald probably figured it best to summon the Bureau to him as if he had nothing to hide about his Fair Play for Cuba activity.

That Oswald called for an FBI agent is strong evidence there was no association between him and the Bureau. A confidential informant could never jeopardize his covert role by publicly dealing with the FBI. But Summers charges that the evidence of a special relationship is evident because it happened on "a Saturday morning, not the most likely time for an agent to respond speedily to a request by an insignificant prisoner. Nevertheless, Oswald asked and the FBI obliged."[15] Quigley was the Saturday duty agent at the New Orleans FBI office. According to another FBI agent who later worked on the Oswald file, Warren de Brueys, "Quigley would never have spoken to Oswald if it had not been a Saturday. One of the responsibilities of the duty agent is to check with the local police and see if there are any cases that might interest the Bureau. Once Oswald asked to talk to the FBI, Quigley had to go over there. If he hadn't, he would have been kicked in the butt for failing to do it—he would have been censured because that was part of his duty. Quigley may not have even been aware we had a file on Oswald in our office, because 99 out of 100 times when they say someone is down there, you just go. If you don't go right away the prisoner might be released, so you always go down and check it out."[16]

Quigley's meeting with Oswald was not a secret one as some have implied. In fact, Quigley typed a five-page, single-spaced report of his hour-and-a-half interview. Oswald repeated the lies he had told Lt. Martello, and then further embellished his story, especially regarding "Hidell." While Oswald said he had spoken to Hidell several times on the telephone, he had never met him, his number had been disconnected, and he did not remember what the number had been.[17] It was a note from Hidell, said Oswald, that told him to pass out the leaflets at the corner where he was arrested. He claimed he attended two Fair Play meetings at different apartments, had been introduced to five different members each time, only by their first name, but could not remember any of them.[18] He said there were no regularly scheduled meetings, but someone would call him when one was planned. Once he said a meeting was held at his own house, but he could not explain how he had informed the other members since he claimed not to know their names or telephone numbers, and he had no telephone. Quigley's report on his bizarre jailhouse interview quickly became part of Oswald's growing FBI file.*

After Quigley left, Oswald called the Murrets to ask for help in getting out of jail. Uncle Dutz was out of town at a Catholic retreat, Aunt Lillian was in the hospital with an ear infection, and the only person at their house was his cousin Joyce Murret, who was visiting from Beaumont, Texas. She went to the jail and there met Lt. Martello. "She was clearly a concerned family member," he recalls. "She stated she wanted to know the charge against Oswald and I told her . . . she became very reluctant to become involved . . . she did not want to get mixed up with it [Fair Play for Cuba] in any way."[19] Joyce told Martello about Oswald's defection to Russia, that he only spoke Russian in his house, and that when she had asked Marina if she liked America, Marina had responded "yes" but told her that "Lee did not."[20]

Joyce Murret departed without bailing Lee out or seeing him. Martello, intrigued by Murret's disclosures, returned for a second interview. That talk was much more productive. When asked if he was a Socialist, Oswald responded "guilty." He said he was a Marxist, fully agreed with *Das Kapital*, but admitted

---

* William Walter, a security clerk in the New Orleans FBI office, claimed five years after the assassination that there was both a security and an informant file on Oswald. He also asserted that while he was on night duty on November 17, 1963, he witnessed an incoming teletype from FBI headquarters in Washington, D.C., warning of a possible assassination attempt against JFK on either November 22 or 23. He contended that the original had been destroyed, and he later produced a version he said was a replica he had personally typed from the purported original (Marrs, *Crossfire*, pp. 228–29). However, Walter's "copy" varied in format and wording from FBI communications. More than fifty other employees of the New Orleans office repudiated his story. Walter claimed that his own wife, who also worked in the New Orleans FBI office, would confirm his story. She did not, and said he never even mentioned the alleged incident during their marriage (HSCA Rpt., p. 192). None of the other fifty-nine FBI field offices ever received such a teletype, although Walter said it was addressed to all of them. The House Select Committee on Assassinations investigated both of his claims and "was led to question Walter's credibility" and finally "rejected[ed] his testimony in its entirety" (HSCA Rpt., pp. 191–92).

Communism in Russia "stunk."[21] He told Martello that he did not teach his wife or child English "because he hated America and he did not want them to become 'Americanized' and that his plans were to go back to Russia." When Martello asked to which country he ascribed allegiance, Oswald replied, "I would place my allegiance at the foot of democracy." "From the way he spoke," recalled Martello, "the impression I received, it appeared to me that he felt that Russia was the lesser of the two evils."[22]

Oswald was furious that Joyce had not obtained his release. He telephoned again. "Come and get me out of here," Lee commanded her.[23] Joyce said she did not have any money and added, "I don't know. I'll have to think this thing over." He told her to get Marina, who had $70 in savings, and bring her to the station. When Joyce got off the phone with him, she instead telephoned her mother. She was afraid to leave her two children while she traveled across town to see Marina. Lillian suggested they call a family friend, Emile Bruneau, a state boxing commissioner, and ask for his help. Bruneau paid Oswald's $25 bail, and he was released late Saturday afternoon.*

When he returned home, Marina was both furious and worried about his all-night absence. Troubled by her memories of Walker, she had checked the closet and was at least relieved to see the rifle leaning against the corner. She was angry when he told her of his arrest, but also so pleased he was home safely that she fed him and then helped him to bed. That night, Dutz Murret returned from his religious retreat. When he heard the news of his nephew's arrest, he was "horrified" and promptly went to the Magazine Street apartment.[24] It was the first time he had visited the Oswalds' home and he was shocked to see a picture of Castro hanging over the mantel.[25] Murret asked Lee if he was a "commie," but Lee denied it. Dutz told him to get a job to support his family and to straighten out his life. He was angry

---

* Since Bruneau apparently knew Nofio Pecora, an associate of New Orleans crime boss Carlos Marcello, some try to stretch the incident to become an organized-crime bailout of Oswald, which in turn earned them a favor. Yet the testimony and evidence show that Bruneau acted, as a personal favor, at the behest of the Murrets and was later reimbursed by Oswald's uncle. Bruneau had no direct contact with Oswald.

over his nephew's demonstrations on behalf of Castro, and the relationship between the Oswalds and the Murrets cooled considerably after Lee's arrest.[26]

Monday, August 12, was the day scheduled for the court hearing for Oswald and Bringuier and his two associates. Early that morning Carlos Bringuier went to the National American Bank to make a deposit. There, he saw Bill Stuckey, a young journalist who had a weekly radio program on Latin American affairs, "The Latin Listening Post," on station WDSU. Stuckey had previously done a newspaper interview about Bringuier and his anti-Castro efforts. "So when I saw Stuckey, I thought it was good public relations to let him know there was a Fair Play for Cuba branch in New Orleans," says Bringuier. "So I told him about the trial later that day."[27] Stuckey was "very, very interested." He said there were many anti-Castro groups in New Orleans, but it had always been difficult to find pro-Castro advocates. "I regarded them [Fair Play for Cuba] as the leading pro-Castro organization in the country," recalled Stuckey.[28]

At the trial later that day, Stuckey sent a cameraman, Johann Rush, to get some film for the evening newscasts for the television branch of WDSU, but the judge refused to allow the short hearing to be filmed. Inside the courtroom, which was split into segregated white and black sections, "Oswald entered the room and sat in the black section," says Bringuier. "As a representative of Fair Play for Cuba, it was a good propaganda move to sit with the blacks, with the oppressed people. It made me angry, because I thought this guy knows what he is doing. He is very clever."[29] Bringuier's attorney did not show up, so he defended himself and his friends, explaining to the judge how Oswald had first pretended to be an ally, and then later they caught him distributing Communist propaganda. Oswald pleaded guilty to disturbing the peace. The judge dismissed the charges against the three Cubans and fined Oswald $10. On the way out of the courtroom, Rush briefly interviewed Oswald, just enough time for Lee to say he was a Marxist.

Oswald was pleased that his efforts for Cuba had finally begun to receive public attention. Such coverage, he thought, would eventually help him gain a visa to Cuba, the place Marina said he spoke of increasingly during August.[30] In a letter, sent on

August 13, to V. T. Lee, Fair Play's president, Oswald wrote that he had "incured the displeasure of the Cuban exile 'worms' here," and that three of them had attacked him. Enclosing a small article about the case from the *Times-Picayune*, Oswald said, "I am very glad I am stirring things up and shall continue to do so." He claimed there was "considerable coverage in the press" and concluded "it will all be to the good of the Fair Play for Cuba Committee."[31] The next day he sent a clipping to Arnold Johnson, of the American Communist party, with an honorary Fair Play membership card, and wrote, "I am doing my best to help the cause of new Cuba . . ."[32]

Three days later he called the local television stations to inform them that he planned a Fair Play demonstration in front of the International Trade Mart for the following day. Friday, late in the morning, he went to the unemployment office, where he offered $2 to anybody who would help him distribute leaflets for half an hour. Two accepted his offer, and they walked to the Trade Mart, where cameraman Johann Rush captured Oswald's demonstration for posterity on film for nearly twenty minutes.* Oswald was ecstatic. His new demonstration had attracted television coverage, and with two "volunteers," it appeared that Fair Play was more than a one-person operation. That night he tried to encourage Marina to go to the Murrets' to watch him on television, but she was appalled that he was seeking publicity for his radical politics and refused to leave the apartment.

Saturday was a surprisingly busy day for Oswald. It began at 8:00 A.M., when Bill Stuckey stopped by his apartment to ask if he wanted to tape a segment for that evening's radio broadcast. Stuckey had received Oswald's address from Bringuier. Oswald, woken from his sleep, had on just a pair of Marine Corps fatigue pants. Still, Stuckey was pleasantly surprised by his "clean-cutness" as he expected "a folk-singer type . . . somebody with a beard and sandals . . ."[33] Oswald showed him his Fair Play membership card and gave him copies of two Castro speeches, a pamphlet titled *Ideology and Revolution* by Jean-Paul Sartre,

---

* One of the youngsters who helped Oswald was later identified as Charles Hall Steele, Jr. He had never met Oswald before that day and never saw him again. The other unemployed helper was never identified, although Steele testified the man volunteered from the unemployment line, the same as he had.

and another called *The Crime Against Cuba* by Corliss La-
mont.[34] Telling Stuckey that Fair Play had twelve to thirteen local members, and emphasizing that he was only the secretary,
he agreed to meet at the WDSU station at five that evening to
tape a show.

Meanwhile, Bringuier was afraid that the televised demonstration of the previous day might enhance the local standing of Fair
Play for Cuba. He called Stuckey. "I told him I was thinking that
it was not good to let a Communist go to a radio station and tell
all his lies."[35] Stuckey offered Bringuier rebuttal time the following week, but Bringuier asked for a live debate instead, something Stuckey said he would consider. Bringuier also embarked
on an effort to infiltrate Fair Play's local chapter to discover
what he could about Lee Oswald. On Saturday, he sent a Cuban
associate, Carlos Quiroga, who spoke excellent English, to Oswald's apartment. Quiroga pretended to have been given a leaf-
let by Oswald and expressed his interest in joining Fair Play for
Cuba. He was the first person who ever responded to Oswald's
public demonstrations, and they spoke for nearly forty-five minutes. "There is almost no question that Oswald must have
known Quiroga was a plant from us," says Bringuier. He was
right. Marina later said, "I asked Lee who that was, and he said
that is probably some anti-Cuban, or perhaps an FBI agent. He
represented himself as a man who was sympathetic to Cuba, but
Lee did not believe him."

Oswald told Quiroga that Fidel Castro was not a dictator and
that if the United States invaded Cuba, he would fight with Castro against America.[36] "Quiroga came back to us and said Oswald was a committed Communist, had a particular dislike for
Somoza [Nicaragua's right-wing dictator], and was quite militant," says Bringuier. "At one point, Oswald's child came onto
the porch and he spoke to her in a foreign language. Quiroga
asked him if that was Russian, and he said, 'Yes, I'm studying
Russian at Tulane University.' He was really a pathological
liar."[37]

That evening Oswald arrived at the WDSU studios, at 520
Royal Street in the French Quarter. There, he taped a thirty-
seven-minute interview, which Stuckey, with Oswald's suggestions, edited to a four-and-a-half minute program that was

broadcast that evening.* Most of the interview consists of Oswald's standard distinctions between Marxism, Socialism, and Communism. However, he also used this platform to more extensively reveal his views on Castro, calling him "an independent leader . . . who had not so far betrayed his country."[38] Oswald kept the discussion simple, said he was honorably discharged as a sergeant from the Marines, and omitted any reference to his defection to Russia. He thought he had "scored a coup."[39]

At the end of the long day on Saturday, Oswald, in a euphoric mood, sat at his desk and wrote again to V. T. Lee. In an airmail envelope marked RUSH PLEASE, he informed Lee that "things have been moving pretty fast."[40] Unable to write without embellishment, he boasted that his demonstration had "considerable [TV] coverage" and that he had been on a fifteen-minute WDSU television program, and "I was flooded with caller and invitations to debates, etc. as well as people interested in joining the F.P.C.C. New Orleans branch."[41]

Stuckey thought Oswald was an "articulate" spokesman for his cause, and he liked the four-and-a-half-minute tape so much that he asked his WDSU news director if he could run the entire thirty-seven-minute interview, but was told no. That is when he considered Carlos Bringuier's idea of a debate with Oswald. On Monday, August 19, Oswald, at Stuckey's suggestion, called the radio station. Stuckey proposed the debate format for that coming Wednesday. Pleased to have another chance at publicity for his Cuban cause, Oswald instantly accepted.† The debate was scheduled for a twenty-five-minute public affairs program, "Conversation Carte Blanche." To counter Oswald, Stuckey selected both Carlos Bringuier and Edward Butler, the executive director of the Information Council of the Americas (INCA), an anti-Communist propaganda organization.

Stuckey provided a copy of the thirty-seven-minute original

---

* The transcript of the entire thirty-seven-minute interview is presented as Stuckey Exhibit 2, WC Vol. XXI, pp. 621–32.

† It was the same day that Radio Havana and the newspaper *Revolución* reported air attacks on oil storage tanks, the third raid in four days, and one blamed on "pirates, organized, armed, and directed by the CIA." American wire services picked up the story the next day.

interview tape to the local FBI office on Monday. While he was later talking to an FBI source, Stuckey said he was put through to either the chief or deputy chief of the New Orleans office.[42] That agent read aloud portions of Oswald's file regarding his dishonorable discharge, the defection to Russia, and his attempt to renounce his citizenship. Intrigued, Stuckey went to the FBI office the next day and examined the file personally. Meanwhile, Butler used his contacts at the House Un-American Activities Committee in Washington independently to uncover information about Oswald's Russian venture.[43]

Oswald appeared at 5:30 P.M. on Wednesday, in his thick flannel Russian suit, carrying a black looseleaf notebook and looking very uncomfortable in the sweltering August heat. He was nervous, though he had practiced throughout the day, walking around the apartment reading notes aloud. When Bringuier arrived, Oswald tried to shake hands, but Bringuier refused, instead trading jibes with him about his Communist beliefs.[44]

At the outset of the show, Stuckey repeated Oswald's statements from the past Saturday's interview, in which he had claimed to have an honorable discharge from the Marines in 1959 and then lived in Fort Worth before moving to New Orleans. He then confronted him with the truth, armed with the information from the FBI file and what Butler had uncovered, about Oswald's undesirable discharge and his Russian defection. Oswald was caught completely by surprise. Despite his attempt to fend off the attacks and bring the program back to a discussion of "the Cuban-American problem," the personal attacks increasingly portrayed him not only as a liar but as a Communist and traitor.[45] By the time the show ended, Oswald was devastated.

Stuckey felt so sorry for him that he took him to Cameaux's, a neighborhood bar, for some drinks. He remembered Oswald was "dejected," and over some beers, he relaxed and opened up a little. He told Stuckey of his early attraction to Marxism and his subsequent disenchantment with Russia, but also about his unhappiness in the U.S.[46] "It was my impression Oswald regarded himself as living in a world of intellectual inferiors," recalled Stuckey.[47] But most revealing was Oswald's statement that the Russians had "gone soft" on Communism and that Cuba was the world's only real revolutionary country.[48]

Marina could tell that Lee was in a terrible mood when he returned home that night. "Damn it. I didn't know they realized I'd been to Russia. You ought to have heard what they asked me! I wasn't prepared and I didn't know what to say."[49] His nearly four months of efforts, distribution of more than a thousand pieces of literature, and his media coverage still had not resulted in any followers. Vincent Lee, Fair Play's national president, had not even answered any of his recent letters. Oswald feared the radio debate had so discredited him that his already lackluster organizing efforts might be permanently damaged.

Bringuier was ecstatic over the evening's results. "After the debate, I thought Oswald was destroyed," he says.[50] Now Bringuier attempted to finish him completely. He drafted a press release calling for a congressional investigation "of Lee Harvey Oswald, a confessed Marxist and an alien [sic] of Castro in the United States" and dropped copies off at newspapers and radio and television stations. He even considered dropping leaflets by plane over New Orleans, but discovered it was illegal.

Marina noticed a fundamental change in Lee after his radio humiliation. He seemed even more disconnected from reality. One of the most worrisome developments was that he began to focus on his rifle again. He brought it out of the closet and at night began taking it onto an unlit screened porch at the front of the apartment. There, Marina remembered watching him "open and close the bolt."[51] Sometimes while she was in the house, she could hear him practice for hours with the bolt action—what experts call dry runs, which greatly increase a shooter's proficiency and speed with a bolt-action rifle.[52] At other times, Marina saw him sitting in the dark aiming his gun at imaginary targets.[53] "Well, it was usually after dark, so if I go over there, you know, just see that he is there, and I come back in the apartment, so I just knew he was there with the rifle," recalled Marina. "He always, most of the time, he said, 'Just leave me alone . . . ' "[54] Once he said, "Fidel Castro needs defenders. I'm going to join his army of volunteers. I'm going to be a revolutionary."[55]

Soon, the dry sighting on the porch was not enough. "Before

it gets very dark outside, he would leave [the] apartment dressed with the dark raincoat, even though it was a hot summer night . . . and he would be hiding the rifle underneath his raincoat," recalled Marina. "He said he is going to target practice . . ."[56] Several times he left the house with the rifle, each time disappearing for several hours.

Marina finally confronted him and asked why he was spending so much time with the rifle. "He was preparing to go to Cuba," she recalled. "He very much wanted to go to Cuba and have the newspapers write that somebody had kidnaped an aircraft." She was shocked that he was thinking of hijacking a plane. "And I asked him, 'For God sakes, don't do such a thing.' "[57]

Oswald now felt that he had to get to Cuba at any cost. The State Department had banned travel there, and *The Militant* ran several prominent stories during the 1963 summer about Americans who visited despite the ban and faced imprisonment upon their return. Oswald did not worry about the sanctions, because he did not intend to return, and hijacking a plane seemed as convenient and revolutionary as any other means. "[In] his imagination, his fantasy, which was quite unfounded, [he thought] he was an outstanding man," recalled Marina. "I always tried to point out to him that he was a man like any other who were around us. But he simply could not understand that. . . . I would say to Lee that [he] could not really do much for Cuba, that Cuba would get along without him, if they had to."[58] Oswald began to study airline schedules departing New Orleans. For Marina, it was frighteningly like his preparation for the Walker shooting.

She argued with him over his hijacking plans. He answered her with details of how he intended to use the rifle to force the pilot to fly to Cuba while Marina held the pistol on the passengers and crew. "It was so ridiculous, it is even embarrassing to mention it right now," Marina recalled. "He told me he would teach me what I am supposed to say, maybe hold the gun and tell the people, you know . . ."[59] Marina refused to listen, and said the very idea threatened her pregnancy. She finally told him to do it alone and not to count on her. He trained on his own for days, running about the apartment, clad only in his underwear, practicing leaps and trying to strengthen his legs and arms, things he considered necessary attributes to hijack a plane. "Junie," Marina whispered to her daughter, "our papa is out of his mind."[60]*

The next thing she knew, her husband abruptly dropped the hijacking talk and told her he instead planned to go to Mexico City and visit the Cuban embassy in order to get a visa to travel to Cuba.[61] Mexico City had the nearest Cuban consulate from which he could obtain a visa, and he planned to go there by bus, swearing Marina to secrecy.[62] Under his new proposal, Marina would return to Dallas with Ruth Paine when she visited New Orleans around September 20. After he got to Cuba, Oswald promised he would either arrange for Marina to join him, or he might return to Russia and meet her there.[63] He began studying elementary Spanish. She knew Cuba was his first choice, but if he failed to get there, she had no doubt he was willing to return to the USSR.[64] But Marina had also come to recognize how changeable he was. None of his convictions, even Cuba, would satisfy him long. "And I am convinced that as much as he knew about Cuba, all he knew was from books and so on. He wanted to convince himself. But I am sure that if he had gone there, he would not have liked it there either. Only on the moon, perhaps."[65]

On August 28 the extent of Oswald's frustration with his political activities showed in a letter he wrote to the Central Committee, the highest governing body of the American Communist party. He was frustrated by Vincent Lee's failure to answer his Fair Play letters and felt that Arnold Johnson was not of a high enough rank to advise him on his new problem. He explained that he had lived in the USSR and had tried to become a Soviet citizen. Since returning from Russia, and having "thrown myself into the struggle for progress and freedom in the United States, I would like to know weather, in your opion, I can continue to fight, handicapped as it were, by my past record . . . to compete with anti-progressive forces above ground or weather . . . I should always remain in the . . . underground" (emphases in

---

*Almost none of the best-selling conspiracy books mention Oswald's hijacking plans.

original).[66] Oswald's excuse for his failures had become the attacks of "anti-progressives" over his Russian defection. When he finally received a reply, three weeks later, he was advised to "remain in the background, not underground."[67]

Although he was distressed over his botched Fair Play efforts, Marina noted that after he decided to go to Cuba, he "was not as brutal and violent . . ."[68] Their only disagreement during this period was over the name for their coming baby, which both were convinced would be a boy. They had earlier agreed that the name would be David Lee. But suddenly Oswald seriously suggested Fidel. Marina was adamantly against it. "There is no Fidel and there will be no Fidel in our family."[69] Oswald then dropped the subject. He had also dropped his Fair Play for Cuba work. Although he wrote more letters to the Socialist Workers party and *The Worker*, they were only requests for information and assistance.[70] Further reports about anti-Castro attacks inside Cuba seemed to strengthen his resolve to go there but did not send him into a fury as sometimes had happened in earlier months. His appetite for serious political books from the public library ceased, and instead he devoured science fiction and spy novels.*

---

* In sharp contrast to Marina's description of this period (late August–early September) as a quiet one for Oswald, Antonio Veciana Blanch, the founder of a radical anti-Castro group (Alpha 66), claimed ten years after the assassination that he had seen Oswald in downtown Dallas meeting with a CIA operative. Veciana, who claimed to have worked for thirteen years for a CIA case officer known only to him as "Maurice Bishop," told the House Select Committee that it was Bishop he saw with Oswald. There are no other witnesses to the meeting, although Veciana claimed it happened in a busy office building. Veciana, a convicted drug dealer, claimed that Bishop (whose real name he never discovered) paid him $253,000 in cash in 1973 to end his relationship with the CIA (*Reasonable Doubt*, p. 328). Veciana could not supply any proof of that payment (HSCA Rpt., p. 137). Some, including Select Committee investigator Gaeton Fonzi, believe that Maurice Bishop was actually David Atlee Phillips, a CIA officer who had been in charge of the Agency's Mexico City station at the time Oswald visited that city later in 1963. The CIA denied that any case officer had ever been assigned to Veciana (HSCA Rpt., p. 134). David Phillips sued a number of journalists who printed the accusation for libel. Some of the suits were unsuccessful and others were settled out of court. There are still doubts not only about Maurice Bishop's identity, but whether he ever existed. In addition, Oswald was in New Orleans every day at the time Veciana claimed to have seen him in Dallas. The Select Committee thoroughly

But while Oswald's political activism appeared diminished, the controversy he had created continued without him. Lt. Francis Martello conducted his own investigation of Fair Play for Cuba and Oswald. "I checked the addresses on his pamphlets. I never could find anything connecting him to 544 Camp Street. I also could not find anything about 'Hidell.' The more I looked, the more I thought this local chapter might just be Oswald."[71] FBI agent Warren de Brueys undertook an extensive investigation. "I checked his employment at the Reily Coffee Co.," recalls de Brueys, "checked with his landlady, as well as with local Cuban sources, and got negative from all of them. Then I contacted our sources for Communist party activity and they were all negative. Nothing indicated he had any connections. He was just a single person, a guy expressing himself and claiming to have a Fair Play for Cuba chapter, but in actuality he was the only member."[72] De Brueys did not consider Oswald a dangerous character or a subversive threat, and his report reflected that judgment. "I thought of Oswald as a weirdo," says de Brueys. "I had several other cases at this time similar to him, where the guys had a fancy, some psychological bent, some aberration, they fancied themselves a poor man's intelligence agent. They tried to involve themselves on the periphery of things. Usually, they were disturbed people of some kind. In the final report you just say that he does not have connections that call for further investigation. You don't say in the report that the guy is a kook, even though I had decided Oswald was a nut."[73]*

Oswald began to compile a file of his life. The general head-

----

investigated Veciana's claims and found several reasons to believe he "had been less than candid," and that it "could not, therefore, credit Veciana's story . . . ." (HSCA Rpt., p. 137).

* De Brueys was later at the middle of a controversy when a Cuban bar owner, Orest Pena, said that Oswald had frequented his place with a Mexican and at other times had met de Brueys there. Pena's story is still cited as evidence of an FBI-Oswald connection. What is often not disclosed is that Pena recanted his story both in an FBI interview and before the Warren Commission. De Brueys and Pena strongly disliked each other, and the postassassination story was evidently Pena's means of revenge. When, in the late 1960s, Pena faced criminal charges connected to an illegal house of prostitution, his defense lawyer was leading conspiracy buff Mark Lane. "I never even met Oswald," de Brueys told the author. "It's preposterous to say he was my informant. It's not my nature to malign a person, but Pena is a propagating liar."

ings included "Military and Far East," "Resident of USSR," "Marxist," "Russian," "organizer," "Street Agitation," "Radio Specker and Lecturer," and "Photograpes."[74] He hand-wrote it on looseleaf paper, as part of a notebook he planned to take to Mexico City to convince Cuban authorities he was a bona fide Communist deserving an immediate visa.

On Labor Day, Oswald called the Murrets and asked if he and Marina could visit. It was the first time he had seen his family since the bailout nearly a month before. It was an uneventful afternoon except for when the Murrets pressed Oswald to teach Marina English, something he still adamantly refused. "I'll tell you right now, I will never teach it to her," he told Lillian and Dutz.[75] That afternoon get-together was the last time the Murrets ever saw or spoke to him.

The Oswalds' final few weeks in New Orleans were uneventful. Lee spent many of the sweltering days naked, inside the house. In the evening, he put on a pair of trousers and sat on the porch, reading one of his library books or tinkering with the rifle. Marina, as well as neighbors, recalled that while he occasionally went to a local candy shop or a nearby Winn-Dixie store for groceries, he was generally at the apartment.[76] Mrs. Jesse Garner, his landlady, used to watch him, dressed only in rubber thongs and bright yellow shorts, stuffing all the garbage cans up and down the block with their refuse, since he was too miserly to buy his own garbage can.[77] Marina often chastised him for his stinginess, but he ignored her.*

He failed to pay Mrs. Garner the September rent of $65. He

---

* Although this was a quiet time, and the one in which Oswald was at home the most, some assert that during the same period he visited the office of a New Orleans assistant district attorney, Edward Gillin. For over an hour, Oswald allegedly praised the wonders of a new drug, LSD, and asked if it was legal to import. Gillin suggested his visitor check with the city's police chemist. After the man left the office, Gillin never again had contact with him, but over the assassination weekend of November 22, 1963, Gillin identified his visitor as Lee Oswald. Since the CIA was experimenting with LSD during the early 1960s, the incident might be evidence of an intelligence link to Oswald. The problem is with Gillin's identification, which has been offered as evidence of another eyewitness account of Oswald's suspicious behavior. "I was then, and still am now, legally blind," Gillin told the author. "I could never have been sure of the identification of Oswald under oath." Gillin had only identified Oswald from the sound of his voice over the television.

intended to save the money for his trip to Mexico. Marina started to worry that once she returned with Ruth Paine to Texas, she might not see him again. She begged to be taken along to Mexico, but he said it was impossible because of her pregnancy. He promised to summon her once he was settled in Cuba.

On September 7, Castro appeared at a Brazilian embassy reception in Havana and submitted to a rare informal interview with Associated Press correspondent Daniel Harker. Castro was unusually outspoken, saying, "Kennedy is a cretin . . . the Batista of his times . . . the most opportunistic American President of all time."[78] Castro denounced recent U.S. attacks on Cuba and then threatened, "We are prepared to fight them and answer in kind. U.S. leaders should think that if they are aiding terrorist plans to eliminate Cuban leaders, they themselves will not be safe."[79] Castro, aware of the CIA attempts to assassinate him, had used a reporter to warn Kennedy that two could play such a dangerous game. Oswald, an avid newspaper reader, almost certainly saw the article.*

Oswald visited the Mexican consulate in New Orleans on Tuesday, September 17. He filled out an application for a tourist card, listing himself as a photographer with an office at 640 Rampart Street.[80] For a fee of 50¢, he was issued a tourist card, No. 24085, which allowed him to stay fifteen days in Mexico.[81]†

On Friday, September 20, Marina came home from a grocery trip to the Winn-Dixie to find that Ruth Paine and her children had arrived at the apartment. Ruth recalled that she had never seen Lee in such a good mood.[82] She spent the weekend, and he lied to her that he intended to look for work in Houston or Philadelphia, and then once he found a job, he would be back to fetch Marina. On Saturday and Sunday, Ruth "was impressed

---

* The interview was prominently covered in the New Orleans *Times-Pica-yune* on September 9, under a three-column headline on page 7.

† The man who was issued tourist card No. 24084, the one directly before Oswald's, was William Gaudet, a newspaper editor. Until 1961, he was a source of information for the CIA's Domestic Contact Division. He did not know Oswald, did not travel to Mexico with him, and had no other association with the case except for the coincidence that they both applied for Mexican tourist cards. The House Select Committee reviewed Gaudet's CIA file and determined he had no clandestine relationship with the Agency (HSCA Rpt. p. 219).

. . . with his willingness to help with the packing [of most of their meager goods]. He did virtually all the packing and all the loading of the things into the car."[83] At the time, she thought his actions were "gentlemanly," but she is now convinced that he probably packed his rifle in one of the bags and did not want anyone else handling it.[84]

Monday, September 23, was the day Marina left for Texas with Ruth. It was a difficult farewell for both Marina and Lee. Ruth remembered, "He kissed her a very fond goodbye, both at home and then again at the gas station [a couple of blocks away, where they changed a flat tire], and I felt he cared and he would certainly see her [again]."[85] Marina remembered his lips trembled when he kissed her, and he fought back tears. He looked at her "as a dog looks at its master."[86] As she drove away with Ruth, Marina looked at him standing alone and wondered if she would ever see him again.

9

"His Mood Was Bad"

The day before Marina left with Ruth to return to Dallas, the Oswalds' landlord, Jesse Garner, saw Lee packing Paine's station wagon. "I asked him if he was moving, since I was concerned that he owed about 15 days' rent," recalled Garner. "Oswald told me he was not leaving but that his wife was going to Texas to have the baby after which she was going to return to New Orleans."[1] Lee had no intention of paying the rent. He needed every cent for his trip to Mexico. Some have suggested it is odd that since he was so anxious to get to Cuba, he did not leave immediately after Marina's departure. But he had to stay in New Orleans until the morning of Wednesday, September 25, when he could collect his $33 unemployment check, the next to last he was scheduled to receive.

Oswald's next-door neighbor Eric Rogers saw him Tuesday, the twenty-fourth, the day after Marina left, running to catch a bus across the street.[2] He was carrying two bags, a small zippered one and his Marine Corps duffel, and he asked the bus driver for directions to the Greyhound bus station.[3] Oswald was making the same preparations he had in Dallas in April before he moved to New Orleans. He deposited his bags at the station, not wanting to be burdened with them for the errands he planned for the next morning, and then returned to the Magazine Street apartment to spend his last night in the city.[4] Lee left the apartment in the early-morning hours of Wednesday, September 25. Jesse Garner noticed the apartment seemed quiet. When she checked it later that morning, Oswald was gone.[5]

At the Lafayette Square substation, Oswald picked up his unemployment-compensation check and mailed a change-ofaddress card, postmarked at 11:00 A.M., listing Ruth Paine's address in Irving, Texas. At a Winn-Dixie on Magazine Street he cashed his $33 check, and was then ready to leave his native New Orleans. At 12:20 P.M. he likely boarded a Continental Trailways bus, No. 5121, bound for Houston.[6] Late that night the telephone rang at the Houston home of Estelle and Horace Twiford. Estelle answered and it was Lee Oswald calling her husband.[7]* Horace Twiford was the national committeeman of the Socialist Labor party for the state of Texas. On September 11, he had sent Oswald a copy of his organization's *Weekly People*, after being notified by the New York Labor party of Lee's request for literature. Twiford was not at home when Oswald called, but his wife wrote the message on some scrap paper. It indicated Oswald was a member of Fair Play for Cuba, that he had some ideas he wanted to discuss with her husband, and that he had only a few hours before he left for Mexico.[8]

Less than four hours later, at 2:35 A.M., Oswald boarded Continental Trailways bus No. 5133 in Houston and left for Laredo, Texas.[9] He was excited to begin the last leg of his trip, and he felt he had no reason to be secretive any longer since he would soon be in Cuba and permanently away from the U.S. The usually introverted Oswald was surprisingly talkative to other passengers, even bragging about the purpose of his trip. A British couple, Meryl and Dr. John McFarland, had also boarded at

---

* Although there were no eyewitnesses to Oswald's departure from New Orleans, bus 5121 is the only one that left New Orleans after Oswald had cashed his check that would get him to Houston that evening. Mrs. Twiford thought the call was a local one. Oswald's address book provides additional evidence he was in Houston. Twiford's name, address, and two telephone numbers were found in Oswald's book after the assassination. One was a disconnected number, which was still listed in the 1963 Houston phone book. The second number in his address book was Twiford's valid one for September 1963. It appears Oswald arrived in Houston, looked up the Twifords in the phone book, and wrote the number in his address book. Then, when he telephoned and discovered it was out of date, he had to call the operator for the new number, and also jotted the second one in his book (CE 18; CE 2335).

Houston. They initially slept on the bus, but when they awoke around 6:00 A.M., they engaged Oswald in a conversation. He told them he was traveling from New Orleans to Cuba via Mexico City, because traveling to Cuba directly from the U.S. was against American law.[10] He bragged that "he was the secretary of the New Orleans branch of the Fair Play for Cuba Organization, and that he was on his way to Cuba to see Castro if he could."[11]

Oswald crossed into Mexico, at Nuevo Laredo, between 1:30 and 2:00 P.M. on Thursday, almost twelve hours after he left Houston.[12] Mexican immigration official Helio Tuexi Maydon stamped Oswald's tourist card, and at 2:15 he boarded another bus, no. 516 of the Flecha Roja line, for an overnight trip to Mexico City, scheduled to arrive mid-morning Friday, September 27.* The final leg of his trip covered 750 miles and cost $5.71. At one stop along the route, Monterrey, two young Australian women, Pamela Mumford and Patricia Winston, boarded for the remainder of the trip. The four seats at the front of the bus were taken by the McFarlands, Oswald, and an elderly Englishman, Albert Osborne, a traveling preacher.† Mumford and Winston could only find seats in the rear of the bus. After some time had passed, Oswald walked to the rear and began talking to them. "He said he had heard us speaking English and wondered where we came from," remembered Mumford.[13] During

---

* While Oswald was on a twenty-hour bus ride that consumed almost all of September 26, a White House spokesman made the first announcement that President Kennedy would make a brief trip to Texas in November. The dates and cities to be visited were not set. Every event in Oswald's life prior to September 26 happened before it was publicly known that the President would visit Texas. Even Oswald's trip to Mexico was planned before the announcement, and if he had been successful in obtaining a visa to Cuba, Kennedy and Oswald would never have crossed paths in another two months. Critics who write about suspicions of a conspiracy before this date never explain how Oswald was supposedly brought into a plot that had no possible sense of time and place, two indispensable ingredients.

† Osborne was contacted after the assassination by the FBI. He was so nervous about having sat next to the man accused of killing JFK that he denied he had, although the other passengers and his travel documents show he did. Osborne told one of the other passengers that in his conversation with Oswald, Lee told him he had been to Mexico before. It is not known if Oswald was talking about his Marine Corps visit to Tijuana or if he was lying about visiting Mexico on other occasions.

their extended conversation, although he never introduced himself by name, Oswald told them that while he was from Fort Worth, he had been in Japan while in the Marines and was sorry he had never been to Australia. Trying to impress them as a world traveler, he said he had been a student in Russia and "at this stage he showed us his passport that had a Russian stamp on it . . . and he didn't mention his Russian wife at all. But we noticed he had a gold wedding ring on his left hand." Before the end of trip, the man they called Texas told them that "on previous trips to Mexico City he had stayed at a place called the Hotel Cuba, and he said he was staying there and recommended it for clean and cheap living."[14] They did not take him up on his suggestion. At the bus stops Oswald ate alone, and they noticed he was lost with the Spanish menus. He just pointed to something on the menu and had to eat a full meal each stop instead of a snack. It made them doubt his claims about being familiar with Mexico.[15] When they finally arrived at the Mexico City bus station, Oswald dropped his friendly veneer and quickly left by himself.* His story to Mumford and Winston about staying at the Hotel Cuba was another of his lies, and Oswald spent nearly an hour checking the rates at the more than forty cheap hotels near the bus depot before selecting the Hotel del Comercio, only four blocks from the terminal.[16] He signed his real name to the hotel register (confirmed later by handwriting experts) and settled into the spartan room No. 18, with bath, at $1.28 per day.†

Establishing Oswald's whereabouts from the time Marina left New Orleans on September 23 until he arrived in Mexico City on the morning of Friday, September 27, is important be-

---

* After the assassination, the McFarlands saw a newspaper photo of the accused presidential assassin and instantly recognized him as the man on the bus. Mumford and Winston were in a Las Vegas hotel room watching television news about the assassination when suddenly Oswald was shown in the Dallas jail. They immediately identified him, startled that he even had on the same sweater he had worn on the bus.

† Oswald traveled, ate, and slept very cheaply in Mexico. The total estimate of his expenses for the Mexican trip is $85. He had enough cash at the beginning of the month to easily pay for the journey (WC Appendix XIV, "Analysis of Lee Harvey Oswald's Finances from June 13, 1962, through November 22, 1963," p. 741).

cause other witnesses are often cited to claim that Oswald was somewhere other than on the bus heading toward Mexico.

Mrs. Lee Dannelly, assistant chief of the administrative division in the Selective Service headquarters in Austin, Texas, was positive that Lee Oswald visited her in the afternoon on Wednesday, September 25. She claimed the young man called himself Harvey Oswald, said he was registered in the Selective Service in Florida, had just come from the governor's office, and was trying to correct his dishonorable discharge from the Marines.[17] A waitress at a nearby coffee shop, Florence Norman, said Oswald had stopped in for several cups of coffee on the same day he visited Mrs. Dannelly.[18] Since Oswald could not be in Austin and also on the bus on its way to Houston, this discrepancy raises the specter of an Oswald imposter. If there was a second "Oswald" it might be evidence of conspiracy.

The Oswald imposter issue is critical from September 1963 through the assassination. After the assassination, scores of people came forward believing they had seen Oswald at places other than where he was (and the same applied to Jack Ruby), almost all of them well intentioned but mistaken. People placed themselves with Oswald from Hawaii to Florida, from bowling alleys to dance parties. Instead of dismissing the sightings of other "Oswalds" at locations where he physically could not be, critics say it is evidence of a "double Oswald," and sometimes even a "triple Oswald."*

What of Dannelly's claim that a Harvey Oswald visited her? She said he had been to the governor's office, but a records check for a six-month period shows no Oswald in the mandatory registration books or any signature that matched Oswald's writing.[19] Dannelly claimed another worker had brought Oswald to her desk, but when asked, the other employee, Jesse Skrivanek, did not remember anyone who looked like Oswald or anyone using that name.[20] Others in the Austin Selective Service office swore they never saw him or heard the name before the

---

* Actually, false identifications are quite common after saturation press coverage of the type that took place after the assassination. Only those instances most often advanced by the critics will be considered in this and the following chapter.

assassination.[21] Actually, there were fifteen Oswalds in the Austin office files, but Dannelly refused to admit she might be mistaken. All of the facts Mrs. Dannelly recounted about Oswald in her story were available locally in the media before she told anyone of the alleged visit. The FBI discovered that the waitress who claimed she too saw Oswald turned out to have Wednesday, the day of the alleged Oswald appearance, as her day off.[22] None of the other employees at the coffee shop recalled ever seeing Oswald or hearing of anyone with that name before the assassination.[23]

Another witness who claimed to have seen Oswald elsewhere at the time he was traveling to Mexico is Sylvia Odio. Summers calls her testimony "the strongest human evidence."[24] Sylvia Meagher dubs it "the proof of the plot."[25] Robert Groden and Harrison Livingstone write that Odio is "among the strongest witnesses to conspiracy in the case . . . ."[26] According to Odio, three men visited her Dallas apartment near 9:00 P.M., near the end of September. Her sister answered the door, and the men claimed to be members of JURE, the Junta Revolucionaria, an anti-Castro group that Odio had helped form several months earlier in Puerto Rico.[27]* Two were Cubans, "the greasy . . . kind of low Cubans, not educated at all," recalled Odio.[28] She later said they "looked very much like Mexicans." One of the Cubans said his name was Leopoldo and asked if she was in the underground, and she said no. "And he said, 'We wanted you to meet this American. His name is Leon Oswald.' He repeated it twice," recalled Odio.[29]† Then they introduced him as someone very interested in the Cuban cause. Leon said very little, "just a few little words in Spanish, trying to be cute . . . like 'Hola,'" she said. The men said they had just come from New Orleans

---

* Odio's father was in a Cuban jail for political actions against the Castro regime. He had been a business tycoon before Castro's revolution, and Odio came from a wealthy and pampered background.

† JURE members used "war names," fictitious names, so that Castro agents could not unmask their real identities. Odio said that the Cubans gave their war names, but she assumed Leon Oswald was a real name for the American. However, she evidently never considered the possibility that Oswald would have been a perfect war name for any anti-Castro Cuban since the name had been in the newspapers, radio, and television in New Orleans as a virulently pro-Castro advocate.

and were in a rush because they were on their way to either Miami or Puerto Rico.[30] They left in a red car.

The next day Leopoldo telephoned her. According to Odio, "He said, 'What do you think of the American?' And I said, 'I didn't think anything.' And he said, 'You know our idea is to introduce him to the underground in Cuba, because he is great, he is kind of nuts.' . . . He [Leon Oswald] told us we don't have any guts, you Cubans, because President Kennedy should have been assassinated after the Bay of Pigs, and some Cubans should have done that, because he was the one that was holding the freedom of Cuba actually. . . . He said he had been a Marine . . . and would be the kind of man that could do anything like . . . killing Castro. He repeated several times he was an expert shotman [sic]. And he said, 'We probably won't have anything to do with him. He is kind of loco.' "[31] Odio said the conversation made her nervous and she soon ended it, and never heard from or saw any of the three men again until after the assassination, when she claimed to realize that Leon Oswald was the man charged with assassinating President Kennedy.

The House Select Committee's report on Odio concluded her "testimony is essentially credible" and "there is a strong probability that one of the men was or appeared to be Lee Harvey Oswald."[32]* The conspiracy critics cite the testimony of Odio's sister, Annie, to support her story. They also refer to a letter Odio wrote to her father before the assassination, in which she discussed the visit.

A reexamination of the Odio story, however, as well as of her credibility, casts doubts on its accuracy. Annie Odio cannot corroborate key parts of her sister's story because she did not hear the American introduced as "Leon Oswald" or the telephone conversation from Leopoldo the following day.[33] As for the preassassination letter to her father, which no longer exists, Odio says she wrote the names of the two Cubans but did not mention the name "Leon Oswald." She was not even sure if she mentioned that an American was in the group.[34]

---

* The House Select Committee report on Odio was researched and written by Gaeton Fonzi, the assassination buff who researched the Banister and Ferrie connections to Oswald.

But there is much stronger evidence that the visitor was not Oswald. Odio could not positively identify him when shown photos during her Warren Commission testimony. She said, "I think this man was the one that was in my apartment. I am not too sure of that picture. He didn't look like that."[35] She said he had a small stubble of beard growth around his mouth, almost "a little moustache," and another thing that "confuses me is the lips that did not look like the same man."[36] But more problematical than the shaky physical identification was the time element she pinpointed. She was certain the men had visited before Tuesday, October 1, because on September 30 she moved to a different apartment.[37] Her sister was living with some American friends and came on the last weekend to help her pack for the move. According to Odio, her sister had arrived on either Thursday, September 26, or Friday, the twenty-seventh. By the time the three men arrived, Odio and her sister had "already started to pack to go" and there were boxes in the living room. Odio remembered she had worked the day the three visitors arrived, and since she did not work Saturday or Sunday, she said "it would be the 26th or the 27th, for sure."[38] Starting on September 26, Oswald began his twenty-hour bus journey from Houston to Mexico City, where he arrived on the twenty-seventh. He did not return to the U.S. for seven days. It was physically impossible for Oswald to visit Odio in Dallas when she claims he did.

If it was not Oswald, then what of Odio's story? Was there an imposter Oswald? There is no doubt that three men visited her, as her sister, Annie, confirms. The FBI thought it had solved the Odio mystery in 1964 when it found three men who might have visited her apartment near the end of September. Loran Hall, a prominent anti-Castroite, bore a marked resemblance to the man Odio described as the leader, Leopoldo. Hall told the FBI on September 16, 1964, that he was in Dallas soliciting funds during September 1963 and had been to the Odio apartment. He named his two companions as Lawrence Howard and William Seymour. The three of them had been arrested in Florida in December 1962, as part of the Kennedy administration's crackdown on anti-Castro paramilitary operations.[39] Howard looked like the second of the Cubans/Mexicans described by Odio. But the most staggering coincidence was that Seymour, who spoke only a few words of Spanish, greatly resembled Oswald. Seymour also constantly wore a beard stubble, the same as what Odio described on "Leon." However, four days later, September 20, 1964, Hall recanted his statement. Seymour and Howard also later denied they were at Odio's apartment.[40] When Odio was shown photos of the three and was asked if it was a case of mistaken identity, she stuck to her story and said she could not identify them.

But even if the visitors were Hall, Howard, and Seymour, what about the introduction of "Leon Oswald" and Odio's explicit details of the following day's telephone conversation about his being a Marine sharpshooter who thought President Kennedy should be dead? For a possible answer to this, Sylvia Odio herself has to be briefly examined. By the time of her Oswald story, she had a history of emotional problems. In Puerto Rico, where she had lived before moving to Dallas in March 1963, she had seen a psychiatrist over her fractious marriage. According to FBI reports, he decided she was unstable and unable, mentally or physically, to care for her children.[41] A doctor who was called to treat her once for "an attack of nerves" discovered she had made it up to get the attention of her neighbors. He described her as a very mixed-up young lady, and was told by others that she had also been under psychiatric care while living in Miami, when she moved to the States in 1961.[42]

In her divorce proceeding in 1963, she lost custody of her four children, because of charges of neglect and abandonment.[43] Near the time of her divorce, her friends recalled that she began having more "emotional problems," suffering total blackouts "when reality got too painful to bear."[44] In Dallas, she sought more extensive psychiatric help from Dr. Burton C. Einspruch. By the time of the assassination, she had been seeing him for more than seven months, at least weekly, sometimes more frequently.[45]

Odio insists she told at least two people, before the assassination, that three men, including Oswald, had visited her apartment. One of the people she told was Lucille Connell. But when the FBI questioned her in 1964, Connell said that Odio only told her about Oswald after the assassination, and then said she not only knew Oswald, but he had given talks to groups of Cuban refugees in Dallas.[46] The second person Odio contended she told before the assassination was her psychiatrist, Dr. Einspruch. When interviewed by the Warren Commission, Einspruch said that during the course of psychotherapy, Odio told him she had seen Oswald at several anti-Castro meetings, and that one of the meetings was held at her house. He made no mention of the three supposed visitors to the Odio apartment. When questioned in 1978 by the Select Committee, Einspruch did not mention Odio's story of multiple Oswald sightings. Instead, he thought she had told him of the three visitors, but he did not remember hearing the name Leon or about the Leopoldo telephone call before the assassination.[47] He also conceded that Odio "has a degree of suggestibility that she could believe something that did not really transpire."

On the day JFK was killed, Odio suffered one of her emotional seizures, passed out, and was hospitalized. "My mind was going around in circles," she recalled.[48] Dr. Einspruch spoke to her the day after the assassination, while she was still hospitalized. That is when he first remembered that Odio, who had a tendency to "exaggerate," connected her visitors to Oswald and the assassination "in a sort of histrionic way."[49] One of Odio's brothers, Cesar, described how his sister suffered a nervous breakdown after the Kennedy assassination, and that she still had the effects nearly a year later.[50] He blamed her divorce and the imprisonment of their parents in Cuba for her emotional collapse. Silvia Herrera, her mother-in-law, went so far as to say that Odio was an excellent actress who could intelligently fabricate such an episode if she wished.[51] A confidential FBI informant, who was an Odio friend, told the Bureau "that one of her main difficulties [is] that she cannot rationalize herself to the fact that she is no longer the daughter of a wealthy individual who will grant her every request, and she will perform various actions in an attempt to become the center of attractions."[52] The informant advised the FBI that Odio's family is "split in their opinion . . . some being of the opinion that she is almost crazy, and the others offering their condolences at her troubles and offering her assistance."[53] Another friend confirmed to the FBI that Odio was extremely lonesome in Dallas, sought to gain attention from others, and had an excellent imagination and a tendency toward exhibitionism.[54]

One of the most unusual aspects of the Odio case is that though she thought she had met the assassin, she never contacted any government or law enforcement agency to tell her story.[55] Carlos Bringuier, the New Orleans anti-Castro leader who was arrested in a street fracas with Oswald, had met Odio once. He considers her failing to report the Oswald sighting a telling factor: "I believe it is possible that she was visited by someone—there were a lot of people with different organizations out there. But after the assassination, I believe her immediate reaction would have been the same as mine, to have jumped up and called the FBI and say, 'Hey, that guy visited me!' Instead [after being released from the hospital], she casually told a neighbor, and that neighbor told the FBI, and that's the only reason it came out. That makes me suspicious of her story. It doesn't sound right, and I know from my own personal experience on what I did and how I felt when I realized I had some contact with the man who killed the President of the United States. I heard the name Lee Harvey Oswald and I jumped from my seat. I didn't finish my lunch—I called the FBI immediately. Maybe with all the news after the assassination she became confused and put Oswald's face and name onto the person she actually met. I have seen this as a lawyer in criminal cases. There is an accident with four witnesses and they give four different versions and they all believe they are telling the truth, and could even pass a lie detector. She thinks she is telling the truth. I hate to say she is lying, but she is mistaken."[56]

Three men did visit Odio, probably on September 26 or 27, 1963. There is not a single piece of corroborating evidence, however, for her postassassination claim that one of the men was introduced as 'Leon Oswald' and that the next day one of the Cubans called to discuss a Marine sharpshooter and his Kennedy death threats.

While Odio thought she had been visited by Oswald in Texas, he was actually undergoing one of his most important encounters since he had tried to renounce his American citizenship in Moscow in 1959. At the Cuban embassy, it was a typical

Friday morning for Silvia Duran, the young Mexican woman who worked as the secretary to the Cuban consul, Eusebio Azcue.[57]* Oswald arrived before noon. Duran remembers him as tentative, but once he discovered she spoke English, he seemed more relaxed. In a monologue that lasted almost fifteen minutes, he proceeded to tell her he was going to the USSR but that on the way he wanted a transit visa to stop in Cuba, for at least two weeks. He then began placing documents on her desk, each accompanied with a short explanation. Duran remembered his Russian residency and work papers, membership cards in the Fair Play for Cuba Committee and the American Communist party,† correspondence with Communist organizations in the U.S., and the clippings from his arrest in New Orleans.[58] He told her he expected to be promptly issued a visa since he "was a friend of the Cuban revolution," and that he wanted to leave by September 30, only three days later. His Russian-born wife was waiting to hear from him in New York, he claimed.[59] Duran, an admitted Marxist, took a liking to Oswald. While his way of making a visa request was unusual, he seemed sincere. Procedurally, Oswald should have begun filling out a lengthy application, but instead Duran called on Eusebio Azcue to see if he might expedite the process for the young American.

Azcue recalled: "She then calls upon me to see whether I, upon examination of those documents, can proceed to issue the visa immediately. I answered negatively. The documents that he submits are not enough. . . . I at that time tell him . . . I must request authorization from the Cuban government. And at that point he agrees to proceed to fill the application out in order to

---

* The Cuban consulate and embassy were in separate buildings but in the same compound. The Soviets had both consular and diplomatic branches in the same building. They will be referred to in this chapter as the Cuban and Soviet embassies. It is not clear in which sequence Oswald visited the two embassies. He told his wife he first went to the Soviet embassy, but the author's interpretation of the Cubans' testimony is that he might have visited them first.

† No membership card for the American Communist party was ever found in Oswald's belongings. However, two of the employees at the Cuban embassy claimed that Oswald had one. After the assassination, the American Communist party denied that he was ever a member. The card may have been counterfeit, made at the same time as his Hidell identifications.

process the visa."[60] Oswald, hoping to be received as a comrade in arms, could not have been pleased by Azcue's refusal to grant an immediate visa. Duran helped him fill out the application, and told him he needed to return with passport-size photographs. Oswald left to get the pictures at a nearby shop recommended by Duran.

When he returned to the Cuban consulate, Duran helped him complete the remainder of the application and stapled photographs to the original and five carbon copies. At that point, she informed him that the fastest way for him to get a visa to visit Cuba would be to obtain Soviet permission first to visit the USSR. While he had been gone, Duran "semi-officially" called the Soviet embassy to see whether she could facilitate his application. The staff was noncommittal but indicated the process could take four months.[61] Oswald began protesting loudly about the extensive paperwork and insisting on his right to get a visa for Cuba immediately.[62] Again, consul Azcue walked out of his office to see about the commotion. Azcue also told Oswald that if he had a Soviet visa, he could grant Oswald a fifteen-day visit for Cuba without having to contact the Cuban government. However, without a Soviet visa, Azcue reminded Oswald, he would have to go through the normal procedures, which could take two to three weeks.[63] Duran remembered Oswald looked angry, and became so noisy that the new Cuban consul, Alfredo Mirabal Diaz, who was scheduled to replace Azcue within a few months, also came out of his office to see what was causing the disturbance. Oswald demanded to use the telephone to call the Soviet embassy.*

"I did not know English," said Mirabal, ". . . and asked my colleague, Azcue, . . . who told me the visitor was in need of an urgent visa, that he was in a great hurry to travel to Cuba."[64] He told Duran that his Mexican tourist visa was only valid for a few more days, and feeling sorry for him, she wrote her name and the embassy's telephone number on a piece of paper, in case he needed further assistance or advice.[65]

---

* There is conflicting evidence as to whether Oswald telephoned the Soviets from the Cuban embassy. The Cuban employees say he did not use the telephone. The CIA refuses to confirm or deny whether it ever recorded a conversation between Oswald and the Soviets made from the Cuban embassy.

When he left the Cuban compound, Oswald quickly walked two short blocks to the Soviet embassy. Once he arrived, he approached the sentry at the entrance to the compound and demanded to see someone from the consulate.[66] It was not every day that a young American who had a rudimentary grasp of Russian, and had lived in the USSR for nearly three years, walked into the Mexico City embassy. Oswald was taken to the consul's office and joined there by Valeriy Vladimirovich Kostikov, a KGB agent operating under the diplomatic cover of a consul corps officer. Kostikov was soon joined by another KGB agent, Oleg Maximovich Nechiporenko.*

Oswald spoke Russian, and again presented his documents, announcing he was a former defector who was married to a Soviet citizen. He told the KGB officers that he was desperate to return to Russia, claiming that the FBI was harassing him because of his leftist politics and his Russian wife.[67] Trying to impress the Soviets that he was an important political activist, Oswald promised that he had interesting information to give them about his time in America. All they had to do was to grant him a visa and pay for his trip.[68] He regaled them about his work on behalf of Communism, and his efforts to infiltrate the anti-Castro Cubans and the right wing. He said it was urgent for him to get to Cuba so he could provide information that could help prevent future CIA attacks.[69] Ernesto Rodriguez, a former CIA contract agent, claimed that Oswald hinted he had information on American efforts to kill Castro.[70] It was vintage Oswald, a mixture of bluster and fabrication. The Soviet agents, having had no previous contact with him, did not know what to believe and what to dismiss. At the time, the KGB agents thought Oswald's rantings were evidence of an "unstable personality." The Soviet officers needed to contact headquarters in Moscow to

---

* The identity of Nechiporenko, who was later expelled from Mexico in 1970 for conspiring to overthrow the Mexican government, only became known at a 1992 press conference in Moscow. He then hired a Californian, Brian Litman, to represent him, and he began working on a book based on his meeting with Oswald. Kostikov's identity has been known since December 1963 and caused initial concern for the Warren Commission since the CIA said he was reportedly chief of KGB terrorism squads in the Western Hemisphere. By 1993 Kostikov had also begun working on a book about his meeting with Oswald (Interview with Brian Litman, April 29, 1993).

determine whether Oswald was somebody to whom the KGB wanted to grant an immediate visa. When Nechiporenko put Oswald off until the next day, he informed Lee that the granting of a visa could take up to four monoths. "This won't do for me," Oswald shouted as he leaned over the table toward Nechiporenko. "This is not my case! For me, it's all going to end in tragedy!"[71] Oswald's hands shook as he stuffed his documents into his jacket, and Nechiporenko observed Lee was "extremely agitated" as he left the Soviet compound.

The cable to Moscow about Oswald, from the KGB agents in Mexico City, ended up on the desk of the agent who had first handled the matter in 1959, Yuriy Nosenko. "Because I had no contact with the local KGB in Minsk, I did not know that Oswald had married or had a child. Then suddenly a special cable arrived from the Soviet embassy in Mexico City seeking our advice. Oswald was there and seeking a visa to reenter the USSR.

"I went to the chief of the department, and he looked and said, 'Oh, this nut. Go back and have the First Department cable the embassy that we are not interested, but have them give him a diplomatic turnaway.' Of course, Oswald didn't know he was being turned away because he was nuts. We considered him nuts. It took us almost no time to say no to his request for a visa."[72]*

The following day, Saturday, September 28, Oswald returned to both embassies. According to Nechiporenko, it appears he first went to the Soviets to see if his visa was ready. He could then take it to the Cubans and get his fifteen-day transit visa. Initially, he spoke briefly to Pavel Antonovich Yatzkov, a KGB captain operating under the cover identity of a consular officer. "He stormed into my office and wanted me to introduce and recommend him to the Cubans," recalled Yatzkov. "He told me that he had lived in the USSR. I told him that I would have to check before I could recommend him. He was nervous and his

---

*Some critics charged Oswald might have entered the Soviet embassy through a separate entrance and met with the KGB officers in a secure room, indicating he had a Soviet intelligence connection. But Oswald actually entered through the embassy's front entrance and met with the KGB officers in a windowed, nonsecure consul's office.

hands trembled . . ."[73] Yatzkov was soon joined by Kostikov, who immediately noticed that Oswald "had the look of someone who was hounded and he was much more anxious than the day before."[74] Oswald, in halting and poor Russian, retold the tale of how the FBI had ruined his life in the U.S. "Throughout the story," recalled Kostikov, "Oswald was extremely agitated and clearly nervous, especially whenever he mentioned the FBI, but he suddenly became hysterical, began to sob, and through his tears cried, 'I am afraid . . . they'll kill me. Let me in!' "[75] Oswald then stuck his hand into the left pocket of his jacket and startled the KGB agents by withdrawing his .38 caliber revolver. He swung it in the air as he cried "See? This is what I must now carry to protect my life."[76] As Oswald sobbed, Yatzkov seized the pistol and emptied its bullets just as Nechiporenko entered the room. "But if they don't leave me alone, I'm going to defend myself," Oswald said. The three KGB agents calmed Oswald. When they finally told him they would not issue a visa, his initial fury turned to depression. "His mood was bad," said Nechiporenko. "Very poor."[77] Nechiporenko, on directions from Moscow, was adamant that Oswald would have to go through normal procedures with the Soviet embassy in Washington.

After Oswald left the compound, the three KGB agents discussed their unusual visitor. They all agreed he was "psychotic." "We were also of the unanimous opinion," recalled Nechiporenko, "that if this was not a person suffering from mental disorders, then he was unbalanced at the very least or had an unstable constitution."[78]

Oswald left the Soviets determined to make a final assault on the Cubans. "We never had any individual that was so insistent or persistent," recalled Azcue. "He always had a face which reflected unhappiness. He was never friendly . . . he was not pleasant."[79] Oswald again demanded that he be issued a visa because of his political credentials, but the consul repeated it was impossible without a Russian visa. Both Azcue and Oswald knew by this time that the Soviets were not going to issue a visa, so Azcue's reasoning was merely a polite way of rejecting him. "He [Oswald] became highly agitated and angry," said Duran.[80] "I hear him make statements that are directed against us," recalled Azcue, "and he accuses us of being bureaucrats, and in a very discourteous manner. At that point I also become upset and I tell him to leave the consulate, maybe somewhat violently or emotionally."[81] He told Oswald that "a person like him, instead of aiding the Cuban revolution, was doing it harm."[82] Azcue moved toward Oswald, prepared to force him physically out of the embassy. "Then he leaves the consulate," recalled Azcue, "and he seems to be mumbling to himself, and slams the door, also in a very discourteous mood. That was the last time we saw him around."[83]*

Many conspiracy writers believe that the visitor to the Cuban and Soviet embassies may have been an Oswald imposter. Garrison calls the embassy visits "the most significant Oswald impersonation."[84]† The issue is a fertile one because of several factors, including a significant CIA blunder that the Agency has never completely clarified. On October 10, 1963, a week after Oswald visited the embassies, the CIA sent a memo about him to the FBI, the State Department, and the Navy.[85] The teletype was replete with errors. It did not even get the names correct, referring to "Lee Henry Oswald" and his wife, "Marian Pusakova." The CIA described the Oswald who contacted the Soviet embassy as "approximately 35 years old, with an athletic build, about six feet tall, with a receding hairline . . ."[86] The description in the teletype was based upon surreptitious photographs the Agency took of almost everyone who entered the Cuban and Soviet embassies in Mexico City. The CIA's Mexico City station had reviewed its surveillance photos and chosen the one it thought was Oswald. It was not.‡ The CIA did not have

---

* The Cubans claim that Oswald's visa application was received at the Ministry of Foreign Affairs in Havana on October 7 and rejected on October 15, since he did not have a visa for his country of destination, the USSR (CE 2445).

† Most proponents of the imposter theory believe that Oswald was only a patsy in the assassination, and was not even a real Communist, but merely someone working for American intelligence, pretending to be a leftist. In this scenario, an imposter made high-profile visits to two Communist embassies so that Oswald's leftist credentials would be enhanced.

‡ The man mistaken in the picture for Oswald has never been publicly identified by the CIA. However, Nechiporenko says it was a former American serviceman, who was psychologically disturbed, and who occasionally wandered by the Soviet embassy (*Passport to Assassination: The Never-Before-Told Story of Lee Harvey Oswald by the KGB Colonel Who Knew Him*, Oleg Maximovich Nechiporenko, Birch Lane Press, 1993, p. 175).

any photographs of Oswald in the file it maintained on him, and did not know what he looked like.*

The official CIA position is that its cameras did not operate around the clock, and upon review, after the assassination, of all the photographs taken of people entering the two embassies, there was no photo of Oswald. Some claim the CIA did have photos or even sound tapes of Oswald. Supposedly, when the CIA station chief for Mexico, Winston Scott, died, his safe was cleaned out, including a right-profile photo of Oswald entering the Soviet embassy. Three former CIA employees told the House Select Committee they had seen such a photo.[87] James Angleton, who was responsible for Nosenko being branded as a KGB plant, personally flew to Mexico after Scott's death and cleaned out his desk and safe.[88] Angleton is now dead, and if there was such a photo, he was the last to know of its whereabouts. As the House Select Committee learned in its investigation, the CIA does not now have any photos of Oswald entering the embassies.

As for sound tapes, the Agency may have recorded as many as eight conversations it originally thought to be of Oswald, either on the telephone to the Soviet embassy or during his visits there. W. David Slawson, a Warren Commission staff counsel, said that the CIA's Winston Scott played part of a poor-quality tape recording that purported to include Oswald, several months after the assassination. But Slawson could not identify Oswald's voice. In 1976, according to *The Washington Post*, David Phillips, a former chief of CIA operations in Latin America, indicated a transcript of an Oswald phone call to the Soviet embassy still existed.[89] Phillips later denied the reported remarks. "The Agency had at one point a recording of Oswald asking to speak to whoever he was going to speak to at the Soviet embassy," Edwin Lopez, a House Select Committee investigator, told the author. "And the Agency had a husband-and-

---

* Oswald's CIA file did not contain *any* photos. However, after the assassination, the CIA discovered it had a photo of him in its Minsk file. In 1961, the Agency's Domestic Contact Division had made copies of some pictures taken by tourists. The CIA wanted the snapshots because an Intourist guide was featured. The unidentified American was not of interest until the Agency realized, several years later, who he was.

wife team [who were Russian] listen to the tape and transcribe
it, and in parentheses, they wrote down—and I talked to both of
them: 'This guy speaks English with a broken Russian accent.'
Now you and I both know that Oswald did not speak in broken
Russian. Well, this is amazing—they have a tape, they sent it up
to Washington at one point after the assassination, I have seen
the cable and all, and guess what happens to the tape—gone! So
all we have left is our transcription, and our conversations with
the husband-and-wife team."[90]

However, the tape referred to by Lopez may not even have
been a recording of Oswald. A retired Agency official familiar
with the Oswald file spoke to the author on the condition he not
be identified. "Even if there had been a sound recording, it
would have been erased routinely a week after it was made. If
we kept everything we recorded, you couldn't find enough ware-
houses to store them. So once something is transcribed, we
don't need the tape, and it's reused. Keeping the tape might be
more of an indication that there was a special interest in this
fellow. However, since there isn't a tape, no one is sure that we
recorded the right person. Just like we made an error in photo-
graphing the wrong man, there's a good chance that we might
have recorded the same man we photographed, thinking the entire time we had surveillance on Oswald. We've really created
our own problems on this one."*

Since there was no photo of Oswald entering the embassies,
or a tape recording proving he was there, conspiracy buffs use
the description in the CIA teletype of October 10, 1963, and the
photo released of the wrong man to claim that Oswald was impersonated. Their argument is bolstered by Cuban consul Azcue,
who testified before the House Select Committee that the man
he argued with for fifteen minutes at the Cuban embassy does
not look like the photographs of Lee Harvey Oswald.[91] He described the man at the embassy as ten years older, with dark

---

* No transcript of any sound tape has ever been released. The CIA is its own
worst enemy on many of these issues. Because it is so protective of sources
and its means of obtaining information, even years after the event, its lack of
full disclosure is often interpreted as evidence of conspiracy. But the CIA's
failure to be forthright is an inherent part of the intelligence trade, and is not
unique to its handling of the Oswald case.

blond hair, and thinner.* Finally, the Select Committee investigator on Mexico City, Edwin Lopez, wrote a 265-page report concluding that it was likely that an Oswald imposter visited the Cuban and Soviet embassies. However, Lopez's report was sealed by the Select Committee, fueling the debate over the issue.[92]

But the evidence is overwhelming that the real Oswald visited both embassies. Except Azcue, the other employees at the Cuban embassy, Silvia Duran and Alfredo Mirabal Diaz, positively identified the visitor as Oswald.[93] In 1978, Cuba finally gave the original of Oswald's visa application to the U.S. government. Handwriting experts for the House Select Committee verified that the two signatures on the applications belonged to him.[94] The six passport-size photographs that Duran told him to have taken, and then stapled to the top of each application, are definitely of Oswald. In the unlikely event an imposter brought back those pictures of the real Oswald, he would have to hope that Duran would not notice he was submitting photos of someone other than himself. Moreover, Oswald argued loudly at the Cuban embassy on at least two occasions after he had brought in his photos, attracting the attention of several employees. The incoming consul at the time, Alfredo Mirabal Diaz, only walked out of his office because of the commotion, and later testified that the man at the Cuban embassy was the same as the man in the visa photos.[95] An imposter, trying to pass off photos of Oswald as himself, would not create two noisy scenes in which people had a chance to study and remember him.

While the Cuban evidence is clear that the real Oswald brought the photos and signed the applications, until recently there had been no Soviet confirmation regarding the visits to its embassy. However, in 1992, one of the KGB agents who met with Oswald finally broke his silence and helped settle any lin-

---

* Azcue admits to being one of the few people who believe Jim Garrison's theory of an imposter Oswald, and cannot say how much this belief colors his memory of the man he encountered at the embassy. The descriptions he gave to the House Select Committee were based on his recall of an event fifteen years earlier. But when told by the committee that the visa-application signatures had been verified as belonging to Oswald, Azcue wavered. "Under such circumstances I would have to accept that I was being influenced or seeing visions."

gering doubts. Oleg Nechiporenko announced that he had met Oswald on September 27 and 28, 1963, in Mexico City, and said "without hesitation" that it was the same man who was arrested two months later for killing President Kennedy. The other KGB agents who met Oswald in Mexico City, Valeriy Kostikov and Pavel Yatzkov, also confirmed they had seen the real Oswald.[96]*

Besides his visits to the embassies, did Oswald do anything else of interest in Mexico? The Warren Commission concluded that since he was dejected and frustrated after his confrontations at the two embassies, he spent the remainder of his time quietly, and alone. The Commission relied on the statements of employees in Oswald's hotel and at nearby restaurants. He was usually gone by the time the maid arrived at 9:00 each morning, and according to the night watchman, he returned nightly around midnight, which the Commission said was "not unusual, in view of the late hour at which Mexico City's activities begin."[97] The Commission had extensive testimony that he ordered food at a small restaurant next to the hotel by pointing at the menu. He spent on average between 40¢ and 48¢ for each meal, often refusing dessert and coffee, because he evidently did not realize it was part of the set price. Oswald's map of Mexico City, found in his possessions after the assassination, had pen markings on it.[98] Two indicate the Cuban and Soviet embassies. Other locations include museums, parks, general sight-seeing landmarks, and even a movie with English subtitles. He later told Marina about his tourist activities, even claiming he had gone to a bullfight.[99] Based upon follow-up investigations by the Mexican police and the FBI, the Commission reviewed further witness statements and was unequivocal in concluding "he was seen with no other person either at his hotel or at the restaurant."[100]

However, Summers, in *Conspiracy*, presents what appears to be credible evidence that Oswald may have had some social contact, with avowed leftists, beyond the embassies, which the Warren Commission did not discover. Silvia Duran, the Cuban

---

* On November 22, the day of the assassination, Kostikov burst into Nechiporenko's office. "Oleg," he shouted, "they just showed the suspect in Kennedy's death on TV. It's Lee Oswald, the gringo who was here in September! I recognized him" (*Passport to Assassination*, p. 101).

embassy employee, admitted to the House Select Committee that she advised Oswald that it would help his visa application if he could get a letter from a Mexican in good standing with the Cuban revolutionary hierarchy.[101] Duran was friends with the chairman of the philosophy department at the National Autonomous University in Mexico City, Ricardo Guerra (he later served as the Mexican ambassador to East Germany).* Guerra sometimes held seminars on Marx at Duran's home.[102] According to Summers, over the September 27 weekend, Oscar Contreras, who was studying to be a lawyer at Mexico City's National University, was sitting with three of his friends drinking coffee in the school's cafeteria after the showing of a film in Guerra's philosophy department. Suddenly, the man at the next table struck up a conversation. He told them his name was Lee Harvey Oswald, a name Contreras and his friends remembered because it was also the name of a popular cartoon rabbit.[103] Contreras adds weight to the imposter Oswald story by claiming the man was five feet six inches at the most, at least three inches shorter than the real Oswald. He told Contreras and his friends that he was a painter from Texas, dissatisfied with the U.S. and harassed by the FBI, and was hoping to go to Cuba but could not get a visa. He had found the right group, as Contreras and his associates were strongly pro-Castro and viewed the U.S. as a great imperialistic power. They also personally knew consul Azcue, and promised to put in a good word for Oswald. But later that night, when Contreras spoke to Azcue and a Cuban intelli-

---

* There is little doubt Duran tried to help Oswald, but she claims it was only at the Cuban embassy and that she did not socialize with him or talk to him outside. A Mexican author, Elena Garro de Paz, said she saw Oswald at a "twist party" at Duran's brother-in-law's house over the weekend of September 27. Garro claims Oswald had two companions and that she overheard consul Azcue, also at the party, tell another person that there was no alternative but to kill President Kennedy. While Duran admits there was a twist party at her brother-in-law's house around this time, she is adamant that Oswald was not there. Azcue is just as firm that he was not at such a party and that he never uttered such an "incredible statement." It is highly unlikely that Duran would have invited Oswald and Azcue to the same party after the almost violent fight they had on Saturday, September 28. No other witnesses at the party support Garro's claim. Another instance, in which a former police official, Salvador Diaz Verson, claimed to see Duran and Oswald at a restaurant, Caballo Blanco Parren, on Saturday, September 28, also remains uncorroborated.

gence agent, he was told to break off contacts with Oswald as the embassy was suspicious he might be a provocation from American intelligence.[104] Oswald supposedly came back to Contreras and his friends and even spent the night at their apartment, most likely Sunday, September 29. They told him the Cuban consul would not change his mind. But when he left in the morning he was still begging for help to get to Cuba. Contreras and his friends did not hear from him again.

Summers wrote that when the CIA received information about Contreras's claim in 1967, it did not adequately pursue it, allowing leads to grow cold in the subsequent decades. Although the House Select Committee failed to find Contreras, Summers located him in Tampico, Mexico, and judged him truthful. When the author tried to interview Contreras in 1992, he refused, dodging telephone calls for several weeks. The author discovered, at a Washington, D.C., archive, Summers's original notes about his September 23, 1978, interview with Contreras.[105] The notes disclosed that Contreras told Summers that while Oswald said he was from Texas in earlier years, he lived in San Francisco at the time he was visiting Mexico City. Summers omitted that from his book. Also, Summers needed a translator to speak with Contreras, but Oswald did not speak Spanish and there is no explanation for how they supposedly communicated. In the same file with Summers's original notes is a summary of another interview conducted with Contreras, by journalist Mark Redhead, in Tampico, on June 3, 1986.* Contreras told Redhead that the account of his story was correct as set forth in Summers's book, except he was adamant he had seen Oswald in 1959 to 1960, not in 1963. The problem is that Oswald was living in Russia during that time. Contreras also claimed that Oswald told him about his police problems in New Orleans, but those events did not take place until nearly four years after Contreras claimed he met Oswald. In his interview notes in 1978, Summers lists the date that Contreras met Oswald as 1963, yet Contreras

---

* The Redhead interview was done for London Weekend Television, which was preparing a televised "Trial of Lee Harvey Oswald." Redhead considered Contreras too unreliable for inclusion in the television program, concluding, "I would not be at all surprised if he didn't just invent it and find the yarn got a bit out of hand."

told Redhead he was not even living in Mexico City in 1963 when Oswald visited.

The Contreras story is clearly false. However, that it was presented as credible and relevant about Oswald's activities in Mexico City, in a best-selling book, is instructive about the pitfalls that beset the research on this subject. There are other stories that emerged from Oswald's trip to Mexico City that often passed as true but, upon closer inspection, are also not credible.

In an article in the *National Enquirer* with a byline by Comer Clark, a British reporter, Castro was said to have claimed in an impromptu 1967 interview that "Lee Oswald came to the Cuban embassy in Mexico City twice. The first time, I was told, he wanted to work for us. He was asked to explain, but he wouldn't. He wouldn't go into details. The second time he said something like: 'Someone ought to shoot that President Kennedy.' Then Oswald said—and this was exactly how it was reported to me—'Maybe I'll try to do it.' . . . Yes, I heard of Lee Harvey Oswald's plan to kill President Kennedy. It's possible I could have saved him. I might have been able to—but I didn't. I never believed the plan would be put into effect."[106] In 1978, Castro denied to the House Select Committee that he had ever been interviewed by Clark.[107] Clark's journalistic past was filled with sensational stories for tabloids, such as "I Was Hitler's Secret Love," "British Girls as Nazi Sex Slaves," and "German Plans to Kidnap the Royal Family."[108] Clark's widow told Anthony Summers that her husband had never mentioned interviewing Castro, and his former assistant, Nina Gadd, finally admitted she ghosted the story based upon a rumor passed to her from a Latin American foreign minister.[109]

Beyond the Clark story, another episode fueled the rumor that the Cubans had known in advance about Oswald's intention to kill JFK. A reliable CIA source reported that a Cuban intelligence agent posted to the Cuban embassy in Mexico City, Luisa Calderon, remarked to an acquaintance about the assassination, "I knew almost before Kennedy."[110] The House Select Committee could not interview Calderon in 1978 because she claimed to be ill. However, in a letter, she said the story was false. Other employees at the embassy also denied any foreknowledge.[111]

The Select Committee concluded Calderon's statement was "braggadocio" and that Oswald did not voice a threat against President Kennedy while at the Cuban embassy.[112]*

On November 25, 1963, only three days after the assassination, a young Nicaraguan, Gilberto Alvarado, went to the American embassy in Mexico. He startled U.S. officials by claiming that in September he had visited the Cuban embassy and overheard a conversation among Oswald, a Cuban, and a black man. According to Alvarado, the Cuban passed money to the black man, who then said, "I want to kill the man." Oswald replied, "You are not man enough—I can do it." The black man said, "I can't go with you. I have a lot to do." Oswald assured him it was all right: "The people are waiting for me back there." Then the Cuban man handed Oswald $6,500 in large-denomination bills.[113] Alvarado also asserted that he had tried to warn the embassy before the assassination, but was ignored.

The CIA gave Alvarado's story its full attention. The information was sent to the FBI as well as to the White House.† But under questioning from Mexican authorities, Alvarado recanted his entire story.[114] Then, when requestioned by the Americans, he said the Mexicans had coerced him to retract. He repeated his original story, but failed a lie detector test. Later he said he was no longer sure of the date, and the person only resembled Oswald. Although Ambassador Thomas Mann, the U.S. representative in Mexico at the time, was not convinced the Alvarado story was completely false, Alvarado is now so discredited that few repeat his story.‡

---

* Another factor that added to the suspicion about the Cuban embassy was that Consul Azcue was recalled to Havana on November 18, just four days before the assassination. But the Cuban government later explained that the move had been planned for more than six months, and that his replacement, Alfredo Mirabal Diaz, had been there for several months.

† President Lyndon Johnson later believed that Castro was behind the assassination. The Alvarado story must certainly have contributed to LBJ's early suspicion.

‡ On December 2, ten days after the assassination, another witness, Pedro Gutierrez, wrote President Johnson that he had seen Oswald receive a large amount of money from an official at the Cuban embassy. At first, this seemed an important confirmation of Alvarado's story, but the Gutierrez claim also crumbled upon subsequent investigation. Then, within days of the Gutierrez allegation, a CIA source pinpointed a Cuban, Gilberto Lopez, who had contact

The final witness whose story sent shockwaves through the U.S. government regarding Oswald's Mexico City trip and a possible Cuban government sponsorship was Autulio Ramirez Ortiz. Ramirez had hijacked an aircraft to Cuba in 1961. When he was later returned to the U.S., he was sentenced to twenty years' imprisonment, and he told the House Select Committee that while in Cuba he had worked in a Cuban intelligence facility. There, he claimed, he found a file labeled "Osvaldo-Kennedy" that contained a photo of Oswald and a recommendation by the KGB; he said the file concluded: "Oswald is an adventurer. Our embassy in Mexico has orders to get in contact with him. Be very careful."[115] Ramirez was not in the U.S. in 1964 and could not testify to the Warren Commission, so the Select Committee was the only government body to interview him, in a session still sealed as confidential. The committee said that although there was independent confirmation of other allegations Ramirez made, the FBI and CIA were unable to substantiate the existence of an "Osvaldo-Kennedy" file. The committee concluded that the "Cuban intelligence system in the 1961–63 period was too sophisticated to have been infiltrated by Ramirez in the manner he had described."[116]*

Completely unaware that he would soon be at the center of such rumors and controversy, Oswald considered his next move. When he had decided to defect to Russia in 1959, he had obtained a Soviet visa in Helsinki within a few days. He had fully expected the same to happen with the Cubans, especially in light of his extensive political activism. His rejection was unexpected and a stunning personal setback. Returning to America was tantamount to admitting defeat, but with limited funds, he could not stay much longer.

---

with the Tampa branch of Fair Play for Cuba, as a conspirator. According to the source, Lopez rushed into Mexico the day after the assassination, went to the Cuban embassy in Mexico City, and was spirited to Havana on a Cubana airlines flight that had waited hours only for him. While the Warren Commission's investigation of this story was weak, the Select Committee extensively researched it. While the Committee was troubled by the CIA's original handling of the Lopez report, it did not discover any evidence that established a link to the assassination.

* Ramirez wrote a manuscript about the episode, titled *Castro's Red Hot Hell*, but it remains unpublished.

On Monday, September 30, Oswald telephoned the Soviet embassy. Colonel Nechiporenko claims he spoke to him at least once, and Oswald asked if there had been any change about granting him a visa.* One final time Nechiporenko told him no. Oswald then walked the several blocks from his hotel to the Chihuahuense travel agency, and spent $20.30 for a ticket on a Transportes del Norte bus from Mexico City to Nuevo Laredo and then by Greyhound into Texas. On the following day, Tuesday, October 1, Oswald paid his hotel bill through that night.[117] On Wednesday, at 8:30 A.M., he left on bus No. 332. Other passengers recall that at the border crossing, he was pulled off and questioned about his Mexican tourist papers, because initially the border guards thought his fifteen-day visa had expired. It was over fifteen days since the visa was issued, but Oswald showed them his entry stamp to prove he had not been in Mexico past the prescribed time. When it was resolved and he returned to the bus, other passengers heard him grumbling about the bureaucrats at the border.[118] At 1:35 in the morning, Oswald crossed the international border. He arrived at Laredo at 3:00 A.M. and did not finish the last leg of his trip until 2:20 in the afternoon on Thursday, October 3. He had returned to Dallas.

---

* Nechiporenko has no doubt the Oswald he spoke to on the telephone was the same man who personally visited the embassy. There is also a possibility that Oswald telephoned again the following day, Tuesday, October 1. The CIA may have intercepted one of these telephone conversations, in which Oswald spoke to a guard, who told him that only by personally visiting the embassy could he obtain any further information. Although many writers on the assassination believe Oswald actually visited the Soviets on October 1, Nechiporenko says he did not (Interview with Brian Litman, April 29, 1993).

10

"When Will All Our Foolishness Come to an End?"

Oswald was ashamed to call Marina when he first arrived in Dallas. He had fully expected he would be calling her from Cuba, and he could not bring himself to talk to her that first day. Instead, he went directly to the YMCA, where he had stayed a year earlier when he had moved to Dallas to find work. He registered as a serviceman to avoid paying the 50¢ membership fee.[1] Later that same day he checked in at the Texas Employment Commission, filed a claim for the last of his unemployment checks, and emphasized that he needed to find work quickly.[2] He listed his address as 2515 West 5th Street in the Dallas suburb of Irving, which was Ruth Paine's house, where Marina was staying.[3]

The following day, Friday, October 4, Oswald reviewed the newspaper's help-wanted ads and applied for work as a typesetter at the Padgett Printing Company. He made a favorable impression on the plant superintendent, Theodore Gangl, who was prepared to hire him. However, before committing himself, he telephoned one of Oswald's references, Jaggars-Chiles-Stovall, and spoke to Robert Stovall. Stovall remembered Oswald well and told Gangl he was "kind of an oddball . . . peculiar . . . and that he had some knowledge of the Russian language . . . may be a damn Communist." Stovall concluded, "If I was you, I wouldn't hire him."[4] Oswald did not get the job.

After his Padgett interview, he finally telephoned Marina. She was elated that he was not in Cuba. He told her to send Ruth

Paine to pick him up and bring him to the Paine home in Irving, but Marina explained that Ruth had just donated blood at the hospital in case it was necessary during the baby's birth, and she was too tired to make the trip. He hitchhiked the twelve miles to the Paine's home and arrived within the hour. Alone with Marina, he began to complain bitterly about his mistreatment by the embassies in Mexico City. He described how they shuttled him back and forth, each waiting for the other to act first, and denounced the "bureaucrats" and the "red tape" that had frustrated his goals.[5] "The same kind of bureaucrats as in Russia. No point going there," he said to Marina.[6] She said he never again talked of "Uncle Fidel," fighting in the Cuban revolution, or of visiting Havana.[7] Marina, who had never relished the idea of moving there, was pleased.

Once he vented his frustration about the embassies, he told her about the rest of his trip. He gave her postcards of bullfights as well as a small silver bracelet inscribed with her name, which he claimed he bought in Mexico, but probably purchased at a Dallas five-and-dime store.[8] Considering his setbacks, he was affectionate and kept saying how much he had missed her, with his only real distraction being the concern for finding work. When Ruth drove him to the bus station on Monday, October 7, after a relatively quiet weekend, he asked if Marina could stay until he found a job and a new apartment. Ruth assured him that Marina could stay as long as she wanted.

Deciding the YMCA was too expensive, Oswald found a room in a boardinghouse in the Oak Cliff section of Dallas, at 621 Marsalis Street. He paid the $7 weekly rent in advance, registered under his real name, and moved in that same day.[9] He searched daily for work, telephoning and visiting the employment commission and prospective employers, but had no success. Mary Bledsoe, who rented him the room, did not like him as a tenant. She said he hardly spoke after he moved in. Bledsoe was also aggravated because he used her refrigerator, ate meals in his room, and made twice daily telephone calls to his wife "in that foreign language."[10] On Saturday, October 12, Lee told Bledsoe that he was going to visit his wife for the weekend and said, "I want my room cleaned and clean sheets put on the bed." "Well, I will after you move," she told him, "because you are going to move. . . . I am not going to rent to you anymore."[11] Oswald, taken by surprise, demanded $2 back, the prorated portion of the $7 he had prepaid for one week. Bledsoe refused. He was angry when he left for Ruth Paine's house, convinced that his landlady's abrupt rejection meant the FBI was back on his trail and had been asking about him.[12] He would not use his real name for his next rental.

For the second weekend in a row, Marina and Lee did not argue, perhaps because the baby was due any day. Both Marina and Ruth noticed the difference. Michael Paine visited Friday and he, too, found Oswald a "reasonable person."* This surprised him, because he had previously concluded Lee was a "bitter person . . . [with] quite a lot of very negative views of people in the world around him, very little charity in his view toward anybody . . ." Before Ruth had even invited Marina to live with her, she had discussed it with Michael. They were concerned that since Lee was so cruel to Marina, he might be violent toward them as well. "We assumed or felt that—if we handled him with a gentle or considerate manner that he wouldn't be a danger to us . . . that he wasn't going to stab Ruth or Marina," said Michael.[13]

Marina was the only one who knew about Lee's Mexico City trip, but she misunderstood how that affected him. She viewed his apparent withdrawal from political action as a turn for the good. To Ruth and Michael Paine, he now seemed just like someone who was trying hard to support his family and find work. "Lee had said over the weekend that he had gotten the last of the unemployment compensation checks that were due him," recalled Ruth, "and that it had been smaller than the others had been . . . and he looked very discouraged when he went to look for work."[14] The Texas Employment Commission arranged interviews for some excellent possibilities, including sales-clerk positions at Solid State Electric and Texas Power and Light that paid $350 and $250 per month, respectively, but the companies were not interested. Even when the commission sent him for low-paying jobs like a clerk-trainee at Burton-Dixie,

---

* Despite the Paines' separation, Michael spent considerable time at the house, still keeping many of his belongings there.

at $1.25 per hour, he was not hired. According to Ruth, Oswald feared that he was losing some job opportunities because he could not drive and could only work at places reached by public transportation. That weekend, she gave him his first driving lesson. He drove three blocks to a parking lot and then around the lot, but Ruth said he was "pretty unskilled."

On Monday, October 14, Ruth, who had errands in Dallas, drove him into the city. Later that day, while having coffee with some neighbors, she had a conversation that would have a profound impact on future events. Ruth, Marina, Dorothy Roberts, and Linnie Mae Randle were discussing Lee's difficulty in obtaining work. Roberts and Randle were also young mothers, and they clearly empathized with Oswald's predicament, especially since Marina's second child was about to be born. Linnie Mae Randle recalled that Wesley Buell Frazier, her younger brother, "had just looked for a job, and I had helped him try to find one. We listed several places that he might go to look for work. When you live in a place you know some places that someone with, you know, not very much of an education can find work."[15] Mrs. Randle said that Buell had applied for jobs at Manor Bakery and Texas Gypsum Company, but both involved driving a truck, so they were not practical for Lee.[16] Then Mrs. Randle mentioned that her brother had finally found a job at the Texas School Book Depository, a warehouse that handled the distribution of mostly educational books.[17] "I didn't know there was a job opening over there. But we said he might try over there. There might be work . . . because it was the busy season . . . ."[18]

It was the group's final suggestion, and Marina later urged Ruth, "Would you please call the Texas School Depository?" "I looked up the number in the book," recalled Ruth, "and dialed it, was told I would need to speak to Mr. Truly, who was at the warehouse. The phone was taken to Mr. Truly . . . and I talked with him . . ." "She said, 'Mr. Truly,' " recalled Roy Truly, " 'you don't know who I am but I have a neighbor whose brother works for you. . . . He tells his sister that you are very busy. And I am just wondering if you can use another man . . . I have a fine young man living here with his wife and baby, and his wife is expecting another baby in a few days, and he needs work desperately.' And I told Mrs. Paine to send him down, and

I would talk to him—that I didn't have anything in mind for him of a permanent nature, but if he was suited, we could possibly use him for a brief time."[19]

The same day Ruth Paine called the School Book Depository, Oswald rented an eight-by-twelve-foot room in a boardinghouse at 1026 North Beckley Street, also in Dallas's Oak Cliff neighborhood, for a dollar more a week, eight dollars, than the Bledsoe room he was forced to vacate.[20] He registered as O. H. Lee.* Unlike Mary Bledsoe, his new landlady, Gladys Johnson, and the manager/housekeeper, Earlene Roberts, found his quiet manner acceptable. Except for weekend visits to his wife, they later reported he never went out at night or had a single visitor.[21] Instead, according to Johnson, he stayed inside his room "95 percent of the time," and the remainder silently in front of the communal television "with the other men renters and he wouldn't speak to them. Maybe they would speak to him but he wouldn't speak, not saying a word to any of the other boarders."[22] Earlene Roberts found him remote as well. "He wouldn't say nothing. I would say, 'Good afternoon,' and he would just . . . give me a dirty look and keep walking and go on to his room. . . . That was the only peculiarity about him."[23]

After Oswald settled into the North Beckley Street rooming house, he telephoned Ruth's home that evening to speak to Marina. Ruth got on the phone at the end of the conversation and told him about Truly and suggested he go to the School Book Depository as soon as possible.[24] The next day, Tuesday, October 15, Oswald went to Dealey Plaza, in downtown Dallas. "So he came in," said Truly, "introduced himself to me, and I took him in my office and interviewed him. He seemed to be quiet and well mannered."[25] Oswald filled the application as he sat with Truly. He told him he had just been honorably discharged from the Marines, where he had office duties. "I asked him if he had ever had any trouble with the police and he said, 'No,'" Truly remembered. "So thinking that he was just out of the Marines, I didn't check any further back. I didn't have anything of a permanent nature in mind for him. He looked like a nice young

* His new alias was probably a simple reversal of his name, but he might also have tried to emulate V. T. Lee, the national president of Fair Play for Cuba.

fellow to me . . . he used the word 'sir,' which a lot of them don't do at this time."[26] Truly had two possibilities for Oswald. One position was in a storage warehouse some distance from Dealey Plaza. The other was as a clerk at the main Depository. Truly decided he seemed earnest enough to hire him as a clerk at the main building, to fill book orders, at $1.25 per hour.[27] Truly told him to report to work the following morning, October 16, which was the start of a new pay period.*

Oswald was elated when he telephoned Marina that night. He told her it was good to be working with books, and the work would not tire him. His primary responsibility was to fill textbook orders, by finding the books in the seven-floor Depository and then bringing them to the first floor, where the orders were processed. The work atmosphere was a relaxed one, and people left Lee alone, which he liked. At the first-floor recreation room where the workers ate lunch and sometimes played dominoes, Oswald sat by himself, reading day-old newspapers.† "He never would speak to anyone," recalled co-worker Bonnie Ray Williams. "He was just a funny fellow. . . . He never did put himself in any position to say anything to anyone." But one person who engaged him in a brief conversation that first week was Buell Frazier, Linnie Mae Randle's brother. When Frazier discovered that Oswald's wife was staying at the Paines' house in Ir-

---

*Some have questioned the coincidence that Oswald obtained a job at a building that gave him a clear shot at the presidential motorcade. Garrison says that Oswald was manipulated, that "guiding hands made sure that he would be at the right place at the right time." That argument ignores the fact that no motorcade route had even been proposed by the date Oswald was hired at the Depository. Moreover, such a theory means that Linnie Mae Randle, who suggested the Depository, and Ruth Paine, who told Oswald about it, were part of the conspiracy, as were Roy Truly and the Texas employers who rejected Oswald for jobs earlier in the week. Even Robert Stovall, Oswald's former employer, who scuttled his hiring at Padgett by a poor recommendation, would have to be part of the plot. That single incident, Oswald obtaining the job at the Book Depository, highlights two key flaws in almost every conspiracy theory—the constant interpretation of coincidence as evidence of conspiracy, and the inordinate number of people who would have had to be involved in any such plot—more than a dozen on just this issue.

† He was too miserly to buy a daily paper, instead picking up the throwaways at work the day after. However, he still maintained subscriptions to journals he thought important—*The Militant*, *The Worker*, *Time*, and some Russian periodicals.

ving, he realized they were neighbors, as Frazier lived only a block from the Paines. "Are you going to be going home this afternoon?" Frazier recalled asking Oswald. "And he told me then . . . that he didn't have a car, you know, and so I told him . . . anytime you want to go just let me know.' So I thought he would be going home every day like most men do but he told me no, that he wouldn't go home every day and then he asked me could he ride home say like Friday afternoon on weekends and come back on Monday morning and I told him that would be just fine with me."[28]

On Friday, October 18, Oswald asked Frazier for his first ride to Irving. When he arrived at the Paines', he was startled by a small surprise birthday party Ruth and Marina had planned.[29] Lee was twenty-four years old. There was a birthday cake, decorations, and wine. Michael Paine was also there. Marina remembered that Lee was so touched that he had tears in his eyes. He was emotional the remainder of the evening, crying and apologizing to Marina for what he had put her through.[30] It was another quiet weekend, until Marina began her labor Sunday evening. Around 9:00 P.M., Ruth drove her to Parkland Hospital, while Lee baby-sat with the household's three children. Ruth returned after checking Marina into Parkland, and although Oswald was in the guest bedroom with a light on, he did not come out to ask any questions.[31] Ruth stayed up, telephoning the hospital until she heard before midnight that Marina had given birth to a second daughter. Ruth told Lee the following morning before he left with Frazier for work.[32]

Frazier drove Oswald to the Depository on Monday, October 21, and then took him back to Irving that evening. Ruth was surprised that he did not want to go to Parkland until she discovered he feared that if the hospital knew he had a job, he would have to pay for Marina's stay. But Ruth had already told the hospital the previous evening that he was employed, and she assured him that his salary was so low that the maternity care was still free.[33] He finally visited Marina later that evening. They named the infant Audrey Marina Rachel Oswald.*

---

* Marina chose Audrey after Audrey Hepburn, and Rachel after a niece. Oswald objected to Rachel saying, "It sounds too Jewish." He wanted Marina, so

Two days after the birth of his daughter, Wednesday, October 23, Oswald returned to his world of political activism. He had promised Marina that he would never again try to kill Walker, but now that he had returned to Dallas, he could not escape thinking about the right-wing general. Walker was more active than ever in politics; he was talking of again running for political office, and the failed assassination attempt had even created a backlash of sympathy for him. On Wednesday, Oswald attended a right-wing rally at which Walker addressed 1,300 people.[34] It is not known if Oswald was stalking him that night, as he had for nearly two months before first trying to kill him.*

The day after Oswald attended the Walker rally, U.S. ambassador to the U.N. Adlai Stevenson was in Dallas for United Nations Day and was attacked by a surging crowd of right-wing protestors. Some spat on him, and another struck him on the head with a placard. Stevenson was rushed from the scene. That incident received widespread media coverage and could only have exacerbated Oswald's inherent fears about the growth of the political right. The Walker surveillance was news that would have greatly upset Marina, but he did not tell her. He did, however, report his activities to Arnold Johnson of the American Communist party. In a letter in which he notified Johnson that he had relocated temporarily to Texas, he said he had been at an "ultra-right meeting" with Walker, and advised that the "political friction between 'left' and 'right' is very great here."[35] He also mentioned the attack on Adlai Stevenson, citing it as evidence of the tensions between right and left.

On Friday, October 25, at Ruth's house for the weekend, Oswald and Michael Paine had a long political discussion. "When I used to see him watch football games on a Saturday or Sunday," Paine recalled, "I used to think, 'Well, that is a hell of a way for a

---

they added it as a second middle name. Today, Oswald's second daughter goes by Rachel.

* Oswald kept his pistol hidden in a leather case at his North Beckley room. His rifle was in the Paines' garage. Michael Paine, who often used a workbench he kept in the garage, thought the dismantled rifle was "camping equipment wrapped in a greenish rustic blanket." Michael, an absolute believer in the privacy of the individual, was tempted to look inside the blanket tied with string, but never did.

revolutionary to behave.' So I talked to him to draw him out, and he did advance his revolutionary beliefs in those discussions with me."[36] Paine, a pacifist and an intellectual, enjoyed debate and discussion, but found it difficult with Oswald. "He was not interested in arriving at the truth, it was quite unfruitful to have real discussion with him," says Paine. "His arrogance was more than just the arrogance of youth. . . . [He thought] he had the word from the enlightenment, that he knew the truth . . ."[37] But in this latest conversation with Oswald, Michael detected a frustration and exasperation he had not previously noticed. "He still thought that as for Russia and the U.S., it was a pox on both your houses," Paine told the author. "But while he believed that change was necessary, he thought it would only come through violence, and he was sincere in that. He was definitely not a proponent of nonviolent change, the Gandhi method. That was repulsive to him. I am practically quoting him, 'that violence was necessary for change.' And I debated him on that. It was a very important point to me."[38]

During the conversation, Oswald mentioned he had attended a speech by General Walker two nights before. Paine told him that he had attended a John Birch meeting that same night. "I knew he visited right-wing groups like John Birch and others," recalls Michael. "Our notions and purposes were quite different, and I don't think he appreciated how different we were on this." Paine visited in the hope of opening a dialogue between left and right. "But he went with the idea to spy on them," says Paine, "that by so doing he might be making the next step toward getting close to this cabal that he was sure controlled everything. He definitely thought he was listening in on the capitalist planning, and he clearly thought this was important work."[39]

Michael planned to attend a meeting of the American Civil Liberties Union that very night. He invited Lee to go with him. "I invited him because I thought I needed to show this kid a group of people who are concerned about the same kind of problems, say the humanity of man to man, and trying to do something about it, in a way that was typically American, through free speech and political action. But he was not much interested in going. It was at the church and that was certainly a mark against it for him. But finally he decided to go with me."[40] As they left the house, Lee leaned over to Marina, who was just back from the hospital, and whispered, "If only Michael knew what I wanted to do to Walker! Wouldn't he be scared!"[41]

At the ACLU meeting, a speaker stated that just because a person was a Bircher, it did not mean they were an anti-Semite. Oswald stood and objected. He told the group about his visit to the Walker meeting at which a John Birch spokesman had made anti-Semitic and anti-Catholic attacks. Paine thought Oswald's remarks were "clear and coherent."[42] After the meeting, Oswald got into a three-way discussion with an elderly man and Frank Krystinik, a co-worker of Michael Paine's. Krystinik almost got into a fight with Oswald when he attacked the free enterprise system, but the older man won Lee over with some kind words about Cuba. In the car on the way home, Oswald told Michael that he thought the older man was a Communist, since he talked favorably about Cuba. "I thought to myself," said Paine, " 'Well, that is rather feeble evidence for proving a Communist. . . . If that is the way he has to meet his Communists, he has not yet found the Communist group in Dallas.' "[43] Paine tried to convince Oswald of the good work with which the ACLU was involved, but Oswald said he could not join such an organization since it "wasn't political."*

The remainder of the October 26 weekend at the Paines' house was uneventful. However, both Michael and Ruth noticed that Lee's more convivial attitude that existed since his return to Dallas was disappearing. He snapped at Marina for failing to get him iced tea or to iron his shirts correctly. Sometimes, he refused Ruth's meals and made Marina prepare another. If he finished eating ahead of the others, he often just left the table, without saying a word, and watched television in the living room. Never did he offer the Paines any money toward Marina's or his daughters' upkeep. It was the same Lee they had come to know, and dislike, a year earlier.[44]

During these first three weeks that Oswald settled back into Dallas, he was not aware that the FBI had taken a renewed

---

*The ever fickle Oswald sent in a $2 membership fee to the ACLU a week later, on November 1. Michael Paine told the author that Oswald became a member "because he mistakenly thought if you joined, you got a free legal defense."

interest in him because of his Mexico City trip. On October 25, the same day Lee attended the ACLU meeting, local Dallas field agent James Hosty learned that "another agency [the CIA] had determined that Lee Oswald was in contact with the Soviet embassy in Mexico City in the early part of October . . ."[45] That notice greatly increased Hosty's interest in Oswald, as he was now possibly an espionage case.

FBI policy is to have a file follow the person, so the local FBI office, where the person under surveillance is living, is always the one with the original file and primary responsibility for the case. Once the New Orleans office discovered that Oswald had filed a change of address from his Magazine Street apartment to Irving, Texas, it notified the Dallas FBI that Oswald might have moved there. Hosty was assigned the case, and he first had to determine whether Oswald had actually moved to Texas. Once he proved Oswald was in his jurisdiction, then the New Orleans office would forward the original file to him.

On October 29, Hosty went to Irving and asked a neighbor of the Paines some questions. He learned that a Russian-born, Russian-speaking woman was living with Ruth Paine. On Thursday, October 31, Hosty ran a credit check on the Paines and conducted some more interviews with those who knew them. "I wanted to make sure before I approached Mrs. Paine that she was not involved in any way with Lee Oswald, in any type of activities which were against the best interest of the United States."[46]

The following day, Friday, November 1, Hosty drove to the Paines' home. Since he did not consider Ruth Paine "a hostile witness," he did not bring along another agent for the interview.[47] In the mid-afternoon, Hosty parked in front of a neighboring house and knocked on the Paines' front door. Ruth had almost been expecting Hosty, because Dorothy Roberts had told her that a man had come around asking questions, and Ruth correctly assumed it was the FBI. During their nearly twenty-five-minute conversation, Hosty discovered that Marina and her children lived at the Paine residence, that Ruth did not know Lee's address in Dallas, and although she had been hesitant to divulge his employer for fear he could lose his job, she finally told Hosty about the School Book Depository.[48] "Towards the conclusion of the interview, Marina Oswald, who had apparently been napping, entered the living room," recalled Hosty.[49] Ruth, in Russian, told Marina that Hosty was from the FBI. "I could tell from her eyes and her expression that she became quite alarmed, quite upset," Hosty remembered.[50] He knew she had recently had a child, and tried to soothe her nerves. After telling her the FBI was not a witch-hunting organization, he slowly turned the conversation to Cuba. When he said he knew of her husband's Fair Play for Cuba work in New Orleans, Marina told Hosty, with Ruth translating, "Oh, don't worry about him. He's just young. He doesn't know what he's doing. He won't do any-thing like that here."[51] Before he left, he wrote his name and telephone number on a piece of paper and gave it to Ruth. Ma-rina urged him, as had Ruth, not to interfere with Lee's new work. The FBI had caused him to be fired from his earlier jobs, she said. "I told her this was not true, that I had never had anyone fired from any job nor did I know of any other FBI agents that had ever done this," Hosty recalled.[52]*

On Friday, during his lunch break, Oswald rented a post-office box at the Terminal Annex across Dealey Plaza, No. 6225, for a two-month period, at $1.50 per month.[53]† He listed his real name, Marina's name, and two organizations, Fair Play for Cuba and the American Civil Liberties Union, as authorized to receive mail. "Hidell" no longer appeared on the application. This was the same day that Oswald sent in his membership fee to the ACLU. He also wrote a letter to Arnold Johnson, of the Ameri-can Communist party, asking, "Could you advise me as to the

---

* On the following Monday, November 4, Hosty telephoned the School Book Depository, under a pretext, and confirmed Oswald was working there. He then sent an airmail communication to the New Orleans FBI bureau and in-formed them that Oswald had relocated to Texas and that the Dallas office should again be the office of origin and the file returned to Hosty's attention. Some who contend that Oswald was an FBI informer overlook the work done by the FBI just to determine where Oswald was living at any given time. If he had been an informer, the FBI would not likely have needed several weeks to find where he was between his departure from New Orleans and his arrival in Dallas.

† According to Marina and those closest to him, Oswald was a notorious penny-pincher. He paid the rent in advance for the post-office box through December 31, 1963, providing some evidence that he planned to be in Dallas at least through that period.

general view that we have on the American Civil Liberties Union? And to what degree, if any, I should attempt to heighten its progressive tendencies?"[54] It was vintage Oswald—talking about "we" as though he were a party member, and again implying that he was at the vanguard of progressive politics.

That Friday, Frazier dropped Oswald off at the Paines' only a few hours after Hosty had left. When Marina told him of the FBI visit, his mood changed dramatically. He became nervous and agitated, and demanded to know everything that was said.[55] He yelled at Marina for not remembering much of the conversation. Ruth gave him the number and address for Hosty and noticed Lee sat quietly through dinner.[56] On Saturday, Lee was still nervous. He pulled Marina aside and instructed her that if the FBI visited again, she was to write down the make, color, and license number of the agent's car.[57] Sunday, Ruth gave Lee another driving lesson. It was the only break in an otherwise sullen weekend.

The following Monday, November 4, the Secret Service in Dallas was instructed by the White House to examine three potential luncheon sites for November 22, the date chosen for the President's Dallas visit.[58] One site, the Women's Building at the State Fairgrounds, lacked the necessary food-handling capacity, and the Market Hall was already booked for that date.[59] That left the Trade Mart, and though it presented additional security problems, Forrest Sorrels, special agent in charge of the Dallas office, was convinced that special precautions could protect the President.[60] Sorrels recommended the Trade Mart be selected for the luncheon.

Meanwhile, Hosty had received a report from his New Orleans counterpart, Milton Kaack, and immediately saw that Oswald's New Orleans FBI interview was filled with lies. It prompted more curiosity about the former defector. On Tuesday, Hosty paid a second visit to the Paines' home. This time he was accompanied by Gary S. Wilson, an agent just out of training school. "We went to the front porch," recalled Hosty. "I rang the bell, talked to Mrs. Paine, at which time she advised me that Lee Oswald had been out to visit . . . his wife . . . over the weekend, but she has still not determined where he was living in Dallas, and she also made the remark that she considered him to be a very illogical person, that he had told her that weekend that he was Trotskyite Communist."[61]

While she talked to Hosty, Ruth thought Marina was in the bedroom, but actually she had slipped out the kitchen door. She went around the side of the house and memorized Hosty's license-plate number, but she could not determine the car's make since she could not read English.[62]* She went back into the house and entered the living room as Hosty was about to leave. Ruth translated as they talked for a few minutes. Marina was much more relaxed than during their first meeting.

Although Marina may not have been upset by Hosty's second visit, Ruth feared that Lee would indeed be. "Marina and I talked about whether to tell Lee that the FBI had been out a second time," recalled Ruth.[63] When Oswald called each day that week and asked if the FBI had visited again, Marina said no. But when Oswald returned to the Paines' house Friday, November 8, Marina told him. He was furious, insulting Marina for even speaking with Hosty. "You fool," he shouted. "You frivolous, simpleminded fool."[64] "He was very angry again," recalled Marina. "He said that he will talk to Mr. Hosty and tell him to stop harassing me."[65]

"He felt the FBI was inhibiting his activities," recalled Ruth. He was "seriously bothered by their having come out and inquired about him. . . . He was worried about losing his job."[66] During the second interview, Hosty had asked Ruth whether Oswald was mentally disturbed. "I did tell Lee this question had been asked," she said. "He gave no reply, but more a scoffing

---

* After the assassination, Hosty's name, office address and telephone number, and license-plate number were found in Oswald's address book. Some, such as Henry Hurt, charge that this "fired speculation that the notation indicated an informant relationship." How Oswald obtained the license-plate number has also stumped many critics, although during her Warren Commission testimony Marina admitted to getting it (WC Vol. I, p. 48). She told Priscilla Johnson McMillan, for her book *Marina and Lee:* "I am a sneaky girl."

Oswald's address page with Hosty's number became controversial after the assassination for another reason. When the FBI gave the Warren Commission copies of Oswald's address book, typed by the FBI, it omitted any references to Hosty. It turned out the person who typed it only concentrated on "leads," and assumed since Hosty was not a lead, the information was unnecessary. Most critics mistakenly conclude it was a deliberate coverup, even though the original address book was available for inspection at the National Archives.

laugh, hardly voiced."[67] Through the dinner and evening, Oswald was in a terrible mood.

The following day, Saturday, Lee asked Ruth to borrow her typewriter. But he took a break while using it to go with Ruth, Marina, and the children to the State Driver's License Examining Station in Oak Cliff. Oswald wanted to apply for a learner's permit. However, Ruth had forgotten it was a local election day and it was closed. They then spent some time at a local five-and-dime store before returning to Irving.*

Oswald stayed at the Paines' through Monday, November 11, Veterans' Day. Ruth gave him his final driving lesson during the weekend. On Sunday, she was up before Marina and Lee and, while walking through the living room, saw a handwritten draft of the note Lee had been working on the day before. Although she had noticed it on Saturday, on this day it was folded so that she could see the words "The FBI is not now interested in my activities . . ."[68] She knew that was not true. Since there was no address, she did not know where the letter was being sent. Opening the rest of it, she was startled. In it, he noted that he and Marina had relocated to Texas, and "This is to inform you of events since my interview with Comrade Kostine in the Embassy of the Soviet Union, Mexico City, Mexico." He wrote: "I could not take a chance on applyig for an extension unless I used my real name, so I returned to the U.S."† Oswald said that while the FBI had been interested in his Fair Play activities in New Orleans, an Agent "Hasty" had warned him not to start

---

* Oswald's driving ability, or lack thereof, became an issue after the assassination when a Dallas car salesman, Albert Bogard, said Lee Oswald visited him on Saturday, November 9, and test-drove a car at high speeds. It could not be the real Oswald since he was occupied with Marina and Ruth in Irving that entire day. Again, the specter of a "second Oswald" was raised. Bogard said he had written Oswald's name on a business card, which he had thrown away, and also claimed to introduce Oswald to his manager, who could not remember such a meeting. None of his fellow workers supported Bogard's story, although one did remember a five-foot-tall "Oswald," not a very good imposter. Bogard was fired soon after he told his story.

† This was another example of Oswald's bravado over the interchangeable use of his real name and his aliases, primarily Hidell. Once rejected by the Soviet and Cuban embassies, he had no intention of staying in Mexico, but he evidently wanted to make the Soviets believe he had a more exotic reason for not staying.

such activities in Texas, and had suggested his wife "could defect from the Soviet Union." The note ended with: "Of course I and my wife strongly protested these tactics by the notorious FBI. I had not planned to contact the Mexican City Embassy at all so of course they were unprepared for me. Had I been able to reach Havana as planned the Soviet Embassy there would have had time to assist me. but of course the stuip Cuban Consule was at fault here I am glad he had since been replaced by another."[69] Ruth, who did not even know Oswald had been in Mexico, thought the letter was mostly a figment of his imagination. She was not only confused about why he would write such a note but also upset that he would do it in her home. Ruth handwrote a copy of the note before Oswald awoke. She intended to confront Lee over it, but failed to do so. She also debated whether she should give it to Hosty.

Oswald had typed a final copy from the draft Ruth saw. He asked Marina to cosign the letter that day, but she refused. Marina noticed he was anxious, putting the letter through the typewriter twice before he had it in decent condition. He typed the envelope at least four times. The only significant change he made to the draft Ruth had seen was a paragraph asking to "please inform us of the arrival of our Soviet entrance visa's as soon as they come."[70] He mailed the letter to the Soviet embassy in Washington on Tuesday, November 12.[71]

Oswald was consumed over the holiday weekend by Hosty's last visit and the draft of the letter to the Soviet embassy, which took him three days. On his Monday holiday, when he was not working on the letter, Marina found him withdrawn, and he spent much of his time alone in the backyard. Oswald was with Marina and Ruth from Friday the eighth until he left with Buell Frazier to drive to work on Tuesday morning. However, after the assassination, some claimed he had been at the Sports Drome Rifle Range that weekend practicing with his Carcano.[72] Other witnesses came forward and said they had also seen him there the following weekend.[73] Since his time was accounted for, critics again raised the issue of an imposter, claiming that someone tried to frame him by sending a sharpshooter, with a similar weapon, to the range so people could later testify that Oswald was a good shot. But a review of the witness statements shows an honest mistake in identification. There was no Oswald in the sign-up sheets at the range—an imposter certainly would have at least printed his name in the register to substantiate the frame.[74] Four witnesses who originally thought it was Oswald could not later identify him when shown photographs.[75] Others said the "imposter" had a new and brightly polished rifle (Oswald's Carcano was dull and weather-beaten) and a Tasco scope (he used an Ordnance scope), and they described the rifle as having the wrong type of wooden stock and a barrel that was too long.[76] Depending on the witness, "Oswald" drove a 1940 or 1941 Ford truck, or an old-model Chevrolet, or a Ford Hardtop, or a dark, modern four-door sedan. One even claimed to have given him a ride home afterward.[77] A part-time worker at the range, Malcolm Price, said the last time he saw "Oswald" was on the Sunday before Thanksgiving, at a holiday "Turkey Shoot."[78] That was after the assassination, the day Oswald was killed by Jack Ruby, not a very good time for the purported conspirators to send an imposter to the practice range. Garland Slack, one of the practice-range witnesses, said that "Oswald" had long hair and big ears. But Slack admitted, 'You see, you read the papers and you get to where you imagine things and you find yourself imagining that you saw somebody . . ."[79]*

---

* The conspiracy critics raise a number of other wrong identifications as imposter cases. Each has even less "evidence" than the one at the practice range. At the Irving Barber Shop, the barber remembered cutting the hair, five or six times, of a man who wore coveralls, had black hair and hairy arms, came with a fourteen-year-old boy, and drove a black Ford. He thought that was Oswald (WC Vol. X, pp. 312–24). At Hutch's Market, in Irving, the manager identified "Oswald" as a daily customer, with slicked-back hair, who tried to cash a check, together with a woman he thought was Marina, and an elderly lady with a white babushka and a fur coat (WC Vol. X, pp. 328–40). Two employees in the Irving Furniture Mart said "Oswald" drove up in a blue-and-white Ford and came in with Marina and two children, looking for the nearest gun store. Marina was taken to the furniture store by the Warren Commission and flatly denied ever having been there. One of the witnesses later identified photos of Oswald's brother, Robert, as the man who supposedly visited, and the other backed off her identification when confronted in person by Marina (WC Vol. X, pp. 254–301). The story that "Oswald" sent a money order from Western Union was discredited when the sole witness was contradicted by his co-workers, was himself unable to identify the man he saw as Oswald, and said he could not remember the name used. He ultimately recanted his story (WC Vol. X, pp. 311–23, 406–24). Finally, there was the story of the Irving

It is likely that on the same day Oswald sent the letter to the Soviet embassy in Washington, he also walked into the FBI office at 1114 Commerce Street, near the Depository, and asked if Agent Hosty was in.* He was at lunch. Oswald did not give his name to the receptionist, Nanny Fenner, but instead just handed her an unsealed envelope with "Hasty" written across the front (the same misspelling of the agent's name as in his letter to the Soviet embassy). She remembered he looked "awfully fidgety" and "had a wild look in his eye." When Hosty returned from lunch, she gave him the envelope and said, "Some nut left this for you."[80] According to Hosty, inside was an undated note that read, "If you have anything you want to learn about me, come talk to me directly. If you don't cease bothering my wife, I will take appropriate action and report this to the proper authorities."[81] Hosty said it was unsigned and concluded it was either from Oswald or from one other person whose case he was investigating, whose wife he had recently spoken to. Only after the assassination, when he confronted Oswald in jail, and Oswald, upon hearing Hosty's name, became very excited and started yelling, was it confirmed that the note was from Lee.[82]†

Sports Shop, where a clerk claimed to have found a tag with the name Oswald, indicating he had a telescopic sight drilled onto his gun. But Oswald's gun came assembled with the scope when he ordered it. The owners of the shop checked their records and found they had never worked on a Carcano. Subsequent investigation found that the clerk, apparently an attention-seeker, had made anonymous calls about Oswald and his gun to the local media and that the gun store tag was in his handwriting, not in Oswald's. He refused to take a polygraph (WC Vol. XI, pp. 226–52).

* No one at the FBI office can remember the exact day Oswald visited. However, the receptionist, Nanny Fenner, believes it was the first business day after the holiday.

† However, special agent Kenneth C. Howe claimed he saw the note, and while he agrees with Hosty about the general contents, he said it was signed by Oswald. The receptionist, Fenner, later claimed that she was able to see the note because it slipped out of the unsealed envelope before she gave it to Hosty. According to her, it was a much more explicit threat, "Let this be a warning. I will blow up the FBI and the Dallas Police Department if you don't stop bothering my wife. [signed] Lee Harvey Oswald" (Senate Hearings on FBI Oversight, Serial 2, Pt. 3, Oct. 21, 1975). But Hosty says the way the note was folded, it would have been impossible for Fenner to see, and if it had made an explicit threat, he would have followed up on it that same day. Instead, it was so general that he tossed it into his mail tray and forgot about it until he saw Oswald at the jail.

The note has taken on added importance because after the assassination, Hosty admits the note was destroyed at the direction of the Dallas special agent-in-charge, J. Gordon Shanklin.[83] According to Hosty, Shanklin first demanded to know why he had a note from Oswald. Hosty explained his contacts with Ruth Paine and Marina. Then two days later, after Oswald had been killed by Jack Ruby, Hosty was again called into Shanklin's office. There, his chief produced the note and, according to Hosty, said, "Oswald is dead now. There can be no trial. Here—get rid of this." Hosty then destroyed the note. Although Shanklin, in testimony before the Senate Intelligence Committee, said he never knew about the note until 1975, Hosty is more credible. Sixteen other employees in the office knew the Oswald note existed.[84] Some, such as agent Kenneth Howe, said they had even shown it to Shanklin. When Hosty retired in 1979, the FBI returned more than $1,000 of the salary that had been withheld from him in 1964, when he was suspended for not having spotted earlier that Oswald was a potential threat and transferred to Kansas City from Dallas.[85]

The destruction of Oswald's note was against FBI regulations and is one of the Bureau's worst breaches of trust in the case. It allowed skeptics to question the FBI's overall role and relationship to him. To compound the problem, the FBI hid the existence of the note from the Warren Commission. Despite extensive testimony before the Commission, Hosty never mentioned it, claiming later that he had never been asked. The information only leaked out in 1975. But the note is not evidence of a conspiracy or cover-up. It is evidence, at least in this instance, of the FBI's negligence and impropriety. Bill Alexander, the assistant district attorney who drew up the murder indictments against Oswald and later prosecuted Jack Ruby, told the author, "I worked with those fellows at the FBI over many years. What they were doing with the Hosty situation is covering their asses. By Sunday, when Oswald was killed, Hoover was already convinced that Oswald was guilty. People like Shanklin were running for cover to make sure no one could point a finger and say, 'You failed to spot Oswald as a threat.' They were afraid the note would be seen as something they were derelict in following up on. And Oswald was dead, so they figured, 'What the hell, we don't need it anymore,' and they destroyed it. It was a pretty stupid thing to do."[86] In the same way that Hoover censured seventeen agents for the preassassination investigation of Oswald to insulate himself from any responsibility, Shanklin thought he could protect himself by disposing of the evidence of his office's contact with Oswald.*

On Tuesday, November 12, the same day Oswald dropped off the note to Hosty, Michael Paine visited Ruth in Irving. One of the first things she did was show him the letter Oswald had drafted for the Soviet embassy. "I never realized how much he could lie," she said. "I want you to read this letter." She wanted to know what to do, especially if she should contact Hosty before his next visit. But Michael was distracted and only glanced at the letter. He mistakenly thought the salutation "Dear Sirs" was "Dear Lisa" and thought Oswald was merely writing to a friend. "Ruth was somewhat irked that I didn't take more interest in the thing . . . and didn't show it to me again and I asked her what was in that letter that I didn't see and she didn't tell me," Michael remembered.[87] Ruth, discouraged, put the letter aside and decided not to call Hosty but instead wait for his next visit. Hosty never came to the house again before the assassination.†

---

* Oliver Stone, in his film *JFK*, implies the Oswald note may have been a warning to the FBI of the plot against the President. If this was just propagated by Hollywood, it could be dismissed as irrelevant. But it was also suggested by Jim Garrison, who wrote: "He [Oswald] may have even filed reports on the plot to kill the President with his contact agent, James Hosty." In this speculative scenario, Oswald is actually a hero who vainly tried to thwart the impending disaster. This contradicts all the available evidence. It also requires the leap of faith that Oswald, armed with the most important information of his life, a plot to kill JFK, merely dropped it off in an unsealed envelope to Hosty, and then failed to ever follow up with a telephone call or another visit. And when finally arrested and charged with the crime, instead of telling the Dallas police and the FBI that he had actually tried to warn them ten days before the assassination, Oswald quietly sat in the station and denied his guilt. Even when Hosty came into the interrogation room, Oswald did not say, "What happened to the warning I gave you?" but rather attacked Hosty for having bothered Marina.

† Hosty, of course, was criticized after the assassination for not taking more interest in Oswald. He later testified to the Warren Commission that once he determined Oswald "was not employed in a sensitive industry," he did not take a priority over the other twenty-five to forty cases assigned to him at any one

On Thursday, November 14, the White House gave its approval of the selection of the Trade Mart as a luncheon site for the President.[88] Once it was chosen, the Secret Service was directed to determine a motorcade route that would allow forty-five minutes for the President to travel from Love Field airport to the Trade Mart.[89] On that same day, agents Forrest Sorrels and Winston Lawson drove over a possible route. They then met with Dallas police, who reviewed the route the following day, November 15.[90] The *Dallas Times Herald* announced the Trade Mart selection on November 15, and the following day listed Main Street as the parade's primary artery.[91] On November 18, Secret Service and Dallas police again drove the route and confirmed its selection.

Lee called Marina on Friday the fifteenth to discuss visiting for the weekend (he always first called to ask permission). She did not think it was a good idea, because Michael was staying that weekend to celebrate his daughter's birthday, and Lee might have worn out his welcome with the three-day holiday weekend just past.[92] Marina also sensed some resentment from Ruth toward Lee, but did not know that Ruth had found a draft of the letter to the Soviet embassy. Lee agreed to stay at his North Beckley Street room. When he later telephoned Marina over the weekend, he told her that he had returned to the driver's license bureau to get his learner's permit, but the line had been too long and he left.[93] Gladys Johnson, his landlady, said that except for a single walk, Oswald did not leave the house and only made calls to Marina.[94]

At Marina's request, on Sunday, November 17, Ruth telephoned the number at North Beckley.

"Is Lee Oswald there?" asked Ruth.

"There is no Lee Oswald living here."

"Is this a rooming house?"

***

time. He first wanted to "determine the nature of his contact with the Soviet embassy . . . and wait until New Orleans forwarded the necessary papers to me" before taking the next step, a full interview of Marina. Hosty currently complains that he was never notified that Oswald had met with Kostikov, a known KGB agent, while at the Soviet embassy. "You can very well see how the whole thing could take on a different complexion if I knew who he was talking to."

218 • CASE CLOSED

"Yes."

"Is this WH3–8993?"

"Yes."

"I thanked him and hung up," recalled Ruth. She turned to Marina and said, "They don't know of a Lee Oswald at that number." Marina was startled.[95] The next day Lee called Marina. Ruth said, "I was in the kitchen where the phone is while Marina talked with him, she clearly was upset, and angry . . ."[96] Marina asked him where he had been the previous night, and he told her he was using a different name because of the FBI, but also became angry with her for calling the rooming house.[97] She found his alias "unpleasant and incomprehensible."[98] "After all, when will all our foolishness come to an end?" demanded Marina. "All of these comedies. First one thing then another. And now this fictitious name."[99] A fight with Marina was the last thing Lee wanted. Their relationship was strained at times since his return from Mexico but better than it had been in New Orleans. It was as though the argument had broken a fragile truce. And now Marina and Ruth knew about his alias. It was only a matter of time until one of them told Hosty, and again he would have to confront the FBI.

Oswald did not call Marina on either Tuesday or Wednesday, the nineteenth and twentieth. The others at the rooming house noticed he sulked and did not use the phone. Oswald was simmering alone and did not want any contact with people, even his family. "He thinks he's punishing me," Marina told Ruth.[100]

That Tuesday, the *Dallas Times Herald* detailed the exact route of the presidential motorcade. It showed that the motorcade would proceed along Main Street, then turn onto Dealey Plaza, a public square that the Texas School Book Depository bordered.* The motorcade would then turn onto Houston Street

---

* Dealey Plaza, named after George Bannerman Dealey, a prominent businessman and founder of the *Dallas Morning News*, is a three-acre public square through which three main streets, Commerce, Main, and Elm, pass. Those parallel streets converge at one end of Dealey under a railroad bridge dubbed the Triple Underpass. The opposite side of the plaza from the underpass is ringed by office buildings, none taller than eight stories. The Book Depository is a free-standing building on the corner of Elm and Houston streets. Two small pergolas are on each side of the plaza, situated between the buildings and the underpass. The one nearest the Depository has a·five-foot-

and make a left along Elm Street before reaching the Stemmons Freeway.[101] The left turn onto Elm Street meant the cars would pass directly in front of the Depository. The city's only other newspaper, the *Dallas Morning News*, provided the same exacting details on both November 19 and 20.[102] There was no change in the motorcade route, and there was no doubt about the Elm Street crossing.* Whether Oswald learned of the route on the day first published, the nineteenth, or on the next day, when he followed his routine of reading day-old newspapers in the first-floor lunch room of the Depository, it is hard to overestimate the impact of that discovery. Oswald, who thought his contribution to his revolutionary cause would be the death of Walker, was suddenly faced with the possibility of having a much greater impact on history and the machinery of government. Failed in his attempts to find happiness in Russia or the U.S., rejected by the Cubans, barely able to make a living in America, frustrated in his marriage, and hounded, in his view, by the FBI, he was desperate to break out of his downward spiral. He had endured long enough the humiliations of his fellow Marines, the Russian and Cuban bureaucrats, the employers that fired him, the radio ambush in New Orleans, the refusal of V. T. Lee and other Communist leaders to acknowledge his efforts and letters. Lee Oswald always thought he was smarter and better than other people, and was angered that others failed to recognize

---

tall fence at one end. In front of that fence is a patch of grass that gently declines to the curb of Elm Street. That section, including the corner of the fence, is called the grassy knoll.

* Some critics charge there were last-minute changes in the parade route and as "proof" cite a November 22 edition of the *Dallas Morning News*, which had a map of the motorcade that showed the cars proceeding straight along Main Street and not turning onto Houston. They contend that those responsible for the motorcade route altered it at the last moment so Oswald could have a clear shot. There was no last-minute change. Anyone familiar with Dallas traffic would immediately know that the *only* access from Main Street onto the Stemmons Freeway, the route the motorcade needed to take to get to the Trade Mart, was to turn right from Main onto Houston Street, then proceed one block to Elm, where a left turn would put the car less than a thousand feet from the Stemmons entrance. If the motorcade proceeded straight along Main Street, it would be forced to cross a concrete divider in order to enter Stemmons. In any case, Main and Elm are parallel roads that run through Dealey Plaza. Both afforded Oswald a clear shot from the Depository. Elm Street provides a direct-line shot, while Main Street provides a longer cross-shot.

the stature he thought he deserved. Now, by chance, he had an opportunity that he knew would only happen once in his lifetime.

On Thursday, November 21, Oswald broke his routine of eating a meager breakfast at the rooming house. Instead, he treated himself to a special breakfast at Dobbs House restaurant. Before 10:00 that morning, he approached Buell Frazier and asked if he could have a ride to Irving that evening as he needed to "get some curtain rods. You know, [to] put in an apartment."[103] His apartment did not need curtains or curtain rods. Both were already in place.[104] It was likely later that day that he used brown paper and tape at the Depository to fashion a bag over three feet long.

Marina saw Frazier's car stop near the Paine home that afternoon near 5:00, and Lee stepped out. He had not called in advance as usual to ask permission before coming to Irving. It was also the first time he had ever broken his routine and arrived on a Thursday instead of a Friday. "He said he was lonely because he hadn't come the preceding weekend, and he wanted to make his peace with me," recalled Marina.[105] She refused his kisses, and turned her back on him when he spoke. "He tried very hard to please me," Marina recalled. "He spent quite a bit of time putting away diapers and played with the children on the street. He was upset over the fact that I would not answer him. He tried to start a conversation with me several times, but I would not answer. And he said that he didn't want me to be angry with him because this upsets him." He seemed different than she had seen him before, and he told her he "was tired of living all alone," and pleaded, "Why won't you come with me?" "Alka," Marina responded. "I think it's better if I stay here."[106] "He repeated this not once but several times," Marina remembered, "but I refused. And he said that once again I was preferring my friends to him, and that I didn't need him."[107] He tried to induce her by saying he had saved money and would buy her a washing machine. Marina told him thank you, but "it would be better if he bought something for himself—that I would manage." One final time, while on the front lawn, he begged her to join him in Dallas. "I'll get us an apartment and we'll all live peacefully at home." She again refused. "I was like a stubborn little mule," she recalled. "I was maintaining my inaccessibility, trying to show Lee I wasn't easy to persuade."[108]*

Ruth, who had been grocery shopping, had pulled up in her car by 5:30. "He was on the front lawn. I was surprised to see him," she recalled. Marina apologized to Ruth that Lee had appeared without any warning, but Ruth said not to worry, that it was his way of making up for their quarrel. "As I entered the house and Lee had just come in, I said to him, 'Our President is coming to town.' And he said, 'Ah, yes,' and walked into the kitchen . . ."[109]

During the rest of the evening the atmosphere in the house was cordial. Ruth did not notice there was any special tension between Marina and Lee. Marina remembered that after her last refusal to join him in Dallas, Lee mostly stopped talking.[110] During dinner, Marina asked him about the President's visit, assuming that talking about politics, his favorite subject, might improve the atmosphere. "And he did not make any comment about it at all," she recalled. "It was quite unusual that he did not want to talk about President Kennedy being in Dallas. . . . That was quite peculiar . . . [and] I asked him . . . if he know which route President Kennedy will take . . . and he said he doesn't know anything about it."[111] After a quiet dinner, he watched television on his own.

At 9:00, he looked into the kitchen, where Marina was washing the dishes. She thought he looked sad.

"I'm going to bed," he said. It was almost two hours before his usual time. "I probably won't be out this weekend."

"Why not?"

"It's too often. I was here today."

"Okay."[112]

That same evening, after Lee had gone to bed, Ruth went into

---

* On July 9, 1964, the Warren Commission held a seven-hour executive session with three psychiatrists, Drs. Dale Cameron, Howard Rome, and David Rothstein. The panel of doctors told the Commission that if Marina had treated Oswald with kindness that night, it might have changed his mind about the assassination. As Dr. Cameron said, "I think what Marina had a chance to do unconsciously that night was to veto his plan without ever knowing of its existence, but she didn't. She really stamped it down hard" (July 9, 1964, executive session transcript). The Commission stayed away from the psychiatric conclusions in its final report.

the garage to paint some children's blocks. The light was on. "It was unusual for it to be on," she recalled. "I realized I felt Lee . . . had gone out to the garage, perhaps worked out there or gotten something."[113]

"I went to sleep about 11:30," Marina remembered. "But it seemed to me that he was not really asleep. But I didn't talk to him."[114] In the middle of the night, she remembered resting her foot against his leg, and he shoved it away with a ferocity that surprised her. "My, he's in a mean mood," she thought. Marina thinks his tension finally gave way to sleep, but not until nearly 5:00 A.M.[115]

The following morning when the alarm sounded, it was Marina, half-asleep, who urged him to get up. Usually, Marina prepared breakfast for him, but that morning she remained in bed. When he was ready to leave, he came to the bedroom door. "He told me to take as much money as I needed and to buy everything, and said goodbye, and that is all," recalled Marina.[116] He walked out the door without kissing her, something he always did before leaving.

When Marina fully awoke, she went to the kitchen, but he was gone and the coffeepot was cold. Returning to the bedroom, she was startled to see that he had left $170 on top of their bureau. It was a remarkable sum for the Oswalds, and she knew it must be almost all their savings. She did not notice something else that would have alarmed her. On the bureau, in a hand-painted demitasse cup that had belonged to her grandmother, Lee had placed his wedding ring. He had never before taken it off.

11

"I'll Never Forget It for as Long as I Live"

Linnie Mae Randle, Buell Frazier's sister, was at her kitchen sink when she glanced out the window at 7:15 Friday morning, November 22. She saw Oswald walk across the street toward her house, carrying a long package parallel to his body. He held one end of the brown-paper-wrapped object tucked under his armpit, and the other end did not quite touch the ground. Randle later recalled it appeared to contain something heavy.[1] He went to Buell's car, opened the right rear door, and laid the package across the backseat. Then he walked to the kitchen window and stared at Linnie Mae until she called out to her brother that he was waiting for his ride.[2]

"That was the first time he had ever done that," recalled Frazier, who always drove the one block to pick Oswald up at Ruth Paine's home. "He never came up to our house before."[3] When Frazier got into the car, he noticed the package and asked what it was. "Those are the curtain rods," Oswald said. "He had never lied to me before so I never did have any reason to doubt his word," said Frazier.[4] When they arrived at the Book Depository, Frazier parked the car in the employee lot behind the warehouse. Usually, they went in together, but on that morning, though they were early, Oswald quickly left the car and walked ahead. Frazier watched him enter the Depository, carrying the package next to his body.*

---

* Critics claim that Linnie Mae Randle and Buell Frazier described a package too short to contain Oswald's rifle. Initially, Randle said the package was ap-

Other employees noticed that Oswald did not follow his normal routine of immediately going to the domino room and reading the day-old newspapers.[5] Later that morning, between 9:30 and 10:00, he was staring out a first-floor window toward Dealey Plaza, when a co-worker, James "Junior" Jarman, approached him. Oswald asked why crowds were gathering outside, and Jarman told him the President was due by in a couple of hours. When asked if he knew which direction the motorcade would take, Jarman said the cars were expected to pass directly in front of the Depository. "Oh, I see," said Oswald.[6]

On the sixth floor of the Depository, five men were laying a plywood floor. The sixth floor was a 96-foot-by-96-foot open storage space, only broken by support posts and stacks of books scattered about. On the south side of the floor, seven large double windows looked directly over Elm Street and Dealey Plaza. On the opposite north end, there were two adjoining elevators and a staircase.[7] At 11:40 one of the workers, Bonnie Ray Williams, spotted Oswald on the east side of that floor, near the windows overlooking Dealey Plaza.[8] About five minutes later, the crew broke for lunch. They got in the two elevators and raced each other to the first floor.[9] "I came downstairs, and I discovered I left my cigarettes in my jacket pocket upstairs," recalled Charles Givens, "and I took my elevator back upstairs to get my jacket with my cigarettes in it. When I got back upstairs, he [Oswald] was on the sixth floor . . . in that vicinity . . . toward the window up front where the shots were fired from. . . . I was getting ready to get on the elevator, and I say, 'Boy, are you going downstairs?' I say, 'It's near lunch time.' He

proximately 27 inches long, and Frazier estimated a little over two feet. The disassembled Carcano is 35 inches long, and the police later found the brown paper bag Oswald had brought into the Depository lying near the corner where three spent rifle shells were discovered (WC Vol. IV, p. 266). The bag was 38 inches long. Both Randle and Frazier said it looked like the same one Oswald carried that morning. The FBI discovered the bag contained microscopic fibers from the blanket with which Oswald kept his rifle wrapped in the Paine garage (WC Vol. IV, pp. 57, 76–80). Frazier later admitted the package could have been longer than he originally thought: "I only glanced at it . . . hardly paid any attention to it. He had the package parallel to his body, and it's true it could have extended beyond his body and I wouldn't have noticed it" (London Weekend Television, "Trial of Lee Harvey Oswald"). Although Oswald claimed to have curtain rods in the bag, none were found at the Depository.

said, 'No, sir.' "[10] Givens did not see anyone else on the sixth floor.[11]* Other co-workers, including Billy Lovelady, Jack Dougherty, Danny Arce, and Bonnie Ray Williams, remembered Oswald remained upstairs when they took the elevators down.[12]

Now all alone, Oswald had enough time to assemble the Carcano and move cartons of books to form a sniper's nest in the southeast corner. That corner had an ideal, unobstructed view of the motorcade route. The cars could be seen as they entered Dealey Plaza on Main Street, turned right onto Houston Street, and headed toward the Depository. In front of the building, the motorcade turned left, providing a clear view from the window as the cars moved toward the Stemmons Freeway entrance.† The sniper's nest was not difficult to construct. Because of the laying of the new floor, workers had moved many of the book cartons, weighing up to fifty pounds each, to the sides of the room.[13] An assortment of boxes were used to hide his position. It protected the sniper from being observed by anyone who wandered onto the sixth floor.[14] Boxes were also arranged as a brace upon which the rifle would rest when shot.‡ The rifle assembly was probably next. An FBI agent, in his first attempt, put the Carcano together, using only a dime as a tool, in less than six minutes, and in under two minutes with a screwdriver.[15]

---

* Some critics cite a February 13, 1964, FBI report that lists an earlier marijuana possession charge by Givens, and the belief that he would alter his story for money, to suggest that he changed his story over several months to place Oswald on the sixth floor shortly after noon. However, Givens had told Dallas police Lt. Jack Revill on the day of the assassination that he had seen Oswald on the sixth floor (WC Vol. V, pp. 35–36).

† Some, like Sylvia Meagher, in *Accessories After the Fact*, wonder why Oswald did not choose the seventh floor, where, she claimed, "there is an enclosure at the southeast corner that would insure privacy." However, the corner enclosure had a door with a glass window, so anyone coming up the stairs would see the sniper. Moreover, the windowsills on the seventh floor are considerably higher than on the sixth, making it difficult to fire a rifle from a seated position. Also, the sixth-floor ledge partially obstructs the line of sight from the seventh floor.

‡ In the Marine Corps, Oswald's best rifle scores were in the seated position, with the rifle braced against his legs. Both the boxes and the edge of the window frame provided a brace inside the sniper's nest, and his improvised sling (adapted from the shoulder strap of an Air Force pistol holster) could be wrapped around his arm to further steady the gun.

Many have tried hard to prove Oswald was not on the sixth floor at this time, relying on his protestations, after his arrest and during his police interrogation, that he had been in the first-floor lunch room with "Junior" Jarman, and had gone to the second floor to buy a Coke near the time of the assassination.[16] Carolyn Arnold, a secretary to the Depository's vice-president, waited fifteen years before telling Anthony Summers in 1978 that at 12:15 she entered the second-floor lunch room and saw Oswald sitting in one of the booths.* "He was alone as usual and appeared to be having lunch," Arnold said.[17] Her interview with Summers was the first time she ever publicly told the story about seeing Oswald in the lunch room.[18] But Arnold had given two different FBI statements shortly after the assassination. In one, she said she "could not be sure" but might have caught a fleeting glimpse of Oswald in the first-floor hallway, and in the second statement said she did not see him at all.[19]† Arnold told Summers the FBI misquoted her, though she had signed her statement as correct.[20] Four other women worked with Arnold and watched the motorcade with her that day. They support her original statements and not the story she told fifteen years later. Virgie Rachley and Betty Dragoo accompanied her when she left the second floor at 12:15. They did not see Oswald in the lunch room.[21]

More important, contemporaneous statements of other workers who were in both lunch rooms say Oswald was in neither. Junior Jarman, with whom Oswald claimed to have had lunch, denied even seeing him during his lunch break.[22] Troy West was inside the first-floor domino room eating lunch from 12:00 to nearly 12:30 and did not see Oswald during that half hour.[23] Danny Arce and Jack Dougherty ate in the first-floor room up to 12:15 and said there was no sign of him. Charles Givens

---

* Workers ate lunch in two rooms at the Depository. One was the first-floor domino room, where the warehouse workers ate, and the other, on the second floor, was usually used by office personnel.

† William Shelley and Eddie Piper also thought they saw Oswald on the first floor shortly before noon. But Shelley later admitted he saw him at 11:45 A.M., before others noticed him on the sixth floor. Piper thought he saw Oswald at noon filling orders on the first floor, but he is clearly mistaken as five witnesses had placed Oswald on an upper floor, left behind by the elevators by that time.

also visited the domino room but did not see Oswald.[24] Joe Molina and Mrs. Robert Reid both ate in the second-floor lunch room and were there at 12:15, when Carolyn Arnold claimed Oswald was there, but neither saw him.[25] Billy Lovelady went to both lunch rooms after 12:00 and did not see him either.[26]

There was actually one Book Depository employee on the sixth floor near noon, but since he did not see anyone, arguments have been made that Oswald was not there. Nineteen-year-old Bonnie Ray Williams returned to the sixth floor to eat his lunch and see whether any other workers had gathered to watch the motorcade. He ate some fried chicken and had a bottle of soda, which he said took "5, 10, maybe 12 minutes."[27] Williams said that while there, he sat in front of the fourth window, some forty feet from the sniper's nest.[28] The books in the southeast corner, however, were "stacked so high" that he "could not possibly see anything . . ."[29] The day after the assassination he told the FBI he left by 12:05 and went to the fifth floor, where he found two friends, Junior Jarman and Harold Norman.* They remained there to watch the motorcade.

While reliable testimony from the Depository places Oswald, alone, on the sixth floor by noon, witnesses in Dealey Plaza also confirmed there was a man in the sniper's-nest window. There is some confusion, however, because some witnesses say they saw one, and sometimes two, men before the shooting who did not look like Oswald.

Ruby Henderson saw two men on the upper floors of the Depository. Summers points out that one of them had dark hair and complexion and might have been Mexican.[30] Summers does not inform the reader that in her FBI statement, Henderson said the men could have been "Mexican, but [also] could have been Negro," and she was not certain of what floor they were on.[31] On the fifth floor, directly below Oswald's sniper's nest, were three young black men—Bonnie Ray Williams, Junior Jarman, and Harold Norman—looking out the windows. Her FBI state-

---

* The critics assert Williams did not leave the sixth floor until 12:20. That is because before the Warren Commission, he said it was approximately 12:20 when he left, but when reminded of his original estimate of 12:05, he acknowledged he did not remember the time (WC Vol. III, p. 173).

ment indicates that Henderson saw two of those three young men on a high floor. She was not describing the sixth floor.

There are other witnesses who claim they not only saw two men, either in the Depository or in Dealey Plaza, but that the men also had a rifle. Julia Ann Mercer said she was caught in a traffic jam at Dealey on the morning of the motorcade and noticed two men in a green Ford pickup. One took a gun case from the rear of the truck and then disappeared into the grassy knoll.[32] She later identified the truck's driver as Jack Ruby, and said Oswald was the man with the rifle.[33] However, subsequent investigation revealed that the truck, which had stalled, belonged to a local construction company; it had three men inside, and they did take tools from the rear of the truck to fix it.[34] They were under constant surveillance by three Dallas policemen, and all of them left when another truck arrived to push the stalled vehicle away.*

In 1978, a Dallas newspaperman encountered the second witness to claim there were two men connected to a rifle in Dealey Plaza. John Powell said he was a prisoner on the sixth floor of the Dallas County Jail, one of the buildings on Houston Street southeast of the Depository, on November 22, 1963.[35] According to Summers, the cell provided "an ideal vantage point for observations of the famous Depository window."[36] Powell insisted that "quite a few" prisoners watched two men in the sniper's-nest window "fooling with the scope" on a high-powered rifle. Summers charged that "during the Warren inquiry, an official failed to respond to a specific reminder that observers in the County Jail had had a perfect view and should be questioned."[37]

But a December 15, 1964, FBI memo reported the results of just such an inquiry. There had been accusations that "seventeen witnesses to the assassination in [the] hospital ward of Dallas County Jail [were] never interviewed."[38] There were several large cells that overlooked Dealey Plaza. One was the jail's mental ward. While it provided a view of the motorcade, the

---

* The Mercer story was fully discredited by December 9, 1963, just over two weeks after the assassination. However, that did not stop Mark Lane from beginning his book *Rush to Judgment* with an excerpt from Mercer's statement. Recent authors who have also cited the Mercer story, unchallenged, include Garrison (1988), Marrs (1989), and Dr. Charles Crenshaw (1992).

FBI's investigation showed the Book Depository "was not visible from this cell area." A second large cell was reserved for those given a three-day sentence for "driving while intoxicated [DWI]." The FBI found there were "no DWI prisoners in this particular cell at the time of the assassination."[39]* The corner of the jail that overlooked the Depository had an iron-mesh grid and the windows were extremely dirty, making any view "very distorted" and almost "impossible" to see.[40] It was the hospital ward and it also contained an overflow of mental patients. The FBI concluded the original source of the jailhouse information was "completely unreliable," having been arrested on several occasions "in the past on lunacy charges." It had "no confidence whatsoever in any information furnished by him."[41]

The third person who claimed to see at least two men with a gun was Arnold Rowland, who testified to the Warren Commission that he saw one man in the far left corner window of the sixth floor (opposite from the sniper's nest) at 12:15. The gunman was reportedly standing at military parade rest with a high-powered rifle across his chest.[42] Then Rowland claimed to see an "elderly Negro" man on the same floor, this time on the other side of the building, in the sniper's nest.[43] But Rowland had previously given seven statements to the Dallas police and FBI and never mentioned the black man.[44] Rowland's wife, who was with him at the time of the assassination, did not see either man, nor did he tell her that he had seen a black man.[45] Immediately after the shooting, Rowland told policeman F. M. Turner and Secret Service agent Forrest Sorrels that he saw a single young white male, with brown hair, holding a rifle.[46] The rest of his testimony is riddled with inaccuracies. Rowland claimed that there were women and children on the nearby Triple Underpass (there were none);[47] that the crowds started to laugh after the first shot (no one else reported such a reaction);[48] and that fifty police converged instantly on the grassy knoll after the shots (there were initially two).[49] According to his wife, Rowland lied under oath about a series of small but telling issues, ranging

---

* It was understandably empty, because under Texas law, any part of a day served constitutes a full day's credit for the sentence, and therefore, prisoners serving three-day DWI sentences reported late on Friday night to gain full credit for that day.

from graduating from high school, to his grades, to the job he held, even to what he claimed he did on the morning of the assassination.[50] "I know there weren't any other people on that floor looking out the windows that could be seen from the outside," Mrs. Rowland insisted under oath.[51] When asked, "Do you feel you can rely on everything that your husband says?" she replied, "At times my husband is prone to exaggerate. Does that answer it?"[52]*

The final witness who claimed to have seen two men with a gun is Carolyn Walther. Walther limited her sighting to the third, fourth, or fifth floor but "positively" not the sixth. She claimed one man had his arms extended and was holding a machine gun outside the window, for all to see. Walther also said a second man, with another gun, stood directly behind the first one.[53] But Carolyn Walther was not alone when she watched the motorcade from her vantage point. A friend, Pearl Springer, was with her and did not notice any gunmen.[54] Nor did Walther ever mention a word to Springer about seeing anyone with a rifle, later claiming, "I just forgot all about it."[55] Fifteen minutes after the assassination, Walther returned to work, still keeping her remarkable story to herself.[56]†

However, there is consistent testimony from other witnesses in Dealey Plaza who saw a man in the sniper's-nest window before the assassination. Robert Edwards and Ronald Fischer, a college student and a county auditor respectively, were at the corner of Houston and Elm, directly in front of the Depository. Just before the motorcade arrived, Edwards glanced at the

---

* Rowland also claimed that while the gunman was standing fifteen feet back of the window, he could see all of the rifle and two thirds of the man. The author stood at the same spot where the Rowlands were on November 22, some 200 feet from the sixth floor of the Depository. At the angle from which Rowland looked at the building, it is impossible to see inside the sniper's nest because of the right wall, and also to see anyone more than a few feet behind the window.

† There were also two amateur films shot of the Book Depository within moments of the assassination. Critics interpret shadows on the film as evidence of two men, one in and one adjacent to the sniper's nest. The films taken by Charles Bronson and Robert Hughes were independently enhanced by the Itek Corporation for CBS, by the House Select Committee on Assassinations, and by public television's *Frontline* program. None showed a second person in the sixth-floor windows.

building and saw a man in the southeast corner of the sixth floor.[57] He nudged Fischer, who looked up and also saw the man. Fischer said, "There were boxes and cases stacked all the way from the bottom to the top and from the left to the right behind him. . . . It looked like there was space for a man to walk through there between the window and the boxes."[58] The man was staring down Elm Street, the path of what would be the line of rifle fire in just a few minutes. "He was just staring out the window," Fischer told the author. "Everyone else was in a good mood with the President coming, but he seemed different, and that's why I stared at him and remembered him later."[59] The figure both men described sounded remarkably like Oswald —white, twenty-two to twenty-four years of age, light complexion, slender, medium-brown hair, and wearing a white T-shirt under a light-colored shirt.[60]*

Some twelve minutes before the motorcade arrived, a man had an epileptic seizure in Dealey Plaza and an ambulance took him to Parkland Hospital. He never registered at Parkland, and as a result, the suspicion arose that the seizure was a staged distraction that allowed a team of assassins to take their positions unnoticed by the crowd. Such conjecture ignores that the FBI located the man on May 26, 1964. He was Jerry Belknap, an epileptic who had suffered seizures since childhood and had evidence he had paid the $12.50 ambulance charge. He left Parkland without registering because he felt better when given water and an aspirin, and there was such a rush of people at the emergency room, he realized he was not going to be quickly treated.[61]

After Belknap was removed from Dealey, the police quickly cleared away the small knot of people that had formed around the scene, and the crowd returned to its festive waiting for the arrival of the President. The large Hertz sign on top of the Depository showed 12:29 when the first car of the presidential motorcade made the turn from Main Street onto Houston and proceeded toward the Depository. It was a security car and included Dallas police chief Jesse Curry, Sheriff Bill Decker, and the local chief of the Secret Service, Forrest Sorrels. Two car

---

* When Oswald was arrested, he had on a white T-shirt under a rust-brown shirt. But he admitted to the police that he had changed his shirt when he returned to his rooming house after the assassination.

lengths behind was the presidential limousine. The driver was the oldest man in the White House security detail, William Greer. Next to him in the front seat was another Secret Service agent, Roy Kellerman. In the car's fold-down jump seats were Texas governor John Connally and his wife, Nellie. In the rear bench seat were President Kennedy and the First Lady, Jacqueline. As the President and his staff had requested, the plastic bubble top was off, leaving the car as an open convertible, and no Secret Service men rode on the running boards attached to the rear. The motorcycle escort was limited to four, and kept at a comfortable distance from the limousine. A 1956 Cadillac convertible filled with Secret Service agents and presidential aides followed JFK's car. The Vice-President's car, with Mrs. Johnson, Texas senator Ralph Yarborough, and some Secret Service agents, was next in line. The remainder of the motorcade included local dignitaries, some press cars, and finally two buses, one for VIPs and one for additional press.

The crowd surged forward as the President passed along Houston Street. The limousine slowed considerably to navigate the 120-degree left turn onto Elm, directly in front of the Depository. Agent Forrest Sorrels, in the car ahead of the President, looked at his watch. It was almost 12:30. He radioed the Trade Mart, "We'll be there in five minutes." In the car behind the President, Agent Emory Roberts independently radioed the Trade Mart, "Halfback to Base. Five minutes to destination." Jackie Kennedy, dressed in a pink wool two-piece suit, with a pillbox hat, was hot under the unfiltered midday sun. After the car had turned onto Elm, she saw the Triple Underpass just a couple of hundred yards away, and thought "it would be cool under that tunnel."[62] Compared to the mobs that had thronged the downtown streets, the crowds had thinned through the plaza. Mrs. Connally turned to the Kennedys and said, "Mr. President, you can't say that Dallas doesn't love you." The President said, "No, you certainly can't." It was 12:30 on the Hertz sign atop the Book Depository.

Most people did not realize the first loud crack was gunfire. Some thought it was a firecracker or a backfire from a police motorcycle. By the second shot, many realized it was too loud to be anything but gunfire. The President's arms jerked up into a locked position level with his neck. Governor Connally pushed back into his jump seat and then fell over into his wife's arms. Seeing his own shirt covered with blood, the Governor shouted, "My God, they are going to kill us all!" The President, strapped into a brace for his bad back, remained propped upright, his head lolling slightly to the left.

The Secret Service agents were slow to react, although some had turned to look at the source of the noise, the Book Depository. Jacqueline Kennedy leaned toward her husband, looking at him quizzically. Incredibly, Greer, sensing something was wrong in the back of the car, slowed the vehicle to almost a standstill and turned in his seat to see what had happened. As he turned, there was a stomach-wrenching sound, as if a grapefruit had been struck with a baseball bat. The final bullet tore off the right side of the President's head, sending a red mist of blood, brain tissue, and skull fragments upward and to the front. As he fell partially across the backseat and toward the floor, Jacqueline began climbing out the rear and onto the trunk. Secret Service agent Clint Hill, riding in the backup car, responded rapidly, running to reach the car just in time to mount the rear bumper and push her back inside. At that moment Greer slammed on the accelerator, and the President's car sped out of Dealey Plaza.*

Witnesses later described the scene that followed as "pandemonium" and "chaos." Some threw themselves on the ground to avoid the gunfire; others screamed or began running. A motorcycle policeman escorting the presidential limousine, Bobby Hargis, "didn't know" where the shots came from, but felt it was either the "railroad overpass or . . . the Texas Book Depository."[63] He stopped his cycle and ran toward the end of the wooden stockade fence on the grassy knoll near the Triple Underpass. Many in the crowd followed him, running—strangely—

---

* All or part of the assassination was filmed by dozens of witnesses at Dealey who had 8mm movie or still cameras. But one film is by far the most crucial. Shot by Dallas dressmaker Abraham Zapruder, the 8mm color film followed the President's car from the moment it made the turn from Houston onto Elm and stayed with it through the entire assassination. Perched on a concrete divider on top of the grassy knoll, Zapruder had an almost unobstructed view of the motorcade. The film is discussed in detail in Chapter 14.

into the area where the gunman might be instead of away from danger.

Because of the ensuing bedlam, Dealey Plaza produced a mass of contradictory statements from scores of witnesses. In even the simplest auto accident, eyewitnesses almost invariably present different, and sometimes completely conflicting, accounts.* There was ample reason for confusion at Dealey. The crowds had concentrated on the presidential motorcade, a mesmerizing event for many. They were not expecting rifle shots over a few seconds, and to complicate matters, the plaza is an echo chamber. In the turmoil that followed, it is little wonder that witnesses standing next to each other often heard and saw things differently. Resolving every conflicting account is impossible. However, the statements can be sifted for internal inconsistencies and judged for credibility. Testimony closer to the event must be given greater weight than changes or additions made years later, when the witness's own memory is often muddied or influenced by television programs, films, books, and discussions with others. Danny Arce, one of Oswald's co-workers and a witness at Dealey, summarized the difficulty: "I have read and heard so many things, it mixes together. You don't know if it's your own memory or it's somebody else's. We all read a lot of things, and sometimes inadvertently adopt things we hear from others. It's hard to separate the two, and can get real confusing trying to figure out what you remember without having your memory colored by everything that has come out."[64]

Yet just as any jury must decide which witnesses are most credible, the same can be done with the seemingly intractable morass at Dealey.

---

*Human observation can be notoriously unreliable. A vivid example of the pitfall of relying exclusively on eyewitness testimony is that when the ocean liner *Titanic* sank in 1912, there were nearly seven hundred people on lifeboats watching it go down. The ship was almost nine hundred feet long, three football fields in size, yet the survivors were split as to whether it sank in one or two pieces.

The Ear-witnesses

How many shots were fired at Dealey Plaza? And from what direction? Estimates at the scene ranged from one to eight shots. However, on this issue, there was more agreement than on any other postassassination matter. Of the nearly two hundred witnesses who expressed an opinion on the number of shots whose testimony or statements are in the National Archives or the twenty-six Warren Commission volumes, over 88 percent heard three shots.[65]* Almost 7 percent heard only two or fewer shots, and fewer than 5 percent heard four or more. Although almost every conspiracy theory that proposes more than one assassin relies on there having been four or more shots, the writers seldom disclose that fewer than one in twenty witnesses heard that many.

While the consistency of opinion on the number of shots is persuasive, the echo patterns in Dealey make locating the direction of the shots more difficult, and the witness statements reflect that. The House Select Committee reviewed more than 178 witness statements and found that 44 percent of the witnesses could not determine where the shots came from. Of the remainder, the largest block, 28 percent, thought the shots came from the Book Depository, 12 percent pinpointed the grassy knoll, and 17 percent believed the shots originated elsewhere (one even thinking they came from within the President's car). And significantly, only four witnesses, 2 percent, thought they came from more than one location.[66]†

The last figure, 2 percent, is a critical blow to most conspiracy theories, since those who charge there was a second gunman usually place the additional shooter in front and to the right of the President's car, on the grassy knoll. But even these writers acknowledge that most of the shots came from the rear. They insist only that the fatal head shot came from the front. How-

---

* Josiah Thompson, in his 1967 book *Six Seconds in Dallas*, did his own tabulation of 190 witnesses, and arrived at 83.4 percent. The author disagrees with Thompson's reading of several witnesses, and also with his omission of one.

† The figures add to slightly more than 100 percent since they are rounded off to the nearest whole number.

ever, only four of 178 witnesses heard shots from more than one location. According to Dr. David Green, an acoustics expert retained by the House Select Committee, it was "hard to believe a rifle was fired from the knoll," since a separate shot from there would have been easy to "localize."[67] Instead, the fact that any witnesses described all the shots as coming from the grassy knoll, when there is incontrovertible evidence that at least two came from the rear, indicates they were just completely fooled by the acoustics at Dealey.

However, the conspiracy critics often manipulate the witness statements to make the Depository seem a less popular choice. Josiah Thompson, author of the best-selling *Six Seconds in Dallas*, is cited by many as saying that 52 percent of the witnesses selected the grassy knoll, 39 percent the Depository, and some 6 percent said both directions.[68] The author reviewed Thompson's work witness by witness and discovered substantive errors. In his "Master List of Assassination Witnesses," Thompson puts witnesses such as Amos Euins, Mrs. Robert Reid, Tom C. Dillard, Jack E. Dougherty, Victoria Adams, Mrs. John Connally, J. W. Foster, Roy Kellerman, James Underwood, and Emmet Hudson in either the undecided or grassy knoll column. Yet, all of them actually described the shots as coming from the vicinity of the Book Depository. For instance, J. W. Foster said the shots originated from "the corner of Elm and Houston." Thompson does not remind the reader that the building at that corner is the Depository. Unless the witness named the Depository, Thompson does not place him in that category. He also lists James Underwood as uncommitted since he said the shots came from "overhead"—but omitted his next sentence, in which he explained that "overhead" meant "the Texas School Book Depository."[69] In other instances Thompson incorrectly puts witnesses in the grassy knoll column. He lists Bobby Hargis, the motorcycle policeman who was the first to run toward the grassy knoll, as saying the shots were from there, when he actually testified: "There wasn't any way in the world I could tell where they were coming from."[70] Abraham Zapruder, William Shelley, and James Tague are similar examples of witnesses confused by the acoustics in Dealey.*

---

* Despite his errors, Thompson is at least one of the more reasonable critics in his interpretation of the numbers. The author was present at a March 3, 1992,

Those who study the plaza are not surprised by its unusual echo characteristics.[71] A number of witnesses reported "reverberation" or sounds that "bounced off the buildings."[72] Others said that sounds were "reflected by the underpass and therefore came back," or that the concrete underpass caused a "concussion" of noises.[73] The worst confluence of echoes affected those witnesses close to the grassy knoll. Abraham Zapruder, the Dallas dressmaker who took the home movie of the assassination, stood atop a concrete divider wall on top of the knoll. "There was too much reverberation," he said. "There was an echo which gave me a sound all over."[74] Lee Bowers was in the second story of a railroad signal tower, 130 feet behind the grassy knoll. He could not tell whether the shots came from the Triple Underpass or the Book Depository. He had worked in that area for more than ten years and knew that echo patterns made it impossible to pinpoint the direction of sounds.[75] Roy Truly, Oswald's supervisor, was standing across the street from the Depository, but said the echo confused him so he believed the gunfire originated from the grassy knoll.[76]

Yet if the overwhelming ear-witness testimony is that only three shots were fired, why did the House Select Committee conclude in 1979 there was a 95 percent certainty that a fourth shot was fired from the grassy knoll, and therefore there was a conspiracy involving a second gunman?

The committee agreed there were three shots from the rear (the Depository), and that two of those struck President Kennedy and Governor Connally.* It based its conclusion that there was a fourth shot on the analysis of a static-filled dictabelt recording of both Dallas police channels in operation on Novem-

discussion in Texas when researcher Joe West said 76 percent of 290 witnesses at Dealey had selected the grassy knoll as the location for the shots. No one present, in a room of fifty other researchers, challenged his "fact." Jim Marrs, in *Crossfire*, writes, "One fact seems inescapable—most of the witnesses in the crowd believed shots came from the Grassy Knoll" (Marrs, p. 39).

* According to the committee, its unidentified grassy knoll assassin, who was much closer to the President than Oswald, fired one shot, and missed not only the President but the rest of the car's five occupants, and even the limousine itself. The bullet that missed the motorcade never struck any of the spectators directly in its flight path, nor was an extra bullet ever found at Dealey Plaza.

ber 22. Channel One was for normal police business, and Channel Two for traffic concerned with the motorcade. A police motorcycle had its radio switch stuck in the "on" position for over five minutes around the time of the assassination.[77] All the sounds within the range of that open microphone were inadvertently recorded. The committee speculated that if the open mike was in Dealey Plaza, it might have recorded the shots.

Yet there are no sounds of gunfire, or even what could be remotely construed as popping sounds, on the dictabelt recordings. The absence of any sounds of gunshots seemed to show the mike was not in Dealey Plaza.* Still, sound experts searched for inaudible "impulse patterns," claiming that such patterns could indicate gunfire, and they found several unusual ones.[78] Then an "acoustical reconstruction" was done at Dealey on August 20, 1978, with a Carcano fired from both the Depository and the grassy knoll. The "impulses" created at the reenactment were then compared to those on the original dictabelt recording. The Select Committee's first experts—Bolt, Beranek and Newman—concluded there was a 50 percent chance of a fourth shot, acoustically located at the grassy knoll.[79] The committee then turned the dictabelt and sound reenactment over to Mark Weiss and Ernest Aschkenasy, of Queens College, for further study. Weiss and Aschkenasy eventually upped the probability to 95 percent. All that was needed to wrap up the scientific breakthrough was "proof" that the open mike was in Dealey Plaza. On December 29, 1978, two days before the committee was scheduled to finish its work, H. B. McLain, an ex–Dallas policeman who was riding to the left rear of Vice-President Johnson's car, testified that his mike was often stuck in the open position, but he did not know if it got stuck that day.[80] That was enough for the final report to conclude that McLain's cycle had the open mike.

However, it was not long after the report was issued that the

---

* In 1991, the *Today* show showed a version of the Zapruder home movie of the assassination, supposedly with sounds from the dictabelt superimposed over it. Four loud shots were clearly audible. *Today* never informed its audience that the four bullet sounds were re-created in a studio and dubbed onto the recording. They do not exist on the original.

Select Committee's rushed work began unraveling. First, when McLain returned to Dallas, he finally heard a copy of the dictabelt recording. "I asked them [the Select Committee] the night before I testified if I could hear the tape," he told the author, "and they said, 'No, you don't need to hear that.' They knew that if I heard that tape I wouldn't testify for them, because I would immediately know that wasn't my cycle. If they had wanted truthful answers they would have played the tape for me first."[81] McLain was adamant once he heard the tape, because immediately after the shots were fired at Dealey, he had raced off on his motorcycle and accompanied the President's car at high speed to Parkland Hospital.[82] The sirens on the Dallas police cycles were footactivated, and the faster the cycle traveled, the louder the siren was. Yet on the dictabelt recording there are no sirens, except nearly two minutes after the supposed shooting, when a siren approaches the vehicle with the open mike and then passes it.[83] If the open mike had been on McLain's cycle, a siren should be heard on the recording from almost immediately after the shots until the arrival at Parkland. Trying to fit McLain into its acoustics conclusion, the committee then suggested he might have sat in Dealey Plaza for two minutes after the shots, forgot to turn on his siren, then raced to catch up with the motorcade, but then fallen back.[84] But that does not fit the photographic or eyewitness testimony about McLain's actions.* Also missing from the tape, if it was stuck open in Dealey Plaza, is any crowd noise. "The crowds were surging forward," says McLain. "They were screaming, hollering, hanging from lampposts. People kept running forward, and we had to run the bikes toward them to push them back. The noise was so great that I had trouble hearing my radio."[85] Instead of crowd noise on the tape, there is the sound of someone softly whistling nearby, and then the single toll of a bell, which was nowhere near Dealey. Finally, when McLain's cycle was speeding toward Parkland, the dictabelt recording reveals the engine on the cycle in question is idling, not racing.[86] Dallas sheriff Jim Bowles has been relentless in pursuing many of the questions unresolved by the Select Committee, and he determined the open mike was on

---

* McLain was photographed accompanying Mrs. Kennedy into the hospital.

a motorcycle stationed at the Trade Mart, where the President's luncheon reception was scheduled.[87]*

If the open microphone was not in Dealey Plaza, it could not have recorded the sounds of the assassination. However, even worse news was due the House Select Committee's acoustics conclusion. In one of the most unusual turns in the case, in July 1979, Steve Barber, a rock drummer living in a small Ohio town, purchased an adult magazine, *Gallery*, which included a plastic insert recording of the dictabelt evidence. "I just played this thing to death," said Barber, "just trying to hear the gunshots and hear for myself what they really said was 95 percent evidence of conspiracy."[88] Barber heard something all the highly paid experts missed. At the point on the tape where the experts decided there were four shots over a six-second period, Barber heard the barely audible words "Hold everything secure . . ." That matched with "Hold everything secure until the homicide and other investigators can get there . . ."—words spoken by Sheriff Bill Decker, in the lead motorcade car, on police Channel Two. The Decker transmission had crossed over to Channel One. But Decker spoke those words nearly one minute after the assassination, when he was instructing his officers what to do at Dealey Plaza. If the cross-talk Barber discovered was correct, it meant the Select Committee's experts had picked up sound impulses of "bullet shots" one minute after the actual assassination.

The National Academy of Sciences appointed a distinguished panel of twelve scientists to study the Select Committee's acoustics work. Dubbed the Ramsey Panel, after its chairman, Professor Norman Ramsey of Harvard, it concluded in 1982 that the committee's work was "seriously flawed"[89] and that Barber's analysis was correct.[90] Moreover, the Ramsey Panel, in a ninety-six-page report, blasted the Select Committee's conclusions about a grassy-knoll shooter and a fourth shot, saying there were "serious errors" in its work and there "was no acoustic basis" for such a claim.[91]†

---

* Bowles later determined the source of the unusual bell tone on the tape. There was a replica of the Liberty Bell at the Trade Mart, and passersby frequently gave it a rap.

† In an understatement, Anthony Summers only admits that "the acoustics evidence . . . has had a rough ride since 1979."

While the Select Committee failed to establish the number of shots at Dealey Plaza scientifically, it also missed other sources of information that could have helped it determine the correct number. Three critical ear-witnesses were Oswald's young co-workers Bonnie Ray Williams, Junior Jarman, and Harold Norman. During the assassination, they were on the southeast corner of the fifth floor, under the sniper's nest. Since the flooring was being replaced on the sixth floor, there was only a thin plywood covering, with cracks in the planks allowing some light between the floors.[92] Sounds passed easily. While they were watching the motorcade below from three separate windows, they heard the first rifle shot. It sounded like an explosion.[93] Bonnie Ray Williams said the shots were "loud. . . . [It] sounded like it was right in the building . . . it even shook the building, the side we were on. Cement fell on my head."[94] Junior Jarman heard the explosions and ran over to his two friends. It was Harold Norman, directly under the sniper's nest, who heard the most important sounds. "When the first shot came, I heard boom, then click-click, boom, click-click, boom," he says. "I could hear the sound of the click [the bolt action], I could hear the sound of the shells hitting the floor, I could hear everything. Three shots. No doubt in my mind."[95] Norman shouted to his friends, "It's coming right over our heads!" "No bullshit!" Williams shouted back.[96] Before anyone discovered Oswald's Carcano on the sixth floor, Norman had correctly described a bolt-action rifle being fired directly over his head.* Robert Jackson and Malcolm Couch, news photographers, looked up at the Depository during the last shot. They noticed two of the young

---

* Many critics ignore the testimony of those three workers because it is so definitive on the number and source of shots. The most Jim Marrs will acknowledge is: "Obviously, there was someone on the sixth floor, but was it Oswald?" Others, like Mark Lane, question why they could hear the bolt action and shells hit the floor but not hear the assassin run across the floor after the shooting. "We were shouting at each other and moving all around," says Norman, "so after that third shot I don't think we could have heard anything upstairs." Also, there is the question of why the three moved to the opposite corner of the building after the shooting. Was it because they thought some shots may have come from that direction, nearer the grassy knoll? "No way," Norman told the author. "We went over there because we saw people on ground going there, and we were wondering, 'Where the hell are they going, the guy who shot is right up here.' "

black men on the fifth floor straining to look at the window above.[97]

The final piece of the acoustical puzzle over the number of shots fired at Dealey Plaza is available now in the confirmation of a story that has long been rumored in Dallas. Since the assassination, local media gossip had it that a journalist had recorded the sounds of Dealey on November 22 and that later the recording was accidentally erased. The author finally located the reporter, Travis Linn, now a professor of journalism. He had always declined previous interviews because "I didn't want to be the subject of twenty thousand telephone calls." But despite his reluctance, he finally agreed to tell, for the first time publicly, the story of the only sound recording known to have been made of the assassination.

"I was a reporter for WFAA radio [there is also a WFAA-TV], which was an ABC and NBC affiliate," says Linn. "As we were making our plans for the day, I was scheduled to go to the Trade Mart, where I was supposed to do radio pool on the speech. I asked one of the TV guys, A. J. L'Hoste, if he would take one of our portable tape recorders up to Dealey Plaza, as he was going up there, and I asked him to set it down on top of a column near the reflective pool at the corner of Houston and Elm [across the street from the Depository]. It would get the natural sound of the motorcade going by. I was at the Trade Mart when the shooting occurred, and after, I was on the air from there, basically repeating what I heard from my own station into the microphone for six other stations for ABC. Finally, we shut down after Kennedy's death had been announced, and I caught a ride up to Dealey. I remembered that I had asked L'Hoste to set up the recorder, but he was gone. And I looked around and found the tape [recorder] on top of one of those pedestals. You couldn't really even see it, as the pedestals are tall, the tape recorder is pretty small, and you would have to look for it. And no one was looking for anything there after the pandemonium of the shooting."[98]

Linn said the German-manufactured recorder was a battery-driven professional unit. It was an early version of a cassette recorder, which had to be rewound manually with a crank. In order to play it on the air, it had to be transferred to a reel-to-reel tape machine.

"So I took it back to the station and dubbed it onto reel-to-reel," he says, "in our beeper room, which is where we took in phone reports and production. And while I was in the process of dubbing it, I was called by my news director to go out, with a TV guy, to Lee Harvey Oswald's apartment. So I yelled, 'Don't erase that tape.' When I got back, the tape had been erased. The way it worked is you got the cassettes, and after you dubbed out of those little cartridges, you then bulk-erased the cartridges and went on to another assignment. And the reel-to-reel was not bulk-erased, but had been recorded over with so many incoming feeds that you could not find anything but little snatches of crowd noises."

When asked if he heard the sounds of shots on the tape when he first played it back, Linn had no hesitation. "When I was dubbing it, I did hear three shots. I can tell you without any doubt that there were three shots and they were rifle shots. I know rifles and pistols. There is no question about those sounds. They were huge over the crowd noise. You've heard a rifle. A rifle fired in that square makes quite a noise. The first two, my recollection is, were closer together, and there was a slightly longer pause until the third one, as if the guy hurried his shots, and then said, 'No, I am going to aim this time.' "[99]

Asked why he had never come forward, Linn said, "Others knew about it at the station. But I was the only one that heard the shots. That's why I figured, 'Let's just forget about it.' In those days after the assassination, the stories were coming in so quick, just bang, bang, bang, that there was no time to think about it. You just don't have time to do thumbsuckers and think of what might have been. I knew within a week that if I had it, that it was very important. But I didn't have it, so what could I do?"*

---

* Linn was not the only one to lose a major story that day. Another was Robert MacNeil, currently of the *MacNeil/Lehrer NewsHour*. He was a young NBC reporter covering the President's trip. After hearing three shots, he jumped from a motorcade car. At first he followed those running toward the grassy knoll, but he soon ran to the nearest building, the Depository. There, he ran into a young man leaving the building and asked, in great agitation, for the telephones, and the man pointed. Oswald later told the Dallas police that as he left the Depository, a young Secret Service agent with a blond crewcut asked him for the telephones. There were no Secret Service agents at Dealey immedi-

The Eyewitnesses

Of the hundreds of witnesses at Dealey Plaza, did any see the assassin fire the shots? There were a good many witnesses who saw the actual shooter, or the rifle itself, and in every instance they identified the same location—the southeast corner of the sixth floor of the Texas School Book Depository. Robert Jackson, a *Dallas Times Herald* photographer, was riding in the motorcade in an open convertible, with four other reporters. They were about one block behind the President's car. During the time the shots were being fired, Jackson and the other reporters began looking around the Plaza for the source, and he glanced up to the top of the Depository. Their car was only twenty-five feet from the front of the building.[100] "I noticed two Negro men in a window straining to see directly above them, and my eyes followed right on up to the window above them and I saw the rifle . . . approximately half of the weapon . . . and just as I looked at it, it was drawn fairly slowly back into the building . . ."[101] Jackson said the rifle was pointing down Elm Street, where the President had just been shot, and he also noticed the wall of boxes in the window, "enough to hide a man."[102]

Malcolm Couch, a cameraman, was in the same car as Jackson. "After the third shot," Couch recalled, "Bob Jackson, who was as I recall on my right, yelled something like, 'Look up in the window! There's the rifle!' And I remember glancing up to a window on the far right, which at the time impressed me as the sixth or seventh floor, and seeing about a foot of a rifle being— the barrel brought into the window."[103] Couch also noticed the rifle was pointed down Elm Street.

James Crawford, a deputy district court clerk, was standing

---

ately after the assassination. MacNeil had short blond hair, and Oswald must have confused the press badge on his jacket as a Secret Service identification. According to Linn, another journalist to have missed a coup was Ron Reiland, the only reporter who got inside the Texas Theater when Oswald was arrested. He photographed the arrest, but mistakenly shot it with a filter over the lens, and nothing developed. When Reiland walked outside, he pulled the filter off and all those photographs, of the crowd spitting and kicking at Oswald, were overexposed.

on the corner across the street from the Depository and not far from Jackson and Couch's car. He also looked around when the shots rang out. "As the third report was sounded," he said, "I looked up and from the far east corner of the sixth floor I saw a movement in the only window that was open on that floor."[104] Crawford turned to his friend Mary Ann Mitchell and said the shots had come from that corner window. He caught a quick glimpse of a "profile, somewhat from the waist up" and noticed something white (likely Oswald's T-shirt), as well as one of the boxes of the sniper's nest. He found a deputy sheriff, Allan Sweatt, and told him to "have the men search the boxes directly behind this window that was open on the sixth floor—the window in the far east corner."[105]

Mrs. Earle Cabell, the wife of the Dallas mayor, was four cars behind the President's in an open convertible. As the shots echoed through the plaza, she was facing the Depository. "Because I heard the direction from which the shot came, I just jerked my head up," she remembered. "I saw a projection out of those windows . . . on the sixth floor."[106] Immediately after, she smelled gunpowder.*

Standing on the sidewalk in front of the Depository was James Worrell, a nineteen-year-old student. The first shot was loud and sounded like it came from over his head, instinctively making him raise his head and look over his body at a ninety-degree angle. "I looked up like that," he said, "just straight up. . . . I saw the rifle, about six inches of it. I saw about four inches of the barrel . . . but it had a long stock and . . . I saw about two inches [of the stock]."[107]† Worrell looked up after the first shot. He saw something few others did, the rifle actually

---

* Others near the School Book Depository also thought they smelled gunpowder, including Tom Dillard, a journalist who was in the same convertible with Bob Jackson and Malcolm Couch (WC Vol. VI, p. 165). Some use the testimony of Senator Ralph Yarborough, who said he smelled gunpowder as he drove through Dealey Plaza, to suggest a shot had been fired closer to the grassy knoll. Although a stiff north-south wind did blow the odor of gunpowder further into the plaza, Yarborough was in the Vice-President's car, two behind the President, and was right in front of the Depository as the shooting began.

† His description of a long wooden stock, with only four inches of barrel exposed at the end of the rifle, exactly describes Oswald's Carcano.

fire, "what you might call a little flash of fire and then smoke."[108] The gun was "pointing right down at the motorcade."

Another witness who had a clear view of the sniper's nest was fifteen-year-old Amos Lee Euins. He was small for his age, and someone had lifted him atop a concrete pedestal by the reflecting pool across the street from the Depository. "I could see everything," he says.[109] "I saw what I thought was a pipe," Euins told the author. "I saw it ahead of time. It looked like a dark metal pipe hanging from the window, and it was an old building, so I figured, 'Hey, it's got a pipe hanging off it.' I never realized it was a gun until the shooting started."[110] Then he jumped off the pedestal and looked up at the sixth-floor window. He saw "the rifle laying across in his hand, and I could see his hand on the trigger part."[111] After the third shot, Euins remembered the sniper "pulled the gun back in the window." While he could not describe the shooter, he ran to a policeman and told him what he saw.

But the person who saw more that day in Dealey Plaza than any other witness was construction worker Howard Brennan. He was sitting on top of a four-foot-high retaining wall on the corner of Houston and Elm, directly across the street from the School Book Depository (Brennan is visible in the Zapruder film —he was just over 100 feet from the window).[112] When he arrived at that corner, he checked his watch and it was 12:18. The first time he noticed a man in the southeast corner of the sixth floor was several minutes later. He guessed he was five feet eight to five feet ten inches tall, white, slender, with dark-brown hair, and between twenty-five and thirty-five years of age.[113] "As I looked at the man," said Brennan, "it struck me how unsmiling and calm he was. He didn't seem to feel one bit of excitement. His face was almost expressionless. . . . He seemed preoccupied."[114]

After the motorcade passed by Brennan's corner, the first shot rang out. He, like many others, thought it was a backfire. "I looked up then at the Texas School Book Depository Building," he recalled. "What I saw made my blood run cold. Poised in the corner window of the sixth floor was the same young man I had noticed several times before the motorcade arrived. There was one difference—this time he held a rifle in his hands, pointing toward the Presidential car. He steadied the rifle against the cornice and while he moved quickly, he didn't seem to be in any kind of panic. All this happened in the matter of a second or two. Then came the sickening sound of a second shot. . . . I wanted to cry, I wanted to scream, but I couldn't utter a sound."[115] A woman next to him screamed when she realized the noises were rifle fire. Brennan's eyes locked on the solitary figure steadying his rifle for the final shot. "He was aiming again and I wanted to pray, to beg God to somehow make him miss the target . . . what I was seeing, the sight became so fixed in my mind that I'll never forget it for as long as I live. . . . Then another shot rang out."[116] Brennan hit the ground, afraid there would be more gunfire. The President's car started to speed away. He looked up at the window a final time. "To my amazement the man still stood there in the window. He didn't appear to be rushed. There was no particular emotion visible on his face except for a slight smirk. It was a look of satisfaction, as if he had accomplished what he set out to do. . . . [Then] he simply moved away from the window until he disappeared from my line of vision."[117]

Brennan said the "last thing I wanted to do was to get involved." But he noticed "that it appeared to me that they [the police] were searching in the wrong direction for the man that did the shooting."[118] Despite his reluctance, he went to a uniformed policeman in front of the Depository and told him what he saw. The policeman left for a few minutes and returned with Dallas police inspector Herbert Sawyer. Brennan repeated his story, and Sawyer walked to a nearby car and reported the first description of the suspect. At 12:45, only fifteen minutes after the assassination, the Dallas police dispatcher broke across Channel One: "Attention all squads—attention all squads. At Elm and Houston reported to be an unknown white male, approximately thirty, slender build, height five feet ten inches, 165 pounds—reported to be armed with what is believed to be a 30-caliber rifle . . . no further description or information at this time."[119]*

---

* The 12:45 identification has been the focus of great controversy. Summers says, "In what today seems an astonishing failure, the Warren inquiry never did

Because Brennan is so specific in his descriptions, the critics go to extensive efforts to discredit him. On the same night of the assassination, at a lineup, Brennan said about Oswald, "He looks like the man, but I can't say for sure."[120] Since he could not positively identify him, did that mean he did not get a very good look at the shooter? Not at all. Brennan could have picked Oswald from the lineup, but did not do so because he feared others might be involved in the assassination, and if word leaked that he was the only one who could identify the trigger man, his life would be in danger.[121] The FBI had already given him a twenty-four-hour guard (which continued for three weeks), heightening his concern. He thought about moving his family out of the area. Besides the danger, Brennan thought "since they already had the man for murder, that he wasn't going to be set free to escape and get out of the country immediately, and I could very easily . . . get in touch with them [the FBI] to see that the man didn't get loose."[122]

"But with all fairness," he told the Warren Commission, "I could have positively identified the man." He said he saw the assassin as well as he saw the three men on the fifth floor, and he identified them as they came out the Depository within a half hour of the assassination.[123] "I knew I could never forget the face I had seen in the window on the sixth floor of the Texas School Book Depository," Brennan said.[124]

The last point on which the critics try to disparage Brennan's credibility is his eyesight. Mark Lane started the attack in his 1966 *Rush to Judgment,* when he wrote, "Perhaps poor eyesight accounted for Brennan's inability to identify the men at the window . . . he was not wearing glasses when he glanced up at the sixth-floor window . . . ."[125] Marrs says, "Much later, it was de-

---

establish the source of this description." But the Commission did settle the issue, despite the best efforts of some to obfuscate it. In his testimony before the Commission, Brennan mistakenly called the plainclothes officer "Sorrels," the name of a Secret Service agent he met about fifteen minutes after he met Inspector Sawyer (WC Vol. III, p. 145). After the assassination, Sorrels did not return to Dealey until nearly 1:00 P.M., so Brennan could not have given him the description broadcast at 12:45. Sawyer testified to the Warren Commission that he was the one who received the description and broadcast the first identification of the assassin (WC Vol. VI, pp. 321–23; WC Vol. XXI, Sawyer Exhibit A, p. 392; Brennan, *Eyewitness to History,* p. 17).

termined that Brennan had poor eyesight . . ."[126] Robert Sam Anson goes one step further, charging that the Warren Commission "purposely excluded" the information about the "near-sighted Howard Brennan . . ."[127] But any who read Brennan's testimony to the Warren Commission would have discovered he was in fact *farsighted.*[128] Although his eyes were later damaged in a sandblasting accident after the assassination, he said, "On that day my vision was perfect." Brennan said his eyesight for anything at a distance was "extraordinary," allowing him when in a car to read license plates of other cars from a couple of hundred feet. He fervently believed God had placed him in the position to witness the assassination because of "my gift of super-eyesight."[129]

But what did other witnesses report seeing in Dealey Plaza, and is there any evidence of a second gunman? Some reported "some commotion," or "a puff of smoke" near the grassy knoll, but not one witness gave a contemporaneous statement about a second gunman at Dealey. However, since that day, new witnesses have stepped forward, sometimes years later, claiming to have seen the real assassin. Some people have actually confessed to being the phantom grassy-knoll shooter. While many reports can be dismissed out of hand (such as the man who identified Frank Sinatra's drummer as the second shooter), the major witnesses for a conspiracy deserve scrutiny.

Jean Hill was standing on the southern side of Elm Street as President Kennedy's car passed. She was with her friend Mary Moorman, who snapped a Polaroid of the rear of the President's car almost at the moment of the fatal head shot.* Over the years, she has become one of the chief witnesses used by critics to establish the presence of a grassy-knoll shooter. Cited in books and articles, and the author of her own book, *The Last Dissenting Witness*, Hill is a frequent television guest and speaker at assassination symposia. Oliver Stone gave her character a prominent role in *JFK*. But what did she originally say that day, and how has her story changed over the years?

---

*For many years, Jean Hill's calling cards bragged she was the "closest witness" to the President at the time of the fatal head shot.

On the day of the assassination, she gave a statement to the sheriff's office and signed it as correct.[130] She said: "Just as Mary Moorman started to take a picture we were looking at the President and Jackie in the back seat and they were looking at a little dog between them." Hill elaborated later to say it was a "white, fluffy dog." When she discovered there was no dog in the President's car, she claimed to be confused by the white roses (they were actually red). She later dropped the dog from her story.

In her November 22 statement, she also said the President looked at her when he was first shot, but then later changed that to say she jumped to the edge of the street and yelled, "Hey, we want to take your picture," and that is why JFK looked over.[131] The Zapruder home movie shows Hill never moved or said a word as the President passed, and she was not even looking at him when he was first shot. Hill said Jackie shouted, "My God, he has been shot!" Jackie and the car's four other occupants deny she said anything. Although Hill claimed she scrutinized the car's passengers, she did not know Mrs. Connally was in the car, actually on the side nearest to her.[132]

According to Hill, there were two shots, then a pause, and "three or four more shots rang out . . ."[133] She testified that the first three shots were from a bolt-action, and the remainder might have been from an automatic.[134] On the day of the assassination, she told the sheriff's department that she saw "some men in plain clothes shooting back . . ." No one returned gunfire. In her original written statement, she saw a "man [near the Depository] running toward the monument" on the other side of the plaza, and started running after him. Over the years that portion of her story has dramatically changed. She soon said that when she chased the man, her attention was drawn "to a trail of blood in the grass."[135] She followed it in the belief that the man had been shot by a policeman, but it turned out to be drops left by a Sno-Cone, flavored crushed ice.[136] Later, she told a reporter that the man looked like Jack Ruby, but backed off the Ruby identification because "quite a few people," including her husband, made fun of her testimony.[137]

Although she considered the man near the Depository suspicious, she admitted she "never saw a weapon the whole time." She told the Warren Commission, "When I ran across the street, the first motorcycle that was right behind [the President's car] nearly hit me," and she explained how she dashed across the road, past the motorcade traffic, to chase the stranger.[138] Summers writes, "Hill had run impetuously across the road, dodging between the cars while the motorcade was still going by. She was ahead of the field in the parking lot . . ."[139] In one version, Hill claims she lost sight of the man as he ran over the railroad tracks.[140] However, another Dealey witness, Wilma Bond, was behind and to the east of Hill, and took a series of still photographs that day. While they show a crowd climbing the small incline leading to the fence on the grassy knoll, just minutes after the shooting, Jean Hill is still either sitting or standing next to Mary Moorman. In one of the photos, the rear of a large bus at the tail end of the motorcade is passing under the Triple Underpass. That means that most of the motorcade had left Dealey Plaza, yet Hill was still in her original position and had not yet taken a step to cross the road to chase the character as she described.

In her original statement, Hill said when she got to the grassy knoll, the police were turning people back, so she returned to Mary Moorman. There was "Mr. Featherstone of the *Times Herald*," and "he brought us to the press room down at the Sheriff's office and ask us to stay."[141] However, she later radically departed from that story and alleged she encountered two men impersonating Secret Service agents. She told Jim Marrs, "I was looking around but I couldn't see anything, when these two guys came up behind me. One of them said, 'You're coming with us,' and I replied, 'Oh, no I'm not. I don't know you.' 'I said you're coming with us,' one of them said and then put this horrible grip on my shoulder. I can still feel the pain when I think about it. I tried to tell them, 'I have to go back and find my friend Mary.' But then the other guy put a grip on my other shoulder and they began hustling me past the front of the Depository. 'Keep smiling and keep walking,' one of them kept telling me. They marched me across the Plaza and into a building. They took me into a little office upstairs and they wouldn't let me out of this room."[142] Featherstone confirmed he was the person who escorted Hill and Moorman to the sheriff's office, just as Hill said in her original statement.

Finally, Hill was interviewed within half an hour of the assassination by a local Dallas television crew. Asked if she saw anybody or if anything drew her attention, she said, unequivocally, "No."[143] She did not see any guns, flashes of light, or puffs of smoke. However, over the years her story changed to include a grassy-knoll shooter. By 1986, she told Jim Marrs, "I saw a man fire from behind the wooden fence. I saw a puff of smoke and some sort of movement on the grassy knoll where he was."[144] In 1989, she added a "flash of light" to her scenario.[145]*

Hill now claims that her Warren Commission testimony "was a fabrication from the first line."[146] She charges that in 1964, when Arlen Specter, now a U.S. senator from Pennsylvania and then a staff attorney for the Warren Commission, took her testimony, he threatened her. "He got angrier and angrier and finally told me, 'Look, we can make you look as crazy as Marguerite Oswald and everybody knows how crazy she is. We could have you put in a mental institution if you don't cooperate with us.' "[147] There is nothing remotely approaching such conduct by Specter in the stenographer's verbatim transcription of the deposition.

Another witness who is used by the critics to support the claim of a grassy-knoll shooter is Jesse Price. He was on the roof of the Union Terminal Annex, on the southern end of the plaza. Price also signed an affidavit the day of the assassination. Marrs, in *Crossfire*, refers to Price's affidavit, and writes, "While sitting on the edge of the building's roof overlooking the plaza, Price heard shots '. . . from by the . . . Triple Underpass.' "[148] What Price actually said in his affidavit had nothing to do with

---

* She pinpointed the shooter at the exact location where some conspiracy buffs believe they have found an image they have dubbed "badgeman." On Mary Moorman's badly faded Polaroid, a half-inch-square portion has been enhanced, and although it only shows shadows and trees, some believe they see the outlines of a rifle and a Dallas police uniform—hence the name "badgeman." Hill is used as the eyewitness confirmation for such a shooter. The author stood at the very spot where a grassy-knoll shooter is supposed to have fired at the President. Although the shooter was purportedly standing on a car bumper, in order to aim over a five-foot fence, he would have been completely exposed at the rear, making it impossible to fire from that location without being seen by witnesses. In addition to more than a dozen who could have seen such a shooter, three witnesses were only a few feet in front of the fence, and they never saw anyone behind the fence.

hearing shots from that location: "The cars had proceeded West on Elm and was [sic] just a short distance from the Tripple [sic] underpass, when I saw Gov. Connelly [sic] slump over."[149] Then Marrs says Price saw a young man, with a white dress shirt, no tie, and khaki-colored pants, running toward the passenger cars on the railroad tracks. According to Marrs, Price saw something in the man's hand, "which could have been a gun."[150] In his affidavit Price actually said, "He had something in his hand. I couldn't be sure but it may have been a head piece [a hat]."* Finally, Marrs cites him to establish that there were many rifle shots at Dealey. Marrs quotes Price as saying: "There was a volley of shots, I think five and then much later . . . another one." The crucial portion that Marrs omitted with ellipsis points says, "maybe as much as five minutes later." Realizing that Price would lose all credibility if the reader knew he thought there was a final shot five minutes after the first, Marrs just omitted the offending language. In conclusion, Marrs says, "Price was never called to testify to the Warren Commission," implying that the Commission wanted to avoid such a witness because it was not seeking the truth about what had happened at Dealey. Judging from Price's affidavit, the reason he was not called is obvious.

Lee Bowers was stationed in the second story of a railroad signal tower, 130 feet behind the grassy knoll. He had a clear view of the parking lot and the back of the fence from which the supposed second gunman fired. Before the assassination, he saw no unusual activity in the area. Three cars drove into the parking lot between noon and the assassination, looking for a space but, seeing it filled, left.[151] Bowers also noted two men behind the fence, some fifteen feet apart, who apparently did not know each other.[152] They were standing near the point where the fence met the Triple Underpass, some fifty feet from where critics believe a second gunman fired. Anyone behind the fence becomes a focus of suspicion, but Bowers testified that at

---

* Over two years later, Price changed his original statement in an interview with Mark Lane, the most energetic of the early conspiracy buffs, saying that instead of a hat, maybe it was a gun. Price not only added new details about the man he saw, but claimed to Lane that the man ran to the School Book Depository instead of away from it, as he had said in his original affidavit.

least one—and maybe both—was still there when the police arrived after the assassination.[153] There has also been import attached to Bowers's statement that at the time of the assassination "there was some commotion" near the parking area. When asked to define "commotion," however, he said, "Nothing that I could pinpoint as having happened."*

Sam Holland, an elderly railway signal supervisor, was standing on top of the Triple Underpass with several other railway workers and a Dallas policeman. He told the Warren Commission, "There was a shot, a report, I don't know whether it was a shot. I can't say that. And a puff of smoke came out about 6 or 8 feet above the ground right out from under those trees."[154] Most critics cite Holland's testimony, saying that "a puff of smoke" is evidence that a shot was fired from the grassy knoll. Yet Holland was not certain the smoke was caused by gunfire. In his affidavit, taken the day of the assassination, he was confused about several issues, thinking that Mrs. Kennedy was trying to climb into the backseat to join her husband, and that a Secret Service agent in the President's car had "raised up in the seat with a machine gun."[155]† Others on the overpass with Holland, such as Frank Reilly, Royce Skelton, and Dallas policeman J. W. Foster, never saw any smoke.[156] Yet Edward Jay Epstein, in *Inquest*, writes, "Five of the witnesses on the overpass said they had also seen smoke rise from the grassy knoll area."[157] Epstein's citation lists only four names, one of which is Holland. The other three, who were all on the overpass with Holland, do not support the proposition that the smoke resulted from gunfire. James Simmons said he thought the shots came from the Book Depository and that he saw "exhaust fumes" from the embankment.[158]

---

* Again, as in the case of Price, Mark Lane talked to Bowers in 1966, and Bowers altered his original testimony, adding "a flash of light." However, there is some doubt as to whether Bowers saw anything during the assassination. He admitted that thirteen railroad tracks converged on his station, and not only was he busy at the time of the assassination, but immediately after hearing the final shot, he had to throw a "red-on-red" signal, which blocked all trains. In order to perform any of his duties at the control panel, Bowers would have had to have his back turned toward Dealey Plaza (Jim Moore, *Conspiracy of One*, pp. 32–33; author's personal observation, March 1992).

† In another car, Secret Service agent Ed Hickey grabbed an AR-15, but no one in the President's limousine drew a firearm.

Clemon Johnson saw white smoke but told the FBI that it "came from a motorcycle abandoned near the spot by a Dallas police-man."[159] Epstein's final citation is from Austin Miller, who thought the smoke he saw was "steam."[160]

In addition, since modern ammunition is smokeless, it seldom creates even a wisp of smoke.[161] Moreover, on the day of the assassination there was a stiff wind blowing north to south, gusting up to twenty miles an hour.[162] A puff of smoke would not rise from a rifle and sit stagnantly in the air when the winds were so stiff. Finally, in 1963, there was a steam pipe along the wooden fence near the edge of the Triple Underpass.[163] A Dallas policeman, Seymour Weitzman, burned his hands on that pipe when searching there immediately after the shots. If there was smoke, it is most likely that it was either exhaust fumes or steam from the pipe.*

Two witnesses whose testimony indicates there was a grassy-knoll shooter appeared publicly for the first time in 1978. Gordon Arnold identified himself as a twenty-two-year-old sol-dier home on leave on November 22. According to his story, he ran into men with CIA identifications behind the grassy knoll before the assassination. During the shooting, he was standing only feet in front of the picket fence when a bullet whizzed past his left ear. He knew it was live ammunition being fired directly behind him, and he hit the ground. Arnold, who claimed he had a camera, said that after the assassination two men in police uniforms approached him. One kicked him while another, bran-dishing a shotgun and crying, confiscated his film. He fled back to Alaska and did not tell his story for fifteen years.[164] He soon became a main figure in a documentary that claimed Kennedy was killed by a team of Corsican mercenaries, and his story is repeated in recent books. The problem is that it appears that Arnold was not even at Dealey Plaza on the day of the assassination. People on the grassy knoll near where Arnold says he was are clearly visible in the pictures taken of the knoll. Although Arnold claims he is not visible because he

---

* When Oliver Stone filmed *JFK* he could not find a rifle that emitted enough smoke to be captured on film when fired from the grassy knoll. Finally, he resorted to a props man pumping smoke from a bellows.

is lying flat on the ground, photo enhancements show no such person.*

Another major witness to appear years after the assassination is Ed Hoffman, a deaf mute, who presents a fascinating tale of multiple gunmen on the grassy knoll. Hoffman said he was on the Stemmons Freeway, some 250 to 300 yards west of the picket fence.[165] Unaware that shots had been fired, he claimed to see a man in a suit and tie in the railyard behind the grassy knoll. He was running with a rifle. That gunman then tossed the rifle to a man disguised as a railyard worker and the second man disassembled the rifle, put it into a sack, and walked away.† Hoffman said that when he saw the wounded President speed past in the motorcade, he ran down the grassy incline from the freeway and tried to communicate to a policeman, who did not understand him.[166]

Although Hoffman did not go public until 1978, he had contacted the FBI in 1967, three and a half years after the assassination, and told a less sensational version. He said he saw two men running from the rear of the Texas School Book Depository, but the FBI concluded he could not have seen them from where he was because a fence west of the Depository blocked his view. He then changed his story to say he saw the men on top of the fence.[167] There are additional problems, though, with his story. Dallas policeman Earle Brown, who was stationed as security on a railroad overpass above Stemmons Freeway, said there was no civilian there.[168] Three other policemen on three-wheel traffic cycles were near where Hoffman claimed to be. They did not see him.[169] Murphy said, "There was no one standing there [on the freeway overpass] prior to the arrival of the motorcade or after the motorcade arrived." But in addition to questions about whether Ed Hoffman was where he said he was

---

* Arnold appeared vindicated when Senator Ralph Yarborough later said he remembered seeing a young man "throw himself on the ground" as soon as the shooting started. However, Yarborough has since clarified that he was referring to Bill Newman, who was at the foot of the grassy knoll with his family and threw himself, his wife, and their two children onto the grass.

† Even those who support Hoffman's story find it difficult to explain how anyone was able to disassemble the rifle in the railyard when more than a dozen people ran into that exact location less than a minute after the last shot.

that day, it appears that even if he was there, his view, 750 to 900 feet away, was blocked. Photographs and independent testimony reveal there were four large railway freight cars over the Elm Street tunnel that day, effectively obstructing any view from Stemmons into the rear of the grassy knoll.[170] Moreover, in 1963, a large Cutty Sark billboard also filled some of the space between the freeway and the railroad tracks.[171] It is almost impossible for Hoffman to have seen what he described.[172]*

There are other eyewitnesses sometimes used to establish a second gunman at Dealey, but each has even greater credibility problems than the primary witnesses discussed above. Malcolm Summers, who was at Dealey, now says that he ran into a man, wielding a gun that looked like a machine pistol, on the grassy knoll. No one else saw such a figure. In an affidavit given the day after the assassination, Summers said he stayed at Dealey for twenty minutes after the shooting, but did not mention confronting anyone with a gun.[173]

A deputy sheriff, Roger Craig, said he saw a green Nash Rambler with a luggage rack, with suspicious men inside, drive away from the Depository soon after the assassination. Craig and others concluded it was the Paines' car (the Paines had a green car, but it was a Chevrolet station wagon). Craig said that back at police headquarters, he entered the room where Captain Will Fritz was questioning Oswald and mentioned the station wagon. According to Craig, Oswald said, "That station wagon belongs to Mrs. Paine. . . . Don't try to tie her into this. She had nothing to do with it."[174] But Captain Fritz branded Craig a liar, saying he had never even been inside the interrogation room.†

A Dallas policeman, Tom Tilson, also claimed, fifteen years after the event, to have witnessed a suspicious car leaving Dealey.[175] Tilson, who was off duty on the day of the assassina-

---

* The author drove to the location on Stemmons where Hoffman claimed to be on the day of assassination. Even without the billboard and railroad cars, the foliage between the freeway and the railyard makes it difficult to see very much. Photographs show the foliage was as dense in 1963 as it is today.

† Some have tried to defend Craig by saying he was in the interrogation room, and they produced a photo of him in Captain Fritz's office, where they say Oswald was interrogated. The picture does not show Craig in the inner office where Oswald was kept, but instead in a separate outer office.

tion, was in his own car with his daughter, Judy. He said he was near Dealey Plaza when he heard about the shooting on his police monitor. Then he noticed a man walk away from the railroad tracks behind the grassy knoll, throw a package into the backseat of a black car, and drive away. Tilson says he caught up to him when the man stopped for a red light, and then followed him at normal speeds over city streets, onto the Dallas–Fort Worth Turnpike. Eventually, Tilson claims his daughter copied down the black car's license plate number, and then he turned off the freeway to call the information into the homicide detectives. There are problems with Tilson's story. About the suspicious man, he said, "If that wasn't Jack Ruby, it was someone who was his twin brother."[176] More than half a dozen witnesses placed Ruby at the *Dallas Morning News* building at that very time (see pages 370–73). A photograph taken by Mel McIntire, snapped at almost the precise moment Tilson says he spotted the fleeing man, reveals no car, black or otherwise, in the location Tilson pinpointed.[177] Dallas police radio logs for the day do not show any alert for such a car as Tilson described, nor is there any record that he gave a license number or made any such call to the homicide detectives. Finally, Tilson himself acknowledges that his daughter, his only witness, no longer confirms his story.[178] He claims to have lost the paper on which his daughter, who was eighteen years old at the time, had supposedly written the car's license, and she "doesn't recall" writing down the number.[179]

Some early eyewitness evidence used to support a conspiracy has been quietly abandoned by the critics and is now discredited. On the day of the assassination, a man near the presidential motorcade opened and closed a black umbrella as the shots rang out. Some, such as Robert Cutler, the publisher of the *Grassy Knoll Gazette*, said the umbrella contained a poisoned flechette (a small dart) that shot into the President's throat and neutralized him so a team of five assassins could finish the job.[180] Jim Marrs and Oliver Stone believe the "umbrella man" gave a signal to the team of assassins waiting in ambush. However, the House Select Committee located the umbrella man in 1978, after publishing a drawing made from photographs taken that day and asking for public assistance in finding him. Louie

Witt did not even know he was the subject of such controversy, still had the same umbrella, and explained he had gone to Dealey to heckle the President with it.[181]

Photographs taken at Dealey Plaza also showed a man standing next to Witt, and soon there were those who said he appeared to be Cuban and that he seemed to occasionally speak into a walkie-talkie. Witt himself said the man was black, and he never had anything that could be remotely confused with a walkie-talkie. Across the street from Witt was a stocky woman in a long coat and with a scarf tied around her head. Dubbed by conspiracy buffs as the "babushka lady," she can be seen in other photos taking her own home movie of the motorcade. But she was never identified after the assassination. In 1970, a Texan, Beverly Oliver, stepped forward and said she was the babushka lady and that her film had been confiscated on the day of the assassination by either the Secret Service or the FBI. But some now doubt that Oliver was even in Dealey Plaza. Her story has changed numerous times. She claimed to have used a camera that did not exist in 1963, and later said that before the assassination she met both Jack Ruby and Lee Oswald, when Ruby introduced his friend as "Lee Oswald of the CIA." Oliver also said she saw David Ferrie at Ruby's Carousel Club so often that she thought he was the assistant manager. The House Select Committee interviewed her in executive session and decided not to use her as a witness. Still, Jim Marrs devoted substantial space to her story and seemingly accepted her claim of being the babushka lady.

Finally, there is controversy over a picture taken by Associated Press photographer Jim Altgens showing the presidential car just as JFK and Governor Connally reacted to their first wounds. Two of the Secret Service agents in the follow-up car have turned around and are looking toward the Book Depository. In the doorway of the Depository is a crowd of people, and one looks like Oswald. Even Marguerite said it looked like her son. How could he be on the sixth floor shooting the President if he was on the ground floor watching the parade? Yet the real question is why, when the original evidence is considered, this ever became such an important issue. Billy Lovelady, a worker at the Depository, testifying before the Warren Commission, immediately identified himself as the man in the doorway.[182] Other co-workers testified they were on the Depository's steps with Lovelady. When shown the same photograph, Danny Arce, Buell Frazier, Harold Norman, Mrs. Donald Baker, and William Shelley all, without hesitation, identified the man as Lovelady.[183] Yet despite the implausibility that it was Oswald, that issue survived until the House Select Committee finally undertook an anthropological photo study and concluded the man in the doorway was indeed Lovelady. But such things die hard. Marrs still only admits that the man in the doorway "may have been Lovelady."[184]

Beyond the eyewitnesses already discussed, the author has discovered several people who saw the assassination and have never before testified or told their stories. In the Terminal Annex building on the southern end of Dealey Plaza was the U.S. Post Office. The first and second floors were parcel post, the third mail processing, the fourth letter mail, and the fifth was both the cafeteria and the postal inspectors' offices. The building's view across Dealey is unobstructed. No one, apparently, including the Dallas police or the FBI, ever interviewed the employees there to discover what they saw. Dozens witnessed the assassination from the building's windows. Most are now retired, some deceased, and their memories nearly three decades after the event are not what they would have been within days of the shooting. But their revelations are still pertinent. The six interviewed for this book each remembered hearing three distinct shots, and most important, three of them watched the assassination with a pair of binoculars.[185] Because of the angle of their building, they looked at the President's car directly in line with the grassy knoll. They saw no gunman, no puff of smoke, or any flash of light. One employee, Francine Burrows, had gone to Dealey Plaza to watch the motorcade. She ran across the grass to get closer to the President. In the Zapruder film, she is seen in a beige raincoat, running toward the limousine near the point of the fatal head shot, and has never been identified until now. Burrows was within twenty-five feet of JFK when he was shot and was also looking directly toward the grassy knoll. She saw nothing there. Instead, she remembers three shots, and says, "I was very close to him when he got shot. And I looked up at that window immediately [the southeast corner of the sixth floor of the Depository]. I knew instinctively that's where the shots came from." She ran back to her office after the third shot, and said she "was in shock, just in shock—I didn't want to discuss it, I just wanted to forget it."[186]

12

"He Looks Like a Maniac"

Oswald had little time for planning, perhaps not much more than twenty-four hours. He had to decide how to slip the gun into the Depository and where to take a sniper's position. His lack of preparation is evident by the fact he only had four bullets with him, though the rifle's clip could hold six. They were all he had left from his last practice session, and he evidently did not have time on Thursday, November 21, to buy more.

Having never before seen a presidential motorcade, Oswald had little idea of what to expect for security, but knew it would be a far more difficult task than taking aim at the retired General Walker. He could not be sure whether the President would have the bubble top on the car,* or if Secret Service agents would ride on the rear of the limousine partially blocking his view. Lookouts might be posted in tall buildings, perhaps even in the Depository, and he could not be certain of finding a deserted floor or area from which to shoot. Yet if he found it impossible to shoot at the President, he could probably abort his plan and return with the rifle to the Paines'. It was not a suicide mission. Oswald also wanted to escape, although he probably had not planned much beyond getting away from the Depository before the police sealed the area.

---

* The bubble top was not bulletproof, but it might have deflected the bullets' trajectory, or the sun's reflection could have obscured his target.

After firing the final shot, he slipped through the narrow gap he had created between the cartons of books. He hurried around the boxes stacked on the sixth floor, toward the rear staircase. Next to the stairs, Oswald dropped the rifle into an opening between several large boxes. It hid the gun from view unless someone stood almost directly over the boxes and peered down. Oswald rapidly descended the stairs until he heard the sound of footsteps running up. He ducked off at the second floor, and dashed into the adjoining lunch room. But suddenly a voice called out, and when he turned, he was face to face with a Dallas policeman with a drawn revolver.*

Marrion Baker was a motorcycle policeman riding in the motorcade about one-half block behind the President's car. Baker had just returned from deer hunting, and he recognized the first shot as coming from "a high-powered rifle . . . and it sounded high . . ."[1] He looked up to where he thought the shots came from, the Book Depository, and saw a flock of pigeons fly off the building. Baker immediately raced his cycle 200 feet and jumped off in front of the Depository's steps and in another 45 feet he was inside the building. He yelled for directions to the stairs or elevator, and the building manager, Roy Truly, rushed him through a pair of swinging doors to the closest elevator. Truly kept pressing the down button and screaming, "Bring that elevator down here!" but nothing happened.† Truly said, "Let's take the stairs." They sprinted to the nearest staircase, that in the

---

* There is a question whether Oswald could have gone downstairs immediately after the assassination, since other Depository workers, including the three men on the fifth floor—Jarman, Williams, and Norman—as well as two fourth-floor office workers, Sandra Styles and Victoria Adams, also ran down the stairs and did not see him. But Oswald immediately took the staircase, whereas the three men admitted they stayed upstairs for ten to fifteen minutes after the shooting (WC Vol. III, p. 182). As for Styles and Adams, although they thought they came down quickly, they actually did not arrive on the first floor until at least four to five minutes after the third shot. The critical testimony is from Victoria Adams, who said that when she got to the first floor, she saw Billy Lovelady and William Shelley. Those two men, by their own testimony, did not return to the Depository for some five minutes after the shooting (see WC Vol. VI, pp. 331, 339, 389).

† Truly later decided that Oswald might have left the elevator's wooden grate open on the sixth floor so the car could not be operated.

rear of the building, and started up, with Baker behind Truly. When Baker reached the second floor, "I was kind of scanning the rooms," he recalled. "I happened to see him through this window in this door. I don't know how come I saw him, but I had a glimpse of him coming down there. . . . I could see him, he was walking away from me . . . [and] I hollered at him at that time and said, 'Come here.' " Baker recalled that Oswald was moving as fast as he was and was "hurrying" through a second door, which would have let him enter the office and conference area where Baker could not have seen him.[2]

Oswald walked back to Baker. Truly, who had started up to the third floor, returned. "Do you know this man, does he work here?" Baker asked Truly. Oswald did not say a word. According to Baker, "He did not change his expression one bit."[3] When Truly said yes, Baker immediately turned and continued upstairs. It was not until he went to police headquarters later that afternoon that he realized he had encountered the suspect within minutes of the last shot.*

Oswald was now left in the empty lunch room, and almost instantly he must have thought of the alibi he later used after his arrest—that he was eating lunch during the shooting. He went to the soda machine and purchased a Coke as he decided how to leave the Depository. He could return to the staircase Baker had just run up and leave from the rear of the building, or he could continue from the lunch room, past the offices, and down another staircase out the front of the Depository.† His choice to leave by the front was propitious. Immediately after the shots,

---

*Baker claimed he encountered Oswald less than two minutes after the assassination, and for some it is difficult to imagine how Oswald could have crossed the sixth floor and been on the second, not out of breath, in such a short time. The Warren Commission did a reconstruction. Officer Baker recreated Oswald's actions (including hiding the rifle) and in two tests made it to the second-floor lunch room, in "normal walking," in 1 minute and 18 seconds, and in a "fast walk" in 1 minute and 14 seconds (WC Vol. III, p. 254). A Secret Service agent, John Howlett, also completed Oswald's route in the necessary time. Neither Baker nor Howlett was out of breath when he reached the spot where Oswald had been stopped (WC Vol. VII, p. 592).

† The front staircase, leading to the Elm Street door of the Depository, did not reach the sixth floor. When Oswald had left the sixth floor he could only descend one staircase, the rear one.

two construction workers, George Rackley and James Romack, volunteered to help the police by keeping a watch on the rear exit. During the five minutes they were there, before they were replaced by police units, no one left from that exit.[4] The building's front was not covered for at least ten minutes, and possibly longer.[5]

On his way past the second-floor offices, Oswald ran into another Depository worker, Mrs. Robert Reid. She had panicked after the shots and ran into the building to her office. In her own reconstruction of her actions after the assassination, Reid returned to the office area in just under two minutes, which would dovetail perfectly with Baker and Truly's encounter with Oswald thirty seconds earlier. She saw Oswald just after he left the lunch room where Officer Baker had confronted him, and he was walking toward the front stairs.[6] "I met him by the time I passed my desk several feet," she recalled, "and I told him, 'Oh, the President has been shot, but maybe they didn't hit him.' He mumbled something to me, I kept walking, he did, too. I didn't pay any attention to what he said . . ."[7] Reid noticed the full bottle of Coke, and thought Oswald seemed calm. Although she considered it "a little strange" that he should be wandering in the second-floor offices just moments after the assassination, she soon forgot about him.

He was outside the Depository less than three minutes after he fired the final shot, and for the first time he saw the pandemonium he had created. His actions after that are unquestionably those of someone in flight. After his arrest, he maintained that when he learned of the shooting, his immediate thought was there would be no more work for the day, so he simply went home. Although politics was his favorite subject, he was not interested, apparently, in whether the President had been hit or if the assassin had been caught. Instead, he headed for his rooming house.

Oswald could have taken either of two buses, one that would drop him off right at his address, the Beckley line, or one that would let him off several blocks away, the Marsalis line. Both buses had stops near the Book Depository, but neither was in sight when he stepped outside. Waiting for a bus at Dealey Plaza was too risky, so he began walking east on Elm Street, away from the Depository, to find a bus.* Near the corner of St. Paul and Elm, a Marsalis bus pulled up. The Beckley bus was not in view.[8] The driver, Cecil McWatters, remembered Oswald because he pounded on the door in the middle of the block in order to board. There were only five other passengers. In a remarkable coincidence, one of the five was Mary Bledsoe, the landlady who had rented a room to him for one week and then refused to allow him to stay further. She was sitting in the right front seat when he boarded. "Oswald got on," she recalled. "He looks like a maniac. His sleeve was out here [indicating]. His shirt was undone . . . he was dirty . . . he looked so bad in his face, his face was so distorted."[9]

Bledsoe looked away because she did not want to make eye contact or speak with him. Just after he boarded, the traffic became heavy, and the number of incoming sirens increased. A couple of minutes passed. The traffic came to a standstill. The driver of the car in front of the bus got out and walked back to inform McWatters that the reason for the delay was that "the President has been shot."[10] He said it loud enough for all on the bus to hear.[11] At that announcement, Oswald stood up, asked for a transfer, and got off the bus.†

Two blocks away, at the Greyhound bus station, taxi driver William Whaley was waiting for his next fare when Oswald approached.

"May I have the cab?" Oswald asked.

"You sure can. Get in."[12]‡

---

*Some thought it peculiar that Oswald walked away from the Depository only to get onto a bus that would come back past the Depository. But Oswald had little choice, since to catch the bus beyond the Depository he would have had to walk a longer distance and through Dealey Plaza.

† The transfer was found on him after his arrest. Every Dallas bus driver has a distinctive paper punch that marks the approximate time of issuance. As a result, after retrieving the transfer, the police quickly knew not only the bus driver but also the time Oswald had taken the bus.

‡ Oswald later admitted it was the first time he had ever taken a taxi. Such an extraordinary departure from normal routine also indicates he was in flight. Before the taxi left the station, an elderly woman approached and asked Whaley to call her another cab. Oswald offered her that cab, apparently in the belief that it would be easier for him just to take another one than to wait for Whaley to help the woman. At the last moment, she must have decided it was also easier just to find another taxi, and she left the cab to Oswald.

Oswald told him to go to 500 North Beckley, which was several blocks away from his rooming house. "The police cars, the sirens was going, running crisscrossing everywhere," recalled Whaley, "just a big uproar in that end of town and I said, 'What the hell. I wonder what the hell is the uproar?' And he never said anything. So . . . I never said anything more to him."

At Oswald's direction, Whaley dropped him off in the 700 block of North Beckley, a walk of five minutes to his rooming house. Around 1:00 P.M., Earlene Roberts, the housekeeper at 1026 North Beckley, was trying to adjust the reception on the television after a neighbor told her the President had been shot. "I couldn't get the picture and he come in and I just looked up and I said, 'Oh, you are in a hurry.' He never said a thing, not nothing."[13] Roberts said he was "walking pretty fast—he was all but running" into his room.[14] Though it was too warm for a jacket, he took one to hide the revolver he had tucked into the waistband of his pants. He zipped the jacket as he rushed out of the house a couple of minutes later.*

While Oswald made good his escape, law enforcement swarmed into Dealey Plaza. Outside the Depository, some witnesses later claimed they ran into Secret Service agents. Since there were no Secret Service agents at Dealey until 1:00 P.M., when Forrest Sorrels returned from Parkland Hospital, could that mean that somebody was impersonating Secret Service agents, indicating a conspiracy? Most of the witnesses later admitted they were mistaken.[15] And immediately after the assassi-

---

* Conspiracy critics often cite the Warren Commission testimony of Earlene Roberts that she heard a car honk while Oswald was inside the house. When she looked outside, she said she saw a police car. Although she did house cleaning for several police officers, she did not recognize the car, and critics charge the unidentified car was passing a prearranged signal to Oswald. But her account is false. Journalist Hugh Aynesworth interviewed Roberts four times, once on the afternoon of the assassination, and three times during the subsequent few months. In the first two interviews Roberts did not tell of any incident with a police car. Aynesworth says that during the last two interviews she "changed her story dramatically," recalling different numbers on the supposed police car each time she was questioned. "She could not have seen out to the curb where she claimed the police car had been," says Aynesworth. "[Although] she had terrible eyesight, she told me specifically that nobody was out there when he [Oswald] ran out." Dallas police records show no car was in her neighborhood at the time she described.

nation, different groups of law enforcement officials (most of them having been there to watch the motorcade from nearby government buildings) spread out in Dealey—they included Alcohol, Tobacco and Firearms (ATF) agents, postal inspectors, officers from the Special Service Bureau of the Dallas Police, county sheriffs, IRS agents, and even an Army Intelligence agent.*

Initially, the police had searched the empty cars in the lot behind the grassy knoll, but they found no evidence of a shooter.[16] Soon, eyewitnesses led the police to focus on the Depository. By 12:45, the building was sealed and a floor-to-floor search had begun.

At 1:12, almost forty-five minutes after the assassination, deputy sheriff Luke Mooney squeezed between two tall stacks of boxes on the sixth floor. "I had to turn myself sideways to get in there—that is when I saw the expended shells and the boxes that were stacked up, looked to be a rest for the weapon. . . . There was a very slight crease in the box, where the rifle could have lain—at the same angle that the shots were fired from."[17] Mooney looked out the window and yelled for Sheriff Decker and Captain Will Fritz of homicide. Lt. Carl Day, chief of the Dallas Police crime scene search unit, photographed the three bullet shells in their original position.[18] Then he dusted them at the scene for fingerprints, but found none.† "That's routine," says Day. "You can handle them and still not leave a mark."[19]

---

* The author has reviewed the 1963 badges for the above organizations, and found that several look alike. Any of those law enforcement officials could have been confused with Secret Service agents. Oswald's mistaken identification of newsman Robert MacNeil as a Secret Service agent shows the tendency in that pandemonium to judge any plainclothes "official" as Secret Service (HSCA Rpt. pp. 183–84; WC Vol. IV, p. 165; WC Vol. VI, p. 312; WC Vol. VII, p. 19; WC Vol. VII, p. 347; Interview with McDermott, March 7, 1992).

† Some claim the shells were neatly arranged in a row by the window ledge, implying they may have been planted. But the photographs and Mooney's testimony indicate the shells were found in a random pattern. FBI tests showed that Oswald's rifle ejected shells at an angle that would have struck the stacked boxes, making their landing pattern unpredictable (WC Vol. III, pp. 401–2). Another shell is indented on the rim, raising doubts that it could have been fired from a rifle in that condition. In experiments by the House Select Committee, rapid firing of the Carcano resulted in some shells being indented in the exact location upon ejection (HSCA Vol. I, pp. 435, 454, 534).

The three empty shells were turned over to the FBI the next day. Ballistics tests later determined they were fired from Oswald's rifle, to the exclusion of any other gun.[20]

Day also dusted the windowsills in the sniper's nest. "All the woodwork there was cracking and had a bad paint job," he recalls. "You can just tell sometimes that a surface won't have a print. There were none. You couldn't put a print on there if you tried."[21] But he had more success with the boxes that comprised the sniper's nest. He expected to find many prints on them. "These things were being moved around all the time, so I thought we might get the shooter's prints mixed in with the workers' in the building," Day told the author. "But there was one print that I knew was fresh and important the moment it came up. At the window the assassin fired from, there were two stacked boxes, one on the floor and the other stacked on top, and that is apparently what he aimed from. A little behind that was a carton of books. That position is where he would have sat and looked out the window. It was plenty heavy enough to support him. When we used metallic powder on that box, toward the top of the corner, was a distinct palm print—right where it looked like he had been leaning his hand as he waited for the motorcade. He might have been a little nervous, because as he leaned his hand there, the oil or moisture in his hand left a very clear, unsmudged print. Usually, you can't get a print that good from cardboard, but he had been sitting there long enough to leave a real fine one. We knew we had a real good print, but we didn't know whether we would match it up to anyone."[22] That print was positively identified as Oswald's left palm.[23]

There was another identifiable Oswald palm print and one from his right index finger on the boxes in that area.[24] However, Day considers the other Oswald prints on the boxes less important. "He could have gotten those while moving the boxes around during his job," he says. "But the palm print was different. It wasn't at a place you would grab if you were moving it, it was real fresh, and it was just in the right spot if you had been sitting on top of that box looking out the window."[25]

Ten minutes after the shells were found, Deputy Sheriff Eugene Boone and Deputy Constable Seymour Weitzman were near the northwest corner of the sixth floor when they spotted the rifle, hidden between boxes only three feet from the rear stairwell.[26] No one touched it until Lt. Day arrived. Day could immediately estimate the chances for recovery of prints, and it was poor. "I looked down between the boxes and saw the rifle had a well-worn leather strap. I knew there could be no finger-prints on that strap, so I picked the gun up by that. The stock was pretty porous and weather-worn, so there was little chance of any prints there. Before pulling the bolt back, I satisfied my-self there were no prints on the little metal lever. Then I held the gun while Captain Fritz pulled the bolt, and a live round fell out. There were no more shells in the magazine."[27]*

Before Day left the Depository, a homemade brown paper sack, with a three-inch-wide strip of tape around the right cor-ner, was found in the rear of the sniper's nest. Because of its shape, Day immediately thought it might be the bag used to carry the rifle.[28] Although he did not find prints on it when he dusted it with metallic powder, the FBI later subjected it to sil-ver nitrate and discovered Oswald's fingerprint and palm print, the only ones on the bag.[29] Most important, the palm print was of Oswald's right hand and was near the bottom of the bag, which concurred with how Buell Frazier and his sister, Linnie Mae Randle, testified he carried the package.[30]†

---

*Seymour Weitzman and Luke Mooney, two Dallas policemen, thought at first glance that the rifle was a 7.65 bolt-action Mauser. Although the officers quickly admitted their mistake, that initial misidentification led to speculation that a different gun was found on the sixth floor and that Oswald's Carcano was later swapped for the murder weapon. There are considerable similarities between a bolt-action Mauser and a Carcano. Firearms experts say they are easy to confuse without a proper exam (HSCA Vol. I, pp. 446–47; HSCA Vol. VII, p. 372.) Yet Mark Lane devoted an entire chapter trying to portray a simple mistake as evidence of conspiracy (*Rush to Judgment*, pp. 95–101). Robert Sam Anson wrote that the scope was set for a left-handed person (*They've Killed the President*, p.76). There is no such thing as a left-handed scope, and tests determined that the very slight misalignment on Oswald's scope may actually have aided him in hitting Kennedy (WC Vol. III, p. 411; HSCA Vol. VII, pp. 371–72). Sylvia Meagher charged that the Carcano had a "hair trigger," which would have hurt Oswald's marksmanship (*Accessories*, p. 102). But the Carcano required three pounds of pull, whereas a hair trigger requires less than sixteen ounces (HSCA Vol. VII, p. 371).

† While fibers discovered in the bag matched those in the blanket with which Oswald kept his rifle wrapped in the Paines' garage, they were too common to be linked exclusively to that blanket (WC Vol. IV, p. 81). The paper

Initially, Day and others thought the soda bottle and chicken remains left by Bonnie Ray Williams might have belonged to the assassin. Day took this physical evidence back to his crime-scene laboratory. Not everything was available that day—Oswald's clipboard was not found on the sixth floor, near the stairwell, until December 2. The three orders attached to the clipboard were all dated November 22, the day of the assassination.[31]

By the time Day left for the lab, the police, with Roy Truly, had gathered every one of the Depository's employees on the first floor. The only one not accounted for was Lee Oswald. The police were not sure whether the assassin merely used the Depository or whether he was an employee. As a result, while they searched there, they also continued to look around Dealey Plaza. Over an hour after the assassination, three men were found inside a railway car several blocks away. They were photographed as they were taken into custody. Later dubbed "the three tramps," they became a mainstay of conspiracy speculation. It was suspicious the police did not take their names, and the men seemed too well dressed to be hoboes. Over the years, everything from computer enhancements to anthropological studies were used to find out who they were. Some labeled Watergate burglars Frank Sturgis and E. Howard Hunt as two of the tramps. The tallest one was identified as Charles Harrelson, a convicted contract murderer.[32] Some self-proclaimed adventurers, like Chauncey Holt, have confessed to being one of the tramps, and spun long tales about their purported roles in the assassination. But in February 1992, researchers discovered that Dallas police files released in 1989 showed that three tramps had indeed been booked on November 22, 1963. The records identified the suspects as Harold Doyle, Gus Abrams, and John Gedney. Two of the men, Gedney and Doyle, were still alive, and it turned out they were real tramps who had been to the local rescue mission the night before the assassination and were sleeping in the railroad car when the police arrested them.[33] The

---

and tape matched those same items maintained at the School Book Depository (WR, pp. 135–36).

men had no connection to the events at Dealey, and the conspiracy press suddenly and quietly abandoned the issue.

While the hunt for the assassin was under way at Dealey, Oswald had left his rooming house. When Earlene Roberts last saw him, he was at a bus stop across the street. Evidently seeing no buses in sight, he walked further into Oak Cliff. Near 1:15, Dallas patrolman J. D. Tippit, having been ordered to drive into Oak Cliff at 12:45 from his outlying area, saw Oswald walking briskly ahead of him, east along Tenth Street.[34]* The description of the presidential assassin had been broadcast four times within thirty minutes. Tippit, a ten-year veteran, decided to stop Oswald. He pulled his patrol car to the curb behind Oswald and called him over.[35]† Oswald turned around and walked back to the car. He leaned close toward the passenger side, exchanging some words through the open vent window. Whatever he said did not satisfy Tippit, who then got out of the car and started to walk around the front toward Oswald. Tippit did not first call in on his radio that he had stopped someone, nor did he draw his gun upon exiting the car. According to Dallas police procedures, this indicated that he was merely suspicious, but not positive he had found a suspect.[36]

As Tippit reached the front left tire, Oswald whipped out his revolver and began shooting. Tippit was killed instantly. Oswald then began running back toward Patton Avenue, emptying shells from the revolver along the way.‡

---

* What had been Oswald's final destination? While no one can be certain, Warren Commission counsel David Belin had a plausible explanation that was in the draft of the Warren Report but did not make it into the final publication. Oswald had walked nearly one mile before Tippit stopped him. At the time, Oswald, who had taken a transfer from the Marsalis bus, was only four blocks away from catching a route 55 bus, due to arrive at 1:40 P.M. That would have taken him to a point on Lancaster Road where a Greyhound was scheduled to leave at 3:30. The southbound Greyhound would have, with connections, gone to Monterrey, Mexico. While he had left Marina $170, almost all their life savings, he had $13.87 on him when arrested, just enough to pay for the trip to Mexico (draft, Chapter 6 of the Warren Report, August 7, 1964).

† Other Dallas police later reported stopping individuals that fit the general description broadcast about the gunman, just as Tippit did with Oswald. It was not an unusual action on the day of the assassination (WC Vol. VII, p. 37).

‡ Could Oswald have physically been at the Tippit scene by 1:15, the time of the shooting? A reconstruction of the time that elapsed since he left the

Helen Markham, standing on a street corner only half a block away, was on her way to catch a bus when she saw Oswald murder Tippit. After the shots, Oswald trotted back toward her and she began screaming. "When he saw me, he looked at me, stared at me," she recalled. "I put my hands over my face . . ."[37] She was traumatized by the scene and had to be given smelling salts at the police station before she could enter the lineup room.[38] There, she quickly selected Oswald.[39]*

Virginia Davis and her sister-in-law, Barbara Davis, were inside their home on the corner of Tenth and Patton when they heard the shots. They went to the front of the house, opened the door and the screen to see what happened, and saw Oswald

_____

Depository shows it is more than possible. He left Dealey by 12:33. Three reconstructions of walking to the point where he boarded the Marsalis bus averaged six and a half minutes (CE 1987). Bledsoe and the bus driver estimated he was on the bus for three to four minutes before leaving (WC Vol. II, pp. 265, 271). He then took another two minutes before reaching the bus station and Whaley's cab. That was approaching 12:45. Whaley's manifest shows he dropped Oswald off in Oak Cliff at 12:45, but that appears too early, and he admitted it was not an accurate record (WC Vol. II, p. 254). Whaley, who had thirty-seven years of taxi experience, claimed he knew every shortcut in the city. He repeated his taxi ride in five and a half minutes, though he believed traffic was actually heavier on the day of reconstruction than on November 22; otherwise, he could have shaved another half minute from the time (WC Vol. VI, pp. 428–29, 434). That placed Oswald in Oak Cliff no later than 12:51 P.M. To walk from where Whaley dropped Oswald off to the boardinghouse at 1026 North Beckley took a maximum of five minutes and forty-five seconds (WC Vol. VI, p. 434). Those who were timed in the reconstruction followed the streets; no one is sure if Oswald, who knew the area, had a shortcut to his room. In any case, he arrived at the rooming house about 12:55 to 12:56, and left again before 1:00. He had fifteen to seventeen minutes to walk nine tenths of a mile to the scene of the Tippit murder, more than enough time (CE 1119-A, p. 158). Witnesses at the scene estimated the shooting occurred anywhere from 1:07 (WC Vol. III, p. 306) to between 1:30 to 2:00 (WC Vol. VI, p. 461). The best way to judge the time is this: The first call reporting the shooting came in to the police at 1:16, when two witnesses, T. F. Bowley and Domingo Benavides, ran to Tippit's car and called it in over his police radio.

* The critics, trying to exonerate Oswald of the Tippit murder, question the accuracy of the witnesses by highlighting any inconsistencies. They claim Markham, who was excitable and at times hysterical, identified Oswald by his clothing and not his face. But when asked if she picked Oswald out of the lineup because of his clothes or face, she said, "Mostly from his face. . . . I told them I wanted to be sure, and looked at his face, is what I was looking at, mostly is what I looked at, on account of his eyes, the way he looked at me" (WC Vol. III, p. 311).

cutting across the corner of their lawn, pulling and shaking the shells from his gun. Virginia watched Oswald look at Markham, who was yelling and pointing toward him, "and [then he] looked at me and then smiled and went around the corner."[40] Barbara Davis heard Markham's piercing screams: "He shot him. He is dead. Call the police."[41] Virginia and Barbara Davis both picked Oswald that same night from a police lineup.[42]

William Scoggins, a Dallas taxi driver, was eating his lunch in his cab, parked less than half a block away. After he heard the shots, he looked up in time to see Tippit fall, and then hid behind the rear of his taxi as Oswald ran toward him.[43] "He never did look at me," recalled Scoggins. "He looked back over his left shoulder . . . as he went by. . . . I could see his face, his features, everything plain, you see. . . . I heard him mutter something like, 'poor damn cop,' or 'poor dumb cop,' but anyway, he muttered that twice."[44] Scoggins also picked Oswald from a police lineup that night.[45]

Perhaps the closest witness to the shooting was Domingo Benavides, who was driving a pickup truck. He estimated he was only fifteen feet from Tippit's car when the officer was shot.[46] He saw Tippit fall over after the first shots and then watched Oswald leave the scene emptying his gun. "I saw him— I mean really got a good view of the man after the bullets were fired . . ."[47]*

After Oswald cut across the Davises' front yard, he went down Patton Avenue one block to Jefferson Avenue. While briskly moving along Patton, he passed near two used-car lots. There, seven people either came outside or to the windows

---

* Benavides was not taken for a lineup before Oswald was killed on Sunday, November 24. The critics interpret the failure of the police to immediately bring him to a lineup to mean that he "could not identify Oswald as the gunman" (Hurt, p. 145). Sylvia Meagher further adds, "Benavides, the man who had the closest view of the murder, did not identify Oswald . . . even when he was shown a photograph of Oswald months later during his testimony for the Commission." Yet in his Warren Commission testimony, Benavides said he recognized Oswald as the shooter from the photos he saw on television (WC Vol. VI, p. 452). CBS newsman Walter Cronkite later asked him whether there was any doubt that Oswald was the shooter. "No, sir, there is no doubt at all," said Benavides. "I could even tell you how he combed his hair and the clothes he wore and what have you. . . . You don't forget things like that" ("The Warren Report," CBS News, Part III, June 27, 1967).

when they heard the shots. Ted Callaway stepped onto the street in enough time to see Oswald run past taxi driver Scoggins, holding the pistol in his right hand, in "what we used to say in the Marine Corps [was] in a raised pistol position."[48] Oswald's elbow was bent and the pistol was pointed up in the air. "I hollered, 'Hey, man, what the hell is going on?' " said Callaway. "He slowed his pace, almost halted for a minute. And he said something to me, which I could not understand. And then kind of shrugged his shoulders, and kept on going."[49] Callaway ran back in the direction from which Oswald had come, and discovering Tippit had been murdered, he grabbed the officer's revolver and had Scoggins drive him around Oak Cliff, searching for the shooter. They did not find him. That night Callaway, however, saw him again. He identified Oswald in a police lineup —"When he came out, I knew him."[50] Sam Guinyard, another worker at the same car lot, picked Oswald from a lineup that same day.[51]

Warren Reynolds was on the far side of Jefferson Avenue in a car lot he owned and had an excellent view from the porch of his office. When he looked outside after hearing shots fired, "I saw this man coming down the street with the gun in his hand, swinging it just like he was running," said Reynolds. "He turned the corner of Patton and Jefferson, going west, and put the gun in his pants and took off, walking."[52] After watching Oswald cut through a gas station, Reynolds futilely searched the parked cars in the rear of the station to see whether he had hidden under any of them.[53] Reynolds had "no question" the man he saw was Oswald.[54]*

Others who saw Oswald flee the Tippit scene, such as William Arthur Smith and B. M. Patterson, positively identified him from photographs.[55] Jack R. Tatum was driving through the intersec-

---

* Reynolds was shot in the temple by an intruder on January 23, 1964, two days after he first spoke to the FBI. He fully recovered and testified to the Warren Commission six months later. The police suspected the perpetrator was actually a Reynolds acquaintance and rival, Darrell Garner. Some critics suggest that the shooting was connected to the Kennedy case, but no one has given a good explanation for why Reynolds was singled out when more than ten other witnesses who saw and testified to the same thing as he did were left unharmed.

tion of Patton and East Tenth Street when the shooting took place. Although he had a "very good look" at the killer, and had "no question whatsoever" that it was Oswald (he later saw him on television), he did not make himself available to the Dallas Police. Tatum told his story for the first time to investigators for the House Select Committee on Assassinations.[56] A high-ranking Dallas police official who was a member of the force in 1963 told the author there was another witness who had positively identified Oswald as the shooter but was never publicly identified. Evidently, the man was married and had been at a house in Oak Cliff visiting his mistress for an afternoon tryst. When he heard the shots, he pulled aside the curtains and got, according to the policeman, "a good, long look at the killer." Although he had no doubt about his identification, the police decided not to use him since they thought they had enough other solid eyewitness evidence of the murder, and the man pleaded that they not involve him, to avoid embarrassing publicity.*

Beyond the eyewitnesses, Oswald left other telling evidence at the scene. Dashing through the gas station across from Reynolds's car lot, he dropped his light-beige jacket. It was retrieved by Captain W. R. Westbrook, under the rear of one of the parked cars.[57] Earlene Roberts saw him put on a jacket when he left the rooming house around 1:00 P.M. All of the Tippit murder eyewitnesses described the shooter with a jacket, and when arrested before 2:00, Oswald had no jacket. As is typical with eyewitness testimony, though all who were asked identified the jacket when it was shown to them during their Warren Commission testimony, each remembered it slightly differently. Markham, Scoggins, and Barbara Davis thought the jacket (Warren Commission exhibit 162) was a little too light.[58] Callaway thought it needed more tan.[59] William Smith, Virginia Davis, Benavides, and Guin-

---

* Those who believe in a conspiracy have searched for conflicting witnesses in the neighborhood, such as cleaning woman Acquilla Clemons, who claimed there was a second man, or even that a car was used in Oswald's escape. Such statements, usually made years after the shooting, have internal inconsistencies which are so great that some of the witnesses must be questioned for their truthfulness in saying they were even in the neighborhood on that day. There is no credible eyewitness testimony that undercuts the evidence that Oswald was the shooter.

yard said the Commission exhibit was exactly like the one they saw in the rear of the gas station.[60] However, the critical testimony came from Marina Oswald. She said her husband only owned two jackets. His dark-blue one was found at the School Book Depository, and she identified the jacket found in the gas station as the other one.[61] She even thought he had worn it to the Paines' house the night before the assassination.[62]*

Oswald also left behind critical ballistics evidence. Benavides and Virginia and Barbara Davis found four shells that Oswald had emptied from his gun while escaping.[63] These shells were matched, to the exclusion of any other gun, to Oswald's revolver, which he had with him when captured just blocks away.[64] His pistol was a .38 caliber, rechambered, by the company he purchased it from, to handle .38 special ammunition, a better bullet than .38 regular ammo. However, that presented unique problems to the ballistics experts when they tried to match the four slugs recovered from Tippit's body. According to ballistics expert Joseph Nicol, "This means that the bullet, instead of touching on all surfaces as it goes down the barrel, actually wobbles a little bit. As a consequence, it is difficult to have it strike the same places every time that it goes through the barrel, so that the match on the projectiles was extremely difficult."[65] On three of the bullets, the best the experts could conclude was that the bullets had the same characteristics as Oswald's revolver, but they could not isolate them only to that gun.[66] However, a fourth bullet had enough unique characteristics that it was matched to his revolver to the exclusion of all others.[67]†

---

* The jacket had a laundry mark on it, and though Marina could not remember Lee ever having his clothes dry-cleaned, she had no doubt it was his. The FBI was unable to find a local dry cleaner that used that mark, raising the possibility that Oswald had purchased the jacket secondhand, with the laundry mark already in it from another city.

† Of the recovered shells, two were manufactured by Winchester-Western and two by Remington-Peters. Of the four bullets removed from Tippit during the autopsy, three were Winchester-Western and only one was Remington-Peters. That indicated that Oswald likely fired five shots and one missed Tippit, leaving an undiscovered Remington-Peters bullet and a Winchester-Western shell. Eddie Kinsley, an ambulance attendant who took Tippit to the hospital, said that upon unloading the body, he kicked a loose bullet, which had evidently struck a button on Tippit's uniform, onto the parking lot. The witnesses

Critics are understandably anxious to deflect attention from the eyewitness, ballistics, and physical evidence in the Tippit murder. They instead delve into Tippit's personal life and charge he was having an affair with a married woman and insinuate the murder was connected to that. Henry Hurt writes, "Was Tippit a player in a plot that called for him to execute Oswald? Was Tippit's job thwarted when Oswald turned the tables and killed him first? Was Tippit to play a role in the Oswald getaway, only to change his mind at the last minute? Was Tippit a pawn in a plot, and was he supposed to be killed after he killed Oswald? Did Tippit have complex personal problems that might have led to his murder by someone completely unrelated to the assassination case?"[68] Others, like John Davis, in his book about a mafia conspiracy to kill JFK, deal with the Tippit murder in only a single sentence in an almost seven-hundred-page book: "Eight minutes later, Dallas Police Officer J. D. Tippit, who was ordered to patrol the area Oswald was now in, was shot dead by someone, perhaps by Oswald, perhaps by someone else."[69]

The Tippit murder is key to understanding Oswald's depth of desperation and recklessness after the Kennedy assassination. The confrontation with Tippit also led indirectly to his arrest. After running through the gas station, he headed west on Jefferson Avenue. Within a few minutes, police squad cars were speeding east on Jefferson toward the site of the Tippit murder. Oswald heard the sirens and ducked into the foyer of Hardy's Shoe Store. Johnny Calvin Brewer, the store's manager, was lis-

---

disagreed over the number of shots (much the same as at Dealey Plaza). Virginia and Barbara Davis heard only two shots, but they were inside their house during the shooting (WC Vol. III, p. 342; WC Vol. VI, p. 456); Guinyard, Markham, and Benavides heard three (WC Vol. III, p. 308; WC Vol. VI, p. 447, WC Vol. VII, p. 396); Scoggins and Tatum said there were four, Reynolds said four to six, and Callaway heard five (WC Vol. III, pp. 325, 352; WC Vol. XI, p. 435; London Weekend Television, testimony of Jack Tatum). Two other ear-witnesses, Jimmy Earl Burt and William Smith, were around the corner from the shooting and each heard six shots (FBI file #100–16601, memo November 16, 1991). When Oswald was arrested he had six bullets in his revolver and five loose ones in his pocket. Eight were Winchester-Western and three were Remington-Peters (WC Vol. III, p. 459).

tening to radio reports about JFK's death when he "looked up and saw the man enter the lobby."[70] It was fifteen feet from the sidewalk to the store's front door, and Oswald came inside the shielded area and turned his back toward the street. Brewer looked at him because "his hair was sort of messed up and [he] looked like [he] had been running, and he looked scared, and he looked funny. . . . He was standing there staring."[71] After the police cars passed, Brewer watched Oswald walk outside, look over his shoulder toward the disappearing squad cars, and then head further west along Jefferson. Brewer, who thought he "looked suspicious," followed him.

Just over fifty yards from the shoe store, Oswald stopped near the front of the Texas Theater. Julia Postal, the ticket clerk, remembered he came "flying around the corner" and had "a panicked look on his face."[72] She turned away for a moment and he ducked inside the theater, past the concession clerk, William "Butch" Burroughs, who did not see him enter.[73]* Brewer ran to Postal and asked if the man who had just dashed into the theater had bought a ticket. She turned around, expecting to see Oswald, and then realized he had sneaked inside when she was distracted.[74] Brewer quickly checked both exits and found they were still locked, meaning Oswald was in the theater. Brewer tried to spot him inside but could not in the dark.[75] At that point, Postal, who had heard a radio report about the President's assassination, told Brewer, "I don't know if this is the man they want in there, but he is running from them for some reason. I am going to call the police, and you and Butch go get on each of the exit doors and stay there."[76] When she called the police, the dispatcher wanted to know why she thought it might be the suspect. She described him. "And he said, 'Well, it fits the description,'" recalled Postal, "and I said I hadn't heard the description." Just after 1:45 P.M., over police Channel One, the dis-

---

* Burroughs, who was rejected by the Army because his intelligence score was too low, said in a 1987 interview that Oswald had been in the theater since 1:00 P.M. and had bought popcorn from him. That was before a dozen witnesses saw Oswald kill Tippit, and then Brewer followed him into the theater. When Oswald sneaked into the theater, Brewer and Postal did not even tell Burroughs, because he was too "excitable."

patcher announced: "Have information a suspect just went in the Texas Theater on West Jefferson."[77]*

When the police entered the rear of the theater, they encountered Johnny Brewer, and at first thought he might be the suspect. Realizing quickly he was not, the police turned up the lights and asked Brewer if he could spot the suspect. "And I or two or three other officers walked out on the stage and I pointed him out . . ."[78]†

After the theater scuffle, in which Oswald unsuccessfully tried to shoot another policeman, he was arrested, hustled into a patrol car, and driven back to the downtown jail. The arresting officers took him into the office of Captain Will Fritz, the chief of homicide. When Fritz arrived he walked over to two homicide detectives, Gus Rose and Richard Stovall, and told them to proceed to 2515 Fifth Street in Irving and "pick up a man named Lee Oswald." Officer Gerald Hill, standing nearby, asked "why he wanted him, and he said, 'Well, he was employed down at the Book Depository and he had not been present for a roll call of the employees.' And we said, 'Captain, we will save you a trip . . . because there he sits.' And with that, we relinquished our prisoner to the homicide and robbery bureau . . ."[79]

It was nearly 3:00 when Ruth Paine heard heavy knocking at the front door. "I went to the door," she recalled. Six men were standing on her front porch. "They announced themselves as

---

* Dr. Charles Crenshaw, in *Conspiracy of Silence*, questions why half a dozen police cars responded to the Texas Theater "all to capture a man suspected of entering the theater without paying" (p. 115). However, from Postal's testimony it is clear the police thought they might either have the Presidential assassin or Tippit's murderer in the theater (no one yet knew they were connected). Most critics fail to mention that before rushing the theater, the police had unsuccessfully raided a nearby public library on the mistaken report the suspect was there (WC Vol. III, p. 298; WC Vol. VII, pp. 29, 36–37, 80, 92–93; WC Vol. XI, p. 436; CE 705, WC Vol. XVII, pp. 415–16).

† Robert Sam Anson, in *They've Killed the President*, made the identification of Oswald much more sinister. He wrote that while the police scanned the theater, "a man sitting near the front spoke up quietly. The man the police were looking for, he said, was sitting on the ground floor, in the center, about three rows from the back." After the arrest, Anson says, "the man in the front row who had fingered him rose from his seat, walked outside, and quietly disappeared." Anson never informed the reader that the man he found so suspicious was actually Johnny Calvin Brewer.

from the Sheriff's office and the Dallas Police. . . . I said nothing. I think I just dropped my jaw. And the man in front said by
way of explanation, 'We have Lee Oswald in custody. He is
charged with shooting an officer.' This was the first I had any
idea that Lee might be in trouble with the police or in any way
involved in the day's events."[80]

Ruth and Marina had been watching the local television coverage of the President's visit when an announcer broke in with
the news that shots had been fired at the motorcade. A half hour
later, while Marina was outside hanging up laundry, Ruth told
her the shots had come from the School Book Depository.[81] Marina's "heart went to the bottom," but she did not say anything.[82]
Ruth had no thought that Lee was involved, but instead was
excited that he worked at the same building from which the
shots came, and that he probably could give them a "first-hand"
account of the day's events.[83] But Marina was horrified at the
news, and feared that Lee might be involved. At her first opportunity away from Ruth, she sneaked into the garage and found
the East German blanket in which Oswald kept the rifle
wrapped. When she saw it lying on the floor, she was relieved,
believing the rifle was still inside. She watched television with
Ruth until the announcement came that the President had died.
Ruth walked about the house crying. Marina did not cry but sat
silently on the sofa, still concerned about Lee.[84]

The police did not have a warrant, but Ruth allowed them to
enter the house. Ruth and Marina accompanied one of them into
the garage. "The officer asked me . . . did Lee Oswald have
any weapons or guns," Ruth recalled. "I said no, and translated
the question to Marina, and she said yes; that she had seen a
portion of it [the rifle]—and looked into—she indicated the
blanket roll on the floor."[85] Ruth, who was standing on the blanket, immediately backed away and the policeman picked it up. It
hung limp in his hand. Marina turned ashen. "Then, of course, I
already knew that it was Lee," said Marina.[86]

At the Dallas Police crime lab, Lt. Carl Day had found partial
prints near the trigger guard and at the main barrel of the rifle.
"There were some looping impressions," Day told the author,
and "incidentally, it later turned out that Oswald had looping
impressions as opposed to arches or whorls. But there was not

enough to positiveiy identify them as his."[87] Then Day moved to the wooden stock. "Down toward the end of the stock, there was a print partially developed," he recalls, "and I could see it running back up under the stock. So I lifted the gun out of the stock. When I dusted that print, it developed. I kept looking at it as it did not stand out real good—it wasn't a great print. So I took the tape and lifted that print off as best I could. It lifted off pretty well, considering it was a dim print."[88] That print was of Oswald's right palm.[89]

Day then prepared to take pictures of the stock, using reflected light and time exposures. But before he could finish, he was told the FBI was sending an agent to collect the rifle and to take it to FBI headquarters in Washington for further tests. "So I put the gun back in the stock," Day says. "I had my orders and I didn't do anything else to it. Around 11:30, the FBI came, Agent [Vince] Drain, and I gave him the gun. I told Vince, 'Here's a print right here,' and I pointed to it. I didn't give him that lifted print on the tape. They said give him the gun, and that's what I gave him. The gun had our powder all over it by then, and I know I wouldn't have liked to receive it in that condition once somebody else had started their work on it. It should have stayed with us."[90]

Day had so completely lifted the palm print that the FBI, in its November 24 examination of the rifle, did not find any evidence of it.[91] Although at least five Dallas police crime lab detectives saw the palm print before it was sent to the FBI, the public did not know that Oswald's print had been found on the rifle until Dallas district attorney Henry Wade told a reporter in an evening press conference on November 24.[92] The FBI then examined Day's lifted print and confirmed it was Oswald's when it discovered that irregularities in the lift corresponded exactly with imperfections on the rifle barrel.[93]

The print was important, because it was the first piece of direct physical evidence that placed the rifle in Oswald's hands. But the failure of the FBI to find a print in its initial examination has led to accusations that the Dallas police must have concocted the evidence in order to close the case against Oswald.[94] Oliver Stone, in JFK, created a scene that showed an unidentified man placing the gun into Oswald's dead hand to obtain a print. Such charges are ignorant of the chain of evidence, of how Day maintained the rifle under lock and key from the moment it was found on the sixth floor until it was turned over to the FBI. But to add to the conspiracy grist, FBI agent Drain claimed that Day never told him about the print when he picked up the gun.[95] J. Edgar Hoover was furious that his vaunted FBI laboratory failed to pick up any trace of one of the most critical prints in the case. Federal agents closely questioned Day about how he lifted the print.

"I respect the FBI," says Day. "I know I told him [Drain]. Now, I don't know if he heard me or paid any attention to me or what. I know what happened. People who claim there was a planted print don't know anything about fingerprinting. You can't even place a print on something from a card, and that's all we had on the first night, when I lifted that print. After lifting the palm print, I could still see traces on the stock with my reflective light. I can't guarantee it was still there when it got to the FBI office. They either overlooked it or it wasn't good enough to see by the time that gun arrived there. We found that print doing solid police work, and nothing anybody says can change that fact."[96]

In 1993, R. W. "Rusty" Livingston, a former Dallas detective assigned to the police's Crime Scene Search division, published a book titled *JFK: First Day Evidence.* Livingston's book included significant new evidence, which he had in his personal possession, and which had never been seen by the FBI, the Warren Commission, or the House Select Committee on Assassinations. Some of the most important material was four photographs of the partial fingerprints found on the Mannlicher-Carcano's trigger guard. Since the Livingston photos were different from the ones previously used by investigators for comparison, Public Television's *Frontline* program had several fingerprint experts examine the newly discovered evidence. Captain Jerry Powdrill, of the Monroe, Louisiana, police department, focused on the clearest of Livingston's four photos. Powdrill found three matching points of identity between the trigger guard prints and Oswald's fingerprints (those taken upon his arrest in New Orleans in August 1963). That was not enough for a positive identification, since law enforcement requires between six and ten matching points. A former FBI fingerprint expert studied the Livingston photos and agreed with Powdrill that they were inconclusive. However, the third expert, Vincent Scalice, made a breakthrough using photo enhancements. Scalice, who had been the fingerprint expert for the House Select Committee on Assassinations, made his own photos of the Livingston prints, at different exposures ranging from light to medium to dark. Studying the varying degrees of contrast between the photos, Scalice identified eighteen matching points between the trigger guard prints and Oswald's fingerprint card. "I have no doubt this is a major breakthrough," Scalice told the author. "For the first time we can say that the developed latent prints on the trigger guard are those of Oswald's right middle finger and right ring finger."

13

"He Had a Death Look"

On November 22, Dr. Pepper Jenkins had lunch in the dining room at Parkland Hospital with several people from his anesthesiology department. "We were grousing as we pushed around some fish croquettes on our plate," he told the author, "because it had already been announced that Kennedy would be having roast beef at his luncheon because he had gotten a special dispensation by the Catholic Church to eat meat, and we were stuck with fish."[1] During the lunch, the hospital began paging: "Dr. Shires [chief of surgery]. Stat" [indicating an emergency]. "And they never page the head of the departments, and never page them stat," recalls Jenkins. "Dr. Ron Jones, one of the senior resident surgeons was at our table, got up and answered the phone."[2]

"I knew that Dr. Shires was out of town," Dr. Jones says. "And the operator told me the President had been shot and was on his way to the hospital. It took a second to recover from that news, and then I immediately walked back to our table to tell the others."

"He was visibly upset when he got off the phone," recalls Jenkins. "We were shocked when he came over and told us the President was being brought into Emergency." Dr. Jenkins left to retrieve an anesthesia machine, while the chief nurse, Audrey Bell, went to prepare trauma room one.

The President's limousine screeched into the rear of Parkland, stopping near the Emergency entrance. Governor Connally appeared unconscious in the middle seat, lying across his wife, his shirt and suit jacket heavily stained with blood. Only President Kennedy's torso was visible as Jacqueline cradled his head in her lap. Blood and brain tissue were scattered over the seats. Secret Service agent Clint Hill, who had barely clung on to the rear of the car during the high-speed dash to Parkland, seemed dazed as he slid off the trunk.

"I was an ob-gyn [obstetrics-gynecology] resident," recalls Dr. Bill Midgett, who has never before spoken publicly about that day. "I was in the emergency room nearest the door, and someone was disrupting my ability to take history from one of my patients because they were screaming for a gurney. I had no idea anyone had been shot. Because I could not carry on the conversation with my patient, I drew a stretcher and went out to find what was going on. The limousine was there when I went outside. There were any number of very serious people standing around with submachine guns, and I honestly thought I was not long for this world. I had no idea what was happening. Then one of the Secret Service men grabbed the other end of the carriage and hustled me toward this big black car, and all of sudden Jackie Kennedy sat up and I knew right away there was terrible trouble. Everyone was still in the car, all huddled down inside."[3]

Governor Connally had to be removed before they could reach the President. Connally suddenly became semiconscious as the car stopped and, with a great show of determination, helped himself from the car before collapsing into the arms of hospital attendants. They raced him inside to trauma room two.

"I stayed at the car," recalls Midgett. "Then it was a matter of Mrs. Kennedy letting go of the President. You couldn't see the President's head at this point." Officer H. B. McLain (the subject of the acoustics controversy) walked over to the rear of the car. "She was laying over him," he recalls. "I gently grabbed her by both shoulders, and said, 'Now c'mon, ma'am, c'mon out of the car, and let them take him inside.' And she sat up and let go of him."[4]

"It was obvious that when she sat up in the car," says Midgett, "she knew that people were there to assist her husband. When I could finally see the President, I thought he was dead. I never saw anyone with a head wound like that, with the amount of brain matter scattered about, that survived. We put the President on the gurney and wheeled him into emergency room one. Mrs. Kennedy would not leave his side. She went in with us as the gurney was rolled into the hospital, walking right beside him, holding his hand. She was absolutely deadpan quiet. One of the nurses offered to clean off her clothing, and she said, 'Absolutely not. I want the world to see what Dallas has done to my husband.' Someone else asked if she wanted to wait outside the emergency room while they worked on her husband, and she said no and went inside with the gurney."[5]

"Everyone claims to be there first," says Dr. Jenkins, "but the only doctor there when I arrived was [Charles] Carrico, and Drs. Baxter and Perry arrived shortly after me. Mrs. Kennedy was also there."[6] The President was on the stretcher on his back, unconscious. He was blue-white, had fixed, dilated pupils and slow, spasmodic breathing. There was initially no pulse. "He had a death look," recalls Jenkins. "He was on the way out."

Two nurses, Diana Bowron and Margaret Henchliffe, cut away the President's clothes and his back brace, which was wrapped with Ace bandages about his waist and thighs.[7]* The doctors immediately noticed an external wound, a small wound in the neck almost directly under the Adam's apple.[8] Dr. Carrico placed his hands under the President's back and felt for any other major wound. He did not find any. He missed the small bullet entrance in JFK's upper shoulder/neck. Nobody at Parkland ever turned him over.

Dr. Carrico inserted a breathing tube into the President's mouth and down his throat, and an automatic respirator was

---

* Examination of JFK's clothes later confirmed that the bullet that struck him in the shoulder/neck came from the rear. The back of his suit jacket had a bullet hole that pushed the threads inward, indicating the entrance point (WC Vol. V, p. 59). The size of the hole corresponded to a 6.5mm bullet. Spectrographic tests showed residues of copper at the edges of the jacket's hole, the same metal that jacketed Oswald's ammunition. JFK's shirt also had one hole in the rear, with the threads pushed in as well (WC Vol. V, p. 60). The front of the shirt had nicks near the collar, with the threads pushed out, confirming an exit (WC Vol. V, p. 61). There was also a nick in his silk tie, near the knot, and because of the thread pattern, it is further evidence the bullet exited at the President's neck (WC Vol. V, p. 62).

hooked up to the tube. Three cutdowns (slicing open the skin to find a vein) were done to give blood and fluids. As for the large wound in the head, Dr. Jenkins believes that few initially saw it. Jenkins had taken the traditional anesthesiologist position at the head of the table. "I was almost standing against his head," he recalls. "And as the room filled up with more people coming in, I knew then, and I know now, that most of them did not even know he had a head injury. He had a shock of hair, a big shock of hair, and he was lying with his head back against me, and by this time we had the EKG [electrocardiogram] hooked up to him, and it showed a dying heart pattern. People only knew that he had been shot, but they didn't know exactly where, and since there was a lot of blood, it was difficult to tell where it was coming from."[9] Dr. Jones's account is typical: "When I came in, I did not know there was a head wound," he says. "I just saw the neck, and was not aware there was a head wound for several minutes."[10]

Dr. Malcolm Perry started a tracheotomy, an operation in which an artificial airway is created by cutting into the throat and inserting a tube directly into the windpipe. "When Dr. Carrico was trying to get the endotracheal tube in, he saw blood in the trachea," Dr. Perry recalls. "So I did what I had done hundreds of times before, I put the tracheostomy right where the tracheal wound was. I had to control the airway, and if I did not put the tube at the point of entry, it would not work as well." That surgical procedure cut directly over the exit wound on the throat, and therefore, within minutes of the President's arrival, that wound was obliterated by Dr. Perry's larger incision.

Drs. Baxter, Peters, and McClelland inserted a tube into the chest cavity to drain any blood or fluid. "I made an incision in the chest and put a tube in the right side," recalls Dr. Paul Peters, "and someone put one in the left. Ron Jones did a cutdown on the left ankle. And there was some admiral behind me and he said, 'Get him some steroids.' "[11]* Dr. Carrico set an intravenous

---

*The admiral was George Burkley, the President's personal physician, who had been in the motorcade and arrived at Parkland several minutes after the President was wheeled inside the trauma unit. JFK needed steroids because of a deficiency in his natural production. Although it was a well-kept secret at the time, the President suffered from Addison's disease, a rare illness named after

solution of 300 milligrams of Solu-Cortef, a cortisone-based steroid.

"As soon as we got the tracheostomy in," says Dr. Charles Baxter, "his pulse, which we had gotten to an erratic level near 100, started to decline. I glanced at his face and his eyes were so bulged out, there was so much hemorrhaging, that it was a little hard to recognize him as the President."[12]

The room was soon packed. "A lot of people came in, looked, and then went out," recalls Dr. Perry, "and others came in and were asked to leave because it was so busy."[13] Clint Hill, the Secret Service agent, walked around the room "wild-eyed and disoriented," holding a cocked pistol.[14] Another agent eventually came to take him outside. Jackie Kennedy continued to stand on the side, staring blankly at the frantic activities to revive her husband. Several times, a nurse or Secret Service agent led her outside, suggesting it was better if she did not remain in the trauma room. On one occasion when she was out of the operating room, Lady Bird Johnson walked around a bend in a corridor, and "suddenly I found myself face to face with Jackie in a small hall. . . . You always think of her . . . as being insulated, protected; she was quite alone. I don't think I ever saw anyone so much alone in my life. I went up to her, put my arms around her, and said something to her . . . like 'God, help us all,' because my feelings for her were too tumultuous to put into words."[15]

But Jackie always returned to the emergency room. "That did quiet down the whole atmosphere," recalls Dr. Jones. "You weren't sure you wanted to do everything you had to in front of her. Once you did it, you weren't sure you should be standing there gazing."[16] "She would stand there with that look she had," says Jenkins. "Then she would walk around with her hands clasped tightly in front of her. And on one of her trips back into the room, she nudged me with her elbow. The table wasn't completely occupied at that time. And she handed me part of his

the English physician who discovered it. That disease slowly destroys the cortex of the adrenal glands, and while it is usually fatal, cortical hormones alleviate many of the symptoms. The President, in shock from the wounds, was in desperate need of the hormones since his adrenal glands were incapable of producing any.

brain—no bone, just tissue. So I handed it to a nurse. I don't think Mrs. Kennedy would have any memory for the whole thing."

The activity in the emergency room was frenetic.* Parkland had the best trauma unit in Dallas, and if the President had any chance of being resuscitated, it was there. "When we were working on Kennedy, he was not the President," recalls Dr. Adolph Giesecke. "He was another life that we were trying our hardest to save. When we were in that room, we were doctors doing what we were trained for, but later we were just regular citizens and the enormity of it hit us."[17]

Despite their efforts, the President still showed only an erratic pulse. Dr. Perry started closed-chest massage. The doctors spoke about cutting open the President's chest and massaging the heart muscle. Dr. Jenkins, standing at the head of the table, noticed a priest, Father Oscar Huber, had appeared at the room's swinging doors. "I asked one of my assistants to take over the breathing apparatus, and I went over to the priest," he says. "I asked him, 'When is the proper time to declare one dead for the last rites?' And I remember him saying, and I doubt it meets Catholic doctrine, 'Well, if we can perform the last rites within an hour or so of the death, it's all right.' And I returned to the head of the table and said to the others, 'I think you better look at this first,' pointing toward the President's head. 'We have no way of resuscitating him. I think it's time to declare him dead.' " Dr. Kemp Clark, the only neurosurgeon in the room, put on a pair of gloves and quickly inspected the head wound. "That was the first time anyone looked at it," says Jenkins.[18]

It took Dr. Clark only a moment to decide the wound was too massive. Dr. Perry was still doing a vigorous chest massage. "It's too late, Mac," Clark said.[19] "The President's pulse had gone from twenty to ten to zero," remembers Baxter, "and Malcolm still pumped on his chest, and I said, 'No, Malcolm, we are through.' Somebody was poised with a knife ready to do open-chest massage, and I almost laid across his chest and said no.

---

* Dr. Malcolm Perry says, "There must be three hundred people who claim they were in there that day, and there's no way that could be true. It's interesting that most of those of us who were intimately involved don't talk about it, and the others do."

There was no way the President could survive no matter what we did."[20] The doctors had worked futilely for more than twenty minutes.

"And I said," recalls Dr. Peters, " 'I think we need to find Mrs. Kennedy,' and someone nudged me and signaled with their head behind me, and I turned and she was right there." Dr. Baxter, the chief of the emergency room, walked over to Jacqueline, and quietly said, " 'Mrs. Kennedy, your husband is dead. We will not pronounce him dead until he has had the last rites.' She had a look in her eyes, on her face, of terror, disbelief, and bewilderment. She was deadpan, with all those emotions in her eyes. It was like this really isn't happening. I could understand every emotion she was going through."[21]

"When we decided to declare him dead," says Jenkins, "people just started to fade away. They just disappeared from the room. Out of respect, no one wanted to stay after that point. With Mrs. Kennedy there, we were not about to start examining the wounds or turning the body over. No one even lifted the head, although a few doctors passed by and quickly looked at the wound."[22] Dr. Baxter agreed: "What happened once we knew we lost him—we were gone. Everyone backed off from that body with the reverence, with the grief, with all the emotions you could imagine. When I had gone into that room, I was emotional. When taking care of him, I was a doctor. As soon as it was over, I was filled with emotions, and I never touched him again, except to pull a sheet over him."[23]

As the room emptied, Dr. Baxter walked over to the President with Mrs. Kennedy. "She kissed his toe, his stomach, his lips, and then slipped off a ring and put it on his little finger," he recalls. "Then she began crying. It was heart-wrenching."[24] Father Oscar Huber entered a minute later. "I stayed because I had to take out the tracheostomy," Jenkins says, "take off the EKG leads we had, take out the IV's and the other apparatus. I wanted to leave, too, but I couldn't get out of the room because I was hemmed in by the priest and Mrs. Kennedy. When the last rites were being performed, I wish I had been elsewhere. Mrs. Kennedy looked just ghastly, pale, with blood all over her dress —it was a terribly personal moment."[25]

Ken O'Donnell, one of the President's aides, tried to persuade

Jacqueline to step outside after the last rites, but she refused to leave her husband's side. She remained while some nurses and residents wrapped the President in white sheets, a plastic mattress cover, and some pillowcases, and awaited the arrival of the casket.[26]

The attending doctors had decided to fix the time of death as 1:00 P.M. and, since the cause of death was the massive head wound, decided that Dr. Clark, a neurosurgeon, should sign the death certificate. Mac Kilduff, a Kennedy aide, went to a side room, where Vice-President Johnson was under heavy Secret Service guard. "Mr. President," he said, and by so addressing LBJ notified him that Kennedy was dead. He informed Johnson that he wanted to announce Kennedy's death, but LBJ told him to wait until his party was away from the hospital. No one was sure who had killed the President or if it was a conspiracy that targeted other members of the government. Johnson decided to return to Washington as soon as possible. Once Johnson was in the car on the way to the airport, Kilduff entered Parkland classrooms 101–102, which had been converted into a temporary press hall. It was 1:33 when he mounted the dais, and there were shouts of, "Quiet!" "President John F. Kennedy died at approximately 1:00 Central Standard Time today here in Dallas." There was a tremendous rush into the hospital corridors by newsmen hurrying to get the word over the wire services.

While the drama with President Kennedy unfolded, another life-and-death battle was being waged with Governor John Connally. He had bullet wounds in his right rear shoulder, under his right nipple, right wrist, and his left thigh. Dr. Robert Shaw, a thoracic (chest) surgeon, took over the Governor's care at 12:45. Within forty-five minutes, Dr. Shaw had moved Connally to surgery and for nearly two hours sutured the Governor's damaged lung and muscles.[27]* "His wounds were life-threatening," recalls Dr. Shaw, "and without prompt care he would have died."[28] When Connally was moved from the trauma room to the operating room, he was transferred from the stretcher on which he

---

* On the following day, minor operations were done on both Connally's wrist and thigh.

had been brought into the hospital to an operating table. That empty stretcher was placed into an elevator by an orderly and then moved into a hospital hallway. Darrell Tomlinson, the hospital's senior engineer, later bumped into it, and when he did, a 6.5mm bullet rolled onto the floor.[29]*

The President's body was placed into a casket and ready for transport back to Washington by 1:40, but by then Dallas city officials informed JFK's staff that the body would have to remain in Texas, where the crime had been committed, for an autopsy.[30] But unknown to the Texan authorities, Vice-President Johnson was determined not to leave the state without the President's body. "When Mr. O'Donnell told us to get on the plane," recalled LBJ, "and go back to Washington, I asked about Mrs. Kennedy. O'Donnell told me that Mrs. Kennedy would not leave the hospital without the President's body, and urged again that we go ahead and take Air Force One and return to Washington. I did not want to go and leave Mrs. Kennedy in this situation. I said so, but I agreed we would board the airplane and wait until Mrs. Kennedy and the President's body were brought aboard the plane."[31]

The ensuing argument between the President's staff and Dallas and Parkland officials was heated. Theron Ward, a Dallas justice of the peace, was at the hospital but was weak in asserting Texas law. "He did nothing," recalled Dr. Earl Rose, the Dallas medical examiner. "He was frozen with fear."[32] Some, such as Dr. Charles Crenshaw, claimed that the Secret Service agents drew their weapons and physically forced their way out of the hospital, stealing the bronze coffin from Texas jurisdiction.[33]

---

* There were two stretchers in the hallway he passed through. Tomlinson was not certain from which one the bullet had dropped. But only one was connected to the assassination, as President Kennedy's stretcher was never in that location. Tomlinson admitted he was not paying much attention when he bumped into it (WC Vol. VI, pp. 49, 56, 130). That slightly deformed whole bullet was later determined to have been fired from Oswald's rifle, to the exclusion of all others. Critics have dubbed it the "magic bullet" because the Warren Commission concluded it was responsible for President Kennedy's throat wound and all the wounds to Governor Connally. Yet the bullet had lost only 3 grains of its total weight of 161 grains, and its main deformity was a flattening, but no crushing of the nose or significant fragmenting. It is discussed in detail in Chapter 14.

"Finally, without saying more, I simply stood aside," said Rose. "The law was broken . . . [but] I felt that it was unwise to do anything more to accelerate or exacerbate the tension. There was nothing else I could do to keep the body in Dallas. I had no minions, no armies to enforce the will of the medical examiner."[34]

The federal agents were indeed prepared to force their way out of the hospital with or without authorization. But most do not realize that Dr. Charles Baxter, chief of the emergency rooms, had authorized the body's removal. "At the time that fight was going on between Earl Rose and the Secret Service," Dr. Baxter told the author, "and I got involved in it, my thinking was twofold. One, the President was above state laws. And second, Earl was sort of a sensationalist, somebody always on the fringes, and I did not want him to do that autopsy. Earl was experienced and good, but I am sure he would have missed points that have since come up."[35]

At 2:04, Jacqueline Kennedy, four Secret Service agents, and Brigadier General Godfrey McHugh left in an ambulance for the airport, with the President's coffin.[36] They arrived at Love Field in ten minutes and loaded the casket onto the rear of *Air Force One* at 2:18.[37]* Instead of immediately departing, Lyndon Johnson, after conferring with Attorney General Robert Kennedy, waited for a local judge to swear him in as President. That brief and somber ceremony took place in the front of the plane at 2:37, while a bloodstained Jacqueline Kennedy looked on in shock. After the ceremony, she returned to the rear of the plane, where she stayed with the casket for the remainder of the trip.

David Lifton, in one of the most unusual conspiracy theories, claims in his book *Best Evidence* that "the President's body was inside the Dallas casket when it was put aboard *Air Force One* at 2:18, but it was no longer inside the casket at 2:47, as the plane rolled down the runway."[38] Lifton contends that the President's body was stolen from the casket while on the plane, di-

---

* Four seats had been removed from the back of the narrow Boeing 707 so the casket could be placed inside the main cabin. The casket was slightly damaged when it was removed from the hearse. Later that night, a mahogany replacement coffin was ordered.

rectly under the eyes of Mrs. Kennedy and the President's personal staff. His theory relies on an elaborate shell game involving rapid exchanges of coffins, a decoy ambulance, and a switched body shroud. He contends that once the body was stolen from *Air Force One*, a covert team of surgeons surgically altered the corpse before the autopsy later that day at Bethesda. The alterations were purportedly done so the autopsy physicians would determine the bullets that hit the President were fired from the rear, from the direction of the Book Depository, thereby sealing the case against Oswald.

Lifton does not think *any* shots from the rear hit President Kennedy. Yet since the medical evidence only supports the conclusion that JFK was struck by shots from behind, Lifton tries hard to devise a theory of "medical forgery" to exonerate Oswald. According to Lifton, the covert team not only hid any evidence of front shots but created rear wounds that had the correct trajectory angles to fit with a sixth-floor assassin from the Book Depository. Lifton's theory involves a massive plot of scores of conspirators in the Navy, Secret Service, and LBJ's inner circle, none of whom he identifies. Among other allegations, he uses eyewitness testimony from bit players at Bethesda —orderlies, technicians, and casket carriers—to allege that Kennedy's body arrived there in a body bag, although it had been sent from Dallas in sheets (in other words, the conspirators were sophisticated enough to steal the body but forgot to put it back in the same bag). He asserts the conspirators also made the mistake of forgetting to put the President back in the same bronze coffin, since he claims a simple gray metal one arrived at Bethesda. Even the President's brain was missing, as the conspirators had to hide it, but another one showed up during the autopsy.

Lifton's purported smoking gun is a November 26, 1963, report by two FBI agents, Francis X. O'Neill and James W. Sibert, in which they said that after the President's body was removed for the autopsy, "it was also apparent that a tracheotomy had been performed, as well as surgery of the head area, namely, in the top of the skull."[39] Since no surgery was performed on the President's head at Parkland, Lifton concludes the surgery must have been done between Parkland and

Bethesda. But that remark was an offhand comment by an attending physician at the autopsy and was misconstrued by the two nonmedical FBI men. "We weren't doctors," O'Neill told the author, "and it was either Humes or Boswell, but I just wrote it down as I understood it. There wasn't any surgery on the head, only my misunderstanding of what the doctors were talking about."[40] All of the physicians at Parkland and Bethesda unequivocally reject the notion there was any surgery on the head.

Dr. Michael Baden, the chief forensic pathologist for the House Select Committee on Assassinations, says, "Lifton just doesn't know what he is talking about. It's a fantasy of his. He thinks he sees signs of surgery in some of the autopsy photos, but he doesn't know how to read those pictures. It's laughable. He's not a doctor and it's clear by his work that he doesn't understand what really happened. He doesn't even take into account rigor mortis [the stiffness caused by death], which starts two hours after death. Surgery done on a corpse would look different than one on a living person. His theory of medical alteration to the President is ridiculous."[41] Even forensic pathologist Dr. Cyril Wecht, the most vocal medical critic of the Warren Commission's conclusions, dismisses Lifton out of hand. "Lifton gets away with crap, and no one challenges him. I could assemble a whole team of the best surgeons in the country and still not be able to accomplish in a day what Lifton says was done in a few hours. I have never bought his stuff. It can't be done."[42]

Beyond its medical impossibility, Lifton's entire scenario rests upon the President's casket being unattended on *Air Force One* for a few minutes, so that the body could be stolen. In a seven-hundred-page book, Lifton spends only two pages on this essential issue. Yet the casket was never unattended. Fulfilling the military duty that a high-ranking officer should remain as an honor guard with the body of a slain Commander in Chief until the burial, General Godfrey McHugh stayed with the casket after it was loaded onto the plane.[43] He went to the cockpit to check on the plane's departure only when Mrs. Kennedy or one of the President's aides was in the rear. During LBJ's swearing-in ceremony, while almost everybody was in the front, McHugh remained with the casket.* There was no opportunity for JFK's body to be stolen anytime before the autopsy.[44]†

During the flight from Texas to Washington, Admiral Burkley, JFK's physician, spoke to Mrs. Kennedy about the autopsy. "I stated an autopsy would be necessary, and that I was perfectly willing to arrange to have it done at any place that she felt it should be done. She said, 'Well, it doesn't have to be done.' I said, 'Yes, it's mandatory that we have an autopsy. I can do it at the Army hospital at Walter Reed or at the Navy hospital at

---

* Moreover, stealing JFK's corpse from its Elgin Britannia coffin was not an easy task. The coffin had an air-lock mechanism that, when turned, hermetically sealed the lid on the casket. It was sealed at Parkland. Aboard *Air Force One* it had been strapped to the floor. To get the body out, the conspirators would have had to unstrap the coffin and unscrew the lock, allowing the unit to unseal itself. After removing the President's body, something of similar weight would likely have to be placed inside, so people handling the casket would not notice it was too light. Finally, the casket would have to be resealed and strapped back into its original position before anyone on the plane noticed the unusual activity.

† Lifton spent an obsessive fifteen years working on his assassination thesis. His book *Best Evidence* eventually became a national best-seller in 1980. Lifton's work has always been unusual. During the mid-1960s, he did his own photo enhancements of the shrubbery on the grassy knoll, and concluded that one tree had been artificial on the day of the assassination, in order to camouflage snipers. In his enhancements, Lifton believed he spotted a man wearing a Kaiser Wilhelm helmet, another with an electronic headset, one with a periscope, and another with a machine gun hidden in a hydraulic lift. He thought one of the men resembled General Douglas MacArthur (*The Scavengers*, pp. 172–73).

Despite his prodigious research, some experts still have little respect for his work. According to Professor David Wrone, a historian and assassination researcher, "In 1967, Lifton had a theory of fake trees, that a construction company put in fake scenery and so forth at Dealey Plaza, and then after the shooting, it was removed. He thought it helped the assassins get close for the shooting and also confused the people. . . . Lifton is a beast . . . [does] gross plundering. It's almost as though he is a religious convert, and he is proselytizing for a false religion" (Interview, February 1, 1992). Robert Blakey, the chief counsel for the House Select Committee, says, "Lifton is just bizarre. . . . On a scale of one to ten, his theory is a zero" (Interview, January 22, 1992). Richard Billings, editorial director of the House Select Committee, said the committee was aware of Lifton's theory and "rejected it as illogical, even absurd." Billings called Lifton a "master nit-picker" and said his theory was "a preposterous notion" and "at best, the book is a monument to one man's ingenuity. At worst, it is an appalling hoax" (February 6, 1991, letter, Billings to Pat Sklar of Times Books).

Bethesda or any civilian hospital that you would designate.'
However, I felt that it should be a military hospital, in that he
had been President of the United States and was, therefore, the
Commander in Chief of the Military. After some consideration,
she stated that she would like to have the President taken to
Bethesda [because he had been in the Navy]. This was arranged
by telephone from the plane, and it was accomplished."[45]*

Air Force One touched down at 5:58 Eastern time at Andrews
Air Force Base. Part of the extensive security to meet the plane
included FBI agents Francis O'Neill and James Sibert. "The casket was lowered from the plane, and then placed into the waiting ambulance," recalls O'Neill. The casket they lowered was
the same bronze one that JFK was placed into at Parkland and
which was loaded onto *Air Force One* in Dallas. There was no
sign of the simple gray casket that Lifton charged contained
Kennedy's body on the arrival at Bethesda. "Bobby Kennedy and
Mrs. Kennedy got into the ambulance," O'Neill told the author.
"Kellerman got into the front seat, and Greer was the driver.
Admiral Burkley was there. I was in the second car of the motorcade, and I observed that ambulance the whole time, every
single moment, from the time it left the aircraft to the time that

---

*There are those who believe even the autopsy physicians were part of a
conspiracy. Yet, since Mrs. Kennedy was given the choice of which hospital
she wanted for the procedure, the conspiracy plan would have required teams
of conspirator doctors at both Walter Reed and Bethesda, as well as at key
civilian hospitals in the area. Moreover, the body almost remained in Dallas for
an autopsy, requiring further conspirators in that medical examiner's office.
Lifton actually believes that "President Kennedy's body was never supposed to
have left Dallas unaltered. However, the plotters lost control of the body. The
reason for that loss of control was a major accident: the shooting of Governor
Connally" (*Best Evidence*, p. 703). Again, Lifton bases his theory on an untenable hypothesis: that plotters who were able to arrange for a secret team of
assassins, frame Oswald, and plan an unprecedented medical forgery to cover
up the crime had forgotten to consider that Governor Connally, sitting only 24
inches directly in front of JFK, might be wounded from a bullet or a fragment.
Even if Connally had not been wounded, it is difficult to imagine how any of
the events in Dallas would have been different. Certainly the President would
have been taken to Parkland (the hospital listed as the primary stop in case of
an emergency) and an effort would have been made to save his life. Yet Lifton
gives no indication whatsoever of how the medical deception involving Kennedy's corpse was to be carried out in Dallas.

ambulance opened its door and I assisted in taking the casket inside."[46]

More than three thousand people were crowded onto the hospital grounds, and they surged around the ambulance as it arrived.[47] Sibert and O'Neill helped take the casket inside, and there, waiting for the President's body, were Dr. James Humes and Dr. J. Thornton Boswell. Humes, a thirty-nine-year-old Navy commander, was director of labs of the Naval Medical School in Bethesda. Boswell, also a commander, was forty-one, and chief of pathology at the Navy hospital. Humes had been notified at 5:15, when he was at home, that he should return to the hospital. Canceling a dinner party for twenty-four guests, he rushed to Bethesda, where Admiral Ed Kenney, the Navy's surgeon general, told him "to be prepared to do an autopsy" on JFK.[48] Humes chose Boswell to be his assistant. Although they had performed several autopsies involving gunshots before, they did not have extensive experience with bullet wounds.[49] Humes spoke to Dr. Bruce Smith, the deputy director of the Armed Forces Institute of Pathology, and asked for a pathologist with experience in gunshot deaths. Smith chose Dr. Pierre Finck.[50] An Army colonel, Finck completed the autopsy team. He was a ballistics expert, and although he had reviewed records of U.S. military personnel who had died of gunshot wounds for nearly ten years, he had never done an autopsy involving a gunshot wound. No forensic pathologist was included on the team.*

When the funeral motorcade arrived at the hospital, Robert and Jacqueline Kennedy were escorted to upstairs waiting rooms while the casket was brought to the morgue. There, Drs. Humes and Boswell, with help from FBI agents O'Neill and Sibert and Secret Service agents Kellerman and Greer, removed the body. O'Neill took responsibility for security, ensuring that no

---

* Hospital pathologists such as Humes and Boswell are not trained in the forensic aspect of autopsies or the search for clues in unnatural deaths, nor do they normally preserve evidence for subsequent medical or legal proceedings. Forensic pathologists are not just concerned with what caused the death but also with the circumstances around the death. "In 1963, there was little appreciation for the difference of the two very different types of autopsies available," says Dr. Baden. "There was the usual hospital one, which is what the President received, and there was the forensic one. Most people mistakenly thought a pathologist was a pathologist."

unauthorized personnel entered the area or had access to the body.[51] "It was a shocking experience," recalled Humes. "We found the unclothed body of President John F. Kennedy, wrapped in sheets in a swaddling manner, the massive head wound wrapped around and around with gauze and bandages."[52] "There was also a plastic liner inside," recalls O'Neill, "and because of the massive amount of blood, some of it was stuck onto the body as well."[53]*

Then Humes started the preparatory work for the autopsy, giving the orders for photographs and X rays. Fourteen X rays and fifty-two photographs were taken of the body. The Navy corpsman who started taking pictures did not have a security clearance, and O'Neill confiscated his film and exposed it (the roll is still in the National Archives). There is an oft-repeated story of an FBI photographer, without any prior autopsy experience, who allegedly took the photographs. "Those reports are an incredible lie," said Humes. "The official photos taken by John Stringer [the medical school's chief of photography] were

---

* Technicians Paul O'Connor and Jerrol Custer claimed that the President's body was brought into the rear of the hospital in a simple gray metal coffin and that he was zipped inside a military body bag. James Jenkins, a laboratory technician, said that a plain gray coffin, containing the body of an Air Force officer in a body bag, arrived at Bethesda before JFK's coffin. That may have created confusion among the technicians.

But O'Connor and Custer also allege the President had no brain when he arrived. Custer even asserted that he put both his hands inside the President's head and it was empty. But they were not part of the team that removed the body, although O'Connor arrived later (Humes interview, November 4, 1992). They were both interviewed by the House Select Committee in 1978, and neither mentioned what they now claim to have witnessed. When O'Connor was interviewed by author Harrison Livingstone in 1990, he admitted, "It has been so many years and so much has happened, I kind of doubt my own ability to remember fine details."

The doctors and FBI agents who removed the body are consistent in their descriptions. They noticed the damage on the bronze casket that had been done in Dallas, and without knowing how Parkland had prepared the President for the trip, they correctly described the white sheets, plastic liner, and rubber bags that were used. As for the brain, it was photographed after being removed during the autopsy by Humes and Boswell (Autopsy report). "There was no body bag near the scene," recalls Dr. Humes. "The President most certainly had a brain when he arrived. I don't know how these stories get started. They are absolutely false" (Interview, November 4, 1992).

never touched, and no one from the FBI even had a camera, let alone the intention to take autopsy photos."[54]

The autopsy photographs and X rays are critical because, despite criticism of the procedure, they provide proof positive of the President's wounds, and have served as the basis for subsequent forensics-panel studies. Because they support the conclusion that the President was shot by two bullets from the rear, there have been attempts to cast doubt on their authenticity. Robert Groden and Harrison Livingstone, in *High Treason*, conclude the X rays are fakes and raise doubts about some of the photos.[55] However, they ignore the extensive work of the House Select Committee in examining that very issue.

John Stringer, who took the photographs, viewed them at the National Archives on November 1, 1966, and verified that the pictures were the ones he had taken. (He again confirmed the photographs in 1993.) Photo experts for the Select Committee concluded the photos were authentic, there was no evidence of fakery, and that alteration of such photos, often taken with two or three exposures from the same camera position, is "essentially impossible."[56] As for the X rays, the tests were also absolute. Human bone structure varies uniquely from one individual to another and can be as good a means of identification as fingerprints.[57] Twenty-two earlier X rays of John Kennedy were compared to those taken at Bethesda. The Committee's experts concluded they were not forgeries and "there was absolutely no question . . . [they were] of John F. Kennedy and no other person."[58] Because of certain peculiarities with JFK's bones and teeth, the experts concluded it was impossible to simulate the twenty-two base X rays used for comparison.[59]*

---

* Groden and Livingstone have asserted as part of their ever-widening plot that the conspirators replaced all the earlier X ray films of John Kennedy taken over the years and maintained at different hospitals and private doctors' offices. They charge that while the X rays of the neck and head are forgeries, the conspirators forgot to replace the photographs of the face, which he admits are real. They claim those photos contradict the X rays since the X rays show the right eye and forehead to be missing, and the photos do not. But the X rays do not show any such damage. "Groden doesn't know how to read those X rays," says Dr. Michael Baden.

The reason Groden and Livingstone offer for the decision of the conspirators not to destroy the photographs, which they say are the medical proof of

Once the autopsy began, it took slightly more than three hours. Bethesda was a teaching hospital, and its morgue had an amphitheater filled with almost forty people. Humes recalled that though they were dealing with the President, the autopsy doctors did not allow the crowd to bother them. "The people who accompanied his body to the morgue," recalled Humes, "were the most disturbed and distressed people I have ever seen. We were unfazed by the commotion . . ."[60] The three pathologists found two wounds caused by high-velocity missiles.

There has been considerable criticism of the autopsy team and the examination they performed on JFK. Dr. Cyril Wecht, the Allegheny, Pennsylvania, medical examiner, called it one of the "worst and most botched autopsies ever—the autopsy work was a piece of crap."[61]* Other forensic pathologists are less vociferous, but they do criticize the fact that Jacqueline and Robert Kennedy remained in the hospital during the proceeding and kept asking when it would finish, placing pressure on the physicians to hurry their work.[62] The Kennedys were willing to let the doctors determine the cause of death but not to let them conduct an extensive autopsy. Dr. Michael Baden says that a proper examination of the President "could have taken two or three days, and yet they only spent a few hours on the autopsy and the rest of the time working with the funeral director to put the body together in case Mrs. Kennedy decided to have an open coffin. A lot of things weren't done, such as inspecting the spine, dissecting the neck organs, tracing out the bullet tracks, and inspecting the clothing. They should have shaved the head—it's necessary for proper examination of a head wound—but Humes didn't do it, to save time."[63] (The Kennedy family did not want the wound shaved, since they intended to have an open casket, and only changed their mind at the last moment).[64]†

_____

the plot, is this: "They did not dare destroy all of them for fear of a Presidential or Congressional order asking to see them." In other words, people who were willing to murder the President of the United States were more afraid of the possibility of a future congressional subpoena.

 * The author, as part of the research for this chapter, observed an autopsy performed by Dr. Wecht.

 † There have been suggestions that Humes was under orders to limit the scope of the autopsy, but he insists that is not true. "Nobody made any decision in the morgue except me. Nobody distracted or influenced me in any way,

The findings of the original autopsy physicians have been studied by subsequent panels of leading national forensic specialists. In 1968, a four-member medical panel appointed by attorney general Ramsey Clark concluded the President was struck by two shots from behind, and reaffirmed the original autopsy report. In 1975, the Commission on CIA Activities Within the U.S. (the Rockefeller Commission) reviewed the case, and also confirmed the autopsy results and the Warren Commission conclusions. In the late 1970s, the House Select Committee appointed a nine-member medical panel of experts with vast experience in gunshot wounds. Its members were the first forensic scientists and medical examiners to have complete access to all the photographs and X rays, as well as financial support to conduct the latest scientific tests, including neutron activation and photo enhancements. The Select Committee panel found faults with the autopsy, but confirmed its findings, and held that JFK was struck only by two bullets from behind.

The Neck Wound

The autopsy doctors were unable to figure out the path for the bullet that had entered at the rear base of the President's neck. They could find no exit for that bullet, even conjecturing that it might have penetrated the back for only a few inches and then fallen out during the emergency treatment in Dallas. They did not know there was an exit hole in the front of his neck because they had not examined the President's clothes and did not see the holes made by the exiting bullet through JFK's shirt collar. Moreover, the tracheotomy done by Dr. Perry at Parkland had obliterated the neck wound and it was not until Dr. Humes spoke with Perry over the phone the following day that he realized what had happened.*

---

shape, or form." The House Select Committee concluded that Humes had the authority for a full autopsy but only performed a partial one (HSCA Vol. VII, pp. 9–10, 13–14, 191–92).

* There was also some question as to why the location of the entry wound at the rear base of the President's neck is several inches higher than is indicated by the bullet holes in his suit jacket and shirt. Photographs taken during the

Early statements by some Parkland physicians that the wound in the front of the neck was a wound of entrance led to considerable confusion. Of all the doctors involved in treating the President at Parkland, only five—Carrico, Perry, Jenkins, Jones, and Baxter—saw the front neck wound in its original condition before the tracheotomy was performed.[65]

At a press conference following the announcement of the President's death, Dr. Perry said in response to a question that the throat wound he saw "appeared to be an entrance wound."[66] "As the press is wont to do," says Dr. Perry, "they took my statement at the press conference out of context. I did say it looked like an entrance wound since it was small, but I qualified it by saying that I did not know where the bullets came from. I wish now that I had not speculated. Everyone ignored my qualification. It was a small wound, slightly ragged at the edges, and could have been an exit or entrance. By Sunday, after working on Oswald, I had learned my lesson, and I handed out a written statement to the press and took no questions. I had got a lot smarter in two days."[67]

What of the opinion of the other four Parkland doctors who saw that wound before the tracheotomy? No one at Parkland ever turned the President over, so they did not see the even smaller hole on his back that was in direct line with the one in the throat.*

Dr. Jones told the author, "The neck wound could have been either an entrance or an exit. I only called it an entrance wound because I did not know about the back wound."[68] Drs. Carrico and Baxter also agreed the wound could have been either an entrance or an exit.[69] But the doctor with the most experience with gunshots at Parkland, Dr. Pepper Jenkins, recalls, "Even at that time, I was convinced it was a wound of exit because it was

---

motorcade show the President's jacket was often bunched and riding up his back as a result of his waving to the crowd. His back brace also pushed his clothing up. Therefore, measuring placement of the holes in the clothing is not an accurate means of determining precisely where the bullet entered the body.

* Although no one at Parkland saw JFK's back wound, Dr. Pepper Jenkins later told Dr. John Lattimer that he had felt it with his finger when he positioned the President's head and neck to facilitate the passage of oxygen (*Kennedy and Lincoln*, p. 153).

bigger than an entrance wound should be. Entrance wounds, as you look at them, are small and round, and may have a halo around them, black, from the bullet. But it makes a clean wound. When a bullet goes through the body, tissue moves in front of it and bursts."[70]

Was the hole in the front of the President's neck, described as only 5mm to 8mm in size, too small to be an exit wound, as some have charged? "There is a mistaken impression that exit wounds are large, gaping wounds," says Dr. Baden. "They can be large, but if the bullet isn't tumbling and doesn't hit anything inside the body beyond soft tissue, they can be very small. I have seen plenty of exit wounds like that in gunshot cases."[71] Moreover, experiments conducted by Dr. John Lattimer, a New York physician who was the first private doctor allowed to view the autopsy X rays and photographs, reveal why the exit wound in the President's neck was small. In reconstructions of the shot, with 6.5mm ammo, Lattimer discovered the exit wound remained small and tight if the bullet exited near the collar band of the shirt, where the buttoned collar and the knotted tie firmly pushed the neck muscles together. As Lattimer moved the shots farther away from the collar band, even by fractions of an inch, the exit wounds became larger.[72] Dr. Carrico said the neck wound was right at the collar band and tie knot.[73]

When the House Select Committee's nine-member forensics panel reviewed the autopsy X rays and photographs, it also examined JFK's clothing, which confirmed the direction of the neck shot. Through enhancements of the original autopsy photos, the panel also noticed that the back wound had a unique "abrasion collar, a roughening of the edges . . . which clearly depicts the entrance."[74] The angle of the abrasion wound showed the bullet was traveling from right to left, the angle of Oswald's line of fire from the sixth floor.[75] The X rays confirmed there was internal injury, a stress fracture to the first thoracic vertebra, caused by the trauma of the bullet passing so close to the spine.[76] The Select Committee's medical panel unanimously determined that the neck wound was caused by a rear shot.[77]

The Head Wound

The autopsy physicians concluded the fatal shot entered the rear of the President's skull and exploded out the right side of his head. Humes said the wound was "blatantly obvious."[78] The evidence of the head wound was a textbook example of entrance and exit for a bullet. Seventy percent of the right hemisphere of the President's brain was blown out, leaving a nearly six-inch hole on the right side of his head. The entry on the back of the head was small, not much larger than the 6.5mm bullet that did the damage.[79] Examination of the inside of the skull indicated the edges of the hole were beveled inward, confirming the entry point. Fragments of the parietal bone missing from the right side of the President's head, found in Dealey Plaza, later confirmed outward beveling, indicating that was the exit point.[80] Less than 1mm of metallic dust particles was evident on the X ray of the President's brain, and followed the bullet's rear-to-front path, leading directly to the exit on the right side.[81] Three fragments were found, one at the entrance point and two near JFK's right eye, further evidence of the bullet's path.[82] There was no photographic, X ray, or personal observation of any other exit on the head except for the large hole on the right side.*

---

* After the autopsy, Humes and Boswell wrote their report from memory, without the benefit of the photographs or X rays. Robert Kennedy, who feared the public display of the X rays and photos would be offensive to the Kennedy family, reached an agreement with the Warren Commission not to publish the materials, and except for Earl Warren, the commissioners did not examine them. When the film was turned over to the custody of the National Archives in 1966, a metal box containing the President's brain was missing from the inventory, together with some tissue slides. Humes had given everything from the autopsy, including the brain, to JFK's personal physician, Admiral George Burkley. "He told me," said Humes, "that the [Kennedy] family wanted to inter the brain with the President's body" (*Journal of the American Medical Association*, May 27, 1992, Vol. 267, No. 20, p. 2803). The House Select Committee concluded that Robert Kennedy likely disposed of the material for fear it would become a lurid public exhibition (HSCA Vol. VII, pp. 367–68).

In the same vein, Humes, who had gotten the President's blood on his autopsy notes, copied them verbatim to clean paper and then burned the original, fearing that the bloodstained notes might become part of a future public display. That same concern prompted the physicians to wash the blood-soaked sheets in which the President's body arrived and to dispose of their own medi-

However, some of the Parkland doctors who treated the President described a gaping wound in the rear of JFK's head (the occipital region), not the right side (the parietal). If true, this not only contradicted the findings of the autopsy team but was evidence that the President was probably shot from the front, with a large exit hole in the rear of the head. Several Parkland doctors also thought they saw cerebellum, tissue from the base of the brain, on the stretcher or in the operating room. Yet, the autopsy photos of the brain show the cerebellum intact. If the Parkland descriptions of the cerebellum were true, this raised legitimate questions over the authenticity of the photographs of JFK's brain, which showed no such damage. Robert Groden and Harrison Livingstone, in their book *High Treason*, devote more than thirty pages to highlighting this conflict between the Parkland and Bethesda descriptions of the head wound.

However, it is questionable to rely on the Parkland doctors for any assertion about the head wound since, by their own admission, they did not examine it in detail. When Dr. Kemp Clark looked at the wound to determine whether the President could be revived, it was the first time it had been examined. "From what I read in later books, everyone looked at it in detail from the beginning, but that is not true," recalls Dr. Jenkins. "We were trying to save the President, and no one had time to examine the wounds. As for the head wound, they couldn't look at it earlier because I was standing with my body against it, and they would only have looked at my pants."[83]

"We never had the opportunity to review his wounds," Dr. Carrico told the author, "in order to describe them accurately. We were trying to save his life."[84] Dr. Adolph Giesecke agrees: "We had no time to examine the wounds. That was to be done by a forensic pathologist, not by us."[85] "I don't think any of us

---

cal garb. But this concern created a situation that led to mistakes. Since Humes and Boswell were not able to use the photographs or X rays when making their autopsy report, they misplaced the entry wound on the back by nearly two inches and the one in the head by four inches. These errors were discovered by the House Select Committee's medical panel. While it did not alter the conclusions about two shots from the rear, it did affect the Warren Commission ballistics tests, which were based on the misinformation about the entry points.

got a good look at the head wound," confirms Dr. Perry. "I didn't examine it or really look at it that carefully."[86] "And when we realized he was dead," Dr. Baxter recalls, "none of us had the heart to go and examine the head wound while Mrs. Kennedy was in the room. We all just made our way out of the room."[87] "When things were over with," Dr. Jones says, "you felt it was her time and you should get out of there and let her be alone with him."[88]

Dr. Baden of the Select Committee concurs: "Parkland was not concerned with whether the bullet was going from front to back or vice versa, they were only treating the symptoms, not the wounds. Some of them could be good surgeons but lousy pathologists. A third of the time, an autopsy shows something was missed by the treating doctors at the hospital. In unnatural deaths, it is common for the treating physicians to mix up stab wounds and gun shots, and they are wrong half the time about exit or entrance. The Parkland doctors did not clean Kennedy off—there is just no way they could have hazarded a real guess about that wound, since it was covered with blood and tissue. If they say they saw cerebellum, they are just wrong because the cerebellum was perfect. And if they say there was a large hole in the rear of the head, they don't know what they are talking about since there is nothing there but the entry injury in the rear cowlick. The mistakes in judgments from Parkland are exactly why we have autopsies.

"One of the most important aspects of the Zapruder film, often overlooked by the critics, are the frames immediately after the President was shot in the head. It's very clear on the enhanced frames that there is a wound over the right ear, but the back of the head is clean. That film is incontrovertible evidence that there was no defect on the rear of the head."[89]

Yet mistaken descriptions of what the Parkland doctors did and saw continue to be published. *High Treason* asserts that some doctors examined the wound with a flashlight and that Dr. Jenkins picked the head up from the stretcher to show other doctors the extent of the rear wound.[90] The eight principal doctors who attended to JFK on that day all told the author that such reports were false. Moreover, Groden and Livingstone cite early interviews and some testimony before the Warren Commission to support their hypothesis that the Parkland doctors saw a different head wound than the one described at Bethesda.* Yet the Parkland physicians, in their discussions with the author, were almost unanimous in supporting the autopsy findings that the massive exit wound was on the right side (parietal) of the President's head, not the rear (occipital), and that there was no sign of damaged cerebellum tissue. They insisted that the explainable differences in the wound descriptions between them and the Bethesda doctors have been exploited by conspiracy writers, who created a controversy where none exists. Some admitted that their early statements about the wounds, which they now consider to be mistaken, may have contributed to the confusion.

Dr. Bill Midgett, who helped wheel the President from the limousine into trauma room one, says, "The President had quite thick hair, and there was a lot of blood and tissue. All of us were so shocked . . . and to have Mrs. Kennedy there—none of us stared very closely to see the wound. But it was more parietal than occipital—that much I could see. I did not turn the President over to look, but there was no cerebellum in that car or on the people."

"We did say there was a parietal-occipital wound," recalls Dr. Carrico. "We did say we saw shattered brain, cerebellum, in the cortex area, and I think we were mistaken. The reason I say that is that the President was lying on his back and shoulders, and you could see the hole, with scalp and brain tissue hanging back down his head, and it covered most of the occipital portion of his head. We saw a large hole on the right side of his head. I

---

* In 1988, four of the Parkland doctors—Pepper Jenkins, Richard Dulaney, Paul Peters, and Robert McClelland—went to the National Archives at the invitation of a PBS documentary show, *Nova*, about the assassination. They were the first Parkland physicians to see the autopsy photographs, and each confirmed the photos represented what they remembered seeing that day, including a picture of the rear of President Kennedy's head, which shows no defect. It has been suggested that the reason the photo shows the rear of the President's head as undamaged is because the doctor (whose fingers are present in the picture) is holding a large flap of skin to cover the rear defect. "False," says Dr. Michael Baden. "There is no flap of skin there. There is a bony protrusion from the right side of the head, but the rear is undamaged, except for the entry hole near the top of the skull" (Interview, January 23, 1992).

don't believe we saw any occipital bone. It was not there. It was parietal bone. And if we said otherwise, we were mistaken."[91] Dr. Giesecke also admits an error in his original testimony when he described the wound as more occipital. "I guess I have to say that I was wrong in my Warren Commission testimony on the wound and in some of my pronouncements since then. I just never got that good of a look at it. But, for instance, Lifton spent six hours with me trying to get me to say the wounds were like he wanted them. The truth is there was a massive head wound, with brain tissue and blood around it. And with that type of wound you could not get accurate information unless you feel around inside the hole and look into it in detail, and I certainly didn't do that, nor did I see anyone else do that."[92]

Dr. Peters had said that the cerebellum was damaged. "I saw the photograph of the brain when I was in Washington for the *Nova* program, and I saw the cerebellum was depressed, but it was not lacerated or torn. It is definitely pressed down and that would be the damage I referred to in 1964. . . . The only thing I would say is that over the last twenty-eight years I now believe the head wound is more forward than I first placed it. More to the side than the rear. I tried to tell Lifton where the wound was, but he did not want to hear."

Dr. Jenkins's original report also stated he saw cerebellum. "The description of the cerebellum was my fault," he says. "When I read my report over, I realized there could not be any cerebellum. The autopsy photo, with the rear of the head intact and a protrusion in the parietal region, is the way I remember it. I never did say occipital."[93]*

"I did not really look at it that closely," says Dr. Perry. "But like everyone else, I saw it back there. It was in the occipital/parietal area. The occipital and parietal bone join each other, so we are only talking a centimeter or so in difference. And you must remember the President had a lot of hair, and it was bloody and matted, and it was difficult to tell where that wound started or finished. I did not see any cerebellum."[94] Dr. Baxter

---

* *High Treason* asserts that Jenkins originally said JFK was shot in the chest. Jenkins laughed when the author read him the Groden and Livingstone charge. "I don't know where they get this stuff from. We put tubes into the President's chest, but there were no chest wounds caused by anything else."

agrees that it was difficult to determine the precise location of the wound when treating the President: "He had such a bushy head of hair, and blood and all in it, you couldn't tell what was wound versus dried blood or dangling tissue. I have been misquoted enough on this, some saying I claimed the whole back of his head was blown away. That's just wrong. I never even saw the back of his head. The wound was on the right side, not the back."[95] Dr. Jones makes the same observation, saying he did not even know there was a head wound for several minutes, and then finally realized it was a "large side wound, with blood and tissue that extended toward the rear, from what you could tell of the mess that was there."[96] Dr. Giesecke agrees "that the occipital and parietal region are so close together it is possible to mistake one for the other."[97]

The only Parkland doctors who still believe they saw a wound in the rear of the head, as well as seeing cerebellum, are Robert McClelland and Charles Crenshaw. "I saw a piece of cerebellum fall out on the stretcher," says McClelland, who claims he was in the best position of any of the doctors to view the head wound.[98] He drew a sketch in 1967 for Josiah Thompson's book *Six Seconds in Dallas*, which showed a gaping wound in the rear of the head.[99]

"I am astonished that Bob would say that," says Dr. Malcolm Perry. "It shows such poor judgment, and usually he has such good judgment."[100] "I don't think Bob McClelland was in the best place to see the head wound," says Dr. Peters. "He wasn't in that position the way I remember it, as he was on the other side of the table. As for Dr. McClelland saying he saw cerebellum fall out on the table, I never saw anything like that."[101] "Bob is an excellent surgeon," says Dr. Jenkins. "He knows anatomy. I hate to say Bob is mistaken, but that is clearly not right. In 1988, when I went to the National Archives, the photos showed the President's brain was crenelated from the trauma, and it resembled cerebellum, but it was not cerebellar tissue. I think it has thrown off a lot of people that saw it. I guess a last point is that Bob and Groden [co-author of *High Treason*] are such good friends, I believe it has changed his attitude."[102] "McClelland may be a fine surgeon, but he is a lousy pathologist," says Baden. "I am sure he thinks he saw that, and has developed it in his mind. But his memory is just completely wrong, and the autopsy photos and X rays prove that."[103]*

Dr. Crenshaw wrote a book in 1992 in which he claimed he examined the wound, that the hole was in the rear of the head, and that the cerebellum was lacerated.[104]† Crenshaw, a junior resident at the time, arrived late at trauma room one and assisted for only a few minutes near the end. He was in no position to make the judgments he sensationally proclaimed in his book. In fact, his role was so minor that most of the other doctors do not even remember him. "I don't remember Dr. Crenshaw in the room," says Dr. Ron Jones. "I don't remember him in there at any time, but he may have been," recalls Dr. Jenkins. "Neither do I," says Dr. Baxter.

"I feel sorry for him," says Dr. Perry. "I had thought about suing him, but when I saw him on television [promoting his book], my anger melted. He has to know that what he said is false, and he knows the rest of us know that. You have to pity him. What a way to end his career. His story is filled with half-truths and insinuations, and those of us who know him know he is desperate. . . . He is a pitiful sight." A senior Dallas doctor who is a close Crenshaw friend told the author, "I think it is a bag of worms of ego, going over the hill, the last hurrah."

While almost all the Parkland doctors who treated JFK sup-

---

* In his original report, McClelland said there was a wound to the left temple, one that does not show up on any autopsy X ray or photograph. This has caused some to charge that Kennedy was shot by a second gunman from another location at Dealey, and that the autopsy team either negligently or intentionally overlooked that wound. "I'll tell you how that happened," Dr. Jenkins explained to the author. "When Bob McClelland came into the room, he asked me, 'Where are his wounds?' And at that time I was operating a breathing bag with my right hand, and was trying to take the President's temporal pulse, and I had my finger on his left temple. Bob thought I pointed to the left temple as the wound."

† Crenshaw also said the autopsy photograph of the tracheotomy opening on Kennedy's neck shows that it was larger than it had been at Parkland, implying that additional surgery might have been done between Parkland and Bethesda. "That's ridiculous," Dr. Malcolm Perry told the author. "I did the procedure. Tracheotomies are not pretty things, as speed is of the essence. Tissue can sag and stretch after death, but the photos I have seen look like the opening I remember making."

port the findings of the autopsy team, their confirmation may not be as important as the studies conducted by subsequent panels of experts. The Clark and Rockefeller commissions, as well as the House Select Committee's medical panel, affirm the original autopsy conclusions about JFK's head wound. The most detailed work was done by the Select Committee. All nine forensic pathologists agreed that the beveling of the skull and the damage to the brain meant the small rear hole in the President's head was an entrance wound.[105] The exit hole was consistent with a wound caused by the two large bullet fragments found in the front of the President's car.[106]*

But if the President was struck in the head by a bullet fired from the rear, then why does he jerk so violently backward on the Zapruder film, which recorded the assassination? To most lay people, the rapid backward movement at the moment of the head shot means the President was struck from the front. "That's absolutely wrong," says Dr. Michael Baden. "People have no conception of how real life works with bullet wounds. It's not like Hollywood, where someone gets shot and falls over backwards. Reactions are different on each shot and on each person."[107]

In the case of President Kennedy's head wound and the reac-

---

* While the Select Committee's forensic panel agreed that a bullet had entered from the rear and exploded out the side of the President's head, there was a lone dissent. Dr. Cyril Wecht said that such a finding did not preclude a shot also entering from the front. Dr. Wecht believed that the large exit wound on the right side "could hide an entrance wound at the same spot." In other words, just as Oswald fired from behind and his bullet exited the President's head, a front shooter fired into the wound created by the rear bullet. That is Wecht's way of explaining why there is not another entry hole on JFK's head. However, the X rays and photographs show no exit for a front bullet. The author raised the issue with Wecht, and he admitted that "the question of where did a front bullet exit is a very good one." He first suggested that the front shot may have been a frangible bullet, which would have exploded upon impact in the brain. However, the X rays do not show any metal fragments in the brain from such a bullet, and when this was pointed out to Wecht, he acknowledged, "Yes, that's true, there should be more fragments." Finally, he suggested that the front bullet may have been plastic, and penetrated the brain but did not exit. He argued that since the brain is not available for examination, his speculation is possible—except that plastic bullets were rarely available until 1968, five years after the assassination.

tion on the Zapruder film, the Itek Optical Systems did a computer enhancement for a CBS documentary. Itek discovered that when the bullet hit JFK, he first jerked forward 2.3 inches before starting his rapid movement backward.[108] Unless the film is slowed considerably and enhanced, the forward motion is not detectable.

The backward movement is the result of two factors. First, when the bullet destroyed the President's cortex, it caused a neuromuscular spasm, which sent a massive discharge of neurologic impulses from the injured brain shooting down the spine to every muscle in the body.[109] "The body then stiffens," said Dr. John Lattimer, "with the strongest muscles predominating. These are the muscles of the back and neck . . ."[110] They contract, lurching the body upward and to the rear.* The President's back brace likely accentuated the movement, preventing him from falling forward. At the same instant the President's body was in a neuromuscular seizure, the bullet exploded out the right side of his head. Dr. Luis Alvarez, a Nobel Prize–winning physicist, focused on that to discover the second factor that drove the President's head back with such force. Dubbed the "jet effect," Dr. Alvarez established it both through physical experiments that re-created the head shot and extensive laboratory calculations. He found that when the brain and blood tissue exploded out JFK's head, they carried forward more momentum than was brought in by the bullet. That caused the head to thrust backward—in an opposite direction—as a rocket does when its jet fuel is ejected.[111] Because the bullet exited on the right side of JFK's head, it forced him to be propelled back and to the left, exactly what is visible on the Zapruder film.†

"So much has been made of Kennedy's movement in the Za-

---

* The author viewed a video taken of the execution of a journalist by army troops in Central America. When the victim, who was lying flat on his stomach on the ground, was shot in the rear of the head, his upper torso and legs arched off the ground, in the opposite direction of the bullet. It was similar to the neuromuscular reaction JFK suffered. Also, when Governor Connally was struck in the rear shoulder by a bullet, he did not fall forward, but is clearly visible on the Zapruder film, his wounded shoulder pushing back into the car seat, toward the direction from which he was shot.

† Dr. Lattimer also conducted twelve physical experiments that confirmed Alvarez's work. In each instance, the jet effect, on mock-ups of human heads

pruder film," says Dr. Baden, "and yet it is one of the least important parts of the case. By his movement alone, you can't tell which direction he was shot from. You then need to examine the bullets, the bones, tissue, X rays, and photographs to determine from where the bullet came. I have personally done thousands of gunshot autopsies. There is no doubt that the bullets that hit John Kennedy, both in the neck and in the head, came from the rear. Nothing hit him from the front."[112]

---

struck from the rear by a 6.5mm bullet, caused the specimens to rocket back toward the shooter.

Another argument that the shot must have come from the front is based on the fact that two motorcycle policemen riding to the rear of the President's car were splattered with blood and brain tissue. But on an enhanced version of the Zapruder film, the two officers drive right into the head spray, which actually shot up and to the front of the President.

14

"My God, They Are Going to Kill Us All"

Two of the most controversial issues in the assassination are whether Oswald could fire three shots in the necessary time and if the nearly whole bullet, Warren Commission Exhibit 399, found on the stretcher at Parkland Hospital could have passed through the President, out his neck, and then caused all of Governor Connally's wounds.

The Warren Commission and the House Select Committee did the best they could with photo and computer technology as it existed in 1964 and 1978. However, scientific advances within the past five years allow significant enhancements of the Zapruder film, as well as scale re-creations using computer animation, which were unavailable to the government panels. As a result, it is now possible to settle the question of the timing of Oswald's shots and to pinpoint the moment when both Kennedy and Connally were struck with a precision previously unattainable.*

---

* At Dealey Plaza, more than 510 photographs that directly relate to the assassination were taken by some seventy-five photographers, but the Zapruder film is by far the most useful in determining what happened, since it records the entire period of the shooting. This chapter is based primarily on the latest enhancements of that film. They include one done by Dr. Michael West, a medical examiner in Mississippi, together with Johann Rush, the journalist who filmed Oswald during his Fair Play for Cuba demonstration at the New Orleans Trade Mart; and another completed by Failure Analysis Associates, a prominent firm specializing in computer reconstructions for lawsuits.

The Formative Years

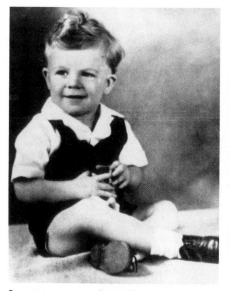

Lee at two years of age. The following year, his mother, unable to cope with him, committed him to an orphanage, where he joined his two older brothers. *(National Archives)*

In this seldom-seen photo, eight-year-old Lee plays with his cap pistol while wearing his brother Robert's military academy hat. At school, he had already developed a reputation as a bully. *(Courtesy of Robert L. Oswald)*

At fifteen, in New Orleans, after fleeing New York with his mother to avoid commitment to a youth center for troubled boys. The psychiatrist who examined Lee concluded he "had potential for explosive, aggressive, assaultive acting out." *(National Archives)*

The Marines

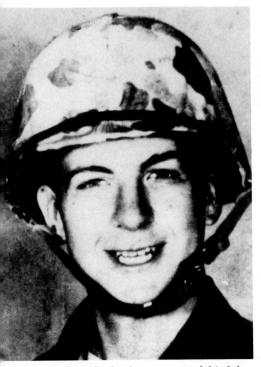

A week after his seventeenth birthday, Lee followed his brother Robert into the Marine Corps, where he was court-martialed twice. *(National Archives)*

A rare photo of Lee hunting while on his first leave from the Marines in February 1958, when he visited his family in Fort Worth, Texas. *(Courtesy of Robert L. Oswald)*

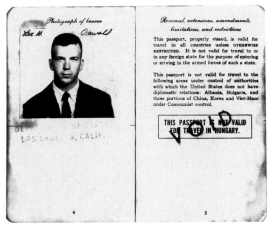

Oswald's passport, issued on September 10, 1959, one day before his release from the Marines. Devoted to Marxism from the age of fifteen, he planned for nearly two years to defect to the Soviet Union. *(National Archives)*

Oswald in Russia

Oswald's failed suicide attempt in Moscow prompted the Soviets to allow him to stay in Russia. In Minsk, he posed with Pavel Golovachev (right), a friend and later a KGB informant on Oswald; Roza Kuznetsova (behind Oswald), an Intourist guide and also a KGB informant; and Ella Germann, Oswald's first love, who devastated him by rejecting his marriage proposal. *(National Archives)*

Oswald kept a "Historic Diary" of his activities while in Russia, which showed not only his fickle nature but his deepening hatred of both the Soviet and American political systems. *(National Archives)*

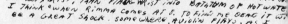

Oswald (with dark glasses) and some of his co-workers at the Minsk radio and television plant. He grew to hate the menial work. *(National Archives)*

Marina and Lee

In March 1961, Oswald met Marina (far right), and they married a month later. With them are Marina's aunt and uncle, Valentina Guryevna Prusakova and Ilya Vasilyevich Prusakov. Some mistakenly conclude that Ilya worked for the KGB, when he was actually the equivalent of a local U.S. policeman. *(National Archives)*

The Oswalds departing from Minsk for America. Although he tried at first to renounce his U.S. citizenship, Lee spent more than a year trying to obtain permission to return home. *(National Archives)*

Dallas: The Walker Shooting

Back in America, the Oswalds' home life turned violent. Lee also created a second identity, complete with false identifications that he made. *Alek* was derived from his Russian nickname "Alik," and *Hidell* was a variation on the name of a Marine he had known. *(National Archives)*

In early 1963, Oswald stalked the Dallas home of right-wing general Edwin Walker, taking surveillance photos such as the one above. *(National Archives)*

The window of the Walker home, showing why Oswald's assassination attempt went awry. His shot nicked the bottom of the wooden frame, deflecting the bullet's path and saving Walker's life. *(National Archives)*

Dallas: The Backyard Photos

This well-known photo of Oswald in the backyard of his Dallas apartment, with his pistol and rifle and holding two leftist newspapers, was one of several taken by his wife, Marina. "I thought he had gone crazy," Marina later said about Lee's request to be photographed in those poses. The Mannlicher-Carcano rifle in Oswald's hand is the same one used to kill President Kennedy. *(National Archives)*

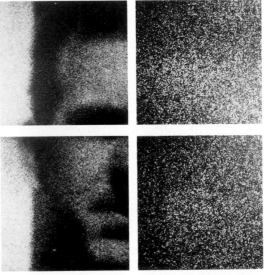

Despite Marina's insistence that she took the photos, conspiracy critics have vigorously contested their authenticity. The House Select Committee on Assassinations finally settled the issue when twenty-two of the nation's leading photo experts submitted the photos to a series of sophisticated tests and concluded there was no evidence of fakery. Above is the grain structure analysis on one of the photos. Under a microscope, composite pictures are easily identified by variations in the grain pattern. *(House Select Committee on Assassinations)*

New Orleans

This unpublished photo of a smug Oswald was taken moments after his court hearing in New Orleans for having disturbed the peace in an altercation with anti-Castro Cubans. *(Courtesy of Johann Rush)*

In August 1963, Oswald passed out pro-Castro leaflets for the New Orleans branch of the Communist Fair Play for Cuba Organization. He was that chapter's only member, though he hired two men from the unemployment line to help him distribute the pamphlets. Marina believed his obsession with Castro had become all-consuming. *(Courtesy of Johann Rush)*

Mexico City

Oswald's application for a travel visa to Cuba, filled out at the Cuban embassy in Mexico City on September 27, 1963. He was furious when the Cuban consul rejected his request. The photo stapled at the upper left-hand corner was given personally by Oswald to the Cuban embassy clerk, belying conspiracy stories that an imposter visited instead. *(House Select Committee on Assassinations)*

Dealey Plaza: The Assassin's View

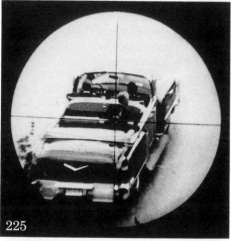

These 1964 reconstructions, done by the FBI for the Warren Commission, approximate the shooter's view through his 4X telescopic sight. These images, keyed by the Commission to frame numbers from the Zapruder film of the assassination, appear much smaller than what the assassin would have seen with the sight filling his entire field of vision. The car is a different model from the presidential limousine, and therefore the two agents are not in the actual positions of President Kennedy and Governor Connally at the time of the assassination. Also, Oswald's first shot was between frames 161 and 166, and his second shot was actually at frames 223–224. The third and final shot was at frame 313. *(National Archives)*

Dealey Plaza: The Shooting

In this picture, President Kennedy's arms have already flexed near his chin, part of a neurological response to the wound through his throat. Governor Connally, struck by the same bullet, is pushing back into his seat, about to fall into the arms of his wife, Nellie. This was Oswald's second shot, the first having missed. *(AP/Wide World Photos)*

This Polaroid was snapped a fraction of a second before the fatal head shot. Conspiracy critics have searched this photo, in the area of the rear retaining wall and the fence, and interpreted shadows, light, and foliage as another assassin firing at Kennedy from the front. *(AP/Wide World Photos)*

Dealey Plaza: The Witnesses

Taken only seconds after the fatal third shot, this photo shows the sniper's nest, with some of the boxes Oswald used to construct it. The tip of the box near the right side of the window served as a brace for the rifle. The men on the lower floor, Bonnie Ray Williams (left) and Harold Norman (right), were startled when they heard the rifle fire directly above them. Norman even heard Oswald operate the gun's bolt action, and the three cartridge cases hitting the floor. *(Dallas Morning News)*

Howard Brennan, the construction worker who saw Oswald shooting during the assassination, here demonstrates where he was at that moment, only ninety-three feet from the sniper's nest. *(National Archives)*

Officer Tippit and Oswald's Arrest

Officer J. D. Tippit's patrol car, in the exact location where he stopped Oswald just forty-five minutes after Kennedy was killed. As Tippit walked around the front of the car, Oswald pulled out his revolver and fired, killing Tippit instantly. *(National Archives)*

The Texas Theater, only blocks away from where Tippit was shot. Oswald, who was followed there by a local shoe-store clerk, ducked inside the movie house without paying for a ticket. The theater's ticket seller then called the police. *(National Archives)*

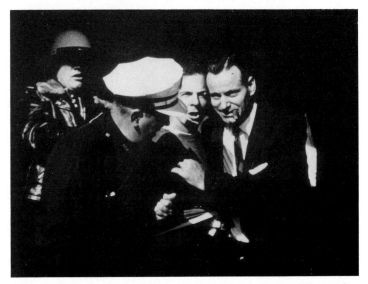

After a scuffle inside the theater, in which he unsuccessfully tried to shoot another policeman, Oswald was dragged out of the movie house by a Dallas policeman and a detective. *(National Archives)*

Jack Ruby

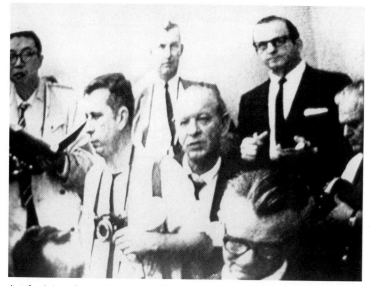

A television shot of the back of the room during Oswald's press conference, held at the jail at midnight on the day of the assassination. Jack Ruby (second from right, in dark suit), a local Dallas nightclub owner, had entered the room by pretending to be a journalist. Ruby, publicity hungry and attracted to high-profile events, was obsessed with the weekend activities surrounding the assassination. *(National Archives)*

Jack Ruby, who had run several failed nightclubs and strip joints during his sixteen years in Dallas, was a petty hustler who had contacts with both the mob and the police. *(National Archives)*

Oswald's Murder

Jack Ruby broke through the crowd just seconds before he fired one fatal shot into Oswald. Ruby, who had just been to the nearby Western Union office, walked inside the jail's basement only half a minute before Oswald passed through while being transferred to the sheriff's office. *(Courtesy of Bob Jackson)*

A mortally wounded Oswald is wheeled into Parkland Hospital. If Oswald had not asked for a change of clothes only minutes before he was to be transferred, he would have left before Ruby was even inside the jail. *(AP/Wide World Photos)*

JFK's Casket Arrives in Washington

One of the most controversial conspiracy theories charges that this bronze coffin containing JFK (here being unloaded from *Air Force One* at Andrews Air Force Base) was empty. Supposedly the President's body had been stolen for surgical alterations while still in Dallas. The casket was never unattended, however, and it was hermetically sealed by an air-lock mechanism in Dallas. It was not reopened until its arrival for the autopsy at Bethesda. *(AP/Wide World Photos)*

The Aftermath

857

Jim Garrison, the New Orleans district attorney, was the only public official to use his office to pursue any of the conspiracy theories in his 1966 investigation into the assassination. Even before Garrison's probe, sensational stories, such as this one in the *National Enquirer,* created enough concern that the Warren Commission examined its charges. The *Enquirer* story was false. Garrison's work was also eventually discredited, although it became the basis for Oliver Stone's $50-million film *JFK* in 1991. *(National Archives; AP/Wide World Photos)*

The first issue is the timing. In 1964, the FBI's test-firing of Oswald's Carcano determined that a minimum of 2.25 to 2.3 seconds was necessary between shots to operate the bolt and re-aim.[1] Since the first bullet was already in the rifle's chamber and ready to fire, that meant Oswald had to operate the bolt action twice (just as Harold Norman heard on the fifth floor). According to the Warren Commission, the fastest he could have fired all three shots was 4.5 seconds. However, that minimum time is now out of date. CBS reconstructed the shooting for a 1975 documentary. Eleven volunteer marksmen took turns firing clips of three bullets at a moving target. None of them had dry practice runs with the Carcano's bolt action, as Oswald had had almost daily while in New Orleans. Yet the times ranged from 4.1 sec-

---

The Failure Analysis work was an extensive undertaking for an American Bar Association (ABA) mock trial of Lee Harvey Oswald (resulting in a hung jury), held at the ABA's 1992 convention. The Failure Analysis project involved 3-D scale generations of Dealey Plaza, physical mock-ups of the presidential car, and stand-in models for the President and Governor, all to determine trajectory angles and the feasibility of one bullet causing both sets of wounds. Failure Analysis also re-created experiments with the 6.5mm ammunition, using more updated information than was available to the Warren Commission, to further test the "single-bullet theory" and the condition of the missile.

At the ABA trial, Failure Analysis presented scientific evidence for both the prosecution and defense of Oswald. The only technical breakthroughs were on the prosecution work, and they are presented in this chapter. The defense presentation was fundamentally flawed and centered on two primary arguments. The first was why Oswald did not take a supposedly better straight shot as JFK's car approached the Depository on Houston Street. Failure Analysis tried illustrating its contention by creating computer animation of Oswald's view of the car. Since Connally was sitting in front of Kennedy in the car, he would have blocked part of the assassin's view along Houston Street, and therefore the computer animation was not an accurate representation of what Oswald saw. Moreover, the Failure Analysis presentation did not take into account that ballistics experts conclude that a target coming toward and below a shooter is a more difficult shot with a telescopic sight, and that Oswald was better hidden from the view of neighboring buildings by choosing a line of fire along Elm Street. The second Failure Analysis defense argument was that a glycerin bullet could have been fired from the grassy knoll and not have exited on the left side of JFK's head. To illustrate the contention, Failure Analysis shot glycerin bullets into full, plastic, water bottles. Yet, the mock jury was never told that glycerin bullets are almost completely unstable at the distance between JFK's car and the grassy knoll. Also, Failure Analysis did not establish whether a glycerin bullet could penetrate a human skull at the Dealey Plaza distance.

onds, almost half a second faster than what the Warren Commission thought was possible, to slightly more than 6 seconds, with the average being 5.6 seconds, and two out of three hits on the target.[2] Based on its 1977 reconstruction tests, the House Select Committee lowered the time between shots on the Carcano to 1.66 seconds, with the shooter hitting all the targets.[3] This reduced the time necessary for three effective shots to 3.3 seconds.

The time necessary to operate the Carcano must be compared to the Zapruder film, which serves as a time clock for the assassination. The FBI concluded that Zapruder's camera operated at 18.3 frames a second.* By figuring when the first and last shots took place, it is possible to know how much total time the shooter had. The third shot is the easiest to pinpoint. On the Zapruder film, the President is hit in the head at frame 313. No matter what number of shots they heard, the witnesses are almost unanimous that the head shot was the final one.[4] That sets the end of the time clock at frame 313.†

Determining the time of the first shot, the start of the assassination clock, is more difficult. The Warren Commission was unsure when the first shot was fired, or if it even hit Kennedy or Connally.[5] Yet because the Commission thought the first shot would be the most accurate, it implicitly favored the theory that the first bullet hit Kennedy in the base of the neck.[6] It relied on several factors in determining the timing of that shot. When the President's car turned in front of the Depository, the

---

* Zapruder said the film in his camera was fully wound when he started filming the motorcade. The FBI's 1964 tests determined that in the first 30 seconds of operation, Zapruder's camera ran between 18 to 18.5 frames per second, with the average at 18.3 While that is a 3 percent variance, it is statistically unimportant when determining the reaction times of Kennedy and Connally to their bullet wounds. The figure 18.3 is used by all researchers.

† Because a Mannlicher-Carcano bullet travels at approximately 2,000 feet per second, the sniper must squeeze the trigger before frame 313 shows the President hit. The bullet flight time, measuring the distance from the Depository's sixth floor to the presidential limousine at the moment of the head shot, would have been 0.13 second, or 2.4 frames on the Zapruder film (HSCA Vol. VI, p. 27). This is essentially true of the other shots as well, but the tenth of a second is statistically insignificant and does not affect the overall calculation for Oswald's shooting.

shooter had to make a fast decision because soon after the turn, the car disappeared under the foliage of a large oak tree. A reconstruction showed the President was blocked from the sniper's view from frame 167 until 210, a period of 2.3 seconds, with only a small break in the foliage at 186.[7] On the Zapruder film, the presidential car is obscured from sight by a freeway sign from frames 200 to 224. Before the President and the Governor disappear behind that sign, neither shows any reaction to being struck by a bullet. However, when the President emerges from behind the road sign at frame 225, the Commission thought he was reacting to a bullet, which means he was wounded somewhere behind the sign. Since the assassin did not have a clear shot until frame 210, when Kennedy emerged from under the tree cover, the Commission concluded that is the earliest he could have been shot. The latest would have been at frame 225, when he appears to be raising his right arm in response to the wound.

The critics have consistently interpreted the Commission's work to give Oswald as little time as possible to fire all three shots. In most conspiracy books, the Commission's position is presented as assuming the first shot was fired between frames 210 and 225, the second shot missed, and the third shot was the fatal head wound at frame 313. In this scenario, Oswald had very little time to fire all three shots, a minimum of 4.8 seconds and a maximum of 5.6 seconds. The Commission admitted this was the "minimum allowable time to have fired the three shots," but concluded that it was "possible" for Oswald to have done it within that time.[8]

However, the assumption that the first shot struck the President is wrong. Ear-witness testimony, in combination with the Zapruder film, suggests the first shot actually missed and was fired before the presidential car disappeared under the tree cover, earlier than frame 166. Buell Frazier, standing on the Depository footsteps, said the President's car barely made the turn from Houston onto Elm when the first shot rang out.[9] Howard Brennan, leaning against a concrete railing at the corner of Houston and Elm, said the car had just passed him when the first shot was fired.[10] Barbara Rowland, half a block from the

Depository, heard it just "as they turned the corner."[11] Royce Skelton was watching from the Triple Underpass and said the first shot came "the same time the car . . . got around the corner . . ."[12] Geneva Hine was in the School Book Depository and remembered the shots started just "after he turned the corner . . ."[13] The driver of the President's limousine, William Greer, said he thought the first shot was the backfire of a motorcycle, and noticed it happened when the President's car "was almost past this building [the Book Depository]."[14] Secret Service agent Paul Landis, in the follow-up car, heard the first shot just after the President's car "had completed [its] turn."[15]

One of the most persuasive witnesses is Secret Service agent Glen Bennett, who was also in the follow-up car. At 5:30 P.M. on the day of the assassination, while on a plane returning to Washington, Bennet jotted notes of what he had seen five hours earlier. The first shot sounded like a "fire-cracker," but it made him look at the President. "At the moment I looked at the back of the President I heard another fire-cracker noise and saw the shot hit the President about four inches down from the right shoulder" [it was actually higher]. Bennett said the third shot "hit the right rear high of the President's head."[16] When he made his notes, it was not known that the President had been hit by a bullet in the rear neck/shoulder.

However, the Commission did not rely on these witnesses in resolving the issue of whether the first shot missed. Since there was also testimony from several witnesses who thought the second shot missed, the Commission refused to decide between them.

New Zapruder enhancements, however, confirm the ear-witness testimony that an early shot missed the President and the Governor. Beginning at frame 160, a young girl in a red skirt and white top who was running along the left side of the President's car, down Elm Street, began turning to her right. By frame 187, less than 1.5 seconds later, the enhancement clearly shows she had stopped, twisted completely away from the motorcade, and was staring back at the School Book Depository. That girl was ten-year-old Rosemary Willis. Some believe the girl's reaction was because her father, Phil Willis, standing only ten feet away, told her to stop and come back toward him.[17]* However, when Rosemary Willis was asked why she had stopped running with the President's car, she said, "I stopped when I heard the shot."[18] The Zapruder film is the visual confirmation that provides the timing. "In that first split second, I thought it was a firecracker. But within maybe one tenth of a second, I knew it was a gunshot. . . . I think I probably turned to look toward the noise, toward the Book Depository."[19]

Just after Rosemary Willis slowed and started turning toward the Depository, the enhanced film shows that President Kennedy, who was waving as the car had turned the corner, suddenly stopped waving. He looked to his right toward the crowd, and then back to his left to Jacqueline, as if to be reassured that everything was all right. As the President began waving again, Mrs. Kennedy's head abruptly twisted from her left to right, the general direction of the School Book Depository.

In addition to the reactions of the Willis girl, the President, and Mrs. Kennedy, Governor Connally's recollection and actions confirm a shot was fired before frame 166. The Governor has always been consistent in his testimony, and because he is a surviving participant, his perceptions must be given considerable weight. "We had just made the turn, well, when I heard what I thought was a shot," he told the Warren Commission. "I heard this noise which I immediately took to be a rifle shot. I instinctively turned to my right because the sound appeared to come from over my right shoulder . . ."[20]

What does the Zapruder film show? The film reveals that the Governor's head turned from mid-left to far right in less than half a second, beginning at frame 162, when the Willis girl started turning around and the President stopped waving.[21]

The film also provides additional evidence of the moment of the first shot, but in an unusual way. Dubbed the "jiggle analysis," it was first postulated by Luis Alvarez, the Nobel Prize–

---

* Phil Willis was responsible for some of the clearest photographs of the presidential car near the time of the shots. He believes he had called out to his daughter and that is why she turned and stopped. However, the enhanced Zapruder film shows he was still taking photos of the motorcade, with his camera in front of his face, when Rosemary slowed and turned. He had not even looked at her by the time she was staring toward the Depository.

winning physicist.[22] He checked the film for evidence that when a shot was fired, the sharp noise made Zapruder jerk the camera, blurring the next frame or two. CBS, in research for a 1967 documentary, tested the theory. Two volunteers were told to hold a movie camera as steady as possible. Despite advance knowledge that shots would be fired, an advantage Zapruder did not have, the men were unable to hold the camera still. Motion was always detectable on the film during the rifle fire.[23] The presence of a jiggle or blur in the film, of course, could be caused by many other factors. However, while sudden movement of Zapruder's camera may not prove a shot was fired, its absence is good evidence there was no shot. Therefore, the question is whether Zapruder had the jerky reaction for an early, missed shot. The House Select Committee determined there were four such noticeable movements, any of which could be evidence of a shot. The first significant blur was at frames 158–160, just at the time Oswald would have had to fire to avoid losing his target under the tree.[24] The largest spastic movement by Zapruder came at frames 313–314, the moment of the head shot.[25]*

An enhanced version of the Zapruder film, together with the ear- and eyewitness testimony, is strong evidence that Oswald fired the first shot near frame 160, shortly after the car had turned the corner onto Elm Street and before the tree blocked his view. Since the last shot to JFK's head was at frame 313, that translates to 8.0 to 8.4 seconds total shooting time (the period between frames 160–166 and 313). That is enough time for even a mediocre shooter to aim and operate the bolt twice.†

After the assassination, two large bullet fragments were found on the front floorboard of the limousine, and a nearly intact bullet on the Parkland stretcher. Neutron-activation tests done on the whole bullet and the fragments show they represent only

---

* The other two movements are evident between frames 189–197 and between 220–228. As is discussed at pages 327–29, the jiggle between 220–228 is caused by the second shot.

† The failure of the Warren Commission to examine the Zapruder film for reactions to an early shot is evident by the fact that when the Commission reprinted still frames from the film in Volume XVIII, it began with frame 171, under the assumption that nothing of interest happened earlier.

two bullets.[26] No part of a third bullet was ever found. So how was it possible that Lee Oswald, who put one bullet into President Kennedy's neck and another into his head, missed not only the occupants of the car with his first shot but even the car itself? What happened to that first bullet?*

The Warren Commission did not try to resolve the issue, although it was close to unraveling the mystery when FBI firearms expert Robert Frazier was asked where the missing bullet could have gone. "I have seen bullets strike small twigs," said Frazier, "small objects, and ricochet for no apparent reason except they hit and all the pressures are in on one side and it turns the bullet and it goes off at an angle. . . . There may have been a shot which deflected from a limb or for some other reason and was never discovered."[27] But the Commission never studied the large oak tree that blocked the sniper's view for almost 2.5 seconds—a simple examination might have revealed if a bullet had struck a limb.†

While the main part of the tree blocked Oswald's view after frame 166, some branches impeded his sight before that. They are evident in photos taken by the Warren Commission in 1964. Robert Kraus, a firearms expert, told the author, "The bullet definitely could have hit something, especially if you are firing close to a tree. Tests have been run over the years, by shooting bullets into baffle boxes into branches, and almost every type of bullet, whether heavy or not, is deflected even by grazing a tree branch. The bullet could have grazed it and put a groove in the branch, or could have drilled right through it without knocking the branch off. Remember, trees aren't brittle, they are living things. If it hit the branch head-on it might have separated the bullet from the jacket."[28]

---

* Upon detailed inspection after the assassination, there were no marks on the car indicating any bullet had struck it. There was, however, a crack on the inside of the windshield and a dent in the chrome stripping along the top of the windshield. Experts concluded that if either of those had been struck directly by a nondeflected stray bullet, the shell would have penetrated the glass or the chrome. Rather, they were damaged from fragments that came from the President's head wound.

† A tall streetlamp also temporarily blocked Oswald's view after the limousine turned the corner. However, it is unlikely that the first shot hit it, since none of the witnesses recall the sound of a bullet striking metal.

Virgie Rachley worked at the Book Depository and watched the motorcade from its front steps. Just after the car passed, she heard the first noise and "I saw a shot or something hit the pavement. . . . It looked just like you could see the sparks from it and I just thought it was a firecracker . . ."[29]* Whatever it was, she was certain she saw it before she heard a second shot.[30]

Five hundred and twenty feet from the Book Depository, in a straight line from the sniper's nest and the tree, James Tague had stopped his car and was standing under the southern end of the Triple Underpass. After the assassination, a deputy sheriff, Buddy Walthers, asked him why he had blood on his face.[31] "I remembered something had stung me during the shooting," recalls Tague. "And he said, 'Where were you standing?' And I showed him, and we crossed the street and on the edge of the curb, along Main Street, we found the bullet mark. And it lined right up with the Texas School Book Depository."[32] A fragment had struck the curb, sending a chip of concrete into Tague's cheek. When asked which shot hit the curb, Tague says, "I actually can't tell you which one. I could try to pick one, but through the years I have maintained accuracy. I don't know which one hit me."[33]

Although Dallas newspapers prominently reported Tague's injury, the FBI and Warren Commission initially ignored him. The Commission did not talk to him until July 1964, and the FBI did not even get a sample of the curbstone until the next month.[34] The Warren Commission concluded, "The mark on the south curb of Main Street cannot be identified conclusively with any of the three shots fired. Under the circumstances it might have come from the bullet which hit the President's head, or it might have been a product of fragmentation of the missed shot upon hitting some other object in the area."[35]

The Commission's guess that a fragment from the head

---

*Another witness, postal inspector Harry Holmes, thought he saw the first bullet hit the pavement near the President's car. Mr. and Mrs. Jack Franzen thought they saw fragments flying inside the car after the first shot. Two other witnesses, motorcycle policeman Starvis Ellis and railroad worker Royce Skelton, saw something strike the pavement near JFK's car, but thought it happened after the first shot.

wound might have caused the curb damage is not realistic. Two large fragments were found in the front of the President's car, one weighing 44.6 grains, and the other 21.0 grains (about a quarter and an eighth of the whole bullet).[36] Smaller lead fragments were found under the carpet and near the front seat. However, those fragments were so spent from the tremendous force expended on Kennedy's head wound that all they did inside the car was crack the windshield and dent a chrome strip. They did not penetrate any of the leather seats or the dashboard or cause any other damage to the car or its occupants. It is highly unlikely that any fragment from the head shot would have enough energy left to travel another 260 feet and knock a chip off a concrete curb.

There is a much simpler explanation of how Tague was wounded, and it resolves the issue of what happened to the missed first shot. Only a bullet fragment hit the concrete near Tague, since when the FBI later performed a spectrographic analysis on the curb, it showed "traces of lead with a trace of antimony."[37] The 6.5mm bullets used in Oswald's gun had full copper jackets (a metal covering on a bullet, designed to increase its penetration). Since there was no copper found on the curb, it meant the fragment that struck was not jacketed. Agent Lyndal Shaneyfelt testified that the lead instead came from the bullet's core.

Art Pence, a competition firearms expert, told the author, "If a 6.5mm bullet struck a hard tree branch, it could tear itself apart by its own rotational speed. It would then fragment, with maybe the largest fragment, the tip, being up to one third of the bullet, flying off. And if the tree was oak"—it was—"it has tremendous compressive strength, and the wood could easily suffer less damage than the bullet that hit it.

"When the lead core separates from the jacket, the core fragment is compact, and more aerodynamically stable, and tends to follow a straight course, whereas the jacket is light and will be very destabilized."[38]*

---

* When Dr. John Lattimer performed shooting experiments with the same 6.5mm ammunition as that used by Oswald, he discovered that the lead core "often" separated from the jacket.

What is likely is that after the bullet fragmented against a tree branch, the stable lead core remained in a straight line from the Depository and struck the curb, over five hundred feet away. The destabilized copper jacket hit the pavement, giving Virgie Rachley the impression of sparks. Neither fragment was ever recovered.*

If the first shot was near frame 160 and the third one at 313, when was the middle shot? And was it possible for that second bullet to have caused both the President's neck wound and all the governor's wounds, the so-called "single-bullet theory"?

On an unenhanced version of the Zapruder film, when the presidential car emerges from behind the road sign at frame 225, President Kennedy's right arm appears to be rising in response to a bullet wound. Governor Connally does not appear to show any reaction to his wounds until his mouth opens at frame 235. That difference of ten frames is just over half a second between the reactions of the two men. However, the Warren Commission was unable to pinpoint the exact frame at which the President and the Governor were hit, instead giving only a range from frames 210 to 225.[39] Conspiracy critics used the earliest possible time, frame 210, and then argued that since Connally did not show a clear reaction until frame 235 (a difference of 25 frames, or 1.4 seconds) his reaction was too slow for him to have been hit by the same bullet that hit Kennedy. If Connally was hit by another bullet, it had to be fired from a second shooter, since the Warren Commission's own reconstructions showed that Oswald could not have operated the bolt and refired in 1.4 seconds. The House Select Committee came to different conclusions, but it did not eliminate the timing problem. It actually increased the time between the moment it said Kennedy was wounded (frame 190) and the moment it saw a marked difference in Connally's posture and facial expressions (frame 226).[40] If the same bullet struck both men, the Select Committee's dif-

---

* There is a photograph of deputy sheriff Buddy Walthers, crouching over a manhole cover in Dealey Plaza, and this led to speculation that another bullet was found. But Walthers denied he ever found or saw any bullet fragment. What he did find was a small bone fragment, part of the President's skull (Sheriff Jim Bowles, interviewed by author, March 1992; Gus Rose, interviewed by Earl Golz, undated).

ference of 36 frames meant the Governor sat unfazed in his seat for nearly two seconds after being wounded.[41] The Warren Commission and Select Committee both explained the delay in Connally's reaction by citing many examples of gunshot victims who had slow reactions and sometimes did not even know they were hit by a bullet. They pointed out that Connally admitted he did not know about his wrist and thigh wounds until the following day.[42] However, both government panels ignored his clear testimony about instantly feeling the impact of the bullet in his right rear shoulder. "It felt like someone had hit me in the back," he recalled. "I knew I had been hit, and I immediately assumed, because of the amount of blood, and, in fact, that it had obviously passed through my chest, that I had probably been fatally hit . . ."[43]

The confusion over the exact timing of the second shot and whether there was an unreasonably delayed reaction by Connally might never have been resolved if further enhancements of the Zapruder film had not become available in 1992. The latest enhancements show that before the President disappeared behind the sign at frame 200, he was waving to the crowd with his right hand. Even when the car and his body are obscured by the road sign, the top of his right hand can sometimes be seen waving. By frame 224, half the car is back in view. The Governor has also emerged and is fully visible, but all that can be seen of the President is his right hand. It is only a few inches above the doorframe. In Zapruder frame 225, the President is almost in full view and his hand is lower, with the elbow resting on the edge of the car. He was bringing it down from a wave. By 226, Kennedy started raising his arm again. At 227, the President's elbow jerked off the car. He was in full reaction to the bullet that hit him from the rear and exited his throat.

Working backward from JFK's reaction, it is possible to pinpoint the precise time of the second shot. The Warren Commission was not aware that the President's spine was damaged by the bullet that entered the base of his neck, since the autopsy physicians did not examine the spine and did not use the X rays in preparing their final report.[44] The damage was first discovered by Dr. John Lattimer when he examined the autopsy X rays in 1972. The bullet passed so close to the spine that it caused "blast injury," trauma near the sixth cervical vertabra, C-6 (in the vicinity of the tip of the transverse process).[45] On the X rays there are small splinters of bone at the point of trauma. The bullet did not even have to hit the spine to cause such an injury —entering the body at nearly 2,000 feet per second and traversing very close would be enough.[46] "The bullet creates a cavity in soft tissue as it passes, and the shock traumatizes the spinal cord," says Dr. Lattimer.[47]

A spinal injury at the level of C-6 is significant because it can cause an instantaneous reaction called "Thorburn's Position."[48] Named after the English physician who discovered it over a hundred years ago, it refers to spinal injury that forces the victim's arms to jerk up into a fixed position, almost parallel with the chin, the hands gathered near the chin and the elbows pushed out to the sides.[49] That is exactly the position the President started assuming at frames 226–227.

Most observers of the Zapruder film, as well as eyewitnesses that day, incorrectly thought the President was grabbing at his throat in response to the bullet that struck him. But the Thorburn Position is a neurological reflex, and upon examination of the enhanced film one can see that the President's hands never touch his throat. Moreover, once C-6 is damaged, the arms would have remained locked in the raised position indefinitely— except the destruction of the right hemisphere of JFK's brain by the head shot released the position. Any doubt he suffered the Thorburn damage to C-6 is resolved in the Zapruder enhancement. In the nearly five seconds that elapsed between the neck and head wound, Mrs. Kennedy leaned over toward him to see what had happened. At one point, she grabbed his raised left arm with her right hand and tried to push it down. It stayed up. Then she reached with both hands and tried again to push it down, but the film clearly records his resistance. His arm did not lower.

Kennedy's Thorburn response, from spinal damage, at frames 226–227, came between one tenth and two tenths of a second after the bullet hit him, which translates to 1.8 to 3.66 Zapruder frames.[50] That means President Kennedy was first wounded at frames 223–224, or just before he was visible from behind the road sign. That is 3.5 seconds after Oswald had fired his first shot near frame 160, more than enough time for him to cock the bolt, re-aim, and fire again.

The focus now moves to Governor Connally. When does he show evidence of being shot? Is there a long enough delay to raise the possibility that a separate bullet, from a second gunman, struck him?

Watching the Zapruder film at its normal speed, or looking at photographs of still frames, provides a misleading impression of when the Governor was hit. Prior to his Warren Commission testimony, the Governor examined the Zapruder film and felt he was struck between frames 231–234 (just before he opened his mouth at frame 235).[51] Mrs. Connally also studied the film before her testimony and thought her husband was hit between 229–233. Two and a half years later, the Governor examined four-by-five-inch transparencies, and after several hours still felt he was hit at frame 234.

The enhanced film shows several physical reactions that reveal exactly when the Governor was hit, and it is within a half second of when he and his wife originally thought the shot struck. At 224, the right front of the Governor's suit lapel flips up from his chest. Confirmed in a 1992 computer enhancement by Jeff Lotz of Failure Analysis Associates, this jacket movement may be one of the most important timing confirmations in the case, as it established the moment the bullet hit him. The movement of the jacket took place at the exact area where the Governor's suit and shirt have a bullet hole, as the missile passed through his right shoulder blade and out under his right nipple.[52]

Since Kennedy and Connally were less than two feet apart in the car, the bullet, with an initial muzzle velocity of more than 2,000 feet per second, passed through them almost simultaneously, at frame 224. Beyond the movement of Connally's suit jacket and the Select Committee's finding that he changed his expression and became rigid at 226, there is other evidence he was struck at this point.[53] A film enhancement of that same frame, done by Dr. Michael West, shows that the Governor's light-colored Stetson hat, which he was holding in his right hand, near his chest, started rising. It flipped quickly up during frames 227 and 228 and then at 229 it started coming down rapidly, and by the next frame it was at its original position. That violent reaction with the governor's hat took less than one third of a second. According to Dr. West, it is "positive proof" of a neurological reaction to physical trauma.[54]*

"It took only an instant for the bullet to pass through Connally's chest, then strike his wrist, and finally settle in his leg," says Dr. West. "His chest wound gave him a pneumothorax [a punctured lung]. When he took his next breath, his lung collapsed, and that is a very painful situation. It sends a nerve signal to the brain's cortex, which in turn will send out his pain transmitters, all in an instant. But the Governor had to take his next full breath after the bullet passed his chest, before all hell broke loose for him."[55]

At frames 235–236, Connally's mouth opened wide, and by 238 his cheeks puffed out and he turned sharply down and to the right. According to Dr. Charles Gregory, one of the surgeons who attended to Connally at Parkland, when the bullet passed through the Governor, it compressed the chest wall, and the epiglottis involuntarily opened, forcing air out of his mouth. Dr. Gregory estimated that such an expulsion of air could come up to half a second after the bullet struck.[56] Dr. Gregory had not seen the Zapruder film when he testified, instead basing his opinion on his medical expertise. His estimate, when applied to the Zapruder film, would indicate that Connally was shot near frame 226. The enhanced Zapruder film shows the Governor was actually struck just one ninth of a second earlier, at frame 224, the same moment President Kennedy was wounded.

Connally's reaction to the shot, while slower than Kennedy's, was still fast. He showed signs of physical stress (his hat flipping up) within a tenth of a second, and reacted visibly to pain

---

* The critics have long charged that the Governor held on to his hat during these frames—proof, they claim, that his wrist could not have been wounded at that point. "If he doesn't drop the hat, it doesn't mean a thing," says Dr. Michael Baden. "Some say that the Governor's radial nerve was damaged, but that's not true. There was no radial damage, but even if that nerve had been hit, he wouldn't have dropped it. His wrist was clearly wounded, with the radius bone broken. No one argues that." Baden says it is a "moot point," since the Zapruder film never shows him dropping the hat.

(his mouth opening and cheeks expanding) only two thirds of a second after he was hit.

What is Governor Connally's own testimony, and does it fit the sequence of the three shots described above? The Governor's memory of what happened is perhaps the most lucid of the witnesses' there.

"When the first shot was fired I thought of nothing else but that it is a rifle shot," he said. "I then had the time to turn to my right, I had time to think, time to react. I turned to my right to see if I could see anything unusual, and especially to see if I could see him out of the corner of my eye, because I immediately thought of an assassination attempt. I didn't see anything but the general blur of waving and of people moving. Nothing really unusual. I did not see the President out of the corner of my eye. I started to turn to look over my left shoulder and had about come to the point where I was looking straight forward again and I felt the impact of the bullet that hit me."[57]

The Governor's description fits exactly with the early missed shot fired near frame 160. That was the sound he heard that made him start to turn sharply to his right. On the film, the Governor was still turning back to his original position, just as he recalled, at frame 224.

Talking of the bullet that wounded him, Connally told the Warren Commission: "Well, in my judgment, it just couldn't be the first one because I heard the sound of the shot. In the first place, I don't know anything about the velocity of this particular bullet, but any rifle has a velocity that exceeds the speed of sound, and when I heard the sound of that first shot, that bullet had already reached where I was, or it had reached that far, and after I heard that shot . . . I started to turn to my left before I felt anything. It is not conceivable to me that I could have been hit by the first bullet, and I felt the blow from something which was obviously a bullet, which I assumed was a bullet, and I never heard the second shot, didn't hear it. I didn't hear but two shots. I think I heard the first shot and the third shot."[58]

The Governor's explanation is sound. Doctors familiar with gunshot wounds say it is normal for the shock caused by the wound to block the sound from the victim.[59] Yet the Warren Commission still decided that the first bullet most likely hit Kennedy and Connally. The Governor, who had described a "very, very brief span of time" between the first shot and the one that hit him, knew that was impossible. While he accepted the Commission's conclusions about Oswald being the lone assassin, he continued to insist that the first bullet fired did not strike him.

Governor Connally had another difficulty with the Warren Commission's conclusion about the sequence of shots. Although convinced he was struck by the second bullet, he thought the President was hit by the first shot. Yet he admitted that when he turned to his right after hearing the first shot, he did not turn far enough to see the President. The Zapruder film shows the first shot did not affect the President, either. If Governor Connally had continued to turn to see the President, he would have seen Kennedy waving to the crowd.

The primary reason that Connally believed the first bullet hit the President was the testimony of his wife, Nellie.[60] She told the Warren Commission that when she heard the first shot, "I turned over my right shoulder and looked back, and saw the President as he had both hands at his neck. . . . Then very soon there was the second shot which hit John."[61] In her testimony, there is a key sentence that the Commission and subsequent researchers have overlooked. Mrs. Connally said, "As the first shot was hit, and I turned to look at the same time, I recall John saying, 'Oh, no, no, no.' Then there was the second shot, and it hit John . . ."[62] However, she could not have heard her husband say, "Oh, no, no, no," at the first shot. He was clear in his testimony: "I immediately, when I was hit, I said, 'Oh, no, no, no.' And then I said, 'My God, they are going to kill us all.' Nellie pulled me over into her lap, she could tell I was still breathing and moving, and she said, 'Don't worry. Be quiet. You are going to be all right.' "[63]

What Mrs. Connally thought was the first shot was actually the second shot, which hit both her husband and the President. When she turned to look at the President, she did indeed see his hands up near his neck, but it was in reaction to the bullet that struck him at frame 224, the same bullet that forced her husband into her arms a few seconds later. The conclusive evidence is again found in the Zapruder film. The enhancement shows Mrs. Connally, despite her recollection of turning to her right after the first shot, actually turning at frames 227–228, a split second after the second shot.

In an October 30, 1966, interview with *Life* magazine, the Governor said, "There is my absolute knowledge, and Nellie's too, that one bullet caused the President's wound, and that an entirely separate shot struck me. . . . I'll never change my mind." The author presented some of the new evidence to Governor Connally during a telephone conversation in May 1992. He was open-minded that new technologies might provide an understanding of the few seconds in Dealey Plaza not available in earlier years. "It may well be that Mrs. Connally was mistaken about seeing the President raise his arms after the first shot," he says. "That might have been after the second shot. And if that is true, it would make it all very, very consistent. The first bullet could have missed us both. The third bullet definitely only hit him. Based upon the angles, the second bullet, which went through his neck, could have gone through my back. The second bullet could have hit both of us."

Was it possible for one bullet to have inflicted the neck wound on President Kennedy and all of the wounds on Governor Connally? Failure Analysis Associates applied the latest computer and film-enhancement technology to answer the question of whether one bullet could have caused the wounds and, if so, where the sniper would have to shoot from for the bullet to do the damage. "The most important factor was to have the President and the Governor in the exact locations they were at the time they were shot," said Dr. Robert Piziali, who oversaw the Failure Analysis tests.[64] Failure Analysis used a technique called "reverse projection" to answer the questions. First it created a full-sized model of the presidential limousine. Then a camera was placed in relation to where Zapruder was standing, and the lens was set to the same focal length, so the view of the car was identical to that afforded in the film. Using the Zapruder film, the images of Kennedy and Connally were sketched into the car, and then people who were the exact height and weight of the two men were placed into the seats in the positions shown on the film. Failure Analysis achieved precision on the placement because it used a sonic digitizer, able to make measurements of the bodies from the two-dimensional Zapruder film, and convert them into three-dimensional space. Once the car was filmed, it was placed into animation, and located at the exact spot on Elm Street that it was when the second shot was fired, at frame 224. Then the wounds on the President and Governor were measured and extended into the animation.

At that point the computer was ready to answer two questions. The first was whether one bullet could cause all the wounds, and the answer was yes.[65] The bullet punctured Kennedy's back, exited his throat, and on a straight-line trajectory entered Connally's right shoulder. It struck Connally's rib, and at a downward angle exited under his right nipple. Because he had turned in his seat, the Governor was slightly to the right. His right forearm was held near the lower portion of his chest. The bullet continued through his right wrist and then into his left thigh.

"One of the silliest arguments critics made over the years," says Dr. Michael Baden, "is that the bullet came out of Kennedy's neck, made a right turn to hit Connally's shoulder, then made another right when it left his chest in order to strike his wrist, and then completely changed directions and made a left to enter his thigh. Some people still believe that, even though photo enhancements long ago showed the Governor was in such a position that his wounds were clearly the result of one bullet passing straight through him."[66]

The second question resolved by the Failure Analysis re-creation is where the sniper would have to be located for the single bullet to have the correct trajectory. Utilizing the information on the wounds and the location of the men and the car, the computer worked backward to provide a "cone" within which the sniper had to be. "In this case," says Dr. Piziali, "the cone is almost centered on the sixth floor of the Texas School Book Depository. The shot could only have come from within that cone."[67]

The final issue on the single bullet is whether Commission Exhibit 399, the bullet found on the stretcher at Parkland Hospital within ninety minutes of the assassination, could have inflicted the wounds to both men and remained only partially deformed. CE 399, denigrated as the "magic bullet" by buffs, is described as "pristine" in conspiracy books. CE 399 is a fully jacketed military bullet, and ballistics expert Howard Donahue says he was "astonished" when he first personally examined it.* He describes it as "obviously somewhat bent and severely flattened, so much so that a small amount of lead had been extruded from the bullet's base."[68]

"It's called a 'pristine bullet,'" said Dr. Michael Baden, "which is a media term that is inaccurate: it's like being a little bit pregnant—it either is pristine or it is not pristine. This is a damaged bullet and is not pristine. It is deformed; it would be very difficult to take a hammer and flatten it to the degree that this is flattened. This is a partially deformed bullet with a heavy jacket."[69]

Yet CE 399 is not fragmented or crushed. In reconstructions, firing shots into a variety of items, the Warren Commission was unable to duplicate a bullet in the same condition. The Commission test bullet most often cited by critics is CE 856, in which a bullet was fired into a cadaver's wrist to simulate Connally's wrist wound. CE 856 emerged with a badly smashed nose.[70] Since the bullet that did the actual wounds to both men also had to pass through the President's neck, the Governor's chest, and then into his thigh, it seemed to indicate that the stretcher bullet could not be the single bullet.

"Nonsense," says Dr. Lattimer. "What that actually shows is that the Warren Commission did not conduct the proper experiments. They fired a 6.5mm shell traveling at over 2,000 feet per second directly into a wrist bone. Of course you are going to get deformation of the bullet when it strikes a hard object at full speed. If Governor Connally's wrist had been hit on the straight

---

*Mandated by the Geneva Convention of 1922, the purpose of enclosing bullets with full metal jackets was to reduce combat fatalities. The bullets were designed to pass through bodies and, if no major organs were struck, only to wound the victim. Before metal jackets, bullets often detoured inside the body. That the 6.5mm Carcano ammunition was designed to do exactly what it did on the President and the Governor is often ignored. Dr. John Lattimer and Dr. John Nichols created experiments to test the bullet's toughness. Nichols shot a 6.5mm slug through four feet of ponderosa pine boards, and Lattimer put one through two feet of elm wood. Both bullets appeared undamaged (Lattimer, Kennedy and Lincoln, p. 272). Moreover, ballistics expert Larry Sturdivan pointed out that another attribute of the Carcano bullet is that it is "one of the most stable bullets we have ever done experimentation with" (HSCA Vol. I, p. 386).

fly by that bullet, CE 399, the bullet would be in much worse shape, and so would his wrist. What the Warren Commission did not understand was that the bullet slowed as it passed through the bodies, and it never hit a hard surface, like bone, on its nose. First it went through Kennedy's neck. When it exited the President, it begun tumbling [rotating] and that is evident by the elongated entry wound on the Governor's back [the bullet entered sideways].* It continued tumbling through his chest, and struck a glancing blow to his rib, knocking out several inches. The gaping exit hole under his right nipple shows the bullet left his chest sideways, entered his wrist while tumbling backwards, and exited with just enough strength to break the skin on his thigh."[71]

Dr. Charles Gregory, the treating physician at Parkland for Connally's wrist and thigh, agreed that based on his examination of the wrist's entry wound, the bullet had been tumbling and entered backward. That the entry wound was large and had an irregular surface, the way in which the muscles were damaged, and that the bullet had picked up organic materials like threads from Connally's suit and carried them into the wound made Gregory conclude: "The only way that this missile could have produced this wound in my view, was to have entered the wrist backwards."[72] As for the thigh wound, he said the bullet "struck the thigh in a reverse fashion and shed a bit of its lead core into the fascia [a layer of fatty tissue] immediately beneath the skin . . ."[73] Gregory was surprised not to find the bullet, since he realized it had barely penetrated the skin of Connally's thigh. He even "suggested to someone to search the Governor's belongings and other areas where he had been to see if it could be identified or found."[74] Gregory did not immediately think about

---

* In his original operating notes on Governor Connally, thoracic surgeon Dr. Robert Shaw described the unprepped wound on the Governor's back as 3 cm long (1.25 inches, the same length as Oswald's 6.5mm bullet). Six months later in his Warren Commission testimony, Shaw recalled the wound as only half that long, but agreed the bullet could have been tumbling. In a March 1992 interview with the author, he remembered Connally's injury as a small puncture wound. Shaw admitted that his changing recollections were influenced by Connally's early opinion that he was hit by a separate bullet from the one that struck JFK.

the stretcher on which the Governor had been brought into the hospital.*

"That bullet slowed in velocity each time it traversed another body part," says Dr. Baden. "There was a debate on our panel [the Select Committee's medical panel] as to whether the bullet even hit Connally's rib or just passed close enough to do the damage. But most of us thought it hit the rib while tumbling, and a sideways hit explains why such a hard bullet is flattened. When it struck the wrist bone, which is small, it was not deformed, since its velocity was so low. By the time it left the wrist, its speed was greatly reduced, and the nature of his thigh wound shows it was a spent bullet by then."[75]†

Dr. Martin Fackler, president of the International Wound Ballistics Association, finds the condition of CE 399 "entirely consistent" with a bullet that inflicted the seven wounds on the two men. "It's a long bullet [1.25 inches] and I would expect it to be flattened on the side, just like you had squeezed it in a vise."[76]

Ballistics experts have calculated the speeds at which the bullet would have entered and exited each wound on the President and the Governor. The 6.5mm slug left Oswald's rifle at 2,000 feet per second and hit Kennedy at the base of the neck between 1,700 and 1,800 feet per second. Passing only through flesh, the bullet lost another one to two hundred feet per second and hit Connally at 1,500 to 1,600. It left his chest and entered the wrist at 900 feet per second. Anything above 700 feet per

---

* Some suggest that CE 399 was planted on Connally's stretcher. CE 399 was found before the surgery on Connally or the autopsy on JFK. At the time it would have to be planted, no one in the supposed conspiracy could know whether the bullets that had been fired at the motorcade were still inside the bodies of the victims. If the conspirators planted a bullet on the stretcher, and then fragments belonging to three different bullets were found in Kennedy and Connally, the plot would have immediately exposed itself by planting a fourth bullet, since there was only time for Oswald to carefully fire three shots.

† Some critics originally charged that the bullet had entered deep into the Governor's thigh and stopped at the femur (thigh) bone. "That's crazy," says Baden. "If it hit the femur, it would never have fallen out. The X ray from the side looks like the fragment left there is on the bone, but that is because you have no sense of depth. However, when you look at an X ray taken on top of the leg, you can see the fragment is barely under the skin and nowhere near the bone."

second is enough to shatter bone. When it left the wrist it was near 400 feet per second, just enough to break the skin and imbed itself into his thigh.[77]

Larry Sturdivan, a scientist at the Army's weapons training center at Aberdeen, said such a missile will "not deform because the pressure, due to the lower velocity, is never high enough to deform the bullet."[78]

"That's the key to understanding why CE 399 emerged in whole condition," says Dr. Baden. "I have seen similar bullets that have inflicted gunshot wounds. The bullet was traveling slow enough that, while its speed and density were still greater than the bone it was hitting, it was not moving so fast as to deform seriously the metal jacket. People want an absolute re-creation of CE 399 in tests, but that is impossible. I have seen cases of machine-gun fire at a stationary person, and the bullet paths and injuries produced are never duplicated. There can be minute differences in the manufacture of the ammunition, the condition of the gun that fires it, and the slightest contraction of any muscle on the victim can cause the bullet to take a different path. Re-creation tests on dead bones may not be as helpful, since they can be different than live bones. Bullets react differently to bones with blood going through them as opposed to bones that are dry. The minutest difference in distance between two bullets fired can affect the path of the bullets, the injuries, and the damage to the bullet. Trying to re-create CE 399 is an exercise in futility."[79]

Although a complete re-creation of CE 399 may be impossible, the question of reduced velocity and damage to the bullet can be tested. For the Warren Commission, the Army conducted separate experiments with 6.5mm bullets, one to determine the effect on a bullet that passed through the President's neck and another to test a bullet going through the Governor's rib. The one that passed through the mock-up of the President's neck (goat skin and meat) was not deformed.[80] The missile that hit the reconstruction for the Governor's rib (an anesthetized goat) did not have the benefit of first being slowed through the President's neck. Yet, still, it only had a slight flattening, similar to CE 399.[81] The remaining question about the condition of the bullet was whether a bullet at a reduced velocity could strike the radius bone in the wrist and emerge in good condition. In 1992 Dr. Piziali, of Failure Analysis, and Dr. Fackler experimented with powder charges. They lowered the velocity on a 6.5mm bullet to 1,100 feet per second and shot it through a cadaver's wrist. "The bullet actually made a slightly greater hole than the one in Governor Connally's wrist," said Dr. Fackler. "That's because the experiment bullet was actually going a little faster than the 900 feet that CE 399 was traveling. The test bullet was non-deformed. It was not flattened in the least and had nowhere near the damage of CE 399."[82]

The final issue in the single-bullet theory involves bullet fragments found in Governor Connally. The FBI randomly weighed 6.5mm Carcano bullets and determined the average weight was 161.2 grains.[83] The stretcher bullet weighed 158.6, meaning only 2.6 grains of its mass were lost.[84] No fragments were left in President Kennedy's neck wound. However, the Governor had three removed from his wrist during surgery, and two small fragments remained in his wrist and one was embedded in his thigh.* According to writers Robert Groden and Harrison Livingstone, in *High Treason*, "There were more than three grains of metal in Connally's wrist wounds alone . . ."[85] That is not true. Dr. Gregory, who performed the surgery on the Governor's wrist, said the fragments he removed "were varying from five-tenths of a millimeter in diameter to approximately 2 millimeters in diameter, and each fragment is no more than a half millimeter in thickness. They would represent, in lay terms, flakes, flakes of metal. I would estimate that they would be weighed in micrograms, which is a very small amount of weight. I don't know how to reduce it to ordinary equivalents for you. It is the kind of weighing that requires a microadjustable scale, which means that it is something less than the weight of a postage stamp."[86] Gregory said the fragments taken from the wrist were so tiny that he did not even plan to take them out, but chanced upon them during surgery.[87] As for the thigh fragment, Dr. Gregory described it as "microscopic, five tenths of a millimeter by 2

---

* Although some interpreted X rays of the Governor's chest to indicate another fragment was in the chest cavity, Dr. Baden says, "That's completely wrong. It's a bone chip, not a metal flake."

millimeters . . . weighing again in micrograms, postage stamp weight . . ."[88]

A reconstruction of weights based upon the fragments removed by Dr. Gregory, as well as the descriptions of those left in Connally, indicates that all the fragments from CE 399 weighed no more than 1.5 grains. That, added to the weight of CE 399 (158.6), is still approximately one grain less than the weight of an average Carcano bullet.[89]

Dr. Gregory, in his Warren Commission testimony, also pointed out that the fragments he recovered from the Governor's wrist were lead, not brass or copper.[90] That is critical because the portion missing from CE 399 is from the soft lead core that protruded from the bottom during its flattening.*

One of the most significant scientific experiments conducted for the single bullet was neutron activation, a nuclear test performed on the fragments. By analyzing the trace elements found in bullet lead, neutron activation makes it possible to determine the probability that different fragments were part of one bullet. In 1974, Dr. Cyril Wecht, the most vocal medical critic of the Warren Commission's conclusions, wrote: "If it had been found that the composition of the lead in the fragment recovered from Governor Connally's wrist wound was indistinguishable from the composition of the lead in the nearly whole bullet found at Parkland Hospital, that fact alone would lend strong support to the single bullet theory."[91]

The House Select Committee engaged Dr. Vincent Guinn, one of the country's most respected experts in neutron activation, to test the stretcher bullet (CE 399), the three fragments removed from Connally's wrist (CE 842), two removed during the autopsy from the President's brain (CE 843), the large mashed fragment found on the front floorboard of the limousine (CE 567), and several small ones found on the rear floor of the limo (CE 840).†

---

* Some question whether less than three grains of lead was enough metal to make the six fragments in Connally. Dr. John Lattimer squeezed an equivalent amount of the lead core from a 6.5mm bullet and was able to create forty-one fragments the size that Dr. Gregory described (*Kennedy and Lincoln*, p. 278).

† Dr. Guinn also examined the deformed bullet found at the scene of the attempted assassination of General Walker (CE 573) and was able to identify it

When the House Select Committee announced it had asked Dr. Guinn to undertake that test, the critics were pleased. It is very easy to exclude different items under neutron activation.[92] Most were convinced that the tests would prove that the fragments from Connally's wrist did not come from the stretcher bullet. But they were shocked when Dr. Guinn reported his results. He discovered that the Western Cartridge Co. bullets made for the Carcano were different from any of the other bullets he had tested during twenty years.[93] According to Dr. Guinn, the most striking feature, and most useful for identification purposes, was that "there seems to be no uniformity within a production lot. That is, even when we would take a box of cartridges all from a given production lot, take one cartridge out and then another and then another . . . all out of the same box —boxes of twenty, these were—and analyze them, they all in general look . . . widely different, particularly in their antimony content. . . . In general if you take most boxes of ammunition . . . take a bunch of them out, you can't tell one from the other. They all look like little carbon copies even to activation analysis, but not so with the Mannlicher-Carcano."[94] This lack of uniformity among the Carcano bullets allowed him to match the fragments with a degree of certainty normally not available, even in a sophisticated test like neutron activation.

Guinn concluded that the all the fragments were Western Cartridge Co. bullets manufactured for the Mannlicher-Carcano rifle. He found they came from only two bullets. "There is no evidence for three bullets, four bullets, or anything more than two . . ." he said.[95] He determined that the fragments from Kennedy's brain matched the three testable fragments found on the floorboard of the limousine, meaning they were all part of the third shot fired.[96] His most important finding was that CE 399, the stretcher bullet, was indistinguishable, both in antimony

as a Western Cartridge Co. 6.5mm Carcano bullet, the same brand Oswald used in the presidential assassination (HSCA Vol. I, p. 502).

Three pieces of evidence did not contain enough lead to be subjected to neutron activation: FBI No. Q-609, the section of the curbstone near James Tague that was struck by a bullet fragment; CE 569, a fragment recovered from the front floorboard of the presidential limousine; and CE 841, tiny particles scraped from the inside surface of the limousine's windshield.

and silver, from the fragments recovered from the Governor's wrist.[97] Guinn's finding ended the speculation that CE 399 had been planted on the stretcher, since there was now indisputable evidence that it had traveled through Connally's body, leaving behind fragments.*

The critics now tried to say that all that Dr. Guinn's test proved is that the stretcher bullet and the Connally wrist fragments came from the same batch of bullets.[98] But the great difference in the composition of the metal among individual bullets meant that Guinn's conclusion was much more specific than that. He considered the test results as definite as any he had seen in two decades of testing. "The stretcher bullet matches the fragments in the wrist," Guinn said, "and that indicates indeed that that particular bullet did fracture the wrist."[99] When asked if there was a chance that another Carcano bullet could have the same composition as Connally's fragments, he said, "Extremely unlikely, or very improbable, however you prefer."[100]

---

* The FBI scraped a microscopic amount from the bullet to conduct its first-ever neutron-activation test in 1964. New to the procedure, the FBI misread the results as inconclusive. However, subsequent experts read the results, and said they also confirm that Connally's fragments came from the stretcher bullet (HSCA Vol. I, p. 560).

15

"I'm a Character! I'm Colorful"

The interrogation of Oswald began soon after homicide captain Will Fritz arrived at the police station. Oswald was taken to the third floor, to a ten-by-fourteen-foot room with glass windows covered by blinds. There, he was questioned at length, at least five separate times, for a total of approximately twelve hours, between 2:30 P.M. on the day of the assassination, Friday, November 22, until just after 11:00 A.M. on Sunday, November 24. None of the interviews were recorded, nor were any transcripts made. Accounts of the questions and answers come from the more than twenty-five participants, including Dallas police detectives, FBI and Secret Service agents, postal inspectors, and assistant Dallas district attorneys.*

---

* Today, the police would videotape the statements of any defendant in such a high-profile case, both for his protection as well as to reduce the likelihood of any police-misconduct charges. However, the Dallas police department's policy in 1963 was not to record interrogations. The department did not even own a tape recorder (WC Vol. IV, pp. 201, 204). Assistant district attorney Bill Alexander, who handled much of the weekend's legal work, gave the author another reason why the interrogations were not recorded: "In Texas, at that time, an oral statement under duress was no good. We had Miranda before the Supreme Court handed it down for the rest of the country. We had to inform him that he did not have to make any statement, and that any he did make had to be voluntary, witnessed, reduced to writing, and could be used against him. So our questions for him were strictly to get information, but there was no way they could be used in court. If he had said 'Yeah, I killed the no-good s.o.b. President,' it would have been inadmissible in any court. Even if we gave

The first priority in the interrogations was to discover whether Oswald had accomplices. "We wanted to know if there was anyone else we should be looking for," recalls assistant district attorney Bill Alexander, an aggressive trial attorney who was at the center of the weekend's activities. He sat in on several hours of questioning. "I had been part of the group that searched his room at the boardinghouse at 1026 North Beckley, and when we first found that Communist propaganda, I thought we might have stumbled across something with international repercussions, a spy ring or something like that. . . ."*

"But even though he didn't tell us much," Alexander told the author, "we felt pretty comfortable, soon after we started questioning him, that there was no one else involved. I still thought we should have thrown Marina into a cell and shaken her down some, and also looked a little harder at the Paines, but no one else agreed with me."[1] Marina and Ruth Paine were brought to the police station. Everyone around Oswald was initially under suspicion.[2] Robert Oswald arrived later that evening, as did his mother, Marguerite.

All those who assisted in questioning Oswald described him as composed and unruffled (except when FBI agent Hosty arrived and identified himself).[3] Detective Richard Sims said, "He

---

him the proper warning, and then reduced his statement to writing, if he then refused to sign it in the presence of a witness, it was useless. That's how strict the Texas law was. He could always say the statement was induced by threats, fraud, or coercion. That would have risked reversal on appeal, so why even take that chance since the physical evidence was so strong? That's why it was not important to record or transcribe the discussions."

In addition, when Oswald later made telephone calls from the jail or met with Marina, his mother, and brother, the Dallas police had no means to monitor the conversations (WC Vol. IV, pp. 238–39).

* At a subsequent search of the Paine house, the police discovered a miniature Minox camera, often dubbed a spy camera because of its size. Rolls of film were also seized and later developed by the FBI. The photos depicted various international locations. On a later FBI inventory of items taken from the Paine household, the Minox camera was listed as a light meter. Critics charged that the government was covering up evidence of intelligence equipment issued to Oswald. The truth is much simpler: The camera and film belonged to Michael Paine. The author was the first person to ask Paine about the camera and to show him copies of pictures from the film that had been confiscated and developed. "Those are my pictures," he says. "I remember taking them. And I had that camera since the 1950s."

was calm and wasn't nervous. . . . He had control of himself."[4] "He was strung very tight," recalls Alexander, "but he was definitely under control, almost arrogant and cocky. He answered almost every question with another question, and never gave that much information. We were very careful not to mistreat him in any way. The world's press was just outside [Captain] Fritz's door, and when we walked him through the hallways, he would have been the first to yell if we had done something to him. But he was so smug in the way he dealt with the questions, at times I had to walk out of the room, because in another few minutes I was going to beat the shit out of him myself."[5] "He struck me as a man who enjoyed the situation immensely," remembered postal inspector Harry Holmes, "and was enjoying the publicity and everything that was coming his way."[6] Detective Jim Leavelle recalls, "I never saw him raise his voice, and he seemed to answer questions easily. He had a smile a lot of the time, kind of a smirk, really, sort of like he knew something you didn't." The description of Oswald at the jail sounds remarkably like the one Carlos Bringuier gave of him after his arrest for the street demonstration in New Orleans some three months earlier: "He was really cold-blooded . . . he was not nervous, he was not out of control, he was confident."

When Marina visited him, however, she felt his eyes betrayed his guilt.[7] She knew that if he had been innocent, he would have demanded his immediate freedom and complained to the highest officials. His compliance, coupled with his assurance that he was not being mistreated, added to her feeling he had committed the crime.* Michael Paine decided not to visit Oswald at the

---

* Today, Marina has changed her mind, telling the author, "I think Lee was completely innocent." She has lived in Texas since the assassination and has been bombarded by the buffs for nearly three decades. "There are just too many things," she says, "like how he could have fired the shots so fast, and lots of questions I don't understand." She admits she has reached her new conclusion about her husband's innocence based not on what she knows from her own experiences with him but on what others have told her about the case and the "evidence." Marina has been susceptible in the past to the arguments of conspiracy buffs, even the most bizarre ones. In the summer of 1980 she joined the successful legal effort of British author Michael Eddowes to exhume her husband's body, under the belief that the man in the grave was actually a Soviet KGB agent who had impersonated the real Oswald, even fooling his mother and brothers. On October 4, 1981, four forensic pathologists

jail, "because when I watched him on television, I was surprised at his chutzpah and was too angry to visit him as I would have antagonized him at that point. But I knew him well enough to see he looked like the Cheshire cat that had just swallowed the canary. He had the smug satisfaction of knowing that he had struck a bold stroke for his cause. He had thrown a definite monkey wrench in the wheels of the capitalist cabal."[8]

Although Oswald disclosed little useful information during the interrogations, he managed to lie about almost every subject. Among other things, he denied owning a rifle,[9] and asserted he had never used an alias at his rooming house and had no knowledge of the name Hidell.[10] He said he had not taken a trip to Mexico City,[11] was not involved in Fair Play for Cuba, and had not been undesirably discharged from the Marines.[12] According to Oswald, he never told Frazier he had curtain rods in any package he carried into the Depository.[13] He lied about how he obtained his pistol and denied ever using post-office boxes or living at Neely Street in Dallas, posing for backyard photos at that address, or making the markings on a map found on him when he was arrested.[14]

When pressed in the interrogations, Oswald remained firm and even dismissed the seriousness of what had happened. "At one time I told him," recalled Captain Will Fritz, "I said, 'You know you have killed the President, and this is a very serious charge.' He denied it and said he hadn't killed the President. I said he had been killed. He said people will forget within a few days and there would be another President."[15]

On Friday, November 22, Oswald sat through four different questioning sessions, interrupted only when police took him for lineups before the Tippit witnesses and Howard Brennan from Dealey Plaza. Late in the first session, he raised the issue of legal counsel. He said he did not want to be represented by any Dallas attorney and asked for John Abt, a New York lawyer prominent in left-wing causes. "When he said he wanted Abt,"

---

at Dallas's Baylor Medical Center used dental and medical records to confirm the exhumed corpse was that of Lee Oswald.

recalls Alexander, "I was vaguely aware of him, and my first thought was 'Hey, this s.o.b. really is a Communist.' "[16]*

By 7:00 P.M. on Friday, Alexander had drafted the murder indictment for Tippit. "We were not an international police force," says Alexander. "We had two murders on our hands and wanted to solve them. I drew up the Tippit charge first because there was no doubt what to write up on that one. We had a good case and had Oswald cold. I said to Captain Fritz, 'Let's go ahead and file because we don't know when the Civil Liberties Union or John Abt or the Communist network is going to run someone in here and find a weak judge who might set a bond, or somebody might come in with a writ.' At that time, any district judge in Texas could grant a writ of habeas corpus [an emergency court order] for any prisoner in the entire state. My fear was that once you were playing with an ideology like Communism, you didn't know what was going to crawl out of the cracks. So I said, 'Let's nail him down so no one can get him away from us.' And by that I also meant the federals, with whom we did not have a good relationship."[17]

Alexander, Captain Fritz, and justice of the peace David Johnston took Oswald into a side room. "A lot of people claimed to be there," Alexander says. "If they were all there, you would have had to rent a convention center. And when David Johnston started to read him the charge, Oswald said, 'This isn't an ar-

* Abt was the lawyer for the Hall-Davis Defense Committee, representing American Communist party chiefs Gus Hall and Benjamin Davis, to which Oswald had offered his photographic services in 1962. Gregory Olds of the Dallas Civil Liberties Union visited the jail on Friday and checked to see whether Oswald wanted a local attorney and left when he was satisfied that Oswald "had not been deprived of his rights . . ." (WC Vol. VII, pp. 323–24). The following day, Saturday, November 23, H. Louis Nichols, president of the Dallas Bar Association, also visited Oswald. Again, Oswald declined help from any Dallas lawyer, and asked Nichols if he could help arrange for Abt to represent him (WC Vol. VII, pp. 323, 329). Oswald telephoned Ruth Paine twice on Saturday, November 23. When Ruth answered the phone, "I was shocked since he was calling as though nothing unusual had happened, and I couldn't believe that he would call me for help after what had taken place" (Interview with Ruth Paine, April 14, 1992). Oswald gave Ruth Abt's home and office telephone numbers, and asked her to call him over the weekend (WC Vol. III, pp. 85–86). Ruth did call, but Abt was not at home, and thereby missed the opportunity to represent the accused presidential assassin.

raignment. This isn't a court. How do I know this is a judge? And who are you?' And I told him in no uncertain terms to shut his mouth, and he was quiet after that. He seemed astonished, like he had gotten off in the wrong territory."[18]*

After the Tippit arraignment, nearly nine hours after the assassination, the police took paraffin casts of Oswald's hands and his right cheek. The theory of the test is that gunpowder residue will react with the paraffin and turn blue on the cast. Oswald's hands proved positive; his cheek, however, was negative,[19] which raised doubts about whether he had fired the rifle earlier that day.[20] Yet paraffin reacts to many items besides gunpowder —including tobacco, cosmetics, pharmaceuticals, soil fertilizer, and various kinds of food. Even the positive result on Oswald's hands was not credible evidence against him, since so many oxidizing agents might have caused the reaction. Law enforcement seldom used paraffin tests in 1963, and the FBI considered them "practically worthless."[21]† As for the negative result on

---

* Alexander later drafted the Kennedy murder indictment and held it for district attorney Henry Wade's signature. Oswald was arraigned on the charge of killing the President at 1:30 A.M. on Saturday. Meanwhile, on Friday, Alexander participated in a midnight raid on the house of J. R. Molina, another worker at the Texas School Book Depository. According to Alexander, Molina was a leftist who was on the Dallas police's intelligence watch list, and it was originally thought he might be connected to Oswald. "We did a deluxe search job on Molina's house," recalls Alexander. "He was polite and very scared. But there was nothing between him and Oswald." Earlier that night, Alexander decided to "shake things up a bit" and spoke to a friend at the *Philadelphia Inquirer*, Joe Goulden, and told him that he intended to indict Oswald for killing the President "in furtherance of a Communist conspiracy." As he told the author, "The *Inquirer* got 200,000 papers on the street before Wade called me up and screamed 'What the hell are you trying to do, start World War III?' " (Interview, March 6, 1992). Shortly after the *Inquirer* incident, Alexander and two local reporters concocted a story that Oswald had been FBI informer S-179 and had been paid $200 a month. Lonnie Hudkins, one of the reporters, printed the story, attributing it to an unidentified source. The fallout was so great that the Warren Commission held a January 22, 1964, executive session to discuss the issue. "I never much liked the federals," Alexander says. "I figured it was as good a way as any to keep them out of my way by having to run down that phony story."

† In an experiment to determine the accuracy of paraffin tests, the FBI had seventeen men fire five shots from a .38-caliber revolver. Eight of the men showed negative results on both hands. Three others were negative on the firing hand and positive on the nonfiring hand. Four men were positive on both hands. Only two men were positive on their firing hand and negative on the

Oswald's cheek, the FBI did reconstruction tests where a shooter fired Oswald's Carcano rifle and there was never a positive result from any paraffin cast taken of the right cheek.[22] The Dallas police had never before even conducted a paraffin test on a shooter's cheek.[23] "I was ordered to take it . . . by Captain Fritz," remembered policeman W. E. Barnes. "I didn't ask the questions why he wanted it. . . . Common sense will tell you that a man firing a rifle has got very little chance of getting powder residue on his cheek."[24]

Following the paraffin test, Captain Fritz spoke to police chief Jesse Curry and district attorney Henry Wade to determine whether they should make Oswald available briefly to the press. More than three hundred reporters had camped out on the third floor of the jail, with cameras, cables, and wires forming a tangled mess.[25] Whenever a witness appeared for a lineup or Oswald was escorted through the hallway, the journalists surged forward, shouting questions and snapping photos. The Dallas police department had never had such a notorious case and was not certain how to handle the press rush.[26] Chief Curry described the scene as "total confusion," while FBI agent James Hosty said it was "very chaotic."[27] When Henry Wade arrived after 11:00 P.M. on Friday, the third floor was so crowded that he had difficulty getting inside.[28]

Chief Curry decided to make Oswald available for a press conference in a small basement assembly room. Shortly after midnight he was brought into the room, which was packed with one hundred police and press.[29] Although Chief Curry had warned the press to maintain strict order, when Oswald arrived they became frantic, and according to Curry, "immediately they began to shoot questions at him and shove microphones into his face."[30] Curry, fearful that the press was about "to overrun him," took Oswald from the room after a few moments.[31] District attorney Wade remained to answer reporters' questions. In answer to one, Wade said that Oswald belonged to the "Free Cuba Com-

---

other. In another test, the FBI took twenty people who had not fired a gun and tested both their hands. All twenty were positive on one or both hands (WC Vol. III, p. 487). Mark Lane said the results of the tests were "consistent with innocence." He never informed the reader that such results were just as consistent with Oswald's guilt (*Rush to Judgment*, pp. 125–26).

mittee." A few reporters corrected Wade, pointing out that early press reports said it was Fair Play for Cuba.[32] Yet one person who spoke from the back row was not even a reporter, but instead a Dallas nightclub owner who had sneaked into the press conference. His name was Jack Ruby.

Ruby was born Jacob Rubenstein, into an Orthodox Jewish home, the fifth of eight children, on March 25, 1911, in Chicago.[33]* The family was very poor and had moved four times by the time Jack was five, always into lower-class, street-tough Jewish ghettos.[34] His father, Joseph, was a heavy drinker who beat his mother, Fanny. Joseph was often arrested on assault-and-battery and disorderly conduct charges, sometimes filed by Fanny.[35] When Jack was ten years old his parents separated.[36]

At school, he had trouble making friends and thought his classmates often picked on him.[37] He frequently skipped classes to stay on the streets, and as a result flunked the third grade. Although he later claimed to have finished the eighth grade, records show he completed only the sixth.[38] By the age of ten, he was scalping sporting tickets and hustling anything he could sell for a few dollars.[39] According to his brother Earl, Jack grew up fast on the streets and was proud of his reputation as "the toughest kid his age."[40]

His mother was high-strung, and though she often beat him, she was incapable of controlling him. By the time he was eleven, in 1922, his mother referred him—because of "truancy and [the fact he was] incorrigible at home"—to the Institute for Juvenile Research of the Jewish Social Service Bureau.[41] A psychiatric report found Jack boastful that "he could lick everyone and anybody in anything," suffered from a hair-trigger temper, was egocentric, and was consumed by dual obsessions with sex and street gangs.[42] An IQ test showed a slightly below normal rating of 94.[43] The report also said that "it is apparent that she [Jack's mother] has no insight into his problem, and she is thoroughly

---

* There is considerable confusion about Ruby's exact birthdate. Birth records were not officially kept in Chicago prior to 1915, and among school records, driver's licenses, and arrest records, there were six different dates, ranging from March to June 1911. March 25 is used by the author since it is the date most often given by Ruby himself in his adult life.

inadequate in the further training of this boy." It concluded that the household atmosphere was so dreadful that his mother must have a "disturbance. She might have been an emotionally and materially grossly deprived individual suffering from a severe character disorder—by the same token she could have been of low intellectual endowment (mentally deficient?) or grossly disturbed emotionally to the point of being psychotic" (remarks in parentheses in original).[44]

The following year, 1923, a juvenile court determined that Jack and two younger brothers and a sister were not receiving proper parental care, and they were placed into a foster home, where they remained for eighteen months.[45]* When they were reunited with their mother, she was still unable to deal with them. Jack continued to run unchecked, with a reputation as an adept street fighter with a flash temper.[46] Nicknamed Sparky because of his volatile nature, he sometimes carried a stick that he used to beat opponents in fights.[47] "He was stronger than any professional fighter," recalls his brother Earl. "And he had the worst temper in the family. But after he exploded and got into a fight, he would be over it in a minute, and often sorry that he had lost his temper."[48] During his teenage years, Ruby was feared in the local neighborhood. He continued scraping a living from the streets, and while the police took note of him, he avoided any major legal problems. However, several of his friends were well on their way to becoming full-time criminals.[49]

In 1933, just before he turned twenty-two, Ruby moved to California with several of his Chicago friends, hoping to make more money.[50] He first went to Los Angeles and then to San Francisco. His sister Eva joined him there the following year, after her divorce from her first husband.[51] In both cities, Ruby still had difficulty making a living—selling tip sheets for horse races at the local tracks, working as a singing waiter in Los Angeles, and selling newspaper subscriptions in San Francisco.[52]

---

* Jack Ruby and his sister Eileen said they were in foster homes for four to five years, and Earl Ruby, though placed in a different home, agreed with the longer period. However, the official foster home records show they were released in eighteen months, on November 24, 1924, but under an order that allowed them to be returned to the foster home if Fanny Rubenstein proved unfit to run the household (WR, p. 782).

352 . CASE CLOSED

By 1937 his new start in California had fizzled, and he returned to Chicago.[53] In July, his mother, who had suffered from
"a psychoneurosis with a marked anxiety state" for more than
ten years, was committed by a court to a mental institution.[54]
She was released three months later, and then readmitted at her
family's request in January 1938.[55]

Ruby, soon after his return, resumed ticket scalping and hus-
tling small merchandise that he could quickly sell for a profit.[56]
He also became involved in the Scrap Iron and Junk Handlers
Union, Local 20467, working as a union organizer.[57] His friend
and union financial secretary Leon Cooke was shot by another
Ruby associate, union president John Martin, in December 1939.
Cooke died of his wounds a month later.* "The mob came in
and took over the union after Cooke was killed," says Earl
Ruby. "It was a legitimate union when Jack was involved, but
the mob was pressuring the union all the time, and then they
eventually grabbed control and forced Jack out."[58] "We checked
him and the union out," says Bill Roemer, the Chicago FBI agent
who spearheaded the federal government's drive against organized crime in that city. "Ruby was a nothing in that union. The
mob came in and took it over later."[59]

Ruby continued to struggle financially. In 1941, he started the
Spartan Novelty Company with his brother Earl and two friends.
Operating out of inexpensive hotels, they sold everything from
punchboards to commemorative plaques of Pearl Harbor and
busts of Franklin Roosevelt.[60] The business quickly floundered,
and from late 1942 to 1943, he worked as a salesman for Globe
Auto Glass and Universal Sales Co.[61]†

During this period, he became a habitué of the Lawndale
Poolroom, as well as a South Side gym where his friend, boxer

---

* Martin was acquitted of murdering Leon Cooke, successfully claiming self-
defense at his trial. Ruby was so upset over the death of his friend that he later
adopted the middle name Leon.

† Author David Scheim claims Ruby was involved in racketeering in the
Chicago nightclub district during this time. "That's absolutely false," Earl Ruby
told the author. "I worked with Jack during that time, and he never had anything to do with nightclubs in Chicago. When you were actually there and
know what went on, it drives you crazy to hear charges like that, which are
just completely wrong." Witnesses might have confused Harry Rubenstein, a
convicted felon who ran several clubs in Chicago, with Jack.

Barney Ross, trained.[62] As part of a group of local toughs, Ruby and his friends also frequently crashed and disrupted rallies of the pro-Nazi German-American Bund.[63] An incessant talker, Ruby bragged that he could hit harder than prizefighter Joe Louis. He exercised at several gyms, and although not a big man (five feet nine inches and 175 pounds), he maintained a reputation as one of the South Side's toughest street brawlers.[64]

Pearl Harbor and the war did not affect his life at first. He originally received a deferment in 1941, but in 1943 he was reclassified 1-A and drafted into the Army Air Force. At the age of thirty-two, he was the oldest in his unit, and he ran some dice and card games, as well as peddling everything from chocolates to cigarettes.[65] Once, when a sergeant called him a "Jew bastard," Ruby beat him mercilessly.[66]* But the men who served with Ruby liked him. He had no disciplinary trouble while in the Army, achieved the rank of private first class, and was honorably discharged on February 21, 1946.[67]

He returned to Chicago but stayed there for just another year and a half, becoming a partner in Earl Products, a company started by his brothers. Again, Jack was selling punchboards, key chains, bottle openers, light tools, and salt and pepper shakers.[68] But he quarreled with his brothers, and they eventually bought out his share for $14,000.[69] He decided to follow his sister Eva to Dallas. She had gone there in 1947 and, with money borrowed from her brothers, opened the Singapore Supper Club, which she ran as a nightclub. When Jack moved to Dallas by late 1947, he helped her manage the club.

Was Ruby brought to Dallas by the Chicago mafia in order to run its operations in Texas? Paul Roland Jones, who represented a group of Chicago criminals, had tried to bribe the Dal-

---

* Although not religious, Ruby was always extremely sensitive to anti-Semitism. "There was hardly anything that would get him angrier faster," Earl Ruby told the author. "Jack was real touchy about anything said bad about Jews, and he would fight with anyone who said it. Once after the war, he returned from downtown Chicago with blood all over one of his good suits. He beat up somebody who called him a dirty Jew. He was always like that." "Jack has always been a fighter for the Jews," said his sister Eva (WC Vol. XIV, p. 484). Lawrence Meyers, a friend, said Ruby was "very proud of being a Jew . . . [and] militantly against anybody bum-rapping Jews" (WC Vol. XV, pp. 634, 636).

las sheriff, Steve Guthrie, in 1946. Guthrie later claimed that Ruby's name had come up in conversations with Jones a number of times. However, a Dallas policeman present during some of the conversations contradicted Guthrie's account and said he never heard Ruby's name mentioned. Ruby is not referred to in twenty-two of the surveillance recordings still available, and Jones described the man he intended to bring to Dallas as someone who looks like a "preacher, not a dago, not a Jew."[70] Bill Alexander, the assistant district attorney who knew Ruby and later successfully prosecuted him for killing Oswald, told the author: "There is no way the Chicago mob would have allowed Ruby to be their representative in Dallas. Just no way. He was not the type of person they would trust with their business."[71] Bill Roemer, the FBI agent who investigated the mafia in Chicago, agreed and also told the author, "Ruby was absolutely nothing in terms of the Chicago mob. We had thousands and thousands of hours of tape recordings of the top mobsters in Chicago, including Sam Giancana [the city's godfather], and Ruby just didn't exist as far as they were concerned. We talked to every hoodlum in Chicago after the assassination, and some of the top guys in the mob, my informants, I had close relationships with them—they didn't even know who Ruby was. He was not a front for them in Dallas."[72]

On December 30, 1947, he legally changed his name to Jack Leon Ruby. During the next sixteen years in Dallas, he owned interests in six nightclubs, losing money in each venture, until he finally managed to turn a small profit at his last one, the Carousel, a strip club.[73] In 1952, however, his financial woes were so great that he had a mental breakdown and had to recuperate for several months.[74] He spoke alternately of killing one of his partners or ending his own life. For a while he thought of returning to Chicago, but decided finally to remain in Dallas. His money problems stayed with him, and by the mid-1950s Ruby had an excise-tax delinquency with the federal government and had to borrow $5,500 from his brother Sam to pay the debt.[75]

Besides his nightclubs, he tried other businesses, ranging from selling sewing machine attachments to costume jewelry.[76] He became the manager for a black youngster dubbed "Little

Daddy Nelson" and spent whatever money he had promoting the act.[77] At various times, he sold pizza crusts to Dallas restaurants, anti-arthritis preparations, twistboards, liquid vitamins, and English stainless steel razor blades.[78] He provided entertainment to Dallas hotels, promoted music records, tried to build and sell log cabins at a Texas lake resort, and even looked into selling jeeps to Cuba.[79] All his business ventures were unsuccessful.

"Jack was always in some kind of debt," says Earl. "He always was owing some money to the government on taxes. By the time he was arrested for shooting Oswald, he owed me over sixteen thousand dollars. He always had some business idea in the works, some new project he had hatched, but just never seemed to make any money at any of them."[80]

Ruby, anxious to be accepted in Dallas, was frustrated by his repeated business failures. Tony Zoppi was a prominent entertainment reporter for the *Dallas Morning News* and knew Ruby well.* "He was a born loser, a real low-level loser," says Zoppi. "He didn't have twenty cents to his name. I knew dozens of guys like him back in New Jersey and in New York. They were fellows always trying to make a name for themselves, always hustling something. He was a hanger-on who was very impressed by famous people, impressed by 'class,' and with anybody that he thought had it. He used to call me up and say, 'Hey, Tony, I run a real classy joint, class all the way, huh? Don't I have class?' But the people that knew him knew that Ruby was a zero. He used to give out passes for his club to everyone he met. He would announce: 'Hi, I'm Jack Ruby,' like it was supposed to mean something. People used to say to me, 'How can you tolerate that guy?' "[81]

"He would do anything to attract attention to himself," said Janet Conforto, his star dancer, also known as Jada. "He craved attention. He really wanted to be somebody, but didn't have it in him. He hung around police headquarters. He was a nuisance

---

* Zoppi's credibility has been called into question largely over arrangements for a trip he claimed that was planned by Ruby to visit Cuba and over the question of whether he saw Ruby on the morning of the assassination. But Zoppi knew Ruby as well as anyone in Dallas, and his characterizations of the nightclub owner are substantiated by many others.

around newspaper offices. He knew a tremendous number of people in Dallas, but he didn't have many friends. Oh, he wanted friends, but he didn't have the capacity to make and hold them. He was insecure . . . and often remarked, 'I'm a character! I'm colorful.' "[82] Bill Willis, a drummer at the Carousel, remembered that Ruby tried to impress people by using large words in his conversations: "They always came out wrong," recalled Willis. "He'd say things like, 'It's been a lovely precarious evening.' Or he'd tell a girl, 'You make me feel very irascible.' "[83]

"He tried too hard to be accepted," says district attorney Bill Alexander. "He had several strikes against him in Dallas. He was a nightclub owner, a Yankee, and a Jew. And no matter how hard he tried—and he did try hard to have people like him—he just wasn't going to get very far in Dallas. He was just a little guy trying to make it here."[84]*

Ruby's inability to launch a successful business was not the only trait that remained constant from his Chicago days. His penchant for violence and fights also carried over. Although his employees generally liked him and found him generous if they were in need, they readily acknowledged he had a volatile and vicious temper.[85] "You could not reason with him when he lost his temper," recalls Zoppi.[86] "He was erratic and hotheaded," said Harry Olsen, a Dallas policeman who knew him. "He would just fly off the handle about anything. . . . Sometimes he would get so mad that he would shake."[87] Ruby often resorted to violence with his employees, and lost the tip of his left index finger when one bit it off during a scuffle.[88] He beat one of his musicians with brass knuckles, cracked another's head with a black-

---

* Another strike against Ruby in 1963 Dallas was that many people thought he was homosexual, something strongly denied by his brother Earl and his friend Tony Zoppi. The rumors persisted because Ruby never married and did have several male roommates, the last of which was George Senator. Senator referred to Ruby as "my boyfriend," but said it was only a sign of friendship. Norman Wright, who had worked for Ruby, said in 1964: "He was always conscious of the fact that a lot of people thought he was sort of a gay boy. . . . One time someone gave him a cigar . . . and he put it in his mouth and lit it and said to me, 'I don't look gay now, do I?' . . . He seemed . . . to go out generally with more men than women . . ." (WC Vol. XV, p. 246). Warren Commission lawyer Burt Griffin, who researched the Ruby issues for the Commission, told the author, "I'm not sure if Senator was honest with us about his relationship with Ruby. People did not advertise their homosexuality in 1963."

jack, knocked another's teeth out, and put the club's handyman in the hospital with a severe beating.[89] To avoid paying the club's cigarette girl $50 in back wages, he threatened to throw her down the stairs unless she relented in her claim.[90] He threatened a stand-upcomedian, Robert McEwan, after McEwan had told several "inoffensive Jewish jokes" in his act, and thereafter enforced a strict ban on any Jewish remarks.[91]*

Not only was Ruby rough with his workers, but he acted as the unofficial bouncer for his clubs, constantly fighting with customers. On at least twenty-five occasions he badly beat them using either his fists or a blackjack, or else pistol whipped them.[92] He often ended his fights by throwing the victim down the Carousel's stairs.[93] He was not above attacking people from behind, kicking men in the groin or face once he had knocked them to the floor, or even striking women.[94] Sometimes the fights were justified. Once when a patron pulled a gun on him, Ruby disarmed him, beat him almost to death, put the gun back into the man's pocket, and then hurled him down the stairs.[95] On other occasions, there was little provocation, but he wanted to prove how tough he was, as when he severely beat a professional boxer.[96] Sometimes the attacks were completely unexpected. Once, a cabdriver came into the club and asked where a patron was who had refused to pay the taxi fare. Ruby punched the cabdriver in the face.[97] He was often malicious, forcing beaten victims to crawl out of the club on hands and knees.[98] Twice he used his gun to chase people from the club. Once he ran after another nightclub owner, Joe Bonds, through a nearby alleyway, shooting at him several times but missing.[99]†

---

* Although Ruby continued to bristle at anything he interpreted as anti-Semitism, all those who knew him described him, while patriotic, as remarkably apolitical (CE 2980, WC Vol. XXVI). His Dallas rabbi, Hillel Silverman, said Ruby was very shallow intellectually and that he would not know the difference between a Communist philosophy and a totalitarian regime. However, Rabbi Silverman said Ruby thought the President of the U.S. was the greatest individual in the world, not because of the person, but because of the position and his respect for the government (CE 1485, WC Vol. XXII). He was also impressed with the Kennedys because, as he told friends, they had glamour and seemed like movie stars (Wills and Demaris, "The Avenger," *Esquire*, May 1967, p. 86).

† Bonds's real name was Joe Locurto. Also from Chicago, he had been Ruby's partner in the Vegas Club in 1953, but their relationship ended when

Beyond Ruby's volatile temper, he also displayed eccentric qualities that made those who knew him sometimes question his stability. Patricia Birch, who had danced for him under the stage name Penny Dollar, recalled he was a fitness fanatic who frequently came into the girls' dressing room without his shirt, hit his chest like a gorilla, and asked if they thought he had a good build. At a party, she witnessed him take off his clothes and roll around the floor naked.[100] Ruby occasionally telephoned some of his dancers and read them obscene poetry or described in detail his private parts.[101] Sometimes, he warmly welcomed guests to his club, and on other nights, for no apparent reason, told the same guests they were not wanted and could not enter the club.[102] During conversations, he sometimes switched in the middle of a sentence to a completely different topic, with no explanation.[103]*

According to his star dancer, Jada, Ruby was "impossible, totally unpredictable. . . . He is completely emotional. One minute he is nice, and the next minute he goes berserk. . . . I don't think he is sane."[104] Wynn Warner, a musician who had worked for him, thought he was a split personality.[105] Edward Pullman, whose wife worked for Ruby, decided he "was insane. He was a psycho. . . . He was not right."[106] Johnnie Hayden, an official of AGVA (American Guild of Variety Artists), said that most of

---

Bonds was sentenced to jail for sodomizing a fifteen-year-old girl. Ruby remained a part owner of the Vegas and considered it his second club. While he ran the Carousel, his sister Eva ran the Vegas.

* Ruby was also the subject of gossip regarding obsessive behavior with his dogs. He had as many as ten at a time and often called them his "children," his only family (CE 2406, p. 650, WC Vol. XXV). His favorite was a dachshund named Sheba, and he referred to the dog as his "wife." He took Sheba to work and kept her with him most of the day (CE 1485, WC Vol. XXII; CE 2411, pp. 621–26, WC Vol. XXV). At the club, there were rumors that Ruby had an unnatural relationship with the dogs, something he vehemently denied on several occasions. One of his Chicago friends, Harry Goldbaum, last visited Ruby in August 1963. They spent an hour in the Carousel's rear office, where Ruby was taking care of three small dogs for a friend. According to Goldbaum, Ruby promised to show him something interesting and began masturbating one of the male dogs, and only stopped when Goldbaum told Ruby it was making him sick (CE 1740, WC Vol. XXIII; CE 2980, p. 5, WC Vol. XXVI). The Warren Commission dealt with his affection for dogs under a separate heading in its final report, but downplayed the more bizarre aspects of the relationship (WR, p. 804).

those who knew him felt Ruby was a "kook" because of his unpredictable, emotional outbursts.[107] William Serur knew Ruby for over ten years and watched him change for the worse. "In the last few years I thought that he might have been suffering from some form of disturbance, mental disturbance, by the way he acted."[108]

Yet Ruby also could present an apparently normal and jovial side, that of a club owner ready to ensure his patrons had a good time. He went out of his way to encourage Dallas policemen to visit his clubs, giving them reduced rates and free drinks.[109] He befriended dozens of them, attended the funeral of one killed in the line of duty, and staged a benefit for the widow of another.[110] Once he jumped in and helped two Dallas policemen who were being beaten by a group of men.[111]* "They dropped by to say hello and screen the crowd," says Bill Alexander, "and it was better than having a bunch of hoodlums there. Remember, Ruby catered to tourists, and nobody was going to get rolled at his place with the type of police contacts he had. He wasn't a cop groupie or buff. He genuinely liked the police, and knew it did some good for him by being friendly with them."[112]†

At the same time he cultivated police contacts, he also maintained friendships with an assortment of criminals. One of his earliest Dallas friends was Paul Roland Jones, who was convicted of narcotics trafficking and for attempting to bribe the Dallas sheriff.[113] One of Ruby's early partners in the Vegas club, Joe Bonds, had a criminal record. He kept close associations to

---

* Dallas police chief Jesse Curry told the Warren Commission that no more than twenty-five to fifty of the force's twelve hundred policemen knew Ruby (WC Vol. IV, pp. 167, 191–92). However, statements and interviews with both former Dallas policemen and Ruby's employees indicate that he was acquainted with several hundred.

† As part of his efforts to ingratiate himself to law enforcement, Ruby contacted the FBI in March 1959 and offered to provide information that came to his attention. Between April to October of that year, he met with Agent Charles Flynn eight times, giving information about thefts and similar offenses. In November, Flynn recommended that no further attempt be made to develop Ruby as a PCI, potential criminal informant, since his information was essentially useless. His FBI file was closed (FBI memo, November 6, 1959; JFK Document 003040; and Executive Session Testimony of Charles W. Flynn, November 16, 1977—JFK Document 014669).

known gamblers, including a good friend, Lewis McWillie.[114]* "It was the nature of his business," says Bill Alexander. "Running those types of nightclubs, he came across plenty of unsavory characters." Although there were rumors Ruby dealt in narcotics or even in prostitution, there is no firm evidence that he did anything more than socialize with some people involved in those vices. Alexander told the author, "The police had a pretty good idea of what happened at Ruby's club, and there was no dope and he certainly didn't allow the girls to do anything illegal from the club, because that would have cost him his license. Ruby was a small-time operator on the fringe of everything, but he never crossed over to breaking the law big-time."[115] His brother Earl agrees: "He had a plush strip-tease club, and the mafia used to go to his place when they were in town. They were big spenders, and I'm sure he wasn't unhappy when they came to his joint to spend their money."[116]

Ruby's solicitation of the Dallas police did not protect him from having legal problems. During fourteen years, he was arrested nine times, for charges ranging from disturbing the peace to assault to carrying concealed weapons.[117] The Texas Liquor Control Board also frequently suspended his license for viola-

---

* McWillie managed the Tropicana Hotel in Havana in 1959 and later managed clubs in Las Vegas. Ruby told the Warren Commission he visited McWillie in Havana for one week in August 1959. The House Select Committee found Ruby made at least two, and probably three, trips to Havana, the longest being for a month and the shortest for one day. He bought two pistols for McWillie, and may have acted as a courier to bring some money out of Havana. Ruby always maintained his time in Cuba was for pleasure and not for business. The polygraph he was administered after he killed Oswald showed he was truthful when he said the time in Cuba "was solely for pleasure." However, a British journalist later claimed that Ruby met Santo Trafficante in 1959, then a prisoner at a Cuban jail. Trafficante, later the mafia don of Tampa, denied under oath that he had ever met Ruby, and no one at the prison confirmed the story.

Robert Ray McKeown, a convicted Texas gun runner, later said that Ruby had contacted him, representing Las Vegas interests that wanted the release of three prisoners in Cuba, including Trafficante, and that Ruby offered $25,000 for a letter of introduction to Castro. McKeown also claimed that Oswald had visited him and offered $10,000 for four high-powered rifles, although he told the FBI in 1964 that he had never met Oswald (CE 1689, p. 23). The Select Committee investigated McKeown's claims and rejected them, concluding he "did not seem to be credible" (HSCA Rpt., p. 152).

tions, primarily for allowing obscene stage shows or for serving liquor after hours.[118]

His legal difficulties, and his associations with criminals, have been the basis of much speculation that Ruby was part of the mafia, and in particular that his killing of Oswald was ordered by the mob to silence the President's assassin. "It is so ludicrous to believe that Ruby was part of the mob," says Tony Zoppi. "The conspiracy theorists want to believe everybody but those whoreally knew him. People in Dallas, in those circles, knew Ruby was a snitch. The word was on the street that you couldn't trust him because he was telling the cops everything. He was a real talker, a fellow who would talk your ear off if he had the chance. You have to be crazy to think anybody would have trusted Ruby to be part of the mob. He couldn't keep a secret for five minutes. He was just a hanger-on, somebody who would have liked some of the action but was never going to get any."[119]

"It's hard to believe," says Bill Alexander, "that I, who prosecuted Ruby for killing Oswald, am almost in the position of defending his honor. Ruby was not mafia. He was not a gangster. We knew who the criminals were in Dallas back then, and to say Ruby was part of organized crime is just bullshit. There's no way he was connected. It's guilt by association, that A knew B, and Ruby knew B back in 1950, so he must have known A, and that must be the link to the conspiracy. It's crap written by people who don't know the facts."[120]

Ruby's lack of influence and power with organized crime is apparent in the problems he had with AGVA, the union responsible for the professional strippers used at his Carousel Club. Ruby's main competition was from the Theater and Colony clubs, owned by two brothers, Abe and Barney Weinstein. In 1961, they had introduced amateur strip-tease dancing. At first, Ruby tried to compete with the Weinsteins' amateur nights, but soon he complained to AGVA that the union's constitution prohibited professional and amateur entertainers from working together, and he demanded the Weinsteins be stopped.[121] The union took no action. AGVA was riddled with corruption and compromised by its mob connections.[122] Tony Zoppi believes the Weinsteins received preferential treatment because they bribed union officials.[123]

Ruby's frustration over the Weinsteins' use of amateur nights peaked during the summer and fall of 1963. It coincided with a series of AGVA complaints about his Carousel Club as well as a contractual dispute he had with his star stripper, Jada, whom he had signed in New Orleans and brought back to Dallas. They argued incessantly. He had hired her in the summer, hoping she could turn around his diminishing fortunes, but fired her by the end of October.[124] In addition to the problems with Jada, he also went through three masters of ceremonies at the same time.[125] He had a growing tax delinquency totaling more than $40,000.[126] Frustrated that AGVA refused to enforce any regulations against the Weinsteins, Ruby accelerated his campaign to compel some union action. He had earlier warned an AGVA official, Irvin Mazzei, that he could use "labor connections in Chicago" to pressure the union.[127] In front of an FBI agent, he physically threatened Vincent Lee, another AGVA official.[128] He called his brother Earl and asked for names of people who could be helpful. "We all knew it wasn't a clean union," recalls Earl. "So I tried to come up with people that might have the right connections, figuring that they could move things along for Jack."[129]

Ruby's long-distance telephone activity jumped significantly during the months when he tried to resolve the AGVA dispute, and some of those he telephoned were people connected to organized crime.[130] Were such calls evidence of a mafia conspiracy to kill JFK? The House Select Committee did an extensive computer analysis of Ruby's five home and business telephone numbers for all of 1963. The Committee checked each number he telephoned, as well as the records of those he called, and determined that most of the increases in his long-distance bill were due to his AGVA problems.[131]

But three of those calls, said the Select Committee, raised the possibility that they might be of significance in the Kennedy case. However, the author's investigation reveals the calls were not as mysterious as the Select Committee assumed.

The first was to Chicago bail bondsman Irwin Weiner, who often represented mob figures. The Committee feared he may have been a link for Ruby to crime bosses. Weiner had refused to cooperate with the FBI in its Warren Commission investigation. "I gave Irwin Weiner's number to my brother," Earl Ruby told the author. "I had gone to school with Weiner; we graduated high school together. I used to see him on visits to California. He was a big bondsman for everyone, and he handled the mafia. It was in the newspapers—you could read about it. I thought he might be able to help Jack with the union. Jack didn't even know Weiner, for God's sake."[132] Weiner later admitted that Ruby called him once, about his AGVA problem; however, Weiner did not offer him any assistance.[133]

The second call was to a trailer park in New Orleans, to the office of Nofio Pecora, a lieutenant to New Orleans godfather Carlos Marcello. This October 30, 1963, call worried the committee since it appeared to be a Ruby contact with a high-ranking aide to Marcello less than a month before the assassination. However, the call was not even intended for Pecora. Harold Tannenbaum, a fellow nightclub owner and friend of Ruby's, lived in that trailer park, the Tropical Court Tourist Park. Tannenbaum had arranged the deal that allowed Ruby to bring Jada from New Orleans to Dallas, and Ruby often called him at his trailer-park home and his French Quarter nightclub to complain about his contractual problems with the temperamental dancer. In 1978, Pecora told the Select Committee that he did not know Ruby, nor did he remember ever speaking to him.[134] However, Pecora, who ran the trailer park from his one-man office, admitted he occasionally took a message for someone in the park, but did not remember doing so for Ruby. But apparently that is exactly what he did. There is no way to know if Ruby first telephoned Tannenbaum's home, since if no one was there, there would be no toll record. The call to Pecora's office lasted less than one minute. Within the hour, Tannenbaum had apparently received the message from Pecora and returned Ruby's call, collect, for twenty-one minutes.[135]

The third call that stumped the Select Committee actually comprised three calls, two on November 7, and one on November 8, all to Robert "Barney" Baker, an aide to Teamster boss Jimmy Hoffa. Baker had only been released from prison in June 1963. The committee was concerned since Hoffa had such a well-known hatred for both John and Robert Kennedy. However, Baker and Ruby did not know each other before Ruby called him on November 7, 1963. When the FBI contacted Baker in 1964, he spoke to them openly. He told the agents that on November 7, Ruby had telephoned, but Baker was not in and his wife had taken a number in Dallas. When Baker got home, he called the number collect. Ruby introduced himself, explained his labor-union problems with his club, and sought Baker's assistance. Baker did not help, nor did he remember the last call the following day.[136] What is critical is that at the time he spoke to the FBI and talked about Ruby's AGVA problems, it was independent of knowing that Ruby had also told the police that the conversations were about union problems. Moreover, Baker, who thought the FBI tapped his phone lines (most Hoffa associates assumed the federal government had them under constant surveillance) reportedly challenged the agents to check their tapes and listen to the conversation if they had any doubts. Unfortunately, there apparently was no surveillance of his line.[137]*

Despite Ruby's intervention with the AGVA board and his pleas to organized-crime figures, no one came to his aid. His dispute with AGVA was still unresolved the weekend the President was assassinated.

---

* The Warren Commission allowed the questions over Ruby's telephone calls to fester, since they did not ask Ruby about some of the people he contacted and did not place those like Weiner, Pecora, and Baker under oath. However, the telephone calls are not evidence of a conspiracy to kill JFK, since most of the calls were made before the President's trip to Dallas was even announced, much less before the motorcade route was set. Even if there was a plot to kill Kennedy and then silence Oswald, it is difficult to imagine that Oswald would have been allowed to get away from the shooting alive. The three days during which he was interrogated was more than enough time for him to expose the conspiracy. If he was really a patsy who did not know anything, there was no reason to kill him. The conspirators could not know where Oswald would be arrested or whether state or federal authorities would have jurisdiction over him. The only way that Ruby was useful to a conspiracy was to penetrate the police security at the local Dallas jail. But that Oswald would be captured and placed there was only one of many things that could have happened to him. Therefore, conspiring with Ruby in September and October made no practical sense. Why inform Ruby about a plot to kill the President when he had no need to know? If he was really given a mafia assignment to kill Oswald, his telephone activity would likely have increased from the afternoon of the assassination until the day Oswald was killed. But Ruby's long-distance calls were all made much earlier, not during the assassination weekend.

16

"I Am Jack Ruby. You All Know Me"

Where was Ruby during the assassination of President Kennedy? What did he do over the weekend of November 22 leading up to his deadly encounter with Oswald on Sunday? It is important to follow Ruby carefully to discover whether there is any evidence of a conspiracy.

Thursday, November 21, the day before the assassination, he left his apartment and arrived at AAA Bonding Service near 10:30 A.M. There, he talked to Max Rudberg about protecting himself from Jada's pending breach-of-contract lawsuit.[1] When he left Rudberg, he spent two hours with Connie Trammel, a young woman he had met several months earlier, who was job hunting in Dallas.[2] Near the end of his time with Trammel, about 1:00, he stopped at the Merchants State Bank and paid the rent for the Carousel.[3] Ruby then went to the district attorney's office, where he saw assistant D.A. Bill Alexander and spoke to him about bad checks that a friend had recently passed while visiting Dallas.[4] After that, he telephoned John Newman, a salesman in the advertising department of the *Dallas Morning News*, and talked to him about some copy for the weekend ads he wanted to run for the Carousel and Vegas clubs.[5]

Sometime on Thursday he also telephoned a local lawyer who was handling his federal excise-tax problem.[6] Before heading to the Carousel, Ruby ran into several people on the street. He gave some of them passes to the club, and tried to make a date with a woman, so he could persuade her to work for him.[7]

The Carousel opened in the late afternoon and closed officially at midnight (but Ruby often kept it open until 2:00 A.M. if business was good), seven days a week.[8] He arrived at the club at 3:00 P.M.* His sister Eva normally ran the Vegas, leaving him responsible only for the Carousel. However, she was recuperating from abdominal surgery, and Ruby had to watch both clubs.[9] He stayed at the Carousel for over four hours and then drove Curtis LaVerne Crafard, known as Larry, a young drifter who was living at the club and acting as its handyman, to the Vegas at 7:30 that evening. Crafard had agreed to help Ruby oversee the Vegas while Eva convalesced. Ruby then returned to the Carousel, where he spoke for nearly an hour with Lawrence Meyers, a Chicago sales manager for a diversified line of consumer goods, who was visiting Dallas.[10] Meyers, who had first met Ruby at the Carousel four years earlier, was a steady customer during his visits to Dallas. Ruby complained about his contractual dispute with Jada as well as the Weinsteins' amateur nights and how they were crippling his business.[11] Meyers planned to meet his brother and sister-in-law, who were in town for a Pepsi-Cola distributors' convention, at a nightclub at his hotel, the Cabana, at 11:00 P.M. He invited Ruby to meet them, and "he said he would if he could."[12]

From about 9:45 to 10:45, Ruby had dinner with Dallas busi-

---

* A number of people thought they saw Ruby in Houston on Thursday afternoon. Despite the numerous witnesses that reported his busy day in Dallas, author David Scheim says, "Ruby was there [Houston], monitoring President Kennedy's movements in preparation for the next day's assassination in Dallas." Claiming that Ruby left Dallas by noon (though he was with Connie Trammel until 1:00 and had later visited a bank and the district attorney's office), Scheim writes that Ruby drove the "243 miles on the freeway to Houston at an 80- to 100-mile-per-hour Texas clip. Such a speed would have been natural for Ruby given his many traffic violations, including four for speeding" (*Contract on America*, p. 261). One of the Houston witnesses claimed Ruby had a scar on the left side of his face. Ruby had no such scar, yet Scheim contends it was "perhaps noticeable only in the background of heavy stubble." The Houston witnesses reported the man they saw was an oil worker, wearing an army jacket and boots, which Scheim calls a "carelessly presented disguise." Scheim says that Ruby returned to Dallas the same afternoon, repeating his high-speed highway trip.

nessman Ralph Paul, his good friend and financial backer. They ate at the Egyptian Lounge, a restaurant and nightclub.* After dinner, he returned to the Carousel, where he acted as the master of ceremonies, and at one point evicted an unruly patron.[13] Shortly before midnight he drove to the Bon Vivant room at the Cabana Hotel, where he joined his Chicago friend Meyers, Meyers' brother, Eddie, and sister-in-law, Thelma. When Ruby found out that Eddie Meyers worked for Pepsi-Cola, he spent the conversation trying to interest him in his twist-board product. It was a $3.95 exercise/diet gimmick composed of a small wooden platform set on ball bearings, on which the user twisted and rotated. He argued it would be a good tie-in for Pepsi.[14] But Myers was not interested and Ruby left the Cabana Hotel by 12:30 A.M. and returned to the Carousel to get the night's receipts.[15]†

---

* The owner of the Egyptian Lounge, Joseph Campisi, was reportedly a ranking member of the Dallas underworld. Ruby was a frequent patron at the Egyptian Lounge, so his Thursday night dinner there was not out of the ordinary (CE 2980, p. 9, WC Vol. XXVI). Campisi did not see Ruby that night (HSCA Vol. I, pp. 363–64, 374). Summers, relying on an FBI report, says Ruby had a brief conversation at the Lounge with someone named "Connors" from the *Dallas Morning News* and "no person of that name worked at the *News* in 1963," implying there is a mystery about the person whom Ruby spoke to (Summers, p. 451). However, the FBI mistakenly listed the name as "Connors." Ruby actually spoke to Don Campbell, a salesmen in the advertising department of the *News*. He invited Ruby to the Castaway Club on Thursday night, but Ruby declined (Testimony of Jack Ruby, WC Vol. V, pp. 183–84; testimony of Don Campbell, *State of Texas* v. *Jack Rubenstein*, CE 2406, p. 26, WC Vol. XXV; Hall (C. Ray) Exhibit 3, p. 3, WC Vol. XX).

† Summers uses another mistake in an FBI report to say Ruby called Larry Crafard from the Cabana as late as 2:30 A.M. (*Conspiracy*, p. 452). That is a misreading of Crafard's statement, which actually says he did not see Ruby again until nearly 2:30 in the morning (Crafard Exhibit 5226, p. 4, WC Vol. XIX). It is important for conspiracy writers to establish that Ruby remained for some time at the Cabana after talking to Meyers, because another guest at the hotel that night was Eugene "Jim" Brading, who had a criminal record and was questioned by the police the day of the assassination, when he was spotted in a building opposite Dealey Plaza "without a good excuse." He was quickly released when he gave a legitimate business purpose for being in downtown Dallas (CD 385, 401, 816; Dallas police report, C. L. Lewis, November 22, 1963; statement of Jim Brading, November 22, 1963). Ruby did not know Brading, and while they were both at the same hotel on November 21, they did not meet. Witnesses at the Cabana say that Ruby left there at 12:30 A.M., and did not return (C. Ray Hall Exhibit 3, p. 3).

After finishing work at the Carousel, he drove to the Vegas club to collect its receipts. By 2:30 A.M., he went to his usual early-morning hangout, the Lucas B&B Restaurant, next door to the Vegas. There he joined Crafard, and they had a meal.[16]* Between 3:30 and 4:00 in the morning, he again returned to the Carousel to drop off Crafard, and then drove to his apartment. His roommate, George Senator, was already asleep when he arrived.[17]

On Friday, November 22, Ruby was up by 9:30 and at the *Dallas Morning News* shortly before 11:00, in order to place his

---

* After the assassination, a B&B waitress, Mary Lawrence, claimed the man with Ruby looked like Oswald (CD 223, pp. 366–67). However, Larry Crafard resembled Oswald. Mary Lawrence described Ruby's restaurant acquaintance as having a small scar near his mouth. Oswald did not have one, while Crafard did. A number of people later identified Crafard as Oswald, leading to the mistaken speculation that Ruby and Oswald knew each other (WR, pp. 360–62). There were also other stories of a Ruby-Oswald relationship. Beverly Oliver, the woman who claims to be the missing "babushka lady" of Dealey Plaza, said that Jada introduced her to Ruby and Oswald over drinks at the Carousel. Oliver claimed Ruby introduced his friend as "Lee Oswald of the CIA." However, within two weeks of the assassination, Jada told the FBI she had never seen Oswald and that she knew of no Ruby-Oswald association (CE 1561, p. 303). She was also extensively interviewed by reporters soon after the assassination and never mentioned seeing Oswald. Although Jada is dead, the author spoke to her son, Joe Conforto, who had been involved in a business with his mother. "She never mentioned anything like that," he said. "It's just not true." Some of Ruby's employees, who initially told the police and FBI they had never seen Oswald, told reporters years later that Oswald had been at the club and used to banter loudly with the stage acts; bump and grind with the strippers; meet with mobsters; hang out with David Ferrie, who supposedly visited from New Orleans for nights of partying; talk loudly about opening a narcotics ring or killing Governor Connally; and, sometimes, get into fist fights. Oswald's wild double life at Ruby's club supposedly took place during the time when Earlene Roberts and his other rooming-house tenants said he was home every night by 6:00 P.M.

The Warren Commission and the Select Committee investigated the rumors, and both concluded there was "no evidence they were ever acquainted." Bill Alexander, who prosecuted Ruby, told the author, "After Ruby killed Oswald, there was a groundswell of these stories, people who claimed they saw them together. I would have had the greatest murder case in the world if any of it was right. It would have made our case easier and I would have pursued it in a moment. But we checked out every one of those stories, took them all seriously, and I know of no credible witness or evidence that connects Ruby to Oswald at any place, at any time, in any way. Not a single one was true."

regular weekend advertisements for his two nightclubs.[18]* On his way into the building, he saw two newspaper employees, waved at one across the ground floor while yelling, "Hi. The President is going to be here today," and spoke to the other about some diet pills he had recommended.[19] He then stopped by the office of Tony Zoppi, the newspaper's entertainment reporter, but he was not in.[20] Ruby next went to the second-floor advertising department, where he met with Don Campbell, the sales agent he had seen at the Cabana Hotel the night before. Campbell worked with him as he wrote his weekend advertisements. Ruby complained about how "lousy" business was and that he was tired of having to act as the unofficial bouncer, even though he was a "very capable fighter."[21]†

Campbell was with Ruby from 12:00 to 12:25 P.M., just five minutes before the President was shot. The *News* building was five blocks from Dealey Plaza. From several second-floor windows of the *News* building, it was possible to observe the Texas School Book Depository, but Ruby apparently never went to those windows. Before 12:40, John Newman, another advertising-department employee, observed Ruby sitting at the same desk where Campbell had left him.[22]‡ He was reading the

---

* A Dallas policeman, T. M. Hansen, said he saw Ruby in front of the Dallas police station and said hello to him at 9:30 A.M. either on Thursday, November 21, or Friday, November 22. He was not certain of the day, but was confident it was one of those two (WC Vol. XV, pp. 442–43). It was most likely Thursday, since George Senator said Ruby left too late on Friday to be at the police station by 9:30.

† Anthony Summers says Ruby "made himself obvious to a number of employees during that morning," implying he made a special effort to establish a memorable alibi (*Conspiracy*, p. 454). "That's nonsense," Tony Zoppi told the author. "Jack was outgoing as hell to everyone he saw. That was his way, and whenever he came to our offices, it was a visit people remembered. He always had some angle or gimmick going. On the Friday the President was shot, I later learned he had stopped by my office to see whether I was going to run a piece on a new master of ceremonies he was hiring, a guy who did ESP with the audience. It was going to be a Dallas first. That was Jack." Also, Ruby had to appear in person and pay cash for his ads, because of past problems with tardy payments (WC Vol. V, p. 184).

‡ An FBI report quoted Georgia Mayor, a *News* employee, as saying Ruby was at a desk from which he could see Dealey Plaza. But Mayor actually saw Ruby at Newman's desk, from which Dealey and the Book Depository were not visible (WC Vol. XV, pp. 536–39; WC Vol. XXV, pp. 390–91). Jim Marrs

Morning News and had the paper open to page 14.[23] The entire page was a black-bordered advertisement, headed in large block letters, "Welcome Mr. Kennedy," and the text accused the President of being a Communist tool. It was signed by "The American Fact-Finding Committee, Bernard Weissman, Chairman."[24] Ruby was very disturbed that the *News* should have run such a demeaning advertisement and was dismayed that it was signed by someone with a Jewish name.* It was the second time he had focused on the ad that day (earlier he had called his sister Eva to complain about it).[25] "Who is this Weissman?" Ruby asked Newman, and he complained about the ad's "lousy taste."[26] "What the hell, are you so money hungry?" Ruby asked Newman. "He was upset that a Jewish name should be part of something he thought was so insulting to the President," says Earl Ruby. "It was something that got under his skin the wrong way."[27]

A few minutes after Newman saw him staring at the ad, two *News* employees ran into the office and announced that shots had been fired at the motorcade and the President may have

---

speculates that in the approximately ten minutes Ruby was alone, he could have "left the newspaper offices, been in Dealey Plaza, and returned unnoticed . . ." (*Crossfire*, pp. 327–28). Not only is the timing of such an excursion almost impossible, but the *News* building was crowded with employees, and no one saw Ruby leave the second floor until after the assassination.

* The ad was paid for by a group of political right-wingers, including Bunker Hunt of the oil-rich Dallas family. While the organization was fictitious, Bernard Weissman did exist. He was a politically conservative twenty-six-year-old, recently discharged from the U.S. Army. He had been in Dallas only three and a half weeks and had agreed to the use of his name in the ad (WC Vol. V, pp. 489, 491, 504, 506–09, 514). Mark Lane later claimed that a secret source notified him that Weissman and Officer J. D. Tippit, who was killed by Oswald, had met with Ruby at the Carousel on November 14, eight days before the assassination (WC Vol. V, pp. 521–22). Weissman not only denied the story but also confronted Lane: "You have never taken the trouble to contact me. . . . I am in the phone book. . . . If you had any courage or commonsense or really wanted to get at the facts, you would have called and asked me, too" (WC Vol. V, p. 522). Lane promised to arrange a meeting in Dallas at which Weissman could confront the story's source. He never heard from Lane again (WC Vol. V, p. 524).

Ruby did know a Tippit on the Dallas police force, but it was G. M. Tippit, a member of the special services bureau, not J. D. Tippit (CE 1620; CE 2430).

been hit.[28] Pandemonium erupted. Newman said Ruby had a look of "stunned disbelief," and he was "emotionally upset."[29]

"I don't recall what was said," Jack Ruby later testified. "And I was in a state of hysteria, I mean. You say, 'Oh my God, it can't happen.' You carry on crazy sayings."[30]

Within minutes, several advertisers telephoned Newman to cancel the ads they had placed for the weekend.[31] Ruby believed the cancellations were motivated by the offending Weissman ad: "The phones were ringing off the desk," said Ruby, "and they were having a turmoil in the *News* Building because of a person by the name of Bernard Weissman placing that particular ad . . . criticizing a lot of things about our beloved President. . . . I heard John Newman say, 'I told him not to take that ad.' "[32]

Ruby asked Newman if he could use his phone, and he again called Eva. She was crying over the news about Kennedy. "This is my sister and she is hysterical," he said, holding the phone out for Newman to hear.[33] Newman said Eva "sounded very upset," and he listened for a moment, without saying a word, while Ruby tried "to calm her down."[34] Jack was distraught that his sister was "crying hysterically." He turned to Newman. "John, I will leave Dallas. John, I am not opening up tonight."[35] According to Newman, Ruby left the *News* no later than 1:30. "I left the building," Ruby recalled, "and I went down and I got my car, and I couldn't stop crying . . ."[36] He said he then drove back to the Carousel.[37]

Seth Kantor, a respected journalist and member of the Washington press corps covering the President's trip to Texas, was at Parkland Hospital after the assassination. He knew Ruby and had worked for the *Dallas Times Herald* before moving to Washington. Kantor was running up some stairs when he felt someone tug at his suit coat. "It was Jack Ruby," said Kantor. "Ruby called me by my first name and I grasped his extended hand. He looked miserable. Grim. Pale. There were tears brimming in his eyes."[38] Ruby commented on how "terrible the moment was" and asked Kantor if he should close his nightclubs because of the tragedy. Kantor said it was a good idea.[39]

Ruby later denied to the FBI and the Warren Commission that he had ever been at Parkland that day. None of the many press photos or television films shot of Parkland show him in the crowd. Although he knew many Dallas policemen and reporters, no one saw him except Kantor.* The Warren Commission believed Ruby and said Kantor was mistaken.[40] However, the House Select Committee determined that Kantor "probably was not" mistaken.[41]

Is Kantor correct when he says Ruby was at Parkland? Kantor claimed he saw Ruby between 1:30 and 2:00.[42] Newman said Ruby left the *News* no later than 1:30.[43] *News* advertising salesman Richard Saunders thought he left the newspaper around 1:10 P.M.[44] According to the Warren Commission, Ruby arrived at the Carousel Club by 1:45, leaving too little time for him to stop by the hospital.[45] But the Commission inaccurately cited the testimony of Andrew Armstrong, a bartender, to support Ruby's arrival at the club.[46] Actually, Armstrong said that Ruby arrived about five minutes after he heard the radio announcement that the President was dead.[47] That would have placed his arrival at the Carousel shortly before 2:00. The club's phone records show a call to Chicago, to his sister Eileen, at 2:05.[48]†

Ruby not only had the time to stop briefly by Parkland (it was a round-trip of eight miles), but had reason to lie about being there, in the same way he later lied about the number of times he was at the jail near Oswald over the weekend. "By the time he testified about it," says assistant district attorney Bill Alexander, who prosecuted Ruby for killing Oswald, "he knew that

---

* Wilma Tice, a former manager of the Dallas Juvenile Department's foster home, went to Parkland out of curiosity. She testified that she overheard someone called "Jack," whom she later identified from newspaper photos as Ruby (WC Vol. XV, pp. 391–94). However, she acknowledged in her Warren Commission testimony that "it could have been somebody else that looked just like Jack, named Jack" (WC Vol. XV, p. 391).

† Another reason the Commission thought Ruby arrived at the Carousel no later than 1:45 was because the club's telephone records showed two toll calls, one at 1:45 and the other at 1:51, that they believed Ruby made. The 1:45 call was to Karen Carlin, a stripper, to tell her the club would probably be closed. However, she testified that she received that call from Armstrong and not from Ruby (WC Vol. XIII, p. 208). The 1:51 call was to Ralph Paul's Bullpen Drive-In restaurant, but it was also made by Armstrong. Paul testified he did not hear from Ruby until he received a call at his house about 2:45 (WC Vol. XIV, p. 151). The Carousel's records show a call to the Bullpen restaurant at 2:42 for less than a minute. When Ruby discovered Paul was not at the restaurant but instead at home, he telephoned him there. The phone record shows he called Paul at 2:43 (CE 2303, p. 27, WC Vol. XXV).

whether he spent a long time in prison or not might depend on whether he shot Oswald on the spur of the moment or whether there was premeditation. Visiting Parkland on Sunday, hanging out at the jail over the weekend, might be natural for a fellow like Ruby. But a jury didn't know him, and who knew how they would look at all that?"[49]

Kantor was not surprised when he saw Ruby at Parkland. "I very well remember my first thought," he told the Warren Commission. "I thought, well, there is Jack Ruby. I had been away from Dallas for eighteen months and one day at that time, but it seemed just perfectly normal to see Jack Ruby standing there, because he was a known goer to events."[50] Kantor later described him as a "town character . . . [who was] self-seeking and publicity hungry."[51]

"If there was one Ruby trait that stands out," says Tony Zoppi, "it is that he had to be where the action was. He was like horseshit, all over the place, wherever anything exciting was happening. That's why the President's assassination and all the followup activity at the jail with Oswald and the press attracted Jack like a magnet. It was a natural for him."[52]

After briefly stopping by Parkland, Ruby continued to the Carousel. He knew Kennedy was dead. "He just got on the telephone," recalled his bartender, Armstrong. "He kept saying, 'It's a shame,' like that and . . . he was crying."[53] He first called his sister Eileen. When she answered the phone, he was crying.

"Did you hear the awful news?" he said.

"Yes."

"Oh my God, oh my God." He repeated it several times. "What a black mark for Dallas. Maybe I'll fly up [to Chicago] to be with you tonight."

"Well, I don't think that will be necessary," she told him.

She asked how Eva was, and he cried more. "Oh, she's terrible. When she heard this news, she's even worse." Eileen told him to stay in Dallas and that she would call him later that night.[54]

Ruby stayed at the club for an hour. All those who saw or spoke to him remember his grief was visible and real. Gladys Craddock, who worked for him as a hostess, said he had great admiration for the Kennedy family.[55] Wynn Warner, a musician who had worked for Jack, said the President's murder shattered his world, especially since it happened in Dallas.[56] It was almost as if the assassination had triggered an emotional collapse for Ruby, who was already under tremendous business pressure. His stability also might have been adversely affected by his severe dieting, aided by an appetite suppressant, Preludin, an "upper," which exacerbated his volatile temperament. Even Ruby later admitted it was a "stimulus to give me an emotional feeling . . ."[57]

"He was heartbroken," recalled his friend Ralph Paul. "[He was] very bad emotionally, and said, 'I can't believe it. . . . It's a terrible, terrible thing.' "[58] Ruby had telephoned Paul to say he was thinking of closing his clubs for three days. Paul informed him that he did not intend to close his restaurant and that Ruby's competition, the Weinsteins, would probably not close. According to Paul, Ruby said, "You can do whatever you want. . . . I don't care about the other clubs."[59]

When he had spoken to his sister Eileen, she felt he just wanted to talk to people. Though he was "crying pretty bad," he called an ex-girlfriend he had not dated in eleven years, Alice Nichols, to express his shock.[60] Alex Gruber was a boyhood friend living in Los Angeles, and Ruby telephoned him. Although Gruber felt Ruby was emotionally distraught and needed to talk, the conversation was brief since Jack broke down sobbing and had to hang up.[61]

In her conversation with him, Eva could hear how distraught he was and told him, "You better come here."[62] When he left the Carousel at 3:15 he went directly to Eva's apartment, but stayed less than half an hour, leaving again to pick up food for the weekend.[63] He stopped by the Ritz Delicatessen, only two blocks from the Carousel, and then went to the club and told Crafard to prepare a sign saying it was closed.[64] Ruby was back at Eva's by 5:30 and stayed for two hours.

Eva said he returned with "enough groceries for 20 people . . . but he didn't know what he was doing then."[65] He told her that he wanted to close the clubs. "And he said, 'Listen, we are broke anyway, so I will be a broken millionaire. I am going to close for three days.' "[66] In dire financial straits, and barely breaking even with both clubs open seven days a week, his decision to close was an important gesture. He called the *News* to cancel his advertisements, but they had already reserved the space for him, so he changed the ads to say the clubs were closed. He made some more telephone calls from Eva's apartment. Those he spoke to later remarked how agitated he was. Cecil Hamlin, a longtime friend, said he was "very emotional . . . and broken up." He was fond of Hamlin's young daughter and told him how upset he was for the Kennedy "kids."

But his sister Eva witnessed the real depth of his anguish, and unwittingly contributed to it. "He was sitting on this chair and crying. . . . He was sick to his stomach . . . and went into the bathroom. . . . He looked terrible."[67] Eva and Jack watched the television news, and were fascinated as details became known about the accused assassin. "One of the things he loved about this President," she said, "he didn't care what you were, you were a human being and Jack felt that this was one time in history that Jews are getting the break. He [Kennedy] put in great Jewish men in office . . ."[68] She told her brother that Oswald was a "barbarian," and said, "That lousy Commie. Don't worry, the Commie, we will get him."[69] She said Jack was sitting with his head in his hands, and said, "Really, he was crazy . . . what a creep."[70] "You see," said Eva, " 'a creep' is a real low life to Jack."[71]

When Jack left, Eva remembered, "He looked pretty bad. . . . I can't explain it to you. He looked too broken, a broken man already. He did make the remark, he said, 'I never felt so bad in my life, even when Ma and Pa died. . . . Someone tore my heart out.' "[72]

Although Ruby was not religious, he had twice telephoned Temple Shearith Israel to check on the time for the evening's services and was told a special memorial for the President would start at 8:00 P.M. He planned to attend. But first, he apparently stopped by the Dallas police headquarters—although he told the Warren Commission he was not there Friday night before 11:15 P.M., and it believed him.[73] At least five witnesses, police and reporters who knew him, reported seeing Ruby on the third floor of the headquarters sometime between 6:00 and 9:00 P.M.[74] John Rutledge, the night police reporter for the *Dallas Morning News*, knew Ruby. He saw him step off the elevator, hunched between two out-of-state reporters with press identifications on their coats. "The three of them just walked past policemen, around the corner, past those cameras and lights, and on down the hall," recalled Rutledge.[75] The next time Rutledge saw him, he was standing outside room 317, where Oswald was being interrogated, and "he was explaining to members of the out-of-state press who everybody was that came in and out of that door. . . . There would be a thousand questions shot at him at once, and Jack would straighten them all out . . . ."[76] Soon, several detectives walked by, and one recognized him. "Hey, Jack, what are you doing here?" "I am helping all these fellows," Ruby said, pointing to the pack of reporters.[77]

"You have to understand," says Tony Zoppi, "that Jack was in his element. He was the center of attention at the hottest place in the city."[78] "That's where the limelight was," recalled Barney Weinstein, Ruby's competitor in the nightclub business. "He just had to get into everything, including the excitement of that weekend Kennedy died."[79]

Victor Robertson, a WFAA radio reporter, also knew Ruby. He saw him approach the door to the office where Oswald was being interrogated and start to open it. "He had the door open a few inches," recalled Robertson, "and began to step into the room, and the two officers stopped him. . . . One of them said, 'You can't go in there, Jack.' "[80]

Ruby probably left police headquarters shortly after 8:30 and proceeded to his apartment. His home telephone records show that, among others, he called his friend Ralph Paul, his brother Hyman, and two sisters, Marion and Ann, about 9:00 P.M.[81] Hyman said Jack was so disturbed about what happened in Dallas that he talked about selling his business and returning to Chicago.[82] Buddy Raymon, a comedian, remembered that when Ruby telephoned him, "he was crying and carrying on: 'What do you think of a character like that killing the President?' I was trying to calm him down. I said, 'Jack, he's not normal; no normal man kills the President on his lunch hour and takes a bus home.' But he just kept saying, 'He killed our President.' "[83] George Senator said it was the "first time I ever saw tears in his eyes."[84]

From his apartment, Ruby finally drove to the temple and arrived in time for the end of a special memorial service for the President. He cried openly at the synagogue.[85]* "They didn't believe a guy like Jack would ever cry," said his brother Hyman. "Jack never cried in his life. He is not that kind of a guy to cry."[86]

By 10:30, he left the temple and arrived at Phil's Delicatessen, near his Vegas Club. There, he stocked up on kosher sandwiches and sodas.[87] While he waited for the sandwiches, he talked to a group of students at the deli, lamenting the President's death, saying the assassination was very bad for Dallas and proudly telling them he had closed his clubs out of respect.[88] When he left the deli, he hoped to stop by KLIF radio, his personal favorite, and drop off some food, but he did not have the station's private night-line number. He then drove to police headquarters, past several nightclubs, and noticed most were open. "I can't understand some of the clubs remaining open," he said. "It struck me funny at such a tragic time . . ."[89]

When he arrived at the third floor of the station, he encountered a uniformed officer who did not recognize him. Ruby saw several detectives he knew, shouted to them, and they helped him get inside. Once there, he said he was "carried away with the excitement of history."[90] Detective A. M. Eberhardt, who knew Ruby and had been at his club, was in the burglary-and-theft section when Jack "stuck his head in our door and hollered at us. . . . He came in and said hello to me, shook hands with me. I asked him what he was doing. He told me he was a translator for the newspapers. . . . He said, 'I am here as a reporter' and he took the notebook and hit it."[91] Eberhardt, who knew Ruby spoke some Yiddish, figured he was translating for Israeli papers. Ruby told them about the sandwiches he had brought, and then the discussion switched to the assassination. He told the detectives "how terrible it was for it to happen in the city. . . . It's hard to realize that a complete nothing, a zero

---

* Summers said that "the rabbi, who talked to him, noticed that Ruby said nothing at all about the assassination," implying that Ruby was not that disturbed over Kennedy's killing (*Conspiracy*, pp. 455–56). Ruby later said, "I wasn't in a conversational mood" (WC Vol. V, p. 187). Rabbi Silverman, however, remembered Ruby appeared to be in "shock or depressed," and that he was in a daze (CE 2281, WC Vol. XXV).

like that, could kill a man like President Kennedy. It's hard to understand how a complete nothing could have done this."[92]

In less than half an hour, Oswald was brought out of room 317 on the way to the basement assembly room for the midnight press conference. Ruby recalled that as Oswald walked past, "I was standing about two or three feet away."[93]*

"I went down to the assembly room in the basement," Ruby said. "I felt perfectly free walking in there. No one asked me or anything."[94] One of the detectives assigned to guard Oswald was Ruby's friend A. M. Eberhardt. He noticed Ruby in the right-hand corner, with a notebook and pencil in his hand.[95] Ruby thought Oswald was smirking at his police guards, and in only a few minutes he was convinced that Oswald was guilty.[96]

When the press conference finished, Ruby walked outside the room and saw Dallas district attorney Henry Wade. " 'Hi, Henry,' he yelled real loud," recalled Wade, "and put his hand out to shake hands with me and I shook hands with him. And he said, 'Don't you know me? I am Jack Ruby, I run the Vegas Club.' And I said, 'What are you doing in here?' He said, 'I know all these fellows.' "[97]

Ruby even introduced himself to justice of the peace David Johnston, who had earlier arraigned Oswald, and gave him a pass to the Carousel.[98] He did the same to Ike Pappas, then a reporter for New York radio station WNEW. In a few minutes he saw that Pappas had an open telephone line and was trying to get Henry Wade's attention. Ruby took it upon himself to interrupt Wade's conversation with several other men, and took the district attorney over to Pappas for the telephone interview.[99] Ruby said, "I felt I was deputized as a reporter momentarily."[100]

He then telephoned KLIF radio station (he had obtained the private night-line number since arriving at police headquarters)

---

*In his first statement to the FBI, Ruby admitted he had his .38 caliber revolver with him on Friday night (CD 1252.9). Later, when he realized that carrying his pistol might be construed as evidence of premeditation, he said he did not have his gun on Friday. However, a photo of the rear of Ruby, taken in the third-floor corridor that night, shows a lump under the right rear of his jacket. If he was a mob-hired killer with a contract on Oswald, he would have shot him at his first opportunity. Certainly, any contract to kill Oswald would not have been one Ruby could fulfill at his leisure. Yet when he had the perfect opportunity, with Oswald only a couple of feet away, Ruby did not shoot him.

and said he was bringing sandwiches over. He also asked if the station wanted a live interview with district attorney Wade. "I heard someone call, 'Henry Wade wanted on the phone,' " recalled Wade, "and I gradually got around to one of the police phones and as I get there it is Jack Ruby. . . . I didn't know a thing, and I just picked up the phone and they said this is so and so [Glenn Duncan] at KLIF and started asking questions."[101] Several minutes later Ruby returned upstairs and ran into one of the KLIF disc jockeys, Russ Knight, who was at police headquarters covering the story. "He [Ruby] overheard me ask where Wade was," recalled Knight, "and then he said, 'I'll show you.' "[102] Ruby took Knight to the basement and pointed out Wade, and introduced them. "Ruby was insistent that I ask Wade if Oswald were insane," said Knight. Wade said Oswald was not insane and that the President's murder was premeditated.[103]

After that interview, Knight walked the four blocks back to KLIF, and Ruby drove there. Ruby had walked in with his sandwiches and sodas by 1:45 A.M. He talked briefly to Knight and several other employees before the 2:00 A.M. newscast. Again, he expressed his sadness over the assassination, and said he was glad the evidence was mounting against Oswald, whom he bragged he had personally seen.[104] At the 2:00 A.M. newscast, Knight talked about his interview with Wade, and said, "Through a tip from a local nightclub owner, I asked Mr. Wade the question of Oswald's insanity."[105] Glen Duncan, a KLIF employee who spoke to Ruby over the phone and at the station, felt he was excited about becoming part of the unfolding story.[106]

Although it was approaching 2:30 in the morning, Ruby decided to drive to the *Dallas Times Herald*. Before leaving KLIF, he went to his car and returned with a pamphlet for Russ Knight titled "Heroism."[107] On the way to the *Herald*, Ruby saw Harry Olsen and Kay Helen Coleman near a downtown parking lot. They waved him over to their car and he joined them. They talked for nearly an hour. Harry Olsen was a Dallas policeman, and Kay Coleman was a stripper who worked at the Carousel under the stage name Kathy Kay.*

---

*Coleman and Olsen were dating, and married several months later (WC Vol. XIV, p. 641).

They were all upset about the killings of JFK and Officer Tippit.[108] Ruby told them, "It's too bad a peon could do something like that, that son-of-a-bitch."[109] Coleman described Ruby as "kind of wild-eyed," and said that Ruby reiterated that he was mad that the other club owners had not closed, and that he "was real upset . . . talked about Mrs. Kennedy and the children and how terrible it was. . . . He would just keep saying over and over how terrible it was, what a wonderful man the President was and how sorry he felt for Mrs. Kennedy and the children."[110] He told Olsen and Coleman that Oswald "looked like a little rat, real sneaky looking."[111]

"And they talked and they carried on," said Ruby, "and they thought I was the greatest guy in the world, and he stated they should cut this guy inch by inch into ribbons, and so on. And she said, 'Well, if he was in England, they would drag him through the streets and would have hung him.' . . . I left them after a long delay. They kept me from leaving. They were constantly talking and were in a pretty dramatic mood. They were crying and carrying on."[112]*

Ruby left Olsen and Coleman and arrived at the *Times Herald* offices just before 4:00 A.M. He often visited the *Herald* at that early morning hour in order to check on his ads for the following day.[113] He talked to several employees, and they remembered him as "pretty shaken up" about the assassination, but also excited over his involvement with Henry Wade and having seen Oswald.[114] Again, he complained about the Weissman ad in the *Dallas Morning News*. "He thought the name Weissman was evidently Jewish," recalled Arthur Watherwax, a printer at the newspaper. "He thought it was a plan that would make the Jews look bad, that it would really reflect on the Jews."[115] Ruby also complained that Oswald was "a little weasel of a guy."[116] Roy

---

* Harry and Kay Olsen denied making the inflammatory remarks about Oswald. However, Joe Tonahill, one of Ruby's attorneys, believed that Ruby, without even realizing it, could have easily been led, through the power of suggestion, to have killed Oswald. "The conversation with Olsen and Kay could have been the beginning of it," he said. "It could have been a lot stronger. . . . Ruby didn't want to talk about that conversation because he had enough sense to know that was premeditation" (Kantor, *The Ruby Cover-Up*, pp. 103–4). Ruby kept the chance meeting with Olsen and Coleman a secret until after his trial was finished.

Pryor, who had known Ruby for years, thought his voice was laced with hatred and revulsion when he spoke of Oswald.[117] At one point, shaking the newspaper emphatically in the air, he said, "Poor Mrs. Kennedy—Jackie and the kids."[118] Watherwax and Pryor thought he was trying to "be a big-shot," especially when he told them, "You see, I'm in good with the district attorney," and how he had corrected Wade at the press conference about his Fair Play for Cuba mistake.[119]*

Ruby left the *Times Herald* offices about 4:30 A.M. and drove back to his apartment. On the way, he began fixating on a billboard he had seen earlier, which demanded, in large block letters: IMPEACH EARL WARREN. He wondered whether there was a connection between that sign and the Weissman advertisement. When he arrived at his apartment, "I very impatiently awakened George Senator," Ruby remembered.[120]

"The next thing I knew," recalled Senator, "somebody was hollering at me, and shaking me up, [and it was] Ruby. He was excited. He was moody; and the first thing come [sic] out of his mouth is . . . 'Gee, his poor children and Mrs. Kennedy, what a terrible thing to happen.' "[121] Next he told Senator about the IMPEACH EARL WARREN sign. He made Senator get dressed and called Larry Crafard, who was sleeping at the Carousel Club, and ordered him to "get that Polaroid with the flashbulbs and meet me downstairs. I'll be right downtown."[122]

At nearly 5:00 in the morning, the three of them drove to the Warren sign, and Ruby had Crafard take some photos.† There was a post-office box number on the billboard, 1754, and Ruby mistakenly thought it was the same post-office box listed in the Weissman advertisement, 1792.[123] "I can't understand why they want to impeach Earl Warren," said Ruby. "This must be the work of the John Birch Society or the Communist Party."[124] The

---

* Before leaving the *Herald* offices, Ruby and several of the employees tried a twistboard he had promised the newspaper's foreman, Clyde Gadash. Some interpret the use of the twistboard as an indication that Ruby was not really that upset over the assassination. However, the *Herald* employees all testified that while he showed them how to use the board and several of them tried it, his general mood was one of sorrow (CE 2816, p. 1510, WC Vol. XXVI).

† When Ruby was arrested for shooting Oswald, three photos of the Warren billboard were in his suit pocket.

three of them drove next to the post office's terminal annex and spoke to the night clerk about the owner of the box. The clerk could not give them any information, but Ruby looked inside the box and was "deeply annoyed" to see there was a large mail response to the ad.[125] He had earlier failed to find Weissman in the phone book, which encouraged his belief that the name was invented in order to blame Jews for the events in Dallas.

It was after 5:30 A.M. when they left the post office and drove to the Southland Hotel's coffee shop. There, a copy of Friday's *Dallas Morning News* was on the counter, and Ruby picked it up and again saw the Weissman advertisement. "He was very, very disturbed," recalled Senator.[126] He kept rereading the ad and mumbling that he could not understand why someone would publish such an insulting tirade against the President. Senator felt Ruby, who had a strange and abnormal stare, was disturbed in a way he had never before seen.[127] "He was deeply hurt about the President, terribly," said Senator. Again, Ruby talked about JFK's children, and he had "tears in his eyes."

Ruby dropped Crafard off at the Carousel at daybreak. Back at his apartment with Senator, he put on the television for a short while before going to bed a little after 6:00 A.M. At 8:30, Crafard woke Ruby by telephoning to say there was no canned food for the dogs at the Carousel. He was furious that Crafard had called so early, and berated him.[128] Crafard had been at the Carousel for nearly six weeks, but Ruby's odd behavior the night before, and now this vicious verbal attack, was too much for the youngster. Later that morning, around 11:00, he took $5 from the club's cash register and left Dallas, hitchhiking back to his sister in Michigan.[129] Crafard, a drifter who did not even know where his wife and two children lived, admitted to the Warren Commission that he had done similar things in the past. He told only the garage attendant next to the club that he was leaving.[130]

Ruby's spirits were not much better when he finally got up Saturday. Shortly after being woken by Crafard, Ruby turned on the television and saw a memorial service broadcast from New York. "I watched Rabbi Seligman," he recalled. "He eulogized that here is a man [JFK] that fought in every battle, went to every country, and had to come back to his own country to be shot in the back. That created a tremendous emotional feeling for me, the way he said that."[131]

Marjorie Richey, who worked for him, telephoned near noon, asking if the club would reopen that night. He said no, and when he spoke of the "terrible" assassination, "his voice was shaking . . ."[132] He drove by the Carousel. At the Nichols Parking Garage next door, at about 1:30 P.M., he told Tom Brown, an attendant, to notify any of his acquaintances who stopped by that the Carousel would stay closed for the weekend.[133] He then went to Sol's Turf Bar, on Commerce Street. Near 2:00, he was spotted there by Frank Bellocchio, the owner of a jewelry firm and a Ruby acquaintance for almost eight years.[134*]

Bellocchio was in a discussion with a friend, in which he blamed Dallas for the assassination, when Ruby got involved. "He was very incoherent," recalled Bellocchio, who tried to make his point about Dallas's responsibility by showing Ruby a copy of Friday's Weissman advertisement.[135] It was like waving a red flag at a bull. Ruby went into a tirade about the ad being the work of radical groups trying to "stir up anti-Jewish feelings," claiming Weissman was fictitious and that the ad was dangerous since Jews in Dallas might be blamed for the assassination. He produced two of his IMPEACH EARL WARREN photos, and

---

* Bellocchio's most contemporaneous statement, taken by the FBI on December 6, 1963, only two weeks after the event, gives the time he saw Ruby as "between 1:00 and 2:00 P.M." Because of Ruby's visit to the Nichols Parking Garage at 1:30, it is possible to place the encounter closer to 2:00 P.M. In his Warren Commission testimony almost seven months later, Bellocchio changed the time of the meeting to 4:00 P.M. (WC Vol. XV, pp. 468–69). He did not change the time because he remembered it differently but rather because a friend who saw him there remembered being there at 4:00. However, Ruby's accountant, Abraham Kleinman, also saw Jack at Sol's, and he was clear it was at 2:30, because he arrived at that time and Ruby left a few minutes later (WC Vol. XV, pp. 386–87). In its final report, the Warren Commission set Ruby's appearance at Sol's Turf Bar as 3:00 P.M., a time mentioned by no one (WR, p. 347). The Commission filled Ruby's time between his appearance at the garage and the time it decided he went to Sol's with an encounter with a policeman and a reporter at Dealey Plaza (WR, p. 346). Yet those two witnesses say Ruby was at Dealey by 3:00, and their testimony is confirmed by an interview the reporter conducted with Dallas police chief Jesse Curry shortly afterward. The Warren Commission's sequence of events has been used by most researchers on the assassination, yet it is clearly mistaken about the early part of Saturday afternoon.

when Bellocchio asked for one, he refused since he said it was part of a "scoop" he was working on.[136]

When Ruby left Sol's it was shortly after 2:30 P.M. He then went past police headquarters, where policeman D. V. Harkness saw him near a large crowd that had gathered for a scheduled transfer of Oswald at 4:00 P.M.[137]* Ruby drove back toward the Carousel and stopped at the Nichols garage to check if he had any messages. Garnett Hallmark, the garage's general manager, spoke to Ruby, who told him he was "acting like a reporter," and then got on the phone in the cashier's office.[138] He called KLIF radio station twice within a few minutes and spoke both times to Ken Dowe, a news announcer. "I understand they are moving Oswald over to the county jail," he told Dowe. "Would you like for me to go over there and get some news stories? Would you like me to cover it, because I am a pretty good friend of Henry Wade's and I believe I can get some news stories." Dowe put him on hold and asked another newsman, Gary De-Laune, "Who the devil is Jack Ruby?" "He is just a guy that calls on the telephone," DeLaune responded, "and he knows everybody in town and maybe he can help us."[139] Dowe told Ruby they appreciated any help he could provide. As far as Jack was concerned, he was now officially representing KLIF as a reporter.[140]

Ruby then went to Dealey Plaza, where he looked at the many memorial wreaths that had been left overnight. As he walked around the plaza, he ran into an acquaintance, Wes Wise, a newsman from KRLD radio. They talked about the assassination. "The only thing I noticed," recalled Wise, "was that when I mentioned that at the Trade Mart I had gone into the room where President Kennedy's rocking chair [was] . . . located and saw the two large presents meant for Caroline and John and

---

* Dallas police chief Jesse Curry wanted to transfer Oswald from his headquarters to the custody of Sheriff Bill Decker's more secure prison, one mile away at Dealey Plaza. However, Captain Will Fritz wanted more time to interrogate him before he lost custody. Curry, hoping Fritz would be ready to relinquish Oswald by the afternoon, initially planned the transfer for 4:00 P.M. on Saturday, November 23. Although there was no public announcement, word quickly spread around headquarters that a transfer was imminent, and a crowd had begun gathering near the jail by 3:00 P.M.

they were Western saddles that were going to be given to Kennedy to give to his children . . . I noticed tears in his eyes."[141]
He informed Wise that Chief Curry and Captain Fritz were at the
Plaza looking at the memorial wreaths, and Wise thanked him
and left to interview them. It was nearly 3:30 when Ruby pulled
up in his 1960 white Oldsmobile to policeman James Chaney,
who was acquainted with him. Ruby asked if the two men standing several hundred feet away were Chief Curry and Captain
Fritz. Chaney said yes. "Good. I just told reporters up the street
that they were down there."[142] Then he abruptly drove away,
because he was about to cry and did not want Chaney to see
him break down.[143]

When he left Dealey Plaza, it appears Ruby once more went to
the third floor of the police headquarters, expecting an Oswald
transfer that never took place. He later denied being there Saturday because, again, he probably feared it might be interpreted
as evidence of premeditation. The Warren Commission said it
"reached no firm conclusion as to whether or not Ruby visited
the Dallas Police Department on Saturday."[144] Yet credible eyewitness testimony shows he was there.

Earlier in the day, Ruby had put his head through the open
window of a remote television truck for NBC affiliate WBAP,
and without asking anyone's permission began watching the
monitors that showed the activity on the third floor of the jail.[145]
He told the reporters he "knew Wade personally and he could
get some information for us or he could get him to come out
and talk to us."[146] Ruby was so bothersome that the WBAP reporters dubbed him "the creep." Later in the afternoon they saw
him on their monitors wandering the third floor of police headquarters and approaching Wade in an office, from which regular
reporters were barred.[147] Only the next day, after Oswald was
shot, did the van's reporters learn "the creep" was Ruby.

On the third floor, several reporters saw him. Philippe Labro,
a reporter for *France-Soir*, a daily French newspaper, ran into
Ruby, who asked who he was and what he did. When Labro told
him, Ruby's response was, "Ooh la la Folies-Bergère," which
Labro was convinced was the only French he knew. He then
gave Labro a pass to the Carousel.[148] Another French correspondent, François Pelou, saw him later hand out sandwiches to

some of the press. Frank Johnston, a UPI photographer, saw him at the same time.[149] Thayer Waldo, a reporter with the *Fort Worth Star-Telegram*, watched Ruby giving out Carousel cards to reporters between 4:00 and 5:00 P.M. He was aggressive in getting the reporters' attention, pulling the sleeves of some and slapping others on the back or arms. When he got to Waldo, Ruby said, "You're one of the boys, aren't you? Here's my card with both my clubs on it. Everybody around here knows me. Ask anybody who Jack Ruby is. As soon as you get a chance, I want all of you boys to come over to my place, the one downtown here is more convenient, and have a drink on me. I'll be seeing you."[150]

Before Ruby left police headquarters, he called his friend and attorney Stanley Kaufman, complaining about the Weissman ad and asking for help in locating Weissman. Kaufman said Ruby "rambled," and that he was "upset" about the effects on the Dallas Jewish community. Jack told him that the ad's black border was a tipoff that those who placed it knew about the assassination, and Ruby assured Kaufman he was helping the police get to the bottom of the Weissman matter.[151]

Ruby left the headquarters just before 6:00 P.M., the same time Chief Curry told the press they expected to transfer Oswald at 10:00 A.M. the next day.[152] Not long after that, he arrived at the Carousel. Andrew Armstrong, the club's bartender, thought he was still "more worried than ever," remarking that he was "in a sad and sorrowful mood . . . and disturbed . . . over the assassination."[153] Armstrong had received calls from patrons who wanted to book reservations for that night's show, and from most of the strippers, trying to find out if the club was going to open. Ruby said no, it would stay closed until Monday.*

He left the Carousel between 7:00 and 7:30 P.M., heading for Eva's apartment, where he stayed for more than an hour.[154]† He

---

* Later that evening, Ruby lost his temper with Armstrong, who refused to stay at the club until 10:00 P.M. just in case any customers arrived who did not know it was closed. Armstrong, who said he was "fed up" with Ruby's unexpected temper tantrums, quit on the spot.

† Eva later testified that her brother was at her apartment only once on Saturday, between approximately 4:00 and 8:00 P.M. However, the first visit to Eva's apartment was a brief one shortly before 8:00, and then later that night

told her of his early-morning expedition to photograph the IM-
PEACH EARL WARREN sign and its links to the Weissman ad. "I
thought my brother Jack was plain nuts," said Eva. "He figured
that a gentile is using that name to blame all this on Jews . . .
and then he analyzed the ad on Saturday and he saw the black
border."[155]

He asked if she would be well enough to attend Tippit's
funeral with him on Monday. Using her telephone, he
made several calls to local acquaintances, and in each
complained about the Earl Warren sign and that competing
nightclubs had stayed open.[156] Russ Knight at KLIF received
a brief call from him, and "he asked me who Earl Warren
was . . ."[157]*

By 9:30 Ruby had returned to his apartment. There, he
received a call from one of his strippers, Karen Bennett
Carlin, whose stage name was Little Lynn. She had driven
into Dallas from Fort Worth with her husband and wondered
if the Carousel was going to open over the weekend,
because she needed money. "He got very angry and was very
short with me," Carlin recalled. "He said, 'Don't you have
any respect for the President? Don't you know the President is dead? . . . I don't know when I will open. I don't
know if I will ever open back up.'"[158] She apologized for
bothering him but still asked for part of her salary, and he
promised to meet them in an hour at the Carousel. When
he had not arrived by 10:30, Carlin's husband, Bruce, again
telephoned the apartment, and emphasized they needed
money for rent and groceries. On this occasion, Ruby spoke to
the attendant at the Nichols garage, Huey Reeves, and persuaded him to lend the Carlins $5 so they could at least return

---

Ruby returned by 10:00 for a longer visit. From there he telephoned Ralph
Paul, who heard Eva in the background. Phone records show the call was
made at 10:44 P.M., from her apartment. Eva was on painkillers and sedatives
for her recent abdominal surgery and admitted the medication may have affected her recall of the exact number and times of his Saturday visits (WC Vol.
XV, p. 342).

* From conversations with others before the Knight call, it is evident that
Ruby knew Earl Warren was someone prominent in government but was not
sure of which position he held until Knight told him.

to Fort Worth, and told Carlin to call him the next day about getting more money.[159]*

Ruby telephoned Eva complaining about his deteriorating mood. "He was very depressed," she recalled. "He was so low."[160] She encouraged him to visit some of his friends, but he was not certain he wanted to leave his apartment. He next telephoned Lawrence Meyers, the Chicago friend he had seen Thursday night. Ruby complained about the "terrible, terrible thing," and then began talking about Mrs. Kennedy and her children. "He was so absolutely repetitious about those poor people," recalled Meyers. "I said . . . life goes on. She will make a new life for herself. . . . Then he was obviously very upset. . . . This night he seemed far more incoherent than I have ever listened to him. The guy sounded like he had flipped his lid, I guess. . . . He became so incoherent, so vehement about those . . . poor children. . . . [He said] 'Those poor people, those poor people, I have got to do something about it.' "[161]

Meyers tried to pacify him, but each attempt only resulted in "another tirade."[162] Ruby turned down an offer to have coffee with Meyers at his hotel, but promised to call the next night at 6:00 P.M. to arrange for dinner.

Shortly after speaking to Meyers, Ruby drove back to his sister's apartment. From there he telephoned Ralph Paul's Bullpen restaurant and spoke to his close friend. Paul remembered that Eva was crying in the background and that Ruby told him he had driven around the city to check on his competitors and none of them were doing any business.[163] A nineteen-year-old waitress at the Bullpen, Wanda Helmick, testified she overheard Paul's end of the conversation and heard him mention something about a gun, and that he also exclaimed, "Are you crazy?"[164] However, Paul adamantly denied he ever made such statements.[165]†

---

* Many who knew Ruby said he was "a soft touch," loaning or giving money frequently to his workers (Wills and Demaris, "The Avenger," *Esquire*, May 1967, pp. 158–59).

† Helmick did not report her information until June 1964, seven months after the incident. None of the other workers at the Bullpen who were near Helmick at the time corroborated her testimony. However, when Paul testified before the Warren Commission in August 1964, Ruby's murder conviction was

Ruby left his sister's apartment and arrived at the Nichols garage shortly after 11:00 P.M. He repaid the attendant the $5 he had loaned to the Carlins. Outside the Carousel, he briefly said hello to Harry Olsen and Kay Coleman, the couple he had spoken to for an hour late the previous night. Inside the club, he made several brief calls to Ralph Paul and made a two-minute call to Breck Wall, a friend and entertainer who had gone to Galveston when his Dallas show had suspended its performances because of the assassination. Wall was also the newly elected president of the Dallas council of AGVA, the union with which Ruby was having difficulties. "He was very upset that he had closed and they [the Weinsteins] had stayed open," recalled Wall. "He thought it wasn't right and he wanted to know when I would return to Dallas and I told him probably Monday or Tuesday and he said, well, when I got in town would I call him. . . . I told him fine and that was it."[166]*

After finishing his calls at 11:48 P.M., Ruby left for the Pago Club, about ten minutes away from the Carousel. He sat at a table by himself, ordered a Coke, and asked the waitress in a disparaging tone, "Why are you open?"[167] Soon, the Pago's owner, Robert Norton, joined him at the table. They talked

---

on appeal, and it is doubtful he would have said anything that could have been used as evidence of premeditation against his friend. Telephone records reveal the conversation at the Bullpen lasted nine minutes, but all Paul remembered was that Ruby said the other clubs in town were doing terrible business. Ruby telephoned the restaurant again at 11:18 and discovered Paul had gone home. He then telephoned Paul three times at home, at 11:19 for three minutes, at 11:36 for two minutes, and at 11:47 for one minute. Paul said he did not feel well, and told Ruby "I was sick and I was going to bed and not to call me" (WC Vol. XV, pp. 672–73).

* In 1964, Wall told the Warren Commission that Ruby did not discuss Oswald during their telephone conversation. In 1988, he told the *Dallas Morning News*, "Then in the course of the conversation, he [Ruby] started talking about Oswald. I don't think he ever said his name. He said 'This guy who killed our President, someone needs to do the same to him'" ("In Their Own Words," November 20, 1988, p. 29). Wall is only one of many witnesses who recalls more information years after the event than he did in his contemporaneous testimony. Unless there is a convincing explanation for the alteration or addition to the original statements, the earliest account must be considered accurate. In this example, Wall's Warren Commission testimony, where he stated that Oswald was not mentioned during his conversation with Ruby, is the most credible.

about the assassination, and Norton expressed strong feelings. "It was terrible and I think it was an insult to our country," he told Ruby. "It was terrible for the man himself. We couldn't do enough to the person that had done this sort of thing."[168] Ruby was uncharacteristically quiet. He complained he was tired and, only fifteen minutes after arriving, left to return to his apartment.[169] George Senator later claimed he was asleep when Ruby returned.[170] Jack telephoned Eva at 12:45 to see how she was feeling and then went to bed himself by 1:30.[171]

On Sunday, Mrs. Elnora Pitts, Ruby's cleaning lady, called between 8:30 and 9:00 A.M., waking him up. She asked if she should stop by to clean the apartment later that day. "He sounded just terrible strange to me," she recalled.[172] He told her to call him back at 2:00 before she came over.* Ruby did not get up until 9:00 to 9:30.[173] Senator noticed he was a "little worse this day . . . the way he talked. He was even mumbling, which I didn't understand. . . . His lips were going. What he was jabbering, I don't know. But he was really pacing."[174] Ruby turned on the television to listen to the latest news and read the morning's *Dallas Times Herald.*† At 10:19, while still lounging in the apart-

---

* Some, like David Scheim, claim the reason Pitts found the man on the phone so strange is that it was an imposter and that the real Ruby was already at police headquarters waiting for Oswald's transfer, due to take place at 10:00 A.M. However, the Warren Commission asked Pitts if she was certain she had spoken to Ruby, and she responded: "Yes, sir. It was him. I'm sure of that . . ." (WC Vol. XIII, p. 232). The evidence that he was at police headquarters early on Sunday is based upon reports of four WBAP-TV technicians, who claimed to see him between 8:00 and 11:00 A.M. None of them, however, knew Ruby. They described him wearing clothes he did not own, and their physical descriptions were not accurate. Videotapes of the scenes early that morning reveal the source of their confusion, a man near the WBAP remote truck who resembled Ruby (KRLD-TV reel 13; CE 3072, WC Vol. XXVI).

A witness at Ruby's apartment complex thought he saw him doing the laundry near 10:00. However, that was George Senator, mistaken for Ruby.

† When the police searched Ruby's apartment after the shooting, they found a copy of the paper at the foot of his bed. It was turned to a page that had an open letter to Caroline Kennedy. Ruby remembered reading the letter on Sunday morning and called it, "the most heartbreaking letter" (WR, p. 354). Next to that letter was an article that concluded Mrs. Kennedy would have to return to Dallas for Oswald's trial (WR, p. 355). According to Senator, "The effect [of those articles] on Jack was it put him in a worse mood than he was, more solemn than ever, and he had tears in his eyes" (*Dallas Morning News*, November 20, 1988, p. 30).

ment in his underwear, he received a call from his dancer Karen Carlin (her phone record revealed the exact time). Although she sensed he "still seemed upset," she told him, "I have called, Jack, to try to get some money, because the rent is due and I need some money for groceries and you told me to call." Ruby asked how much she needed, and she said $25. He offered to go downtown and send it to her by Western Union, but told her it would "take a little while to get dressed . . . ."[175]

According to Senator, he got ready slowly. "Jack was never a fast dresser or never a fast washer. . . . He sure had a moody and very faraway look to me. It was a look that I had never seen before on him . . ."[176] Ruby left the apartment a few minutes before 11:00 A.M. His route downtown took him past Dealey Plaza, where he saw the many new wreaths left overnight in memory of the President. Again, he cried.[177] As he drove near the jail, he noticed a large crowd and assumed Oswald had already been transferred.[178]

At the police station, if everything had gone according to plan, Oswald would have been moved to the sheriff's custody nearly an hour earlier.[179] By 9:00 A.M., the police had cleared the basement. Guards were posted at the two driveway ramps, and at the five doorways into the garage. Then the press was allowed to set up to film the transfer.[180]*

A crowd of several hundred had gathered before 10:00, in front of the jail, to watch the event.[181] However, the transfer had undergone a series of last-second changes and delays. Although they had received anonymous telephone threats on Oswald's life, the police had considered and rejected a secret nighttime transfer. Their plans stayed in a state of flux as they decided on the best compromise between security and press access.[182] Only an hour and a half before the planned move, the police decided to make the arrangements themselves, instead of the usual policy of allowing the sheriff's department to take responsibility.[183] An hour before the transfer, Fritz decided to bring Oswald

---

*Despite these precautions, it was never clear whether the door near the public elevators was properly locked. The basement was also accessible from an unguarded hallway inside the police and courts building. Newsmen running to photograph Oswald passed through this door without ever being asked for credentials (CE 2027, 2062, WC Vol. XXIV).

through the basement, so the press could have more room to take pictures.[184]

The original plan to transfer Oswald in an armored truck went awry when two armored vehicles arrived that were unusable. One was too small to hold guards, and the other was too tall to fit under the jail's eight-foot driveway clearance.[185] Captain Fritz decided to use the larger armored truck as a decoy and move Oswald in an unmarked police car.

One of the biggest delays to the scheduled transfer was caused by the arrival of postal inspector Harry Holmes for a final interrogation. "I had been in and out of Captain Fritz's office on numerous occasions during this 2½-day period," recalled Holmes. "On this morning, I had no appointment. I actually started to church with my wife. I got to church and I said, 'You get out, I am going down and see if I can do something for Captain Fritz. I imagine he is as sleepy as I am.'"[186] When Holmes arrived at police headquarters, Fritz asked if he wanted to participate in the final interrogation of Oswald. Holmes's extensive questioning about Oswald's use of his post-office boxes made the session run long. Captain Fritz remembered, "We went, I believe, an hour overtime with the interrogation, but we tried to finish by 10:00 . . ."[187] Holmes remembered that near the end of the session, Chief Curry "was beating on the door."[188] The questioning lasted more than one and a half hours and did not end until shortly after 11:00 A.M.[189]

Ruby parked across the street from the Western Union station, only one block from police headquarters, near 11:05.* At Western Union, he filled out the forms for sending $25 to Karen Carlin. Then he patiently waited in line while another customer completed her business. According to the clerk, Ruby was in no hurry.[190] It was impossible for him to know that Oswald had not been transferred, since there was no television or radio at the Western Union office. There was a public telephone, but Ruby did not use it.[191] When he got to the counter, the cost for send-

---

* His favorite dog, Sheba, was left in the car. "People that didn't know Jack will never understand this," Bill Alexander told the author, "but Ruby would never have taken that dog with him and left it in the car if he knew he was going to shoot Oswald and end up in jail. He would have made sure that dog was at home with Senator and was well taken care of."

ing the moneygram totaled $26.87. He handed over $30 and waited for his change while the clerk finished filling out the forms and then time-stamped the documents. Ruby's receipt was stamped 11:17.[192]* When he left Western Union, he was less than two hundred steps from the entrance to police headquarters.

On the third floor of the headquarters, police had informed Oswald shortly after 11:00 A.M. that they would immediately take him downstairs and move him to the sheriff's jail. He asked if he could change his clothes. Captain Fritz sent for some sweaters, and when they were brought to him, he put on a beige one, and then changed his mind and switched to a black sweater. Then he announced he was ready to leave.[193] If Oswald had not decided at the last moment to get a sweater, he would have left the jail almost five minutes earlier, while Ruby was still inside the Western Union office.

Now, Ruby walked the one block along Main Street and stopped near the eight-foot-wide rampway. It was guarded by policeman E. R. Vaughn. At 11:20, about fifty-five seconds before Oswald was shot, Lt. Rio Pierce drove a black car up the Main Street ramp as part of the decoy plan. That ramp was normally a one-way entrance into headquarters, but Pierce had to use it as an exit since the large armored truck that was originally scheduled to move Oswald was blocking the Commerce Street ramp. Officer Roy Vaughn stepped away from the center of the rampway, into the middle of Main Street, to stop the traffic so Pierce could safely exit.[194]

Ruby slipped inside while Vaughn was distracted. He walked down the ramp and arrived at the back of a crowd of police and press only seconds before Oswald was brought past. If the car that was scheduled to move Oswald had been in its correct position at the bottom of the ramp, it would have blocked Ruby from gaining access.[195]†

---

* The time clock at that office was coordinated nationwide with all Western Union offices. It was connected with the U.S. Naval Observatory Clock in Washington D.C., and each day at 11:00 A.M., the time was synchronized (WC Vol. XIII, p. 224).

† Vaughn passed a lie detector test that he did not see Ruby walk past him. Dallas policeman Don Flusche, who was parked across the street from the

Oswald was taken downstairs from the third floor to the basement. Cramped inside the garage confines were almost thirty reporters and seventy police. The glare from the bright television lights made it difficult to see. As Oswald walked into the garage, the large clock on the wall turned to 11:21.[196]

Jimmy Turner, a television director at WBAP, was waiting for Oswald to come out the door when he saw a man walking at the bottom of the Main Street ramp. He noticed Ruby's dark suit and hat, and later said the man on the ramp was the same one who shot Oswald.[197] When Turner first saw Ruby at the ramp, it was only thirty seconds before the shooting. Then Ruby walked closer to where Oswald was to emerge. "There was only a matter of four seconds, or five seconds, when he arrived there," Turner said, "until Oswald reached the point where he was assassinated."[198] Even Ruby told the Warren Commission that he could never have planned to have made it there at the instant Oswald walked past, unless they believed it was "the most per-

ramp, knew Ruby, yet did not see him enter, either. The House Select Committee decided that Ruby had not entered by the Main Street ramp because there were no witnesses to his entrance (although those in the garage admitted they had concentrated on the jail door where Oswald was about to exit and not on the driveway ramps) (HSCA Rpt., pp. 156–57). The committee concluded that the most likely entrance was "an alleyway located next to the Dallas Municipal Building and a stairway leading to the basement garage of police headquarters" (HSCA Rpt., p. 157). The committee finally viewed Ruby's act as premeditated. It could not accept the use of the Main Street ramp entrance because it was only happenstance that Vaughn was momentarily distracted when Pierce's car drove up that ramp a minute before Oswald walked into the garage. Within thirty minutes of the shooting, Ruby told three Dallas policemen that he had walked to the top of the Main Street ramp and that he had entered when Pierce's car distracted Vaughn (WC Vol. XII, pp. 434–38; WC Vol. XV, pp. 188–89; McMillon Exhibit 5018). At that time, there was no way that Ruby could have known about Pierce's car, much less that the Main Street ramp had been changed from an entrance to an exit, unless he saw it. However, in arriving at its conclusion, the committee did not believe the police testimony since the officers had not said it in their initial written reports. It ignored the fact that Secret Service agent Forrest Sorrels also said he heard Ruby tell Captain Fritz, later on the same day of the shooting, that he had come down the ramp (*Dallas Morning News*, March 25, 1979).

Because of his frequent visits to police headquarters, Ruby was intimately familiar with the building and could have known about the alternate route described by the Select Committee. Nevertheless, it appears the committee is mistaken in its conclusion.

fect conspiracy in the history of the world . . . if it had been three seconds later I would have missed this person." Ruby later concluded, "The ironic part of this is had I not made an illegal turn behind the bus to the parking lot, had I gone the way I was supposed to go, straight down Main Street, I would never have met this fate because the difference in meeting this fate was thirty seconds one way or the other."[199]*

"Just as they reached the edge of the ramp," recalled policeman Don Archer, who was stationed directly across from where Ruby broke through, "I caught the movement of a man, and my first thought was, as I started moving, my first thought was that somebody jumped out of the crowd, maybe to take a sock at him. . . . And as I moved forward I saw the man reach Oswald, raise up, and then the shot was fired." As he fired, Ruby yelled, "You killed my President, you rat!"[200]

Oswald was fatally shot through the abdomen. Several policemen immediately tackled Ruby. "The next thing, I was down on the floor," remembered Ruby. "I said, 'I am Jack Ruby. You all know me.' "[201]

An ambulance arrived within three minutes and took Oswald to Parkland Hospital, the same trauma unit that only forty-eight hours earlier had treated President Kennedy and Governor Connally. Homicide detective Chuck Dhority was one of those in the ambulance. "He [Oswald] looked up at me one time," recalled Dhority, "and kind of gurgled, with his eyes open, but that was all that come out of him."[202] The Parkland surgeons could not save him. "It's pretty hard to imagine one bullet doing more

---

* Still, did the police let Ruby know when Oswald would be transferred, as some have contended, and that the rest of the morning's events were only contrived to provide him a defense to show the murder was not premeditated? Such a plot would have centered around Karen Carlin, whose plea for money took him to the Western Union office and near the jail. Some of the others guilty of complicity would include George Senator, for confirming the Carlin story and Ruby's departure time from the apartment; postal inspector Harry Holmes, for delaying the transfer with his questions; police chief Curry and Captain Fritz, for selecting the basement and abandoning the armored cars; Lt. Rio Pierce, for driving his car up the ramp a minute before Oswald was taken from the jail; and Officer Roy Vaughn, for turning his back when Ruby walked down the ramp. And what of Oswald himself, whose last-minute request for a clothing change delayed his transfer by at least five minutes? Was he coordinating a suicide wish with Ruby's arrival?

damage than that," says Dr. John Lattimer. "It perforated the chest cavity, went through the diaphragm, spleen, and stomach. It cut off the main intestinal artery, and the aorta, and the body's main vein, as well as breaking up the right kidney. That wound was definitely fatal."[203]*

Ruby was rushed inside the jail and taken to a third-floor interrogation room. "I hope I killed the son of a bitch," he muttered on the way upstairs. "It will save you guys a lot of trouble."[204] One of the police pushing him along was Detective Barnard Clardy. Ruby looked at him and said, "I'm Jack Ruby. Don't you know me? Don't you know me?" Clardy assured him he did know him.[205] When they got to the third floor, Ruby, who was excited from the shooting, talked to anybody who came by. "If I had planned this I couldn't have had my timing better," he bragged. "It was one chance in a million."[206] He told the police that he had wanted to get off at least three shots, but could only fire one before he was tackled. Within a few minutes, several asked him why he did it. He explained that he did not want Mrs. Kennedy to have to return to Dallas for a trial and "go through this ordeal for this son-of-a-bitch."[207]† Secret Service agent Forrest Sorrels was one of the first to see him. Ruby told Sorrels "he had been to the Western Union office to send a telegram, and that he guessed he had worked himself into a state of insanity, where he had to do it. And to use his words after that, 'I

---

* In 1992, Dr. Charles Crenshaw, who had been a junior resident and part of the team that tried to save Oswald at Parkland, claimed he had answered a telephone call and it was from President Lyndon Johnson, demanding a deathbed confession from Oswald. No other doctors support his story. That was the same day that President Kennedy's memorial service was held in Washington, with an enormous contingent of foreign heads of state. A review of the telephone logs from the White House do not show that the President called Parkland Hospital at any time that day (LBJ Library, Austin, Texas; interview with David Perry, May 24, 1993).

† After his trial, Ruby was furious with his defense staff for their handling of his case and actually thought they were part of a conspiracy to frame him. In apparent retaliation against one of his original attorneys, Tom Howard, he claimed that Howard was responsible for concocting the story that he had shot Oswald because of concern over Mrs. Kennedy. "That's crap," assistant district attorney Bill Alexander told the author. "I saw Ruby at the jail before Tom Howard ever arrived, and he was telling people then that he had shot Oswald because he was so upset about Mrs. Kennedy. No one told Jack to say that."

guess I just had to show the world that a Jew has guts.' . . . He wanted [us] not to hate him for what he had done."[208]

Assistant district attorney Bill Alexander arrived when Ruby was changing from his clothes into the jail's white coveralls. "I said, 'Goddamn it, Jack, what did you do this for?' " recalls Alexander. "And he said, 'Well, you guys couldn't do it. Someone had to do it. That son of a bitch killed my President.' The excitement of the shooting had really buoyed him up. He thought he was going to go through the booking, and then he would be released. He just thought, How mad can you get with the guy who just killed the President's assassin? Jack actually thought he might come out of this as a hero of sorts, getting the acknowledgment he always wanted in Dallas. He thought he had erased any stigma the city had by knocking off Oswald."[209] Jim Martin, an attorney who spoke to Ruby during his first hours in jail, said, "He never expected to spend a night in jail."[210]*

"Jack was one of the most talkative guys you would ever meet," says Tony Zoppi. "He'd be the worst fellow in the world to be part of a conspiracy, because he just plain talked too much."[211] "Jack Ruby would be the last one that I could ever trust to do anything," said Rabbi Silverman.[212] While in jail, Ruby often granted press interviews, and talked to police and investigators and with others.† He wrote frequent letters. Rabbi Silverman met with him at least once a week for nearly a year.[213] The first visit was the morning after Oswald was killed. "I entered his cell," recalls the rabbi. "I knew him very well. . . . He was a very volatile, a very emotional, unbalanced per-

---

* The initial reaction of the several hundred people gathered across the street from the jail indicated Ruby might be treated as a hero. When the word spread that Oswald had been shot inside police headquarters, the crowd spontaneously broke into cheers and applause. Ruby later received thousands of letters while in jail, most praising his murder of Oswald.

† One of the best indicators that Ruby had not killed Oswald at the behest of organized crime was that one of Ruby's earliest visitors while he was in jail was Joe Campisi, reputedly Dallas's number-two mafia figure. Campisi, owner of the Egyptian Lounge restaurant, knew Ruby well and visited the jail together with his wife. The author spoke to a number of experts on organized crime; none of them recalled an instance in which a mob boss issued a murder contract and then visited the arrested hit man in jail. "If the mob had hired Ruby for a hit," a retired FBI agent told the author, "they would have run twenty miles away from him. Campisi would never have gone near that jail."

son. He thought he was doing the right thing. He loved Kennedy. This man killed Kennedy. He happened to be there. . . . He was impetuous. He pulled the trigger."[214] Ruby told his friend Breck Wall that "I was right to kill Oswald."[215] When he saw his brother Earl, he told him that when he arrived in the basement and saw Oswald, he noticed "there was a smirk on his face, and he thought, Why you little s.o.b.," and pulled out his gun and shot him.[216] Jack's sister Eva may have had the best insight into his motivation: "The truth is this . . . he said he did it for Jackie and the kids, but I think he's just looking for a reason." Eva realized that shooting Oswald was a momentary explosion caused by his violent temper. There was perhaps no single motivation.*

Earl Ruby hired flamboyant San Francisco attorney Melvin Belli, the "King of Torts," to defend Jack. Belli agreed to do it for nothing: The publicity and the book that would result would be enough.[217] In Texas, there was a crime called murder without malice, equivalent to manslaughter in most states. The maximum penalty for such a conviction was five years. However, Belli gambled that he could acquit him completely and argued that Ruby's family had a history of mental illness and that he was insane when he shot Oswald.

"Belli took a good five-year murder-without-malice case," says Bill Alexander, "and made it into a death penalty for his client. He came down here thinking he was going to teach us 'hicks' in Texas a lesson. He probably thought we had never heard the word *psychiatrist* before. Well, he put on this god-awful defense, and day by day Jack melted—he just looked worse and worse. He was a pitiful object by the time the trial was over. Instead of [Jack's] being a hero, Belli was bringing out all this stuff about Jack's mother in an insane asylum and how Jack

---

* Ruby's friends were all surprised when they learned that he had killed Oswald, but some did not think it was out of character. "At the club, after the first shock," said Carousel drummer Bill Willis, "we all said, 'Well, it figures. Jack thought while he was downtown he might as well kill Oswald, too.'" Max Rudberg, a Ruby friend, said, "Well, everyone was saying the son-of-a-bitch needs killing, and Jack was anxious to please. . . . He couldn't possibly pass it by." Milton Joseph, a local jeweler, had no doubt that Ruby killed Oswald to be in the limelight (Wills and Demaris, "The Avenger," pp. 85, 158; see also CE 1460, 1480).

himself was sick. He just wanted to get on the stand and say, 'I shot the guy because he killed my President,' but Belli hacked away at his family in public. It was humiliating for Ruby. I actually felt sorry for him. It took away whatever dignity he had left."[218]

On March 14, 1964, after deliberating less than an hour, the jury returned a guilty verdict of premeditated murder, later sentencing Ruby to be executed for the crime. After his arrest, there had been a steady mental deterioration and the conviction hastened his decline. The very item that kicked off his original interest on the weekend of the assassination, the Weissman advertisement, and his belief that it could have been published to embarrass Jews, grew into an obsession. His sister Eva was distraught over his disintegration. He often told her to kill herself because "he thinks they are going to kill out all the Jews and he has made remarks that 25 million Jews have been slaughtered, on the floor below, in the jail. Sometimes it's planes going over and they are dropping bombs on the Jews."[219] He told Eva that he could hear and see Jews boiled in oil and that he had recurrent visions of his brother Earl and his children being dismembered.[220] The police guards used to watch him put his ear to the jail wall and say, "Shhh! Do you hear the screams? They are torturing the Jews again down in the basement."[221]

He thought he had been blamed for killing President Kennedy, that Lyndon Johnson was a Nazi, and there was a conspiracy to eliminate all Jews, to which he had fallen a victim by killing Oswald. Jack tried to kill himself on several occasions. Once, he tried to split his skull by pounding his head against the wall.[222] Once he tried hanging, and once he tried to electrocute himself with a light fixture. He kept a picture of President Kennedy in his cell and kissed it during the day.[223] "He is mentally deranged," Eva told the Warren Commission.[224]

Ruby was in this state of mind when the Warren Commission interviewed him on June 7, 1964. During the course of the questioning he pleaded to take a polygraph to prove "I am as innocent regarding any conspiracy as any of you gentlemen in this room. . . . All I want to take is a polygraph test and tell the truth about things and combat the lies that have been told about me. . . . There was no conspiracy."[225] He told the Commission that he was "a scapegoat [used] . . . to create a falsehood about some of the Jewish faith, especially at the terrible heinous crime such as the killing of President Kennedy."[226] He warned Chief Justice Warren that "the Jewish people are being exterminated at this moment," that "my people are going to suffer about things that will be said about me," and "I don't want my people to be blamed for something that is untrue . . ."[227]

Ruby also repeatedly asked the Commission, "Do I sound screwy?" and sometimes lost control and cried.[228] Conspiracy theorists have focused on the fact that Ruby asked nine times to be taken to Washington. They assert that he could not tell the truth about some secret conspiracy to kill JFK while he was in Texas.[229] When Ruby's entire testimony is read, however, it is evident his pleas were exactly the opposite, a desire to be taken to Washington to vindicate himself of the rumors that he was part of a conspiracy. "If you don't take me back to Washington tonight to give me a chance to prove to the President that I am not guilty, then you will see the most tragic thing that will ever happen," he told Earl Warren. Ruby thought his life was in danger, as part of an extermination program against Jews, primarily undertaken by the John Birch Society.[230] The "great conspiracy" he spoke about was his belief that his lawyers and the district attorney had plotted to portray him as insane and to prevent him from getting another trial.[231]*

"In his demented frame of mind," said Rabbi Silverman, "he thought Washington was the only place where he could tell the world that he had nothing to do with Oswald and nothing to do with the conspiracy, not that there was any other story. . . . The man was schizophrenic. He was psychotic."[232] Ruby was convinced he could get a fair polygraph only in Washington, and he was ready to leave for the nation's capital immediately. The Warren Commission decided not to take him.

The Commission did have a polygraph exam administered on July 18, 1964. According to the Commission's experts, Ruby told the truth when he said he never knew Oswald, that he took the

---

* In one of the last notes he smuggled out of prison, Ruby wrote that he was worried "that I am being framed for the assassination that my motive was to silence Oswald." It is proof that, even in his final days, he was still protesting the implication that he had killed Oswald "to silence" him.

Main Street ramp to enter the jail's basement, that he shot Oswald on his own, and had not decided to do it until the last moment on Sunday.[233]*

On October 5, 1966, the Texas Court of Criminal Appeals granted him a new trial on the grounds that his statements to Dallas policemen immediately after the shooting should not have been allowed, and that the original court should have granted a change of venue to another jurisdiction since a fair trial was all but impossible in Dallas. By December 5, Wichita Falls, Texas, was selected as the site for the retrial.

When the sheriff from Wichita Falls arrived in December 1966 to move Ruby for his new trial, he refused to take him because he seemed too sick. The Dallas jail had been treating him with Pepto-Bismol for a stomach problem.[234] At Parkland Hospital, he was first diagnosed with pneumonia, but a day later the doctors realized he had cancer in his liver, brain, and lungs. Although he had probably had it for fifteen months, none of the jail physicians had seen his condition as a serious one.[235] Ruby died, officially of a blood clot, on January 3, 1967, more than three years after he shot Oswald.

---

* The House Select Committee had its own panel of experts review the polygraph. They reported they were "unable to interpret the examination" due to "numerous procedural errors" (HSCA Rpt., p. 159).

17

"A Religious Event"

Although a suspect in the presidential assassination was arrested within ninety minutes of the shooting and the physical evidence seemed overwhelming, Ruby's Sunday murder of Oswald stimulated many suspicions and rumors. In the days following Oswald's death, unfounded but spectacular stories of left-wing and right-wing plots, the complicity of Cuban and Soviet leaders, even speculation about Lyndon Johnson hatching a plan to seize the presidency, swept the country. A Gallup poll taken a week after the assassination showed that only 29 percent of Americans believed that Oswald alone killed JFK.[1]

To quell the unchecked speculation, government officials announced public investigations into the assassination. On the first business day after the murder, Monday, November 25, Texas attorney general Waggoner Carr declared that Texas would hold a public court of inquiry. With the help of the FBI, Carr planned to question primarily local witnesses and file his findings with a federal commission.[2]

Lyndon Johnson tentatively approved the Texas commission in conversations with Carr. Since the crime had happened in Dallas, the Carr panel was to include only Texans and no federal officials. Johnson had also decided to release the FBI's initial report on the assassination the day it was finished, though it would contain raw and largely unsubstantiated data. Nicholas Katzenbach, acting attorney general while Robert Kennedy mourned with his family, worked feverishly behind the scenes to change LBJ's mind and return control of the investigation to Washington.

The next day, Tuesday, Congress jumped in. Senator Everett Dirksen of Illinois, to widespread bipartisan support, suggested the Senate Judiciary Committee examine the case. By Wednesday, the House vied for the limelight when Congressman Charles Goodell of New York proposed that a joint committee of senators and congressmen investigate the assassination.

Lyndon Johnson silently abandoned his support for the Texas commission and intervened on Friday, November 29, with Executive Order No. 11130, which created a fact-finding panel he hoped would have a "national mandate."[3] The implications of the investigation were far-reaching. There was even a possibility of war if either Cuba or the Soviet Union was found to have sponsored JFK's death, and Johnson appointed a seven-man panel of distinguished public servants he thought had unimpeachable credentials. Seventy-two-year-old Earl Warren, chief justice of the U.S. Supreme Court, was chosen as chairman.*

When Katzenbach and solicitor general Archibald Cox first approached Warren to head the federal panel, he refused. Johnson summoned Warren for a private meeting. "He said there had been wild rumors," recalled Warren, "and that there was the international situation to think of. He said he had just talked to Dean Rusk, who was concerned, and he also mentioned the head of the Atomic Energy Commission, who had told him how many millions of people would be killed in an atomic war. The only way to dispel these rumors, he said, was to have an independent and responsible commission, and that there was no one to head it except the highest judicial officer in the country. I told him how I felt. He said that if the public became aroused against Castro and Khrushchev there might be war.

" 'You've been in uniform before,' he said, 'and if I asked you, you would put on the uniform again for your country.'

" 'I said, 'Of, course.'

---

* The panel's official name was The President's Commission on the Assassination of President John F. Kennedy. However, almost immediately it was referred to as the Warren Commission.

" 'This is more important than that,' he said.

" 'If you're putting it like that,' I said, 'I can't say no.' "[4]

Of the six other panelists, two were ranking senators, John Sherman Cooper, a Kentucky Republican, and Richard Russell, a Georgia Democrat. Two were senior House representatives: Congressman Hale Boggs, a Louisiana Democrat and the majority whip, and Gerald Ford, a Michigan Republican. The final members were prominent attorneys—John J. McCloy, former president of the World Bank and high commissioner of Germany after World War II, and Allen Dulles, the CIA's former spymaster. The members and their mandate were so prestigious that other proposed state and federal investigations promptly gave way to the presidential panel.

The Commission's powers were broad and virtually unprecedented. It had subpoena power, as well as the right to grant immunity to compel testimony otherwise protected under the Fifth Amendment's self-incrimination article. All federal and state agencies were ordered to comply fully with its requests. The Commission's general counsel was former U.S. solicitor general J. Lee Rankin, and fourteen lawyers comprised a legal staff; under his supervision. There were also twelve investigators. The legal staff divided the case into five general subjects: the assassination's basic facts; the identity of the assassin; his background and motives; possible conspiracy; and Oswald's death. The staff attorneys determined the facts and were responsible for draft findings. Major disputes were brought to the attention of the seven commissioners.

The Warren Commission had its first meeting on December 5, 1963, only two weeks after the assassination, and four days later the FBI presented its five-volume report that summarized the Bureau's preliminary findings.[5] Marina Oswald, the first witness, appeared on February 3, 1964. The Commission and its staff took testimony from 552 witnesses during the next six months.* Warren was so sensitive to possible government abuse that he established strict rules for the questioning of witnesses, includ-

---

* Only 94 personally appeared before any commissioners. The largest number, 395, were questioned by the legal staff; 61 supplied affidavits; and 2 gave statements (WR, p. xiii).

ing no private interrogations without a stenographer present and no polygraphs. He later regretted that he agreed to Ruby's insistent pleas for the test, which he referred to as "Big Brother paraphernalia."

The FBI's field investigation was, by itself, enormous. It conducted some 25,000 interviews and submitted over 2,300 investigative reports, totaling more than 25,000 pages.[6] At the same time, the Secret Service conducted another 1,500 interviews and submitted 800 reports. Though many critics of the Warren Commission acknowledge that a mammoth examination was accomplished in a relatively brief period, they charge the Commission favored witnesses and documents that supported its early conclusion that Oswald alone killed the President. Yet this view underestimates the independence the legal staff had within the Commission's hierarchy. The staff could call any witness it wanted, and none of its more than 400 requests were ever denied by the commissioners.[7]

The original deadline of June 30, 1964, turned out to be impractical. LBJ, fearful that rumors might start that he had political reasons for delaying the report, wanted the work finished before the presidential nominating conventions. Warren told the other members, in a January 21 executive session, that it "would be very bad for the country to have this thing discussed" during the coming campaign.[8] Tempers often flared during the final months as Warren pushed the probe at a pace that meant fourteen-hour days, seven days a week, for the legal staff. The 888-page final report was released three months late, on September 24, 1964.

Although the Commission had done an extraordinary job of marshaling information and presenting it in a cohesive and organized manner, in only ten months it was not possible to delve into many issues that would later come to the forefront as nagging and persistent problems. Since it was so limited in manpower, the Commission was almost entirely dependent on agencies such as the FBI to conduct the actual investigation. Rankin had referred to "tender spots," potential embarrassments to the FBI or CIA that might hinder the sharing of information. J. Edgar Hoover was convinced within days of the assassination that Oswald alone had killed Kennedy. He knew, of course, that if

Oswald was part of a conspiracy, the Bureau's reputation would suffer for not having uncovered the plot prior to JFK's trip to Dallas. Because of his iron-clad control over the Bureau, his feelings on the case colored the work the field agents did. Since Hoover thought the answer to the assassination was straightforward, he believed the Warren Commission could only cause problems by delving into many other areas. The FBI did not treat the Commission as its partner in search of the truth.

"I don't have any doubt that the FBI viewed the Commission the same way they later viewed civilians requesting documents," says James Lesar, the nation's leading attorney in pursuing assassination-related documents under the Freedom of Information Act (FOIA). The FBI even created files on the Commission's staff members.* Richard Helms [former CIA director] later admitted that he only told the Warren Commission something if they asked for it. "I am sure the Bureau had the same attitude," says Lesar. "Basically, any request that comes in from a government commission or a citizen, the Bureau looks at very carefully to see if they can avoid responding. The relationship between the Commission and the Bureau was partly adversarial, because no one wanted to bring that tension out into the open. The Commission gave in to the FBI. In the executive sessions, they said they were going to investigate Hoover, but they knew they wouldn't."[9]

The FBI's early insistence that Oswald was the lone assassin was actually a sore point with the Commission's staff. On January 22, 1964, Lee Rankin complained to the commissioners, "They [the FBI] would have us fold up and quit. . . . They found the man [Oswald]. There is nothing more to do. The Com-

---

*The extent to which the FBI was ready to investigate staff members is apparent in the case of Norman Redlich, a New York University law professor who, after Rankin, was the senior attorney on the legal staff. In February 1964, Redlich was publicly assailed for his membership on a civil-liberties panel and for having co-authored an article with a Communist sympathizer. Actually, Redlich had never worked with the other author, but a magazine had merged their two separate articles together and given them joint credit. Yet the FBI still conducted a full field investigation of Redlich, including interviews with his vacation neighbors in Vermont, the elevator operators in his New York apartment building, and even the obstetrician who had delivered him.

mission supports their conclusions, and we can go home and that is the end of it."[10]

The FBI, anxious to downplay its contacts with Oswald, withheld information from the Commission, including Agent James Hosty's receipt of a note from Oswald. It also deleted Hosty's name, address, and telephone number, which were in Oswald's address book, when the information was sent to the Commission staff. The CIA withheld information as well, most critically that the Agency and the mafia had embarked on a joint effort to kill Fidel Castro.

"It's a serious point," says former staff lawyer Burt Griffin, now a judge. "I don't know if anyone will ever get the answer. I am not convinced, as I look back on it now, that Lee Rankin did not know about the CIA conspiracies to kill Castro. I don't have any evidence, but as I look back on the failure to bring us together to speculate, he never encouraged us to think speculatively, and the way Rankin operated with his door always closed, maybe he knew something and it was this secret. Only Johnson, obviously, the Chief Justice, Allen Dulles, and Bobby Kennedy knew about the CIA plots against Castro. Its disclosure would have had very important implications. It might have allowed us to say something reasonably definitive about Oswald's motive. It would have put a new dimension on his Cuban activities and opened new areas of exploration. The fact that we could not come up with a motive for Oswald was a great weakness in the report."[11]

CBS news anchor Walter Cronkite summarized the concern of many when he noted that the FBI and CIA, by withholding information that later became public, "weakened the credibility of the Warren Report."[12] But beyond the problems caused by its tug-of-war with the investigative branches, the Commission created many of its own difficulties. At the time, the Commission wanted to use the autopsy photos and X rays as the best evidence of how the President was shot, but the Kennedy family refused to release them. Warren feared that if the Commission had the photos, they might be leaked to the press, and as a result he was hesitant to pressure Robert Kennedy on the matter. But Howard Willens, a staff attorney, had worked for Robert Kennedy and persisted to obtain them. In June 1964, RFK allowed only Warren and Rankin to review them. In his memoirs, Warren wrote, "[T]hey were so horrible that I could not sleep well for nights." None of the other commissioners or staff ever saw the autopsy photographs or X rays, nor did the panel utilize independent forensics experts.* Reproduced in the final report are schematic drawings of the President's neck and head wounds, but both were made by an artist who was unfamiliar with the autopsy and never saw the photographs. The artist's sketches were based upon Drs. Humes and Boswell's original measurements of the wounds.[13] Those drawings were mistaken in the placement of both entry wounds, and that later developed into a significant issue for the conspiracy press.[14]†

In other areas, the Commission's work seemed to stop just short of thoroughness. In replicating the firing of the Carcano, and figuring trajectory angles, the Commission used FBI tests that had a platform at the incorrect height when compared to the sixth floor of the Book Depository. The tests also calculated the minimum firing time and accuracy by shooting at stationary targets as opposed to a moving one such as Oswald had faced.

The Commission did not have the technology in 1964 to positively establish the single-bullet theory. But unless one bullet caused the wounds to both Governor Connally and President Kennedy, the Commission could not figure out how Oswald could have fired the three shots within the approximately five seconds they mistakenly allotted to him. Though advances in neutron activation and photographic and computer techniques now confirm that the theory is correct, the Commission had no way of being certain the single bullet was viable. The members were almost evenly split in their feelings about the theory, and Senator Russell threatened not to sign a final report that abso-

---

* The Commission did call in outside experts for both ballistics and finger-prints.

† In 1967, former commissioner John McCloy told CBS News, "I think that if there's one thing that I would do over again, I would insist on those photographs and the X rays having been produced before us. In the one respect, and only one respect there, I think we were perhaps a little oversensitive to what we understood as the sensitivities of the Kennedy family against the production of colored photographs of the body" ("The Warren Report," CBS News, Part IV, June 28, 1967).

lutely concluded the single bullet was correct.[15]* They fought over the right adjective to use to describe the probability that the single bullet was right. McCloy suggested "persuasive" evidence, while Russell wanted "credible" evidence, and Ford pushed for "compelling."[16] The Warren Commission Report settled on "There is very persuasive evidence." This type of compromise opened more doors to critics.

Few of the witnesses who contradicted the official version of events testified before the Commission. If they had been examined, their testimony would have been explainable, but because the Commission ignored them, critics had ammunition for future claims of deliberate omission. Also, the Commission underplayed Jack Ruby's underworld associations and did not effectively portray him as the unbalanced and volatile person he was, leaving itself open to criticism that it had failed to pursue the Ruby clues because it feared where those might lead.

Since all the commissioners had full-time careers that entailed substantial responsibilities, they could only spend part of their time at the hearings. Senator Russell had the poorest attendance record, hearing only 6 percent of the testimony. Only three of the seven commissioners heard more than half the testimony.[17]

But the most controversial aspect of the Commission's work may be its conclusion about the possibility of any conspiracy. The final report stated, "The Commission has found no evidence that either Lee Harvey Oswald or Jack Ruby was part of any conspiracy, domestic or foreign, to assassinate President Kennedy."[18]

"There is no question Oswald was the shooter, and Oswald was the lone shooter," says former staff lawyer Burt Griffin. "We were wrong, in my opinion, in issuing the statement that there was no evidence of a conspiracy. That was the wrong statement. I frankly was very critical of using that language. There is plenty of evidence in the testimony and the documents that could lead

---

* The three commissioners who had the most difficulty with the single-bullet theory, Russell, Cooper, and Boggs, were also the three who had the least contact with the probe, attending on average only 25 percent of the hearings among them.

a reasonable person to pursue a conspiracy theory. There is nothing that then establishes a conspiracy theory, but there is plenty there that would allow a reasonable person to speculate about a conspiracy theory. Statements like that sweeping 'no conspiracy' one does a disservice to our overall work. I think I was in a minority of one on that statement."[19]

Despite its shortcomings, early reviews in the United States generally lavished praise on the Warren Report. In Europe, however, where political conspiracies and government changeovers by violence are an integral part of much longer histories, the Commission's work was viewed as the official, sanitized version. Many leading European commentators questioned its conclusions without ever reading the report.

In the U.S., the honeymoon for critical acceptance was short-lived. By the time the Warren Commission published its report in September 1964, a network of amateur sleuths was prepared to check its accuracy against the research they had compiled since the day of the murder. An eclectic mixture of people across the country, many of whom were admitted leftists and were suspicious that a Communist was blamed for the murder in a right-wing city, had independently begun collecting everything printed on the subject. They also interviewed eyewitnesses and others connected to the case. Each soon carved out a specialty. As they heard about one another, some began sharing information and ideas. Mary Ferrell, a Dallas legal secretary, started a card file on Oswald's background. Raymond Marcus, who ran a small retail sign business, began a newspaper file about the direction of the bullets. Vincent Salandria, a Philadelphia lawyer, collected newspaper articles that discussed police agencies that might have been involved in the assassination. Marjorie Field, the wife of a Beverly Hills stockbroker, saved everything that appeared in *The New York Times*. Josiah Thompson, an assistant philosophy professor specializing in the Danish philosopher Kierkegaard, began studying ballistics and firearms to better understand what had happened in Dealey Plaza. Shirley Martin, an Oklahoma housewife, drove to Dallas, with her four children, to interview witnesses. Sylvia Meagher, an administrator at the World Health Organization, started a clipping file on anything that contradicted the Dallas police's version. Lillian

Castellano, a Los Angeles bookkeeper, pursued the government and media with her belief that the President was shot from the front by an assassin hidden in a storm drain near the car. David Lifton, a Los Angeles student, focused on the foliage at Dealey Plaza, who hid in it, and whether it was all real or moved in as part of the plot.

Professor Josiah Thompson said their work was an "obsession" and that "there's a fantastic way in which the assassination becomes a religious event. There are relics, and scriptures, and even a holy scene—the killing ground. People make pilgrimages to it."[20] This burgeoning amateur network supplied the original basis for challenging the Warren Report. These researchers not only shared their work with each other but, anxious to gain a public hearing for their findings, provided it freely to journalists and other professionals.

The earliest books focused on apparent contradictions and unanswered questions in the report, such as the misidentification of the rifle found at the Depository as a Mauser instead of a Mannlicher-Carcano, or whether the man photographed standing in the doorway of the Depository during the assassination was Lee Oswald or his co-worker Billy Lovelady. Although the issues raised now seem rudimentary, they were the first to undermine the authority the press had bestowed on the Warren Commission.

None of the early critics created a cogent alternate account to compare to the one set forth of Oswald acting alone. The books accomplished their goals if they merely raised doubts about the official version. Their view was that a cover-up of key information had taken place, by the FBI, the CIA, or others in the federal government, and the general tenor was that the extreme right had probably hatched the plot. The rumors of Soviet or Cuban complicity were never popular with the critics, since they figured it made no sense for the U.S. government to cover up evidence if it pointed to the guilt of Communist regimes. Many of the books acknowledged they did not have the answers, and called for a new investigation.

In its own reexamination of the case in the late 1970s, the House Select Committee investigated the first generation of critics and found their work wanting in terms of fairness and accuracy. Robert Blakey, the Select Committee's chief counsel, said that many early critics "had special axes to grind. As a result of our investigation, the Committee found that 'criticism leveled at the Commission . . . [was] often biased, unfair and inaccurate . . . [and] . . . the prevailing opinion of the Commission's performance was undeserved.' "[21]

Thomas Buchanan, an American Communist living in Europe, wrote *Who Killed Kennedy?* based on press accounts, and published it before the Warren Report was even in print.[22] The FBI, which studied Buchanan's work, concluded he was responsible for "false statements, innuendoes, incorrect journalism, misinformation, and . . . false journalism," and that his book stated as facts items "which the Commission's investigation has disproved completely."[23] A German leftist, Joachim Joesten, published a vitriolic book also based on newspaper accounts, *Oswald: Assassin or Fall-guy?*, but its questions were answered when the Commission's report was released.[24]

In 1966, Harold Weisberg published *Whitewash*, the first in-depth attack on the Warren Report.[25] Weisberg, who later published another five books on the case, was a former Senate investigator who had been dismissed for possibly leaking information to the press. Robert Blakey said his "rhetoric was so obscure, his arguments so dependent on accusation rather than logic, the effect of [his] work was to make complex issues confusing."[26]

That same year, the first major commercial success for a Commission critic was *Rush to Judgment*, by New York attorney Mark Lane.[27] Dan Rather, of CBS, dubbed Lane "the gadfly of the Warren Commission," but Governor John Connally called him a "journalistic scavenger."[28] Lane, a former New York State legislator associated with some prominent left-wing causes, had represented Marguerite Oswald. He unsuccessfully argued with the Commission to be allowed to represent the deceased Oswald at the hearings and to be permitted to cross-examine the witnesses who appeared. Reportedly, *Rush to Judgment* has sold more than a million copies in various editions.

Lane's attack on the Commission was an admitted brief for the defense by a skilled advocate. Using only the evidence that buttressed his arguments, he persuasively argued that the Commission's work was seriously flawed. And while he was careful in his book about whom he accused and about the scope of the conspiracy he said he had discovered, in his dozens of college lectures and radio and television appearances he went much further, charging complicity at the highest levels of government. The Select Committee concluded: "Lane was willing to advocate conspiracy theories . . . [without checking] them, [and his] . . . conduct resulted in public [misperception . . .]." Blakey said he was "the best example of a critic who fit the Committee's 'unfair and inaccurate' description . . ."[29] Walter Cronkite, in a four-part 1967 CBS documentary, concluded there were a number of examples in Lane's work of "lifting remarks out of context to support his theories. Perhaps the most charitable explanation is that Mark Lane still considers himself a defense attorney . . . [whose] duty is not to abstract truth but to his client [Oswald]."[30]*

A rash of books appeared on the heels of Lane's success. Philosophy professor Richard Popkin, in *The Second Oswald*, was the first to use mistaken sightings of Oswald to develop the theory of an imposter.[31] Raymond Marcus, the owner of the retail sign business, published *The Bastard Bullet*, an attack on the single-bullet theory.[32] Leo Sauvage, a professional journalist, wrote *The Oswald Affair*, which raised more questions about the Commission's evidence-gathering.[33] In his self-published *Forgive My Grief*, Penn Jones, Jr., the editor of a small Texas

---

* Harold Weisberg believes Lane is interested only in self-promotion and money, and says that Lane largely "cribbed" from his book *Whitewash*. Assassination researcher David Wrone told the author, "I took every footnote in his *Rush to Judgment*. There's 4,500 of them. I checked them against the text and so forth, for accuracy, fidelity, and all of that. . . . His chapter on Perrin, [Nancy] Perrin Rich, who was Jack Ruby's nightclub lady—I mean, that's a terrible one. . . . She gave three separate and distinct accounts of the assassination that are mutually exclusive. And he selected the one that fit his scenario. The woman is disturbed. This is an outrage. One time I was going to do a smallish book on Lane, but I thought, you don't honor slime."

Lane has said that if only 10 percent of his footnotes were accurate, that would still mean the Warren Commission had serious problems (January 25, 1967, UCLA Student Union address). Warren Commission staff attorney Wesley Liebeler said, "It's just incredible to listen to him. He talks for five minutes, and it takes an hour to straighten out the record."

newspaper, introduced the issue of "critical" witnesses who were supposedly dying mysteriously.[34]*

Despite their differences, those books were uniformly virulent attacks on the Warren Commission, and their advocacy often diminished their effectiveness. At their best, the critics had only exposed the Commission as incompetent, but they had not established it was wrong in its conclusions.

1966 also saw the publication of Edward Jay Epstein's *Inquest*, which was originally his master's thesis at Cornell.[35] Temperate in tone, it was a careful study of the inner workings of the Commission. Relying on fresh documents, as well as interviews with five of the commissioners and twelve members of the legal staff, Epstein charged the Commission had sought the "political truth" rather than the factual truth about the case. A "central question" that bothered Epstein was that the FBI's report to the commissioners indicated the bullet that struck the President in the neck/shoulder only penetrated a short distance and did not exit, whereas the autopsy and the Commission concluded that it was the single bullet that went on to wound Connally. When Epstein raised the problem, it appeared valid since the autopsy photos and X rays were still locked away. It was an issue that festered until the House Select Committee's forensics panel reviewed all the autopsy X rays and photographs and confirmed that the FBI report was simply mistaken.

Since Epstein had academic credentials, appeared to make an objective examination, and drew moderate conclusions, his book was critically accepted as an important one.† *Inquest*

---

    * Popkin later claimed to have "cracked the case" by uncovering "zombie assassins" programmed by the CIA. Marcus became convinced he could see four to five assassins in the photos of foliage at Dealey Plaza. Jones later self-published another three books on the assassination, as well as a conspiracy newsletter. He developed a theory that on November 21 in Dallas, Richard Nixon met with J. Edgar Hoover and oil tycoons as part of an "assassination staff" (*Truth Letter*, Vol. II, No. 11, February 15, 1970). Eventually, Jones argued that John Connally, President Johnson, the FBI, the CIA, the Dallas police, and the news media were all part of the conspiracy.

    As for the supposed mystery deaths of key witnesses, it has become one of the entrenched myths in the Kennedy assassination. See Appendix B, "The Non-Mysterious 'Mystery Deaths,'" for a detailed discussion.

    † However, Epstein did have his critics. Six months after Epstein published *Inquest*, Professor A. L. Goodhart wrote an article in *The Law Quarterly Re-*

prompted the mainstream press to reexamine its favorable conclusions about the Warren Report. As a result, a series of critical articles through 1966 and 1967 cast further doubt on the Commission's credibility.[36]

Authors like Lane and Epstein were assisted by an informal alliance of self-appointed researchers, whom writer Calvin Trillin dubbed "the buffs" in a 1967 *New Yorker* article.[37] "You can compare this to a company that has a public relations program," said David Lifton in 1967, "and a research and development program. The two puncture points at the top—what gets public notice—are Lane's book and Epstein's book. The 'R&D' program is being done by a bunch of amateurs."[38] David Lifton and Marjorie Field had provided Buchanan material for his book. Shirley Martin had sent copies of her taped interviews to Lane. Sylvia Meagher did the index for *Inquest*, and reviewed Sauvage's book.

There was no equivalent of the conspiracy network to support the Warren Report. When the Commission disbanded, the members failed to arrange to defend their work or answer questions. Although a few books were published in support of the report, they had little impact in slowing the critical onslaught. Gerald Ford's *Portrait of the Assassin* was the first pro-Commission book, published in 1965.[39] However, it consisted largely of reprints of testimony from the Commission's volumes and did not answer any of the early critiques. By 1967, Charles Roberts, in *The Truth About the Assassination;* Richard Lewis, in *The Scavengers;* and John Sparrow, in *After the Assassination,* wrote slim volumes that contributed little new information about the case; Lewis's book was largely a hard personal attack on the critics themselves and their motivation.*

---

view that cast doubts on the quality of his work. Wesley Liebeler, a staff attorney on the Commission, was infuriated that one of his internal memos that criticized "the writing of the report" was misused by Epstein to challenge the conclusions of the investigation. Joseph Ball, another staff attorney, said Epstein spoke to him only once, for ten minutes in a hotel lobby, and that the quotations attributed to him were "wrong or false." The Goodhart article was also critical of Epstein for having taken remarks of general counsel J. Lee Rankin out of context to imply the Commission was ready to squash any evidence that Oswald had been an FBI informant.

* In later years, the most energetic defender of the Warren Commission was former staff counsel David Belin. Belin wrote two books defending the Com-

Those pro–Warren Commission writers felt compelled to defend almost everything the Commission had done, and therefore weakened their own effectiveness. But they were overshadowed in 1967 by the publication of two significant books, both written by graduates of the buff network, that added to the growing mistrust of the Commission. In *Six Seconds in Dallas*, Josiah Thompson tried to determine what happened at Dealey Plaza by focusing on ballistics, trajectory angles, medical evidence, and eyewitness testimony. Thompson had an advantage since he was the first conspiracy writer who had studied the original Zapruder film, and his book was the first to include drawings of critical frames.* His book focused exclusively on how the assassination of the President physically happened, and he did not bother with other issues. Ruby was mentioned only once and Tippit not at all. Thompson concluded there was a cross-fire in Dealey Plaza from shooters perched in the Book Depository, on the grassy knoll, and in the Records Building on Houston Street.

The second book that further damaged the Commission was Sylvia Meagher's *Accessories After the Fact*.[40] Meagher probably knew the twenty-six volumes of the Warren Commission hearings and exhibits better than any other critic. A year earlier, she had published an index to all twenty-six volumes. It was re-

---

mission's work and its conclusion that Oswald acted alone. He also served on the Rockefeller Commission's re-examination of the case in the 1970s. Belin, through many articles, lectures, and debates with critics, was virtually the lone public voice for the Commission by the 1980s.

* Critics other than Thompson had to rely on the poor reproductions of still frames of the Zapruder film in Volume XVIII of the hearings of the Warren Commission. *Life* magazine had purchased the exclusive rights to the film for a reported $150,000, and Thompson had worked as a consultant to *Life* on the film. He later tried to purchase the right to use reproductions of several frames in his book, but *Life* refused to sell him the rights, so he had drawings recreated from memory. *Life* sued for copyright infringement. In a landmark case, a New York court held that Thompson's drawings were "fair use" of the film, and that he was even entitled to reproduce actual frames from the film in his paperback edition (*Time Inc.* v. *Bernard Geis Associates*, U.S. District Court for the Southern District of N.Y. No. 67 4736, appellate decision, 293 Federal Supplement 130). In 1975, *Life* gave the film back to the Zapruder family instead of donating it to the National Archives. As a result, the Zapruder family, in recent years represented by Henry Zapruder, Abraham's son, has sold use rights for books, documentaries, and films at significant fees, sometimes for tens of thousands of dollars.

ceived as an important contribution for research since the volumes originally had only a name index, making it almost impossible to work effectively with the more than 1 million–plus words.* Her book concentrated on any testimony or exhibits that raised doubts about the final report. Meagher was a committed leftist, and her politics are clear throughout the book. She admitted that when JFK's death was announced, and before Oswald was arrested, she derisively told her co-workers, "Don't worry . . . you'll see, it was a Communist who did it." When Oswald was taken into custody and she heard of his pro-Castro activities and his Russian wife, she knew he was "framed." In *Accessories*, she charged that large numbers of the Dallas police were members of "right-wing extremist organizations," and spoke derisively of the forces behind the assassination, including "American Nazi thugs."[41] Meagher fueled the speculation about Penn Jones's list of mystery deaths by stating "the witnesses appear to be dying like flies." Her invective about the Commission was as harsh as that of anyone since Lane's *Rush to Judgment.*

Subsequent events, however, had significant impact on the development of the post–Warren Commission review of the assassination. On July 4, 1967, Lyndon Johnson signed into law the Freedom of Information and Privacy Act (FOIA). It was revolutionary legislation that allowed private citizens to apply for the release of federal government files, even including those main-

---

* Because it is the only index of its kind, Meagher's has been used extensively, even by the House Select Committee in its reinvestigation. However, the author, in reading the twenty-six volumes, made a new card index and compared it to Meagher's publication. Her subject index reflects her bias that Oswald was innocent. For instance, under her listing for Oswald's potential for violence, Meagher does not find a reference until Volume II, and lists a total of only twenty-three incidents in the volumes that relate to that subject. The author, however, discovered the first supporting reference was in the first volume, and there were more than fifty citations just in the fifteen volumes of testimony. There are quite a few other examples in which Meagher's index underplays evidence that incriminates Oswald but meticulously lists references that tend to exonerate him or raise doubts. That prejudice is critical since the index was marketed as a scholarly undertaking and is universally used by researchers. It means those who use the index are following each other in making the same mistakes and unwittingly ignoring evidence that buttresses the Commission's conclusions.

tained by the FBI, CIA, and other sensitive organizations. The government agencies could only refuse to release the documents if they fell under privacy or security exemptions that were set forth in the law. Since its inception, and a subsequent amendment in 1974, over a million pages of documents have been released about the Kennedy assassination. However, the federal agencies were initially very reluctant to comply with FOIA, and researchers were often forced to resort to lawsuits to win the release of even the simplest documents.

"I think the FBI's attitude was that they hated the Freedom of Information Act from the very beginning," says James Lesar, whose pro bono lawsuits for documents relating to the Kennedy case, many on behalf of Harold Weisberg, have been responsible for prying more sensitive material out of the government than those of anyone else. "The FBI was originally so against the idea of FOIA that it classified early FOIA requestors as a '100 file,' a domestic subversive. They also tried to make the process unpleasant. One of the little things they did at first was to provide you with atrocious copies. They would wait for the copy machine to run low or something, and provide terrible copies. But they eventually wearied of that."

The FBI was repeatedly unmasked for lying to those who filed FOIA requests. "For instance," Lesar recalls, "one ploy was that they said they had to search all their files page by page, because they had no index. And all the while they had a 48,000-card index in the Dallas field office. Technically, FBI headquarters [in Washington] didn't have the index.*

"In other instances, they would say there wasn't anything in the field offices that wasn't also kept in headquarters, that the field offices just had duplicates of what was in headquarters. That's been proven false in several cases. The originating field office can maintain as much as four times as many documents as headquarters."

The FBI was not alone in its dislike of FOIA. "The CIA, NSA, military intelligence," says Lesar, "were all very close to the FBI

---

* Researchers did not discover the existence of the card index until Weisberg sued for the Dallas field office files in 1978, and the index was disclosed in 1980 (Interview with James Lesar, December 1, 1992).

in their distaste for FOIA. However, they have much better tools to fight FOIA requests, because they have national security and the compromise of sensitive sources as strong reasons for withholding information."

The attitude of government agencies toward FOIA prompted suspicion about motives, especially since researchers sometimes had to fight for apparently innocuous documents. "The problem is that the FBI has generally fought everything to the hilt, even if nobody could see any relevancy to it," says James Lesar. "Sometimes, they do it in subjects at which there is nothing at stake."[42] Harold Weisberg was in litigation with the FBI for over a decade regarding the release of the spectrographic tests conducted on the curbstone at Dealey Plaza that was chipped by a bullet fragment. Although the Warren Commission discussed and relied on the results of the Bureau's spectrographic test in its final report, the FBI steadfastly refused to give Weisberg the underlying data. To many, that obstinacy added to the growing public perception that the government had something to hide in the Kennedy case. But to Lesar it does not necessarily indicate cover-up as much as the bureaucratic mindset for agencies like the FBI. "The basic overall strategy," says Lesar, "assuming there is one, is that the FBI is trying to drive up the cost of getting information, making it so difficult that you don't want to do it again. I tend to think it's part of their overall litigation strategy. At times, they do it for political reasons, but other times it is part of their effort to resist disclosure, no matter what is being requested. Government officials seem to live in constant terror. In general, the government's only interest in its records occurs when somebody asks for them, and at that point they go into paralysis. They suspect that somewhere there must be something that spells trouble. It's just part of their psychology. It's built into them."

Nevertheless, the Freedom of Information Act gave added impetus to the effort to extend the examination into the assassination. In spite of the difficulties encountered by those using FOIA, the momentum against the Warren Commission led to the introduction in 1966 of a congressional resolution to reexamine the case.[43] Yet the passage of FOIA and the new resolution were overshadowed by another event that had started in July 1966, which temporarily electrified the critics and the nation. Jim Garrison, the flamboyant New Orleans district attorney, convinced there were suspects in his city who had been part of a conspiracy to kill JFK, had launched the first official investigation into the assassination since the Warren Commission.

18

"Black Is White, and White Is Black"

The curious phenomenon that became Jim Garrison's assassination probe can only be comprehended by trying to understand the man who was single-handedly responsible for the investigation. At six feet seven inches, with a bass voice and sharp tongue, Jim Garrison was an impressive figure. Born Earling Carothers Garrison in 1921 in Iowa and reared in New Orleans by his divorced mother, he served in the National Guard during World War II. After his discharge in March 1946, he attended Tulane Law School, graduated in 1949, and then moved to Seattle and Tacoma, where he was an FBI agent for two years. Bored with the Bureau, he returned to New Orleans and in July 1951 asked to be placed again on active service with the National Guard. He was relieved from duty fifteen months later. Doctors at Brooke Army Hospital in Texas found he suffered from a "severe and disabling psychoneurosis." According to the Army's evaluation, Garrison's neurosis "interfered with his social and professional adjustment to a marked degree. He is considered totally incapacitated from the standpoint of military duty and moderately incapacitated in civilian adaptability." The recommendation was long-term psychotherapy.[1]*

After his release from the Guard in October 1952, he worked

---

* Garrison later claimed he had only been sick with amoebic dysentery and the Army incorrectly diagnosed him with acute anxiety.

first for a private law firm and then became an assistant district attorney, a post he held until 1958.[2] He impressed others at the New Orleans DA's office with a quick wit and was even considered the sharpest of more than twenty lawyers. However, he also developed a reputation for making snap judgments and oversimplifying complex issues. And it soon became clear he had an ego that revealed a tendency toward arrogance.[3] "Garrison also had a small streak of paranoia, thinking he was up against everyone else, no matter what the case was," says Hubie Badeaux, former chief of the New Orleans police intelligence division. "And when he got into the Kennedy assassination, that trait came to the forefront."[4]

In a town that loved colorful characters, Garrison fit right in. When he left the DA's office in 1958, he again entered private practice. He legally changed his name to Jim and developed a flamboyant reputation for expensive suits and cigars and multihour, four-martini lunches at the city's best restaurants. He unsuccessfully campaigned to be a judge of the criminal court during the 1959 election. Two years later he was one of four candidates running against the incumbent district attorney, Richard Dowling. Given virtually no chance of winning, he took the campaign's first television debate by storm and gained enough momentum to win by 6,000 votes. In May 1962, Garrison and his staff were sworn into office. His conduct quickly became a preview of what would happen once he launched his JFK investigation four years later. He often brought sensational charges that garnered headlines, but he seldom prosecuted the cases, much less ever obtained a conviction.

The first warning signs that he might be willing to trample someone's civil liberties in exchange for media ink came soon after he took office. He brought malfeasance indictments against the former district attorney and one of his senior assistants. It was front-page news. But the charges were dismissed for lack of evidence, and "for stating no criminal offense recognizable in law."[5] Garrison promised to appeal, but never did. Instead, he embarked on a cleanup of vice in the French Quarter, and while his work again resulted in no trials or convictions, he received national press attention for his nightly raiding parties. "The Bourbon Street cleanup was a sham," says Milton Brener, an assistant district attorney responsible for narcotics and vice, who worked under Garrison. "Any clubs that closed up only did so because of harassment."[6]

Garrison was soon fighting with the local criminal judges, who under New Orleans law had to approve some of the DA's budget, but balked at his Bourbon Street publicity raids and lavish plans for redecorating his office. In what would become vintage Garrison, he complained, "There is a conspiracy among the judges to wreck my administration," and he accused the judges of being compromised by "racketeer influences."[7] The justices were so infuriated that all eight issued a charge of criminal defamation against him, a misdemeanor. Garrison was brought to trial in January 1963, acted as his own lawyer, and was convicted and sentenced to pay a $1,000 fine. (In 1965, the U.S. Supreme Court reversed the conviction, holding the Louisiana defamation statute was an unconstitutional infringement of free speech.)

While the appeal was pending, he pursued what appeared to be a vendetta against the judiciary, forcing malfeasance indictments through the grand jury against a leading judge, Bernard Cocke. In two trials, in which Garrison tried the cases himself when his assistants refused, Cocke was acquitted. "I had felt that such almost childishly punitive measures and blatant abuse of the Grand Jury," said Milton Brener, "would cause wide public condemnation. Again, I had overestimated the public and underestimated Garrison."[8]

In 1963, he charged nine policemen with brutality, but quietly dropped the case within two weeks, after intense media interest. In 1964, he held a press conference and announced that members of the state parole board were accepting bribes in exchange for granting early paroles. Garrison personally represented the city at the judicial hearing, but his case was so weak that it ended with no indictments or arrests. Next, he turned his attention to the state legislature, saying, "I am convinced that public bribery occurred in passage of House Bill 894. . . . We know bribery occurred. We want to find out where."[9] He never pursued an investigation. The legislature unanimously censured him for his unsupported accusations.[10]

William Gurvich, who was later Garrison's chief investigator on the Kennedy case, said, "He believes everyone reads the headlines concerning arrests and charges but few people read denials or correcting statements."[11] "He wouldn't worry about whether the charges were true or not," Milton Brener told the author. "The press just loved him. When he made public statements, his only concern was whether it was going to get him a headline. He liked being the hero."[12]

"If Garrison's repeated and dramatic assaults on high office produced little by way of results," said Brener, "he nevertheless captivated the public with his daring. He was now [in 1965] unquestionably one of the most powerful political figures in the State . . ."[13]

1965 was an election year for both the mayor and the district attorney. Early that year, signs appeared around the city proclaiming VOTE FOR GARRISON but not listing the office, fueling speculation he might run for mayor. He had occasionally spoken of higher office, but instead he ran for reelection. His opponent, criminal judge Malcolm O'Hara, urged voters to reject a man whose "ugly force . . . compels him to destroy everyone who fails to bow to his will. It used to be called a Napoleonic complex."[14] Garrison won a solid 60 percent of the vote.

Although he had earlier attacked vice in the French Quarter, he now lobbied for a full pardon for a Bourbon Street stripper, Linda Brigette, who had been convicted for lewd dancing. Aaron Kohn, an ex–FBI agent who headed the Metropolitan Crime Commission, criticized Garrison since Brigette danced for a club connected to New Orleans mob boss Carlos Marcello. Shortly afterward, three New Orleans gangsters were arrested in a New York restaurant with some of the country's leading mafia figures. The publicity put pressure on Garrison to take action against the local mob. He reluctantly convened a grand jury to investigate mafia influence in the city, although his position was clear when he announced that Marcello was a "respectable businessman" and that "there is no organized crime in this city."[15] Garrison's grand jury was supposed to investigate mob influence in the bail bond, pinball, and liquor industries, as well as gambling and prostitution. It asked Marcello questions for just over ten minutes, and did not return an indictment.[16]

While Garrison was ostensibly building a reputation as a corruption fighter, there is evidence he was developing a special relationship with Carlos Marcello. During his earlier raids on Bourbon Street clubs he had assiduously avoided those dominated by the local godfather.[17] The man he hired as his chief investigator, Pershing Gervais, had previously been fired from the police for stealing payoff money, and later admitted he was friendly with Marcello.[18] "Gervais was as crooked as could be," says Milton Brener.[19] During his second term as DA, Garrison dismissed eighty-four cases against Marcello associates.[20]*

"He [Garrison] spent more and more time at the Playboy Club and the New Orleans Athletic Club," said crime commissioner Aaron Kohn, "and hardly ever went to the office."[21] But Garrison soon focused on a new probe that made the public lose sight of his laxity on the mafia. JFK's murder was something that had been on his mind since his first term, but he now decided to pursue the case. The investigation, which began in secret shortly after the second term commenced, was initially based on two different leads.

The first involved David Ferrie, an eccentric self-styled adventurer, whom Garrison later called "one of the most important

---

*In 1967, *Life* magazine reported Garrison had been given three free trips and a $5,000 line of credit at the Sands Hotel, which was partially owned by mob figures, and that a Marcello lieutenant, Mario Marino, signed one of his bills (Blakey, *Fatal Hour*, p. 54). Marino later took the Fifth Amendment when questioned about it ("The Mob," Part II, *Life*, September 8, 1967, pp. 94–95; September 29, 1967, p. 35). After his second term as district attorney, Garrison moved into a lavish home built by Frank Occhipinti, a Marcello business partner. Garrison bought it for a bargain $65,000, and Occhipinti was his neighbor (Warren Rogers, "The Persecution of Clay Shaw," *Look*, August 26, 1969, pp. 54, 56). Marcello bagman Vic Carona died of a heart attack while he was visiting Garrison's house ("The 'Little Man' Is Bigger Than Ever," *Life*, April 10, 1970, p. 33). In 1971, Garrison was indicted on federal charges of accepting $50,000 in bribes to protect the mob's gambling interests. Six co-defendants testified against him, and government surveillance tapes exposed him accepting four bribes. He represented himself in the trial, claiming it was a plot to punish him for his JFK investigation, and won an acquittal. *The New York Times* later reported there might have been bribes of $10,000 and $50,000 to fix the trial's outcome (September 21, 1973, p. 25). Milton Brener told the author, "Garrison was on the take. The evidence was there, no question about it." Even after he became an elected judge, Garrison was still occasionally seen having lunch at La Louisiana restaurant with some of Marcello's brothers (Scheim, *Contract on America*, p. 50).

men in history." On November 24, 1963, two days after the President was killed, Jack Martin, a private investigator, called an assistant district attorney in New Orleans with the startling information that Ferrie had been in Dallas about two weeks before, had been corresponding with Oswald, and had taught Oswald how to shoot."[22] Garrison's investigators ransacked Ferrie's apartment, picked him up several days later, and turned him over to the FBI for questioning. The Bureau quickly determined that Martin's information was false and that Ferrie had not been to Dallas in six years.[23] Martin turned out to be totally unreliable, a drunk who had spent time both in prison and mental institutions. According to Hubie Badeaux, who was acquainted with Martin, he had a local reputation for "crazy and wild stories."[24] On November 26, two days after his original call, he admitted to the FBI that the entire story was a "figment of his imagination." He had fabricated the tale about Ferrie and Oswald when he heard a radio report that Oswald had been in the Civil Air Patrol in the mid-1950s, an organization to which Ferrie had belonged.[25] It turned out Ferrie and Martin knew each other well. They had not only worked together in the past but were the only two members of their own radical offshoot of the Catholic church. Martin acknowledged he was drunk when he made the first call to the district attorney's office, and confessed that his motivation was revenge for Ferrie's having excluded him from several recent cases.

Although there was no evidence that connected Ferrie and Oswald, Garrison was certain the "FBI blew the investigation . . . only I didn't know it at the time."[26] Garrison became suspicious of a trip Ferrie had taken with two younger friends—from New Orleans to Houston and Galveston—leaving Friday night, November 22, 1963. "It wasn't even Dave's idea to go to Houston," says Alvin Beauboeuf, one of the two teenagers who accompanied him to Texas. "It was my idea. I used to competitively roller-skate for years, and I had never ice-skated. So I told Dave, 'You are from Ohio, you ice-skate, and I would like to go.' And it was just like Dave to say, 'Let's go.' "[27] (Since the ice rink in Baton Rouge had closed, the one in Houston was the nearest to New Orleans).

To Garrison, however, the trip to the Winterland Ice Skating

Rink was highly suspicious. Breck Wall, the Dallas head of AGVA who spoke to Ruby on the night of Saturday, November 23, was in Galveston performing in a show. Ferrie, Beauboeuf, and the second teen, Melvin Coffey, had stopped in Galveston. Although they did not know each other, the fact that Ferrie and Wall had been in the same city was too much of a coincidence to the DA.[28] Garrison also claimed Eva Grant, Ruby's sister, had been in Houston on Saturday when Ferrie arrived. She was not.[29]

There was more. Since Ferrie did not ice-skate with his friends but may have made some telephone calls from a pay phone, Garrison believed that the trip to the rink was obviously a cover, and the rink was actually the message center for the conspiracy.[30] He insisted that Ferrie, a licensed pilot, was waiting for a message that would allow him to spirit one or more of the assassins out of the country. The FBI later checked Ferrie's plane and found it was not airworthy.[31]

The second lead that revived Garrison's interest in the assassination was a story told by Dean Andrews, a three-hundred-pound, forty-four-year-old jive-talking attorney with a reputation for exaggeration and showmanship. After the assassination, he told the FBI that he recognized Oswald from the newspaper photos as a person he had done legal work for (supposedly trying to overturn Oswald's undesirable Marine Corps discharge) during the summer of 1963. "Oswald came into the office accompanied by some gay kids . . . a maximum of five times, counting [the] initial visit," Andrews told the Warren Commission.[32] He never identified any of the people he said had accompanied Oswald to his office, nor did he have any records substantiating the consultations, because, he said, his office had been rifled and the papers were missing.[33]*

---

* He claimed Oswald's acquaintances were later part of a group of fifty cross-dressers the police arrested, and that Oswald was usually with a "Mexicano . . . [with] a butch haircut," who was wearing "colored silk pongee shirts." When the Commission asked Andrews for the names of any of Oswald's associates, he said, "Today their name is Candy; tomorrow it is Butsie; next day it is Mary. You never know what they are. Names are a very improbable method of identification. More sight. Like you see a dog. He is black and white. That's your dog. You know them by sight mostly" (WC Vol. XI, p. 327).

But Andrews had even more interesting things to say about Oswald—and indeed others. He claimed that on November 23, the day after the assassination, a man called "Clay Bertrand" telephoned him while Andrews was in the hospital recovering from pneumonia. Bertrand allegedly asked if he would defend Oswald for killing the President. Andrews, who had a reputation as an ambulance-chaser, had a ramshackle office near the New Orleans port. Much of his work was immigration cases for the city's poorest clients, and he could not explain why anyone would want him to represent the accused assassin. He described Bertrand as "the one who calls in behalf of gay kids normally, either to obtain bond or parole for them. I would assume he was the one that originally sent Oswald and the gay kids, these Mexicanos, to the office . . ."[34] He could not provide any more information about Bertrand, had no files on him, and no means of contacting him. "He is mostly a voice on the phone. . . . Oh, I ran up on that rat about six weeks ago and he spooked, ran in the street. I would have beat him with a chain if I had caught him. . . . I probably will never find him again."[35] To the FBI, Andrews had described Bertrand as six feet one, with brown hair. He told the Warren Commission that Bertrand was five feet eight, with sandy hair, blue eyes, a ruddy complexion, weighing 165 pounds, and said he was "bisexual. What they call a swinging cat."[36] Asked about the height and hair discrepancy, he shrugged and said, "I don't play Boy Scout and measure them."

The problem was there was no Clay Bertrand. In April, five months after the assassination, the FBI had confronted Andrews with the fact it had combed New Orleans and failed to find anyone who had ever heard of the name. He then confessed his entire Bertrand-Oswald story was fictitious. Yet when he appeared before the Warren Commission three months later, in July, he revived the original tale. When pushed by Commission counsel Wesley Liebeler about the existence of a Bertrand and the call asking him to defend Oswald, Andrews again backed off, saying, "I would tell that I was smoking weed. You know, sailing out on cloud nine. . . . Yes, I would just say I have a pretty vivid imagination and let's just forget it. . . . I was full of dope . . ."[37] When Liebeler asked him if he would lie under oath, he snapped, "Be my guest. I'll swear to anything."*

"People did not take Dean Andrews seriously," says Milton Brener, an assistant district attorney. "He talked like a Damon Runyon character, only more pronounced. He enjoyed saying the most outrageous things, and while he was entertaining, he had little regard for fact."[38] Garrison, however, not only believed that Andrews was truthful but also that Bertrand was a key to the assassination puzzle. In October 1966, Garrison began calling Andrews, as well as some of Ferrie's friends, into the office for discussions. Andrews further embellished his story. He now remembered the name of Oswald's Mexican associate—Manuel Garcia Gonzales. There was no such person. Later, when Andrews admitted it was a hoax, he said he told Garrison the first name that came to his mind because "I don't know what he's up to. He's pickin' me like chicken, shuckin' me like corn, stewin' me like an oyster . . . I'm trying to see if this cat's kosher, you know?"[39] Garrison, who did not even know if there was such a person as Gonzales, eventually became convinced that he was one of the assassins in Dealey Plaza.

In late November 1966, Garrison shocked the rest of his staff when he announced that he had decided that Clay Bertrand was actually Clay Shaw, a prominent civic figure and the man who had almost single-handedly led the historic restoration of the French Quarter. Shaw, the former president of the prestigious International Trade Mart, was an active member of the city's social elite as well as a poet and a playwright. He was also, in his personal life, a homosexual. Garrison knew he was gay, and that provided a link to Ferrie, also homosexual. One of Garrison's assistants pointed out that Shaw was six feet four and had shocking-white hair, while Andrews had described Bertrand as five feet eight and with sandy hair. That was a false description to protect his client, retorted Garrison. Moreover, he said, "they

---

* Much later, Andrews finally admitted that "Clay Bertrand" was a pseudonym he heard at "a fag wedding" and that he invented the hospital phone call to "get on the publicity gravy train and ride it to glory. . . . I was just huffing and puffing. I let my mouth run away with my brain" (Phelan, *Scandals, Scamps, and Scoundrels*, p. 161).

[homosexuals] always change their last names, but never their first names."[40]

Shaw was brought in for questioning in late December 1966, and it was evident he did not know anything. Garrison was disappointed and told his investigators to "forget Shaw."[41] Also in December 1966, Garrison told newsmen, "for background," that he had a suspect [Ferrie] in the Kennedy assassination and an arrest was imminent.[42] *Life* magazine quietly assigned several journalists to the story. In January 1967, *Life*'s Richard Billings asked Garrison if he had unmasked the mysterious Clay Bertrand, and the district attorney told him, "His real name is Clay Shaw, but I don't think he's too important."[43]

In early 1967, Garrison's office had to file public papers to explain why it needed additional funds. Reporters for the New Orleans *States-Item* obtained the papers, which listed the office's investigation into the Kennedy case. The *States-Item* broke the story on February 17.* Within a day, reporters from more than thirty countries descended on the district attorney's office. The buffs also flocked to New Orleans. To them, Garrison was a godsend. He could break the case, since he had the power of subpoena, not to mention a courtroom that protected him from libel for anything he said. Mark Lane, who billed himself as the "unpaid chief investigator for the DA," advised Garrison on the evidence and had complete access to the district attorney's files; with William Turner, of *Ramparts*, he compiled information for an "official history" of the case.[44] Edward Jay Epstein and Jones Harris, a New York buff, also had access to all the files, as well as to Ferrie's belongings.[45] Penn Jones, with Allan Chapman, who believed a worldwide conspiracy of intellectuals controlled the television networks, reported on developments in Texas. Harold Weisberg pored over the Warren Commission vol-

___
* After it became public, a group of wealthy New Orleans residents formed a committee called Truth and Consequences to finance Garrison's investigation so he would not have to make public requests for funds. Between February 1967 and October 1968, they contributed $77,000 (Warren Rogers, "The Persecution of Clay Shaw," *Look*, August 26, 1969, p. 58). Today, the impropriety of private funding of a public prosecutor, with the inherent possibility for improper influence or conflicts of interest, is a violation of the American Bar Association's ethical rules.

umes, while Raymond Marcus and Richard Sprague concentrated on the films and photographs taken at Dealey Plaza (the Zapruder film was not yet available). Vincent Salandria, Richard Popkin, and comedian Mort Sahl gave general advice. William Gurvich, Garrison's chief investigator, later said, "His true investigative staff . . . [when] I was with him were not the police officers, but the authors of the books that are critical of the Warren Report."[46] Garrison dubbed himself "the wagon boss of the buffs."[47]*

Once the investigation was public, Garrison began to put more pressure on Ferrie, calling in more of his associates for questioning. When he learned that Ferrie had known ex–FBI agent Guy Banister (who died of a heart attack in 1964), he extended the probe toward Banister and the anti-Castro Cubans. So far, Garrison had found only one person willing to testify. He was David Lewis, a shipping clerk who claimed to have seen Oswald, Ferrie, Banister, and anti-Castro activist Carlos Quiroga at a meeting in New Orleans. The only problem was that Lewis was adamant it was in early 1962, when Oswald either was in Russia or had just returned to Texas.[48] But Garrison was so desperate to build a case against Ferrie that he tried to intimidate and cajole witnesses to provide the necessary testimony.

"I was offered a bribe from his office, by Lynn Loisel [an investigator on the DA's staff], in front of a witness and on tape," says Al Beauboeuf, who had accompanied Ferrie on the ice-skating trip on the weekend of the assassination and knew firsthand that Garrison's sinister interpretation was unwarranted. "And I took a lie detector test and passed it. But they wanted

---

* When Garrison's investigation ended ignominiously several years later, most of his supporters backed away from him. Some, like Harold Weisberg and Edward Epstein, even condemned him. However, in the beginning, most were convinced Garrison was on the right track. "The case has been solved," said Popkin (Anson, *They've Killed the President*, p. 111). Weisberg wrote, "He and his staff are dedicated, and sincere and, I am convinced from my own work, right" (Weisberg letter to editor, *Playboy*, October 18, 1967). Lane boosted both himself and Garrison, saying, "Besides Jim Garrison, I am perhaps the only person in the world who knows the identity of the assassins" (Bob Katz, "Mark Lane Fingers the Dead," *Mother Jones*, August, 1979, p. 27). Closer to the trial, Lane predicted, "When it is presented in court it will shake this country as it has never been shaken before" (UPI).

me to change my testimony. You could tell that Garrison had a theory but had no evidence to back it up."[49]

On the transcript of the taped conversation, Loisel assured Beauboeuf's attorney, "The boss is in a position to put him [Beauboeuf] in a job, you know, possibly of his choosing, of Al's choosing. Also they would be, we would make a hero out of him instead of a villain, you understand. Everything would be to your satisfaction. We can change the story around, you know, enough to positively, beyond a shadow of a doubt, you know, eliminate him into any type of conspiracy, or what have you. . . . I would venture to say, well you know, I'm fairly certain, we could put $3,000 just like that [snaps his fingers], you know. I'm sure we'd help him financially."[50]

Loisel laid out the conspiracy plot he wanted Beauboeuf to support. He discussed "cross fire" and escape routes, and said either Ferrie and Shaw, or Oswald and Shaw, were arguing in the apartment, and Beauboeuf overheard them. "But anyway, that's what we have in mind—along that line," said Loisel.[51]

"It was very obvious," says Beauboeuf, "they just wanted me to come forward and they would tell me what to say. I told them no way, and when they heard we had recorded Loisel, they went nuts. Louis Ivon [another Garrison staff investigator] came to my house and put a gun down my throat and threatened to kill me because I had exposed them. . . . They also had pictures they threatened to give out like they were going out of style if I came out in the open . . . that I might make headlines as Ferrie's lover.

"Garrison tried to bribe a lot of people, but I was the only one who had proof. He wouldn't let up. He was unbelievable. Finally, I made a deal with him to sign a statement that it was all blown out of nowhere, just in order to get him off my back. Then he left me alone."[52]*

Early in February, Garrison was introduced to Gordon Novel, an anti-eavesdropping expert he wanted to use to ensure his office was not bugged by the FBI. He soon discovered that Novel knew Ferrie and claimed to have knowledge of his anti-

---

* Beauboeuf signed a statement absolving the district attorney's office of any misconduct.

Castro connections. Garrison decided to use Novel as a witness, and called him repeatedly to the DA's office. In a meeting with Novel, Garrison suggested that Ferrie was stonewalling the investigation by lying, and that one solution might be for Novel to shoot Ferrie with a tranquilizer dart and then inject him with sodium pentothal to obtain the details of the assassination plot.[53] At one point, Novel also saw apparent forgeries of letters, purportedly from Oswald to Ferrie, in the district attorney's office.[54]

On February 21, Novel, appalled by Garrison's tactics, left for Ohio, where he had once lived.* The investigation received a greater jolt the next day, when David Ferrie was found dead in his apartment. Garrison announced it was a suicide, interpreting a rancorous letter to a friend as a suicide note.† The autopsy revealed something quite different—he had died of a berry aneurysm, the bursting of a blood vessel in the skull (forensic pathologists again confirmed the results in 1992).[55] The coroner was unequivocal that the death was natural, primarily because Ferrie had a history of high blood pressure and a berry aneurysm cannot be induced. But Ferrie was under tremendous strain from Garrison's probe, and he looked so bad in the days before his death that his acquaintances believed the pressure was too much for him. "When I saw Ferrie two days before he died," recalls Carlos Bringuier, the Cuban storeowner who had the street confrontation with Oswald during the summer of 1963,

---

* Garrison was so furious with Novel that he filed burglary charges against him for a conspiracy to steal weapons. The governor of Ohio, James Rhodes, agreed to extradite Novel to Louisiana, but Garrison never completed the paperwork within the sixty-day time limit, so the extradition case was dismissed (*The New York Times*, July 4, 1967). Yet in a subsequent interview with *Playboy*, Garrison asserted, "The reason we were unable to obtain Novel's extradition . . . is that there are powerful forces in Washington who find it imperative to conceal from the American public the truth about the assassination" (*Playboy*, October 1967, p. 172). In public speeches, Garrison accused LBJ of pressuring Ohio's officials in the Novel case, and he told *Playboy* that "there is no doubt that Gordon Novel was a CIA operative." He was not. Novel filed an unsuccessful $10 million libel suit against Garrison and *Playboy*.

† Novel, because of the investigative abuses he had witnessed at Garrison's office, became convinced that the DA's staff actually typed the angry, unsigned letter, on Ferrie's typewriter, so it might appear to be a suicide (Interview with Gordon Novel by Sal Panzeca and Robert Wilson, April 16 and 17, 1967).

"he looked real sick. He told me, 'I feel very sick. I should be in bed. My physician told me to stay in bed. I have a big headache. Garrison is trying to frame me.' "[56] Al Beauboeuf says, "Dave lost his self-respect, lost his dignity, with those charges. Garrison had set up a camera across the street from his apartment, and they followed him everywhere. They kept pressure on him all the time. They just brought him down to the point where they killed him."[57]

But Garrison used Ferrie's death as evidence he was on the right track. Ignoring the coroner's report, he said, "[Ferrie] knew we had the goods on him and he couldn't take the pressure. . . . A decision had been made earlier today to arrest Ferrie. Apparently, we waited too long."[58] There had been no plans to arrest Ferrie.

"Garrison was looking anywhere for a lead; he seemed desperate at times," recalls Bringuier. "He called me in several times, and he and I were playing a game of chess. I knew any minute he could turn against me. I was trying to avoid a confrontation with him, because I knew he would stop at nothing to make his case. People like Garrison and his staff could be very dangerous. I was warned to be very careful, that I could be killed by them.

"He called in Quiroga [Bringuier's friend] and left him alone in a room, and the Garrison team brought in a rifle with a telescopic sight and left it in the room for an hour or two. They wanted to see if Quiroga was stupid enough to touch it, and then they would have brought the gun and buried it somewhere in a hole and then found it and charged Quiroga with being part of the conspiracy. You cannot imagine what they were willing to do to succeed in their case. I knew Garrison was bribing witnesses and fabricating evidence. If I was sent to jail, I had decided to go on a hunger strike. I had not come to America and worked fifteen hours a day to allow Garrison to destroy my life and ruin everything I worked for.

"When I spoke to him, that's when I realized what a crazy investigation it was. And I let him know what I thought. And he said, 'Maybe somebody is fooling you,' and I said, 'Maybe somebody is fooling me, or maybe somebody is fooling you, but we will see who is the fool.' And he got mad with me, and asked if I would take a lie detector test. And I said, 'Yes, I'll take it right now.' They took me next door and they gave me a couple-hour test, a real fishing expedition. When I left the office that day, it was 1967, and I had read the book *1984*, and I thought it was just like *1984*."[59]

With Ferrie's death, some of Garrison's staff urged him to abandon the investigation. But he refused. Instead, he focused on Dean Andrews's story about Clay Bertrand, although he only had his personal hunch that Clay Shaw was Clay Bertrand. He was not bothered that one of his best assistant district attorneys, Andrew "Moo" Sciambra—like the FBI—had talked to every informant in the French Quarter and found no one who had ever heard the name Clay Bertrand.[60]

On February 24, only two days after Ferrie died, a pack of reporters stopped Garrison as he left a luncheon and asked if he was close to solving the assassination. "My staff and I solved the case weeks ago," he boasted. "I wouldn't say this if I didn't have evidence beyond the shadow of a doubt. We know the key individuals, the cities involved and how it was done. There were several plots, but that's more than I wanted to say. Ferrie might not be the last suicide in the case. The only way they are going to get away from us is to kill themselves." A few minutes earlier he told another group of reporters, "The key to the whole case is through the looking glass. Black is white and white is black. I don't want to be cryptic, but that's the way it is."[61]

On Wednesday, March 1, 1967, Garrison arrested Clay Shaw and charged him with being part of a conspiracy to kill President Kennedy. Only two days after Shaw's arrest, Garrison agreed to meet Jim Phelan, of *The Saturday Evening Post*, in Las Vegas, at the Sands Hotel. He liked an earlier article Phelan had written about his Bourbon Street cleanup and had decided to give him the exclusive story behind Shaw's arrest.

In Vegas, Phelan said, the man he encountered "was a Garrison I had never seen before, arrogant, prejudicial, blindly confident that whatever he suspected had happened, had to have happened. . . . [He] told me that some of his assistants had opposed the arrest of Shaw, that he ordered it as 'a command decision,' and that 'this is not the first time I've charged a person before I've made the case.' "[62]

Phelan asked Garrison what the motivation was behind the conspiracy. "They had the same motive as Loeb and Leopold when they murdered Bobbie Franks in Chicago back in the twenties," he replied. "It was a homosexual thrill-killing, plus the excitement of getting away with a perfect crime. John Kennedy was everything that Dave Ferrie was not—a successful, handsome, popular, wealthy, virile man. You can just picture the charge Ferrie got out of plotting his death." When Phelan pressed him, Garrison said: "Look at the people involved. Dave Ferrie, homosexual. Clay Shaw, homosexual. Jack Ruby, homosexual." Garrison thought he had uncovered Ruby's gay name— "Pinkie." "And then there's Lee Harvey Oswald," he said. "A switch-hitter who couldn't satisfy his wife." If they were all homosexuals, in Garrison's opinion, it was too much of a coincidence.*

A preliminary hearing for Shaw had been scheduled for Tuesday, March 14. Near the end of his ten-hour series of interviews with Phelan, the district attorney feared the *Post* article was in jeopardy because Phelan was still skeptical about the weak supporting evidence. Garrison then walked to the dresser in his hotel room and picked up a thick manila envelope. "I'm going to give you something no one knows about but my top people," he said. "I've got a witness who ties this whole case together. He's my case against Shaw. Here's the evidence my witness is going to present in the Shaw hearing next week."[63]

Garrison's star witness was a twenty-five-year-old Baton Rouge insurance salesman, Perry Raymond Russo, who brought himself to the attention of the district attorney by writing a letter to the DA's office after Ferrie's death. He had also given a February 24 television interview to WDSU-TV in New Orleans, in

---

* Garrison also thought that Ferrie and the other plotters were responsible for several unsolved homosexual murders in New Orleans and intended to charge them for those crimes as well (William Gurvich conference with Edward Wegmann, August 29, 1967, Tape 2, p. 9). Despite the fact that he was married, Garrison himself was the subject of numerous stories in New Orleans about his sexual preference. A prominent New Orleans attorney told the author how Garrison had tried to sexually molest his brother, then thirteen, in 1968 at the New Orleans Athletic Club. Nationally syndicated columnist Jack Anderson wrote about Garrison's assault of the youngster in a February 1970 column.

which he said he knew Ferrie and that Ferrie did not like Kennedy. As for Oswald, Russo later said, "I never heard of him until the television on the assassination."[64] On February 25, assistant district attorney Andrew Sciambra interviewed Russo. In a 3,500-word memo, Sciambra reported the results to Garrison. Russo again said Ferrie never issued a direct threat against Kennedy. When Sciambra showed Russo photos of Oswald and Shaw, Russo thought he might have seen Shaw twice, once at a gas station and once at the Nashville Street Wharf. As for Oswald, Russo drew a beard on the photo and said it resembled one of Ferrie's roommates [he confused Oswald with Jim Lewallen, a Ferrie roommate].[65]

Two days later, on February 27, at Garrison's request, Russo submitted to sodium pentothal at Mercy Hospital in New Orleans. While interrogating Russo, who was in a semiconscious state, Sciambra introduced the name Clay Bertrand for the first time. Russo had never heard the name before. On March 1, Russo was placed under hypnosis by Dr. Esmond Fatter, whom Garrison had hired, though he had no background in using hypnosis to elicit criminal testimony. What Phelan saw in the transcript shocked him. Fatter, in his interrogation of Russo, used a memorandum supplied by Garrison's office. While Russo was in a trance, it was Fatter who insinuated the idea of a conspiracy and Clay Shaw. At one point, Fatter said, "Picture that television screen again, Perry, and it is a picture of Ferrie's apartment and there are several people there and there is a white-haired man. Tell me about it."[66] What Phelan did not know is that two days before Fatter placed Russo under hypnosis, Garrison had taken Russo to Shaw's house, where Russo rang the bell and introduced himself as an insurance salesman. Having seen a photo of Shaw on February 25, and having met him in person on February 28, Russo was ready to incorporate him in his dream state at Fatter's suggestion.

Shortly after introducing the image of Shaw during the hypnotic trance, Fatter said, "Let your mind go completely blank, Perry. . . . See that television screen again, it is very vivid. . . . Now notice the picture on the screen. There will be a Bertrand, Ferrie, and Oswald and they are going to discuss a very important matter and there is another man and girl there and they are talking about assassinating somebody. Look at it and describe it to me."[67]

Russo had never talked about a plot to kill anyone. He then responded for the first time, "They planned to assassinate President Kennedy." As the session continued, he elaborated that there would be a cross fire, and gave more details about the meeting he "witnessed."*

Phelan could not believe that Garrison had provided him with the two documents, the first of which—the Sciambra memorandum of the original meeting with Russo—utterly impeached the credibility of his star witness. Garrison, who had just received the packet from his office, had impulsively given it to Phelan without first reading the material himself. When Phelan returned it, he asked why the plotters would discuss the details of their plan to kill JFK in front of a stranger who could turn them in to the FBI. "Garrison pondered that in silence," recalled Phelan, "and then shook his head. 'Say, that's a good question,' he said."[68]

The March 14 preliminary hearing to determine if there was "probable cause" to hold Shaw for trial was held before a three-judge panel. Russo told his newly developed story about being at a party at Ferrie's apartment, where Oswald, Ferrie, and Shaw discussed the details of an assassination plot. Shaw was brought into the courtroom, and Russo placed his hand over Shaw's head and identified him as "Clay Bertrand," the name he said Shaw used at Ferrie's party.

Garrison also produced a surprise second witness, Vernon Bundy, a black heroin addict, who was in prison for a parole violation. He testified that when he was shooting heroin along the lakefront during 1963, he saw Shaw meet Oswald and give him some money. The first time he ever publicly presented the story was at the preliminary hearing.

The judges took less than half an hour to rule that Shaw should be held for trial on the charge of conspiring to kill the President. However, it was not long before the DA's witnesses

---

* Dr. Fatter later told Jim Phelan that he "certainly would hate to see anyone taken to trial on what Russo had said in a trance" (Letter to author from Phelan, April 6, 1993).

were under attack. On June 19, NBC News aired the devastating results of an investigation into Garrison's work. The show disclosed the extent to which the district attorney's office had tried to bribe and intimidate witnesses into giving favorable testimony. Not only did NBC reveal the incident with Al Beauboeuf, but Fred Lemanns, who owned a Turkish bath, said Garrison offered him money to open a new club if he would testify that Shaw had visited the baths with Oswald and had used the name Bertrand. Russo admitted to reporter Walter Sheridan that his testimony against Shaw was a mixture of truth, fantasy, and lies, but he feared that if he changed his testimony, Garrison would charge him with perjury. "The hell with truth," Russo said. "The hell with justice. You're asking me to sacrifice myself for Clay Shaw [by telling the truth], and I won't do it."[69]

During the preliminary hearing, Russo had identified two other people as having been at the now infamous Ferrie party—Niles Peterson and Sandra Moffitt. Niles told NBC he was at the party but said no one was there who even resembled Oswald or Shaw. Moffitt denied being there, and said she had never even met Ferrie until 1965.

In addition, NBC had uncovered two fellow inmates of Vernon Bundy, John Cancler and Miguel Torres. Separately, they admitted that Bundy had boasted he was going to give perjured testimony against Shaw because "it's the only way I can get cut loose [get out of jail]." Torres also disclosed that the DA's office had offered him a deal if he would testify he had been at sex orgies at Shaw's house and knew Shaw used the name Bertrand.[70]

Furthermore, NBC revealed that both Russo and Bundy had failed friendly polygraph tests administered by Garrison. Finally, they asked Dean Andrews if Shaw was Clay Bertrand. "Scout's honor," he said. "He is not."

Within several weeks of the NBC show, William Gurvich, Garrison's chief investigator, resigned and headed for Washington, where he told Robert Kennedy that Garrison's case was a sham and there was no basis to arrest Shaw. He repeated those convictions on national television and accused Garrison of using methods that were "illegal and unethical." He said he hoped to testify before a grand jury.[71]

Garrison dismissed the NBC investigation as part of a coordinated effort at "thought control." He said he was not surprised by the program since NBC's parent company was RCA, "one of the top ten defense contractors," and they "are desperate because we are in the process of uncovering their hoax."[72] Garrison then launched a public relations offensive, a media blitz that included a Mort Sahl–arranged appearance on Johnny Carson's *Tonight Show*, the longest interview in *Playboy*'s history, and dozens of radio and television spots. NBC gave him an unprecedented half hour of unedited national airtime to respond to its exposé. Buttressed by the buffs, he captivated a public all too willing to believe that JFK had been killed by a complex conspiracy and that one brave prosecutor was fighting the cover-up forces. " 'He must have something,' people used to say all the time," former assistant district attorney Milton Brener told the author. "People everywhere thought he just wouldn't have brought those charges unless he had something. But that's exactly what he was doing, just pulling the charges out of the thin blue air."[73]

Garrison had now gone far beyond the motivation of a "homosexual thrill-killing" to explain the conspiracy, and he regaled audiences with his constantly changing and expanding theories. Depending on which show he was on, he said the assassination "was a Nazi operation, whose sponsors included some of the oil-rich millionaires in Texas," or at other times it included the Minutemen, the CIA (with Jack Ruby as the operations paymaster), the FBI, White Russians, or anti-Castro Cubans.[74] Audiences responded positively to his charges of Nazi involvement, and Garrison elaborated on that concept over several months. He developed a standard college speech titled "The Rise of the Fourth Reich, or How to Conceal the Truth About the Assassination." Garrison warned that America was "in great danger of slowly evolving in to a proto-fascist state" and that "our government *is* the CIA and Pentagon . . ." He claimed that Jack Ruby was a self-hating Jew who had smuggled guns with neo-Nazis and that "Oswald would have been more at home with *Mein Kampf* than *Das Kapital.*"[75] Lyndon Johnson, the Warren Commission, and even Robert Kennedy became part of the cover-up, and he accused RFK of making "very positive efforts" to obstruct his investigation. "It is quite apparent to me," said Garrison, "that for one reason or another, he does not want the truth to be brought out."[76]

He also went after those who had abandoned him or tried to expose the investigation. Garrison charged William Gurvich and Tom Bethell, another aide who quit in disgust, with theft of part of his files; John Cancler, the inmate who spoke to NBC, was hit with contempt of court; Gordon Novel, who resisted extradition from Ohio, had burglary charges placed against him; and Walter Sheridan, the reporter behind the NBC investigation, and Richard Townley, who had assisted in its preparation, were accused of attempted bribery of a witness for offering to pay Russo for his expenses to come to California for an interview.[77]*

Garrison filed perjury charges against a number of witnesses who refused to give the testimony he wanted, not only to punish them, but also because, under Louisiana law, if he obtained a conviction they would be barred from testifying at the Shaw trial. He brought perjury indictments against Dean Andrews; Kerry Thornley, Oswald's Marine buddy who said he had not seen Oswald in New Orleans in 1963; Layton Martens, a young friend of Ferrie's who said he could not connect Shaw to Ferrie; and David Chandler of *Life* magazine, originally a Garrison confidant who later became disillusioned.†

When assistant district attorney James Alcock objected that there was no legal ground for the arrests, Garrison retorted: "Don't be so legalistic."[78] Some of those indicted lost their jobs, and others spent thousands of dollars defending themselves on frivolous charges.[79] The only one convicted was Dean Andrews,

---

* Garrison was so furious with the exposé by NBC that he told Gurvich he wanted Sheridan "arrested, handcuffed, and beaten and drug [sic] into jail" (Edward Wegmann, Esq., memorandum, June 4, 1968, p. 1).

† In an almost forgotten part of the case, Garrison had also charged another man, Edgar Eugene Bradley, with conspiracy to kill the President. Garrison had received a letter saying Bradley had made inflammatory remarks about JFK. Bradley had lived and worked in North Hollywood, California, since 1962 and had never lived in New Orleans. But when Garrison learned he had been in El Paso, Texas, on the day of the assassination, he issued an arrest warrant. No evidence or witnesses were ever produced at a subsequent extradition hearing, and California governor Ronald Reagan refused to send Bradley to New Orleans.

for having concocted the fictitious Clay Bertrand. But success-fully prosecuting the cases was not Garrison's concern. Filing the charges—aside from the intimidation it created—enhanced the image that he was fighting a secret network of conspirators pressed into service to disrupt his investigation. He soon added the media, which he had so successfully used, to his hit list. Much of the national press was part of a "CIA-inspired cam-paign" against him, he said.[80] "Anytime you attacked him or crit-icized him, you were part of the conspiracy to destroy him," recalls Milton Brener.[81] The late 1960s, with the country in a rebellion against authority and many wary of government du-plicity over the war in Vietnam, gave rise to a climate that was receptive to Garrison's assertions that the greatest government deception of a generation had taken place in the Kennedy assas-sination.

As he fended off criticism, he also worked at creating a case against Clay Shaw. During the months following Shaw's arrest, hundreds of would-be witnesses were interviewed by the DA's staff. Celebrated cases tend to bring forward people who want to be in the limelight, and the Shaw matter was no exception. Some were outright con artists, who wrote Garrison with excep-tional tales about Oswald's CIA connections and how Shaw fit into the plot, and when the DA then sent them air tickets to come to New Orleans, they merely cashed the tickets and were never heard from again.[82]

Following up on those who did arrive in New Orleans and tell their stories, Garrison sent his investigators across the country to determine which, if any, he could use against Shaw. A man calling himself Julius Caesar appeared, wearing a toga and san-dals, and put Oswald, Ferrie, and Shaw together in an elaborate plot that fit Garrison's scenario. When the press discovered he was an ex–mental patient, Garrison abandoned him.[83] Cedric Younger von Rolleston, an itinerant artist, arrived from New York, where he said he had "worshiped" the younger Oswald, who was then a "thirteen-year-old boy," and that he had met Ruby at the Dallas jail, been cut in on the postassassination plot, and delivered money to Shaw. After Garrison decided Rolles-ton's story did not fit into his theory, he refused to talk to him, and even made him pay his own hotel bill. Rolleston told the press he did not know Shaw after all.[84] At the time Richard Nagell offered his help—through the mail—he was confined to the psychiatric section of the federal prison in Springfield, Missouri. Nagell claimed his role in an extensive conspiracy was to execute Oswald, on Soviet orders, in order to prevent the assassination. He changed his mind and instead robbed a bank in El Paso, Texas, in September 1963, so that he would be sent to jail and avoid his conspiratorial duties. Garrison sent an investigator, William Martin, to speak to Nagell. When he found Nagell unreliable, Nagell complained that Martin was part of the CIA plot against him.[85] Garrison later personally met Nagell, who charged that Clay Shaw, Guy Banister, and David Ferrie all manipulated Oswald on behalf of the CIA. Even Garrison found his tale "not easy to digest."[86]*

"You cannot imagine what a circus it was," says Carlos Bringuier. "And as for Garrison, as time passed, he seemed to get wilder in what he said."[87] "I knew that the facts meant absolutely nothing to him," says Milton Brener. "I knew he was determined to get a conviction on Shaw no matter what he had to do to get the evidence. His judgment was absolutely skewed. It was a farce, but a tragic farce. It's astounding and frightening, but the whole thing was made out of nothing but his imagination."[88]

Garrison, heavily influenced by the buffs, envisioned a vast conspiracy of which Shaw was only a small part. Before Shaw's trial, he made statements about numerous issues for which he had no supporting evidence. Nevertheless, many of his pronouncements survived the prosecution of Shaw and became part of the folklore about the assassination. Among others, he gave his stamp of approval to the following stories: former Dallas sheriff Roger Craig's tale of a getaway car at Dealey Plaza;

---

* Nagell was the subject of a conspiracy book, *The Man Who Knew Too Much*, written by Richard Russell and published in 1992 by Carroll & Graf. Russell, a researcher on the assassination for nearly two decades, considers Nagell a reliable source despite his history of mental problems and uses his stories to spin a far-flung plot involving the CIA and KGB. Russell, in his 824-page book, never mentions that Nagell had told Garrison that Clay Shaw was part of a plot with Oswald. Nagell also believes that Oswald was placed into a hypnotic trance by David Ferrie and turned into a "Manchurian Candidate" who then carried out the assassination.

witnesses were being killed as part of an organized cover-up (the odds that all the deaths were coincidental were 30 trillion to one, he said); Ferrie and Banister both knew Oswald; Ruby and Oswald knew each other and both had worked for the CIA; Oswald's Fair Play for Cuba work was only a front for American intelligence; there was an imposter Oswald and he was often present in New Orleans; the Mannlicher-Carcano was planted at the Depository about twenty minutes after the assassination; Ruby may have been injected with cancer cells to kill him (scientifically impossible); and a woman who had successfully predicted the assassination was later killed because she knew too much.*

Every time the media seemed to get close to unraveling Garrison's case as a fraud, he diverted attention by rolling out another conspiracy story. On Johnny Carson's *Tonight Show*, he produced, with a flourish, grainy photographs of five men talk-

---

*Rose Cheramie, a prostitute and heroin addict, was found lying unconscious on a road near Eunice, Louisiana, on November 20, 1963, and taken to a hospital. As Garrison developed the story, Cheramie had warned the hospital staff that JFK would be killed in Dallas. From the medical records, the House Select Committee discovered that she had been in heroin withdrawal and physical shock when she was checked into the hospital. Dr. Victor Weiss, a treating physician, told investigators that he did not hear her say anything about the assassination until November 25, the day after Ruby killed Oswald (HSCA Vol. X, p. 200).

The only person who later claimed that Cheramie had mentioned the assassination before November 22 was the state trooper, Francis L. Fruge, who brought her to the hospital on November 20. Fruge initially claimed that Cheramie said she was personally going to kill JFK. When he spoke to Cheramie on November 25, Fruge said that she brought in Ruby and Oswald. Fruge later worked with Garrison's probe and his story of what Cheramie said before the assassination expanded dramatically.

According to Fruge, Cheramie said that she had been a stripper for Jack Ruby, that she knew that Oswald and Ruby were homosexual lovers, and that she had been thrown out of the car by Ruby, who she was working with on a narcotics deal. Cheramie is the one who provided Garrison the supposed gay nickname for Ruby, "Pinkie." She died on September 4, 1965, when she was again lying on the roadway and was struck by a car. The subsequent investigation revealed it was an accident, although buffs list it as a mystery death. Further inquiry revealed Cheramie had never worked for Ruby, had been confined to mental hospitals in the past, and had a history of providing the FBI and U.S. Customs with elaborate and false stories about narcotics deals (HSCA Vol. X, p. 203). Yet Oliver Stone still opened his movie *JFK* with the Cheramie story.

ing to police in Dealey Plaza after the assassination. "Here are the pictures of five of them being arrested. . . . Several of these men . . . have been connected by our office with the Central Intelligence Agency," he said.[89] It was a photo of bystanders, none of whom were arrested, and Garrison's staff had not identified any of them when he appeared on Carson. Another time he startled the press with the announcement that Oswald's address book contained Ruby's unlisted phone number. According to Garrison, it was in code in Oswald's book and he had deciphered it. He mistakenly assumed two Russian Cyrillic letters in Oswald's book referred to a post-office box, then converted "P.O." to "W.H." and scrambled the numbers, 19106, until he had 6901, then subtracted 1300 to get WH1-5601, Ruby's number. When asked how he came to subtract 1300, he said it was simply the block on Dauphine Street where Clay Shaw lived.[90] When a reporter challenged him that his formula was completely arbitrary and clearly worked backward to reach Ruby's number, he angrily said, "Well, that's a problem for you to think over, because you obviously missed the point."[91] Garrison later took the number 1147 that appeared in Oswald's address book, multiplied it by 10, rearranged the numbers, subtracted 1700, and remultiplied. He said it resulted in 522-8874, the CIA's phone number in New Orleans, although he failed to mention it was listed in the phone book.[92]*

Perhaps the most outrageous aspect of the sideshow that Garrison conducted with the media—while Clay Shaw was forced to wait for his day in court—was his evolving pronouncements on the number of assassins at Dealey Plaza. When he started his investigation he thought there were only two, one in the Depository and one on the grassy knoll.[93] After he spoke to Harold Weisberg, he put a shooter at the Dal-Tex building and cleared Oswald of firing any shots.[94] To *Playboy*, he proffered a second

---

* Among his other accusations, Garrison also charged that Shaw had been a CIA operative. Gurvich, Garrison's investigator, said, "He [Garrison] has nothing to prove, not even concocted evidence, that Shaw was connected with the CIA" (Gurvich conference with Edward Wegmann, August 29, 1967, Tape 3, p. 4). Shaw was questioned about his foreign travels by the CIA's Domestic Contact Division, the same as thousands of other Americans during that period, but he had no other relationship to the Agency.

"Oswald" at Dealey Plaza, based on his talks with Richard Popkin.[95] Garrison added four more assassins in a CBS interview after speaking to Raymond Marcus, who told him that blown-up photos of the trees revealed the men.[96] Allan Chapman convinced him that another shooter was hidden inside a storm drain. To *The New York Times* Garrison flatly announced the fatal shot was "fired by a man standing in a sewer manhole."[97] Soon, he made the three tramps, as well as Jerry Belknap, the epileptic who had a seizure and was taken away by ambulance only minutes before the shooting, part of the killing team.[98] Jones Harris convinced him that a pickup truck shown in a photo hid two more assassins.[99] After Garrison received an anonymous letter saying that Kennedy might have been shot with "frangible" bullets (those that fragment upon impact), he told *Playboy* "some of the gunmen appear to have used frangible bullets."[100] Eventually, Garrison placed sixteen assassins at five locations in Dealey Plaza.[101]*

His preoccupation with conspiracies was not confined to Kennedy's assassination. "He saw conspiracies everywhere," recalls Milton Brener. "And there's a word for that, and it's called *paranoid*. I know that word is discredited because it's overused, but if it ever fit somebody, it fit him."[102] Since early 1967, Garrison had carried a pistol clipped onto his belt. He once showed James Phelan a bullet from his pistol and said, "That's a magnum load, and my gun can't handle it. If I used it, the gun would blow up on me. I can't figure out who inserted that shell into my gun." Then he put the shell back into his pistol.[103] After telling the press that Havana had sent a hired assassin who was stalking him,[104] he hired bodyguards and used a code language when talking about the case over the phone.[105] Gurvich said Garrison wanted "to raid the local FBI office" to uncover "the secret recording room" that he believed monitored all his conversations.[106] Near the start of the Shaw trial, Garrison took a taxi

---

* Although the buffs usually encouraged Garrison's proclivity to widen his conspiracy charges, sometimes they prevented him from making major mistakes. At one point in the investigation, he had a warrant drafted for the arrest of Robert Perrin, who supposedly could testify about Ruby's gun-smuggling activities to Cuba. The night before he made the arrest notice public, Weisberg proved to him that Perrin had died in 1962.

home one night, and threw the money at the driver as he ran into the bushes near his house, crouching there for several minutes and surveying the area before running up to his front door.[107]

During the long delay leading to Shaw's trial, Garrison hoped he could find witnesses who would tie the defendant to either Oswald or Ferrie. On January 21, 1969, the trial finally began, nearly two years after Shaw was arrested. Despite his promises of spectacular disclosures, Garrison presented the same basic prosecution he had in the 1967 preliminary hearing. Yet this time the problems in his case were readily apparent. Russo testified again that he had seen Ferrie, Oswald, and Shaw at the party, but said they might not have been planning a conspiracy but instead just "shooting the bull."[108] Then Dean Andrews took the stand and admitted that Clay Bertrand was an invented character. Trying to prevent his case from falling apart, Garrison introduced the Clinton, Louisiana, witnesses, who said they had seen Shaw driving a car with Oswald and Ferrie sometime in the late summer or early fall of 1963.*

Then he produced a surprise witness, a tense New York accountant, Charles Spiesel. He testified he had attended a party several months before the one Russo described, and Ferrie, Oswald, and Shaw had been there and had openly discussed their plans to kill Kennedy in front of him. Under cross-examination, Spiesel admitted he himself had been the victim of a vast conspiracy for sixteen years, in which the New York police and his own psychiatrist had invaded every part of his existence, interfering with his thought processes as well as his sex life. He claimed that strangers had hypnotized him some fifty or sixty times "against my will," and because "new police techniques" allowed the conspirators to enter his house disguised as his relatives, he had fingerprinted his daughter when she returned from school to ensure it was she. Garrison had been aware of Spiesel's past but put him on the stand over his staff's objection.[109]

Yet as the case against Shaw collapsed, Garrison increasingly concentrated on what appeared to be a second prosecution, one

---

* See Chapter 7 for a further discussion of the Clinton witnesses.

against the Warren Report and its conclusion of a lone assassin. Although they were not relevant in determining Shaw's guilt or innocence, he called Marina Oswald, Bethesda pathologist Pierre Finck, and witnesses from Dealey Plaza. He successfully subpoenaed the Zapruder film and showed it ten times to the Shaw jury.* A court had rejected his attempt to have the autopsy X rays and photos released.†

Late in the evening of Saturday, March 1, two years to the day since Shaw's arrest, the jury retired for deliberations. It returned forty-five minutes later with an acquittal on its first ballot.‡

For Shaw, whose life was devastated by the charges of having conspired to kill the President of the United States, it appeared he was finally free of the district attorney. Yet two days later, Garrison arrested Shaw for perjury, claiming that when Shaw testified he did not know Ferrie or Oswald, he had lied. It took another two years of legal fighting before a federal court, on June 7, 1971, finally issued a permanent injunction against Garrison from prosecuting Shaw, on the grounds that the charges had been brought in bad faith. At the federal court, Garrison once again offered Perry Russo as a witness, but Russo finally refused to repeat the fabrication about the Ferrie party. He later voluntarily approached Shaw's attorneys and gave them a tape-recorded statement confessing that Garrison's staff had told him what to say: "It was sort of a script and I was playing my part. I guess I played a too good one, huh?"[110] All his earlier testimony about Shaw was a lie. "I never dreamed he [Garrison] only had me," he said. "I guess I always knew he [Shaw] had nothing to do with anything." At times Garrison promised Perry "that after Shaw was convicted we'd all be rich," and other times he "told

---

* The conspiracy critics working with Garrison made copies of the Zapruder film, and bootleg versions soon flooded the "research" community.

† During 1968, attorney general Ramsey Clark, one of the few federal officials who openly criticized Garrison's investigation and tactics, had convened a panel of forensic pathologists to review the medical evidence to offset Garrison's complaint that he was not able to obtain the autopsy X rays and photographs. The Clark Panel, as it was known, confirmed the medical conclusions of the Warren Commission, but its findings were largely lost in the coverage of the events in New Orleans.

‡ A juror later said they would have returned in twenty minutes, but several of them had to go to the bathroom.

me about people who had been convicted of perjury and said mine would be worse because a lot of people had been affected by what I said."[111]*

Garrison appealed the federal court injunction to the Supreme Court, where he again lost. His response was a nine-page press release again charging that the CIA had murdered JFK, that Oswald had been a mere "scapegoat," and that the Supreme Court's decision "puts the final nail in John Kennedy's coffin."[112] He lost his bid for reelection as district attorney to a young lawyer, Harry Connick, and complained that the FBI and CIA had assisted in his defeat.

Although he never convicted Clay Shaw, he did bankrupt him. Garrison told *Playboy* he thought the CIA might have paid Shaw's legal bills, but Shaw actually spent over $200,000, his life savings, on the four years of legal battles. Borrowing money from friends, he had his attorneys file a multimillion-dollar abuse-of-process suit against Garrison and the investigation's financial backers, Truth and Consequences. But before it got to trial, Shaw died in 1974 of cancer, a broken man.

"At the time Clay Shaw died," says Cynthia Wegmann, an attorney and the daughter of one of those who defended him, "Louisiana had a quirk in its laws. For the suit to survive the death of the plaintiff, he had to have surviving children or parents. Shaw had no children, and his mother died shortly before he did, so his case was dismissed. Louisiana later changed its law so the estate of the deceased person could continue the suit. Almost everybody familiar with the case is convinced that if Shaw's suit had continued, it would have succeeded, thereby stopping Garrison from writing anything else about him."[113]

"What he did to Clay Shaw is a travesty of justice," says Irvin Dymond, Shaw's chief defense attorney. "It should never have been allowed to happen in this country. The abuse of power from a megalomaniac prosecutor destroyed Shaw's life. It was

---

*Since the film *JFK*, in which Russo had a small walk-on role, was produced in 1991, he has revived his original tale. However, during an interview with the author, Russo admitted, "I believe that Shaw was innocent. I do not disagree with the jury. I agree with it. The bottom line is that history must recall that Shaw is innocent. If I was on the jury, I would have come to the same conclusion."

one of the low points in the history of our judicial system, and I don't know how Garrison can hold his head up without shame."[114]

"I thought he was slightly nuts to begin with," recalls Milton Brener, "and then I think he went completely off his rocker in the Kennedy investigation. He was unsettled. You could see the wild look in his eye."[115]

But Garrison never abandoned his zealot's beliefs. Until his death in 1992, he continued beating the media drum that he was right all along and that only the efforts of the military-industrial complex prevented him from succeeding. In 1988, he published *On the Trail of the Assassins*, in which he regurgitated all of his theories developed in 1966 and 1967, though they were clearly outdated. He spoke about Shaw as though the jury's acquittal was a mere oversight in an otherwise iron-clad case.

Despite his efforts, and his election as an appellate judge, he could not redeem his reputation. The evidence of his abusive prosecution had hurt the conspiracy movement and ruined him as a credible voice. Garrison died, at the age of seventy, on October 21, 1992. However, he had lived to see director Oliver Stone use more than $50 million of Warner Bros.' money to rehabilitate his theory and again tarnish the name of an innocent man, Clay Shaw, for yet another generation.

19

"What Happened to the Truth?"

As the extent of Garrison's folly in New Orleans became known, the conspiracy press, which had gained tremendous public acceptance during 1966 and 1967, began to falter. Garrison's excesses reflected poorly on other theorists, especially since the leading critics were an integral part of his early efforts. Anthony Summers later wrote, "What angers investigators about . . . Jim Garrison is that his cockeyed caper in 1967 was more than an abuse of the justice system. It was an abuse of history, and—more than any other single factor—[responsible] in discrediting . . . genuine researchers for a full decade, a decade in which witnesses died, and evidence was further obscured."[1]

During the late 1960s and early 1970s, some buffs, including Penn Jones,[2] Harold Weisberg,[3] and even Garrison himself,[4] published books, but they had dismal sales. The most popular works on the assassination were now those that exposed the New Orleans fiasco, most notably James Kirkwood's *American Grotesque*[5] and *Counterplot*, by Edward Jay Epstein, who had turned on Garrison.[6]*

"Although a dedicated group of people kept researching the case, it wasn't until 1974 that several things took place that

---

*Epstein has increasingly become a gadfly among the conspiracy critics, writing national magazine articles in 1992 and 1993 attacking both Garrison's failed efforts and Oliver Stone's excesses in *JFK*.

started to again ignite public interest," says James Lesar, the Freedom of Information Act attorney for many assassination researchers. Harold Weisberg had sued to obtain the transcript of the January 27, 1964, executive session of the Warren Commission, which discussed a newspaper article that asserted Oswald had been an FBI informer.* "We got that in the summer of '74 [June 14]," says Lesar, "and it made headline news that November. *The Washington Post* ran a big story, on page three, and that was picked up by Senator Pell. That was the beginning, more or less, of the buildup for an eventual congressional investigation."[7]

A few months after the release of the transcript of the executive session, conferences on the assassination were held in both New York and Boston. They received considerable attention, were moderate in tone, and instead of jumping to conclusions, both demanded new government investigations. In March 1975, Geraldo Rivera aired, for the first time, the Zapruder film on ABC's *Goodnight America*. Millions were shocked by its graphic detail, and especially the image of Kennedy's head snapping back and to the left after the final shot. Without an understanding of the medical evidence or the physics involved, it appeared as though the President reacted to a bullet fired from the front, rather than the rear as the Commission had concluded.

"I also think the disclosures about Watergate had an effect," says Lesar. "It reminded people of how duplicitous government leaders could be, and it created the right atmosphere for a renewed look at the assassination."[8]

In 1975, the work of the Senate's Select Committee to Study Governmental Operations with Respect to Intelligence Activities revealed yet another persuasive reason for a new investigation. It had discovered that the CIA, with the assistance of the mafia, had repeatedly tried to assassinate Cuba's Fidel Castro during the early 1960s.[9]† There was an added outrage. The CIA had not

---

* At the time, the Commission was extremely concerned about the story, and discussed ways to approach J. Edgar Hoover about Oswald. See page 348, about how the report was a hoax concocted by reporter Lonnie Hudkins et. al.

† The mafia leaders who cooperated with the government were Sam Giancana and Santo Trafficante, the godfathers of Chicago and Tampa, respectively. Robert Maheau, an ex–FBI agent who had become a private investigator

kept President Kennedy fully informed about the assassination plots, and most of the Warren Commission members had never heard anything about them, though commissioner Allen Dulles had been director of the CIA when many of the attempts were made. That the CIA hid its operations to murder the Cuban leader from the Warren Commission, as well as the details from its own President, raised questions about what it might have withheld on Lee Oswald and the Kennedy assassination.

In April 1975, Virginia congressman Thomas Downing, a committed believer in a conspiracy, introduced a resolution calling on Congress to reinvestigate the assassination of John Kennedy.[10] In the same Congress (the 94th), Texas representative Henry Gonzales had introduced a resolution calling for a new investigation not only of JFK, but also of the shootings of Robert Kennedy and the Reverend Martin Luther King, Jr., and of the attempted assassination of Governor George Wallace. By July, those congressional efforts were bolstered when a newsman broke the story that FBI agent James Hosty had received a note from Oswald shortly before the assassination and had destroyed it. Was this not further evidence of a cover-up? Yet despite the growing demand for a new investigation (over a hundred congressman said they would back a resolution), it failed to get out of the committee, killed by a tie vote.

The next year, 1976, when it appeared the momentum for a new investigation was faltering, Coretta Scott King, the widow of Martin Luther King, Jr., met with the Congressional Black Caucus to inform them of new evidence that might affect the conclusion that James Earl Ray was the lone assassin of her husband. A group of congressmen began working to meld the Downing and Gonzales drafts to empower a select committee to investigate the deaths of both King and JFK. Their efforts resulted in House Resolution 1540, introduced on September 14, 1976, and passed by a vote of 280 to 65 on September 30.

The committee was established, with Congressman Downing as its first chairman. The Black Caucus suggested Mark Lane as general counsel, but eventually Richard Sprague, a prominent

---

with underworld connections, and Johnny Roselli, a captain in the Las Vegas syndicate, acted as conduits between the government and the mob.

Philadelphia prosecutor, was selected. He had never read the Warren Report or any of the critics' books, and appeared to approach the case without prejudgment. But he did not last long. He angered and offended Congress by submitting a 1977 budget of $6.5 million, considered excessive, and by announcing he would make extensive use of polygraphs and stress analyzers on potential witnesses.[11] Henry Gonzales, who had replaced Downing at the start of 1977 as the chairman, tried to dismiss Sprague, but Sprague insisted the entire committee vote him out. In the ensuing standoff, Gonzales resigned. By February 1977, it appeared there would be no new investigation of the JFK assassination.

In March, however, Speaker Tip O'Neill named a new chairman, Louis Stokes, Democrat of Ohio. Stokes persuaded Sprague to resign, and was also able to get Congress to extend the committee's life, at least through the end of the year, with a budget of $2.5 million. G. Robert Blakey was appointed chief counsel. He was a highly regarded attorney and academician, a Cornell University law professor who had spent four years in the organized-crime section of the Kennedy Justice Department.* He was to coordinate an extensive reexamination of the Warren Commission's evidence, and pursue the major issues raised by the critics during the preceding fourteen years. But Blakey's specialty and overriding interest was the mafia.

Except for a few weeks of public hearings, with carefully chosen witnesses, most of the committee's work was conducted in private, as are most congressional inquiries. Its investigators signed strict nondisclosure forms.† Under Blakey's guidance,

---

* After serving with the committee, Blakey became a professor at Notre Dame, and was also known as the "father of RICO," the Racketeer Influenced and Corrupt Organizations Act, which he drafted, one of the most important laws ever devised in the fight against organized crime.

† The committee eventually sealed more than eight hundred cubic feet of documents, much of it for privacy or security reasons. Following the release of Oliver Stone's 1991 film *JFK*, Congress passed historic legislation establishing a process that will lead to the release of most of those documents, as well as the small percentage of remaining Warren Commission papers, and whatever files other federal agencies still maintained about the case. The purpose of the legislation was to dispel the notion fostered in Stone's movie that the government was party to a cover-up. By January 1994, more than 500,000 pages of documents had been released pursuant to the legislation, and no information

the committee accomplished some important work, debunking many nagging issues. Its forensic panel, which had complete access to the autopsy X rays and photographs, together with the firearms and photographic panels, found unequivocally that JFK had been wounded only twice and that both shots came from Oswald's rifle, fired from the southeast sixth-floor corner of the School Book Depository.[12]

In December 1978, after spending nearly $5.8 million, the Select Committee reviewed a draft of a lengthy final report on both the JFK and King assassinations. While it found that there was likely a conspiracy in the King case, it concluded the Warren Commission was basically correct and that Oswald alone had killed Kennedy and Tippit. But late that month, acoustics experts Mark Weiss and Ernest Aschkenasy came forward with their interpretation of the Dallas dictabelt recording from the police motorcycle "proving," with a supposed 95 percent certainty, that a fourth shot was fired from the grassy knoll. On December 29, Weiss, Aschkenasy, and Dallas police officer H. B. McLain, who mistakenly thought his cycle had the open microphone, testified in a public hearing. The more than six-hundred-page draft was put aside, and a majority of the committee approved a preliminary nine-page "Summary of Finding and Recommendations" that concluded, based on the flawed acoustics findings, that there was a conspiracy to kill JFK involving a second gunman.*

That flip-flop in the closing days of the committee's existence overshadowed all its less sensational, but often solid, conclusions. Instead of quietly resolving the conspiracy questions left over from the Warren Commission, the acoustics blunder opened the door to much greater speculation about a plot. And since the committee had decided there was a conspiracy, it felt

---

that contradicted or undermined the conclusions that both Oswald and Ruby acted alone surfaced in the new files. In November 1993, the author testified before the Legislation and National Security Subcommittee of the House of Representatives, providing not only a summary of the contents of some of the newly released documents, but also proposing methods for expediting the release of the remaining government files.

* Blakey later told a journalist, "If the acoustics come out that we made a mistake somewhere, I think that would end it [the talk of a conspiracy in the case]" (G. Robert Blakey, interviewed by Earl Golz, January 5, 1980).

obliged, in its final report issued in July 1979, to assess the probable identity of the conspirators.

For some time, Blakey had had a suspicion about possible organized crime involvement, partly because of the mob's well-known hatred for attorney general Robert Kennedy, and partly because of the way Ruby had killed Oswald, which he says "had all the earmarks of a mob hit."[13]* Although it could never prove Oswald had personal contact with any mobster, the Select Committee nevertheless, under Blakey, concluded that while the "national syndicate of organized crime, as a group, were not involved in the assassination, it could not preclude the possibility that individual members may have been involved."[14] Suspicion focused on Teamster boss Jimmy Hoffa, Tampa godfather Santo Trafficante, and New Orleans boss Carlos Marcello. The committee's conclusion infused new life into the arguments for a conspiracy, which now had the imprimatur of a government investigation that had not only concluded there was a conspiracy, but even highlighted the suspects. To the buffs, Garrison's investigation was now only a distant, bad memory.

For many, the CIA remained a leading suspect,† but now the mafia moved to the forefront as the most credible plot-master. The same year that the Select Committee completed its work, Seth Kantor's book, *Who Was Jack Ruby?*, concluded Ruby was a mafia hit man.[15] In 1979, *The Washington Post* ran a long article headlined DID THE MOB KILL KENNEDY?[16] And Blakey published his own best-seller, *The Plot to Kill the President*, in 1981.[17] By

---

* Though the mob hated Robert Kennedy because he was relentlessly pursuing them, the committee implied that individual mobsters may have assassinated JFK in the hope that by their removing him, Robert would lose his power to prosecute them.

† Books like *High Treason*, by Robert Groden and Harrison Livingstone, and *Conspiracy*, by Anthony Summers, charged that the CIA, or a rogue group of agents, was responsible for the assassination. In *First-Hand Knowledge* (1992), ex–CIA contract agent Robert Morrow weaves an intricate intelligence plot, of which he claims to have been a part. Oliver Stone, in his film *JFK*, regurgitated almost all of Garrison's original contentions against the intelligence community. Yet not only have the underlying facts to such accusations been disproved, but the CIA theories necessarily involve the greatest number of conspirators, sometimes numbering in the hundreds. As the House Select Committee concluded, "The more complicated a plot becomes, the less likely it will work" (HSCA Rpt., p. 179).

the end of the decade, there were many successful conspiracy books, including two that embellished the mafia theme, John Davis's *Mafia Kingfish*[18] and David Scheim's *Contract on America*.[19]

What did the Select Committee uncover in its multiyear investigation? Is there credible evidence that Hoffa, Trafficante, and Marcello were involved in the assassination of President Kennedy?

As for Hoffa, the committee found evidence that he had spoken about wanting Robert Kennedy dead, but it could find nothing to show his interest went beyond the talking stage or extended to JFK. The witness was Edward Partin, a Hoffa lieutenant and convicted felon turned federal informant. Hoffa completely trusted Partin, and if there had been a plot to kill the President, he would almost certainly have known of it. According to Partin, in the summer of 1962, Hoffa said he would like to kill Robert—not John—Kennedy. Partin said Hoffa discussed either shooting RFK or using plastic explosives to blow up his house.[20] But Partin also said that was the extent of Hoffa's interest, and he never took any further steps. Moreover, in early 1967, when presented with a concrete plan to murder RFK, Hoffa rejected the opportunity. Teamster official Frank Chavez told Hoffa about the details of a plot to eliminate Robert Kennedy, and Hoffa strongly rebuked him, saying that such an action was dangerous and should never be contemplated.[21] The committee "strongly doubted . . . that Hoffa would have risked anything so dangerous as a plot against the President at a time that he knew he was under active investigation by the Department of Justice." It "concluded, therefore, that the balance of the evidence argued that it was improbable that Hoffa had anything to do with the death of the President."[22]

The sole evidence the Select Committee found implicating Santo Trafficante in a plot against JFK was provided by a Cuban exile, José Aleman. He boasted to committee investigators that although he only casually knew Trafficante, the mob boss had confided to him, over a year before the assassination, in a September 1962 conversation, that the President was "going to be hit."[23] He claimed he had reported that information to the FBI in

1962 and 1963, but a review of Bureau reports on his contacts did not record any such disclosures.[24] And in his public testimony before the Committee, Aleman recanted and said it was only "his impression" that Trafficante meant the President was going to be hit.[25] The House Select Committee acknowledged that the Aleman story was weak: "Further, the committee found it difficult to comprehend why Trafficante, if he was planning or had personal knowledge of an assassination plot, would have revealed or hinted at such a sensitive matter to Aleman. It is possible that Trafficante may have been expressing a personal opinion, 'The President ought to be hit,' . . . In sum, the committee believed there were substantial factors that called into question the validity of Aleman's account." As for Trafficante, the committee concluded that "it is unlikely that Trafficante plotted to kill the President, although it could not rule out the possibility of such participation on the basis of available evidence."[26]

Carlos Marcello, as the godfather of New Orleans, received special attention from the Select Committee since Oswald had spent the summer of 1963 in that city. About the same time Aleman says he spoke to Trafficante, another witness who casually knew Marcello claims he also heard about a threat to kill JFK. Edward Becker was a speculator in the oil business. Becker says he tried to interest Marcello in distributing an oil additive he had invented. During their discussions, Becker mentioned Bobby Kennedy, and the godfather lost his temper. Carlos supposedly jumped up from the table and cried out, *"Livarsi 'na pietra di la scarpa!"* (Sicilian for "Take the stone out of my shoe!") and spoke of using a "nut" for an assassination.[27] Becker said Marcello added, "If you want to kill a dog, you don't cut off the tail, you cut off the head."[28] Another man present, Carl Roppolo, denied Marcello ever said anything like that, and was not even sure if there was a meeting with Becker. The House Select Committee concluded it was extremely unlikely that Marcello, who knew he was under a federal criminal investigation and had a reputation for being very close-mouthed, would discuss a plot to kill the President with anyone but his closest lieutenants. The committee also discovered that Becker "had a questionable reputation for honesty and may not be a credible source of information."[29]* "Anybody that told that story about Carlos swearing in Italian about getting a stone out of his shoe has seen *The Godfather* too many times," says Hubie Badeaux, the former New Orleans police intelligence chief who was personally acquainted with Marcello. "Carlos doesn't talk like that. He talks with 'dees, dems, and dose,' just like in Brooklyn. Carlos wouldn't know what the shit you are talking about. He's not even from Sicily, for God's sake, he's from North Africa, Tripoli. I don't even know if he speaks Sicilian worth a damn. If he was going to talk about Kennedy, there is no way on this earth he would talk to a geologist [Becker] about that. What the hell is the geologist going to do but get him in trouble? He doesn't need his help. And for Carlos, who hardly ever talks, that would have been a goddamn oration. That story does not fit Carlos Marcello. You have to know Marcello and know how he talks to understand how stupid that story is."[30]

After the Select Committee had finished its work, a 1979 FBI bribery investigation of Marcello, code-named BRILAB, resulted in eight months of surveillance tapes of him. Most of them were played in a 1981 trial in which Marcello was found guilty of racketeering and conspiracy.[31] Three tapes were withheld in the trial. Those tapes contain some conversations between Marcello and the undercover agents about the Kennedy family or the JFK assassination, and critics long contended they have been withheld because Marcello incriminates himself in those conversations and the government is covering it up.[32] Since the Select Committee had disbanded by the time the tapes were made, Professor Blakey did not hear them. In 1980, however, the FBI briefed him on their details. He found hardly anything in the conversations suspicious.[33]†

---

* Although the committee did not believe Becker's story, it remained suspicious about Marcello because it mistakenly thought Oswald, in 1963, associated with David Ferrie (who had done investigative work for Marcello) and used an office at 544 Camp Street, where Guy Banister also had an office. Thus, the committee thought it had a link between Oswald and Marcello. But as shown in Chapter 7, Oswald did not associate with Ferrie or Banister, nor did he use an office at 544 Camp Street.

† The only thing on a tape that bothered Blakey was actually a nonconversation. Picked up by a ceiling bug in Marcello's Town & Country office, an unidentified acquaintance asked Marcello how he intended to deal with the Se-

Thirteen years after the Select Committee issued its report, Frank Ragano, an attorney who had represented both Hoffa and Trafficante, has told a story that some consider strong evidence implicating Hoffa, Trafficante, and Marcello in an assassination plot.[34] Early in 1963, when he was about to fly to New Orleans to meet Trafficante, Ragano claims, "Jimmy told me to tell Marcello and Trafficante they had to kill the President."[35] When he arrived in New Orleans, Ragano said he met with Trafficante and Marcello and "I told them, 'You won't believe what Hoffa wants me to tell you. Jimmy wants you to kill the President.' They didn't laugh. They looked dead serious. They looked at each other in a way that made me uncomfortable. Their looks scared me. It made me think they already had such a thought in their mind."[36]

Ragano admits he does not have any knowledge of whether Marcello and Trafficante then executed a plan to kill the President. But at the very least, if true, his account shows Hoffa wanted JFK dead in early 1963, and Marcello and Trafficante were apparently not opposed to the idea. There are, however, difficulties with his story.

On April 11, 1967, two FBI agents interviewed Ragano at their Tampa office, regarding the Bureau's continuing criminal investigation of his client Trafficante. He dismissed the allegations about Trafficante's possible involvement in the assassination as "ridiculous" and, to prove his point, told the agents about a trip he had made to New Orleans earlier that year, during the Garrison probe. He recounted that when he was in a car with Trafficante and Marcello, a radio broadcast commented on the Garrison investigation. According to Ragano, "Santo turned and remarked to Marcello, 'Carlos, the next thing you know they will be blaming the President's assassination on us.' "[37] Twenty-five years after that FBI interview, Ragano publicly told his new and more sensational story. He made his disclosure less than three weeks after the movie *JFK* had created a national fervor on the

lect Committee's suspicions about him in its final report. Marcello told the man to be quiet, and according to the FBI description, the tape records the sounds of a chair being pushed away from a desk, and the two men walked out of the room. Blakey found it suspicious that Marcello wanted to go outside to answer the question about the Select Committee conclusions.

subject, and at a time he was coincidentally trying to sell a book manuscript, his autobiography.* There is no corroboration for his new tale.

In addition, Ragano recalled a quite different reaction from Marcello and Trafficante when he relayed another murder request from Hoffa, this one to "hit" Teamster boss Frank Fitsimmons. The two mob bosses refused, saying that Fitsimmons was too powerful and they "could never touch him." The same mafia leaders who shied away from a contract on the teamster's leader supposedly were interested in the most powerful target of all, the President.

Those who have investigated and studied the mafia do not believe there is any credible evidence that the mob was involved in the JFK assassination. "I spent thousands and thousands of hours listening to surveillance tapes on the top mobsters in the country," says Bill Roemer, who led the FBI's fight in Chicago against the mafia. "We put a microphone in the general headquarters of the Chicago mob in 1959, and it stayed in place until 1965. We also put a microphone into the special headquarters of Sam Giancana. We listened to them—Giancana, all the top leaders of the Chicago mob—as they talked to other mobsters. They constantly talked about how they hated Bobby Kennedy. They always said it would be nice if something could be done. But they never talked or showed any interest in assassinating him. That was, as far as I could see, the furthest thing from their mind. And then when the assassination of the President happened, they discussed it relentlessly, but there was never any sign they had anything to do with it—nothing to indicate that the Marcello clan or anyone they knew was connected in any

---

* Ragano has recently added a new wrinkle to his story, claiming that Trafficante admitted four days before he died that it had been a mistake "to get rid of John—they should have got rid of Bobby instead" (*Frontline*, November, 1992). There is no corroborating witness for the purported conversation. Dragging Trafficante's name into the assassination may be Ragano's revenge for a time when Trafficante refused to help him. When Ragano was convicted of tax evasion and was disbarred in 1976, he was soon destitute. When he approached his old friend and client Trafficante for a loan, he was flatly turned down. "I was flabbergasted," admitted Ragano. "I thought he was different. Then it finally dawned on me he was no different than the rest of them. He abandoned me, and I thought ours was a special relationship."

way. You have to remember something important. Giancana and the people around him were complete virgins when it came to electronic surveillance. Hoover had brought us into the fight against organized crime in 1957, and he ordered us to try and get microphones in, and the first we ever got in was in July 1959 . . . I was the police agent on that. And they had no idea we put that in. And one time they did wonder about it, it was after '63, but they were so dumb they talked about it in front of the microphone: 'I wonder if this place is tapped. Let's get hold of Dick Cain'—who was their wiretap expert—'and bring him in here tomorrow and see if anything is there.' That night we went up and took it out and then let it smolder for a couple of weeks, and then put it back in.

"We did not wiretap the phone. They wouldn't talk on the phone. That's the place they thought they were vulnerable. They never, in those days, thought we could put a microphone in their headquarters. They thought we didn't even know where their headquarters were. But we got them in there for six years, talking about every crime you could imagine. In all that time there was not an inkling that the JFK assassination was connected to any part of the mob."[38]

Roemer spent thirty years in the FBI penetrating the mafia and was intimately familiar with its operations and way of thinking. "The mob would never go after someone as high-ranking as RFK or JFK," he says. "They don't go after reporters, they don't go after judges, they don't go after FBI agents or cops—they will only go after those people when they have stolen money from them and double-crossed them. It's counterproductive. It would be the end of the mafia if they went after the attorney general or the president and anything went wrong. It's not the way these businessmen would have acted. The risk would be far too great."[39]

At most, the conspiracy books, and the House Select Committee, have established that the mafia hated the Kennedys, may have talked about removing them from office or even killing them, and celebrated the news that the President was dead. "They would have congratulated Oswald if they had a chance," says Hubie Badeaux. But none of the books can credibly link Oswald to any mafia plot. The mafia theorists no longer argue the evidence presented in the Warren Commission or the activities of Lee Harvey Oswald. In *Mafia Kingfish*, for instance, Oswald is not even mentioned until 130 pages into the book, and Tippit only once. The attempt on General Edwin Walker's life is given only passing mention, since there was no motivation for the mob to want Oswald to kill the general. In developing the details about the mafia and men like Marcello, Trafficante, and Hoffa, these books and theorists ignore Oswald's history and personality, leaving the reader with no understanding of how or why he ended up in the School Book Depository shooting at the President.

The mistaken belief that Oswald associated with Ferrie and Banister during the summer of 1963, both of whom did investigative work for the New Orleans godfather, has been used to link him to Marcello—as has been the fact that Oswald's uncle, Dutz Murret, was a local gambler. Oswald seldom saw Murret in New Orleans, but some writers, including Blakey, suggest that Marina may have confided to him that Oswald had tried to kill General Walker. Then, presumably, Murret turned his nephew over to Marcello, who, according to Becker, was looking for "a nut" since 1962. But Marina adamantly denies ever telling Murret or anyone—not even Ruth Paine—about the Walker assassination attempt before JFK was killed.

One of the most persuasive arguments against Oswald's involvement with the mafia is the absence of any evidence of conspiratorial contact between them. Oswald was living in Dallas in 1962 and early 1963 when Aleman, Becker, and Ragano claim the mafia leadership in New Orleans developed a plan to kill Kennedy. Though Oswald went to New Orleans during the summer of 1963, he left there before Kennedy's trip to Texas was even announced. Moreover, if the Cuban embassy in Mexico City had granted Oswald a visa to travel to Cuba in September 1963, he would have been in Havana when JFK visited Dallas. The job at the Book Depository was not arranged by the mob but, instead, by Ruth Paine and her friends. During the two months before the assassination, according to his landlady and roommates, Oswald stayed at home every night, never received any calls, and only made one a night to his wife. After the motorcade was officially announced only days before the visit, there was no flurry of telephone calls. When and how were last-minute preparations made with Oswald? There were none. Mobsters may have discussed killing JFK, but their plans did not involve Lee Oswald. He beat the mafia to Kennedy.

Although the mob thesis is the current favorite, critics have flooded the field with new and ever-changing theories. Some are even based on elaborate personal stories told by people who have stepped forward and implicated themselves in a purported assassination plot. That trend, which gained momentum after the Select Committee's Report, had actually begun with Garrison's weakening of the research standards. The New Orleans district attorney believed almost anyone who had a story to tell about the assassination—the more elaborate the better. Although Garrison's results were condemned, his methods were perpetuated by others in the field.

Dallas researcher David Perry has compiled the names of twenty-eight men identified by buffs as having been a second (or third, or fourth) assassin or as having "confessed" to being a second assassin.[40] "This is a major part of the problem with the Kennedy assassination right now," says Perry. "You have people coming forward with phony stories, and some critics are so willing to believe they have solved the case that they print it without properly checking their facts. There are also some forged documents being produced and this could do real damage to the historical record. And unfortunately, a lot of the research that is getting printed in books is secondary work, just one author citing another. That means that stories that are wrong are getting repeated over and over, and in many cases they are getting embellished in each retelling. Eventually, people believe these stories just because they see them in print so often. It's disastrous."[41]

It is not surprising that theories frequently contradict each other and are internally inconsistent. Almost none of them focus on Oswald. "People have lost sight of what really happened in this case," says ex–Dallas assistant district attorney Bill Alexander. "All those conspiracy books telling the same basic story, or relying on some fellow who just confessed to the crime of the century, have made everything so damn confusing that a lot of good people have just thrown their hands up in the air and said,

'Forget it.' That's why so many people believe there's probably a conspiracy. It seems like there is so much written about it, they figure some of it must be right."[42]

In *Appointment in Dallas*, Hugh McDonald tells the story of "Saul," a man who claimed to be the second shooter at Dealey Plaza as part of a CIA plot. Even McDonald prudently prefaced his work with the caveat "I had no proof per se of the truth of Saul's statement."[43] In *Reasonable Doubt*, Henry Hurt laid out the intricate details of a plot involving Oswald, the CIA, and anti-Castro Cubans, based largely upon the unverified word of Robert Easterling, a person committed to a mental institution. Richard Russell, in *The Man Who Knew Too Much*, does the same with Richard Nagell, who not only spent time in and out of a mental ward but was so unreliable that not even Garrison used him. In his latest book on the assassination, *Plausible Denial*, Mark Lane relies in part on the word of Marita Lorenz, who claims to be a former mistress of Fidel Castro. She spins an incredible tale of CIA complicity, and recounts cross-country car trips with conspirators as well as meetings with Ruby and the CIA's E. Howard Hunt. The problem is, as Edwin Lopez, a former researcher for the House Select Committee, says, "Mark Lane was taken in by Marita Lorenz. Oh God, we spent a lot of time with Marita. . . . It was hard to ignore her because she gave us so much crap, and we tried to verify it, but let me tell you—she is full of shit. Between her and Frank Sturgis,* we must have spent over one hundred hours. They were dead ends. . . . Marita is not credible."[44] For a time, convicted Texas hitman Charles Harrelson (incidentally, the father of actor Woody Harrelson) said he was one of the assassins, disguised as a tramp. Adventurer Chauncey Holt, who says he knew Oswald, Ruby, and mobster Meyer Lansky, claimed to have delivered phony Secret Service identifications to Dealey Plaza while also disguised as a tramp. Holt, represented by a Texas attorney, tried to sell a book about it all. Harrelson and Holt became part of the same story when the January 14, 1992, *Globe* had banner

---

* Sturgis, an ex–CIA contract employee, was arrested as one of the Watergate burglars. He was mistakenly identified by many buffs as one of the three tramps detained at Dealey Plaza.

headlines: REVEALED: JFK'S REAL KILLER; MYSTERY TRAMP CHARGES: *CHEERS* STAR'S DAD SHOT KENNEDY—AND I GAVE HIM THE GUN.

Ricky White said his father, Roscoe, a Dallas policeman, was the grassy-knoll shooter and claimed the evidence was in his father's diary. When asked to produce the diary, Ricky declared it had, conveniently, "disappeared." Other documents that "prove" White was an assassin have been unmasked as forgeries. Meanwhile, a group of Texas investors formed a corporation, MATSU, and has repeatedly tried to market the Roscoe White story as a book or film.[45] Oliver Stone reportedly considered paying $750,000 for the White story but eventually decided to buy the rights to Garrison's 1988 book *On the Trail of the Assassins* for $250,000.[46]

Jailed drug dealer Christian David spun an exciting tale of three Corsican hitmen who shot Kennedy. A British producer believed David, and his story became the basis for a television documentary, *The Men Who Killed Kennedy*, although it was later discovered that the accused men were either in the French navy or in prison on the day David claimed they were in Dallas.

Oliver Stone's film *JFK*, released late in 1991, was the culmination of more than a decade of work by the conspiracy press.* It portrayed Garrison as a hero standing up bravely to the forces that killed the President. *JFK* is a blatant mix of fact and fiction and is a microcosm of what has happened throughout the assassination-research community.† An increasing amount of pub-

---

* Stone's film was not the first inspired by the assassination. In 1973, Mark Lane co-wrote *Executive Action*, a semidocumentary in which a wealthy right-winger is the chief conspirator. *The Parallax View* (1974) shows how an innocent man could be framed as a lone gunman. In *Winter Kills* (1979), based around a Kennedyesque family, the slain President's father was responsible for the assassination.

† In *JFK*, Stone created a fictional character, a mysterious intelligence officer named "Mr. X," who meets Garrison and tells him about the motivation of the military-industrial complex to kill Kennedy. Mr. X was loosely based on an adviser to the film, Fletcher Prouty, an ex–Army colonel who was the chief Pentagon liaison officer to the CIA at the time of the assassination. He was in Christchurch, New Zealand, on November 22, 1963. Prouty claimed that the local newspaper published an "extra" edition containing details about Oswald's life before he was even charged with a crime in Dallas (Prouty, *JFK* [New York: Birch Lane Press, 1992], p. 306). The implication is that some intelligence agency, probably the CIA, released an early, prepackaged set of

lished work is a dangerous mixture of good information with a liberal dose of falsehoods. Sifting out the truth is increasingly difficult for those not well versed in the facts.

Even the few critics who approach the subject from an academic's viewpoint, such as University of Wisconsin professor David Wrone, decry the field's decline in quality fueled by the public acceptance of more sensational theories: "To my mind, this assassination syndrome, this terrible collapse of the critical people—witness Lane, and Lifton, and Garrison and the rest— it's a suggestion that we are really in trouble as a society. These theorists take us away, fly us away to this unknown land of Oz, wherever they take us. They divert our attention from the reality. Every book that asks the question 'Who shot John Kennedy?' or tries to answer the question 'Who shot John Kennedy?' has fallen short of the mark, and sometimes egregiously so. Now, as you know, there are a bunch of books that are just old-fashioned nut books, like the umbrella man. And then there are a number of books which appear deceptively within the pale."[47]

There is an increasing emphasis by the critics on commercialization, disguised often as research. An annual convention in Dallas, dubbed an information symposium, is actually a three-day gathering where buffs pay $150 per person to shop at tables of assassination memorabilia and also listen to published authors and other self-appointed experts speak on topics such as "Strange and Convenient Deaths," "Media Cover-up—Then and Now," "FBI/Hoover Cover-up." Dealey Plaza witnesses important to the conspiracy, such as Jean Hill and Ed Hoffman, are treated as celebrities, complete with autograph sessions. For only $20 a person, there are daily bus tours of the assassination sites, including Dealey Plaza, the Texas Theater, and Neely Street (the site of Oswald's backyard photographs). Besides the

---

details about the assassin to the media. But there is nothing mysterious about the "extra" edition of the *Christchurch Star*. Because of the nineteen-hour time difference, it was 7:30 A.M. on November 23 in New Zealand when JFK was assassinated. Oswald was arrested when it was shortly after 9:00 A.M. in Christchurch. Culling information from press stories around the time of Oswald's defection, plus information released by the Dallas police, the *Star* managed to get a thin "extra" on the street within three hours, by noon (Prouty, *JFK*, p. 306).

annual convention, a Dallas "JFK Assassination Information Center" has opened in a shopping mall, where everything from bumper stickers to T-shirts are sold.* There are plans to expand to other cities. Within the research community, some have profited from selling bootleg copies of the Zapruder film and the autopsy photographs. In the wake of Oliver Stone's *JFK*, the gun Jack Ruby used to kill Oswald sold at auction for $200,000 and the new owner is offering a "limited edition" of 5,000 bullets shot from Ruby's pistol, for $500 each. Ruby's hat sold for $12,100. The coroner's tag that had been placed on Oswald's big toe after his death sold for $6,000. Oswald's signature commands a higher price than President Kennedy's. Oswald's KGB file was recently the subject of frenetic efforts by several journalists who hoped to purchase exclusive access. Some witnesses now refuse to speak to researchers unless they are paid.

"You have to understand," says Bill Alexander, "what you are dealing with is a thriving industry. People are making lucrative livings off of selling conspiracy theories to the public. What happened to the truth? Hell, it got lost under a lot of dollar signs. No one wants to hear what really happened because it would be the end of their very profitable little business."[48]

There are, however, researchers who sincerely believe they are seeking the truth, and others who hold on to the concept of a conspiracy with an almost religious fervor. The ready acceptance of a conspiracy by most Americans, though few have bothered to read the Warren Report, does not surprise those who study the phenomenon. Historian Henry Steele Commager said, "I do think there has come up in recent years . . . something that might be called a conspiracy psychology. A feeling that great events can't be explained by ordinary processes. . . . We are on the road to a paranoid explanation of things. . . . The conspiracy theory, the conspiracy mentality, will not accept ordinary evidence. . . . There's some psychological requirement that forces them to reject the ordinary, and find refuge in the extraordinary."[49]

William Manchester, historian and author of *Death of a Presi-*

---

* Oliver Stone used Larry Howard, the director of the Dallas center, as a consultant on *JFK*. Howard and the center received $80,000.

dent, said, "Those who desperately want to believe that President Kennedy was the victim of a conspiracy have my sympathy. I share their yearning. To employ what may seem an odd metaphor, there is an esthetic principle here. If you put six million dead Jews on one side of a scale and on the other side put the Nazi regime—the greatest gang of criminals ever to seize control of a modern state—you have a rough balance: greatest crime, greatest criminals.

"But if you put the murdered President of the United States on one side of a scale and that wretched waif Oswald on the other side, it doesn't balance. You want to add something weightier to Oswald. It would invest the President's death with meaning, endowing him with martyrdom. He would have died for something.

"A conspiracy would, of course, do the job nicely. Unfortunately, there is no evidence whatever that there was one."[50]

The decision to release the remaining JFK files from federal agencies is not likely to resolve the issue for those committed to believing that Kennedy was killed as the result of a conspiracy. "I know everything in those files," G. Robert Blakey told the author, "and there is no smoking gun in there. People who expect major revelations will be disappointed. Everything of importance got into our report."[51] As the critics dissected the Warren Commission documents looking for small contradictions or unanswered questions, they will pore over the hundreds of thousands of pages due for release. Over ten conspiracy books followed on the heels of Stone's *JFK*. After the remaining federal files are released, a slew of books will probably follow, each focusing upon "new" evidence, further removing the facts from the real story. Oswald is likely to become a footnote to the ever-widening theories fueled by fresh documents.

The search for a darker truth than the lone assassin seems unquenchable. The desire to find a conspiracy in the Kennedy assassination will continue to be answered for years by more "confessions," witnesses who change their testimony to recall disturbing events, the appearance of papers of dubious authenticity, and by writers and researchers who present cases of guilt by association supported by rumor and innuendo. But for those seeking the truth, the facts are incontrovertible. They can be tested against credible testimony, documents, and the latest scientific advances. Chasing shadows on the grassy knoll will never substitute for real history. Lee Harvey Oswald, driven by his own twisted and impenetrable furies, was the only assassin at Dealey Plaza on November 22, 1963. To say otherwise, in light of the overwhelming evidence, is to absolve a man with blood on his hands, and to mock the President he killed.

THE BALLISTICS
OF ASSASSINATION

One man, acting alone, killed the President. That was the Warren Commission's conclusion in 1964. Ever since, the technical plausibility of such marksmanship has been under attack. Did Oswald have the skill? Enough time? Could one bullet have so extensively wounded both Kennedy and Connally? Today, the ballistics can be subjected to advances in computer analysis. By tracking the trajectories of the shots in reverse from the wounds, the source of the shots can be determined with precision. The following graphics are based on forensic evidence analyzed by these new techniques, using timing from the frames of the now-famous 8mm film of the assassination taken by Abraham Zapruder. The crucial seconds in Dealey Plaza are reconstructed, step by step. Then Oswald's escape from the Texas School Book Depository is plotted from eyewitness accounts.

This is the single bullet that wounded both JFK and Connally

ACTUAL SIZE

End view

Graphics by John Grimwade   Edited by Clive Irving   Research by Joyce Pendola

MARKSMANSHIP

Did Oswald have time to fire three shots? Enhancements of the Zapruder film lead to the answer. His first shot missed. He had at least 3 seconds to reload, aim, and fire the second shot, which hit both Kennedy and Connally. He then had another 5 seconds—ample time—for the third shot, which killed the President.

Bolt Action

The bolt action can easily be executed in a fraction of a second.

1. Push bolt up... **2.** Pull back (to eject case and position next cartridge)...
3. Push forward... **4.** Push down (to lock bolt).

The Gunsight

Through the 4X telescopic sight, the target filled Oswald's vision. The President appeared to be only about 25 yards away at the time of the third shot.

4 rounds in a six-bullet clip

The Ammunition

The rifle fired 6.5mm full-metal-jacketed bullets with a muzzle velocity of over 2,000 feet per second.

The Gun

Oswald's Italian World War II Mannlicher-Carcano was purchased from a mail-order house in Chicago. The rifle cost $12.78, the 4X telescopic sight $7.17. In the Marines, Oswald was proficient with an M-1 rifle at distances of up to 200 yards—without the benefit of a telescopic sight. He had practiced to become equally effective with the Mannlicher-Carcano. The sling, adapted from the belt of a Navy pistol holster, provided additional steadiness. A brown bag, 3 inches longer than the disassembled rifle, was found in the sniper's nest.

The Sniper's Nest

Oswald's exact stance when shooting is not known. The top of one cardboard box had a fresh palm print, and another, a slight crease where the rifle (weighing 8 pounds) rested when firing. Three empty cartridge cases were found on the floor. From Oswald's sixth-floor position, the motorcade would have been within his chosen and optimum field of fire along Elm Street for about 15 seconds.

Left index finger and right palm prints on paper bag

Book cartons

Right palm print

Right index fingerprint

Book cartons

Left palm print on corner of box

Partially open window

Right palm print on end of wooden stock

Crease in box

Right middle and right ring fingerprints on trigger guard

Three cartridge cases found on floor

N

THE THREE SHOTS

The first of Oswald's three shots missed. The origin of the second and third shots is established by the projection of the cones (right). The 120-degree turn from Houston Street onto Elm Street slowed the motorcade to under 10 mph. In Oswald's line of fire the President was a simple shot.

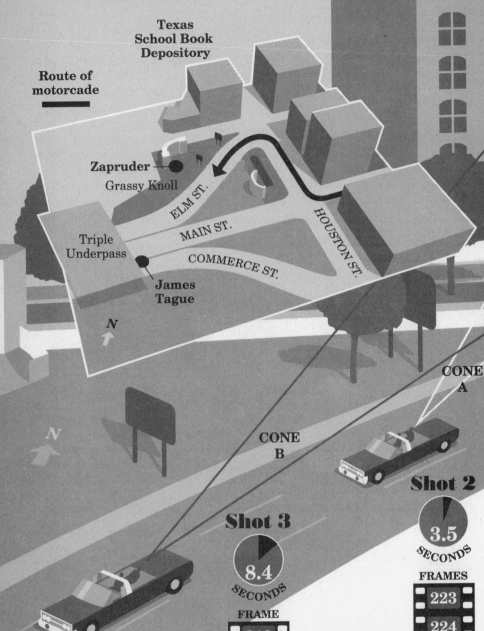

Texas School Book Depository

Route of motorcade

Zapruder
Grassy Knoll

ELM ST.

MAIN ST.

Triple Underpass

COMMERCE ST.

HOUSTON ST.

James Tague

N

N

CONE A

CONE B

Shot 2
3.5 SECONDS

FRAMES
223
224

Shot 3
8.4 SECONDS

FRAME
313

Oswald's
sniper's
nest

The "Cones"

Using computer enhancements of
the Zapruder film, Failure
Analysis Associates calculated the
trajectories of the two bullets that
struck their target. They fixed the
position of the limousine and the
postures of Kennedy and Connally
at the precise moments of impact.
Working backward and allowing
for a margin of error, a computer
then calculated a line through the
entry and exit wounds. The
trajectory could then be splayed
into a "cone." Cone A shows the
origin of the second shot, and
Cone B of the third shot.

The First Shot

During the first shot (dotted line) there
were oak trees and a traffic-light support
post between Oswald and Elm Street.
That shot was almost certainly deflected
by a branch, and its only trace was a nick
made on a concrete curb near the Triple
Underpass. A chip of concrete from that
shot cut James Tague on the cheek.

Shot 1

0

SECONDS

FRAMES

160

to

166

The Zapruder frames

The moments of impact of
Oswald's second and third
shots can be established by analyzing
frames of the Zapruder film. The second
shot (Cone A) hit both the President and
Governor Connally just as their limousine
emerged into Zapruder's view from behind
a freeway sign. Careful analysis points to
the impact of Oswald's second shot at
frames 223–224. The third shot (Cone B),
in full view of Zapruder, hit Kennedy in
the back of his head at frame 313.

THE SINGLE BULLET

Oswald's second shot, the first to strike, is the most contentious. It is variously called the "magic" or "pristine" bullet by conspiracy theorists, who contend that no single bullet could have so seriously wounded both men. The bullet needed no magic and was not pristine. Its trajectory, based on the Failure Analysis computations and the Zapruder film, is reconstructed here.

BULLET SPEED
1,700–1,800 feet per second

KENNEDY

Entry wound
in the back
6.5 mm in diameter

Exit wound
in throat

Bullet tumbling

Bullet grazed tip of
a vertebra in the neck,
slightly splintering the bone.

Cavity momentarily
caused by bullet's
passage

By frame 226 the President began to show a neurological reflex—known as the Thorburn position—to spinal injury. His arms jerked up to a fixed position, hands nearly at his chin, elbows pushed out.

FRAME

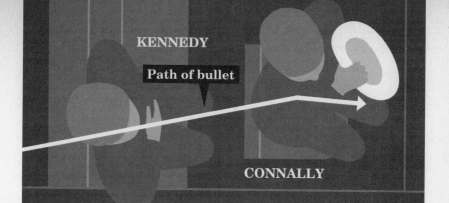

KENNEDY

Path of bullet

CONNALLY

View from above

The trajectory, plotted in accordance with the exact postures of both men, was not significantly altered until the bullet was slightly deflected by Connally's rib.

CONNALLY

Entry wound in right shoulder was 1¼" long—the exact length of the bullet—indicating the bullet was tumbling end over end.

1,500–1,600 feet per second

Exit wound below the right nipple was large—nearly 2" in diameter—and ragged; the bullet was still tumbling.

Stetson hat

Traverses chest and shatters fifth right rib.

900 feet per second

Entry wound at top of right wrist was ragged and irregular. The bullet, now traveling backward, fractured the radius bone.

When the bullet came to rest in Connally's left thigh, having lost more than 80 percent of its velocity, it was just able to penetrate skin.

400 feet per second

THE ESCAPE

Oswald came very close to being captured as he fled from the Book Depository. But within 3 minutes after his final shot, he walked, unmolested, out of the front entrance, while the rear was guarded.

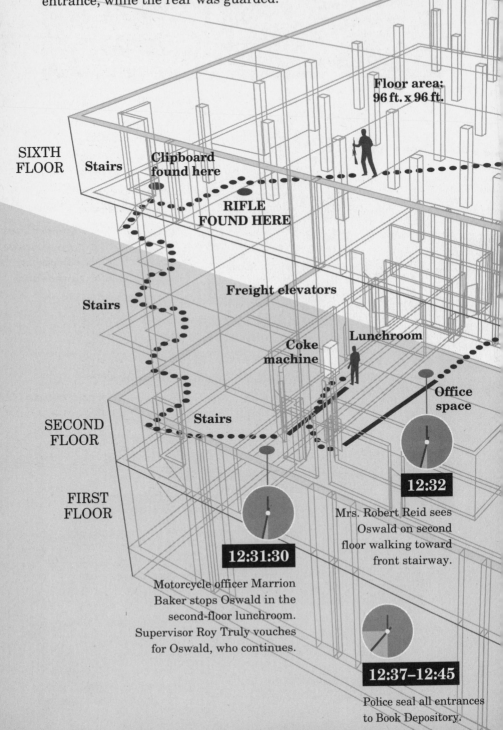

Floor area: 96 ft. x 96 ft.

SIXTH FLOOR

Stairs

Clipboard found here

RIFLE FOUND HERE

Stairs

Freight elevators

Lunchroom

Coke machine

Office space

SECOND FLOOR

Stairs

12:32

Mrs. Robert Reid sees Oswald on second floor walking toward front stairway.

FIRST FLOOR

12:31:30

Motorcycle officer Marrion Baker stops Oswald in the second-floor lunchroom. Supervisor Roy Truly vouches for Oswald, who continues.

12:37–12:45

Police seal all entrances to Book Depository.

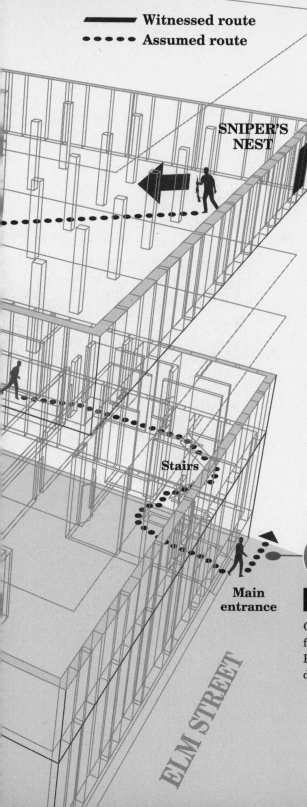

Witnessed route

⋯⋯ Assumed route

SNIPER'S NEST

Stairs

Main entrance

ELM STREET

12:30

Oswald shoots JFK.

12:36

Sergeant D.V. Harkness, relying on eyewitnesses, cites Book Depository as possible sniper's nest.

12:45

Police radio a description of suspect based on the account of witness Howard Brennan.

12:33

Oswald leaves via Elm Street front entrance, meets Robert MacNeil (of NBC), directs him to a phone.

THE SINGLE BULLET TESTED

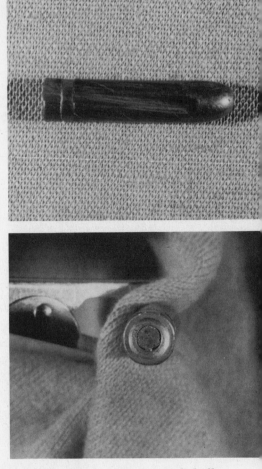

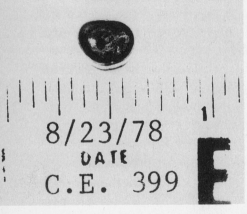

Left: A side and rear view of Warren Commission Exhibit 399, the single bullet that wounded President Kennedy through his neck as well as inflicting all of Governor Connally's injuries.

Right: The bullet (also shown in side and rear views) from a 1992 reconstruction done by Failure Analysis Associates. In that test, the bullet's charge was reduced so it would strike a cadaver's wrist at 1100 feet per second, approximating the speed of CE 399 when it struck Governor Connally's wrist. Emerging in even better condition than 399, it provided the final physical evidence necessary to prove the single-bullet theory.

(National Archives and Failure Analysis Associates)

APPENDIX B

The Non-Mysterious "Mystery Deaths"

Penn Jones, former editor of the Texas weekly *Midlothian Mirror*, originated the popular theory that witnesses to the Kennedy assassination who knew too much were being silenced by an unidentified murder squad. Jones, who believes there were nine assassins at Dealey Plaza, is the author of four self-published books on the case. By 1967, he had compiled a list of eighteen people connected to the assassination who had suffered unnatural deaths. Initially, *The London Sunday Times* used Jones's list of eighteen to conclude that the odds against them being dead through foul play within three years of the assassination was one hundred thousand trillion to one.[1] But *The Times* had not taken into account the huge number of people included in the Warren Commission investigation and discovered, after publishing its first edition, that its calculation of the odds was "a careless journalistic mistake."[2] Although it almost immediately issued a retraction, critics often cite the original, incorrect figure.* And Jones continued to expand his list. By 1983, he said there were "over 100 murders, suicides, and mysterious deaths, the strange fate of those who saw Kennedy shot."[3] Sylvia Meagher, in *Accessories After the Fact*, concluded that "the witnesses ap-

---

* In the eighteen names Jones provided the newspaper, he had included Lee Oswald, J. D. Tippit, Jack Ruby, and David Ferrie among the material witnesses (HSCA Vol. IV, pp. 464–65).

pear to be dying like flies."[4] In *Crossfire*, one of two books upon which the movie *JFK* was based, author Jim Marrs provided the most comprehensive list. He named 103 mystery deaths.[5]* In 1991, when NBC's *Today* show ran a week of segments on Oliver Stone's *JFK*, it concluded by scrolling dozens of names from Marrs's mystery list on the screen, accompanied by somber music.

Marrs's figure is culled from among more than 10,000 people who were connected in any way to the Warren Commission investigation, the House Select Committee during the late 1970s, press coverage of the case, and the network of private citizens who are full-time assassination researchers. It would be surprising if 101 people out of some 10,000 had not died in unnatural ways. Yet upon closer inspection, most of the 101 did not even die mysteriously.

No major writer or investigator on the case—even those trying to expose dangerous conspiracies—has died an unusual death. All of the earliest critics, like Mark Lane, Edward Epstein, Harold Weisberg, David Lifton, Josiah Thompson, and Mary Ferrell, are alive and well. Even Penn Jones, who first published information about the deaths, was never bothered and is now seventy-eight years old. No one tried to eliminate Jim Garrison or any of his staff during their judicial probe, nor was Oliver Stone bothered when he "exposed" the government and sanctified Garrison. The key witnesses who claimed to see a second gunman at Dealey Plaza—Jean Hill, Malcolm Summers, Gordon Arnold, and Ed Hoffman—are all alive. Fundamental

---

* Actually there are only 101. Marrs lists Teresa Norton as a Ruby employee, and says she was "fatally shot" in August 1964. He also lists Karen "Little Lynn" Carlin, another Ruby employee, as being a "gunshot victim" in 1966. Teresa Norton was another name used by Karen Carlin—they are the same person. Sylvia Meagher, Robert Sam Anson, and David Scheim all reported that Carlin died in August 1964 in a Houston hotel fire. But there is no record of such a fire, much less a death certificate. Moreover, Carlin testified a second time to the Warren Commission on August 24, 1964, after the date she was supposed to have died. Marrs provides no citation for the 1966 date, and does not list a location, month, or day. Until there is proof of her death, Marrs's list of 103 must be reduced by two. (A woman purporting to be Karen Carlin contacted conspiracy theorist J. Gary Shaw in 1992 and told an intricate story of conspiracy. There is no substantiation yet that the 1992 woman is the real Carlin.)

conspiracy witnesses like Beverly Oliver, who linked Ruby and Oswald, and others like Delphine Roberts, who tied Oswald to Guy Banister and David Ferrie, are still living. Almost thirty men named as the "second shooter" by conspiracy buffs are alive. Frank Ragano, sixty-nine years old, has reportedly sold his manuscript that says he passed the "hit" from Hoffa to Marcello and Trafficante. Carlos Marcello, the New Orleans crime boss who some say carried out an assassination contract for the CIA, enjoyed his retirement until his natural death in 1993, at the age of eighty-three.

What are the causes of death that apparently qualify for the mystery list? And how soon after the assassination were the victims disposed of?

Over half, 53 of the 101, actually died of natural causes—heart attacks (24), cancer (14), complications from surgery (1), and other quite ordinary causes of death, ranging from pneumonia to aneurysms to strokes, with heart failure often listed in a newspaper obituary as the official cause of death (14).[6]

It would seem necessary that key "witnesses" to conspiracy be eliminated as soon as possible after the assassination, yet the list covers more than two decades. The last death is that of Roy Kellerman, the Secret Service agent in charge of JFK's limousine. He died of heart failure at the age of sixty-nine in 1984, twenty-one years after the assassination—Marrs lists the cause of death as "unknown."[7] Fifty-one of the 101 did not die until the 1970s, well over a decade after the assassination. As might be expected, more than 60 percent of the post-1970s victims died of old age and natural causes (ages, when available from records, are provided in the entries below). Only 14 of the 101 died within a year of the assassination.

Most of the 101 have nothing but the most tenuous connection to the case. In many instances, the persons listed were strong believers in Oswald's guilt, which should have assured their survival—at least from murder by conspirators.

The Natural Deaths

1964

• C. D. Jackson (heart attack)—his only connection to the case was that he was the *Life* magazine executive who decided to purchase the Zapruder film.

• Bill Chesher (heart attack) was unconnected to the case, but Penn Jones later claimed, without giving supporting evidence, to have a reliable source who asserted that Chesher could link Oswald and Ruby.

• Guy Banister (heart attack) was the New Orleans private investigator repeatedly and incorrectly linked to Oswald. Marrs writes that Banister was the "ex–FBI agent in New Orleans connected to Ferrie, CIA, Carlos Marcello, and Oswald."

1965

• Paul Mandel (lung cancer) was a *Life* reporter who wrote a single article on the assassination.

• David Goldstein (heart attack) is listed by Marrs as a "Dallasite who helped FBI trace Oswald's pistol."[8] Actually, Goldstein was simply the owner of a Dallas gun shop, Dave's House of Guns. He supplied a half-page affidavit, as did every other Dallas gun-store owner, that he did not sell a Smith and Wesson .38-caliber revolver, serial number 65248, the gun Oswald used to kill Tippit.[9]

• Mrs. Earl Smith (heart failure) had nothing to do with the Kennedy case. She is listed solely because she was a friend of Dorothy Kilgallen, a syndicated columnist who wrote about the Ruby trial (see pg. 494).

• Tom Howard (heart attack) was one of Jack Ruby's defense attorneys. "He had a history of heart disease," says assistant district attorney Bill Alexander.* "He had a heart attack several years earlier, and was a heavy drinker."

---

* Bill Alexander, who prosecuted Ruby, was familiar with everyone connected to the Ruby trial. The author asked him to comment on the Ruby-related deaths, and he is quoted whenever they appear.

1966

• Hank Suydam (heart attack) was a *Life* editor who worked on a couple of the Kennedy articles.

• Earlene Roberts (heart failure and pneumonia) had a history of heart disease. She was the cleaning woman at 1026 North Beckley and saw Oswald near 1:00 P.M. on the day of the assassination.

• Dallas police captain Frank Martin (cancer). Marrs writes that Martin witnessed Oswald's murder and told the Warren Commission, "There's a lot to be said but probably be better if I don't say it."[10] In almost the next sentence Martin told the Commission what he was withholding, that the police were not experienced in handling a prisoner like Oswald, and he was critical there "was no organization at all."[11]

• Judge Joe Brown (heart attack) was the presiding judge in the Ruby trial. "Brown never exercised," Bill Alexander recalls, "ate like a hog, and panted when he walked—some mystery death."

• Clarence Oliver (heart attack) is listed by Marrs as "D.A. investigator who worked Ruby case" and cause of death is "unknown."[12] "What hogwash," says Alexander. "Oliver had come to the DA's office from the police in the late 1950s, and he was in the office when the Ruby trial took place, but he did not work any part of it. The only thing he knew about the Ruby investigation was what he read in the newspapers. And as for the 'unknown' listing—hell, there's a death certificate for him on file, and he had a series of heart attacks before his final one."

1967

• Jack Ruby (blood clot). Marrs says "He [Ruby] told his family he was injected with cancer cells."[13] That is medically impossible. Ruby was deranged at the end of his life and believed not only that he was being killed by injections, but also that 25 million Jews were being slaughtered on the jail floor below him.

• Jimmy Levens (cancer) was a Fort Worth nightclub owner who casually knew Ruby and had no other connection to the case.

• Harold Russell (heart failure) supplied an affidavit to the FBI, which was made part of the Warren Commission volumes, saying that he saw Oswald fleeing the scene of the Tippit murder.[14] He had no involvement in the case thereafter. Marrs says he was "killed by cop in bar brawl."[15] Actually, Russell was in a fight at a party in Oklahoma when he was struck and subdued by police who arrived at the scene. He died of heart failure several hours later, at a local hospital.

1968

• Dallas County deputy sheriff Hiram Ingram (cancer) had no association to the case. He is only listed because he was a friend of Roger Craig, the deputy sheriff who told the elaborate tale about a phantom getaway car at Dealey Plaza.

• Dr. Nicholas Chetta (heart attack) was the New Orleans coroner who performed the autopsy on David Ferrie. His finding of a berry aneurysm has been confirmed by subsequent forensic pathologists.

• A. D. Bowie (cancer) is listed by Marrs as the "assistant D.A. prosecuting Ruby." "Wade had him sit at the table during the trial, but there was no reason for him to do that since he knew nothing about the case or the testimony," Bill Alexander recalls. "He died before he was forty, when a lump the size of an egg came up under his armpit—he had cancer of the lymph glands and went fast."

1969

• Charles Mentesana (heart attack) was one of several news cameramen who filmed Lt. Carl Day carrying the Carcano rifle out of the Book Depository.

• Mary Bledsoe (heart attack) was Oswald's landlady for one week in Dallas and was on the bus he boarded after the assassination. Her testimony helped prove he was in flight after the shooting, certainly not someone the conspirators would apparently kill at the age of seventy-two, six years after the assassination.

1970

• Abraham Zapruder (complications from heart disease) took the most famous home movie of the assassination. He sold the film to *Life* magazine and was uninvolved in the investigation.
• Bill Decker (cancer), the Dallas sheriff in 1963.

1971

• Charles Cabell (heart attack), deputy director of the CIA, was no longer with the Agency at the time of the assassination. Marrs says only that he "collapsed and died after physical at Fort Meyers."[16]
• Clayton Fowler (heart attack) was one of Ruby's defense attorneys. Marrs marks the cause of death as "unknown."[17] "That's crazy," says Bill Alexander. "Fowler was a World War II fighter pilot who had lost a piece of his leg below the knee. Almost every year they had to cut off a bit more gangrenous tissue. They called him Red because he drank too much and his face looked like a baboon's ass. He had high blood pressure, bad circulation, and arteriosclerosis."

1972

• J. Edgar Hoover (heart attack, age seventy-seven), director of the FBI.[18]

1974

• Clay Shaw (cancer) was the victim of Garrison's abuse of process. Marrs lists the death only as "possible cancer," despite the unambiguous death certificate and statements from his treating physicians.
• Earl Warren (heart failure, age eighty-two) was Supreme Court chief justice and chairman of the Warren Commission.
• Earle Cabell (heart disease) was the mayor of Dallas in 1963; his only connection was that he was in one of the motorcade cars.

1975

• Allan Sweatt (heart disease) was a Dallas deputy sheriff who had worked briefly on the case.

• Clyde Tolson (heart disease, age seventy-one) was J. Edgar Hoover's chief assistant.[19]

• Earl Wheeler (heart failure, age sixty-seven) was a liaison between the CIA and JFK, but had no connection to the case.[20]

1976

• Dr. Charles Gregory (heart attack) was one of the surgeons who operated on Governor John Connally. Gregory's medical testimony was some of the most important supporting the Warren Commission and the single bullet.

• Ralph Paul (heart attack) was Jack Ruby's business partner in his nightclubs and spoke frequently with Ruby during the weekend of the assassination. Knowing Ruby was his only affiliation with the case.

• James Chaney (heart attack) was part of the motorcade's motorcycle escort—none of the other escort policemen are listed.

• William Harvey (complications from heart surgery, age sixty), dubbed "America's James Bond," was a CIA official who knew of the attempts to kill Castro but had no relation to the Oswald file.

1977

• Ken O'Donnell (aneurysm and liver complications) was one of JFK's aides and was in the car behind the President in the motorcade. After his Warren Commission testimony, he had no connection with the case.[21]

• Paul Raigorodsky (heart disease) had no relation to the assassination. The only reason he seems to be on the mystery-deaths list is that he was a business acquaintance of George de Mohrenschildt, Oswald's Dallas friend.

• Louis Nichols (heart disease and cancer, age seventy-one), a former FBI official, had briefly worked on the case.[22]

• Alan Belmont (cancer, age seventy) was a retired FBI official who provided a general overview of the Bureau's investigation to the Warren Commission.[23]

• Donald Kaylor (heart attack) was a chemist in the FBI's fingerprint section, with no specific assignment to the Kennedy case.

• J. M. English (heart attack) was former director of the FBI Forensic Sciences Laboratory.

1978

• Garland Slack (heart disease) was one of several witnesses who mistakenly identified a man at a Dallas shooting range as Oswald. He was not involved in the case after making his 1964 statement.

• C. L. Lewis (cancer) was one of the dozens of Dallas deputy sheriffs who worked on the case.

1979

• Billy Lovelady (heart attack) was the Book Depository employee photographed in the building's doorway during the assassination and mistaken by many buffs for Oswald.

1980

• Jesse Curry (heart attack), the Dallas police chief.

• Dr. John Holbrook (heart attack), a psychiatrist, was a prosecution witness at the Ruby trial, testifying that Ruby was not insane at the moment he shot Oswald. "He supported the Warren Commission case," says Bill Alexander. "These fellows [the buffs] are getting their sides mixed up in who is supposed to be getting knocked off."

1981

• Marguerite Oswald (cancer, age seventy-three), Lee's mother.[24] Immediately after her son's arrest she hired Mark

Lane to represent her, and over the years she gave and sold dozens of press interviews about many aspects of the case.

• Frank Watts (cancer, age eighty-three) was the chief felony prosecutor for the Dallas district attorney. "He was in his eighties, for God's sake," Alexander remarks. "He had nothing to do with Ruby. He sat at the table with us during the trial and did not question one witness."

1982

• Peter Gregory (heart failure) was a member of the conservative Russian émigré community in Dallas and one of those who first befriended Oswald after his return from Russia. He testified before the Warren Commission but had no involvement with the investigation after his testimony.

• Dr. James Weston (heart attack) was a pathologist who examined the JFK autopsy X rays and photos for the House Select Committee. Marrs himself writes he "died while jogging, ruled natural causes."[25] Weston was one of nine forensic pathologists on the Select Committee's medical panel and was in the majority of eight who confirmed the medical findings of the Warren Commission. All of the other doctors are still alive at this writing—and perhaps the surprise survivor (from Marrs's point of view) is Cyril Wecht, who for twenty years has led a vocal one-man campaign to prove medically that the assassination is a conspiracy. Wecht is alive and well and is the medical examiner for Allegheny County, Pennsylvania.

• Will Griffin (cancer) was an FBI agent who was one of scores assigned to taking witness statements for the Warren Commission in 1963 and 1964.

• W. Marvin Gheesling (heart failure) was an FBI official who had a minor supervisory role in the 1964 investigation.

1984

• Roy Kellerman (heart failure, age sixty-nine) was a Secret Service agent in the presidential motorcade.[26] He was retired and living in Florida when, Marrs says, he died of "unknown" causes. His death and its cause were actually reported in numerous newspapers.

The Unnatural Deaths

While the fifty-three listed above died of natural causes, the following forty-eight died unnatural deaths. Who were they and why are they on the mystery-deaths list?

1963

• Karen Kupcinet (murdered in Los Angeles two days after the assassination) was the daughter of a Chicago television host. According to Penn Jones, unidentified sources reported that she screamed into the telephone, before the assassination, that the President was going to be killed. There is no corroboration for the report, yet Marrs still begins his list with her death.

• Also, according to Penn Jones, Jack Zangetty (Marrs lists it as Zangretti; murdered) was the manager of a motel complex in Oklahoma. Jones asserts that Zangetty told friends about three assassins scheduled to kill JFK, that Ruby would kill Oswald, and that the Sinatra family was involved. There is no support for Jones's claim, and the author could find no record of such a death.

1964

• DeLesseps Morrison (plane crash) was the mayor of New Orleans during 1963. He had no association to the case.

• Hugh Ward (same plane crash as Morrison) was a private investigator who was also unconnected to the case. He probably qualifies for the list since he was acquainted (because they had the same profession) with Guy Banister.

• Betty MacDonald (suicide) had worked for Jack Ruby, and was an alibi for Darrell Garner in the shooting of Warren Reynolds (see Chapter 12).

• Hank Killiam (murdered) was the husband of a Ruby employee. He also reportedly knew a fellow roomer at Oswald's Beckley Street boardinghouse.

• Dr. Mary Sherman (house fire) had no connection to the case, though she was acquainted with David Ferrie. Marrs says she was "possibly shot." According to the medical records, she was killed in an accidental fire, and there was no gunshot wound on her body.

• Bill Hunter (accidental shooting) and

• Jim Koethe (murdered). Both were reporters who had stopped by Ruby's apartment on November 24, 1963, after the shooting of Oswald. There, they spoke to one of Ruby's attorneys, Tom Howard, Ruby's roommate, George Senator, and a friend of his, Jim Martin. That was the extent of their association with the case. Both wrote about the November 24 visit and described it innocuously. Hunter was killed in California when someone dropped a pistol and it accidentally discharged. The Dallas police believed Koethe's murder was the result of a fight with a gay lover.[27]

• Eddy Benavides (murdered) was the brother of Domingo Benavides, one of thirteen witnesses who placed Oswald at the Tippit murder scene. But Eddy had nothing to do with case. Domingo's Warren Commission testimony was important in identifying Oswald as the murderer of J. D. Tippit. Domingo has continued to give interviews and is alive and well.

• Gary Underhill (suicide) was, according to Penn Jones, a CIA agent who claimed the CIA was involved in JFK's death. The evidence that Underhill was an agent is from an undisclosed source known only to Jones, and there is no corroboration that he ever said that there was CIA complicity in the assassination.

• Mary Meyer (murdered) was allegedly one of JFK's mistresses. Except for her reported liaison with the President, she was not associated with any aspect of the case.

1965

• Maurice Gatlin (injuries from a fall) was a pilot who is probably on the list because he was once hired by Guy Banister for an unconnected investigation.

• Dorothy Kilgallen (drug and alcohol overdose) was a nationally syndicated reporter. Marrs claims she "had private interview with Ruby" and was going to break open the case.[28] Her "private" interview with Ruby was when she spoke to him for a few minutes during a recess in the courtroom during his trial, surrounded by other reporters.[29] There was no scoop pending by the time Kilgallen drank herself to death.

• Rose Cheramie (struck by car) was the heroin addict who was mistakenly said to have foreknowledge of the assassination. She made up her story *after* Ruby had shot Oswald (see Chapter 18).

• Mona Saenz (struck by a Dallas bus) worked at the Texas Employment Commission where Oswald had applied for work while living in Dallas.

• William Whaley (car accident) was the Dallas cabdriver who drove Oswald from the bus station to Oak Cliff immediately after the assassination. Marrs lists under cause of death "the only Dallas taxi driver to die on duty." Whaley had a head-on collision, in which his taxi passenger was critically injured, when the eighty-three-year-old driver of the other auto had a fatal heart attack and lost control of his car.

1966

• Marilyn "Delilah" Walle (shot to death by her husband) was a former Ruby employee.

• Lee Bowers (car accident) was in the train switching station at Dealey Plaza and testified to seeing "some commotion" near the picket fence. Bowers told his story not only to the Warren Commission but also to Mark Lane for his book and film documentary.*

• Albert Bogard (suicide) was the Dallas car salesman who claimed Oswald had test-driven a car with him, although none of his co-workers supported the story. He was fired shortly after he told the story and had no other relationship to the case.

---

* Since Bowers's car drove off the highway into a concrete abutment, there was suspicion he might have been forced off the road. Researcher David Perry, in "The Lee Bowers Story," (published in the *Third Decade*, an assassination newsletter), conclusively proved that Bowers's death was accidental.

• James Worrell (car accident) was a Dealey Plaza witness who testified in detail about the Carcano rifle he saw fire the shots from the southeast corner of the sixth floor of the Book Depository.[30] His testimony supports the Warren Commission conclusion about the location of the assassin.

• William Pitzer (suicide) was a naval lieutenant commander who Marrs identifies as the "JFK autopsy photographer."[31] A friend of Pitzer's claims he was in the autopsy-room gallery at Bethesda filming the event with a home movie camera, but no one at the autopsy remembers him. He is not on the official list of those present. His purported film has never been produced. The story was exploited by Robert Groden and Harrison Livingstone in *High Treason*, and Marrs picked it up for his mystery-deaths list.

1967

• Eladio Del Valle (murdered) was an anti-Castro militant killed in Florida. He was warned shortly before his death that a murder contract was put on his head by Castro agents. Garrison wanted to question him as part of his anti-Castro investigation.

• David Ferrie (brain aneurysm) was mistakenly and repeatedly linked to Oswald. Marrs lists the cause of death for the eccentric adventurer as "blow to neck, ruled accidental." The coroner's report and death certificate show it was an aneurysm, with no foul play involved.

• Leonard Pullin (car crash) was a civilian employee in the Navy who helped film the assassination documentary *The Last Two Days*. He was a cameraman, not a reporter, and never claimed to have any special information.

1968

• Philip Geraci (accidental electrocution) was the fifteen-year-old youngster who spoke to Oswald at Carlos Bringuier's store in New Orleans when Oswald tried to infiltrate the anti-Castro movement.

1969

• Clyde Johnson (murdered in personal dispute) was considered and rejected as a witness in Clay Shaw's trial. Johnson, who claimed he could put Shaw and Oswald together, was so unreliable that not even Garrison used him. Marrs implies that he was killed before he could testify.[32] The Shaw trial finished on March 1, and Johnson was not killed until July.

• John Crawford (plane crash) was, according to Marrs, a "close friend to both Ruby and Wesley [Buell] Frazier, who gave ride to Oswald on 11/22/63."[33] When Frazier was asked about Crawford, he had never heard the name.[34] In Ruby's personal papers there is no evidence he knew Crawford. The story was apparently started by Penn Jones.

• Buddy Walthers (gunshot) was a Dallas deputy sheriff who helped search Dealey Plaza the day of the assassination. He was shot and killed when he and his partner, Al Maddox, tried to arrest a fugitive, James Walter Cherry.

• Henry Delaune (murdered) had no relationship to the case, but is evidently listed because he was the brother-in-law of the New Orleans coroner, Nicholas Chetta, who ruled on David Ferrie's death.

1970

• George McGann (murdered) was head of the Dixie mafia, and while he had no connection to the assassination, he is listed because of his marriage to Beverly Oliver, the woman who now claims she was the "babushka lady" at Dealey Plaza.

• Salvatore Granello (murdered) was a mobster who was linked to the CIA plot to kill Castro.*

• Darrell Garner (drug overdose) was a business rival suspected of shooting Warren Reynolds, a witness to Oswald flee-

---

* Granello is one of three mobsters listed only because they had some association with the CIA-sponsored effort to kill Castro in the early 1960s. As Select Committee chief counsel G. Robert Blakey, said: "It's established beyond all reasonable doubt that the Cubans were connected to the mob, and the mob was connected to the CIA, but the President they were planning to assassinate was Castro, not Kennedy."

ing the scene of the Tippit murder. Garner had no relation to the assassination investigation, and he is evidently listed only because he was the prime suspect in the wounding of a man who also happened, coincidentally, to be a witness in the Kennedy case (see Chapter 12).

1971

• James Plumeri (murdered) was another gangster who was part of the CIA effort to kill Castro.

1972

• Hale Boggs (plane crash) was the House majority leader and former Warren Commission member. As with many people on the list, it is not clear why he qualifies. Since he was supposedly a member of the "Warren Commission cover-up," any team of assassins eliminating dangerous witnesses would be expected to let Boggs live.

1973

• Thomas Davis (electrocuted while cutting a power line during a robbery) was a convicted bank robber who may have run guns to Cuba during the 1950s. He also knew Ruby.

1974

• Dave Yaras (murdered) grew up in Chicago with Ruby and was later a local hoodlum. Ruby had only sporadic contact with him over fifteen years, and none during 1963.

• Joseph Milteer (died from injuries suffered from a heater explosion) was a right-winger in Miami who told a police informant in November 1963 that Kennedy would be killed when he came to Miami (November 18, only days before his Texas trip). For a time, critics claimed Milteer was identified in one of the photographs taken at Dealey Plaza, but photo analysts for the Select Committee proved it was not him. Beyond his boastful claim in November, there is no link between Milteer and the events in Dallas.

1975

• Sam Giancana (murdered) was the godfather of the Chicago mafia. The thousands of hours of surveillance tapes on Giancana, starting in the late 1950s, show that he knew nothing about the assassination or about any alleged mob plot.

1976

• Johnny Roselli (murdered) was a mafia liaison with the CIA in its effort to assassinate Castro.

1977

• Carlos Soccaras (suicide) had no relationship to the assassination, but he raised money for anti-Castro Cubans.

• William Pawley (suicide, age eighty) was an extremely wealthy adventurer who helped found the Flying Tigers in Asia during World War II and later was U.S. ambassador to Brazil, also holding high positions in the State and Defense departments.[35] He strongly opposed Castro, and solicited American support for the anti-Castro Cubans. He had no association with the assassination.

• George de Mohrenschildt (suicide), Oswald's closest Dallas friend, is included although he gave extensive testimony to the Warren Commission, as well as press interviews in succeeding years.

• Lou Staples (suicide), a former Dallas radio announcer who conducted several radio programs about the assassination, was living in Oklahoma when he killed himself.

• James Cadigan (died of injuries suffered in a fall at his home, at age sixty) and

• William Sullivan (shot accidentally at age sixty-five by a hunter who mistook him for a deer) were both retired FBI employees.[36] Cadigan was a document expert whose involvement with the case ended with his 1964 Warren Commission testimony, and Sullivan was an official later in charge of counterespionage.

• Francis Gary Powers (helicopter crash) was the U-2 pilot shot down over the Soviet Union in 1960. Oswald had been assigned to a U-2 base and was in Russia when Powers was downed.

• Joseph Ayres (shooting accident at a firing range while on vacation with his family) was the chief steward on JFK's *Air Force One*.[37]

Acknowledgments

The goal of this book was to reexamine all the evidence on the JFK assassination. Any of a dozen issues could have been the subject of a separate book, including, among others, Oswald's time in Russia, Jack Ruby's story, or the actual assassination. Although I had studied the subject and conducted preliminary research for several years, the last two, after Random House agreed to be the publisher, were particularly hectic. There are nearly a million pages of government documents on the assassination, two thousand books, and hundreds of researchers and original witnesses connected to the investigation. In addition, considerable time was spent obtaining information about files still classified by the U.S., Russian, and Cuban governments. Much of the research would not have been possible without the help of many people and organizations (some of whom preferred not to be named).

In obtaining documents, I was aided by an excellent staff at the National Archives, particularly Michael McReynolds, director of Textual Reference, and Sue McDonough, archivist; Master Sgt. Tom Pennington, historian of the 89th Military Air Wing; Geir Gunderson, archivist, Gerald Ford Presidential Library; June Payne, researcher, John F. Kennedy Library; Mike Simpson, public affairs officer, Secret Service; Alfredo Murphy, U.S. Department of Justice; Gary Boutwell, Freedom of Information and Privacy Office, FBI; and Cindy Smolovik, archivist, City of

Dallas. A special thank you to both Cynthia Wegmann, Esq., New Orleans, who allowed me to review her father's voluminous papers on the Garrison case, and to Peter Earnest, chief of the CIA's Office of Public and Agency Information, who was always very generous in his assistance.

For help in obtaining information in other countries, I am indebted to Rene Mujica of the Cuban mission to the United States; Yuriy Kobaladze, press bureau chief of the KGB, Moscow; Kravchenko Pyotr Kuzimich, foreign minister, Belorussia; General Dmitri Volkogonov, Moscow; Anatoliy Petrovich Privalov, KGB Veterans of Foreign Espionage, Moscow; Nicholas Vykhodtsev, manager, Alice 24-Hour Information Service, Moscow; Gerald Nadler, *The Washington Times*, Moscow; and Ambassador Akira Sono, Tokyo.

Almost two hundred people were interviewed for this book. While I am grateful to all of them for the time they took to speak with me, a few made an extra effort. Carlos Bringuier clarified the anti-Castro issues as well as the problems in New Orleans in 1963; Dr. John Lattimer and Dr. Michael Baden resolved many persistent medical discrepancies; and Earl Ruby provided valuable insights into his brother Jack.

Yuriy Nosenko, the 1964 KGB defector, is familiar with the KGB's handling of Oswald in Russia. He is living under an assumed name in the United States since his life is still at peril because of a standing KGB death warrant. Only twice before had he agreed to private interviews, and they had not been about Oswald. A journalist from one of the earlier meetings had later disclosed the U.S. state in which Nosenko was living, forcing him to move. Despite the risks in granting another interview, he agreed with the argument of my first letter to him, emphasizing his duty to the historical record. The extended time he spent with me, combined with his recall for details, was more than I originally expected.

Bill Alexander, Esq., was the assistant district attorney in Dallas at the time of the assassination. He was an integral part of the investigation after Oswald's arrest and later prosecuted Jack Ruby for Oswald's murder. He is a significant source of untapped information about the case but has seldom given interviews. I am grateful for the several days he gave me in Dallas, in addition to the many retired Dallas police sources he led me to. His recollections of the assassination weekend helped me better understand many of those about whom I had to write.

Dallas sheriff Jim Bowles made himself and his staff, particularly Jim Ewell and Wilma Snelen, available for days at a time. Sheriff Bowles's crusade to uncover the truth in the assassination's acoustics issues is some of the case's best private research. He shared his work selflessly with me, and I am indebted for his considerable assistance.

Some private corporations aided my many research requests. I am especially thankful to Mary Latham of Itek Optical Systems and Janet Steele of Bell & Howell.

Dr. Robert Piziali, of Failure Analysis Associates, and Dr. Michael West have done some of the most sophisticated computer-enhancement work on the Zapruder film. They not only gave me access to their enhancements and underlying tests, but also patiently guided me through the intricacies of the ballistics issues.

Steve Goldberg, Esq., Los Angeles, was always available with astute legal advice, and Rev. Dave Murph, Dallas, aided with his expertise on Oswald in New Orleans. Jim Moore gave me a useful tour through the Texas School Book Depository and around Dealey Plaza. David Whipple, president of the association of retired intelligence agents, Hamilton Brown, who holds the same position for retired Secret Service agents, and Les Stanford, for Alcohol, Tobacco, and Firearms, were diligent in finding those long retired from their respective agencies.

I owe a special thanks to David Perry, an insurance investigator who has studied the assassination for nearly two decades. He is one of a small number of researchers who approaches the subject in a scholarly manner, attempting to debunk the more outlandish stories while simultaneously seeking the truth in the case. While he may disagree with the conclusions I have reached in this book, he will recognize the benefit of purging many falsehoods that clutter the field. He was unstinting in his assistance, often spending hours on the most arcane requests, ranging from the mystery deaths to the height of the fence on the grassy knoll to 1963 Dallas street maps and the like. He has a fine eye for credible sources and solid information.

Harold Weisberg was one of the earliest critics of the Warren

Report. Using the Freedom of Information Act in many lawsuits, he has obtained thousands of government documents on the case. He told me, "I feel that just because I fought to get these documents released, that is no reason I should not share them with others." He allowed me full run of his basement, filled with file cabinets, and he and his wife, Lil, graciously received both me and my wife, Trisha, at their home for several days. His attitude toward the sharing of information is refreshing, and although I disagree with him about almost every aspect of the case, I thank him for his generosity in the use of his papers and his time.

The same applies to Mary Ferrell, a retired legal secretary in Dallas who has one of the largest private archives on the assassination. She also gave advice and allowed me to review some of her extensive collection when I visited Dallas. Paul Hoch, in Berkeley, California, is the unofficial archivist for the conspiracy press. An academic, with a thorough understanding of the documents in the case, Hoch provided insights that helped me avoid pitfalls in the research. Gus Russo, in Baltimore, Maryland, is a private researcher who was kind to provide many telephone numbers and addresses from his extensive database.

The Assassination Archives and Research Center (AARC) in Washington, D.C., directed by attorney James Lesar, has all the documentation available at the National Archives, but instead of microfilm, everything at the AARC is in an easier format for research—paper copies. There is also an extensive video and photographic library. Members have unlimited use of the center. With annual dues of $25 and a high-speed photocopy machine on the premises, there is no better place for anyone interested in researching the subject.

Charles Schwartz saved me after several computer crashes, as I made the mistake of trying to learn new software while I wrote the first draft of the manuscript. His patience in taking panicked telephone calls at all hours of the night is greatly appreciated. John and Catherine Martin were kind enough to allow my wife and me to be their houseguests on our often unplanned and lengthy research trips to Washington. They always found room for us, and their home was an oasis of peace and quiet.

Pam Bernstein, my agent and friend, has left William Morris to establish her own agency. I miss her sage advice. She helped place this project and negotiate a contract that allowed me to undertake the extensive research. Since her departure, I have been fortunate to be represented by one of the best agents in the business, Owen Laster. His encouragement and guidance were always appreciated.

At Random House, Beth Pearson oversaw the editorial production of the book. Her great enthusiasm for the subject, combined with her keen eye for detail, greatly helped maintain the accuracy of the text. Her efforts and long hours ensured the project met a tight deadline.

Harold Evans, editor in chief of Random House, is a former editor of *The Sunday Times of London* and has a "nose for news." He recognized this was a good story and gave me free rein to do the research and come up with the answers. It is rare that a publisher will commit to a project without specific guarantees from the author about the book's conclusions and the ability of the writer to gather the data. My charge from Random House? Reexamine the evidence and find the truth—a task facilitated by the fact that they did not care if I came back with a book that concluded the Kennedy assassination was a conspiracy or the result of a lone assassin, so long as my work was supported by credible evidence. I am indebted to Harold Evans for that vote of confidence.

My editor, Robert Loomis, has forever spoiled me for any future book because his effort on this one was beyond the ordinary assistance that can be expected from someone who must attend to a dozen manuscripts at a time. He believed in this book from the beginning and championed it at Random House. Our extensive discussions fundamentally affected its organization and tone several times, each for the better. His imprint is evident throughout, and the book's quality is due largely to his commitment and support. There would be no book without his early confidence.

My wife, Trisha, is truly my muse. She is my inspiration at every stage of my work, even enduring my frequent self-doubt when I constantly tormented her with my worries about organizing the masses of information into a solid manuscript by the deadline. She invaluably assists me on each of my projects. Depending on the subject, she endures the daily invasion of figures and trappings from another period. I know she will be happy to no longer live with the shadow of Lee Oswald. There would be no book without her.

Notes

Abbreviations Used for Citations:

WR: Warren Commission Report (Doubleday edition)

WC Vol.: The 26 volumes of Hearings and Exhibits accompanying the Warren Report, referred to by volume and page number

CE: Warren Commission Exhibit

CD: Warren Commission Document

HSCA Rpt.: House Select Committee Report on Assassinations (U.S. Government Printing House edition)

HSCA Vol.: The 12 Kennedy volumes of Hearings and Appendices of the House Select Committee on Assassinations, referred to by volume and page number

1 "WHICH ONE ARE YOU?"

1. Testimony of M. N. McDonald, WC Vol. III, p. 300.
2. See, e.g., testimony of C. T. Walker, p. 39; George Applin, Jr., p. 89; Ray Hawkins, p. 94, WC Vol. VII.
3. Testimony of M. N. McDonald, WC Vol. III, p. 301.
4. Testimony of Gerald Hill, WC Vol. VII, pp. 52, 61.
5. Testimony of Bob Carroll, WC Vol. VII, p. 21.
6. Testimony of C. T. Walker, WC Vol. VII, p. 40.
7. Ibid., pp. 40–41.
8. Testimony of Gerald Hill, WC Vol. VII, p. 58.
9. Ibid.
10. Ibid., p. 59.
11. WR, p. 377; testimony of Marina Oswald, WC Vol. I, pp. 60–61.
12. Jim Marrs, *Crossfire: The Plot That Killed Kennedy* (New York: Carroll & Graf, 1990), p. 92.
13. Anthony Summers, *Conspiracy: The Definitive Book on the J.F.K. Assassination* (New York: Paragon House, 1989), pp. 310–11.

14. Robert Lee Oswald, *Lee: A Portrait of Lee Harvey Oswald* (New York: Coward-McCann, 1967), p. 34.
15. Testimony of Robert Oswald, WC Vol. 1, pp. 315–16.
16. Testimony of John Pic, WC Vol. XI, pp. 33, 78.
17. WR, p. 377.
18. Testimony of Marguerite Oswald, WC Vol. I, p. 255; WR, p. 377.
19. Oswald, op. cit., p. 18.
20. Gerald Ford and John Stiles, *Portrait of the Assassin* (New York: Simon & Schuster, 1965), p. 71.
21. Testimony of Robert Oswald, WC Vol. I, pp. 272–73.
22. WR, p. 671.
23. Testimony of Robert Oswald, WC Vol. I, pp. 277–79.
24. Ibid., p. 280.
25. Testimony of John Pic, WC Vol. XI, p. 27.
26. WR, pp. 672–73.
27. Testimony of Marina Oswald, WC Vol. I, pp. 26–27, 72–73; WR, p. 672.
28. Oswald, op. cit., p. 39.
29. WR, p. 673.
30. Testimony of Philip Eugene Vinson, WC Vol. VIII, p. 77.
31. Ibid.
32. Ibid., p. 79.
33. FBI report of addresses of Lee Harvey Oswald from time of his birth (CD 205), CE 1963, WC Vol. XXIII, p. 544; FBI report, December 16, 1963, of interview with W. M. Young (CD 205), CE 2212, WC Vol. XXV; testimony of John Pic, WC Vol. XI, p. 28.
34. Oswald, op. cit., pp. 40, 44.
35. Testimony of John Pic, WC Vol. XI, p. 29.
36. Testimony of Lillian Murret, WC Vol. VIII, p. 128.
37. Testimony of John Pic, WC Vol. XI, p. 74.
38. Ibid., p. 75.
39. Ibid., p. 77.
40. Ibid.
41. Testimony of Lillian Murret, WC Vol. VIII, p. 119.
42. Testimony of Marilyn Murret, WC Vol. VIII, p. 163.
43. FBI report, December 13, 1963, of interview with Mrs. W. H. Bell (CD 205), CE 2219, WC Vol. XXV, p. 527.
44. Testimony of Myrtle Evans, WC Vol. VIII, p. 51.
45. Ibid.
46. Ibid., p. 52.
47. Testimony of Hiram Conway, WC Vol. VIII, p. 86.
48. Ibid., p. 90.
49. FBI report, April 3, 1964, of investigation concerning Lee Harvey Oswald's possible attendance at a day nursery in Dallas, Texas, during the school year 1944–45 (CD 861), CE 1874, WC Vol. XXIII, p. 7.
50. FBI report, June 4, 1964, of interview with Mrs. Clyde Livingston (CD 1245), CE 2220, WC Vol. XXV, p. 119.
51. Oswald, op. cit., p. 49.
52. Ibid., pp. 50–51.
53. Ibid., p. 53; testimony of John Pic, WC Vol. XI, pp. 38–39.

54. Testimony of John Pic, WC Vol. XI, p. 40.
55. Ibid., p. 42.
56. Letter to Commission, February 4, 1964, from the mayor of New York, transmitting school records of Lee Oswald (CD 364), CE 1384, WC Vol. XXII, pp. 688–700.
57. Carro Exhibit 1, WC Vol. XIX, p. 1.
58. Testimony of John Carro, WC Vol. VIII, p. 205.
59. Ibid., p. 206.
60. Oswald, op. cit., pp. 57–58.
61. Testimony of Dr. Renatus Hartogs, WC Vol. VIII, p. 217.
62. Ibid., p. 220.
63. Ibid., p. 223.
64. Ibid.
65. Hartogs Exhibit 1, WC Vol. XX.
66. CE 1384, p. 700.
67. Testimony of John Carro, WC Vol. VIII, p. 207.
68. Oswald, op. cit., p. 63.
69. Testimony of John Carro, WC Vol. VIII, pp. 207–8.
70. Oswald, op. cit., p. 60.
71. Testimony of John Carro, WC Vol. VIII, p. 209.
72. Testimony of Lillian Murret, WC Vol. VIII, p. 124.
73. Testimony of Myrtle Evans, WC Vol. VIII, p. 54.
74. Ibid., p. 57.
75. Testimony of Julian Evans, WC Vol. VIII, p. 70.
76. Ibid.
77. Ibid., p. 73.
78. Testimony of Ruth Paine, WC Vol. III, p. 22.
79. Testimony of Edward Voebel, WC Vol. VIII, p. 3.
80. Ibid., p. 13.
81. Ibid., p. 9.
82. Testimony of William E. Wulf, WC Vol. VIII, p. 18.
83. Ibid., p. 18.
84. Ibid., pp. 18, 19, 21.
85. Letter from Louisiana Department of Public Safety to Commission, February 4, 1964, transmitting information concerning Lee Oswald's education and background in Louisiana (CD 365), CE 1413, WC Vol. XXII, p. 10.
86. Ibid.
87. Ibid., p. 11.
88. WR, p. 384.
89. Testimony of Marguerite Oswald, WC Vol. I, pp. 198, 200; Carro Exhibit 1, WC Vol XIX, p. 319; FBI report, December 18, 1963, of interview with Dr. Benjamin Powell (CD 189), CE 2240, WC Vol. XXV, p. 140.
90. FBI report, November 26, 1963, reflecting affidavit of Palmer McBride (CD 75), CE 1386, WC Vol. XXII, pp. 251, 252.
91. Ibid., p. 252.
92. Ibid., p. 253.
93. Testimony of George de Mohrenschildt, WC Vol. IX, p. 247.
94. Notes of interview of Lee Oswald conducted by Aline Mosby in Moscow, November 1959 (CD 352), CE 1385, WC Vol. XXII, p. 703.

95. Copies of Lee Oswald's classification card, dated August 30, 1956, Fort Worth public schools, high school department, and Oswald's permanent high school record, Fort Worth public schools, Arlington Heights High School (CD 373), CE 1873 J, K, WC Vol. XXIII, pp. 671–73.
96. Testimony of Marguerite Oswald, WC Vol. I, p. 234.
97. CE 2240, p. 2.
98. Testimony of Viola Peterman, WC Vol. VIII, p. 64; testimony of Dr. Renatus Hartogs, WC Vol. VIII, p. 223.
99. Testimony of Robert Oswald, WC Vol. I, pp. 375–76.
100. Testimony of Marguerite Oswald, WC Vol. I, p. 227.
101. CE 1385, p. 705.
102. Testimony of John Pic, WC Vol. XI, p. 4.
103. Oswald, op. cit., p. 57.

2 "THE BEST RELIGION IS COMMUNISM"

1. Folsom Exhibit 1, WC Vol. XIX, pp. 1, 7.
2. Testimony of Maj. Eugene Anderson, WC Vol. XI, p. 302.
3. Testimony of Lt. Col. Allison Folsom, WC Vol. VIII, p. 304.
4. Testimony of John E. Donovan, WC Vol. VIII, p. 296.
5. Testimony of Lt. Col. Allison Folsom, WC Vol. VIII, p. 304.
6. Testimony of Sgt. James A. Zahm, WC Vol. XI, p. 308; see also Folsom, WC Vol. VIII, p. 305.
7. Folsom Exhibit 1, WC Vol. XIX, pp. 3, 36.
8. FBI report, June 26, 1964, of interview with Allen R. Felde (CD 1229), CE 1962, WC Vol. XXIII, p. 3.
9. Testimony of Daniel Powers, WC Vol. VIII, p. 268.
10. Ibid., pp. 272–73.
11. Testimony of Kerry Thornley, WC Vol. XI, p. 106.
12. Testimony of John Donovan, WC Vol. VIII, p. 295.
13. Testimony of Daniel Powers, WC Vol. VIII, p. 270.
14. Folsom Exhibit 1, WC Vol. XIX, p. 3.
15. Ibid., p. 111.
16. Affidavit of Paul Edward Murphy, WC Vol. VIII, p. 320.
17. Folsom Exhibit 1, WC Vol. XIX, p. 5.
18. Ibid., p. 3.
19. Letter from Lee Oswald to Robert Oswald, November 26, 1959, CE 295, WC Vol. XVI, p. 816.
20. Folsom Exhibit 1, p. 8.
21. Affidavit of Paul Edward Murphy, WC Vol. VIII, p. 320.
22. Testimony of George de Mohrenschildt, WC Vol. IX, p. 243.
23. Ibid., p. 242.
24. Based on interview with confidential intelligence source.
25. Notes of interview of Lee Oswald conducted by Aline Mosby in Moscow, November 1959 (CD 352), CE 1385, WC Vol. XXII, p. 705.
26. Edward Jay Epstein, *Legend: The Secret World of Lee Harvey Oswald* (New York: McGraw-Hill, 1978), p. 68.
27. Testimony of Daniel Powers, WC Vol. VIII, p. 287.
28. Testimony of John Donovan, WC Vol. VIII, p. 300.

29. Epstein, op. cit., p. 70.

30. Testimony of John Donovan, WC Vol. VIII, p. 297.

31. Testimony of Nelson Delgado, WC Vol. VIII, p. 265.

32. Testimony of Daniel Powers, WC Vol. VIII, p. 275.

33. Affidavit of Peter Connor, WC Vol. VIII, p. 317.

34. Affidavit of John Rene Heindel, WC Vol. VIII, p. 318.

35. Testimony of Lt. Col. Allison Folsom, WC Vol. VIII, p. 308.

36. Folsom Exhibit 1, WC Vol. XIX, pp. 3, 10.

37. Epstein, op. cit., p. 79.

38. Testimony of Daniel Powers, WC Vol. VIII, p. 278.

39. Affidavit of John Rene Heindel, WC Vol. VIII, p. 318.

40. Epstein, op. cit., p. 81.

41. Folsom Exhibit 1, WC Vol. XIX, p. 3.

42. Epstein, op. cit., p. 82.

43. Testimony of Robert Oswald, WC Vol. I, pp. 294, 327.

44. Folsom Exhibit 1, WC Vol. XIX, p. 3.

45. Affidavit of Donald Camarata, WC Vol. VIII, p. 316.

46. Affidavit of James Botelho, WC Vol. VIII, p. 315.

47. Affidavit of Richard Call, WC Vol. VIII, p. 323.

48. Affidavit of Mack Osborne, WC Vol. VIII, p. 322.

49. Testimony of Nelson Delgado, WC Vol. VIII, pp. 233, 240, 241, 243.

50. Ibid., p. 243.

51. Ibid., p. 262.

52. Kerry Thornley, *The Idle Warriors* (New York: IllumiNet, 1991).

53. Testimony of Kerry Thornley, WC Vol. XI, p. 107.

54. Ibid., p. 87.

55. Ibid., pp. 94, 95, 102.

56. Ibid., pp. 101–2.

57. Ibid., pp. 101–2, 108.

58. Affidavit of James Anthony Botelho, WC Vol. VIII, p. 316; testimony of Kerry Thornley, WC Vol. XI, p. 84.

59. Application form filled out by Lee Harvey Oswald on March 4, 1959, for entry to the Albert Schweitzer College, CE 228, WC Vol. XVI, pp. 621–25.

60. Folsom Exhibit 1, WC Vol. XIX, p. 28.

61. Ibid., p. 84.

62. Oswald, *Lee: A Portrait*, pp. 94–95.

63. FBI report, January 17, 1964, of interview with Saner Davis (CD 329, p. 172), WC Vol. XXV, p. 141; Folsom Exhibit 1, WC Vol. XIX, pp. 86–91.

64. Folsom Exhibit 1, WC Vol. XIX, p. 4.

65. U.S. passport application of Lee Oswald, dated September 4, 1959 (CD 1114, X-80[3]), CE 1114, WC Vol. XXII, pp. 77–79.

66. Passport of Lee Oswald, issued September 10, 1959, CE 946, WC Vol. XVIII, pp. 160–71.

67. Testimony of Marguerite Oswald, WC Vol. I, pp. 201–2, 212.

68. Testimony of Marguerite Oswald, WC Vol. I, pp. 201–2.

69. FBI reports, December 4, 1963, concerning passenger records of steamship on which Oswald sailed from New Orleans to Le Havre, France (CD, pp. 304–6), CE 2665, WC Vol. XXVI, p. 305.

70. Undated letter from Lee Oswald to Marguerite Oswald, with envelope postmarked September 19, 1959, CE 200, WC Vol. XVI, p. 580.
71. Testimony of Kerry Thornley, WC Vol. XI, pp. 94, 97–98.

3 THE WAR OF THE DEFECTORS

1. Tom Mangold, *Cold Warrior: James Jesus Angleton—The CIA's Master Spy Hunter* (New York: Simon & Schuster, 1991), p. 165.
2. Interview with Yuriy Nosenko, September 1, 1992.
3. Mangold, op. cit., pp. 167–68; Nosenko interview, September 1, 1992.
4. David Wise, *Molehunt: The Secret Search for Traitors That Shattered the CIA* (New York: Random House, 1992), pp. 75–77; Nosenko interview, September 1, 1992.
5. Mangold, op. cit., p. 168.
6. Ibid., p. 169.
7. Nosenko interview, September 1, 1992.
8. Ibid.
9. Ibid.
10. Ibid.
11. Ibid.
12. Ibid.
13. Ibid.
14. Ibid.
15. Epstein, *Legend*, pp. 34–35.
16. Nosenko interview, September 1, 1992.
17. Epstein, op. cit., p. 47.
18. Mangold, op. cit., p. 145.
19. Nosenko interview.
20. Ibid.
21. Ibid.
22. Ibid.
23. Mangold, p. 402.
24. Ibid., p. 204.
25. Ibid., p. 231.
26. Ibid., note 53, p. 402.
27. Nosenko interview.
28. Ibid.
29. Ibid.
30. Ibid.
31. Mangold, op. cit., p. 189.
32. Nosenko interview.
33. Ibid.
34. Ibid.
35. Mangold, op. cit., p. 190.
36. Ibid., p. 93.
37. Ibid., pp. 197–98.
38. Ibid., p. 198.
39. Ibid., pp. 200, 400, note 33.
40. Nosenko interview.

41. Mangold, op. cit., p. 401.
42. Summers, *Conspiracy*, pp. 164, 172.
43. Epstein, op. cit., p. 38.
44. Marrs, *Crossfire*, p. 131.
45. HSCA Rpt., p. 102.
46. Ibid.
47. HSCA Vol. II, p. 484.
48. Mangold, op. cit., p. 398, n. 22.
49. Ibid., p. 196.
50. Nosenko interview.
51. Aline Mosby interview of Lee Oswald, November 1959, CE 1385, WC Vol. XXII.
52. Passport of Lee Oswald, issued September 10, 1959, CE 946, WC Vol. XVIII, pp. 163–65.
53. Passport of Lee Oswald, CE 946, p. 9.
54. Summers, op. cit., p. 120.
55. HSCA Rpt., p. 212.
56. Nosenko interview.
57. Ibid.
58. Ibid.
59. Lee Oswald's Historic Diary, CE 24, WC Vol. XVI, entry for October 16, 1959.
60. Letter from Lee Oswald to Robert Oswald, November 8, 1959, CE 294, WC Vol. XVI, p. 814.
61. CE 1385.
62. Letter from Lee Oswald to Robert Oswald, November 26, 1959, CE 295, WC Vol. XVI, p. 816.
63. Testimony of Priscilla Johnson, WC Vol. XI, p. 449.
64. CE 1385, p. 703.
65. Ibid. p. 704.
66. Ibid., pp. 702, 706.
67. Oswald's Historic Diary, CE 24, entry for October 16, 1959.
68. Note to Lee Oswald from Rima Shirokova (FBI item 291), CE 1399, WC Vol. XXII, p. 738.
69. Nosenko interview; HSCA Volume II, p. 460.
70. Jim Garrison, *On the Trail of the Assassins* (New York: Warner Books, 1991), p. 56.
71. Nosenko interview.
72. Ibid.
73. Based on interviews with confidential intelligence sources.
74. Priscilla Johnson McMillan, *Marina and Lee* (New York: Harper & Row, 1977), p. 81; confidential sources.
75. Oswald's Historic Diary, CE 24, entry for October 21, 1959.
76. Nosenko interview.
77. Oswald's Historic Diary, CE 24, pp. 94–95.
78. Nosenko interview.
79. Sergey Mostovshchikov, "KGB Case No. 31451 on Lee Harvey Oswald," *Izvestiya*, August 8, 1992, p. 7.

80. Nosenko interview; McMillan, op. cit., p., 81; Soviet file document on Lee Oswald, CE 985, WC Vol. XVIII, p. 461.
81. Mostovshchikov, "KGB Case No. 31451 on Lee Harvey Oswald," August 8, 1992, p. 7.
82. Nosenko interview.
83. Oswald's Historic Diary, CE 24, entry for October 28, 1959.
84. Testimony of Richard Snyder, WC Vol. V, p. 266.
85. McMillan, op. cit., p. 82.
86. Oswald's Historic Diary, CE 24, entry for October 31, 1959.
87. Letter from Lee Oswald to Robert Oswald, CE 294.
88. Letter from Lee Oswald to Robert Oswald, CE 295.
89. Ibid.
90. Ibid.
91. Oswald's Historic Diary, CE 24, entry for November 17–December 30, 1959.
92. Oswald's Historic Diary, CE 24, entry for January 4, 1960; CE 985, WC Vol. XVIII.
93. Nosenko interview.
94. Ibid.
95. Ibid.
96. Ibid.
97. Ibid.
98. Ibid.
99. Ibid.

4   "THE LESSER OF TWO EVILS"

1. Lee Oswald's Historic Diary, CE 24, WC Vol. XVI, entries for January 4, 5, 7, 1960.
2. Ibid., entry for January 8, 1960.
3. Testimony of Marina Oswald, WC Vol. V, p. 590; testimony of Max Clark, WC Vol. VIII, pp. 347, 350; testimony of Paul Gregory, WC Vol. IX, p. 147; see also R. Johnson Exhibit 1, WC Vol. XX, pp. 1, 6.
4. McMillan, *Marina and Lee*, p. 88.
5. Sergey Mostovshchikov, "KGB Case No. 31451 on Lee Harvey Oswald," *Izvestiya*, August 11, 1992, p. 3.
6. Henry Hurt, *Reasonable Doubt* (New York: Henry Holt, 1985), pp. 210, 214.
7. Marrs, *Crossfire*, p. 134.
8. Interview with Ernst Titovets, December 14, 1992.
9. Oswald's Historic Diary, CE 24, entries for January 11 and 13, 1960; interview with Priscilla Johnson McMillan, September 29, 1992.
10. WR, p. 698.
11. Interview with Ernst Titovets.
12. Oswald's Historic Diary, CE 24, entry for January 13, 1960.
13. Mostovshchikov, "KGB Case No. 31451 on Lee Harvey Oswald," August 8, 1992, p. 7.
14. Ibid.
15. Ibid.

16. Mostovshchikov, "KGB Case No. 31451 on Lee Harvey Oswald," August 11, 1992, p. 8.
17. Mostovshchikov, "KGB Case No. 31451 on Lee Harvey Oswald," August 8, 1992, p. 7.
18. Letter from Yuriy Nosenko to author, March 1993.
19. Interview with Ernst Titovets.
20. Ibid.
21. Oswald's Historic Diary, entry for August–September, 1960.
22. Testimony of Max Clark, WC Vol. VIII, p. 350.
23. Testimony of Valentina Ray, WC Vol. VIII, p. 425.
24. Testimony of George de Mohrenschildt, WC Vol. IX, p. 234.
25. Lee Oswald's handwritten account of amorous affairs in the USSR, found among Oswald's personal effects (p. 22 of diary from FBI exhibits, vol. 3, p. 46), CE 2759, WC Vol. XXVI, p. 144.
26. Oswald's Historic Diary, entry for January 1, 1961.
27. Ibid., entry for January 2, 1961.
28. Ibid., entry for January 4–31, 1961.
29. McMillan, op. cit., pp. 88–89.
30. Mostovshchikov, "KGB Case No. 31451 on Lee Harvey Oswald," August 11, 1992, p. 3.
31. Oswald's Historic Diary, CE 24, entry for August–September, 1960.
32. Typed narrative concerning Russia by Lee Oswald, CE 92, WC Vol. XVI.
33. Notes written by Lee Oswald on Holland America Line stationery, CE 25, WC Vol. XVI, pp. 113–14.
34. Declaration of Lee Oswald requesting that his U.S. citizenship be revoked, CE 931, WC Vol. XVIII.
35. Letter from Lee Oswald to Robert Oswald, November 8, 1959, CE 294, WC Vol. XVI, p. 814.
36. CE 931.
37. Letter to Lee Oswald from the American embassy in Moscow, February 28, 1961, CE 933, WC Vol. XVIII, p. 135.
38. Foreign Service dispatch from the Department of State to the American embassy in Moscow, March 24, 1961, CE 940, WC Vol. XVIII, p. 151.
39. Ibid.
40. State Department memorandum from John T. White to Edward J. Hickey, March 31, 1961, CE 970, WC Vol. XVIII, p. 367; Department of State Instruction to the American embassy in Moscow, April 13, 1961, CE 971, WC Vol. XVIII, p. 368.
41. Oswald's Historic Diary, CE 24, entry for March 17, 1961.
42. Summers, op. cit., p. 157.
43. Marrs, op. cit., p. 125.
44. WR, p. 257.
45. Testimony of Lt. Col. Allison Folsom, WC Vol. VIII, p. 307.
46. Epstein, *Legend*, p. 86.
47. Testimony of Richard Snyder, WC Vol. V, p. 291.
48. Testimony of Priscilla Johnson McMillan, WC Vol. XI, p. 455; notes of interview of Lee Oswald conducted by Aline Mosby in Moscow, CE 1385, WC Vol. XXII, p. 706.

49. Oswald's Historic Diary, CE 24, entry for November 17 to December 30, 1959.
50. WR, p. 257.
51. Oswald's Historic Diary, CE 24, entry for August–September, 1960.
52. Mostovshchikov, "KGB Case No. 31451 on Lee Harvey Oswald," August 11, 1992, p. 3.
53. Interview with Ernst Titovets.
54. Interview with Marina Oswald, October 4, 1992; HSCA Vol. II, p. 208.
55. HSCA Vol. II, p. 311.
56. Hurt, op. cit., pp. 215, 217.
57. Oswald's Historic Diary, CE 24, entry for May 1961.
58. Ibid., entry for June 1961.
59. McMillan, op. cit., p. 102.
60. Ibid., p. 101.
61. Ibid.
62. Testimony of George de Mohrenschildt, WC Vol. IX, p. 229.
63. Testimony of Jeanne de Mohrenschildt, WC Vol. IX, p. 312.
64. Mostovshchikov, "KGB Case No. 31451 on Lee Harvey Oswald," August 13, 1992, p. 6.
65. McMillan, op. cit., p. 103.
66. Oswald's Historic Diary, CE 24, entry for June 1961.
67. Letter from Lee Harvey Oswald to the American embassy in Moscow, dated May 1961, CE 252, WC Vol. XVI, pp. 705–8.
68. Mostovshchikov, "KGB Case No. 31451 on Lee Harvey Oswald," August 13, 1992, p. 6.
69. McMillan, op. cit., pp. 160–61.
70. Ibid.
71. Ibid., p. 121.
72. Mostovshchikov, "KGB Case No. 31451 on Lee Harvey Oswald," August 11, 1992, p. 8.
73. Ibid.
74. FBI reports, December 1–7, 1963, of interviews with and data concerning Marina Oswald (CD 6, pp. 250–98), CE 1401, WC Vol. XXII, p. 278.
75. Passport of Lee Oswald, issued September 10, 1959, CE 946, WC Vol. XVIII, p. 6.
76. Operations memorandum from State Department to the American embassy in Moscow, dated August 18, 1961, CE 979, WC Vol. XVIII, pp. 347, 357.
77. Testimony of Abram Chayes, WC Vol. 5, p. 339.
78. McMillan, op. cit., p. 135–36.
79. Testimony of John McVickar, WC Vol. 5, p. 321.
80. Testimony of Virginia James, WC Vol. XI, p. 185.
81. Letter from Lee Oswald to Robert Oswald, dated July 14, 1961, CE 301, WC Vol. XVI, p. 833.
82. Copies of letters dated from July 15, 1961, to October 4, 1961, from Lee Oswald to the American embassy in Moscow, as preserved in State Department files (CD 115), CE 1122, WC Vol. XXII.
83. Oswald's Historic Diary, CE 24, entry for July 15, 1961.
84. Ibid., entry for July 16–August 20, 1961.

85. Ibid., entry for August 21–September 1, 1961.
86. Ibid., entry for September–October 18, 1961.
87. CE 1122.
88. McMillan, op. cit., p. 159.
89. Oswald's Historic Diary, CE 24, entry for November–December, 1961.
90. McMillan, op. cit., p. 159.
91. Internal memorandum of the Commission, dated June 8, 1964, and attached documents, re "Senator John G. Tower's contacts with Lee Harvey Oswald" (CD 1119), CE 1058, WC Vol. XXII, p. 11.
92. Oswald's Historic Diary, CE 24, entry for December 25, 1961.
93. "Inside the KGB," NBC, May 25, 1993; interview with Yuriy Nosenko, September 1, 1992.
94. Operations memorandum from the American embassy in Moscow to the Department of State, August 28, 1961, CE 944, WC Vol. XVIII.
95. Testimony of John McVickar, WC Vol. V, p. 322.
96. Operations memorandum, March 16, 1962, from the American embassy in Moscow to the American embassy in Brussels, re: Marina Oswald and use of third-country shelter (CD 115), CE 1095, WC Vol. XIX, pp. 1-2; affidavit of Byron Phillips, March 13, 1962, taking responsibility for support of Marina Oswald upon her entry into the United States (CD 363), CE 2653, WC Vol. XXVI, p. 3.
97. Testimony of Virginia James, WC Vol. XI, p. 186.
98. Copy of letter, dated May 9, 1962, from Robert H. Robinson, Immigration and Naturalization Service, to Michael Cieplinski, State Department, concerning Marina Oswald, CE 1777, WC Vol. XXIII, p. 383.
99. WR, p. 770.
100. Telegram from the American embassy, Moscow, advising of the departure of the Oswalds (CD 1114–15), CE 1099, WC Vol. XXII, p. 48.
101. Mostovshchikov, "KGB Case No. 31451 on Lee Harvey Oswald," August 8, 1992, p. 7.
102. McMillan, op. cit., p. 185–86.
103. Summers, op. cit., p. 185.
104. Ibid., pp. 185–86.
105. Ibid., p. 186.
106. CE 29 (Marina Oswald's passport), WC Vol. XVI; CE 946 (Lee Oswald's passport), WC Vol. XVIII.
107. HSCA Vol. II, pp. 288–89.
108. McMillan, op. cit., pp. 191–92.
109. Ibid., p. 215–16; testimony of Marina Oswald, HSCA Vol. II, p. 220.
110. Testimony of Marina Oswald, HSCA Vol. II, p. 280.
111. Testimony of Robert Oswald, WC Vol. I, p. 331.
112. Self-questionnaire by Lee Oswald, CE 100, WC Vol. XVI, pp. 436–39.
113. Foreign Service dispatch from the American embassy in Moscow to the State Department, dated July 11, 1961, CE 935, WC Vol. XVIII, pp. 137–39.
114. CE 25, p. 120.
115. Notes for a speech by Lee Oswald, CE 102, WC Vol. XVI, pp. 441–42.
116. CE 25, p. 117.
117. Ibid., p. 1.
118. See generally CE 24, 25, and 92.

5 "I'LL NEVER GO BACK TO THAT HELL"

1. Testimony of Robert Oswald, WC Vol. 1, p. 312.
2. McMillan, *Marina and Lee*, p. 220.
3. Testimony of Robert Oswald, WC Vol. I, 332.
4. Testimony of Pauline Virginia Bates, WC Vol. VIII, p. 336.
5. Ibid., p. 335.
6. Ibid., p. 336.
7. Testimony of John W. Fain, WC Vol. IV, pp. 423–24.
8. Ibid., p. 416.
9. Ibid., p. 416–17.
10. Ibid., p. 418.
11. HSCA Rpt., p. 190.
12. Copy of an FBI report by Special Agent Fain, May 12, 1960, CE 823, WC Vol. XVII.
13. McMillan, op. cit., p. 225.
14. Ibid., p. 227.
15. Oswald, *Lee: A Portrait*, p. 121.
16. Testimony of Tommy Bargas, WC Vol. X, pp. 161–63; application for employment at Leslie Welding Co., dated July 13, 1962, filled out by Lee Oswald (part of FBI item D-18), CE 1943, WC Vol. XXIII, p. 741.
17. Testimony of Tommy Bargas, WC Vol. X, p. 165.
18. Oswald, op. cit., p. 121.
19. McMillan, op. cit., p. 229.
20. Ibid., p. 231.
21. Testimony of George de Mohrenschildt, WC Vol. IX, pp. 225–26.
22. Testimony of John Fain, WC Vol. IV, p. 420.
23. Ibid., p. 421.
24. Ibid., p. 424.
25. McMillan, op. cit., p. 232.
26. Soviet embassy file re: Lee Oswald, CE 986, WC Vol. XVIII, p. 486.
27. Testimony of Marina Oswald, WC Vol. I, p. 10.
28. Testimony of Marguerite Oswald, WC Vol. I, p. 139.
29. Testimony of Paul R. Gregory, WC Vol. IX, p. 150.
30. Ibid., pp. 155–56.
31. Ibid., p. 154.
32. McMillan, op. cit., p. 245.
33. Testimony of Katherine Ford, WC Vol. II, p. 297.
34. Testimony of George Bouhe, WC Vol. VIII, p. 372.
35. Ibid.
36. Testimony of Elena Hall, WC Vol. VIII, p. 394.
37. Testimony of Anna Meller, WC Vol. VIII, p. 383.
38. Ibid., p. 384.
39. Testimony of Katherine Ford, WC Vol. II, p. 308.
40. Ibid.
41. Testimony of Anna Meller, WC Vol. VIII, p. 381.
42. Testimony of George Bouhe, WC Vol. VIII, p. 374.
43. Testimony of Paul R. Gregory, WC Vol. IX, pp. 148, 150; McMillan, op. cit., p. 239.

44. Testimony of Anna Meller, WC Vol. VIII, p. 382.
45. Testimony of George Bouhe, WC Vol. VIII, p. 371.
46. Testimony of Anna Meller, WC Vol. VIII, p. 382–83.
47. McMillan, op. cit., p. 249.
48. Testimony of Max Clark, WC Vol. VIII, p. 351.
49. Testimony of George de Mohrenschildt, WC Vol. IX, pp. 225–26.
50. Ibid., p. 227.
51. Testimony of Mrs. Igor Vladimir Voshinin, WC Vol. VIII, p. 435.
52. Testimony of George de Mohrenschildt, WC Vol. IX, p. 227.
53. Summers, *Conspiracy*, pp. 194–95.
54. Ibid., pp. 197–98.
55. Testimony of George de Mohrenschildt, WC Vol. IX, p. 236.
56. HSCA Rpt. pp. 217–19.
57. Testimony of Mrs. Igor Vladimir Voshinin, WC Vol. VIII, p. 433.
58. Testimony of Igor Voshinin, WC Vol. VIII, pp. 467–68.
59. Testimony of George Bouhe, WC Vol. VIII, p. 377.
60. Testimony of Igor Voshinin, WC Vol. VIII, p. 464.
61. Testimony of Gary Taylor, WC Vol. IX, p. 99.
62. Testimony of Paul Raigorodsky, WC Vol. IX, pp. 19, 20.
63. Testimony of Igor Voshinin, WC Vol. VIII, pp 462, 464.
64. Testimony of Mrs. Igor Voshinin, WC Vol. VIII, p. 434.
65. Testimony of Igor Voshinin, WC Vol. VIII, p. 466.
66. Testimony of Declan Ford, WC Vol. II, p. 327.
67. Testimony of George de Mohrenschildt, WC Vol. IX, p. 223.
68. Ibid., p. 208.
69. Testimony of Ilya Mamantov, WC Vol. IX, p. 122.
70. Testimony of George de Mohrenschildt, WC Vol. IX, p. 227.
71. Ibid., p. 238.
72. Testimony of Mrs. Igor Voshinin, WC Vol. VIII, p. 436; testimony of George de Mohrenschildt, Vol. IX, p. 261.
73. Testimony of George de Mohrenschildt, WC Vol. IX, p. 241.
74. Ibid., pp. 236–37.
75. Ibid., p. 237.
76. Testimony of Marina Oswald, WC Vol. I, p. 6; testimony of George de Mohrenschildt, Vol. IX, p 230.
77. Testimony of Elena Hall, WC Vol. VIII, pp. 393–96.
78. Ibid., p. 395.
79. Ibid., pp. 396–97.
80. WR, p. 719.
81. Garrison, *On the Trail of the Assassins*, p. 60.
82. Summers, op. cit., p. 201–3.
83. Testimony of Robert Stovall, WC Vol. X, p. 168.
84. Ibid., pp. 168–69.
85. Ibid., p. 169.
86. Interview with David Perry, September 28, 1992.
87. McMillan, op. cit., p. 116.
88. Ibid., p. 212.
89. Testimony of Marina Oswald, WC Vol. I, p. 22.
90. Testimony of Katherine Ford, WC Vol. II, p. 305.

91. Oswald, op. cit., p. 47.

92. Group of retouched negatives, CE 800, WC Vol. XVII, pp. 684–85.

93. Weinstock Exhibit 1, WC XXI.

94. FBI report, December 5, 1963, of interview with Gladys Yoakum (CD 7), CE 2699, WC Vol. XXVI, p. 73; FBI report, December 6, 1963, of interview with Troy Bond, principal, evening school at Crozier Tech High School, Dallas, Texas (CD 6), CE 1130, WC Vol. XXII, p. 110.

95. Four photographs of CE 795, a spurious Selective Service card in the name "Alek James Hidell," CE 796–799; and three photographs of CE 806, a counterfeit certificate of service card in the name "Alek James Hidell," CE 808–810, WC Vol. XVII.

96. McMillan, op. cit., p. 254.

97. Ibid.

98. Affidavit of Alexander Kleinlerer, WC Vol. XI, p. 120.

99. Ibid.

100. McMillan, op. cit., p. 263.

101. Testimony of George de Mohrenschildt, WC Vol. IX, p. 232.

102. Ibid., p. 233.

103. Ibid.

104. Testimony of Katherine Ford, WC Vol. II, p. 299.

105. Ibid., p. 302.

106. Testimony of Mrs. Frank Ray, WC Vol. VIII, p. 418.

107. Testimony of Marina Oswald, WC Vol. I, p. 10.

108. Ibid., p. 12.

109. Testimony of Mrs. Mahlon Tobias, WC Vol. X, p. 235.

110. Ibid., p. 242.

111. Ibid., pp. 242–43.

112. Ibid., pp. 243–44.

113. Testimony of Marina Oswald, HSCA Vol. II, pp. 238, 299, 308.

114. Testimony of George de Mohrenschildt, WC Vol. IX, p. 238.

115. Ibid., p. 244.

116. Testimony of Anna Meller, WC Vol. VIII, p. 391.

117. Testimony of Katherine Ford, WC Vol. II, p. 307.

118. Testimony of Marina Oswald, WC Vol. V, p. 597.

119. Testimony of Katherine Ford, WC Vol. II, p. 309.

120. WR, p. 721.

121. Ibid.

122. Testimony of George Bouhe, WC Vol. VIII, p. 369.

123. Ibid., pp. 369–70.

124. Testimony of Marina Oswald, WC Vol. I, p. 33.

125. Soviet embassy file on Lee Oswald, CE 986, WC Vol. XVIII, p. 495.

6 "HUNTER OF FASCISTS"

1. Emergency Loan Record Payout Schedule, CE 1120, WC Vol. XXII.

2. Cadigan Exhibit 12, WC Vol. XIX.

3. Testimony of Alwyn Cole, WC Vol. IV, pp. 375–77; testimony of James C. Cadigan, WC Vol. VII, p. 424.

4. Testimony of Marina Oswald, WC Vol. V, pp. 594, 597; McMillan, *Marina and Lee*, p. 317.
5. Testimony of Marina Oswald, WC Vol. I, pp. 10–11.
6. McMillan, op. cit., p. 318.
7. FBI file, Volkmar Schmidt, p. 1.
8. McMillan, op. cit., p. 321.
9. Interview with Michael Paine, April 11, 1992.
10. 1962 election statistics compiled by David B. Perry, letter dated September 30, 1992.
11. Testimony of George de Mohrenschildt, WC Vol. IX, p. 210.
12. McMillan, op. cit., p. 322.
13. Testimony of Marina Oswald, WC Vol. V, p. 400.
14. Letter from Marina Oswald to Russian embassy, February 17, 1963, CE 986, WC Vol. XVIII, p. 501.
15. Testimony of Everett Glover, WC Vol. X, p. 27.
16. Ibid., p. 30.
17. Ibid., p. 29.
18. Testimony of Ruth Paine, WC Vol. II, pp. 443–44, 446.
19. McMillan, op. cit., p. 326.
20. Ibid., p. 328.
21. Testimony of Katherine Ford, WC Vol. II, p. 318.
22. Testimony of Marina Oswald, WC Vol. XI, p. 299.
23. Testimony of Ruth Paine, WC Vol. II, p. 443–44.
24. CE 986, p. 503.
25. Ibid., pp. 506–13.
26. *The Militant*, March 11, 1963 (Vol. 27, No. 10), p. 7.
27. Photographs of General Walker's home, CE 3, p. 1; CE 5, WC Vol. XVI, pp. 5, 7–8.
28. Photograph of a mail order for a rifle in the name of "A. Hidell," and the envelope in which it was sent, CE 773, WC Vol. XVII, p. 120.
29. Robert Sam Anson, *"They've Killed the President!": The Search for the Murderers of John F. Kennedy* (New York: Bantam, 1975), p. 75.
30. Mark Lane, *Rush to Judgment* (New York: Fawcett Crest, 1967), p. 105.
31. Testimony of Robert A. Frazier, WC Vol. III, p. 411.
32. Ibid., p. 414.
33. Ibid., p. 413.
34. Interview with Art Pence, February 21, 1992; testimony of Ronald Simmons, WC Vol. III, pp. 442–43.
35. Interview with Art Pence.
36. Ibid.
37. Testimony of Robert Frazier, WC Vol. III, pp. 400, 437, 449.
38. Ibid., p. 413.
39. Oswald's work time sheets, CE 1855, WC Vol. XXIII.
40. Testimony of Marina Oswald, WC Vol. I, p. 14.
41. McMillan, op. cit., p. 337.
42. Testimony of Marina Oswald, WC Vol. I, p. 13.
43. Ibid., p. 15.
44. Ibid., WC Vol. XI, p. 299.
45. Oswald notes from Holland America trip, CE 25, WC Vol. XVI.

46. Notes by Oswald re: Communist party of the U.S., CE 97, WC Vol. XVI, p. 424.
47. Notes by Oswald titled "A System opposed to the Communists," CE 98, WC Vol. XVI, p. 433.
48. CE 97, pp. 426, 427.
49. Testimony of Ruth Paine, WC Vol. II, p. 448.
50. Ibid., p. 449.
51. Ibid., p. 450.
52. Testimony of Marina Oswald, WC Vol. I, p. 15.
53. Testimony of Marina Oswald, WC Vol. I, p. 15; HSCA Vol. II, pp. 314–15.
54. Testimony of Marina Oswald, HSCA Vol. II, p. 240.
55. McMillan, op. cit., p. 341.
56. HSCA Rpt., p. 55.
57. Testimony of Sgt. Cecil W. Kirk, HSCA Vol. II, pp. 361–63, 365, 368–70.
58. Testimony of Calvin McCamy, HSCA Vol. II, p. 418.
59. HSCA Vol. VI, pp. 182–206.
60. HSCA Vol. VI, p. 66.
61. Testimony of Joseph McNally, HSCA Vol. II, p. 385.
62. Summers, op. cit., p. 207.
63. Testimony of Marina Oswald, WC Vol. XI, p. 296.
64. McMillan, op. cit., p. 340.
65. Testimony of James Hosty, WC Vol. IV, p. 442.
66. Ibid., WC Vol. IV, p. 444; copy of an FBI report by agent John Fain, September 10, 1963, CE 829, WC Vol. XVII, p. 771.
67. Testimony of James Hosty, WC Vol. IV, p. 443.
68. Testimony of Robert Stovall, WC Vol. X, p. 172.
69. Ibid., p. 173.
70. Testimony of Dennis Ofstein, WC Vol. X, pp. 204–5.
71. Testimony of John Graef, WC Vol. X, p. 190.
72. Testimony of Dennis Ofstein, WC Vol. X, p. 203.
73. Testimony of Michael Paine, WC Vol. II, p. 422.
74. Interview with Michael Paine, April 11, 1992.
75. Testimony of Michael Paine, WC Vol. II, p. 400.
76. Ibid.
77. Ibid., p. 403.
78. Ibid., p. 442.
79. FBI report, February 18, 1964, of interview with Marina Oswald, CE 1156, WC Vol. XXII, p. 440.
80. McMillan, op. cit., p. 348.
81. CE 1156, p. 442.
82. Report of investigation into possible target practice by Lee Oswald in Dallas, Texas, area (CD 778), CE 2694, WC Vol. XXVI, p. 10.
83. Testimony of Marina Oswald, WC Vol. I, pp. 14–15, 94.
84. Testimony of Jeanne de Mohrenschildt, WC Vol. IX, p. 317.
85. McMillan, op. cit., p. 350.
86. Ibid.
87. Ibid., p. 351.
88. Testimony of Marina Oswald, WC Vol. I, p. 36.
89. Ibid., WC Vol. 1, p. 16.

90. Interview with Marina Oswald, August 21, 1992.
91. Testimony of Marina Oswald, WC Vol. 1, pp. 16–17.
92. McMillan, op. cit., p. 353.
93. Testimony of Marina Oswald, WC Vol. I, p. 16.
94. Dr. John Lattimer, *Kennedy and Lincoln: Medical and Ballistic Comparisons of their Assassinations* (New York: Harcourt Brace Jovanovich, 1980), p. 134.
95. Testimony of Edwin A. Walker, WC Vol. XI, p. 405.
96. Ibid., p. 410.
97. Ibid.
98. Testimony of Marina Oswald, WC Vol. 1, p. 17.
99. Ibid.
100. Ibid., p. 16.
101. Testimony of Marina Oswald, HSCA II, p. 318.
102. McMillan, op. cit., p. 357.
103. Testimony of Marina Oswald, WC Vol. 1, pp. 17–18.
104. McMillan, op. cit., p. 358.
105. Testimony of Marina Oswald, WC Vol. XI, pp. 292–94.
106. Ibid., p. 18.
107. McMillan, op. cit., p. 359.
108. Testimony of Marina Oswald, WC Vol. I, p. 18.
109. Testimony of George de Mohrenschildt, WC Vol. IX, p. 249.
110. Testimony of Marina Oswald, WC Vol. XI, p. 292.
111. McMillan, op. cit., p. 367.
112. Testimony of Marina Oswald, WC Vol. V, p. 388.
113. Ibid., p. 389.
114. Ibid.
115. Ibid., p. 390.
116. Testimony of Ruth Paine, WC Vol. II, p. 457.
117. Ibid., p. 459.

7 "HANDS OFF CUBA"

1. Testimony of Lillian Murret, WC Vol. VIII, p. 133.
2. Ibid., p. 135.
3. Testimony of J. Rachal, WC Vol. XI, p. 475.
4. Testimony of Lillian Murret, WC Vol. VIII, p. 135.
5. Ibid.
6. Ibid., p. 136.
7. Burcham Exhibit 1, WC Vol. XIX, p. 192.
8. Oswald's undated application for employment at Goldrings, New Orleans, CE 1945; application dated August 6, 1963, for employment at Cosmos shipping, CE 1946; application for employment at unknown place, CE 1947; Lykes Brothers Steamship Co. "Passenger Immigration Questionnaire—Leaving United States," September 16, 1959, CE 1948, WC Vol. XXIII.
9. Postcard marked April 1963, from Lee to Marina Oswald, CE 69A, WC Vol. XVI, p. 230.
10. Testimony of Lillian Murret, WC Vol. VIII, p. 136.

11. Ibid.
12. Oswald's application for employment with William B. Reily, May 9, 1963, CE 1398, WC Vol. XIX, pp. 736–37.
13. Testimony of Myrtle Evans, WC Vol. VIII, p. 58.
14. Ibid., pp. 59–60.
15. Testimony of Ruth Paine, WC Vol. II, p. 471.
16. Ibid., p. 470.
17. Soviet embassy file on Oswald, CE 986, WC Vol. XVIII, pp. 516–17; Lee (V. T.) Exhibit 8-A, WC Vol. XX, p. 531.
18. Dobbs Exhibits 7 and 8, WC Vol. XIX, pp. 573–74.
19. Lee (V. T.) Exhibit 2, WC Vol. XX, pp. 512–13.
20. Testimony of Marina Oswald, HSCA Vol. II, p. 252.
21. Testimony of Marina Oswald, WC Vol. I, p. 24.
22. Testimony of Marina Oswald, WC Vol. I, p. 496; testimony of Ruth Paine, WC Vol. III, p. 104.
23. Testimony of James Hosty, WC Vol. IV, p. 454.
24. FBI report, December 4, 1963, of interview with Myra Silver, re: investigation of the printing of pro-Castro materials on order by Lee Oswald, CE 1410, WC Vol. XXII, pp. 796–98.
25. FBI report, December 3, 1963, of interview with John Anderson in New Orleans, re: investigation of the printing of pro-Castro materials on the order of Lee Oswald, CE 1411, WC XXII, pp. 800–01.
26. Ibid., p. 802.
27. Lee (V. T.) Exhibit 3, WC Vol. XX, pp. 514–16.
28. Ibid. pp. 514–15.
29. Testimony of Marina Oswald, WC Vol. I, p. 22.
30. Letter from Marina Oswald to Ruth Paine, May 25, 1963, CE 408, WC Vol. XVII, p. 88.
31. Testimony of Marina Oswald, WC Vol. I, p. 25.
32. Letter from Marina Oswald to Ruth Paine, June 5, 1963, CE 409-B, WC Vol. XVII, p. 100; McMillan, *Marina and Lee*, p. 397.
33. Testimony of Mrs. Jesse Garner, WC Vol. X, p. 275.
34. McMillan, op. cit., p. 397.
35. Ibid., p. 399.
36. CE 409-B, p. 101.
37. Testimony of Marina Oswald, WC Vol. V, p. 401.
38. Ibid.
39. HSCA Vol. II, p. 255.
40. Cadigan Exhibits 23 and 24, WC Vol. XIX, pp. 296–97.
41. McMillan, op. cit., p. 402.
42. Cadigan Exhibit 22, WC Vol. XIX, p. 295.
43. Testimony of Charles Le Blanc, WC Vol. X, p. 214–15.
44. Ibid., p. 215.
45. Ibid., p. 216–17.
46. Statement of Arturo Mendez Rodriguez, CE 1898, WC Vol. XXIII, p. 702.
47. Testimony of Charles Le Blanc, WC Vol. X, p. 216.
48. Testimony of Adrian Alba, WC Vol. X, p. 223.
49. Ibid., p. 224.
50. Summers, *Conspiracy*, p. 283.

51. HSCA Rpt., p. 194.

52. Interview with Adrian Alba, March 20, 1992.

53. HSCA Rpt., p. 194.

54. McMillan, op. cit., p. 405.

55. Ibid., p. 413.

56. Johnson (Arnold) Exhibit 1, WC Vol. XX, pp. 257–58.

57. Letter from FBI to Commission, August 4, 1964, with attached memos of July 16, 1964, and July 22, 1964, re: investigation into allegations that Oswald distributed leaflets in vicinity of Navy at New Orleans (CD 1370,a,b), CE 1412, WC Vol. XXII, pp. 805–6.

58. Ibid., p. 806.

59. Lee (V. T.) Exhibit 5, WC Vol. XX, p. 525.

60. McMillan, op. cit., p. 410.

61. Lee Oswald passport application of June 24, 1963, CE 781, WC Vol. XVII, pp. 666–67.

62. Ibid., p. 666.

63. Testimony of Marina Oswald, HSCA Vol. II, p. 226.

64. Testimony of Marina Oswald, WC Vol. I, p. 68.

65. Ibid., p. 21.

66. Undated letter from Marina Oswald to the Russian embassy, with translation, CE 12, WC Vol. XVI, pp. 26–29.

67. Ibid., p. 29.

68. Letter from Lee Oswald to Russian embassy, July 1, 1963, CE 13, WC Vol. XVI, p. 30.

69. Unpublished Warren Commission Document No. 928, May 6, 1964, memorandum from Richard Helms, Deputy Director of Plans of the CIA, titled "Contacts Between the Oswalds and the Soviet Citizens, June 13, 1962, to November 22, 1963."

70. CE 986, pp. 527–28.

71. Letter of Ruth Paine to Marina Oswald, July 11, 1963, CE 410, WC Vol. XVII, pp. 102–4.

72. Letter from Ruth Paine to Marina Oswald, July 11, 1963, CE 411, WC Vol. XVIII, p. 105.

73. WR, p. 726.

74. Burcham Exhibit 1, WC Vol. XIX, pp. 211–13; Hunley Exhibits 2, 3, 5, WC Vol. XX, pp. 205, 207, 211; Rachal Exhibits 1, 2, 3, WC Vol. XXI, pp. 282–86; CE 1902–1914, FBI interviews with Roy Richardson, Robert Hedrick, Teddy Guichard, S. K. Manson, G. M. Watson, George Reppel, Philip Blappert, Fred Madden, and Fred Olsen; also, reports of investigations on Oswald's employment in New Orleans, WC Vol. XXIII, pp. 705–14.

75. Letter draft from Ruth Paine to Marina Oswald, July 21, 1963, CE 416, WC Vol. XVII, pp. 119–23.

76. Folsom Exhibit 1, WC Vol. XIX.

77. Ibid., p. 10.

78. Ibid., p. 65.

79. Letters dated August 22 and July 6, 1963, from Eugene Murret to Lee Oswald, CE 2648, WC Vol. XXV, p. 919.

80. Statement of Robert J. Fitzpatrick, S.J., CE 2649, WC Vol. XXV, pp. 924–28.

81. Ibid., p. 926.
82. Lee (V. T.) Exhibit 5, WC Vol. XX, pp. 524–25.
83. Marrs, *Crossfire*, p. 147.
84. John H. Davis, *Mafia Kingfish: Carlos Marcello and the Assassination of John F. Kennedy* (New York: New American Library, 1989), pp. 146–47.
85. HSCA, ref. 11, SR-11-N-244, November 19, 1962, p. 6 (JFK Document 014904).
86. Hurt, *Reasonable Doubt*, pp. 263–64.
87. Ibid, p. 263.
88. HSCA Vol. X, pp. 126–27.
89. Ibid.
90. Secret Service report, December 9, 1963, reflecting investigation of allegation that Oswald rented an office in New Orleans for conduct of Fair Play for Cuba Committee activities (CD 87, SS control No. 517), CE 1414, WC Vol. XXII, pp. 828–31; Secret Service report, December 3, 1963, of investigation concerning Lee Harvey Oswald's activities in New Orleans, (CD 407, pp. 1–24), CE 3119, WC Vol. XXVI, p. 769.
91. CE 1414, WC Vol. XXII, pp. 830–31; deposition of Sam Newman, November 6, 1978, HSCA, p. 22 (JFK Document 014020).
92. CE 1414, pp. 828–30.
93. WR, p. 292.
94. HSCA Vol. X, p. 130.
95. Interview with Hubie Badeaux, March 24, 1992.
96. HSCA Vol. X, p. 130.
97. Ibid., pp. 128–29.
98. Ibid.
99. Summers, op. cit., p. 295; Summers documentary interview notes with Delphine Roberts, files of Anthony Summers, maintained at the Assassination Archives and Research Center, Washington, D.C.
100. Summers, op. cit., p. 296.
101. Interview with Delphine Roberts, March 17, 1992.
102. Ibid.
103. Interview with John Lanne, March 9, 1992.
104. Interview with Delphine Roberts, Jr., March 17, 1992.
105. Ibid.
106. Summers, op. cit., p. 296.
107. CE 3119, p. 769.
108. Outside Contact Report, Ross Banister, February 20, 1978, HSCA, p. 3 (JFK Document 012308).
109. HSCA Vol. X, p. 123.
110. Summers, op. cit., pp. 301–2.
111. "Ferrie in Fatigues at CAP Activity—DA," New Orleans *TimesPicayune*, May 30, 1968.
112. FBI Report No. 89-69-682, November 27, 1963, interview of David Ferrie by special agents Ernest Wall and Theodore Viater.
113. Minutes of the Meeting of the Membership Committee of the Civil Air Patrol with the Commander, Chaplain, and D. W. Ferrie, held June 5, 1959.

114. Letter from Major James T. McCarley, CAP Deputy for Personnel, to Deputy Commander, CAP, Louisiana Wing, November 3, 1959.
115. Ibid.
116. Garrison, *On the Trail of the Assassins*, p. 125.
117. Summers, op. cit., p. 306.
118. Garrison, op. cit., p. 123.
119. Ibid.
120. Summers, op. cit., p. 307; Garrison, op. cit., p. 124.
121. Summers, op. cit., p. 307.
122. Philip Melanson, *Spy Saga: Lee Harvey Oswald and U.S. Intelligence* (New York: Praeger, 1990) pp. 43, 46–50.
123. HSCA Rpt., p. 142.
124. Ibid., pp. 142, 145.
125. Ibid., p. 142.
126. Summers, op. cit., p. 304.
127. Garrison, op. cit., p. 125.
128. Review of U.S. Weather Bureau Records, including microprint records of climatological observations of regional weather centers, from the National Climatic Data Center; James Kirkwood, *American Grotesque: An Account of the Clay Shaw–Jim Garrison Affair in the City of New Orleans* (New York: Simon & Schuster, 1968), pp. 442–43.
129. Memorandum from Andrew Sciambra to Jim Garrison, June 1, 1967, p. 1.
130. Summers, op. cit., p. 305.
131. Memorandum from Andrew Sciambra to Jim Garrison re: interview of Corey Collins, January 31, 1968, p. 1.
132. Memorandum from Andrew Sciambra to Jim Garrison re: interview of Lea [sic] McGee [sic], June 17, 1967, pp. 1–2.
133. Corey Collins statement, p. 2.
134. Affidavit of John Manchester, as prepared by Andrew Sciambra, undated, 1967, p. 1.
135. Affidavit of Henry Burnell Clark, September 12, 1967.
136. Memo re: McGehee interview, p. 2.
137. Ibid.
138. Handwritten statement of Andrew Dunn, July 13, 1967, pp. 1–2.
139. The New Orleans *States-Item*, February 7, 1967, p. 1.
140. Manchester affidavit, pp. 1–2.
141. Corey Collins statement, pp. 1–3.
142. *States-Item*, Feb. 7, 1967, p. 1.
143. Affidavit of Henry Burnell Clark, September 12, 1967, pp. 1–2.
144. Ibid., p. 2.
145. Memorandum from Andrew Sciambra to Jim Garrison re: interview with Bobbie Dedon, August 4, 1967.
146. *States-Item*, Feb. 7, 1967, p. 1.
147. Summers, op. cit., p. 306.
148. Memorandum from Andrew Sciambra to Jim Garrison re: interview with Henry Earl Palmer, May 29, 1967, pp. 1–3.
149. HSCA Rpt., p. 142.
150. Interview with Irvin Dymond, March 17, 1992.
151. Testimony of Marina Oswald, HSCA II, p. 262.

8 "OUR PAPA IS OUT OF HIS MIND"

1. McMillan, *Marina and Lee*, p. 425.
2. Letter from Arnold Johnson to Lee Oswald, July 31, 1963, CE 1145, WC Vol. XXII, pp. 166–67.
3. Ibid., p. 167.
4. McMillan, op. cit., p. 438.
5. Testimony of Philip Geraci, WC Vol. X, p. 77.
6. Testimony of Carlos Bringuier, WC Vol. X, p. 35.
7. Ibid., p. 36.
8. Interview with Carlos Bringuier, March 16, 1992.
9. Testimony of Philip Geraci, WC Vol. X, p. 77.
10. Interview with Carlos Bringuier.
11. Ibid.
12. Ibid.
13. Testimony of Carlos Bringuier, WC Vol. X, p. 38.
14. Testimony of Francis Martello, WC Vol. X, pp. 54–55.
15. Summers, *Conspiracy*, p. 280.
16. Interview with Warren de Brueys, March 20, 1992.
17. FBI report by Agent Milton Kaack, October 31, 1963, CE 826, WC Vol. XVII, p. 759.
18. Ibid.
19. Interview with Warren de Brueys, March 16, 1992; testimony of Warren de Brueys, WC Vol. X, p. 55.
20. Testimony of Warren de Brueys, WC Vol. X, p. 55.
21. Ibid., p. 56.
22. Ibid., p. 59.
23. Testimony of Lillian Murret, WC Vol. VIII, p. 145.
24. Ibid.
25. Testimony of Charles Murret, WC Vol. VIII, p. 187.
26. Ibid., pp. 187–88.
27. Interview with Carlos Bringuier.
28. Testimony of William Stuckey, WC Vol. XI, p. 159.
29. Interview with Carlos Bringuier.
30. Testimony of Marina Oswald, HSCA Vol. II, p. 252; WC Vol. I, p. 24.
31. Lee (V.T) Exhibit 6, WC Vol. XX, pp. 526–27.
32. Johnson (Arnold) Exhibit 3, WC Vol. XX, p. 261.
33. Testimony of William Stuckey, WC Vol. XI, p. 162.
34. Ibid., p. 161.
35. Testimony of Carlos Bringuier, WC Vol. X, p. 39.
36. Interview with Carlos Bringuier.
37. Testimony of Carlos Bringuier, WC Vol. X, p. 39.
38. Stuckey Exhibit 2, WC Vol. XXI, p. 623.
39. McMillan, op. cit., p. 439.
40. Lee (V. T.) Exhibit 7, WC Vol. XX, p. 529.
41. Ibid., pp. 529–30.
42. McMillan, op. cit., p. 440.
43. Testimony of William Stuckey, WC Vol. XI, p. 168.
44. Ibid., pp. 168–69.

45. Stuckey Exhibit 3, WC Vol. XXI, pp. 633–41.
46. Testimony of William Stuckey, WC Vol. XI, p. 171–75.
47. Ibid., p. 175.
48. Copy of a FBI report by Special Agent Kaack, October 31, 1963, CE 826, WC Vol. XVII, pp. 763–64.
49. McMillan, op. cit., p. 441.
50. Interview with Carlos Bringuier.
51. Testimony of Marina Oswald, WC Vol. I, pp. 54, 65.
52. Ibid., pp. 21, 54, 65.
53. Testimony of Marina Oswald, HSCA Vol. II, pp. 229–30.
54. Ibid., p. 230.
55. McMillan, op. cit., p. 452.
56. Testimony of Marina Oswald, HSCA Vol. II, p. 231.
57. Testimony of Marina Oswald, WC Vol. I, p. 22.
58. Ibid., pp. 22–23.
59. Testimony of Marina Oswald, HSCA Vol. II, p. 257.
60. McMillan, op. cit., p. 444.
61. Testimony of Marina Oswald, HSCA Vol. II, p. 257; WC Vol. I, p. 23.
62. Testimony of Marina Oswald, HSCA Vol. II, p. 258.
63. Testimony of Marina Oswald, WC Vol. I, p. 23.
64. Testimony of Marina Oswald, HSCA Vol. II, p. 260.
65. Testimony of Marina Oswald, WC Vol. I, p. 22.
66. FBI report, December 6, 1963, re: post-office form addressed to "Worker," New York, N.Y., reflecting a new address for Lee Oswald, and concerning other information on Oswald, CE 1145, WC Vol. XXII, p. 168.
67. Johnson (Arnold) Exhibit 4-A, WC Vol. XX, p. 265.
68. Testimony of Marina Oswald, HSCA Vol. II, p. 261.
69. McMillan, op. cit., p. 449–50.
70. Dobbs Exhibit 10, WC Vol. XIX, p. 577; Johnson (Arnold) Exhibit 5, WC Vol. XX, p. 266–268.
71. Interview with Francis Martello, March 16, 1992
72. Interview with Warren de Brueys, March 20, 1992.
73. Ibid.
74. Notes by Lee Oswald on his background, CE 93, WC Vol. XVI, pp. 337–46.
75. Testimony of Lillian Murret, WC Vol. VIII, p. 146.
76. FBI statement of Mr. and Mrs. Alexander Eames, CE 1154, WC Vol. XXII, p. 191.
77. Testimony of Mrs. Jesse Garner, WC Vol. X, p. 268.
78. CIA Item 451, Subject: "Review of Selected Items in the Lee Harvey OSWALD File Regarding Allegations of CASTRO Cuban Involvement in the John F. Kennedy Assassination; Reference, Letter by David W. Belin to CIA, 15 April 1975," p. 2.
79. Ibid., p. 3.
80. Lee Oswald's application for tourist card to visit Mexico, CE 2481, WC Vol. XXV, pp. 677–78.
81. Lee Oswald's Mexican tourist card (FBI item J-3) CE 2478, WC Vol. XXV, pp. 674–75.
82. Testimony of Ruth Paine, WC Vol. III, p. 5.
83. Ibid., p. 7.

84. Interview with Ruth Paine, April 11, 1992.
85. Testimony of Ruth Paine, WC Vol. III, p. 10.
86. McMillan, op. cit., p. 463.

9 "HIS MOOD WAS BAD"

1. Affidavit of Jesse Garner, WC Vol. X, p. 276.
2. Testimony of Eric Rogers, WC Vol. XI, p. 462.
3. FBI report, December 11, 1963, of interview with Earl Spencer Anderson, CE 2126, WC Vol. XXIV, p. 698.
4. WR, p. 731.
5. Affidavit of Jesse Garner, WC Vol. X, p. 276.
6. WR, p. 731.
7. Affidavit of Estelle Twiford, WC Vol. XI, pp. 179–80.
8. Ibid.
9. Secret Service report, August 28, 1964, of schedule of buses traveling from Dallas and Houston to Laredo, Texas, CE 2534, WC Vol. XXV, pp. 749–50.
10. Affidavit of John Bryan and Meryl McFarland, WC Vol. XI, p. 214.
11. Ibid., p. 215.
12. Letter of June 23, 1964, from State Department to Commission, transmitting note and enclosures received from Mexican government, with translation (CD 1154), CE 2123, WC Vol. XXIV; FBI report of March 16, 1964, of investigation into Oswald's trip to Mexico, with a translation of a report prepared by a Mexican immigration inspector and an interview of the inspector (CD 675), CE 2193, WC Vol. XXV, pp. 1–2; FBI report of May 4, 1964, concerning Lee Oswald's trip to Mexico (CD 940), CE 2566, WC Vol. XXV, pp. 2–3.
13. Testimony of Pamela Mumford, WC Vol. XI, p. 217.
14. Ibid., p. 218.
15. Ibid., pp. 219–21; McMillan, *Marina and Lee*, p. 467.
16. FBI report, May 18, 1964, re: Lee Harvey Oswald's visit to Mexico (CD 1084e), pp. 1–178, CE 2121, WC Vol. XXIV, p. 586.
17. FBI statement of Lee Dannelly, CE 2137, WC Vol. XXIV, p. 732.
18. FBI statement of Ronnie Duger, CE 2137, WC Vol. XXIV, p. 736.
19. FBI statement of Larry Temple, CE 2137, WC Vol. XXIV, p. 734.
20. CE 2137, WC Vol. XXIV, p. 735; CE 2138, FBI statement of Jesse A. Skrivanek, WC XXIV, p. 739.
21. FBI statement of Lt. Col. William B. Sinclair, CE 2137, WC Vol. XXIV, p. 736.
22. FBI statement of Lorine Shuler, CE 2138, WC Vol. XXIV, p. 740.
23. Ibid.; FBI statement of William Covington, CE 2138, p. 741.
24. Summers, *Conspiracy*, p. 386.
25. Meagher, *Accessories After the Fact*, p. 376.
26. Groden and Livingston, *High Treason*, p. 399.
27. Testimony of Sylvia Odio, WC Vol. XI, p. 368–69.
28. Ibid., p. 370.
29. Ibid., pp. 370–71.
30. Ibid., p. 372.

31. Ibid., pp. 372–73, 377.
32. HSCA Vol. X, p. 31.
33. Testimony of Sylvia Odio, WC Vol. XI, p. 371–72.
34. Ibid., p. 373; HSCA Vol. X, p. 29.
35. Testimony of Sylvia Odio, WC Vol. XI, p. 385.
36. Ibid.
37. Ibid., p. 386.
38. Ibid.
39. "U.S. Nabs Anti-Castro Fighters," *Miami Herald*, Dec. 5, 1962, p. 21A.
40. CD 1553; HSCA Vol. X, p. 23.
41. FBI memorandum, "Re: Lee Harvey Oswald, Internal Security—R—Cuba, Miami, Florida," dated September 12, 1964, p. 9.
42. Ibid., p. 10.
43. Ibid., pp. 2–3, 9.
44. HSCA Vol. X, p. 24.
45. Burt Griffin memo to W. David Slawson, May 16, 1964, House Select Committee on Assassinations (JFK Document 002969); deposition of Dr. Burton C. Einspruch, July 11, 1978, House Select Committee on Assassinations, p. 5 (JFK Document 010069).
46. FBI report, DL 44-1639, November 29, 1963.
47. Deposition of Dr. Burton C. Einspruch, July 11, 1978, House Select Committee on Assassinations (JFK Document 010069), pp. 9, 14–17.
48. HSCA Vol. X, p. 27.
49. Deposition of Dr. Burton C. Einspruch, July 11, 1978, House Select Committee on Assassinations (JFK Document 010069), p. 17.
50. FBI memorandum, "Re: Lee Harvey Oswald, Internal Security—R—Cuba, Miami, Florida," dated September 12, 1964, pp. 1–2.
51. Ibid., pp. 3–4.
52. Ibid., p. 13.
53. Ibid.
54. Ibid., p. 2.
55. HSCA Vol. X, pp. 28–29.
56. Interview with Carlos Bringuier, March 16, 1992.
57. FBI report, May 18, 1964, re: Lee Harvey Oswald's visit to Mexico (CD 1084e), pp. 1–178, WC Vol. XXIV, p. 588.
58. FBI report, May 18, 1964, re: Lee Harvey Oswald's visit to Mexico (CD 1084e), pp. 1–178, CE 2121, WC Vol. XXIV, pp. 588–89; letter of June 15, 1964, from State Department to Commission, enclosing copy of note from the Cuban Ministry of Foreign Affairs to the Swiss Ambassador in Cuba, with translation (CD 1110), CE 2445, WC Vol. XXV, p. 586; FBI report of investigation of December 16, 1963, of schedule of Continental Trailways buses from New Orleans to Houston; excerpts of Secret Service report dated August 28, 1964, of schedule of buses from Dallas and Houston to Laredo, Texas (CD 231, 1084e), CE 2464, WC Vol. XXV, p. 634.
59. CE 2121, p. 589.
60. Testimony of Eusebio Azcue, HSCA Vol. III, pp. 130–31.
61. CE 2121, p. 589.
62. Testimony of Eusebio Azcue, HSCA Vol. III, p. 131.
63. Ibid.

64. Testimony of Alfredo Mirabal, HSCA Vol. III, pp. 173–74.

65. CE 2121, p. 590.

66. Oleg Maximovich Nechiporenko, *Passport to Assassination: The Never-Before-Told Story of Lee Harvey Oswald by the KGB Colonel Who Knew Him* (New York: Birch Lane Press, 1993) p. 66.

67. Nechiporenko, pp. 67–68.

68. Statement of David Phillips, 1978.

69. Interview with Gerald Nadler, April 3, 1992; Jean Davison, *Oswald's Game* (New York: Norton, 1983), p. 209.

70. Davison, op. cit., p. 209.

71. Nechiporenko, *Passport to Assassination*, p. 70.

72. Interview with Yuriy Nosenko, September 1, 1992.

73. Rankin memorandum, Warren Commission Documents, July 2, 1964, No. 1216.

74. Nechiporenko, *Passport to Assassination*, p. 76.

75. Ibid., p. 77.

76. Ibid.

77. Gerald Nadler, "The KGB Spies Who Came in for the Gold," *The Washington Times*, March 27, 1992, p. A9; interview with Gerald Nadler, April 3, 1992.

78. Ibid., p. 105.

79. Testimony of Eusebio Azcue, HSCA Vol. III, pp. 132–33.

80. CE 2121, p. 589.

81. Testimony of Eusebio Azcue, HSCA Vol. III, p. 133.

82. CE 2121, p. 590.

83. Testimony of Eusebio Azcue, HSCA Vol. III, p. 133.

84. Garrison, *On the Trail of the Assassins*, p. 326.

85. CD 631.

86. Ibid.

87. Summers, op. cit., p. 522.

88. Ibid.

89. Ibid., p. 363.

90. Interview with Edwin Lopez, January 30, 1992.

91. Testimony of Eusebio Azcue, HSCA III, p. 136.

92. Interview with Edwin Lopez.

93. CE 2121, pp. 588–89; testimony of Alfredo Mirabal, HSCA Vol. III, p. 174.

94. HSCA Vol. III, p. 172.

95. Testimony of Alfredo Diaz, HSCA Vol. III, p. 174.

96. Gerald Nadler, "The KGB Spies Who Came in for the Gold," *The Washington Times*, March 27, 1992, p. 1; interviews with Gerald Nadler, April 3 and 5, 1992.

97. WR, p. 735.

98. Photos of guide map of Mexico City, CE 2488, WC Vol. XXV, pp. 689–704.

99. Testimony of Marina Oswald, WC Vol. 1, p. 27; FBI report, April 22, 1964, giving approximation of expenditures that Lee Oswald made during his travel and stay in Mexico (CD 905b), CE 1166, WC Vol. XXII; photo of pamphlet titled "Fiesta Brava," published by Pemex Travel Club, Mexico (CD 1458), CE 2489, WC Vol. XXV, p. 705.

100. WR, p. 735.

101. HSCA Vol. III, pp. 106–7; JFK Document 014975, interview of employees of the Cuban consulate in Mexico City, p. 421.
102. HSCA Rpt., pp. 124–25.
103. Summers, op. cit., p. 351.
104. Ibid., p. 352.
105. The research files compiled by Anthony Summers for *Conspiracy* are available for reading and photocopying at the Assassination Archives and Research Center, Washington, D.C. Summers donated them to the center after finishing the work on his book.
106. Comer Clark, "Fidel Castro Says He Knew of Oswald Threat to Kill JFK," *National Enquirer*, October 15, 1967.
107. HSCA Vol. III, pp. 196–97; JFK Exhibits F-429-B and F-429-C.
108. HSCA Rpt., p. 122.
109. Summers, op. cit., p. 364.
110. "Analysis of the Support Provided to the Warren Commission by the Central Intelligence Agency," HSCA Appendix XI.
111. HSCA Rpt., p. 123; JFK Documents 014974 and 014975, classified staff report of "Lee Harvey Oswald and Mexico City," prepared by Ed Lopez and Dan Hardway, containing interviews of employees of the Cuban consulate in Mexico City.
112. HSCA Rpt., p. 123.
113. Senate Intelligence Committee, *Performance of Intelligence Agencies*, pp. 28–41.
114. Ibid.
115. JFK Document 005134; Autulio Ramirez Ortiz, *Castro's Red Hot Hell* (unpublished).
116. HSCA Rpt., p. 121.
117. FBI report of interviews of manager and other personnel of Hotel del Comercio at Mexico City (CD 1084e), CE 2540, WC Vol. XXV, p. 9.
118. Letter, dated June 29, 1964, from the FBI to the Commission, with attached report of reinterviews of Mr. and Mrs. Juan M. de Cuba (CD 1187), CE 2459, WC Vol. XXV, pp. 2–3; CE 2460, WC Vol. XXV, p. 6; FBI report, June 11, 1964, of interview of Eulalio Rodriguez-Chavez (CD 1166), CE 2456, WC Vol. XXV, p. 3; CE 2532, re: Oswald's Mexico trip, p. 9; CE 2121, pp. 61, 76.

10 "WHEN WILL ALL OUR FOOLISHNESS . . . ?"

1. Testimony of Colin Barnhorst, WC Vol. X, pp. 289–90.
2. Burcham Exhibit 1, WC Vol. XIX, pp. 192–93; Cunningham Exhibit 1A, WC Vol. XIX, pp. 399–400.
3. Burcham Exhibit 1, p. 192.
4. Testimony of Robert Stovall, WC Vol. X, pp. 170–71.
5. Interview with Marina Oswald, December 8, 1992.
6. McMillan, *Marina and Lee*, p. 471.
7. Interview with Marina Oswald.
8. Photograph of Marina Oswald's bracelet, CE 2484, WC Vol. XXV, p. 681.
9. Testimony of Mary E. Bledsoe, WC Vol. VI, pp. 401–2.
10. Ibid., pp. 425–27.

11. Ibid., p. 406.
12. McMillan, op. cit., p. 472.
13. Testimony of Michael Paine, WC Vol. II, pp. 422–23.
14. Testimony of Ruth Paine, WC Vol. VI, p. 33.
15. Testimony of Linnie Mae Randle, WC Vol. II, p. 246.
16. Testimony of Ruth Paine, WC Vol. IX, p. 393.
17. Testimony of Ruth Paine, WC Vol. III, p. 34.
18. Testimony of Linnie Mae Randle, WC Vol. II, p. 247.
19. Testimony of Roy Truly, WC Vol. III, p. 213.
20. Testimony of Gladys Johnson, WC Vol. X, pp. 293–94, 302.
21. Ibid., pp. 296, 298.
22. Ibid., pp. 296, 298, 306.
23. Testimony of Earlene Roberts, WC Vol. VI, p. 437; McMillan, op. cit., p. 479.
24. Testimony of Ruth Paine, WC Vol. III, pp. 34–35.
25. Testimony of Roy Truly, WC Vol. III, p. 213.
26. Testimony of Roy Truly, WC Vol. III, p. 213–14.
27. Gerald R. Ford and John R. Stiles, *Portrait of the Assassin* (New York: Simon & Schuster, 1965), p. 282.
28. Testimony of Wesley Buell Frazier, WC Vol. II, p. 216.
29. Testimony of Ruth Paine, WC Vol. III, p. 40.
30. McMillan, op. cit., p. 475.
31. Testimony of Ruth Paine, WC Vol. III, p. 39.
32. Ibid., pp. 39–40.
33. Ibid., p. 40.
34. Interview with Michael Paine, April 18, 1992; testimony of Michael Paine, WC Vol. II, p. 403.
35. Johnson (Arnold) Exhibit 7, WC Vol. XX, pp. 271–73.
36. Interview with Michael Paine, April 11, 1992.
37. Interview with Michael Paine, April 18, 1992; testimony of Michael Paine, WC Vol. II, p. 401.
38. Interview with Michael Paine, April 18, 1992.
39. Ibid.
40. Ibid.
41. McMillan, op. cit., p. 485.
42. Testimony of Michael Paine, WC Vol. II, p. 408.
43. Ibid.
44. McMillan, op. cit., pp. 489–90.
45. Testimony of James Hosty, WC Vol. IV, p. 447.
46. Ibid., p. 448.
47. Ibid., p. 449.
48. Interview with Ruth Paine; testimony of James Hosty, WC Vol. IV, pp. 450–51.
49. Testimony of James Hosty, pp. 450–51.
50. Ibid., p. 450.
51. McMillan, op. cit., p. 495.
52. Testimony of James Hosty, WC Vol. IV, p. 452.
53. Holmes Exhibit 1, WC Vol. XX, p. 172.
54. Johnson (Arnold) Exhibit 7, WC Vol. XX, pp. 272–73.

55. McMillan, op. cit., p. 496.
56. Interview with Ruth Paine, April 11, 1992.
57. McMillan, op. cit., p. 497.
58. Testimony of Forrest Sorrels, WC Vol. VII, p. 334.
59. WR, p. 31.
60. Testimony of Forrest Sorrels, WC Vol. VII, p. 335.
61. Testimony of James Hosty, WC Vol. IV, p. 453.
62. McMillan, op. cit., p. 498.
63. Testimony of Ruth Paine, WC Vol. III, p. 101.
64. McMillan, op. cit., p. 499.
65. Testimony of Marina Oswald, HSCA Vol. II, p. 263.
66. Testimony of Ruth Paine, WC Vol. III, p. 101.
67. Ibid., p. 102.
68. Ibid., pp. 51–52.
69. Draft of letter from Lee Oswald to the Russian embassy, CE 103, WC Vol. XVI, pp. 443–44.
70. Soviet embassy file on Lee Oswald, CE 986, WC Vol. XVIII, pp. 538–39.
71. Letter from Lee Oswald to the Russian embassy, November 9, 1963, CE 15, WC Vol. XVI, p. 33.
72. Testimony of Floyd Davis, WC Vol. X, p. 357.
73. Testimony of Sterling Wood, WC Vol. X, p. 392.
74. Testimony of Floyd Davis, WC Vol. X, p. 365.
75. Ibid., pp. 359, 367.
76. Testimony of Malcolm Price, WC Vol. X, pp. 370–74; testimony of Garland Slack, WC Vol. X, pp. 381–82.
77. Testimony of Floyd Davis, WC Vol. X, p. 361; testimony of Malcolm Price, WC Vol. X, p. 370; testimony of Gordon Slack, WC Vol. X, p. 382; interview with David Perry, March 8, 1992.
78. Testimony of Malcolm Price, WC Vol. X, p. 376.
79. Testimony of Gordon Slack, WC Vol. X, p. 383.
80. Senate Intelligence Committee, *Performance of Intelligence Agencies,* Appendix B; Hearings on FBI Oversight before House Subcommittee on Civil and Constitutional Rights, Serial 2, Pt. 3, October 21 and December 11–12, 1975.
81. Ibid., pp. 129–30, 145–47.
82. Ibid., pp. 132, 160.
83. HSCA Rpt., p. 195.
84. FBI memorandum, To: Mr. Held, From: H. N. Bassett, Subject: Assassination of President John F. Kennedy, August 17, 1976, p. 1.
85. Wire-service story, "Back Pay Can't Erase Censured Agent's Years of Pain," by Earl Golz, December 8, 1980.
86. Interview with Bill Alexander, March 6, 1992.
87. Testimony of Michael Paine, WC Vol. II, p. 406.
88. Secret Service memo to Commission of July 10, 1964, concerning Trade Mart decision (CD 1251), CE 1360, WC Vol. XXII, p. 613.
89. Testimony of Winston Lawson, WC Vol. IV, p. 325.
90. Statement of Special Agent Winston Lawson concerning his official duties from November 4 to November 22, 1963, in preparation for President Kennedy's trip to Dallas, CE 769, WC Vol. XVII, p. 3.

91. Letter from Secret Service to the Commission, March 26, 1964, CE 1022, WC Vol. XVIII, p. 2; "Increased Seating Readied for Kennedy Luncheon," *Dallas Times Herald*, November 16, 1963, CE 1361, WC Vol. XXII, p. 613.
92. Interview with Marina Oswald, August 21, 1992; testimony of Marina Oswald, WC Vol. I, p. 54.
93. Testimony of Ruth Paine, WC Vol. II, p. 515.
94. Testimony of Gladys Johnson, WC Vol. X, p. 298.
95. Interview with Ruth Paine, April 18, 1992; testimony of Ruth Paine, WC Vol. III, p. 44.
96. Testimony of Ruth Paine, WC Vol. III, p. 45.
97. Testimony of Marina Oswald, WC Vol. I, pp. 53–54, 63–66; testimony of Ruth Paine, WC Vol. III, p. 45.
98. Testimony of Marina Oswald, WC Vol. I, p. 66.
99. Ibid., p. 63.
100. Testimony of Ruth Paine, WC Vol. III, p. 46.
101. "Yarborough Gets JFK Table Spot," *Dallas Times Herald*, November 19, 1963 (CD 320), CE 1362, p. 614.
102. "Yarborough Seating Pondered," *Dallas Morning News*, November 19, 1963 (CD 320), CE 1363, WC Vol. XXII, p. 615; "Yarborough Invited to Travel with JFK," *Dallas Morning News*, November 20, 1963 (CD 320), CE 1364, WC Vol. XXII, p. 616.
103. Testimony of Wesley Buell Frazier, WC Vol. II, p. 222.
104. Testimony of Gladys Johnson, WC Vol. X, p. 297; testimony of A. C. Johnson, WC Vol. X, p. 302.
105. Testimony of Marina Oswald, WC Vol. I, p. 65.
106. McMillan, op. cit., p. 521.
107. Testimony of Marina Oswald, WC Vol. I, p. 66.
108. McMillan, op. cit., p. 523.
109. Testimony of Ruth Paine, WC Vol. III, pp. 46, 49.
110. Testimony of Marina Oswald, WC Vol. I, p. 66.
111. Testimony of Marina Oswald, HSCA Vol. II, pp. 268–69.
112. McMillan, op. cit., p. 524.
113. Testimony of Ruth Paine, WC Vol. III, p. 47.
114. Testimony of Marina Oswald, WC Vol. I, p. 66.
115. Ibid., p. 69; McMillan, op. cit., p. 524.
116. Testimony of Marina Oswald, WC Vol. I, p. 72.

11 "I'll Never Forget It . . ."

1. FBI statement of Linnie Mae Randle, CE 2008, WC Vol. XXIV, p. 407.
2. Ibid.
3. Statement of Wesley Buell Frazier, London Weekend Television, "The Trial of Lee Harvey Oswald."
4. Testimony of Wesley Buell Frazier, WC Vol. II, p. 228.
5. Testimony of Charles Givens, WC Vol. VI, p. 352.
6. Testimony of James Jarman, WC Vol. III, p. 201.
7. See generally the diagram of the sixth floor, Texas School Book Depository, CE 483, WC Vol. XVII, p. 201.
8. Statement of Bonnie Ray Williams, CE 1381, WC Vol. XXII, pp. 681–82.

9. Testimony of Charles Givens, WC Vol. VI, p. 354.

10. Ibid., p. 349.

11. Ibid., p. 353.

12. Interview with Danny Arce, March 8, 1992; testimony of Bonnie Ray Williams, WC Vol. III, p. 168; testimony of Danny Arce, WC Vol. VI, p. 365; testimony of Billy Lovelady, WC Vol. VI, p. 337; affidavit of Jack E. Dougherty, November 22, 1963.

13. Jim Moore, *Conspiracy of One* (Fort Worth, Texas: The Summit Group, 1991) p. 44.

14. Testimony of Gerald Hill, WC Vol. VII, p. 46.

15. Testimony of Cortlandt Cunningham, WC Vol. II, p. 252.

16. Testimony of Capt. Will Fritz, WC Vol. IV, p. 224.

17. Summers, *Conspiracy*, p. 77.

18. Summers, op. cit., pp. 77, 554.

19. Testimony of Mrs. R. E. Carolyn Arnold, CE 1381, WC Vol. XXII, p. 635; FBI statement of Mrs. R. E. Arnold, November 26, 1963, File # DL-80-43.

20. CE 1381, p. 635; Summers, op. cit., p. 76.

21. Statements of Mrs. Donald Sam Baker (nee Virgie Rackley), CE 1381, WC Vol. XXII, p. 635, and Mrs. Barney R. (Betty) Dragoo, p. 645.

22. Testimony of James Jarman, WC Vol. III, p. 201.

23. Testimony of Troy West, WC Vol. VI, p. 361–62.

24. Testimony of Charles Givens, WC Vol. VI, p. 352; testimony of Danny Arce, WC Vol. VI, p. 365; testimony of Jack Dougherty, WC Vol. VI, p. 378.

25. Testimony of Joe Molina, WC Vol. VI, p. 372; testimony of Mrs. Robert Reid, WC Vol. III, p. 271.

26. Testimony of Billy Lovelady, WC Vol. VI, p. 338.

27. Testimony of Bonnie Ray Williams, WC Vol. III, p. 170.

28. Ibid.; diagram of the sixth floor of the Depository, CE 483, WC Vol. XVII, p. 201.

29. Testimony of Bonnie Ray Williams, WC Vol. III, pp. 169–70.

30. Summers, op. cit., p. 43.

31. FBI statement of Ruby Henderson, CE 2089, WC Vol. XXIV, p. 524.

32. Sheriff's statement of Julia Ann Mercer, CE 2003, WC Vol. XXIV, p. 216.

33. Marrs, *Crossfire*, p. 19.

34. Statement of Dallas police officer Joe Murphy, December 9, 1963, CD 205.

35. Earl Golz interview with John Powell for the *Dallas Morning News*, December 19, 1978.

36. Summers, op. cit., p. 43.

37. Ibid., p. 44.

38. Memo, SAC Dallas to Director, FBI, December 15, 1964.

39. Ibid., p. 2.

40. FBI memo, ibid.; interview with Dallas sheriff Robert Knowles, March 3, 1992.

41. Memo, SAC Dallas to Director, FBI, December 15, 1964, p. 2.

42. Testimony of Arnold Rowland, WC Vol. II, pp. 169–70.

43. Ibid., p. 176.

44. Ibid., pp. 185–87.

45. Testimony of Mrs. Arnold Rowland, WC Vol. VI, pp. 181–85.

46. Testimony of F. M. Turner, WC Vol. VII, p. 220; testimony of Forrest Sorrels, WC Vol. VII, p. 351.
47. Testimony of Arnold Rowland, WC Vol. II, p. 178.
48. Ibid., pp. 179, 189.
49. Ibid., p. 181.
50. Testimony of Mrs. Arnold Rowland, WC Vol. VI, pp. 177–80.
51. Ibid., p. 185.
52. Ibid., p. 190.
53. FBI statement of Carolyn Walther, CE 2086, WC Vol. XXIV, p. 522.
54. FBI statement of Pearl Springer, CE 2087, WC Vol. XXIV, p. 523.
55. Earl Golz interview notes with Mrs. Eric Walther, November 21, 1978, maintained in the archives of the Assassination Research Center, Washington, D.C.
56. FBI statement of Carolyn Walther, CE 2086, WC Vol. XXIV, p. 522.
57. Testimony of Robert Edwards, WC Vol. VI, pp. 201–2.
58. Testimony of Ronald Fischer, WC Vol. VI, p. 194.
59. Interview with Ronald Fischer, January 19, 1992.
60. Testimony of Ronald Fischer, WC Vol. VI, p. 194; testimony of Robert Edwards, WC Vol. VI, pp. 203–4.
61. CD 1245.
62. Testimony of Jacqueline Kennedy, WC Vol. V, p. 179.
63. Testimony of Bobby Hargis, WC Vol. VI, pp. 294–95.
64. Interview with Danny Arce, March 9, 1992.
65. Author's review of Warren Commission volumes and statements from Dealey Plaza witnesses by FBI, sheriff's office, and Dallas police.
66. HSCA Rpt. p. 87.
67. Ibid., p. 90.
68. Josiah Thompson, *Six Seconds in Dallas*, (New York: Berkley, 1976), p. 26.
69. Testimony of James Underwood, WC Vol. VI, p. 169.
70. Testimony of Bobby Hargis, WC Vol. VI, p. 294.
71. Moore, *Conspiracy of One*, p. 33.
72. Testimony of Tom Dillard, WC Vol. VI, p. 165; testimony of James Underwood, WC Vol. VI, p. 169; testimony of Ronald Fischer, WC Vol. VI, p. 195; testimony of Joe Murphy, WC Vol. VI, p. 259; testimony of D. V. Harkness, WC Vol. VI, p. 309.
73. Testimony of James Crawford, WC Vol. VI, p. 174; testimony of S. M. Holland, WC Vol. VI, p. 243.
74. Testimony of Abraham Zapruder, WC Vol. VII, p. 572.
75. Testimony of Lee Bowers, WC Vol. VI, p. 287.
76. Testimony of Roy Truly, WC Vol. III, p. 283.
77. "Analysis of Recorded Sounds Relating to the Assassination of President John F. Kennedy," Bolt, Beranek and Newman Inc., in "A Study of the Acoustics Evidence Related to the Assassination of President John F. Kennedy," appendix to the hearing before the Select Committee on Assassinations, Vol. VIII, sec. 4.1.
78. HSCA Rpt., p. 68.
79. Ibid., p. 72.
80. Testimony of H. B. McClain, HSCA Vol. V, p. 637.

81. Interview with H. B. McClain, March 3, 1992.
82. Ibid.
83. Report of the Committee on Ballistics Acoustics, Commission on Physical Sciences, Mathematics, and Resources; National Research Council; National Academy Press, Washington, D.C., 1982, p. 7.
84. HSCA Rpt., pp. 75–76.
85. Interview with H. B. McClain, March 3, 1992.
86. James C. Bowles, "The Kennedy Assassination Tapes: A Rebuttal to the Acoustical Evidence Theory," unpublished, pp. 50–51.
87. Ibid.
88. "Who Shot President Kennedy?," Nova Productions, 1988.
89. Letter to the author from Professor Norman Ramsey, April 3, 1992.
90. Report of the Committee on Ballistics Acoustics, Commission on Physical Sciences, Mathematics, and Resources; National Research Council; National Academy Press, Washington, D.C., 1982, pp. 23–26.
91. Ibid., pp. 34, 38.
92. Testimony of Harold Norman, WC Vol. III, p. 195.
93. Interview with Harold Norman, January 19, 1992.
94. Testimony of Bonnie Ray Williams, WC Vol. III, p. 175.
95. Interview with Harold Norman; testimony of Harold Norman, WC Vol. III, pp. 191, 194–96.
96. Interview with Harold Norman; testimony of Bonnie Ray Williams, WC Vol. III, p. 175.
97. Testimony of Robert Jackson, WC Vol. II, p. 159; testimony of Malcolm Couch, WC Vol. VI, p. 157.
98. Interview with Travis Linn, April 15, 1992.
99. Ibid.
100. Testimony of Malcolm Couch, WC Vol. VI, p. 158.
101. Testimony of Robert Jackson, WC Vol. II, p. 159.
102. Ibid., p. 160.
103. Testimony of Malcolm Couch, WC Vol. VI, pp. 156–57.
104. Testimony of James Crawford, WC Vol. VI, p. 173.
105. Ibid., p. 174.
106. Testimony of Mrs. Earle Cabell, WC Vol. VII, p. 486.
107. Testimony of James Worrell, WC Vol. II, p. 193.
108. Ibid., p. 200.
109. Interview with Amos Lee Euins, January 19, 1992.
110. Ibid.
111. Testimony of Amos Lee Euins, WC Vol. II, p. 204.
112. Photo of the Book Depository as marked by Howard Brennan, CE 477; photo of Howard Brennan taken on March 20, 1964, showing his position on the day of the assassination, CE 478; negative of a slide taken from the Zapruder film, CE 479, WC Vol. XVII, pp. 196–98.
113. Howard Brennan and J. Edward Cherryholmes, *Eyewitness to History: The Kennedy Assassination: As Seen by Howard Brennan* (Waco, Texas: Texian Press, 1987) p. 7; testimony of Howard Brennan, WC Vol. III, p. 143.
114. Brennan and Cherryholmes, op. cit., pp. 8–9.
115. Ibid., p. 13; testimony of Howard Brennan, WC Vol III, pp. 144–45.

116. Brennan and Cherryholmes, op. cit., p. 13.
117. Ibid., pp. 14–15.
118. Testimony of Howard Brennan, WC Vol. III, p. 145.
119. Transcript of Dallas police channels for November 22, 1963, CE 705, WC Vol. XVII, p. 397.
120. Brennan and Cherryholmes, op. cit., p. 25.
121. Testimony of Howard Brennan, WC Vol. III, p. 148.
122. Brennan and Cherryholmes, op. cit., p. 160.
123. Testimony of Howard Brennan, WC Vol. III, p. 158.
124. Brennan and Cherryholmes, op. cit., p. 18.
125. Lane, *Rush to Judgment*, p. 75.
126. Marrs, *Crossfire*, p. 26.
127. Anson, *"They've Killed the President!,"* p. 18.
128. Testimony of Howard Brennan, WC Vol. III, p. 147.
129. Brennan and Cherryholmes, op. cit., pp. 6–7.
130. Decker Exhibit 5323, statement of Jean Hill to sheriff's department, WC Vol. XIX, p. 479.
131. Testimony of Jean Hill, WC Vol. VI, pp. 206–7.
132. Ibid., p. 208.
133. Decker Exhibit 5323, statement of Jean Hill to sheriff's department, WC Vol. XIX, p. 479.
134. Testimony of Jean Hill, WC Vol. VI, p. 207.
135. Marrs, op. cit., p. 323.
136. Testimony of Jean Hill, WC Vol. VI, p. 212.
137. Ibid., pp. 212, 214.
138. Ibid., p. 212.
139. Summers, op. cit., p. 51.
140. Ibid.; Hurt, *Reasonable Doubt*, p. 119.
141. Decker Exhibit 5323, statement of Jean Hill to sheriff's department, WC Vol. XIX, p. 479.
142. Marrs, op. cit., p. 323.
143. Interview with Gary Mack, February 23, 1992.
144. Marrs, op. cit., p. 38.
145. *USA Today* television program, February 20, 1989.
146. Marrs, op. cit., p. 484.
147. Ibid., p. 483.
148. Ibid., p. 39.
149. Decker Exhibit 5323, affidavit of J. C.Price, WC Vol. XIX, p. 492.
150. Marrs, op. cit., p. 39.
151. Testimony of Lee Bowers, WC Vol. VI, pp. 285–86.
152. Ibid., p. 287.
153. Ibid., p. 288.
154. Testimony of S. M. Holland, WC Vol. VI, pp. 243–44.
155. Decker Exhibit 5323, affidavit of Sam Holland, WC Vol. XIX, p. 480.
156. Testimony of Frank Reilly, WC Vol. VI, p. 227; testimony of J. W. Foster, WC Vol. VI, pp. 249–52; Decker Exhibit 5323, affidavit of Royce Skelton, WC Vol. XIX, p. 496.
157. Edward Jay Epstein, *Inquest: The Warren Commission and the Establishment of the Truth* (New York: Viking, 1966), p. 70.

158. FBI report of interview with James Simmons, CE 1416, WC Vol. XXII, p. 833.

159. FBI report of interview with Clemon Johnson, CE 1422, WC Vol. XIX, p. 836.

160. Decker Exhibit 5223, statement of Austin Miller, WC Vol. XIX, p. 485.

161. Interview with Art Pence, February 21, 1992.

162. Testimony of Mrs. Robert Reid, WC Vol. 3, p. 273; testimony of Luke Mooney, WC Vol. III, p. 282; testimony of Tom Dilliard, WC Vol. VI, p. 165; testimony of James Romack, WC Vol. VI, p. 280; WC Vol. VII, p. 517.

163. Testimony of Seymour Weitzman, WC Vol. VII, pp. 107, 109; interview with Jim Moore, March 13, 1992.

164. Gordon Arnold, interviewed by Earl Golz, August 27, 1978, for the *Dallas Morning News*.

165. Interview with Jim Moore, March 13, 1992.

166. Marrs, op. cit., pp. 81–86.

167. FBI statement of Ed Hoffman, June 28, 1967, Dallas field office files.

168. Testimony of Earle Brown, WC Vol. VI, p. 236.

169. Testimony of Joe Murphy, WC Vol. VI, pp. 256–58.

170. Testimony of Eugene Moore, WC Vol. III, p. 294; testimony of Earle Brown, WC Vol. VI, p. 233; interview with Jim Moore, March 4 and 13, 1992.

171. Interview with Jim Moore.

172. Ibid.

173. Decker Exhibit 5323, affidavit of Malcolm Summers, WC Vol. XIX, p. 500.

174. Marrs, op. cit., p. 330.

175. Earl Golz, "Ex-Officer Suspects He Chased '2nd gun,'" *Dallas Morning News*, August 20, 1978, p. 42A.

176. Marrs, op. cit., p. 326.

177. "Scenes from an Assassination," *Dallas Times Herald*, November 20, 1978.

178. Interview with David Perry, March 2, 1992.

179. Duke Lane, "The Black Car Chase and the Cowtown Connection," unpublished, 1993.

180. *Entre Nous* newsletter, Vol 14, #2, " Will the Real Umbrella Man Please Stand Up?," p. 15.

181. Testimony of Louie Witt, HSCA Vol. IV, pp. 428–33, 441–52.

182. Testimony of Billy Lovelady, WC Vol. VI, p. 338.

183. Testimony of Danny Arce, WC Vol. VI, p. 367; testimony of Wesley Buell Frazier, WC Vol. II, pp. 233, 234, 236, 242; testimony of Harold Norman, WC Vol. III, p. 202; testimony of Mrs. Donald Baker, WC Vol. VII, p. 515; and testimony of William Shelley, WC Vol. VI, pp. 328–29.

184. Marrs, op. cit. p. 46.

185. Interviews with Tom Weaver, March 8, 1992, and John Crawson and Bernie Schram, March 6, 1992.

186. Interview with Francine Burrows, March 6, 1992.

12 "HE LOOKS LIKE A MANIAC"

1. Testimony of Marrion Baker, WC Vol. III, p. 246.
2. Ibid., p. 252, 253.
3. Ibid., p. 252.
4. Testimony of George Rackley, WC Vol. VI, pp. 276–77; testimony of James Romack, WC Vol. VI, pp. 280–82.
5. Testimony of D. V. Harkness, WC Vol. VI, p. 311; testimony of J. Herbert Sawyer, WC Vol. VI, p. 320.
6. Testimony of Mrs. Robert Reid, WC Vol. III, pp. 278–79.
7. Ibid., p. 274.
8. Testimony of Cecil McWatters, WC Vol. II, p. 265.
9. Testimony of Mary Bledsoe, WC Vol. VI, p. 409.
10. Testimony of Cecil McWatters, WC Vol. VI, p. 265.
11. Ibid., p. 272.
12. Testimony of William Whaley, WC Vol. II, p. 256.
13. Testimony of Earlene Roberts, WC Vol. VI, p. 438.
14. Ibid., p. 439.
15. HSCA Rpt., p. 183.
16. Testimony of Luke Mooney, WC Vol. III, p. 283; testimony of Eugene Boone, WC Vol. III, p. 292; testimony of Bobby Hargis, WC Vol. VI, pp. 295–96; testimony of D.V. Harkness, WC Vol. VI, p. 310; testimony of Seymour Weitzman, WC Vol. VII, p. 107; testimony of J. M. Smith, WC Vol. VII, pp. 535–37, 568.
17. Testimony of Luke Mooney, WC Vol. III, p. 284.
18. Testimony of Carl Day, WC Vol. IV, p. 250.
19. Interview with Carl Day, January 19, 1992.
20. Testimony of Robert Frazier, WC Vol. III, pp. 414–28; testimony of Joseph Nicol, WC Vol. III, pp. 505–7; CE 558, WC Vol. XVII, p. 556.
21. Interview with Carl Day.
22. Ibid.
23. A carton labeled box "A" found on the sixth floor of the Book Depository, CE 641; photo of Oswald's left palm print card (CE 628) with a circle around a portion of the palm print, CE 642; photo of the latent palm print on CE 641, CE 643, WC Vol. XVII, pp. 292–93; testimony of Sebastian Latona, WC Vol. IV, p. 31.
24. Testimony of Sebastian Latona, WC Vol. IV, pp. 32, 35.
25. Interview with Carl Day.
26. Testimony of Will Fritz, WC Vol. IV, p. 206; testimony of Luke Mooney, WC Vol. III, p. 293.
27. Interview with Carl Day.
28. Testimony of Carl Day, WC Vol. IV, p. 267.
29. WC Appendix X, "Expert Testimony," pp. 565–66; WC Vol. IV, p. 5.
30. WR, p. 135; testimony of Wesley Buell Frazier, WC Vol. II, p. 228.
31. Testimony of Nat Pinkston, WC Vol. VI, pp. 333–35.
32. Marrs, *Crossfire*, pp. 333–337.
33. Police arrest records of Gus W. Abrams, Harold Doyle, and John Gedney, November 22, 1963, Dallas Municipal Archives and Records Center.
34. Call of Tippit into Oak Cliff: testimony of Jesse Curry, WC Vol. IV, pp.

178–79, 184–86, 193; testimony of James Putnam, WC Vol. VII, pp. 75–77; testimony of Calvin Owens, WC Vol. VII, pp. 81–82; Oswald walking east on Patton: testimony of Helen Markham, WC Vol. III, p. 317; testimony of William Scoggins, WC Vol. III, p. 325. (Some thought Oswald was walking west, the opposite direction, but later admitted that Oswald had turned around to look at the police car, which put him in a westerly direction.)

35. WR, p. 165.
36. Testimony of C. T. Walker, WC Vol. VII, p. 42.
37. Testimony of Helen Markham, WC Vol. III, p. 308.
38. Ibid., p. 320; interview with Jim Leavelle, March 7, 1992.
39. Testimony of Helen Markham, WC Vol. III, p. 311.
40. Testimony of Virginia Davis, WC Vol. VI, p. 457.
41. Testimony of Barbara Jeanette Davis, WC Vol. III, p. 343.
42. Testimony of C. W. Brown, WC Vol. VII, p. 250.
43. Testimony of William Scoggins, WC Vol. III, p. 325.
44. Ibid., p. 327.
45. Ibid., p. 334.
46. Testimony of Domingo Benavides, WC Vol. VI, p. 446.
47. Ibid., p. 449.
48. Testimony of Ted Callaway, WC Vol. III, p. 352.
49. Ibid., pp. 353–54.
50. Ibid., p. 355.
51. Testimony of Sam Guinyard, WC Vol. VII, p. 400.
52. Testimony of Warren Reynolds, WC Vol. XI, p. 435.
53. Ibid., p. 436.
54. Ibid., p. 435.
55. Testimony of William Smith, WC Vol. VII, p. 85; testimony of B. M. Patterson, WC Vol. XV, pp. 744–45.
56. London Weekend Television, "Trial of Lee Harvey Oswald," testimony of Jack Tatum.
57. Testimony of W. R. Westbrook, WC Vol. VII, p. 115; testimony of Thomas Hutson, WC Vol. VII, pp. 30, 33.
58. Testimony of Helen Markham, William Scoggins, and Virginia Davis, WC Vol. III, pp. 312, 328, 347.
59. Testimony of Ted Callaway, WC Vol. III, p. 356.
60. Testimony of Domingo Benavides, WC Vol. VI, p. 453; testimony of Virginia Davis, William Smith, and Sam Guinyard, WC Vol. VII, pp. 45, 85, 264, 401.
61. Testimony of Marina Oswald, WC Vol. I, pp. 121–22.
62. Ibid., p. 122.
63. Testimony of Barbara Davis, WC Vol. III, pp. 345–46; testimony of Domingo Benavides, WC Vol. VI, pp. 448–50, 460. The shells were marked at the scene by Dallas policeman J. M. Poe (WC VI, p. 49; WC VII, pp. 272, 275, 276), but he later could not identify his marking because during the chain of evidence four FBI sets of initials had been added, obliterating most of his original markings (WC III, p. 511).
64. Testimony of Cortlandt Cunningham, WC Vol. III, pp. 470, 473; testimony of Joseph Nicol, WC Vol. III, p. 511.
65. "The Warren Inquiry," CBS News, Part III, June 27, 1967.

66. Testimony of Cortlandt Cunningham, WC Vol. III, p. 483.
67. Testimony of Joseph Nicol, WC Vol. III, pp. 512–13; "The Warren Inquiry," CBS News, Part III, June 27, 1967.
68. Hurt, *Reasonable Doubt*, p. 158.
69. Davis, *Mafia Kingfish*, p. 210.
70. Testimony of Johnny Calvin Brewer, WC Vol. VII, p. 3.
71. Ibid., p. 4.
72. Testimony of Julia Postal, WC Vol. VII, pp. 10, 14.
73. Testimony of William Burroughs, WC Vol. VII, p. 15.
74. Testimony of Julia Postal, WC Vol. VII, p. 11.
75. Testimony of Johnny Calvin Brewer, WC Vol. VII, p. 5.
76. Testimony of Julia Postal, WC Vol. VII, p. 11.
77. Radio log of Channel One of the Dallas Police Department for November 22, 1963, CE 705, WC Vol. XVII, p. 418.
78. Testimony of Johnny Calvin Brewer, WC Vol. VII, p. 6.
79. Testimony of Gerald Hill, WC Vol. VII, p. 59.
80. Testimony of Ruth Paine, WC Vol. III, pp. 78–79.
81. Interview with Ruth Paine, April 18, 1992.
82. Testimony of Ruth Paine, WC Vol. IX, p. 433.
83. Testimony of Ruth Paine, WC Vol. III, p. 69.
84. Ibid., pp. 68–69.
85. Ibid., p. 79.
86. Testimony of Marina Oswald, WC Vol. I, p. 74.
87. Interview with Carl Day.
88. Ibid.
89. Testimony of Sebastian Latona, WC Vol. IV, p. 24.
90. Interview with Carl Day.
91. Testimony of Sebastian Latona, WC Vol. IV, p. 24.
92. Transcript of press conference with Henry Wade, CE 2168, WC Vol. XXIV, p. 821.
93. Testimony of Sebastian Latona, WC Vol. IV, p. 24.
94. Hurt, op. cit., pp. 106–9.
95. Ibid., p. 109.
96. Interview with Carl Day.

13 "HE HAD A DEATH LOOK"

1. Interview with Dr. Pepper Jenkins, March 10, 1992.
2. Ibid.
3. Interview with Dr. Bill Midgett, April 16, 1992.
4. Interview with H. B. McClain, March 3, 1992.
5. Interview with Dr. Bill Midgett, April 16, 1992.
6. Interview with Dr. Pepper Jenkins, March 10, 1992.
7. Testimony of Diana Bowren, WC Vol. VI, pp. 134–35.
8. "Three Patients at Parkland," *Texas State Journal of Medicine*, Vol. 60, January 1964, p. 61.
9. Interview with Dr. Pepper Jenkins, March 10, 1992.
10. Interview with Dr. Ron Jones, April 14, 1992.
11. Interview with Dr. Paul Peters, March 10, 1992.

12. Interview with Dr. Charles Baxter, March 12, 1992.
13. Interview with Dr. Malcolm Perry, April 2, 1992.
14. Charles Crenshaw, *JFK: Conspiracy of Silence* (New York: Signet, 1992), p. 80.
15. Statement of Mrs. Lyndon B. Johnson, WC Vol. V, p. 566.
16. Interview with Dr. Ron Jones, April 14, 1992.
17. Interview with Dr. Adolph Giesecke, March 5, 1992.
18. Interview with Dr. Pepper Jenkins, March 10, 1992.
19. Interview with Dr. Malcolm Perry, April 2, 1992.
20. Interview with Dr. Charles Baxter, March 12, 1992.
21. Ibid.
22. Interview with Dr. Pepper Jenkins, March 10, 1992.
23. Interview with Dr. Charles Baxter, March 12, 1992.
24. Ibid.
25. Interview with Dr. Pepper Jenkins, March 10, 1992.
26. Testimony of Doris Mae Nelson, WC Vol. VI, p. 146; testimony of Kenneth O'Donnell, WC Vol. VII, p. 452; Price (Charles J.) Exhibit 12, pp. 203–4; Price Exhibit 21, p. 216.
27. Interview with Dr. Robert Shaw, March 11, 1992.
28. Ibid.
29. Testimony of Darrell C. Tomlinson, WC Vol. VI, pp. 129–31.
30. WR, p. 58.
31. Statement of President Lyndon B. Johnson, WC Vol. V, p. 563.
32. Dennis L. Breo, "JFK's Death, Part II: Dallas MDs Recall Their Memories," *Journal of the American Medical Association*, Volume 267, No. 20, May 27, 1992, p. 2806.
33. Crenshaw, op. cit., pp. 118–19.
34. Dennis L. Breo, "JFK's Death, Part II: Dallas MDs Recall Their Memories," p. 2806.
35. Interview with Dr. Charles Baxter, March 12, 1992.
36. Testimony of Roy Kellerman, WC Vol. II, p. 97.
37. Ibid., pp. 97–98.
38. David S. Lifton, *Best Evidence: Disguise and Deception in the Assassination of John F. Kennedy* (New York: Macmillan, 1980), p. 678.
39. FBI report, November 26, 1963, File # 89-30, by Francis X. O'Neill, Jr., and James W. Sibert, p. 3.
40. Interview with Francis O'Neill, November 5, 1992.
41. Interviews with Dr. Michael Baden, January 28, 1992, and November 7, 1992.
42. Interview with Dr. Cyril Wecht, February 4, 1992.
43. William Manchester, *Death of a President* (London: Michael Joseph, 1967) pp. 361–62; Godfrey T. McHugh, letter to the editor, *Time*, February 16, 1981.
44. Ibid., pp. 361–62.
45. Admiral George G. Burkley, recorded interview by William McHugh, October 17, 1967, pages 16–17, John F. Kennedy Library Oral History Project.
46. Interview with Francis O'Neill, November 5, 1992.
47. *The Washington Post*, November 23, 1963, p. A11.

48. Dennis L. Breo, "JFK's Death, Part II: The Plain Truth from the MDs Who Did the Autopsy," *Journal of the American Medical Association*, Volume 267, No. 20, May 27, 1992, pp. 2795–96.
49. Ibid.
50. Interview with Dr. James Humes, November 2, 1992.
51. Interview with Francis O'Neill, November 5, 1992.
52. Testimony of Dr. James Humes, WC Vol. II, p. 349; Dennis L. Breo, "JFK's Death: The Plain Truth from the MDs Who Did the Autopsy," p. 2797.
53. Interview with Francis O'Neill, November 5, 1992.
54. Dennis L. Breo, "JFK's Death: The Plain Truth from the MDs Who Did the Autopsy," p. 2798.
55. Groden and Livingstone, *High Treason*, p. 82.
56. "Report of Autopsy Color Photographs' Authenticity," by Frank Scott, August 15, 1978, HSCA Vol. VII, pp. 69–70.
57. HSCA Vol. VI, pp. 239–40; HSCA Vol. VII, p. 43.
58. Authentication of John F. Kennedy Autopsy Radiographs and Photographs, HSCA Vol. VII, Addendum A, pp. 43–45; HSCA Vol. I, p. 152.
59. Testimony of Dr. Lowell Levine, HSCA Vol. I, p. 173.
60. Dennis L. Breo, "JFK's Death: The Plain Truth from the MDs Who Did the Autopsy," p. 2798.
61. Interview with Dr. Cyril Wecht, February 4, 1992.
62. Dennis L. Breo, "JFK's Death: The Plain Truth from the MDs Who Did the Autopsy," p. 2799.
63. Interview with Dr. Michael Baden, February 1, 1992.
64. Interview with Dr. John Lattimer, February 6, 1992.
65. Interview with Dr. Ron Jones, April 14, 1992.
66. Transcript of news conference, "At the White House with Wayne Hawks," November 22, 1963, archives of Lyndon Baines Johnson Library, p. 6.
67. Interview with Dr. Malcolm Perry, April 2, 1992.
68. Interview with Dr. Ron Jones, April 14, 1992.
69. Testimony of Dr. Charles Carrico, WC Vol. VI, p. 5; interview with Dr. Carrico, March 8, 1992.
70. Interview with Dr. Pepper Jenkins, March 10, 1992.
71. Interview with Dr. Michael Baden, February 1, 1992.
72. John Lattimer, *Kennedy and Lincoln*, pp. 232–39; testimony of Dr. Michael Baden, HSCA Vol. I, pp. 305–6.
73. Interview with Dr. Charles Carrico, March 8, 1992.
74. Testimony of Dr. Michael Baden, HSCA Vol. I, pp. 189–91.
75. Ibid., p. 192.
76. Ibid., p. 199.
77. Ibid., p. 230.
78. Dennis L. Breo, "JFK's Death: The Plain Truth from the MDs Who Did the Autopsy," p. 2798.
79. Testimony of Dr. James Humes, WC Vol. II, p. 359.
80. Ibid., pp. 354–55.
81. Testimony of Dr. James Humes, WC Vol. II, p. 353; Dennis L. Breo, "JFK's Death: The Plain Truth from the MDs Who Did the Autopsy," p. 2798.
82. Ibid.; testimony of Dr. James Humes, WC Vol. II, p. 354.
83. Interview with Dr. Pepper Jenkins, March 10, 1992.

84. Interview with Dr. Charles Carrico, March 8, 1992.
85. Interview with Dr. Adolph Giesecke, March 5, 1992.
86. Interview with Dr. Malcolm Perry, April 2, 1992.
87. Interview with Dr. Charles Baxter, March 12, 1992.
88. Interview with Dr. Ron Jones, April 14, 1992.
89. Interviews with Dr. Michael Baden, February 1, 1992, and November 7, 1992.
90. Groden and Livingstone, op. cit., p. 46.
91. Interview with Dr. Charles Carrico, March 8, 1992.
92. Interview with Dr. Adolph Giesecke, March 5, 1992.
93. Interview with Dr. Pepper Jenkins, March 3, 1992.
94. Interview with Dr. Malcolm Perry, April 2, 1992.
95. Interview with Dr. Charles Baxter, March 12, 1992.
96. Interview with Dr. Ron Jones, April 14, 1992.
97. Interview with Dr. Adolph Giesecke, March 5, 1992.
98. Interview with Dr. Robert McClelland, March 9, 1992.
99. Thompson, *Six Seconds in Dallas*, p. 140.
100. Interview with Dr. Malcolm Perry, April 2, 1992.
101. Interview with Dr. Paul Peters, March 10, 1992; Dr. Peters also drew a diagram that showed the doctors' positions around the table and provided it to the author.
102. Interview with Dr. Pepper Jenkins, March 10, 1992.
103. Interview with Dr. Michael Baden, February 1, 1992.
104. Charles Crenshaw, op. cit., p. 88.
105. HSCA Vol. VII, pp. 110, 115.
106. Ibid., p. 128.
107. Interview with Dr. Michael Baden, January 23, 1992.
108. "John Kennedy Assassination Film Analysis," Francis Corbett, Itek Corporation, 1975.
109. HSCA Vol. VII, pp. 174–75; Lattimer, op. cit., p. 255.
110. Lattimer, op. cit., p. 255.
111. Luis W. Alvarez, "A Physicist Examines the Kennedy Assassination Film," *American Journal of Physics*, Vol. 44, No. 9, September 1976, p. 819.
112. Interview with Dr. Michael Baden, January 23, 1992.

14   "MY GOD, THEY ARE GOING TO KILL US ALL"

1. Testimony of Lyndal Shaneyfelt, WC Vol. V, p.153.
2. "The Warren Report," CBS News, Part I, June 25, 1967, p. 14.
3. HSCA Rpt., p. 83.
4. Author's review of witness statements published in the twenty-six volumes of the Warren Commission and available in the National Archives.
5. WR, pp. 111–12.
6. Ibid., p. 114.
7. Testimony of Lyndal Shaneyfelt, WC Vol. V, pp. 146–51.
8. WR p. 115.
9. Testimony of Wesley Buell Frazier, WC Vol. II, p. 234.
10. Testimony of Howard Brennan, WC Vol. III, p. 143.
11. Testimony of Barbara Rowland, WC Vol. VI, p. 184.

12. Testimony of Royce Skelton, WC Vol. VI, p. 237.
13. Testimony of Geneva Hine, WC Vol. VI, p. 395.
14. Letter from the Secret Service to the Commission, dated June 11, 1964, with attached statements of Secret Service personnel concerning the events surrounding the assassination, CE 1024, WC Vol. XVIII, p. 723.
15. Ibid., p. 754.
16. Ibid., p. 760.
17. Interview with Jim Moore, March 9, 1992.
18. David Lui, "The Little Girl Must Have Heard," *The Dallas Times Herald*, June 3, 1979, H-3.
19. Rosemary Willis interview with Marcia Smith-Durk, 1979.
20. Testimony of John B. Connally, WC Vol. IV, pp. 132–33.
21. HSCA Vol. VI, p. 29.
22. Luis Alvarez, "A Physicist Examines the Kennedy Assassination Film," *American Journal of Physics*, Vol. 44, No. 9, September 1976, pp. 815–19.
23. "The Warren Report," CBS News, Part I, June 25, 1967, pp. 17–18.
24. Ibid., p. 29.
25. Ibid., p. 28.
26. Testimony of Dr. Vincent Guinn, HSCA Vol. I, pp. 504, 555–56.
27. Testimony of Robert Frazier, WC Vol. V, pp. 172–73.
28. Interview with Robert Kraus, March 29, 1992.
29. Testimony of Virgie Rachley, WC Vol. VII, p. 509.
30. Ibid., p. 513.
31. Interview with James Tague, January 19, 1992.
32. Ibid., January 20, 1992.
33. Ibid., January 19, 1992.
34. Warren Commission memorandum, Arlen Specter to Lee Rankin, June 11, 1964; WC Vol. XXI, p. 472.
35. WR, p. 117.
36. Testimony of Robert Frazier, WC Vol. III, pp. 432, 435.
37. Testimony of Lyndal Shaneyfelt, WC Vol. XV, p. 700.
38. Interview with Art Pence, February 21, 1992.
39. WR, p. 105.
40. HSCA Rpt., p. 46.
41. HSCA Vol. VI, p. 43.
42. Testimony of Governor John Connally, WC Vol. IV, p. 135.
43. Ibid., p. 133.
44. Interview with Dr. Michael Baden, January 21, 1992; interview with Dr. Michael West, November 7, 1992.
45. Testimony of Dr. Malcolm Perry, WC Vol. III, p. 389; Lattimer, *Kennedy and Lincoln*, pp. 241–43;
46. Interview with Dr. Michael West, November 7, 1992.
47. Interview with Dr. John Lattimer, May 25, 1993.
48. Lattimer, op. cit., pp. 243–44; interview with Dr. Lattimer, February 6, 1992.
49. Interview with Dr. John Lattimer, February 6, 1992.
50. Interview with Dr. Michael West, November 7, 1992; interview with Dr. Robert Piziali, November 9, 1992.
51. Testimony of Governor John Connally, WC Vol. IV, p. 145.

52. Testimony of Robert Frazier, WC Vol. V, p. 63; front view of coat worn by Governor Connally at time of assassination, CE 683; front view of shirt worn by Governor Connally, CE 686, WC Vol. XVII.

53. HSCA Rpt., p. 46.

54. Interview with Dr. Michael West, February 6, 1992.

55. Ibid.

56. Thompson, *Six Seconds in Dallas*, p. 89.

57. Governor John Connally press conference, December 1963.

58. Testimony of Governor John Connally, WC Vol. IV, pp. 135–36.

59. Interviews with Dr. Michael Baden and Dr. Michael West, November 7, 1992.

60. Interview with Governor John Connally, May 27, 1992.

61. Testimony of Nellie Connally, WC Vol. IV, p. 147.

62. Ibid.

63. Testimony of Governor John Connally, WC Vol. IV, p. 133.

64. Testimony of Dr. Robert Piziali, American Bar Association, mock trial of Lee Harvey Oswald, August 10, 1992.

65. Interview with Dr. Robert Piziali, November 9, 1992; testimony of Dr. Piziali, American Bar Association, mock trial of Lee Harvey Oswald, August 10, 1992.

66. Interview with Dr. Michael Baden, November 7, 1992.

67. Testimony of Dr. Robert Piziali, American Bar Association, mock trial of Lee Harvey Oswald, August 10, 1992.

68. Bonar Menninger, *Mortal Error: The Shot That Killed JFK* (New York: St. Martins Press, 1992), p. 37.

69. Testimony of Dr. Michael Baden, HSCA Vol. I, pp. 305–6.

70. Bullet that caused damage shown in CE 854, 855, and 856, WC Vol. XVII, p. 850.

71. Interview with Dr. John Lattimer, February 6, 1992.

72. Testimony of Dr. Charles Gregory, WC Vol. IV, pp. 121, 124.

73. Ibid., p. 125.

74. Ibid.

75. Interview with Dr. Michael Baden, February 1, 1992.

76. Testimony of Dr. Martin Fackler, American Bar Association, mock trial of Lee Harvey Oswald, August 10, 1992.

77. Testimony of Dr. Alfred Oliver, WC Vol. V, pp. 76-83; testimony of Dr. Martin Fackler, American Bar Association, mock trial of Lee Harvey Oswald, August 10, 1992.

78. Testimony of Larry Sturdivan, HSCA Vol. I, p. 393.

79. Interview with Dr. Michael Baden, February 1, 1992.

80. Testimony of Dr. Alfred Oliver, WC Vol. V, pp. 76-78; photos of holes in goat skin produced by bullets before passing through 13.5 to 14.5cm. of animal tissue (left) and upon leaving the tissue (right) CE 850, WC Vol. XVII, p. 846.

81. Testimony of Dr. Alfred Oliver, WC Vol. V, pp. 78-81; bullet that was first fired through goat, CE 853, WC Vol. XVII, p. 849.

82. Testimony of Dr. Martin Fackler, American Bar Association mock trial of Lee Harvey Oswald, August 10, 1992.

83. Testimony of Robert Frazier, WC Vol. III, p. 430.

84. Testimony of Dr. Robert Piziali, American Bar Association, mock trial of Lee Harvey Oswald, August 10, 1992.
85. Groden and Livingstone, *High Treason*, p. 72.
86. Testimony of Dr. Charles Gregory, WC Vol. IV, p. 120.
87. Ibid., p. 123.
88. Ibid., p. 125.
89. Testimony of Dr. Robert Piziali, American Bar Association, mock trial of Lee Harvey Oswald, August 10, 1992.
90. Testimony of Dr. Charles Gregory, WC Vol. IV, p. 122.
91. Dr. Cyril Wecht, *Modern Medicine*, October 28, 1974.
92. Testimony of Dr. Vincent Guinn, HSCA Vol. I, p. 492.
93. Ibid., pp. 494-95.
94. Ibid.
95. Ibid., p. 504.
96. A Report to the House of Representatives, Select Committee on Assassinations, on the subject of "1977 Activation Analysis Measurements on Bullet-Lead Specimens Involved in the 1963 Assassination of President John F. Kennedy," by Dr. Vincent P. Guinn, September, 8, 1978, JFK-Exhibit F-331, pp. 533–34.
97. Testimony of Dr. Vincent Guinn, HSCA Vol. I, p. 504; "1977 Activation Analysis Measurements on Bullet-Lead Specimens Involved in the 1963 Assassination of President John F. Kennedy," JFK-Exhibit F-331, p. 533.
98. Hurt, *Reasonable Doubt*, pp. 85-86.
99. Testimony of Dr. Vincent Guinn, HSCA Vol. I, p. 565.
100. Ibid., p. 555.

15 "I'M A CHARACTER! I'M COLORFUL"

1. Interview with William Alexander, March 12, 1992.
2. Ibid., March 6, 1992.
3. Testimony of Will Fritz, WC Vol. IV, p. 240; testimony of Richard Sims, WC Vol. VII, pp. 180, 182; interview with William Alexander, March 12, 1992.
4. Testimony of Richard Sims, WC Vol. VII, pp. 180–82.
5. Interview with William Alexander, March 6, 1992.
6. Testimony of Harry Holmes, WC Vol. VII, p. 269.
7. Testimony of Marina Oswald, HSCA Vol. II, p. 301; McMillan, *Marina and Lee*, pp. 547–48.
8. Interview with Michael Paine, April 11, 1992.
9. Testimony of Will Fritz, WC Vol. IV, p. 214.
10. Ibid., p. 210.
11. Testimony of James Hosty, WC Vol. IV, p. 468.
12. Testimony of Will Fritz, WC Vol. IV, p. 209.
13. Ibid., pp. 214, 218.
14. Ibid., pp. 223–24, 226, 228, 230.
15. Ibid, p. 225.
16. Interview with William Alexander, March 12, 1992.
17. Ibid., March 12 and 13, 1992.
18. Ibid., March 13, 1992.

19. Testimony of Cortlandt Cunningham, WC Vol. III, p. 485.
20. Lane, *Rush to Judgment*, p. 126.
21. Testimony of Cortlandt Cunningham, WC Vol. III, p. 495.
22. Ibid., p. 494.
23. Testimony of Carl Day, WC Vol. IV, p. 276; testimony of Lyndal Shaneyfelt, WC Vol. IV, p. 288; interview with Carl Day, January 19, 1992.
24. Testimony of W. E. Barnes, WC Vol. VII, pp. 281, 283.
25. Testimony of Henry Wade, WC Vol. V, p. 218.
26. Testimony of Jesse Curry, WC Vol. IV, p. 152.
27. Ibid.; testimony of James Hosty, WC Vol. IV, 462.
28. Testimony of Henry Wade, WC Vol. VII, p. 238.
29. WR, p. 208.
30. Testimony of Jesse Curry, WC Vol. XV, p. 131.
31. Ibid., p. 175.
32. Interview with William Alexander, March 12, 1992; testimony of Jack Ruby, WC Vol. V, p. 189.
33. FBI report of investigation conducted on November 24, 1963, of Dallas area police record concerning Jack Ruby and others (CD 45), CE 1234; FBI report, December 6, 1963, of interview with Edward J. Nerad, chief administrative officer, Family Court of Cook County, Chicago, Ill. (CD 86), CE 1254; Selective Service records pertaining to Jack Ruby's military career (CD 221), CE 1274; FBI report, June 9, 1964, concerning records pertaining to Jack Ruby provided by Chicago Board of Education (CD 1090a), CE 1290; records pertaining to Jacob Rubenstein provided by Illinois Institute for Juvenile Research (CD 1291), CE 1297 p. 1, WC Vol. XXII; and CE 1654, WC Vol. XXIII.
34. Interview with Earl Ruby, November 17, 1992; statement of Marian Carroll and Ann Volpert, CE 1185, WC Vol. XXII, pp. 304–5.
35. Interview with Earl Ruby, November 17, 1992; testimony of Earl Ruby, WC Vol. XIV, p. 367; testimony of Hyman Rubenstein, WC Vol. XV, p. 18; statement of Mary Lawrence, CE 1256, WC Vol. XXII, p. 365.
36. Testimony of Eva Grant, WC Vol. XIV, p. 439; FBI letter to Commission, dated February 18, 1964, transmitting records of Fannie Rubenstein in Elgin State Hospital, CE 1281, p. 11, WC Vol. XXII.
37. CE 1291, p. 2; CE 1297, p. 22, WC Vol. XXII.
38. Interview with Earl Ruby, November 17, 1992; testimony of Hyman Rubenstein, WC Vol. XV, p. 10; testimony of Eva Grant, WC Vol. XIV, p. 439; CE 1290; CE 1297, pp. 17, 22, 26; WC Vol. XXII.
39. Testimony of Hyman Rubenstein, WC Vol. XV, p. 10; Sam Ruby Exhibit 1, p. 185; C. Ray Hall Exhibit 1; FBI report, November 27, 1963, of interview with Sam Gordon (CD 4), CE 1195; FBI report, November 27, 1963, of interview with Sollie Ziv (CD 4), CE 1197; FBI report, November 29, 1963, of interview with Harry M. Epstein (CD 4), CE 1200; FBI report, January 31, 1964, of interview with Martin Brauner (CD 441), CE 1282, WC Vol. XXII.
40. Interview with Earl Ruby, November 17, 1992.
41. CE 1291, p. 1, WC Vol. XXII.
42. CE 1291, pp. 1, 4, 5; CE 1297, pp. 2–3, 7; WC Vol. XXII.
43. CE 1291, WC Vol. XXII.

44. Ibid., pp. 4–5.
45. FBI report, December 9, 1963, of information on Jack Ruby and his family supplied by Michael F. Heneghan, chief probation officer, Family Court of Cook County, Chicago, Ill., CE 1255, p. 364; CE 1254, WC Vol. XXII.
46. FBI report, November 26, 1963, of interview of Ben Epstein (CD 4), CE 1193; FBI report, November 29, 1963, of interview of Ralph Kaplan (CD 4), CE 1194; CE 1195; CE 1197; FBI report, October 4, 1963, of interview of Phil Udell (CD 84), CE 1246; FBI report, June 5, 1964, of interview with Ira Colitz (CD 1061), CE 1289, p. 3; WC Vol. XXII.
47. Testimony of Hyman Rubenstein, WC Vol. XV, p. 28; FBI report, November 29, 1963, of interview with Erwin Horwitz (CD 4), CE 1191; CE 1194; FBI report, November 29, 1963, of interview with Harry Solavit (CD 4), CE 1198; WC Vol. XXII.
48. Interview with Earl Ruby, November 17, 1992.
49. Ibid.; testimony of Eva Grant, WC Vol. XIV, pp. 443–45; testimony of Hyman Rubenstein, WC Vol. XV, p. 21.
50. Testimony of Eva Grant, WC Vol. XIV, p. 44; C. Ray Hall Exhibits 1 and 3, p. 13; FBI report, December 4, 1963, of interview of Bennie Barrish (CD 84), CE 1239, WC Vol. XXII.
51. WR, p. 786.
52. Testimony of Eva Grant, WC Vol. XIV, p. 442; C. Ray Hall Exhibit 3, p. 13.
53. C. Ray Hall Exhibits 1 and 3, p. 13, WC Vol. XX.
54. CE 1281, pp. 3–8, 35, WC Vol. XXII; WR, p. 783.
55. CE 1281, pp. 28, 43.
56. CE 1200; FBI report, November 29, 1963, of interview with Mike Nemzin (CD 4), CE 1203; FBI report, November 29, 1963, of interview with Ben Kay (CD 4), CE 1207; FBI report, November 26, 1963, of interview with Art Petacque (CD 4), CE 1208; CE 1246; FBI report, December 2, 1963, of interview with Barney Ross (CD 86); CE 1261; FBI report, December 20, 1963, of interview with Arthur Douglas Cohen (CD 106), CE 1299; WC Vol. XXII.
57. Testimony of Eva Grant, WC Vol. XIV, p. 445; FBI report, November 29, 1963, of interview with Abe Cohn (CD 4), CE 1190; FBI report, November 26, 1963, of interview with Theodore Shulman (CD 4), CE 1206, WC Vol. XXII; C. Ray Hall Exhibit 3, p. 15.
58. Interview with Earl Ruby, November 17, 1992.
59. Interview with Bill Roemer, January 23, 1992.
60. Letter to Commission, dated January 27, 1964, from Abraham L. Kaminstein, Register of Copyrights, concerning copyright claim filed by Jack Rubenstein, with attachments (CD 376), CE 1280, WC Vol. XXII; FBI report, April 2, 1964, of interview with Saul Molodofsky (CD 856), CE 1702, WC Vol. XXIII, p. 179.
61. CE 1274, WC Vol. XXII.
62. Testimony of Hyman Rubenstein, WC Vol. XV, p. 21; CE 1191; CE 1193; FBI report, November 29, 1963, of interview of Maury Cahn (CD 4), 1199; CE 1207; FBI report, November 29, 1963, of interview of Harry Jack Goldbaum (CD 4), CE 1217; CE 1239; FBI New York office report of investigation conducted on November 25, 1963, concerning Jack Ruby's friendship

with Barney Ross and Ruby's trip to New York in August 1963 (CD 84), CE 1244; CE 1289, WC Vol. XXII.

63. Interview with Earl Ruby, November 17, 1992.

64. CE 1193; FBI report, November 27, 1963, of interview with Joe Kellman (CD 4), CE 1216; FBI report, December 3, 1963, of interview with Israel Horowitz (CD 86), CE 1258; CE 1299, WC Vol. XXII.

65. FBI report, June 22, 1964, of interview with Stephen Andrew Belancik (CD 1234b), CE 1294, WC Vol. XXII.

66. FBI report, June 24, 1964, of interview with Irving Zakarin (CD 1234d), CE 1295, WC Vol. XXII.

67. Military records of Jack Ruby (CD 83), CE 1707, p. 2, WC Vol. XXII.

68. Interview with Earl Ruby, November 17, 1992.

69. Testimony of Earl Ruby, WC Vol. XIV, pp. 370, 422–23.

70. FBI reports, August 10, 13, and 19, 1964, concerning the examination of phonograph records and papers pertaining to the Dallas crime investigation of 1946–48 (CD 1429), CE 2416, WC Vol. XXV, pp. 511–15.

71. Interview with William Alexander, March 14, 1992.

72. Interview with Bill Roemer, January 23, 1992.

73. WR, pp. 794–796.

74. C. Ray Hall Exhibit 3, p. 14.

75. WR, p. 795.

76. FBI report of interview with Herman Ross on November 25, 1963 (CD 4), CE 1516; FBI report, December 13, 1963, of interview with John N. Crawford (CD 104), CE 1619, WC Vol. XXIII.

77. Testimony of Hyman Rubenstein, WC Vol. XV, p. 26.

78. Interview with Earl Ruby, November 17, 1992; FBI report, November 27, 1963, of interview with Michael Shore (CD 4), CE 1507, WC Vol. XXII; FBI report, November 25, 1963, of interview with Leon Worth (CD 4), CE 1531; FBI report of interview conducted on December 9, 1963, with Joseph Leipsic (CD 86), CE 1552; FBI report, December 8, 1963, of interview with Norman Smith (CD 86), CE 1742, WC Vol. XXIII; Sam Ruby DE 1, p. 187; testimony of Edward J. Pullman, WC Vol. XV, p. 224.

79. Testimony of Jack Ruby, WC Vol. V, p. 202; testimony of Robert C. Patterson, WC Vol. XIV, pp. 129–30; Sam Ruby Exhibit 1, p. 187; C. Ray Hall Exhibit 3, p. 15; FBI report, November 27, 1963, of interview with Edwin Carrell (CD 4), CE 1503, WC Vol. XXII; FBI report, November 29, 1963, of interview with Lacy Brooks (CD 84), CE 1534; FBI report, December 5, 1963, of interview with Robert Gurley (CD 86), CE 1555; FBI report, December 19, 1963, of interview with L. W. Newberry (CD 105), CE 1638; FBI report, December 19, 1963, of interview with Mrs. Wiley Dismukes (CD 105), CE 1639; FBI report, December 19, 1963, of interview with Wiley Dismukes CE 1640; FBI report, December 6, 1963, of investigation into Ruby's allegedly owning property near Lake Grapevine, Texas (CD 105), CE 1641; FBI report, December 19, 1963, of interview with T. A. Yates (CD 105), CE 1642; FBI report of investigation on December 21, 1963, into Ruby's interest in transporting jeeps to Cuba (CD 360), CE 1688; FBI investigation into Ruby's transporting jeeps to Cuba and interviews with Robert Ray McKeown, January 28, 1964, and A. J. Ayo, (CD

441), CE 1689; FBI report, April 1, 1964, of interview of Prentis I. Vaughn (CD 856), CE 1694, WC Vol. XXIII.

80. Interview with Earl Ruby, November 17, 1992.

81. Interview with Tony Zoppi, April 8, 1992.

82. "Ruby Unpredictable, Insecure Says Strip-Teaser in El Paso," *El Paso Herald Post*, January 1, 1964.

83. Garry Willis and Ovid Demaris, "The Avenger: 'You All Know Me! I'm Jack Ruby!,'" *Esquire*, May 1967, p. 84.

84. Interview with William Alexander, March 6, 1992.

85. FBI report, November 25, 1963, of interview with Sgt. Jerry Hill (CD 4), CE 1502, WC Vol. XXII; FBI report, November 24, 1963, of interview with Benny H. Bickers (CD 4), CE 1517; FBI report, December 6, 1963, of interview with Philip Lance (CD 7), CE 1532; FBI report, December 6, 1963, of interview with Mrs. Philip Lance (CD 7), CE 1533; FBI report, December 5, 1963, of interview with Janet Adams Conforto (CD 86), CE 1561; FBI report, December 5, 1963, of interview with Winnie Fay Floyd (CD 106), CE 1651; FBI report, December 5, 1963, of interview with Vernon Roy Smith (CD 106), CE 1653; FBI report, December 5, 1963, of interview with Richard William Proeber (CD 223), CE 1657; FBI report, January 20, 1964, of interview with Mrs. Bobby Bradford (CD 360), CE 1681; WC Vol. XXIII.

86. Interview with Tony Zoppi, November 19, 1992.

87. Testimony of Harry Olsen, WC Vol. XIV, p. 626.

88. FBI report, January 3, 1964, of interview with Charles Edward Morgan (CD 360), CE 1548; FBI report, December 8, 1963, of interview with Jack Rowe (CD 86), CE 1568; FBI report, December 19, 1963, of interview with Dan Alvin Gunn (CD 105), CE 1633; FBI report, January 4, 1964, of interview with Willis D. Dickerson (CD 302), CE 1676, WC Vol. XXIII.

89. FBI report, November 26, 1963, of interview with Frank Ferraro (CD 4), CE 1514; FBI report, December 4, 1963, of interview with Robert Gurley (CD 86), CE 1554; FBI report, December 6, 1963, of interview with Joe Peterson (CD 86), CE 1564; FBI report, December 6, 1963, of interview with Breck Wall (CD 86), CE 1566; FBI report, January 16, 1964, of interview with John Wilson (CD 302), CE 1672; FBI report, January 6, 1964, of interview with Willis Dickerson (CD 302), CE 1676; FBI report, January 21, 1964, of interview with Gordon Sims (CD 360), CE 1683, WC Vol. XXIII.

90. CE 1683.

91. FBI report, December 3, 1963, of interview with Robert McEwan (CD 86), CE 1740, WC Vol. XXIII, pp. 348–49.

92. FBI report, December 5, 1963, of interview with Robert Lee Shorman (CD 86), CE 1250; FBI report, undated, of interview with Rick Morrison (CD 104), CE 1483; FBI report, December 8, 1963, of interview with Mrs. Fannie Birch (CD 86), CE 1496; FBI report, January 22, 1964, of interview with John Van Kampen (CD 360), CE 1497; FBI report, December 24, 1963, of interview with Barry Herbert James Deavenport (CD 223), CE 1498; FBI report, December 20, 1963, of interview with Mrs. Patricia Kohs (CD 105), CE 1499, WC Vol. XXII; CE 1548; FBI report, November 29, 1963, of interview with Mrs. Leonard Repsky (CD 4), CE 1671, WC Vol.

XXIII; FBI report, November 26, 1963, of interview with Alexander Gruber (CD 4), CE 2243; FBI report, November 30, 1963, of interview with Billy Joe Willis (CD 4), CE 2414; WC Vol. XXV; memo, September 16, 1964, from CIA to Commission reporting that CIA files have no information on Ruby or his associates (CD 1493); letter, May 19, 1964, from Commission to CIA, requesting said information; memo, February 24, 1964, from Commission to CIA concerning Ruby, CE 2980, p. 4, WC Vol. XXVI.

93. CE 1496, 1497, 1499, WC Vol. XXII; CE 1671, WC Vol. XXIII; CE 2414, WC Vol. XXV.

94. CE 1499, WC Vol. XXII; CE 1671, WC Vol. XXIII; FBI report, December 3, 1963, of interview with Mrs. Joe Garcia (CD 86), CE 2495, WC Vol. XXV.

95. FBI report, December 12, 1963, of interview with William Earl O'Donnell (CD 104), CE 1624, p. 2, WC Vol. XXIII.

96. CE 2243.

97. CE 1499.

98. FBI report, December 3, 1963, of interview with John C. Jackson, CE 1478, WC Vol. XXII.

99. CE 1502; Crafard Exhibit 5226, p. 355, WC Vol. XIX.

100. CE 1499.

101. FBI report, November 28, 1963, of interview with Elaine Rogers (CD 4), CE 1459; FBI report, November 28, 1963, of interview with Marilyn Miranda Moone (CD 4), CE 1460, WC Vol. XXII.

102. CE 1496.

103. FBI report, November 29, 1963, of interview with Wayne Keller, CE 1486, WC Vol. XXII.

104. "Ruby Unpredictable, Insecure Says Strip-Teaser in El Paso," *El Paso Herald Post*, January 1, 1964.

105. FBI report, December 4, 1963, of interview with Wynn Warner (CD 86), CE 1484, WC Vol. XXII.

106. Testimony of Edward Pullman, WC Vol. XV, p. 228.

107. FBI report, December 6, 1963, of interview with Johnnie Hayden (CD 86), CE 1449, p. 170, WC Vol. XXII.

108. Testimony of William Serur, *State of Texas* v. *Jack Rubenstein*, CE 2411, p. 626, WC Vol. XXV.

109. Testimony of Larry Crafard, WC Vol. XII, p. 434; testimony of George Senator, WC Vol. XIV, pp. 213–14; testimony of Andrew Armstrong, WC Vol. XIII., p. 324; C. Ray Hall Exhibit 3, p. 17; CE 1502, WC Vol. XXII; FBI report, December 17, 1963, of interview with Theodore Louis Fleming (CD 105), CE 1632; FBI report, December 16, 1963, of interview with Mrs. Mary Pullman (CD 105), CE 1636; FBI report, December 23, 1963, of interview with Hugh Gene Smith (CD 106), CE 1646; FBI report, December 24, 1963, of interview with James Rhodes (CD 223), CE 1659; FBI report, December 21, 1963, of interview with Jean Flynn (CD 106), CE 1663; FBI report, November 29, 1963, of interview with Joe Howard Linthicum (CD 84), CE 1739; FBI report, December 10, 1963, of interview with Bryce Brady II (CD 86), CE 1741; FBI report, December 20, 1963, of interview with Joey Gerard (CD 223), CE 1744; FBI report, December 31, 1963, of interview with Leo Ukie Sherin (CD 302), CE 1747; FBI report, December

4, 1963, of interview with John Wayne Barnett (CD 84), CE 1749, WC Vol. XXIII.

110. Testimony of A. M. Eberhardt, WC Vol. XIII, p. 193; testimony of Eva Grant, WC Vol. XIV, p. 485.

111. Interview with Tony Zoppi, November 19, 1992.

112. Interview with William Alexander, January 29, 1992.

113. WR, p. 801.

114. FBI report, November 25, 1963, of interview with Joe Campisi (CD 4), CE 1748; FBI report, December 3, 1963, of interview with Robert Donald Lawrence (CD 86), CE 1752; FBI report of June 10, 1964 of investigation of Isadore Max Miller (CD 1102d), CE 1754; FBI report, January 22, 1964, of interviews with Isadore Miller and Sam Hicks (CD 360), CE 1755, WC Vol. XXIII.

115. Interview with William Alexander, March 6, 1992.

116. Interview with Earl Ruby, November 17, 1992.

117. FBI report, November 24, 1963, of information provided by George Snyder, records bureau, Dallas Police Department, relating to arrest record of Ruby (CD 4), CE 1528, WC Vol. XXIII.

118. FBI report, November 25, 1963, of interview with John McKee, president, Dallas Crime Commission (CD 4), CE 1233; FBI report, November 28, 1963, of interview with Lynn Burk (CD 4), CE 1510, WC Vol. XXII.

119. Interview with Tony Zoppi, November 19, 1992.

120. Interview with William Alexander, January 29, 1992.

121. Testimony of Norman Wright, WC Vol. XV, p. 248.

122. HSCA Rpt., p. 156, note 5; HSCA Vol. IX, pp. 22, 418–23; Alan Adelson, *The Ruby-Oswald Affair* (Seattle, Washington: Romar Books, 1988), p. 59.

123. Adelson, *The Ruby-Oswald Affair*, p. 59; interview with Tony Zoppi, November 19, 1992.

124. Testimony of Marjorie Richey, WC Vol. XV, pp. 199–200; testimony of Thomas Palmer, WC Vol. XV, p. 210–11; testimony of Nancy Powell, WC Vol. XV, pp. 411–12; CE 1561.

125. Testimony of Larry Crafard, WC Vol. XIV, pp. 67–68; testimony of Eva Grant, WC Vol. XIV, p. 456; testimony of William D. Crowe, WC Vol. XV, pp. 99–100; testimony of Marjorie Richey, WC Vol. XV, pp. 200–01; FBI report, November 28, 1963, of interview with Salvatore Vincent Giambone (CD 4), CE 1508, WC Vol. XXII; FBI report, November 25, 1963, of interview with Wally Weston (CD 4), CE1530; FBI report, December 13, 1963, of interview with Walter Brown (CD 86), CE 1560; FBI report, November 26, 1963, of interview with John Joseph McNaughton (CD 86), CE 1563, WC Vol. XXIII.

126. IRS memo of March 13, 1962, relating to compromise offer to Ruby, CE 1727, pp. 324–30; IRS memo of November 26, 1963, attaching sensitive case reports on Ruby dated November 27 and December 6, 1963, CE 1728; IRS notice of levy against Ruby, dated November 26, 1963, for $44,413.86, sent to Sheriff Decker, Dallas, CE 1729; IRS notice of levy, same as CE 1729, sent to Chief Curry, Dallas, CE 1730; IRS notice of levy, same as 1729–30, but dated December 9, 1963, to Curry, CE 1731, WC Vol. XXIII.

127. FBI report, November 29, 1963, of interview with Irvin Charles Mazzei (CD 84), CE 1543, WC Vol. XXIII, p. 191.
128. FBI internal memorandum, Special Agent Ralph J. Miles, August, 11, 1953.
129. Interview with Earl Ruby, November 17, 1992.
130. HSCA Vol. IV, pp. 496–99.
131. Ibid., p. 497.
132. Interview with Earl Ruby, November 17, 1992.
133. HSCA Rpt., p. 155; interview with Earl Ruby, November 17, 1992.
134. HSCA Rpt., pp. 155–56.
135. FBI report of March 17, 1964, of examination of telephone records for the Carousel Club for September 26–November 22, 1963 (CD 722), CE 2303, WC Vol. XXV.
136. HSCA Rpt., on Organized Crime, pp. 822–23.
137. Interview with confidential FBI source, October 12, 1992.

16 "I AM JACK RUBY. YOU ALL KNOW ME"

1. FBI report, December 5, 1963, of interview with Max Rudberg (CD 86), CE 2265, WC Vol. XXV; Garry Wills and Ovid Demaris, "The Avenger: 'You All Know Me! I'm Jack Ruby!,' " *Esquire*, May 1967, p. 158.
2. FBI report, December 20, 1963, of interview with Connie Trammel (CD 106), CE 2270, WC Vol. XXV.
3. FBI report, December 18, 1963, of investigation into records at Merchants State Bank (CD 223), CE 1669, WC Vol. XXIII.
4. FBI report, November 26, 1963, of telephone interview with assistant district attorney Bill Alexander (CD 4), CE 2245, WC Vol. XXV; interview with Bill Alexander, March 6, 1992.
5. Newman Exhibit 2, WC Vol. XX, p. 652.
6. FBI report, November 30, 1963, of interview with Graham Koch (CD 84), CE 2251, WC Vol. XXV.
7. FBI report, December 20, 1963, of interview with C. William Selah (CD 106), CE 2269; FBI report, December 16, 1963, of interview with Ralph Gismont (CD 104), CE 2288; FBI report, December 16, 1963, of interview with Kathleen C. Root (CD 104), CE 2319 WC Vol. XXV.
8. Crafard DE 5226, p. 150, WC Vol. XIX.
9. Testimony of Eva Grant, WC Vol. XV, p. 323.
10. Testimony of Lawrence Meyers, WC Vol. XV, pp. 626, 628.
11. Ibid., pp. 625–27.
12. Ibid., p. 626.
13. FBI report, December 21, 1963, of interview with Robert G. Landers (CD 106), CE 2434; FBI report, December 21, 1963, of interview with Charles Miller (CD 106), CE 2435, WC Vol. XXV.
14. Testimony of Lawrence Meyers, WC Vol. XV, p. 628.
15. Ibid.; WR, p. 334.
16. Crafard Exhibit 5226, WC Vol. XIX.
17. Ibid.
18. Testimony of Jack Ruby, WC Vol. V, p. 183; testimony of John W. Newman, WC Vol. XV, p. 539; Hall (C. Ray) Exhibit 3, p. 4, WC Vol. XX.

19. Hall (C. Ray) Exhibit 3, p. 4, WC Vol. XX; FBI report, November 28, 1963, of interview with Gladys Craddock (CD 4), CE 1479, WC Vol. XII; FBI report, July 31, 1964, of interview with Gladys Craddock (CD 1400c), CE 2321, WC Vol. XXV.
20. Interview with Tony Zoppi, November 23, 1992; Hall (C. Ray) Exhibit 3, p. 4, WC Vol. XX.
21. Testimony of Don Campbell, *State of Texas* v. *Jack Rubenstein*, CE 2405, pp. 24–26; FBI report, December 4, 1963, of interview with Don J. Campbell (CD 86), CE 2436; WC Vol. XXV.
22. Testimony of John Newman, WC Vol. XV, pp. 538–39.
23. Ibid., p. 539.
24. Tear sheet from *Dallas Morning News* of November 22, 1963, entitled "Welcome Mr. Kennedy," CE 1031, WC Vol. XXI.
25. Testimony of Eva Grant, WC Vol. XV, pp. 323–24.
26. Testimony of John Newman, WC Vol. XV, pp. 544–45.
27. Interview with Earl Ruby, November 17, 1992.
28. Testimony of John Newman, WC Vol. XV, p. 540.
29. Ibid., pp. 541–42.
30. Testimony of Jack Ruby, WC Vol. V, p. 184.
31. Testimony of John Newman, WC Vol. XV, p. 541.
32. Testimony of Jack Ruby, WC Vol. V, p. 184.
33. Testimony of Eva Grant, WC Vol. XV, p. 324.
34. Testimony of John Newman, WC Vol. XV, p. 542.
35. Testimony of Jack Ruby, WC Vol. V, p. 185.
36. Ibid.
37. Ibid.; testimony of John Newman, WC Vol. XV, p. 544.
38. Kantor, *The Ruby Cover-Up*, p. 89.
39. Ibid., pp. 89, 424.
40. WR, pp. 336–37.
41. HSCA Rpt., p. 158.
42. Testimony of Seth Kantor, WC Vol. XV, p. 81.
43. Testimony of John Newman, WC Vol. XV, p. 544.
44. Testimony of Richard Saunders, WC Vol. XV, pp. 578, 583.
45. WR, p. 337.
46. Ibid., pp. 336–37.
47. Testimony of Andrew Armstrong, WC Vol. XIII, p. 331.
48. FBI report dated March 17, 1964, of examination of telephone company records for Carousel Club from September 26–November 22, 1963 (CD 722), CE 2303, p. 27, WC Vol. XXV.
49. Interview with William Alexander, March 6, 1992.
50. Testimony of Seth Kantor, WC Vol. XV, p. 80.
51. Kantor, *The Ruby Cover-Up*, p. 424.
52. Interview with Tony Zoppi, November 23, 1992.
53. Testimony of Andrew Armstrong, WC Vol. XIII, p. 331.
54. Testimony of Eileen Kaminsky, WC Vol. XV, p. 283.
55. CE 1479.
56. FBI report, December 4, 1963, of interview with Wynn Warner (CD 86), CE 1484, p. 191, WC Vol. XII.
57. Testimony of Jack Ruby, WC Vol. V, p. 199.

58. Testimony of Ralph Paul, WC Vol. XIV, pp. 151–52.

59. Ibid., p. 151.

60. Testimony of Jack Ruby, WC Vol. V, p. 185; testimony of Alice Nichols, WC Vol. XIV, pp. 123–24.

61. FBI report, June 11, 1964, of interview with Alexander Philip Gruber (CD 1144), CE 2284, WC Vol. XXV, p. 208.

62. Testimony of Eva Grant, WC Vol. XV, pp. 324–25.

63. Ibid., p. 325.

64. Testimony of Larry Crafard, WC Vol. XIII, pp. 455–57.

65. Testimony of Eva Grant, WC Vol. XV, pp. 326–27.

66. Ibid., p. 328.

67. Ibid., WC Vol. XIV, p. 468.

68. Ibid., pp. 469, 484.

69. Ibid., WC Vol. XV, p. 331.

70. Ibid., p. 331.

71. Ibid., WC Vol. XIV, p. 468.

72. Testimony of Eva Grant, WC Vol. XIV, p. 468, and WC Vol. XV, p. 332.

73. Testimony of Jack Ruby, WC Vol. V, p. 188.

74. Testimony of Augustus M. Eberhardt, WC Vol. XIII, p. 187; testimony of Victor Robertson, WC Vol. XV, pp. 351–52; testimony of Roy E. Standifer, WC Vol. XV; testimony of Ronald L. Jenkins, WC Vol. XV, pp. 601–2; FBI report, December 10, 1963, of interview with Ronald Jenkins (CD 85), CE 2254, pp. 424–25; Testimony of John Rutledge, *State of Texas* v. *Jack Rubenstein*, CE 2410, pp. 106–8, WC Vol. XXV.

75. Testimony of John Rutledge, *State of Texas* v. *Jack Rubenstein*, CE 2405, p. 105, WC Vol. XXV.

76. Ibid., pp. 106–7.

77. Ibid., p. 108.

78. Interview with Tony Zoppi, November 19, 1992.

79. Garry Wills and Ovid Demaris, "The Avenger: 'You All Know Me! I'm Jack Ruby!,' " *Esquire*, May 1967, p. 85.

80. Testimony of Victor Robertson, WC Vol. XV, p. 351.

81. FBI report, June 12, 1964, of examination of Jack Ruby's telephone records for November 22–24, 1963 (CD 1193), CE 2300; FBI report, March 17, 1964, of examination of Jack Ruby's telephone records from September 26–November 22, 1963 (CD 722), CE 2302, p. 14, WC Vol. XXV.

82. Testimony of Hyman Rubenstein, WC Vol. XV, pp. 31–32.

83. Wills and Demaris, *Esquire*, p. 153.

84. Affidavit of George Senator, November 24, 1963.

85. Wills and Demaris, *Esquire*, p. 47.

86. Ibid.

87. Testimony of Jack Ruby, WC Vol. V, pp. 187–88.

88. FBI report, November 25, 1963, of interview with Marguerite Vea Riegler (CD 4), CE 2247; FBI report, April 3, 1964, of interview with Rita Leslie Siberman (CD 856), CE 2278; FBI report, April 3, 1964, of interview with Robert Louis Sindelar (CD 856), CE 2279; FBI report, April 17, 1964, of interview with Dennis Patrick Martin (CD 856), CE 2280, WC Vol. XXV.

89. Testimony of Jack Ruby, WC Vol. V, p. 188.

90. Ibid.

91. Testimony of A. M. Eberhardt, WC Vol. XIII, p. 187.

92. Ibid., pp. 187–88.

93. Testimony of Jack Ruby, WC Vol. V, p. 188.

94. Ibid., p. 189.

95. Testimony of A. M. Eberhardt, WC Vol. XIII, p. 189.

96. Testimony of Jack Ruby, WC Vol. V, p. 189; testimony of Arthur Watherwax, WC Vol. XV, p. 568.

97. Testimony of Henry Wade, WC Vol. V, p. 224.

98. Testimony of David Johnston, WC Vol. XV, pp. 505–9.

99. Testimony of Icarus Pappas, WC Vol. XV, pp. 364–65.

100. Testimony of Jack Ruby, WC Vol. V, p. 189.

101. Testimony of Henry Wade, WC Vol. V, p. 224.

102. Testimony of Russell Lee Moore, WC Vol. XV, p. 255.

103. Ibid., pp. 255–56.

104. Testimony of William Glenn Duncan, WC Vol. XV, pp. 487–88; testimony of Russell Lee Moore, WC Vol. XV, p. 257.

105. Testimony of Russell Lee Moore, WC Vol. XV, p. 257.

106. Testimony of William Glenn Duncan, WC Vol. XV, pp. 487–88.

107. Testimony of Russell Lee Moore, WC Vol. XV, p. 259.

108. Testimony of Harry Olsen, WC Vol. XIV, p. 633.

109. Ibid., p. 632.

110. Testimony of Kay Helen (Coleman) Olsen, WC Vol. XIV, pp. 647, 649.

111. Ibid., p. 647.

112. Testimony of Jack Ruby, WC Vol. V, p. 191.

113. WR, p. 344.

114. Testimony of Arthur W. Watherwax, WC Vol. XV, pp. 566–68; FBI memo, August 24, 1964, transmitting reports dated August 7 and August 21, 1964, of interviews with Roy A. Pryor and Kenneth E. Griffith (CD 1442), CE 2297, WC Vol. XXV; testimony of Arnold Clyde Gadash, *State of Texas* v. *Jack Rubenstein*, CE 2816, WC Vol. XXVI, pp. 1508–9.

115. Testimony of Arthur Watherwax, WC Vol. XV, p. 568.

116. Testimony of Roy A. Pryor, WC Vol. XV, p. 559.

117. Ibid.

118. Ibid., p. 561.

119. Ibid., pp. 558–59; WR, p. 344.

120. Testimony of Jack Ruby, WC Vol. V, p. 203.

121. Testimony of George Senator, WC Vol. XIV, p. 218.

122. Ibid.

123. Testimony of Jack Ruby, WC Vol. V, p. 203.

124. Testimony of George Senator, WC Vol. XIV, p. 219.

125. Testimony of Jack Ruby, WC Vol. V, p. 203; testimony of George Senator, WC Vol. XIV, p. 220.

126. Testimony of George Senator, WC Vol. XIV, p. 221.

127. Ibid.

128. Testimony of Curtis LaVerne Crafard, WC Vol. XIII, pp. 466–68.

129. Ibid., pp. 468–69.

130. Ibid., p. 469.

131. "In Their Own Words," *Dallas Morning News*, November 20, 1988, p. 25.

132. Testimony of Marjorie Richey, WC Vol. XV, p. 196.

133. FBI report of November 29, 1963, of interview with Thomas Raymond Brown (CD 4), CE 2341, WC Vol. XXV.

134. Bellocchio Exhibit 1, WC Vol. XIX.

135. Testimony of Frank Bellocchio, WC Vol. XV, p. 470.

136. Bellocchio Exhibit 1, WC Vol. XIX; testimony of Frank Bellocchio, WC Vol. XV, p. 470–72.

137. Testimony of D. V. Harkness, WC Vol. VI, p. 314.

138. Testimony of Garnett Hallmark, WC Vol. XV, pp. 489–90; Hallmark Exhibit 1, p. 1, WC Vol. XX.

139. Testimony of Ken Dowe, WC Vol. XV, p. 434.

140. Testimony of Jack Ruby, WC Vol. V, p. 189.

141. Testimony of Wesley Wise, *State of Texas* v. *Jack Rubenstein*, CE 2413, p. 500, WC Vol. XXV.

142. FBI report, November 28, 1963, of interview with James M. Chaney, CE 2324, WC Vol. XXV.

143. Hall (C. Ray) Exhibit 3, p. 9, WC Vol. XX.

144. WR, p. 347.

145. Testimony of Frederic Rheinstein, WC Vol. XV, pp. 355–56.

146. Ibid., p. 357.

147. Ibid., pp. 355–56.

148. FBI report of information received February 17, 1964, concerning interview of Phillipe Labro in Paris (CD 856), CE 2276, WC Vol. XXV.

149. FBI report, December 3, 1963, of interview with Frank Bernard Johnston (CD 85), CE 2326, p. 428, WC Vol. XXV.

150. Testimony of Thayer Waldo, WC Vol. XV, pp. 588–89.

151. Testimony of Stanley Kaufman, WC Vol. XV, pp. 519–20.

152. Testimony of Thayer Waldo, WC Vol. XV, p. 588.

153. Testimony of Andrew Armstrong, WC Vol. XIII, p. 340.

154. Ibid., pp. 340–41.

155. Testimony of Eva Grant, WC Vol. XIV, p. 469.

156. See, e.g., FBI report, November 25, 1963, of interview with Thomas J. O'Grady, CE 2325; testimony of D. V. Harkness, *State of Texas* v. *Jack Rubenstein*, CE 2407, WC Vol. XXV.

157. Testimony of Russell Lee Moore, WC Vol. XV, p. 262.

158. Testimony of Karen Bennett Carlin, WC Vol. XIII, pp. 209–210.

159. Ibid., p. 211.

160. Testimony of Eva Grant, WC Vol. XV, p. 342.

161. Testimony of Lawrence Meyers, WC Vol. XV, pp. 632–34.

162. Ibid.

163. Testimony of Ralph Paul, WC Vol. XV, p. 672.

164. Testimony of Wanda Helmick, WC Vol. XV, p. 399.

165. Testimony of Ralph Paul, WC Vol. XV, pp. 672, 675.

166. Testimony of Breck Wall, WC Vol. XIV, p. 605.

167. FBI report, July 23, 1964, of interview with Laura Bryum and report, July 29, 1964, of interview of Virginia Thompson Humphries (CD 1366), CE 2337, WC Vol. XXV.

168. Testimony of Robert Norton, WC Vol. XV, p. 552.

169. Ibid., p. 551.

170. Testimony of George Senator, WC Vol. XIV, p. 236.

171. Testimony of Jack Ruby, WC Vol. V, p. 198, and WC Vol. XIV, p. 529; testimony of Eva Grant, WC Vol. XV, p. 343.
172. Testimony of Elnora Pitts, WC Vol. XIII, p. 231.
173. Testimony of George Senator, WC Vol. XIV, p. 236.
174. Ibid.
175. Testimony of Karen Bennett Carlin, WC Vol. XIII, pp. 211–12.
176. Testimony of George Senator, WC Vol. XIV, p. 239; "In Their Own Words," *Dallas Morning News*, November 20, 1988, p. 30.
177. "In Their Own Words," *Dallas Morning News*, November 20, 1988, p. 31.
178. Testimony of Jack Ruby, WC Vol. V, p. 199.
179. Testimony of Jesse Curry, WC Vol. IV, p. 187; see also WC Vol. IV, p. 242; WC Vol. VII, pp. 257, 357; WC Vol XII, pp. 2, 7, 9, 35, 97, 109, 162, 319.
180. Testimony of Buford Beaty, WC Vol. XII, 166; R. Pierce, WC Vol. XII, pp. 338–40; D. F. Steele, WC Vol. XII, p. 354; Gano Worley, WC Vol. XII, pp. 384–86; Patrick Dean, WC Vol. XII, pp. 421–26; Fred Bieberdorf, WC Vol. XIII, pp. 85–86; Harold Fuqua, WC Vol. XIII, p. 143; Edward Kelly, WC Vol. XIII, pp. 146–47; Louis McKinzie, WC Vol. XIII, pp. 149–56; A. Riggs, WC Vol. XIII, pp. 166–75; John Servance, WC Vol. XIII, pp. 175–81; E. Pierce, WC Vol. XIII, pp. 156–66; FBI report, December 11, 1963, of interview with Carl Linsey Thompson (CD 85), CE 2010; FBI report, December 4, 1963, of interview with Donald T. Suits (CD 85), CE 2032; FBI report, December 27, 1963, of interview with Gene Miller (CD 223), CE 2066, WC Vol. XXIV.
181. Testimony of Charles Batchelor, WC Vol. XII, pp. 9, 14.
182. Testimony of Jesse Curry, WC Vol. XII, p. 40; see also WC Vol. XII, pp. 4, 5, 7, 48, 53–54; WC Vol. XIII, pp. 60, 62.
183. Testimony of Charles Batchelor, WC Vol. XII, p. 7.
184. Testimony of Jesse Curry, WC Vol. XII, pp. 35–36.
185. Testimony of Charles Batchelor, WC Vol. XII, p. 15.
186. Testimony of Harry Holmes, WC Vol. VII, pp. 296–97.
187. Testimony of Will Fritz, WC Vol. XV, pp. 148–49.
188. Interview of Harry Holmes by postal inspector David McDermott, June 29, 1989, p. 3 (unpublished transcript).
189. Testimony of Forrest Sorrels, WC Vol. XIII, p. 63; interview of Harry Holmes by postal inspector David McDermott, June 29, 1989, p. 2.
190. Testimony of Doyle Lane, WC Vol. XIII, p. 226.
191. Ibid., p. 222.
192. Testimony of W. W. Semingsen, WC Vol. X, p. 406.
193. Testimony of Forrest Sorrels, WC Vol. VII, p. 357.
194. Testimony of Eugene Roy Vaughn, WC Vol. XII, p. 361.
195. Testimony of James Leavelle, WC Vol. XIII, p. 17.
196. Testimony of Willie Slack, WC Vol. XII, pp. 349, 391–92; WC Vol. XIII, pp. 92, 98, 101.
197. Testimony of Jimmy Turner, WC Vol. XIII, p. 136.
198. Ibid., pp. 136–37.
199. Transcript of interview with Jack Ruby, 1967, copyright Alskog, Inc.
200. Testimony of Jack Ruby, WC Vol. V, p. 200; testimony of Don Ray Archer, WC Vol. XII, p. 399.
201. Ibid.

202. "In Their Own Words," *Dallas Morning News*, November 20, 1988, p. 32.
203. Interview with Dr. John Lattimer, February 6, 1992.
204. Testimony of Henry Wade, WC Vol. V, p. 245; testimony of Louis Miller, WC Vol. XIII, p. 308.
205. Testimony of Barnard Clardy, WC Vol. XII, p. 412.
206. Ibid.
207. Testimony of Forrest Sorrels, WC Vol. XIII, p. 68.
208. Ibid., pp. 68, 71.
209. Interview with William Alexander, March 12, 1992.
210. Gary Wills and Ovid Demaris, *Jack Ruby: The Man Who Killed the Man Who Killed Kennedy* (New York: New American Library, 1967), pp. 72–73.
211. Interview with Tony Zoppi, November 17, 1992.
212. Statement of Rabbi Hillel Silverman, March 30, 1992, *Geraldo*.
213. Interview with Rabbi Hillel Silverman, January 15, 1993.
214. Ibid.
215. Wills and Demaris, *Jack Ruby*, pp. 72–73.
216. Interview with Earl Ruby, November 19, 1992.
217. Ibid.
218. Interview with William Alexander, March 6, 1992.
219. Testimony of Eva Grant, WC Vol. XIV, p. 471.
220. Ibid.
221. Wills and Demaris, *Jack Ruby*, p. 255.
222. Adelson, *The Ruby-Oswald Affair*, p. 133; Kantor, *The Ruby Cover-Up*, pp. 316–19.
223. Testimony of Eva Grant, WC Vol. XIV, pp. 484–85.
224. Ibid., p. 471.
225. Testimony of Jack Ruby, WC Vol. V, pp. 204, 212.
226. Ibid., p. 211.
227. Ibid., pp. 210–12.
228. Ibid., pp. 194, 196, 198, 209, 210.
229. See, e.g., Henry Hurt, *Reasonable Doubt*, p. 189.
230. Testimony of Jack Ruby, WC Vol. V, p. 210.
231. Ibid., Ruby, p. 192; Adelson, *The Ruby-Oswald Affair*, p. 72.
232. Statement of Rabbi Hillel Silverman, March 30, 1992, *Geraldo*.
233. WR, pp. 809–16.
234. Adelson, op. cit., p. 36.
235. Ibid., pp. 38–39.

17 "A RELIGIOUS EVENT"

1. Calvin Trillin, "The Buffs," *The New Yorker*, June 10, 1967, p. 42.
2. *Texas Supplemental Report on the Assassination of President John F. Kennedy and the Serious Wounding of Governor John B. Connally*, Austin, Texas, 1964, pp. 1–2, 8, 20.
3. WR, p. x.
4. William Manchester, *Death of a President*, (London: Michael Joseph, 1967), p. 717.
5. WR, p. xi.
6. Ibid., p . xii.

7. Edward J. Epstein, *Inquest* (New York: Bantam, 1966), p. 58.

8. Commission meeting of January 21, 1964.

9. Interview with James Lesar, December 1, 1992.

10. Warren Commission executive session of January 22, 1964.

11. Interview with Burt Griffin, January 23, 1992.

12. "The Warren Report," CBS News, Part IV, June 28, 1967.

13. Dennis L. Breo, "JFK's Death: The Plain Truth from the MDs Who Did the Autopsy," *Journal of the American Medical Association*, May 27, 1992, Vol. 267, No. 20, p. 2800.

14. See, e.g., CE 385, WC Vol. XVI.

15. Epstein, *Inquest*, p. 122.

16. Ibid., p. 122.

17. Ibid., p. 89.

18. WR, p. 21.

19. Interview with Burt Griffin, January 23, 1992.

20. Calvin Trillin, op. cit. p. 45.

21. Robert Blakey, *Fatal Hour* (New York: Berkeley Books, 1992), p. 44.

22. Thomas C. Buchanan, *Who Killed Kennedy?* (New York: Putnam, 1964; London: Secker & Warburg, 1964).

23. Testimony of Alan Belmont, WC Vol. V, p. 30.

24. Joachim Joesten, *Assassin or Fall-guy?* (New York: Marzani and Munsell, 1964).

25. Harold Weisberg, *Whitewash: The Report on the Warren Report* (Frederick, Maryland: Harold Weisberg, 1965).

26. Robert Blakey, *Fatal Hour*, p. 44.

27. Mark Lane, *Rush to Judgment* (New York: Holt, Rinehart & Winston, 1966).

28. "The Warren Report," CBS News, Part IV, June 28, 1967; John Connally press conference, November 1966.

29. Blakey, *Fatal Hour*, p. 44.

30. "The Warren Report," CBS News, Part IV, June 28, 1967.

31. Richard Popkin, *The Second Oswald (New York: Avon Books, 1966)*.

32. Raymond Marcus, *The Bastard Bullet: A Search for Legitimacy for Commission Exhibit 399* (Los Angeles: Rendell Publishers, 1966).

33. Leo Sauvage, *The Oswald Affair: An Examination of the Contradictions and Omissions of the Warren Report* (Cleveland: World Publishing Co., 1966).

34. Penn Jones, Jr., *Forgive My Grief* (Midlothian, Texas: The Midlothian Mirror, 1966).

35. Epstein, *Inquest*.

36. "The Warren Commission Report on the Assassination Is Struck by a Wave of Doubts," *Look*, July 1966; "A Matter of Reasonable Doubt," *Life*, November 1966; "The Crossfire That Killed President Kennedy," *Saturday Evening Post*, December 2, 1967.

37. Calvin Trillin, op. cit.

38. Ibid., p. 45.

39. Gerald Ford and John Stiles, *Portrait of the Assassin* (New York: Simon & Schuster, 1965).

40. Sylvia Meagher, *Accessories After the Fact: The Warren Commission, the Authorities, and the Report* (New York: Bobbs-Merrill, 1967).

41. Ibid., pp. xxi, xxvi; Sparrow, *After the Assassination*, p. 72.

42. Interview with James Lesar, December 1, 1992.

43. Statement of Thomas Kupferman, 89th Congress, 2nd Session, September 28, 1966, *Congressional Record*, Vol. 118, pp. 24157–59.

18 "BLACK IS WHITE, AND WHITE IS BLACK"

1. Associated Press wire-service story, "Garrison Record Shows Disability," December 29, 1967; Warren Rogers, "The Persecution of Clay Shaw," *Look*, August 26, 1969, p. 54.

2. Jim Garrison, *On the Trail of the Assassins* (New York: Warner Books, 1991), p. 9.

3. Milton E. Brener, *The Garrison Case: A Study in the Abuse of Power* (New York: Clarkson N. Potter, Inc., 1969), pp. 2, 10.

4. Interview with Hubie Badeaux, November 30, 1992.

5. Brener, op. cit., p. 15.

6. Interview with Milton Brener, December 11, 1992.

7. Brener, op. cit., p. 16.

8. Ibid., p. 21.

9. Ibid.

10. Interview with Milton Brener, December 11, 1992.

11. Kirkwood, *American Grotesque: An Account of the Clay Shaw–Jim Garrison Affair in New Orleans* (New York: Simon & Schuster, 1970), p. 178.

12. Interview with Milton Brener, December 11, 1992.

13. Brener, op. cit., p. 33

14. Hugh Aynesworth, "The Garrison Goosechase," *Dallas Times Herald*, December 21, 1982.

15. Warren Rogers, "The Persecution of Clay Shaw," *Look*, August 26, 1969, p. 56; Aynesworth, "The Garrison Goosechase."

16. Aynesworth, "The Garrison Goosechase."

17. Walter Sheridan, *The Fall and Rise of Jimmy Hoffa* (New York: Saturday Review Press, 1972), p. 417.

18. "The Mob," Part II, *Life*, September 8, 1967, p. 96; Sheridan, op. cit., p. 417.

19. Interview with Milton Brener, December 11, 1992.

20. David Chandler, "The 'Little Big Man' Is Bigger Than Ever," *Life*, April 10, 1970, p. 33.

21. Aynesworth, "The Garrison Goosechase."

22. Brener, op. cit., p. 45.

23. FBI internal memorandum report, to SAC New Orleans, re: David Ferrie, 1964.

24. Interview with Hubie Badeaux, March 24, 1992.

25. U.S. Secret Service report, New Orleans, December 13, 1963, file CO-2-34,030, p. 5. (HSCA JFK Document 003840).

26. James Phelan, *Scandals, Scamps and Scoundrels: The Casebook of an Investigative Reporter* (New York: Random House, 1982), p. 147.

27. Interview with Alvin Beauboeuf, March 15, 1992.

28. Phelan, op. cit., p. 148.

29. Letter from Eva Grant to Edward Wegmann, Esq., March 16, 1968.

30. Phelan, op. cit., p. 148.

31. Testimony of Frederick O'Sullivan, WC Vol. VIII, p. 30.

32. Ibid., pp. 326, 328.

33. Ibid., p. 331.

34. Ibid.

35. Ibid., pp. 332, 334.

36. Ibid., p. 335.

37. Ibid., p. 333.

38. Interview with Milton Brener, January 22, 1993.

39. "The JFK Conspiracy: The Case of Jim Garrison," NBC News, Part 2, June 19, 1967.

40. Aynesworth, "The Garrison Goosechase."

41. Epstein, *Counterplot* (New York: Viking Press, 1988), p. 51.

42. Blakey, *Fatal Hour*, p. 51.

43. Richard N. Billings, "Garrison and the JFK Plot," *Long Island Press*, May 15, 1968.

44. Epstein, *Counterplot*, p. 76.

45. Anson, *"They've Killed the President!,"* p. 111.

46. Gurvich conference with Edward Wegmann, August 29, 1967, Tape 2, unpublished transcript, p. 10.

47. Blakey, *Final Hour*, p. 49.

48. Statement of David Lewis, district attorney's files, month undated, 1966.

49. Interview with Al Beauboeuf, March 15, 1992.

50. "The JFK Conspiracy: The Case of Jim Garrison," NBC News, Part 2, June 19, 1967.

51. Hugh Aynesworth, "The JFK 'Conspiracy,' " *Newsweek*, May 15, 1967, p. 38.

52. Interview with Alvin Beauboeuf, March 15, 1992; "The JFK Conspiracy: The Case of Jim Garrison," NBC News, Part 2, June 19, 1967.

53. Interview with Gordon Novel by Salvatore Panzeca and Robert Wilson, April 16 and April 17, 1967.

54. Ibid.

55. Autopsy Protocol, Nicholas J. Chetta, Coroner, Orleans Parish Coroner's Office, No. W67-2-255.

56. Interview with Carlos Bringuier, March 16, 1992.

57. Interview with Al Beauboeuf, March 15, 1992.

58. Aynesworth, "The Garrison Goosechase."

59. Interview with Carlos Bringuier, March 16, 1992.

60. Epstein, *Counterplot*, p. 50.

61. Aynesworth, "The Garrison Goosechase."

62. Phelan, op. cit., p. 155.

63. Ibid., p. 151.

64. Transcript of preliminary hearing, pp. 182–83, 206.

65. Andrew Sciambra memorandum to Jim Garrison.

66. Phelan, op. cit., p. 153.

67. Ibid., p. 153.

68. Ibid., p. 156.

69. "The JFK Conspiracy: The Case of Jim Garrison," NBC News, Part 2, June 19, 1967.

70. "The JFK Conspiracy: The Case of Jim Garrison," NBC News, Part 2, June 19, 1967.

71. "The Warren Report," CBS News Part II, June 27, 1967 p. 16.

72. New Orleans *Times-Picayune*, June 20, 1967.

73. Interview with Milton Brener, December 11, 1992.

74. UPI, November 1, 1967; *Playboy* interview, pp. 174–75; *Tonight Show*, January 31, 1968.

75. *Playboy*, pp. 159–60, 176.

76. UPI wire-service story, "Garrison Claims Robert Kennedy Is Obstructing His Investigation."

77. Kirkwood, *American Grotesque*, pp. 177–78.

78. Rogers, "The Persecution of Clay Shaw," *Look*, p. 56.

79. Aynesworth, "The Garrison Goosechase."

80. *Times-Picayune*, July 12, 1968.

81. Interview with Milton Brener, December 11, 1992.

82. Phelan, op. cit., p. 169.

83. Aynesworth, "The Garrison Goosechase."

84. Ibid.

85. Epstein, *Counterplot*, pp. 84–85.

86. Jim Garrison, *On the Trail of the Assassins*, pp. 212–16.

87. Interview with Carlos Bringuier, March 16, 1992.

88. Interview with Milton Brener, December 11, 1992.

89. *Tonight Show*, NBC, January 31, 1968.

90. Aynesworth, "The Garrison Goosechase."

91. "The JFK Conspiracy: The Case of Jim Garrison," NBC News, Part 2, June 19, 1967.

92. Epstein, *Counterplot*, pp. 39–40.

93. *New York World Journal Tribune*, March 5, 1967; Epstein, *Counterplot*, p. 78.

94. Epstein, *Counterplot*, p. 78.

95. *Playboy*, p. 170.

96. "The Warren Report," CBS News, Part II, June 27, 1967, p. 12.

97. *The New York Times*, December 11, 1967.

98. Epstein, *Counterplot*, p. 81.

99. *Playboy*, p. 165.

100. Ibid., pp. 167–68.

101. Epstein, *Counterplot*, p. 78.

102. Interview with Milton Brener, December 11, 1992.

103. Phelan, op. cit., p. 149.

104. Aynesworth, "The JFK Conspiracy," *Newsweek*, May 15, 1967, p. 40.

105. Rogers, "The Persecution of Clay Shaw," *Look*, p. 56.

106. Edward Wegmann memorandum, June 4, 1968, p. 5.

107. Interview with Layton Martens, March 19, 1992.

108. Phelan, op. cit., p. 172.

109. Ibid., pp. 172, 174.

110. Transcript of April 16, 1971, interview of Perry Russo by William Gurvich, Edward Wegmann, and Irvin Dymond, p. 3.

111. Ibid.
112. Phelan, op. cit., p. 174.
113. Interview with Cynthia Wegmann, March 17, 1992.
114. Interview with Irvin Dymond, March 20, 1992.
115. Interview with Milton Brener, December 11, 1992.

19 "WHAT HAPPENED TO THE TRUTH?"

1. Anthony Summers, in a special forward to the 1992 paperback release of *Conspiracy* by Paragon Press, New York.
2. Penn Jones, *Forgive My Grief III* (Midlothian, Texas: Penn Jones, 1969).
3. Harold Weisberg, *Whitewash IV: JFK Assassination Transcript* (Frederick, Maryland: Harold Weisberg, 1974).
4. Jim Garrison, *A Heritage of Stone* (New York: Putnam, 1970).
5. James Kirkwood, *American Grotesque: An Account of the Clay Shaw–Jim Garrison Affair in the City of New Orleans* (New York: Simon & Schuster, 1970).
6. Edward Epstein, *Counterplot* (New York: Viking Press, 1969).
7. Interview with James Lesar, December 1, 1992.
8. Ibid.
9. *Alleged Assassination Plots Involving Foreign Leaders*, Interim Report of the Select Committee to Study Governmental Operations, with Respect to Intelligence Activities, U.S. Senate (Washington, D.C.: U.S. Government Printing Office, 1975).
10. See Introduction by Thomas Downing in Peter Model, with Robert J. Groden, *JFK: The Case for Conspiracy* (New York: Manor Books, 1976).
11. Blakey, *Fatal Hour*, pp. 71–72.
12. HSCA Rpt., p. 47.
13. Interview with Robert Blakey, January 22, 1992.
14. HSCA Rpt., p. 147.
15. Seth Kantor, *Who Was Jack Ruby?* (New York: Everest House, 1978).
16. Carl Oglesby and Jeff Goldberg, "Did the Mob Kill Kennedy?" *The Washington Post*, February 25, 1979. pp. BI, B4.
17. G. Robert Blakey and Richard N. Billings, *The Plot to Kill the President* (New York: Times Books, 1981).
18. John Davis, *Mafia Kingfish: Carlos Marcello and the Assassination of John F. Kennedy* (New York: McGraw-Hill, 1988).
19. David Scheim, *Contract on America: The Mafia Murders of John and Robert Kennedy* (New York: Shapolsky Books, 1988).
20. HSCA Rpt., p. 176.
21. House Select Committee interview with Walter Sheridan, July 10, 1978 (JFK Document 009777); HSCA Rpt., p. 178.
22. HSCA Rpt., pp. 178–79.
23. HSCA JFK Ex. F-602. HSCA Vol. V, p. 31.
24. HSCA Rpt., pp. 174–75.
25. Testimony of José Aleman, HSCA Vol. V, pp. 301–14.
26. HSCA Rpt., p. 175.
27. HSCA Rpt., p. 169.
28. Davis, *Mafia Kingfish*, p. 122.

29. HSCA Rpt., p. 172; HSCA Report on Organized Crime, pp. 390–98.
30. Interview with Hubie Badeaux, March 24, 1992.
31. Transcript of the *State of Louisiana* v. *Carlos Marcello, Charles Roemer, et al.*
32. Davis, op. cit., pp. 530–31.
33. Ibid., p. 531.
34. *Frontline*, November 1992, one-hour documentary on Frank Ragano.
35. Jack Newfield, "Hoffa Had the Mob Murder JFK," *New York Post*, January 14, 1992, pp. 4–5.
36. Ibid., p. 5.
37. Memorandum to Director, FBI, from SAC, Tampa, April 11, 1967, p. 5.
38. Interview with Bill Roemer, January 23, 1992.
39. Ibid.
40. David Perry, "Rashomon to the Extreme," October 19, 1992, five pages (unpublished).
41. Interview with David Perry, August 23, 1992.
42. Interview with Bill Alexander, March 14, 1992.
43. Hugh C. McDonald, *Appointment in Dallas: The Final Solution to the Assassination of JFK* (New York: The Hugh McDonald Publishing Corp., 1975), p. 6.
44. Interview with Edwin Lopez, February 6, 1992.
45. Interview with David Perry, September 8, 1992.
46. Interview with David Perry, March 2, 1992.
47. Interview with Professor David Wrone, January 17, 1992.
48. Interview with Bill Alexander, March 16, 1992.
49. "The Warren Report," CBS News, Part IV, June 28, 1967, pp. 16–17.
50. Letter to the Editor of *The New York Times*, by William Manchester, February 5, 1992.
51. Interview with Robert Blakey, January 22, 1992.

Appendix B

1. HSCA Vol. IV, p. 463; David Wallechinsky and Irving Wallace. *The People's Almanac* (New York: Doubleday and Co., 1975).
2. HSCA Vol. IV, pp. 464–65.
3. Penn Jones, Jr., "Mystery Deaths," *The Rebel*, November 22, 1983.
4. Sylvia Meagher, *Accessories After the Fact: The Warren Commission, the Authorities, and the Report* (New York: Vintage Books, 1992, p. 301).
5. Jim Marrs, *Crossfire: The Plot to Kill Kennedy* (New York: Carroll & Graf Publishers, 1989).
6. Review of newspaper files for *Dallas Morning News*, New Orleans *Times-Picayune*, and *The New York Times*.
7. Marrs, *Crossfire*, p. 566.
8. Ibid., p. 559.
9. Affidavit of David Goldstein, WC Vol. VII, p. 594.
10. Marrs, op. cit., p. 560.
11. Testimony of Captain Frank Martin, WC Vol. XII, p. 284.
12. Marrs, op. cit., p. 560.
13. Ibid., p. 561.

14. Affidavit of Harold Russell, WC Vol. VII, p. 594.
15. Marrs, op. cit., p. 561.
16. Ibid., p. 562.
17. Ibid.
18. *The Washington Post*, May 3, 1972, p. A1.
19. *The Washington Post*, April 15, 1975, p. C6.
20. *The Washington Post*, December 19, 1975, p. B18.
21. *The Washington Post*, September 10, 1977, p. D6.
22. *The Washington Post*, June 10, 1977, p. C8.
23. *The Washington Post*, August 2, 1977, p. C4.
24. *Houston Post*, January 18, 1981, p. A13.
25. Marrs, op. cit., p. 566.
26. *The Washington Post*, March 30, 1984, p. B16.
27. Interviews with James Leavelle, March 11, 1992, and David Perry, March 2, 1992.
28. Marrs, op. cit., p. 559.
29. Interview with David Perry, March 2, 1992, referring to conversation with Hugh Aynesworth.
30. Testimony of James Worrell, WC Vol. II, pp. 193, 200.
31. Marrs, op. cit., p. 560.
32. Ibid., p. 562.
33. Ibid.
34. Interview with David Perry, December 13, 1992.
35. *The Washington Post*, January 9, 1977, p. B6.
36. *The Washington Post*, August 13, 1977, p. E4; and November 19, 1977, p. C8.
37. *The Washington Post*, August 20, 1977, p. E6.

Bibliography

Books and Articles

Instances in which a second edition is listed refer to the paper-back used by the author for research.

Adelson, Alan. *The Ruby-Oswald Affair.* Seattle: Romar Books, 1988.

Alvarez, Luis W. "A Physicist Examines the Kennedy Assassination Film." Lawrence Berkeley Laboratory, University of California, preprint LBL-3884, July 1975.

Anson, Robert Sam. *"They've Killed the President!": The Search for the Murderers of John F. Kennedy.* New York: Bantam, 1975.

Aynesworth, Hugh. "The Garrison Goosechase." *Dallas Times Herald,* December 21, 1982.

Baden, Dr. Michael M. *Unnatural Death: Confessions of a Medical Examiner.* New York: Random House, 1989.

Belin, David W. *November 22, 1963: You Are the Jury.* New York: Quadrangle/The New York Times Books, 1973.

———. *Final Disclosure,* New York: Scribners, 1988.

Belli, Melvin M. (with Maurice C. Carroll). *Dallas Justice: The Real Story of Jack Ruby and His Trial.* New York: David McKay Co., 1964.

Bishop, Jim. *The Day Kennedy Was Shot*. New York: Funk & Wagnalls, 1968.

Blakey, G. Robert, and Richard Billings. *The Plot to Kill the President*. New York: Times Books, 1981; published as *Fatal Hour: The Assassination of President Kennedy by Organized Crime*, by Berkley Books, 1992.

Bloomgarden, Henry. *The Gun: A Biography of the Gun That Killed John F. Kennedy*. New York: Macmillan, 1965.

Brener, Milton E. *The Garrison Case: A Study in the Abuse of Power*. New York: Clarkson N. Potter, 1969.

Brennan, Howard L., and J. Edward Cherryholmes. *Eyewitness to History: The Kennedy Assassination as Seen by Howard Brennan*. Waco, Texas: Texian Press, 1987.

Breo, Dennis L. "JFK's Death" (Parts I–III). *The Journal of the American Medical Association*. Vol. 267, No. 20; Vol. 268, No. 13.

Buchanan, Thomas G. *Who Killed Kennedy?* New York: Putnam, 1964; MacFadden-Bartell, 1965.

Bringuier, Carlos. *Red Friday: Nov. 22, 1963*. Chicago: Chas. Hallberg & Co., 1969.

Crenshaw, Dr. Charles A. *JFK: Conspiracy of Silence*. New York: Signet, 1992.

Curry, Jesse. *JFK Assassination File: Retired Dallas Police Chief Jesse Curry Reveals His Personal File*. Dallas: American Poster and Publishing Co., 1969.

Davis, John H. *Mafia Kingfish: Carlos Marcello and the Assassination of John F. Kennedy*. New York: McGraw-Hill, 1988; Signet, 1989.

Davison, Jean. *Oswald's Game*. New York: W. W. Norton, 1983.

Eddowes, Michael. *The Oswald File*. New York: Clarkson N. Potter, 1977.

Epstein, Edward Jay. *Inquest: The Warren Commission and the Establishment of the Truth*. New York: Bantam, 1966.

———. *Counterplot*. New York: Viking Press, 1968.

———. *Legend: The Secret World of Lee Harvey Oswald*. New York: Reader's Digest Press/McGraw-Hill, 1978.

———. *Deception: The Invisible War Between the KGB and the CIA*. New York: Simon & Schuster, 1989.

Ford, Gerald R., and John R. Stiles. *Portrait of the Assassin.* New York: Simon & Schuster, 1965.

Garrison, Jim. *A Heritage of Stone.* New York: Putnam, 1970.

————. *On the Trail of the Assassins.* New York: Sheridan Square Press, 1988; Warner Books, 1991.

Gertz, Elmer. *Moment of Madness: The People vs. Jack Ruby.* New York: Follett Publishing Co., 1968.

Groden, Robert J., and Harrison Livingstone. *High Treason: The Assassination of President John F. Kennedy and the New Evidence of Conspiracy.* New York: Conservatory Press, 1989; Berkley Books, 1990.

Guinn, Vincent P. "JFK Assassination: Bullet Analyses." *Analytical Chemistry,* Vol. 51 (April 1979).

Hurt, Henry. *Reasonable Doubt.* New York: Henry Holt & Co., 1985; Owl Books, 1987.

James, Rosemary, and Jack Wardlaw. *Plot or Politics? The Garrison Case and Its Cast.* New Orleans: Pelican Publishing, 1967.

Joesten, Joachim. *Oswald: Assassin or Fall-guy?* New York: Marzani and Munsell, 1964.

Jones, Penn, Jr. *Forgive My Grief* (Vols. I–IV). Midlothian, Texas: The Midlothian Mirror, 1966–1974.

Kantor, Seth. *Who Was Jack Ruby?* New York: Everest House, 1978; published as *The Ruby Cover-Up,* by Zebra, 1992.

Kirkwood, James. *American Grotesque: An Account of the Clay Shaw–Jim Garrison Affair in New Orleans.* New York: Simon & Schuster, 1970.

Kurtz, Michael. *Crime of the Century.* Knoxville, Tenn.: University of Tennessee Press, 1982.

Lane, Mark. *Rush to Judgment.* New York: Holt, Rinehart & Winston, 1966; Fawcett Crest, 1967.

————. *A Citizen's Dissent.* New York: Holt, Rinehart & Winston, 1968.

————. *Plausible Denial: Was the CIA Involved in the Assassination of JFK?* New York: Thunder's Mouth Press, 1991.

Lattimer, Dr. John K. *Kennedy and Lincoln: Medical & Ballistic Comparisons of Their Assassinations.* New York: Harcourt, Brace, Jovanovich, 1980.

Lewis, Richard W. *The Scavengers and the Critics of the Warren Report.* New York: Dell, 1967.

Lifton, David S. *Best Evidence: Disguise and Deception in the Assassination of John F. Kennedy.* New York: Macmillan, 1981; Carroll & Graf, 1988.

Livingstone, Harrison Edward. *High Treason 2: The Great Cover-Up—The Assassination of President John F. Kennedy.* New York: Carroll & Graf, 1992.

McDonald, Hugh, as told to Geoffrey Bocca. *Appointment in Dallas: The Final Solution to the Assassination.* New York: Zebra Books/The Hugh MacDonald Publishing Co., 1975.

McMillan, Priscilla Johnson. *Marina and Lee.* New York: Harper & Row, 1977.

Manchester, William. *The Death of a President.* London: Michael Joseph, 1967.

Mangold, Tom. *Cold Warrior: James Jesus Angleton—The CIA's Master Spy Hunter.* New York: Touchstone, 1991.

Marrs, Jim. *Crossfire: The Plot That Killed Kennedy.* New York: Carroll & Graf, 1989, 1990.

Meagher, Sylvia. *Subject Index to the Warren Report and Hearings and Exhibits.* New York: Scarecrow Press, 1966.

———. *Accessories After the Fact: the Warren Commission, the Authorities, and the Report.* New York: Bobbs-Merrill, 1967; Vintage, 1992.

Melanson, Philip H. *Spy Saga: Lee Harvey Oswald and U.S. Intelligence.* New York: Praeger, 1990.

Moore, Jim. *Conspiracy of One: The Definitive Book on the Kennedy Assassination.* Fort Worth, Texas: The Summit Group, 1990, 1991.

Mostovshchikov, Sergey. "KGB Case No. 31451 on Lee Harvey Oswald." *Izvestiya*, August 7, 8, 11, 13, 1992.

Nechiporenko, Oleg Maximovich. *Passport to Assassination: The Never-Before-Told Story of Lee Harvey Oswald by the KGB Colonel Who Knew Him.* New York: Birch Lane Press, 1993.

Oswald, Robert L., with Myrick and Barbara Land. *Lee: A Portrait of Lee Harvey Oswald.* New York: Coward-McCann, 1967.

Phelan, James. *Scandals, Scamps and Scoundrels: The*

Casebook of an Investigative Reporter. New York: Random House, 1982.

Popkin, Richard H. *The Second Oswald*. New York: Avon Books, 1966.

Roemer, William F., Jr. *Roemer: Man Against the Mob*. New York: Ivy/Ballantine, 1991.

Scheim, David. *Contract on America: The Mafia Murders of John and Robert Kennedy*. New York: Shapolsky Books, 1988.

Sparrow, John. *After the Assassination*. New York: Chilmark Press, 1967.

Sprague, Richard E. "The Assassination of President John F. Kennedy: The Application of Computers to the Photographic Evidence." *Computers and Automation*, May 1970.

Stafford, Jean. *A Mother in History: Mrs. Marguerite Oswald*. New York: Farrar, Straus & Giroux, 1966.

Summers, Anthony. *Conspiracy*. New York: McGraw-Hill, 1980; Paragon House, 1989.

Thompson, Josiah. *Six Seconds in Dallas: A Microstudy of the Kennedy Assassination*. New York: Bernard Geis Associates, 1967; Berkley, 1976.

"Three Patients at Parkland." *Texas State Journal of Medicine*, Vol. 60 (January 1964).

Trillin, Calvin. "The Buffs." *The New Yorker*, June 10, 1967.

Weisberg, Harold. *Whitewash* (Vols. I–IV). Self-published, 1965–1974.

———. *Post-Mortem*. Self-published, 1975.

Wills, Garry, and Ovid Demaris. "The Avenger: 'You All Know Me! I'm Jack Ruby!' " and "The Disposal of Jack Ruby." *Esquire*, May and June, 1967.

Wrone, David R. "The Assassination of John Fitzgerald Kennedy: An Annotated Bibliography." State Historical Society of Wisconsin, 1973.

Government Reports

"Alleged Assassination Plots Involving Foreign Leaders," Interim Report of the Select Committee to Study Governmental

Operations, with Respect to Intelligence Activities, U.S. Senate. Washington, D.C.: U.S. Government Printing Office, 1975.

Hearings Before the Sub-Committee on Civil and Constitutional Rights of the Committee on the Judiciary, House of Representatives, on FBI Oversight, 1976.

Investigation of the Assassination of President John F. Kennedy, Book V, Final Report of the Select Committee to Study Governmental Operations, with Respect to Intelligence Activities, U.S. Senate, 1976.

Panel Review of Photographs, X-Ray Films, Documents and Other Evidence Pertaining to the Fatal Wounding of President John F. Kennedy on November 22, 1963, in Dallas, Texas. The Clark Panel, 1968.

Report of the Committee on Ballistic Acoustics, National Research Council, Washington, D.C. Prepared for the Department of Justice, 1982.

Report of the President's Commission on the Assassination of President John F. Kennedy, and 26 accompanying volumes of Hearings and Exhibits, 1964; Report, without supporting volumes, also published by Doubleday, 1964.

Report of the Select Committee on Assassinations, U.S. House of Representatives, and 12 accompanying volumes of Hearings and Appendices on Kennedy investigation, 1979; Report, without supporting volumes, also published by Bantam, 1979.

Report to the House of Representatives, Select Committee on Assassinations, on the subject of 1977 Neutron Activation Analysis Measurements on Bullet-Lead Specimens Involved in the 1963 Assassination of President John F. Kennedy, by Vincent Guinn, September 1978.

Report to the President by the Commission on CIA Activities Within the United States, June 1975.

Texas Supplemental Report on the Assassination of President John F. Kennedy and the Serious Wounding of Governor John B. Connally, November 22, 1963, by Texas Attorney General Waggoner Carr, Austin, Texas, 1964.

"The Assassination of President Kennedy," New Orleans Metropolitan Crime Commission, November 26, 1963, New Orleans, La.

Television Network Transcripts

CBS News Inquiry, "The Warren Report," (Parts 1–4), June 25, 26, 27, 28, 1967.

CBS News Inquiry, "The American Assassins: Lee Harvey Oswald and John F. Kennedy," November 25, 26, 1975.

CBS, *48 Hours*, "JFK." February 5, 1992.

NBC, "The JFK Conspiracy: The Case of Jim Garrison." June 19, 1967.

Nova, "Who Shot President Kennedy?," November 15, 1988.

Trial Transcripts

1964 transcript of *State of Texas* v. *Jack Rubenstein.*

1969 transcript of *State of Louisiana* v. *Clay Shaw.*

Unpublished Manuscripts

Bowles, James C. *The Kennedy Assassination Tapes: A Rebuttal to the Acoustical Evidence Theory.* 1979.

"John Kennedy Assassination Film Analysis." Itek Corporation, undated.

"Nix Film Analysis." Itek Corporation, May 18, 1967.

Perry, David. *Rashomon to the Extreme.* 1992.

West, Dr. Michael, and Dr. John Lattimer. *The Shots Seen Round the World.* 1992.

Interviews conducted by the author and unpublished government and private documents reviewed for the book are cited as they appear in the Source Notes, starting at page 507.

Index

ABOUT THE AUTHOR

Gerald Posner, a former Wall Street lawyer, is the co-author of *Mengele: The Complete Story* (1986), critically acclaimed as the definitive biography of the "Angel of Death." His other books have included a 1988 exposé of the international heroin trade *(Warlords of Crime: Chinese Secret Societies—The New Mafia)*, a first novel in 1989 *(The Bio-Assassins)*, and, in 1991, a collection of interviews with the sons and daughters of leaders of the Third Reich *(Hitler's Children)*.

Mr. Posner's articles have appeared in numerous magazines and newspapers, including the *New York Times*, *The New Yorker*, and *U.S. News & World Report*. He lives in New York City with his wife, Trisha.